Alan Rogers' ~~Guides~~

BRITAIN and IRELAND
2003

Quality Camping and Caravanning Parks

Compiled by: Alan Rogers Guides Ltd

Cover design: Paul Effenberg, Vine Cottage
Maps created by Customised Mapping (01985 844092)
contain background data provided by GisDATA Ltd.
Maps are © Alan Rogers Guides and Gis DATA Ltd 2002

Clive Edwards, Lois Edwards & Sue Smart have asserted
their rights to be identified as the authors of this work.

First published in this format 2002

© Alan Rogers Guides Ltd 2002

Published by: Alan Rogers Guides Ltd, Burton Bradstock, Bridport, Dorset DT6 4QA

British Library Cataloguing-in-Publication Data:
A catalogue record for this book is available from the British Library.

ISBN: 0 901586 87 0

Printed in Great Britain by J H Haynes & Co Ltd

Contents

Introduction

It is thirty-five years since Alan Rogers himself, now sadly no longer with us, published the first campsite guide that bore his name, so we've been indulging in a little nostalgia and celebrating our 35th anniversary most notably by moving into new larger offices, by having our guides published in Dutch as well as in English, and by opening new offices in Holland at Amersfoort.

When Alan published the first of his guides in 1968 he introduced it with the words "I would like to stress that the camps which are included in this book have been chosen entirely on merit, and no payment of any sort is made by them for their inclusion".

As campers and caravanners ourselves, it was this objective approach that attracted us to become regular readers of his Guides and which eventually lead to our taking over the editing and publishing of the Guides when Alan retired in 1986.

Whilst the content and scope of the Guides have expanded considerably in the fifteen years since we took over, mainly due to the huge growth in the number of campsites throughout the UK and Europe during those years, our selection of sites to be featured still employs exactly the same philosophy as Alan defined over thirty years ago.

The Alan Rogers' Approach to Selecting Sites

Firstly, and most importantly, our selection is based entirely on our own rigorous inspection. Parks cannot buy their way into our guides - indeed the extensive Site Report which is written by us, not by the site owner, is provided free of charge so we are free to say what we think and to provide an honest description. This is written in plain English and without the use of icons or symbols.

The criteria which we use when selecting sites are numerous, but the most important by far is the question of good quality and standards. Whatever the size of the site, whether it's part of a campsite chain, or even a local authority site, makes no difference in terms of it being required to meet our exacting standards in terms of its quality. In other words, irrespective of the size of the site, or the number of facilities offered, the essentials (the welcome, the pitches, the sanitary facilities the cleanliness and the general maintenance) must all be of a good standard.

Our selection of sites is designed to cater for a wide variety of preferences, from those seeking a small peaceful campsite in the heart of the countryside, to those looking for an 'all singing, all dancing' site in a popular seaside resort, and for those with more specific needs such as sports facilities, cultural or historical attractions, even sites for naturism.

We rely on our small, dedicated team of Site Assessors, all of whom are experienced campers, caravanners or motorcaravanners, to visit and recommend parks and to follow up readers' recommendations, following which our Sites Director makes the final decision on those to be included in the following year's guide. Once a park is included, it will be regularly inspected to ensure that standards are being maintained.

We also appreciate the feedback we receive from many of our readers, and we always make a point of following up complaints, suggestions or recommendations for possible new sites. Given the occasion of our 35th anniversary we felt we might include a selection of some of the comments we've had from readers during the past year:

"Very useful - excellent guide! Wouldn't go without it."

"A pleasure to use and very reliable."

"A wealth of information you can't find anywhere else."

"Superb, up to date, accurate and informative. An absolute must with the trailer tent."

"Reassuring guides - taking the anxiety out of first night arrivals."

"Makes it a lot easier to find a campsite that suits you, especially when you have two toddlers like us... good reading - keep writing!"

"Totally brilliant! As a first timer to camping abroad it has become my bible."

"Saw it for the first time today and bought it! Best buy we have made."

"Excellent value given the level of detail and knowledge."

For latest information visit www.**alanrogers**.com

Of course we get a few grumbles too - but it really is a few, and those we do get usually arrive at the end of the high season and relate mainly to overcrowding or to poor maintenance during the peak school holiday period. The most frustrating complaints we get are from readers who have been using a guide that's several years out of date! Of course we don't expect readers to buy a new guide every year, but it can be rather galling to receive a complaint about a campsite which hasn't been featured in our guides for some time! Please bear in mind that although we are interested to hear about complaints, we have no contractual relationship with the parks featured in our guides and are therefore not in a position to intervene in any dispute between a reader and a park. If you have a complaint, the first step should be to take the matter up with the park operator, preferably at the time, as in most cases we'd expect any of the professional owners or managers of parks we feature to do their best to address any justifiable complaint positively and quickly.

How to use the Guide

A few words of explanation regarding the layout may be useful:

Regions and counties

For England we have used official Tourist Board Regions and the counties. For Wales and Scotland, where there are many official regions, we have adopted our own regional structure based on the needs of the average holidaymaker. For Ireland (North and South) we use the counties.

The Site Reports

These are really self-explanatory, but please remember that all prices shown are per night, and all telephone numbers assume that you are 'phoning from within the country where the site is situated - thus if you want to telephone a site from abroad you will need to prefix the number with the appropriate International Dialling Code.

Example of an entry:

County or area

Park name
Address

number

Main text	**Facilities:**
A description of the park in which we try to give an idea of the general features of the site - its size, its situation, its strengths and weaknesses. This column should provide a picture of the site itself with reference to the facilities provided if they impact on its appearance or character. We retain reference to pitch numbers, electricity (with amperage), hardstandings etc. in this section as pitch design, planning and terracing affects the site's overall appearence. Similarly we continue to include reference to caravan holiday homes, etc. but no longer indicate if they are available to let (this type of information will appear in our new guide for 'Mobile Homes & Chalets'). Importantly at the end of this column we indicate if there are any restrictions, e.g. no tents, adults only etc.	*The second column in smaller print contains all the more specific information on the site facilities.* *Please see the following notes.* **Charges** **Tel/Fax:** **Reservations:** **Open** **Directions:** *Please see the following notes.*

General information
Grouped under the headings of charges, opening dates, address, telephone and reservations.

Charges are the latest provided by the parks. In those few cases where 2002 or 2003 prices are not given, we try to give a general guide. The pricing structures vary considerably and we try to be as uniform and succinct as possible in what is included since some parks have a simple tariff, while others have a vast complex of possibilities. The same is true of reservations and what is written cannot wholly replace the official park tariff and reservation form.

Please note that the opening dates are those advised to us during the early autumn of the previous year - park operators can, and sometimes do, alter these dates before the start of the following season - often for good reasons - so if you intend to visit a park shortly after its published opening date, or shortly before its closing date, it really is wise to check that it will actually be open at the time required. Similarly some parks operate a restricted service during the low season, only opening some of their facilities (e.g. swimming pools) during the main season - where we know about this, and have the relevant dates, we indicate it, but if you are at all doubtful again it is wise to check.

We note an ever increasing number of 'special' pitches under a variety of fancy names (for example, Executive, Panorama, Super). These provide a range of extra facilities such as waste water disposal, TV and phone connections, patios, etc. and they are often booked up well in advance. We would suggest that readers interested is such pitches should contact the park concerned to check exactly what is provided and to pre-book if that is what they want. Disabled readers are also advised to telephone the park of their choice before turning up to ensure that facilities are appropriate to their particular needs.

Special thanks are due to Chris and Gerry Bullock for being out and about, continuing their work on facilities provided by parks for disabled visitors. See page 310 for their comments and recommendations. The Disabled Discrimination Act (DDA) 2000 requires parks to make reasonable adjustments for wheelchair users and persons with disabilities.

Quick Reference Sections
Our Guide includes several Quick Reference Sections, (see pages 303-308) which should enable you to quickly identify parks that:

| Are open all year | Do not accept children | Do not welcome dogs, |

and where there are facilities for:

| Fishing | Bicycle hire | Launching small boats |
| Horse riding | Golf | |

Maps
These start on page 321. The approximate position of each campsite is indicated on the map by the symbols: ● or ■ and the name of the site. The colour of the campsite name indicates whether it is open all year or not. The maps are to help you find the approximate location of campsites, not to navigate by! Each Site Report includes succinct directions as to how to find the site, based on the assumption that you will be using a proper road map, such as those produced by Ordnance Survey, the AA or RAC, etc. We include an Ordnance Survey Grid Reference in our Report in respect of sites in mainland Britain.

Index
Not one, but three - on page 329 you will find each campsite indexed by its number, and on page 334 by region, and on page 327 you will find an index of the villages or towns nearest to where the sites are situated.

Our Site Assessors
Finally we'd like to say a special thank you to to our Site Assessors for all their efforts and hard work:

Rosemary and George Boyce	Lorraine Houghton	Thelma and Jack Mitchell
Gordon and Joyce Pearce	Gerry Ovenden	Keith Smart
Gerry and Chris Bullock	Clare Edwards	Pauline and Chalky White
Donald and Rita Laycock	Carole and George Bolton	

We are, of course, also out and about ourselves, visiting parks, talking to owners and readers, and generally checking on standards, new developments, etc. For our 2003 edition we're delighted to feature sixty new parks, whereas about a dozen have been removed as they no longer meet the standards we require for their continued inclusion. We would like to wish all our readers thoroughly enjoyable Camping and Caravanning in 2003, favoured by good weather.

Alan Rogers

Lois Edwards MAEd, FTS
Clive Edwards BEd, FTS
Sue Smart   Directors

South West

Isles of Scilly, Cornwall, Devon, Somerset, Bath, Bristol,

South Gloucestershire, Wiltshire and Dorset

Address: Woodwater Park, Exeter, Devon EX2 5WT

Tel: 0870 442 0830 Fax: 0870 442 0840

E-mail: post@swtourism.co.uk

Internet: http://www.westcountrynow.com

If you've only ever thought of the West Country as a heavenly place for summer holidays it's time to think again. More than 400 attractions now stay open all year, so whatever the season, there's always a reason to visit the West Country. In a region where British winters are mildest, you can walk for miles in lovely countryside, along spectacular coastal paths and rolling moorland. If you need reviving drop into a country inn. You'll find the warm climate is mirrored by warm hospitality from people with time to chat.

Good food is an art in the West Country. Rich pastures provide the grazing for quality meats, while fresh fish and seafood is landed at quaysides along 600 miles of coast. Local cheeses and tasty Cornish pasties will tempt the taste buds and who can resist a West Country cream tea?

Spring comes early in the West, where the gentle climate encourages a profusion of flowers to bloom early. Cornwall's Festival of Spring Gardens takes place during early March through April and May, with over 70 gardens open to the public on different days.

Cornwall

While you're in Cornwall, take time out to visit some of area's other attractions like the Pilchard Works at Newlyn in Cornwall or the Wheal Martyn China Clay centre at St Austall and see the stunning scenery of Land's End. Artists have always loved the quality of light in the West and you will be equally inspired by the art exhibitions and the architecture of the Tate Gallery in St Ives.

Devon

Home to the English Riviera with the cosmopolitan atmosphere of Torquay, Paignton and Brixham on the palm fringed south coast. Nearby Salcombe and Dartmouth with the Royal Britannia Naval College, now open to the public, stands proud over the Dart Estuary are popular for watersports. Further west is the dramatic moorland of Dartmoor with wild ponies and granite tors. Clovelly, Ilfracombe and Lynton on the North coast are a stark contrast to the green moorland with long golden beaches and pretty harbours. For shopping and heritage visit the cities of Plymouth for The Hoe, Barbican area and National Marine Aquarium or the cathedral city of Exeter with it's beautiful Tudor buildings.

Somerset

The west is covered by Exmoor where you can travel by steam train from Bishop's Lydeard to the coast at Minehead. Visit lush gardens at Hestercombe and historic Forde Abbey. Glaston-bury Tor and Abbey have links to past dating thousands of years and while the caves and Gorge at Cheddar are spectacular. Weston Super Mare bustles with the noise of families as they enjoy the carnival atmosphere while the city of Taunton has a great range of shops, theatres and cafes.

Dorset

Land of Thomas Hardy and one of the best coastlines in the country for fossils which can be found along the three mile stretch of Chesil Beach or the cliffs of Lyme Regis. The seaside town of Weymouth is popular due to it's bustling nightlife and charming Georgian town houses.

Wiltshire

Where the West Country begins - is less than an hour from London. The cities of Bristol and Bath and beyond them, Exeter, Plymouth and Penzance, are all served by fast, direct rail services from London, the Midlands and the North.

To find out about exhibitions and events currently happening in the West Country, contact the Tourist Information Centre in the town or city you plan to visit. To get the number of the local TIC call 0870 442 0880.

River Valley Country Park

Relubbus, Penzance TR20 9ER

River Valley is a quiet park in the natural environment of a pleasant river valley. Run by Brian and Eileen Milson, it provides 150 large touring pitches well spaced in nooks and bays around the perimeters of small meadows or in natural clearings. All are clearly defined with shrubs, hedges or trees which have been planted to supplement where needed and in the more open areas to edge the pitch space thus giving your own individual area and increasing the sense of space. Most pitches have electrical connections (15A), some have hardstanding and there are special sections for families, couples, tents, dogs, etc. There are now 38 caravan holiday homes, some privately owned, in more or less separate areas, beside the river at the far end of the park or on the hillside at the back. There is no children's playground, but tame ducks on the river will entertain. A fence separates the park from the river and there is a pleasant walk for 2.5 miles alongside it, popular for dog walks. St Michael's Mount is only 3 miles and can be reached by footpath. Much of the valley is a protected nature reserve and the park encourages wildlife by not using weed killers and by leaving parts uncut - badgers, foxes, herons, kingfishers and glow-worms are regular visitors. A member of the Best of British group.

Facilities: Three good quality, carefully maintained toilet blocks are well placed for all pitches. Two male and two female family shower rooms are in the block at the far end. Some private cabins for ladies and a make-up room with hair dryers. Separate laundry facilities and baby bath. Covered dishwashing sinks. Motorcaravan service point (fresh water top up and waste water emptying). Shop/reception. **Off site:** Bicycle hire 5 miles, riding or golf 3 miles.

Charges 2002

Per unit incl. 2 adults	£6.00 - £11.00
extra adult	£1.00 - £3.25
child	£0.50 - £1.50
awning/pup tent	£1.00 - £3.00
dog	£1.00 - £3.00
electricity	£1.50 - £1.50

Min. charge 2 adults per vehicle. **Tel:** 0845 60 12 516. Fax: 01736 763398. E-mail: rivervalley@surfbay.dircon.co.uk. **Reservations:** Any period with deposit (£20). **Open** 23 March - 31 October and Christmas.

Directions: From A30 at St Michaels Mount roundabout, take A394 towards Helston. At next roundabout take B3280 to Relubbus. In approx. 3 miles in village turn left just over a small bridge. O.S.GR: SW566320.

Situated in one of the most picturesque Valleys in Cornwall

Located along the bank of a clear shallow stream, River Valley offers you a sense of utter peace and tranquillity.

Discover River Valley

- 150 Touring, Motorhome or Tent pitches
- 18 Acres of partly wooded countryside
- Luxury Caravan Holiday Homes available
- Shop and Launderette
- Wooden Lodges available

River Valley Country Park, Relubbus, Penzance, Cornwall, TR20 9ER
Tel 0845 60 12516 Fax 01736 763398
www.rivervalley.co.uk rivervalley@surfbay.dircon.co.uk

The low season 'go as you please' solution. With over 300 sites across Europe, all at just £8.50 per night, there's no need to commit yourself to a fixed itinerary.

Move freely from site to site as you wish, and enjoy incredibly low ferry prices as well. This discount scheme offers fantastic savings.

Enjoy the freedom - Enjoy the flexibility - Enjoy the ferry prices - Enjoy the savings

Call us now on 0906 22 44 800 for your Camping Cheque guide

(calls cost no more than £2 and entitle you to receive the 3 Seasons magazine 3 times yearly)

www.campingcheque.co.uk

Cardinney Camping Park

002 Crows an Wra, St Buryan, Penzance TR19 6HX

A friendly Geordie welcome awaits from the owner, Kevin Lindley, when you visit Cardinney, which is perfectly situated for visiting the famous Lands End beauty spots and tourist attractions and also within easy driving distance of small Cornish beaches and coves. With open unspoilt views, the level field is semi-divided into three camping areas and is neatly kept with some landscaping. Bushes have been planted, along with a central Cornish stone wall, allowing for 105 individual, marked, level pitches, 56 with 10A electricity and some with hardstanding, and a number of seasonal pitches. The combined café and bar acts as reception and a social point providing breakfasts, takeaway food at most times and good cheer in the evenings. Somewhat behind the site a National Trust viewpoint gives panoramic views to the Isles of Scilly, Cape Cornwall and the Lizard point and the ancient Iron Age settlement of Carn Euny is 20 minutes walk.

Facilities: The facilities are simple compared to many of the more sophisticated sites in Devon and Cornwall, the toilet block originally built over 30 years ago but adapted over the years. It includes a deep sink for babies, laundry facilities and one outside dishwashing sink with hot water. Games room with TV, pool table and video games. At times care and maintenance can be a little haphazard. **Off site:** Coastal, cliff top walks, surfing beaches and Minnack Open Air Theatre nearby. Fishing 3 miles, bicycle hire 5 miles, riding 7 miles.

Charges 2002

Per unit incl. 2 adults	£5.00 - £8.00
extra adult	£2.00
child (2-15 yrs)	£1.00
electricity	£1.75

Pets free. Less for stays over 2 weeks. **Tel:** 01736 810880. Fax: 01736 810998. E-mail: cardinney@ btinternet.com. **Reservations:** Made with £10 per week deposit. **Open** 1 February - 30 November.

Directions: Park is signed before Crows an Wra on main Penzance - Lands End A30 road, 5 miles west of Penzance. O.S.GR: SW426285.

Kelynack Caravan & Camping Park

052 Kelynack, St Just, Penzance TR19 7RE

An unspoilt, traditional campsite in a natural environment, Kelynack offers 11 caravan holiday homes to rent, space for 7 caravans (5 with 10A electricity) and a tent field taking 17 tents or small motor-caravans. The owner's Cornish cottage, two donkeys and a Bunk Barn overlook the camping field which is level with roughly mown grass and water points. The caravan pitches and mobile homes are found on the lower side of this small valley site, edged by bubbling clear streams and trees, part of which is a natural focus for children complemented by some play equipment. A covered area hidden near the stream, built of Cornish wood and slate, provides campers with a sheltered area to barbecue and to eat. This is an 'environ-mentally sensitive area' and part of the Heritage Coastline. Steve Edwards, the owner, is very conscious of this and the prehistoric heritage evident in the local monuments, tombs, stone circles and prehistoric villages. The mining of tin and copper has also left its mark, as has the sea. The dramatic coastline and cliffs are said to be one of the best climbing areas in the UK. Now tourism is the main emphasis, but ask Steve about the 'energy lines' - you could just be completely revitalised after your stay at this delightfully simple, but well cared for site.

Facilities: A central, clean and sturdy toilet block provides for all needs, including 2 en-suite units. Showers cost 20p for 6 minutes. Fully equipped laundry room with tourist information and washing up sink. Small shop for basics at reception. Gas supplies. Play area, table tennis. Bunk barn with 3 bunk rooms, shared shower room and kitchen. **Off site:** Pub within walking distance. Indoor pool, mountain bike hire, golf, shops and pubs at St Just, 1 mile. Coastal bus service passes near to the park in summer months. Sennen Cove with its magnificent surfing beach and Theme Park at Lands End are a short drive.

Charges 2002

Per person	£3.50
child 5-12 yrs	£1.75
child under 5 yrs	free - £1.75
electricity	£1.50

Tel: 01736 787633. Fax: 01736 787633. E-mail: steve@kelynackholidays.co.uk. **Reservations:** 25% deposit on booking, non-returnable, balance on arrival. **Open** April - October.

Directions: One mile from St Just on B3306 Lands End road. O.S.GR: SW374301.

Polmanter Tourist Park

Halestown, St Ives TR26 3LX

Polmanter is a good example of a sympathetic conversion of a farm from agricultural to leisure use and the Osborne family have developed the park well. The converted farm buildings provide a cosy bar lounge overlooking the heated swimming pool, toddler's pool and sunbathing area. Good value meals are served in the bar and there is a family area with high chairs. The new conservatory between the bar and the pool provides extra space for families (open all day, with a hot drinks machine). Occasional entertainment is organised in season. The 240 tourist pitches (no statics) are well spaced in several fields with growing shrubs and hedges giving individual pitch areas and connecting tarmac roads. There are 16 hardstandings, 190 electric hook-ups (16A) and 80 deluxe pitches with electricity, water and waste water. It is a busy park with a happy atmosphere within 1.5 miles of St Ives - a footpath leads from the park (20 minutes downhill) or there is a bus service from the park in high season (hourly, 10 am. - midnight). The park gates are closed midnight - 6.30 am. with outside parking. A member of the Best of British group.

Facilities: The toilet blocks vary - as the park has grown, so extra blocks have been added. There are now four, the latest being modern and good, the others refurbished and tiled. All can be heated and still incorporate the ideas of the first block, which include a wall cupboard for clothes in each shower to keep them dry. Two fully equipped en-suite family shower rooms, plus a baby changing room. Extra dishwashing sinks in the new block and good laundry provision. Well stocked, self service shop (shop and pool Whitsun - mid Sept). Bar, with food and family area (Easter, then Whitsun - mid Sept). Takeaway (4.30 - 7 pm). Swimming pool. Tennis courts. Play areas. Sports field. Games room with two pool tables, table tennis and games machines. **Off site:** Golf 1 mile, fishing, riding, bicycle hire and boat launching facilities within 2 miles. Indoor pool at St Ives. Note: Dogs are banned from the St Ives beaches in high season.

Charges 2002

Per unit incl. 2 persons, electricity	£12.50 - £17.50
incl. mains services and awning	£14.50 - £19.50
extra adult	£2.50 - £4.50
child (3-15 yrs)	£2.00 - £3.50
dog	£1.00

Tel: 01736 795640. Fax: 01736 793607. E-mail: reception@polmanter.com. **Reservations:** Made with £30 deposit. For 15/7-26/8 only: multiples of 7 nights with arrival on Fri, Sat or Sunday for electric pitches, multiples of 7 nights but any day arrival for non-electric pitches. **Open** Easter - 31 October (full facilities to 10 Sept).

Directions: Take B3074 to St Ives from the A30, then first left at a mini-roundabout taking 'Holiday Route' (B3311) to St Ives (Halestown). At T-junction turn right for Halestown, right again at the Halestown Inn then first left. O.S.GR: SW509392.

Little Trevarrack Tourist Park

Laity Lane, Carbis Bay, St Ives TR26 3HW

Little Trevarrack is a traditional Cornish park covering 16 acres with views from the top of the site across St Ives Bay towards Hayle and the surrounding countryside. It is now being updated by Neil Osborne, the son of the owners of Polmanter Park. There are 254 pitches, in five open fields (top ones with gentle slopes), 168 with 16A electricity. Bushes have been planted which will in time form hedging to provide individual type pitches. A new toilet block and children's play area have been built. Reception is clearly marked in the 'Kids Play Zone' which is situated at the site entrance. Carbis Bay is less than a mile and in high season a bus runs hourly into St Ives (10.00- 23.30 hrs). This is a developing site which will provide a quiet, peaceful base from which to explore St Ives and the southern tip of Cornwall.

Facilities: The new toilet block is central, modern and well equipped. An older, original block is open for the peak season only. Dishwashing sinks under cover. Laundry behind reception in the Kids Play Zone. Small shop in reception providing basics (but Tesco is nearby, also fish and chips and pasta restaurants). Children's play area and playing field. No kites allowed. Dogs are banned from the St Ives beaches in high season.

Charges 2002

Per unit incl. 2 persons	£8.50 - £13.00
extra adult	£2.00 - £3.50
child (3-15 yrs	£1.75 - £2.50
dog (max. 2)	£1.00
electricity	£2.50

Tel: 01736 797580. **Reservations:** Made with deposit of £25 per week booked. **Open** 15 May - 15 September.

Directions: Follow signs for St Ives and take A3074 at Carbis Bay. Site is signed on left opposite junction to Carbis Bay beach. Follow road for 150 yds, cross small crossroads and site is on right. O.S.GR: SW52737.

Cornwall
Ayr Holiday Park
003 Higher Ayr, St Ives TR26 1EJ

On first arrival Ayr Park seems to be all caravan holiday homes, but behind them, with marvellous views over St Ives Bay and Porthmeor beach, is a series of naturally sloping fields providing 40 touring pitches. Level, hard-core, terraced areas and hardstandings provide places for motor-caravans and caravans with 35 electrical connections (16A). With an extra field for tents open in July and August, the facilities could be a little hard-pressed, but were coping well when we visited in high season. St Ives centre and supermarkets are within easy walking distance, also the new Tate Gallery. There is direct access to the coastal footpath.

Facilities: The modern, well maintained toilet block, consisting of various parts, has controllable showers (some accessed direct from the outside and some with toilet), dishwashing sinks under cover and good laundry facilities. Motorcaravan waste point. Games room with pool table and TV, hot drinks and snack machines. Adventure play area and football field. One dog per pitch, up to medium size, is permitted but contact the park as dogs are not allowed on St Ives beaches in high season. **Off site:** Spa shop nearby.

Charges 2002

Per adult	£2.40 - £3.90
Per child (5-16 yrs)	£1.10 - £1.85
pitch	£4.75 - £10.20
car	£1.20
awning	£2.10 - 4.20
motorcycle	£1.20
dog	£1.10
electricity	£2.30

Tel: 01736 795855. Fax: 01736 798797. E-mail: reception@ayrstivesholidays.co.uk. **Reservations:** Made with £35 deposit. **Open** Easter/1 April - 31 October.

Directions: 300 yds after leaving the A30 turn left on A3074 at mini-roundabout following signs for St Ives for heavy vehicles and day visitors (not town centre direction). After approx. 2 miles this joins the B3311 and then the B3306 about 1 mile from St Ives (an octagonal building on your left). Still heading for St Ives turn left at a mini-roundabout following camping signs through residential areas. Park entrance is 600 yds at Ayr Terrace. O.S.GR: SW515388.

Cornwall
Trevalgan Holiday Farm
004 Trevalgan Farm, St Ives TR26 3BJ

We already have two very different sites in the St Ives area and Trevalgan is different yet again. Based on a working farm, it is a friendly, no frills site on the cliffs 1.5 miles west of St Ives, providing 120 clearly marked pitches (43 with 16A electricity) in a level stone walled field. The pitches vary in size as the park is very popular with walkers. There is direct access to the coastal path and it is a 45 minutes walk to St Ives. Tractor rides are possible in high season, plus farm and hill trails and there is a farm pets corner with baby chickens, two donkeys etc. It is in all quite an original type of park. A member of the Countryside Discovery group.

Facilities: A purpose built toilet block has curtained washbasins, plus a baby room, laundry and washing up, and even a hot drinks machine. Small shop (1/6-15/9). 'Farm House Kitchen' with takeaway (July/Aug), popular for breakfast or suppers. Gas available. Games field, play area and crazy golf. Games room in a barn with table tennis, pool, fruit machines and a comfortable upstairs TV room. **Off site:** Fishing 3 miles, bicycle hire, riding, golf, all within 2 miles. In July/Aug. bus service once a day from the park to St Ives (10 am. returning at 5 pm).

Charges 2002

Per pitch incl. 2 persons	£7.00 - £13.00
extra adult	£2.50 - £4.00
electricity	£2.50
dog	£0.50

Tel: 01736 796433. Fax: 01736 799 798. E-mail: trevalgan@aol.com. **Reservations:** Contact park. **Open** Easter - 30 September.

Directions: Approach site down a narrow Cornish lane from the B3306 St Ives - Lands End road, following sign. O.S.GR: SW490400.

Mullion Holiday Park
Helston TR12 7LJ

For those who enjoy plenty of entertainment, both social and active in a holiday environment, Mullion would be a good choice. The site is situated on the Lizard peninsula with its sandy beaches and coves. It is a holiday home park with all the trimmings - indoor and outdoor pools, super children's play areas, clubs, bars, and a wide range of nightly entertainment. These facilities form the core of the park and are well organised and managed. The touring area past the holiday homes has a more relaxed atmosphere and is set on natural heathland with clumps of bramble and gorse which provide breaks and recesses making for a more informal layout. Linked by a circular gravel road, all 160 pitches are numbered, 10 with hardstanding and 105 with electricity connections (16A). Land drainage could be a problem if there is heavy continuous rain. A resident warden is now based at the entrance to the touring section. Eurotents for hire. There is much to see in the area including Goonhilly Satellite Station and Flambards Village, the theme park, Lizard Point and Lands End.

Facilities: Central modern toilet block with additional 'portacabin' style facilities for high season. Dish-washing sinks under cover, two laundry sinks and two washing machines. Large launderette in main complex. Freezer pack service. Large supermarket with off licence. Pub with family room, restaurant and takeaway (half board or breakfast options). Moonshine Club with live shows and cabarets, big screen satellite TV. Excellent outdoor children's play areas (fenced). Toddlers' soft play area. Amusement arcade, bowling alley. Heated outdoor pool and paddling pool (26/5-8/9). Indoor fun pool with slide, both supervised. Sauna and solarium. Crazy golf, pitch and putt. Mountain bike hire. Barbecue.

Charges 2002

Per pitch (incl. free club membership)	£10.00 - £19.50
electricity	£2.95
awning	£3.00
dog (one only)	£5.00
'super hook-up' incl. TV point, fresh water	£4.75

Half board or breakfast options available. **Tel:** 0870 4445344. Fax: 01326 241141. E-mail: touring@ weststarholidays.co.uk. **Reservations:** Contact site. High season and Spr. B.H. bookings must be Sat. - Sat. **Open** 18 May - 13 September.

Directions: From Helston take A3083 for The Lizard and continue for 7 miles. Site on left immediately after the right turning for Mullion. O.S.GR: SW698185.

See also Sandford Park, page 97

Boscrege Caravan Park

Ashton, Helston TR13 9TQ

A pretty little site hidden deep in the countryside, Boscrege will suit those who want a quiet peaceful base for their Cornish holiday. The main large touring field nestles at the foot of Tregonning Hill with its striking hill top cross, and has neatly cut grass with a gentle slope from the top. The pitches are generously spaced around the edge, backing on to hedging and leaving plenty of room in the centre for ball games. Two small, attractive paddock areas, one with caravan holiday homes, the other for tourers, complete the total provision of 46 pitches, 36 with 10A electricity. It is a welcome retreat for couples and families with young children.

Facilities: The traditional style toilet block is nicely fitted out and recently tiled including a smaller basin for children (M/F). Dishwashing sinks, laundry sink, washing machine and dryer. Reception keeps emergency supplies (nearest shop at Godolphin). Two play areas for smaller children and central ball area. Meadows adjacent to the park may be used for recreation. Amusement machines and pool table.

Charges 2002

Per unit	£6.50 - £13.50
electricity	£2.50
extra small tent	£2.50

No charge for dogs (max. 3). **Tel:** 01736 762231. E-mail: enquiries@caravanparkcornwall.com. **Reservations:** Made with deposit of £35 per week or part week. **Open** Easter/1 April - 31 October.

Directions: From Helston take A394 for Penzance. At top of Sithney Common Hill turn right just before Jet garage on B3302 (Hayle) road. Pass Sithney General Stores on left and take next left for Carleen and Godolphin. Continue on this road to Godolphin village and turn left at side of Godolphin Arms signed Ashton. Proceed up hill and at top where road turns sharply left go straight over into lane leading to Boscrege. O.S.GR: SW593305.

Silver Sands Holiday Park

Kennack Sands, Ruan Minor, Helston TR12 7LZ

Silver Sands is a small, peaceful 'away-from-it-all' park in a remote part of the Lizard peninsula, the most southerly part of mainland Britain and an 'area of outstanding natural beauty'. The park is only reached after passing Culdrose Naval Base and the Goonhilly Earth Station down a single track road. Silver Sands is tucked away behind two other parks which provide static holiday homes with very little else. A half mile footpath leads down through a small valley to the twin beaches of Kennack Sands (one is dog-free) divided by a small headland. This is generally an unspoilt walking area with the coastal path passing through and under the care of English Nature. The park itself has 16 caravan holiday homes, along with 14 touring pitches with 5A electrical hook-ups for caravans and motorcaravans. They are large, attractively situated and divided into individual bays by growing flowering shrubs and bushes. An adjoining tent field has similar pitches (4 with electricity) where the shrubs are growing and the pitches in bays are slightly sloping. Reception, housed in an elderly static van, has a good supply of tourist information. A member of the Countryside Discovery group.

Facilities: The sanitary block is old and quaint, but it is well maintained. It includes, a laundry room, baby changing unit, dishwashing sinks and a microwave. Some play equipment and an undeveloped three-acre field can be used for walking, kite flying, etc. **Off site:** Shop 20 yards on the next site and pub within walking distance. Fishing 1 mile, bicycle hire 5 miles, boat launching 2 or 7 miles, riding 5 miles, golf 6 miles.

Charges 2002

Per unit incl. 2 persons	£5.70 - £7.70
extra adult	£2.00 - £3.20
Per child (3-13 yrs)	£1.10 - £1.80
extra car or boat	£1.00 - £1.40
dog	£1.00 - £1.60
electricity	£1.60

Reductions for some bookings. No credit cards. **Tel:** 01326 290631. Fax: 01326 290631. E-mail: enquiries@silversandsholidaypark.co.uk. **Reservations:** Made with 25% deposit, min. £30; balance on arrival. **Open** 1 May - 15 September.

Directions: From Helston take A3038 Lizard road. After Culdrose turn left on B3293 passing Goonhilly after 4 miles. At the next crossroads turn right (signed Kennack Sands, continue for 1.5 miles then left to Gwendreath on single track road - site is 1 mile. O.S.GR: SW732170.

Trelowarren Touring Caravan & Camping Park

Mawgan, Helston TR12 6AF

039

There is a sense of timelessness about Trelowarren. Perhaps it is the mature parkland or the mellow manor house, home to the Vyvyan family since 1427, but whatever, it is a beautiful, tranquil park set on the eastern side of the Lizard Peninsula, close to the banks of the Helford river. Access from the main road is via a single track road for one mile but it is well worth it. Set in 20 acres, there are three distinctive areas for camping all with neatly cut grass and providing 125 places for caravans and motorcaravans and 75 for tents. First is the walled gardens, originally designed for ripening fruit, with some pitches on a slight slope, then the apple orchard edged by the woods with a secluded area known as the quarry at the lower end, with some level but mainly sloping pitches. The third area is more open, with views across the valley and running parallel to the orchard, separated by Cornish stone walling. It has some mature trees and the main toilet block. There are 25 level hardstandings in this area which will fit the largest motorhomes. Just past the walled garden area, through a small door is the stable courtyard with the stylish Yard restaurant with its French chef, a Cornwall Craft Association Exhibition Centre, Art Gallery and Pottery and Weaving Studio not to mention the gardens and nurseries to visit and woodland walks (way-marked). Trelowarren becomes a most attractive place to spend some time with something for everyone in a relaxing, yet interesting and peaceful environment. There is also a lovely welcome from Ginger and Angeline who manage the park which sets the tone for your visit. The little pub is also very friendly and Ginger's milk bottle collection is quite amazing.

Facilities: The main sanitary facilities in original stone buildings are modern and attractively equipped with some washbasins in cubicles for ladies, and a bath. Five washing up sinks are under cover. Laundry room, complete with original stone walls and floor, providing three sinks, a washing machine and dryer. En-suite facility for disabled visitors. Baby room with three sinks. Extra small basic sanitary block with toilets, washbasins in walled garden area. Motorcaravan service point. Takeaway (1/7-3/9) and attractive little 'Inn'. Craft and Countryside Centre next door with licensed courtyard restaurant which is open at lunch-times and evenings. Games room with TV and pool table. **Off site:** Range of woodland walks to the Helford river and Tremayne Quay. Nearby Goonhilly Earth Station and the National Seal Sanctuary.

Charges 2002

Per person	£3.50 - £4.00
child (3-16 yrs)	£1.50 - £1.95
extra car or boat	£1.00
electricity	£1.80
dog	£1.00

Pitch and awning incl. No credit cards. **Tel:** 01326 221637. 01326 221427. E-mail: info@trelowarren. com. **Reservations:** Made with deposit (£15 p/week). **Open** 1 April/Easter - 30 September.

Directions: From Helston take A3083 for the Lizard. Just after Culdrose Naval Air Station turn left on B3293, signed St Keverne. Avoid turnings to both Gweek and Mawgan and watch for the Trelowarren signs on the left before reaching Goonhilly Earth Station. O.S.GR: SW719239.

Cornwall
Chacewater Park

001 Cox Hill, Chacewater, Truro TR4 8LY

For those who want to be away from the hectic coastal resorts and to take advantage of the peace and quiet of an 'adults only' park, this will be an excellent value-for-money choice. Chacewater has a pleasant rural situation and the site is run with care and attention by Richard Peterken and his daughters Debbie and Mandy. It provides 100 level touring pitches, all with electricity (10A) and 80 with hardstanding, in two large field areas (with a slight slope) edged with young trees or in smaller bays formed by hedging. There are 29 fully serviced pitches with electricity, water, drainage and sewage connections and one area for dog owners. The modern, new reception is not at the entrance but through the park to one side in a pleasant courtyard area and it also provides a small library and basic requirements. Truro is only 5 miles and there is a good choice of beaches north or south within 5-10 miles.

Facilities: The main toilet block provides well equipped showers and two en-suite units, along with dishwashing sinks under cover and a laundry room. Second fully equipped block near reception providing roomy showers open direct to outside. Gas supplies. Icepack service. Only adults are accepted (over 30 yrs). One dog only (by arrangement). **Off site:** Golf, riding and bicycle hire, all within 3 miles. Cornish tramways/railway coast to coast trail to walk or cycle nearby.

Charges 2002

Per unit incl. 2 persons from	£9.00
extra person	£4.00
electricity	£0.95
dog (one only)	£1.00

Weekly rates for pre- booked pitches. Discounts for senior citizens excl. August. Weekly rates for pre-booked pitches. **Tel:** 01209 820762. Fax: 01209 820544. E-mail: chacepark@aol.com. **Reservations:** Made with £15 deposit per week or part week, balance on arrival. **Open** 1 May - 30 September.

Directions: Chacewater can be approached either from the A390 road or from the A30. Park is 0.5 miles west of the village - follow signs. O.S.GR: SW742439.

Cornwall
Calloose Caravan Park

011 Leedstown, Hayle TR27 5ET

A family touring park quietly situated in an inland valley covering 12 acres Calloose is under new ownership. It is about 4 miles from Hayle, with an extra half a mile to the beaches beyond, 9 to St Ives on the north coast and 6 to Helston and Praa Sands on the south. Attractively landscaped with almost a tropical feel, units are personally sited. The terrain is mainly flat but is dry, with two slightly raised areas on terraces. There are 120 tourist pitches (96 with 10A electricity, 8 with water and 28 gravel hard-standings) close together with individual markers, and 17 caravan holiday homes. In the main meadow areas, pitches are arranged round the perimeter with some free space in the middle. A heated swimming pool and separate paddling pool are neatly landscaped with a sunbathing terrace and access for disabled people. A large recreation block with a themed bar and family room serves bar meals. Entertainment is organised every evening in the main season including weekly barbecues in peak season. All public areas have wheelchair access. A popular park, booking is essential. The new owners plan to open for Christmas and New Year.

Facilities: Both toilet blocks are well kept, providing washbasins in cubicles, a family shower room, baby room, en-suite unit for disabled visitors, dishwashing sinks under cover. Laundry room and first aid room. Well stocked shop and off-licence (including gas). Swimming pool (40 x 20 ft. open mid-May to mid-Sept). Bar with bar meals (daily in the main season, slightly restricted in early season). Takeaway (mid-May - late Sept). TV lounge, pool table, games room with skittle alley and arcade machines. All-weather tennis court. Crazy golf (floodlit). Table tennis. Adventure playground. Sun lounger and mountain bike hire and extensive local information available in reception. Four acres of recreation fields include dog exercise fields, a full size football pitch and mountain bike scramble track. **Off site:** Village with shops, pubs, etc. is within walking distance. Golf 4 miles, fishing 2 miles, riding 5 miles.

Charges 2002

Per unit incl. 2 persons	£7.00 - £13.00
extra person (over 3 yrs)	£1.00 - £3.00
pup tent (max 1.8 x1.2m)	£1.00 - £2.00
dog	£1.00 - £2.50
electricity	£2.00
'super' pitch plus	£2.00

Tel: 01736 850431. Fax: 01736 850431. **Reservations:** Made with £20 deposit per pitch, balance on arrival. **Open** 1 April - early November, plus Xmas and New Year.

Directions: From crossroads of B3280 and B3302 in Leedstown take the B3302 towards Hayle. First right, then left on 0.5 miles access road to park. O.S.GR: SW599353.

Carnon Downs Caravan & Camping Park

Carnon Downs, Truro TR3 6JJ

018

Carnon Downs is an excellent all year park run personally by Simon Valence whom some may know from his days at Leverton Park. This is a thoughtfully laid out, level park with attractive hedging and flowering shrubs providing some pleasant bays for caravans. Gravel roads connect 120 pitches, 100 with electricity (10/15A) and 20 with hardstanding. Of these 20 are fully serviced, with 8 new ones being exceptionally large. Tent pitches, some with electricity, are well spaced around the outside of two level fields, the centre of one for goal posts and adventure-type play equipment, the other containing the mobile home used as reception. Here you will receive a warm welcome, a neatly presented layout plan of the park and a touring information pack including comprehensive details on walks and cycle paths leading from the park. Some of the park's amenities are to be found in the round-house next to the TV and information room. The round-house used to house the donkeys that turned the mill which once operated on the site! Although one side of the park is next to the A39 road, it is well screened with a band of mature woodland so noise should be minimal. This quiet, quality family park is well situated to explore the tip of Cornwall. A member of the Best of British group.

Facilities: An excellent new heated block provides 12 en-suite units and dishwashing. Two other well maintained toilet blocks can also be heated and provide good facilities including some washbasins in cubicles. Showers are unisex, and once you have got used to the idea, it works well. One block includes three very good family bath/shower rooms, one suitable for use by disabled people or mothers and toddlers. Two good laundries, one in each block with freezers. Mother and toddler room (heated), including two baby sinks and a full sized bath. Motorcaravan service point (ask at reception). Gas, newspapers and caravan accessories. General room with TV, library, table tennis and tourist information. Recycling centre. Caravan storage. **Off site:** Brewsters' pub 100 yds across the road. Fishing 3 miles, riding or bicycle hire 2 miles, golf 1 mile. Walks direct from site.

Charges 2002

Per unit incl. 2 persons and electricity	£7.25 - £13.50
extra adult	£2.00
child (5-14 yrs)	£1.70
electricity	£2.25
all service hardstanding	£2.00

Small 2 man tent plus car less £1.00, walker or cyclist (single) less £3.00, double less £2.00. **Tel:** 01872 862283. E-mail: info@carnon-downs-caravan-park.co.uk. **Reservations:** Made with £20 deposit p/week. **Open** all year.

Directions: From Truro take A39 Falmouth road. There is direct access from the Carnon Downs roundabout after 3 miles. O.S.GR: SW805406.

Summer Valley Touring Park

Shortlanesend, Truro TR4 9DW

051

Approached down a short single track roadway from the Truro - Perranporth road this is a quiet and mature, but very pleasant, small rural park suitable for visiting both the north and south coast of Cornwall. South facing, the park consists of a large well kept grass area with reception and facilities to one side. A tarmac road circles this and mature trees edge the whole site providing shelter but still allowing rural views. Caravans go on the central area which slopes gently and is divided down the centre with more mature trees and shrubs. The pitches around the perimeter area are semi-divided by shrubs and used more for tents. In total there is provision for 60 units of all types, 45 with electricity connections (10/16A). The owners live on site and provide a warm welcome. A Countryside Discovery site.

Facilities: A good quality, solid toilet block is well maintained with ladies to the left and men to the right. Fully equipped, it has some washbasins in cabins and one shower/toilet en-suite each. Washing up and laundry sinks are part of the same building with a washing machine, dryer, spin dryer and iron. A pleasant little sitting room off to the side provides a small library and tourist information. Licensed shop with freezer pack service and reception (reduced hours out of main season). Gas supplies. Small play area hidden in a corner but part of the central area is left for ball games. **Off site:** Village of Shortlanesend within walking distance with post office and pub. Fishing 2.5 miles, golf 3 miles, riding 5 miles, and bicycle hire 2.5 miles. Perranporth beach 6 miles (dogs are allowed away from the village end).

Charges 2002

Per unit incl. 2 adults	£7.00 - £9.50
extra adult	£1.50
child 3-16 yrs	£1.00
electricity	£1.50
dog	£0.25

Tel: 01872 277878. E-mail: sv@summervalley.co.uk. **Reservations:** Made with deposit of £25 per week; balance on arrival. **Open** 1 April - 31 October.

Directions: From Truro take B3284 north, signed Perranporth. Follow for 2.5 miles and site is signed on left just through the village of Shortlanesend. O.S.GR: SW 800479.

Cornwall

Trethem Mill Touring Park

St Just-in-Roseland, St Mawes, Truro TR2 5JF

009

St Mawes is a very popular, pretty village on the Roseland peninsula, which is itself an 'area of outstanding natural beauty'. Only three miles away, Trethem Mill is well placed for either sailing, walking the coastal path, visiting the gardens of Trelissick or Heligan, or simply lazing on the nearby beaches. The Akeroyd family are proud of their park and work hard to keep it really well maintained. Trethem is a 'strictly touring' park with 84 pitches, of which 50 have 16A electricity and with several classified as all-weather. The pitches are large, most on slightly sloping ground, with the lower field more level and sheltered. All are individual or in bays, divided by hedging (some yet to grow) giving your own area. Generally there is a good spacious feel to the site, with a tarmac circular access road. The park has been carefully landscaped and is a mass of colour, the area around reception being particularly pretty where a small watermill has been built amongst the flowers - the sound of gently flowing water is very relaxing - and there are pet animals (do not feed)! Trethem Mill aims to attract couples and families seeking peace and tranquillity, without a bar and on site entertainment.

Facilities: The centrally located toilet block has been refurbished to a very high standard and it is kept spotlessly clean. Heated in cooler weather, it is well equipped, complete with baby room. Laundry and dishwashing sinks. Reception/shop, only small but very well stocked and licensed. Freezer for ice packs (free). Motorcaravan services. Children have a games room, and a well equipped, fenced adventure playground (closed at 9 pm). Large field alongside the park is used as a recreation and ball game area. Extra field for dog walk. **Off site:** Fishing 1.5 miles, boat launching 2 miles, bicycle hire 4 miles, riding 8 miles, golf 6 miles.

Charges 2003

Per unit incl. 2 adults	£8.00
Per person, cyclist or hiker	£5.00
extra adult	£3.00
child (4-16 yrs)	£2.00
electricity	£2.00
dog	£1.00
extra car or pup tent	£1.00

Tel: 01872 580504. Fax: 01872 580968. E-mail: reception@trethem-mill.co.uk. **Reservations:** Made with £30 deposit. **Open** 27 March - 13 October.

Directions: From Tregony follow A3078 to St Mawes. Approx. 2 miles after passing through Trewithian, watch for caravan and camping sign. O.S.GR: SW862364.

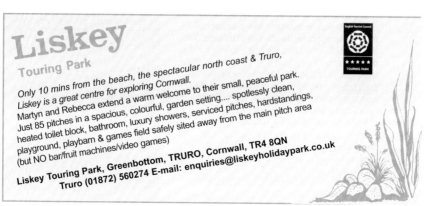

Pennance Mill Farm Chalet & Camping Park

Maenporth, Falmouth TR11 5HY

045

Pennance Mill Farm has been in the hands of the Jewell family for three generations. Listed as a typical Cornish farmstead, you can still watch the cows being milked and enjoy tractor rides. The camping park is friendly and relaxed, situated in three sheltered south-facing and fairly level meadows with views over the fields and providing for 70 pitches, 50 of which have 16A electricity. An old mill wheel reminds one of the site's origins and you book in at the farmhouse. Continuing on past the site for half a mile, you come to the sandy beach at Maenporth. Across the road and up a footpath you can reach Maen Valley Holiday Park where you can use their shop and club bar, enjoy good value food and where there is a nice atmosphere and some entertainment.

Facilities: There are two toilet blocks, the first near the entrance is the original one but it is well kept and provides a washing machine, dryer and laundry sinks. The new block in the top meadow is heated and well equipped and includes covered washing up sinks. Small farm shop including some basic provisions (open 9.00-10.30 and 5.30-6.30). Gas available. Children have a small play meadow with a swing and climbing frame, and table tennis. **Off site:** Within walking distance are tennis courts, a golf course and pitch and putt.

Charges 2002

Per pitch with two persons	£9.00 - £10.50
extra adult	£3.00 - £3.50
child over 3 yrs	£1.00
awning	£1.00
dog	£0.70
electricity	£2.00

Tel: 01326 317431. **Fax:** 01326 317431.
Reservations: Contact park. **Open** Easter - November.

Directions: From Truro, follow signs for Falmouth on A39. At first roundabout pass Asda then turn right at next roundabout signed Maenporth and industrial estates (on Bickland Water Road). Pass Maen Valley Holiday Park after 1.5 miles and continue down the hill to site on your left as the road bends to the right. O.S.GR: SW789307.

Liskey Holiday Park

Greenbottom, Truro TR4 8QN

013

Liskey is a quiet, family run park, pleasantly landscaped with rockery plants and well manicured grass - first impressions of loving care are carried all through the park. The main, slightly sloping camping area is beautifully landscaped with trees, shrubs and heathers and the level, well spaced pitches have good views across the countryside. The 4 seasonal and 81 touring pitches have 10A electricity and 12 are fully serviced with level hardstanding and a gravel area for awnings. Sixteen holiday homes are in a separate area. There is a great feeling of spaciousness, mainly because the enthusiastic new owners do not try to fit in too many units. Breathable groundsheets are welcome on the grassy pitches. A pub with good food and real ale is only 600 yards and buses to Truro pass the gate. Liskey is a good place for the family that can amuse itself without the need for discos and gaming machines.

Facilities: The central, very clean and well maintained toilet block can be heated. A second block is planned. Some washbasins are in cubicles. Family bathroom (50p). Well equipped laundry room and dishwashing sinks under cover. Motorcaravan service point. Shop for basics at reception, plus excellent maps. Adventure playground. Volleyball and basketball nets. Table tennis. Winter caravan storage. **Off site:** Coarse fishing 400 yards, bicycle hire 3 miles, riding 2 miles, golf 1 mile. Within 5 miles are beaches and facilities for tennis and boat launching. Truro supermarkets 3 miles.

Charges 2002

Per unit incl. 2 persons	£8.50 - £11.00
extra person (over 3 yrs)	£2.00
electricity	£2.00
serviced pitch	£3.00

Low season discounts for over 50s, fully retired. **Tel:** 01872 560274. **Fax:** 01872 561413. E-mail: enquiries@liskeyholidaypark.co.uk. **Reservations:** Made with £3 deposit per night booked or payment in full if less than 5 days. **Open** 1 March - 31 October.

Directions: From the A30 take A390 to Truro. At the next roundabout turn right (signed Threemilestone) and, immediately at mini-roundabout, right again towards Chacewater. Park is 600 yds on right past small business unit. O.S.GR: SW772452.

Cornwall
Silverbow Park
Goonhavern, Truro TR4 9NX

012

Silverbow has been developed by the Taylor family over many years and they are justifiably proud of their efforts. A select, spacious park, they seek to encourage couples and quiet families with young children (no teenagers over 12). The Taylors believe Silverbow is a way of life and staying is an experience - they have certainly created a relaxed and tranquil atmosphere. Hard work, planting and landscaping has provided a beautiful environment set in 21 acres which has, in the past, taken part in the well known 'Gardens Scheme'. There are 90 tourist pitches of a good size, plus 69 'super' pitches with electricity, water and drainaway, which are even larger. Many are on a slight slope with some attractive views. There are also 15 park-owned, high quality leisure homes. Much free space includes an excellent sports area with two all-weather tennis courts, two outdoor badminton courts, as well as wild meadow and wooded areas ideal for walks. A natural area with ponds has been created to encourage wildlife (Silverbow was the first in Cornwall to gain the coveted '5-year' Bellamy gold award for conservation).

Facilities: Three toilet blocks, all of excellent quality, have private cabins for each sex, four family shower/toilet rooms, two accessible for wheelchairs, and one bath on payment for each sex. Enclosed washing-up sinks. Laundry room. Recycling bins. Free freezer service. Shop (mid May-mid Sept). Attractive, kidney shaped, heated swimming pool and small paddling pool (open mid-May - mid-Sept) sheltered by high surrounding garden walls. Games room with pool table, table tennis and tourist information. Children's adventure playground and general play field. Tennis (free coaching in season) and badminton courts. Short mat bowls. Mountain biking from the park (but no bikes on site). **Off site:** Gliding, riding and fishing nearby. Concessionary green fees available at Perranporth golf club. Pub within walking distance. Park is 2.5 miles from the long sandy beach at Perranporth (30 minutes walk away from traffic) and 6 miles from Newquay.

Charges 2002

Per unit incl. 2 adults	£6.00 - £14.00
extra adult under 50 yrs	£3.00 - £6.00
child (2-12 yrs) or adult over 50 yrs	£2.00 - £4.00
dog	free - £1.50
full service pitch incl. electricity	£3.00

Children over 12 yrs with or without parents not accepted. Discounts available. **Tel:** 01872 572347. **Reservations:** Made with £20 p/week deposit (Sat. - Sat. only 17/7-21/8). **Open** 4 May - 28 September.

Directions: Entrance is directly off the main A3075 road 0.5 miles south of Goonhavern. O.S.GR: SW781531.

Penrose Farm Touring Park

Goonhavern, Truro TR4 9QF

014

Penrose Farm is a quality, family park for tourers only, on the edge of the village of Goonhavern. The park is level and sheltered, the 100 pitches spread over five fields with flower beds and bushes set amongst them. These flowers and those at the entrance are very colourful and give the park a neat, orderly and well cared for feel. The present, enthusiastic owners, Alan and Sharman, enjoy getting to know their customers, many of whom come every year, and take pride in the pitches and facilities they provide. Children not only have an excellent adventure playground but also an indoor animal centre with guinea pigs, rabbits, chickens, fish, terrapins and birds to admire. There are 52 pitches with 16A electricity and 8 pitches with hardstanding (4 with electricity). Alan always ensures that each unit has plenty of space and does not feel overcrowded. It is only a short walk to the village and its popular pub, and buses to Newquay stop in the village. The superb beach at Perranporth is only 2.5 miles. To retain its quiet family image, there are no plans for bars or entertainment and only couples and families are admitted.

Facilities: The fully equipped toilet block also provides four excellent family rooms containing an adjustable shower, washbasin, WC and hairdryer. One of these rooms is also accessible for wheelchairs. The owners have a love of plants and all these amenities are enhanced with beautiful pot plants and flowers. Well equipped laundry. Dishwashing sinks provided. Small shop for gas and basics (Easter, then May - Sept). Adventure playground. Caravan storage. Bicycle hire can be arranged. **Off site:** Fishing or riding 0.5 miles, golf 1 mile.

Charges 2002

Per unit incl. 2 persons	£8.00 - £12.00
extra person (5 yrs and over)	£3.00
awning	free
extra car	free
dog	free
electricity	£2.00

Families and couples only. Less 50p for over 60s if booked. **Tel:** 01872 573185. **Reservations:** Made with £30 deposit. **Open** 1 April - 31 October.

Directions: Take A30 from Exeter past Bodmin and Indian Queens. Just after wind farm take B3285 to Perranporth. Park is on the left as you enter Goonhavern village. O.S.GR: SW790535.

Trethiggey Touring Park

Quintrell Downs, Newquay TR8 4LG

053

Trethiggey is a garden-like park with a ten month season, set some three miles back from the busy Newquay beaches and night life. The 157 pitches are in sharp contrast to some of the large, open fields of some of the bigger sites, broken up by trees, shrubs and plants to provide a pleasant 'green' atmosphere. With natural areas including a small wildlife pond and a fishing lake to enjoy, conservation is high on the agenda. There are 94 numbered pitches with electricity (6-12A) and 32 with hardstanding. Interspersed amongst the touring pitches are 12 caravan holiday homes and a tent field is open in the main season. Some level pitches are formally arranged with others more informal on gently sloping grass. Facilities keep the informal touch with reception alongside the Trethiggey Trading Post which provides basic supplies, an off licence and a small library. A snack bar with covered eating area operates in the school holidays for breakfasts and simple evening meals, curries etc. with children catered for.

Facilities: The single, traditional style toilet block can be heated and is fully equipped, including an 'easy access' toilet/washbasin for disabled people, a wet suit washing point, laundry and dishwashing sinks. Games room also here with TV, two amusement machines and a pool table. When we visited, a new toilet block was being completed near the tent area to providing en-suite toilet/washbasins, showers, unit for the disabled and a laundry room to increase facilities for high season. Shop. Snack bar/takeaway. Pay area, games room and recreation field. Coarse fishing. **Off site:** All the delights of Newquay within 3 miles with nightly mini bus service (book in shop). Pub within walking distance.

Charges 2002

Per adult	£3.40 - £6.00
child	free - £2.00
electricity	£2.30
awning	free - £1.00
car	free - £1.00
dog	£1.50

Min. stay is 3 nights at B.Hs. **Tel:** 01637 877672. Fax: 01637 879706. **Reservations:** Made with £15 deposit per pitch, per week. **Open** 2 March - 2 January.

Directions: Site is a few hundred yards south of roundabout where A393 crosses the A3058 at Quintrell Downs (beside the A3058). O.S.GR: SW846596.

Newperran Tourist Park

Rejerrah, Newquay TR8 5QJ

016

This is a large, level park in rural Cornish countryside. Being on high ground makes it quite open but also gives excellent views of the coast and surrounding district. Keith and Christine Brewer are the new owners with plans to improve and develop the site in the next few years. Newperran is only 2.5 miles from Perranporth beach, but there is a free heated swimming pool on site. Those who prefer traditional camping to a holiday camp atmosphere should appreciate this park. This is not to say that it is without facilities; it certainly has its full share of amenities, but it is a quiet park used mainly by families and with few evening activities. It does have a licensed bar and restaurant open every evening, more in high season. The park consists of a number of flat, well drained, hedged meadows divided into 250 individual pitches. Some fields have larger and reservable plots, with more free space in the middle. There are 113 electrical connections (10A) including 13 'all-service' pitches.

Facilities: Sanitary facilities comprise four clean blocks, two heated. Most washbasins are in cabins, there are two bathrooms, baby room with sink and changing mat, hairdressing room and a unit for disabled visitors. Dishwashing sinks. Launderette. Good self-service licensed shop. Licensed bar and restaurant with takeaway (both B.Hs and main season, as required in low season). Outdoor swimming pool with paddling pool (Whitsun - Sept). TV room. Adventure playground and separate toddlers play area. Crazy golf. **Off site:** Riding or golf 2 miles. Fishing 1 mile. Goonhavern village within walking distance with pubs and post office.

Charges 2002

Per adult	£3.60 - £6.15
child (3-16 yrs)	£1.80 - £3.10
car	£0.80 - £0.90
dog	£0.65 - £1.10
electricity	£2.40
serviced pitch	£6.00

Tel: 01872 572407. Fax: 01872 571254. E-mail: holidays@newperran.co.uk. **Reservations:** Advised in high season; made with £25 p/w deposit and £2.50 fee. **Open** Easter - mid-September.

Directions: Turn off A3075 to west at camping sign 7 miles south of Newquay and just north of Goonhavern village. O.S.GR: SW794546.

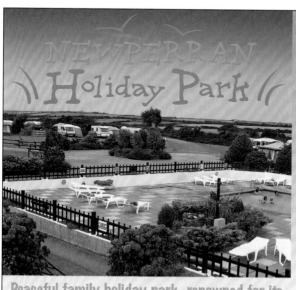

Peaceful family holiday park, renowned for its spacious, flat perimeter pitching, with breathtaking open countryside and sea views.

- Modern heated toilet block
- free showers · bathrooms
- baby rooms
- disabled facilities
- premium all-service pitches
- launderette
- shop/off licence
- cafe/bar · TV room
- games room · crazy golf
- adventure playground
- toddlers play area · aviary
- outdoor heated swimming pool with sunbathing terraces

Rallies Welcome

Rejerrah, Newquay,
Cornwall TR8 5QJ
Tel: 01872 572407
Fax: 01872 571254
www.newperran.co.uk

Trevella Caravan & Camping Park

Crantock, Newquay TR8 5EW

One of the best known and most respected of Cornish parks with its colourful flower-beds and driveway (a regular winner of a 'Newquay in Bloom' award), Trevella is also one of the first to fill up and has a longer season than most. Well organised, the pitches are in a number of adjoining meadows, most of which are on a slight slope. Of the 250 pitches for touring units (any type), some 200 can be reserved and these are marked, individual ones. Over 200 pitches have electricity (10A), with 33 'premium' serviced pitches (with hardstanding, electricity and TV hook-ups, water, waste water, sewage). Trevella is essentially a quiet family touring park with an accent on orderliness and cleanliness; on-site evening activities are limited. Access is free to three fishing lakes, two on site, with some fishing instruction and wildlife talks for youngsters in season. There is a pleasant walk around the lakes, a protected nature reserve, and it is also possible to walk to Crantock beach but check the tides first. A member of the Best of British group.

Facilities: The sanitary facilities are kept very clean, three blocks providing sufficient coverage with individual washbasins in private cabins for ladies, hair dressing room and a baby room. Launderette. Well stocked supermarket and heated outdoor pool (both Easter - October). Freezer pack service. Nicky's Kitchen offers hot dishes and snacks to take away or eat there, open late. Games room with pool tables and table tennis. Separate TV room. Crazy golf, large adventure playground, separate play and sports area and a pets corner. Fishing (permits from reception). **Off site:** Shuttle bus service to Newquay in high season. Nearest beach is 0.5 miles on foot, 1 mile by car and Newquay is 2 miles. Pubs and restaurants at Crantock, 1 mile. Riding 1 mile, golf 3 miles

Charges 2002

Per unit incl. 2 adults and electricity	£9.70 - £14.80
incl. mains services and awning	£12.95 - £18.05
extra adult	£3.25 - £5.75
child (3-16 yrs)	£1.50 - £2.75
dog	£0.60 - £1.20

Families and couples only. **Tel:** 01637 830308. Fax: 01637 830155. E-mail: trevella@AOL.com.
Reservations: Made with £20 deposit and £2 booking fee (16/7-27/8: Fri/Fri or Sat/Sat only). **Open** Easter - 31 October.

Directions: To avoid Newquay leave A30 or A392 at Indian Queens, straight over crossroads with A39 and A3058, left at A3075 junction and first right at camp sign. O.S.GR: SW802598.

See advertisement on pages 24-25

Trevornick Holiday Park

Holywell Bay, Newquay TR8 5PW

Trevornick, once a working farm, is now a busy and well run family touring park providing a very wide range of amenities close to one of Cornwall's finest beaches. A modern reception with welcoming staff sets the tone for your holiday. The park is well managed with facilities and standards constantly monitored and staff happy to help. It has grown to provide caravanners and campers (no holiday caravans but some tour operator tents) with 450 grass pitches (350 with 10A electricity and 55 fully serviced) on five level fields and two terraced areas. There are few trees, but some good views. Providing 'all singing, all dancing' facilities for fun packed family holidays, the farm buildings now provide the setting for the Farm Club. Furnished in keeping, it has licensed facilities and food, children's rooms and a cafeteria 'De caff' with terrace and takeaway, plus much entertainment from bingo, quizzes to shows, discos and cabaret. The rest of the development provides a pool complex, an 18 hole golf course, with a small, quiet clubhouse offering bar meals and lovely views out to sea and three fishing lakes. An innovative idea is the 'Hire shop' where it is possible to rent anything you might have forgotten from sheets, a fridge, travel cot etc. to a camera or a wet suit to catch the famous Cornish surf!

Facilities: Five toilet blocks of a standard modern design provide coin-operated showers (20p), a family shower room, two bathrooms (50p), baby bath, dishwashing, laundry facilities, and provision for disabled visitors. Well stocked supermarket with fresh bread made on site (both from late May). Hire shop. Bars (with TV), restaurant, cafe and takeaway. Entertainment (every night in season). New pool complex planned for 2003. Sauna and gym. Super Fort Knox style adventure playground, crazy golf, Kiddies Club and indoor adventure play area (supervised for 2-8 yr olds at a small charge). Bicycle hire. Coarse fishing with three lakes. Dogs are accepted in one field only. **Off site:** Next door is the Holywell Bay 'fun' park (site pass gives reduced rates) and the sandy beach is five minutes by car. Boat launching 4 miles, riding within 1 mile.

Charges 2002

Per adult	£3.35 - £6.15
child (4-14 yrs)	free - £4.00
car	£1.00
electricity	£3.00
'super' pitch incl. electricity	£7.50
dog	£2.00

Families and couples only. **Tel:** 01637 830531. Fax: 01637 831000. E-mail: info@trevornick.co.uk.
Reservations: Made with £20 deposit per week (Sat. to Sat. only July/Aug). **Open** Easter - mid September.

Directions: From A3075 approach to Newquay - Perranporth road, turn towards Cubert and Holywell Bay. Continue through Cubert to park on the right. O.S.GR: SW776586.

See advertisement on pages 24-25

Cornwall
Hendra Holiday Park

Newquay TR8 4NY

Hendra is a long-established holiday park for the family that likes to be entertained, as the entertainment programme here is very comprehensive. There are comedians, bands, cabaret, dancing, bingo, discos, plus entertainment and clubs for children. The 700 pitches are on various well mown, slightly sloping grass fields with country views and mature trees, some more sheltered than others. There are tarmac roads and lighting and 200 pitches have electrical connections (16A). Some landscaped hardstanding 'super' pitches have individual water, electricity, light, sewer drainage and satellite TV connections (dogs are not accepted on these pitches). Many pitches also have water, drainage and hardstanding. There are caravan holiday homes for hire but they are separate from the tourers. The entrance and reception are very attractive with a mass of well tended flower beds which, along with the other facilities, form an attractive, village-like centre to the park. The 'star of the show' at Hendra is the Oasis complex consisting of a 30 m. indoor, heated fun pool with three flumes, river rapids, water falls and beach. The complex is open to the public - really a mini water-park. The new outdoor heated pool is free to campers. Hendra welcomes families and couples.

Facilities: The three toilet blocks provide vanity style washbasins, free showers and some facilities for babies and disabled visitors. Large launderette. Motorcaravan services. Gas supplies. Well stocked shop. Various bars and restaurants, open all season (limited hours in early season), breakfast included. Pizzeria (main season only). Takeaway. Outdoor swimming pool. Indoor pool complex (cost £2.20 per family group, max. 4 persons, under 5s free; timed sessions if very busy). Play areas. Tennis. Minigolf. Bowling. Large playing fields, adventure play areas, table tennis, pool tables and a very large array of slot machines. **Off site:** Fishing or riding 1 mile, bicycle hire or golf 2 miles. Park is only 1.5 miles from Newquay and its fabulous surfing beaches - a bus to the town passes the gate.

Charges 2002

Per adult	£3.30 - £5.90
child (3-14 yrs)	free - £3.65
vehicle	£1.00
awning	free
'super' pitch (electricity, water, chemical disposal, TV point, hardstanding, no dogs)	£7.95
hardstanding pitch (electricity, water, drainage)	£3.95
electricity only	£2.95
dog	£2.00

Families and mixed couples only. **Tel:** 01637 875778. Fax: 01637 879017. E-mail: hendra.cornwall@dial.pipex.com. **Reservations:** Made with deposit (£20) and fee (£3). **Open** 23 March - 31 October.

Directions: Park is on left side of A392 Indian Queens - Newquay road at Newquay side of Quintrell Downs. O.S.GR: SW833601.

See advertisement on pages 24-25

Cornwall
Newquay Holiday Park

Newquay TR8 4HS

This park lies peacefully on a terraced hillside only just outside the town, two miles from the beaches and town centre. Its main feature is an attractively laid out group of three heated swimming pools with a giant water slide (lifeguards in attendance) and surrounding 'green' sunbathing areas. Mainly a touring park, it has 348 marked pitches for any type of unit in a series of hedged fields, some sloping. Some fields are just for caravans, others are for tents, plus 138 caravan holiday homes (for hire). Most pitches are individual ones marked out by lines on ground but with nothing between them. Electricity points (16A) are provided for caravans and tents, plus 10 special 'star' pitches with hardstanding, water and drainage. Entertainment is provided each night with live music, discos etc. in the site's Fiesta Club which also has a bar, TV lounge and games room with pool and snooker tables (all open when the site is open). A bus service runs to Newquay from the main road at the site entrance.

Facilities: Two good-sized, modern toilet blocks provide fairly basic free hot showers (pre-mixed hot water which runs for four minutes and stops). An extra block is opened for the main season when facilities may be under pressure. Baby bath. Covered external dishwashing sinks. Full launderette with free ironing. Well stocked self-service shop (gas available at reception). Bar/lounge with Sky TV. New café/restaurant with all day food also 'pub grub' in evenings (all season and good value). Outdoor pool complex with slide (and lifeguards). Pitch and putt and crazy golf. New playground for little ones and adventure play area for older children, children's club and recreation field for football and volleyball. Amusement arcade. Dogs or other pets are not accepted.

Charges 2002

Per unit incl. 2 persons	£6.00 - £18.50
with electricity	£7.50 - £21.50
extra person (over 3 yrs; up to 4 people)	free - £2.00
awning	free - £0.50
serviced pitch supplement	£1.00

Families and mixed couples only. **Tel:** 01637 871111. Fax: 01637 851973. E-mail: bookings@newquay-hol-park.demon.co.uk. **Reservations:** Advised for peak season and made with £25 deposit p/wk. **Open** Easter - October.

Directions: Park is east of Newquay on A3059 road 1 mile east of junction with A3058. O.S.GR: SW853626.

Cornwall
Trekenning Tourist Park
Newquay TR8 4JF

031

Trekenning is owned by John Fynn, his daughter Tracey and son-in-law Skegs and they have succeeded in developing a popular park with good facilities, a nice change from the 'all singing, all dancing' Newquay sites. Easy access just off the A39 roundabout at St Columb Major leads to a large sloping field with neatly cut grass and all the facilities in the opposite corner, colourful with potted plants. In total there are 75 pitches, 68 with 10A electricity. Some have been levelled, others are tucked away at a lower level shaded by tall trees. A well hidden tent field with just a water point is edged by a wooded small stream. The star of the show is undoubtedly the kidney shaped pool and paddling pool which are in a garden-like setting with gazebos and sun loungers, with a terraced lawn and patio at the top. This leads to the games room and cosy 'olde worlde' upstairs bar. Entertainment is provided every night in the main season (for example, singers, quiz nights, 'Connect-4' nights, discos on Fridays). The A39 runs parallel to one side of the site, so there may be road noise.

Facilities: Two sanitary blocks, one providing normal showers and vanity style washbasins, the other with two en-suite bathrooms and six large family showers, well refurbished. Laundry room. Covered dishwashing sinks. Shop for basics. Free freezer service. Play area. Outdoor pool (Whitsun - end Aug). Games room with table tennis and pool and some amusement machines. Characterful bar with food and takeaway (B.Hs and July/Aug). **Off site:** Fishing 1 mile, riding and golf 2 miles, bicycle hire 6 miles.

Charges 2002

Per adult	£3.50 - £5.40
child (3-15 yrs)	free - £3.90
electricity	£2.90
extra vehicle	£1.10
dog	£2.00

Tel: 01637 880462. Fax: 01637 880500. E-mail: enquiries@trekenning.co.uk. **Reservations:** Made with £20 deposit. **Open** Easter/1 April - 2 November.

Directions: Take A3059 turning to Newquay from St Columb Major then turn immediately left; park is signed (this was the old road). O.S.GR: SW907625.

Cornwall
Southleigh Manor Naturist Holiday Club
St Columb Major TR9 6HY

024N

Southleigh is a secluded, popular naturist site in the mature grounds of a large house, well located for touring Cornwall. Naturist owners, Kathy and Bob, extend a warm welcome to all visitors, who include good numbers from Europe, creating an international, relaxed atmosphere. The sheltered, south-facing touring area slopes gradually, providing 41 spacious pitches on well manicured lawns. All have 10A electricity and a limited number have hardstanding. There are nine touring vans to let. Social events are organised including barbecues, quiz nights and a weekly (Wednesday) boule tournament followed by locally made hot pasties. There is the opportunity to enjoy Cornwall's naturist beaches and many tourist attractions, which combine to provide a relaxed holiday atmosphere. Occasional aircraft noise.

Facilities: The purpose built toilet block has identical, well equipped, unisex units at each end, well maintained, with a laundry room in the middle. Showers cost 20p. Small shop - bread, milk, papers and tourist information (late May - 31 Aug). Bar area and bistro with good food. Pool table. Small outdoor swimming pool (heated most of the season). Sun room/leisure suite including sauna and spa bath in the house. Boules, volleyball, table tennis and minigolf. Play area with tree house and gaily painted train. **Off site:** Fishing 4 miles, bicycle hire 7 miles, riding 2 miles, golf 5 miles. Eden Project 15-20 minutes.

Charges 2002

Per unit incl. 2 adults	£13.50 - £15.00
extra adult	£2.75 - £2.85
child (14 yrs and under)	£1.30 - £1.50
extra pup tent	£1.25
electricity	£1.95
dog	£0.95
Club membership per couple/family per stay	£2.50

No credit cards. **Tel:** 01637 880938. Fax: 01637 881108. E-mail: enquiries@southleigh-manor.com. **Reservations:** Contact site for details. **Open** week before Easter - end October.

Directions: From north on A30 Bodmin - Truro road, after village of Victoria pass crossroad (Roche Cross) and go under iron railway bridge and then first right on A3059 towards St Mawgan and St Columb. Site is on left in 3 miles. From A39, take A3059 at Newquay/St Columb roundabout and site is on right, almost immediately. O.S.GR: SW904622.

Cornwall
Sea View International
Boswinger, Gorran Haven, St Austell PL26 6LL

015

Sea View is one of the best examples of a well cared for, quality park and this is reflected in the number of awards it has won. In the hands of the third generation of the Michell family, the park is constantly being improved with the aim of providing quality camping for the discerning camper. Although somewhat exposed, the park is colourful with flower beds and flowering shrubs and has well manicured grass of exceptional quality. The area around the pool is particularly attractive, with free sun-beds on tiled terraces surrounded by flowers creating private little areas, all with magnificent views of the sea and the distant headland. An attractive covered, flowered walkway with hanging baskets, connects two excellent toilet facilities, topped by a handsome clock tower. There are no bars, restaurant or evening entertainment which seems to be the main reason many return year after year. Many of the 163 large, level pitches have views, all have 16A electricity and 47 are fully serviced, including 12 hardstandings suitable for large motorhomes. There are 38 caravan holiday homes for hire in a separate area. Anyone not restricted by school holidays will find May and June a particularly good time to visit, the gardens of Heligan and Trelissick and Lanhydrock House being at their best at that time. A member of the Best of British group.

Facilities: Excellent toilet blocks are central, well maintained, with good quality fittings and central heating. Large showers, baby baths, facilities for disabled visitors (two showers and WCs), and a hairdressing area, plus bathrooms (on payment). Smart dishwashing area with two small campers' kitchens (one with a microwave, one with a mini-grill and hob) and a well equipped laundry. Motorcaravan service point with car washing facilities. Shop and off-licence with gas (June-end Sept). Takeaway (Whit-mid Sept). Swimming pool (all season, heated end May-mid Sept). Barbecue area with tables and seats at the top of the park has a descriptive weather map updated daily. Excellent large play field for leisure activities including tennis, volleyball, badminton, football, putting, table tennis, crazy golf, petanque, fenced play area for under-sevens. Adventure playground. Bicycle hire. Certain breeds of dog are not accepted. **Off site:** Fishing 0.5 miles, boat launching 2 miles, riding 1 mile, golf 9 miles. The area is full of places to visit from theme parks to the seal sanctuary, not forgetting the safe beaches, one of which is only a half mile walk from the park.

Charges 2002

Per unit incl. 2 persons and electricity	£5.00 - £19.00
incl. mains services and awning	£6.00 - £20.00
extra adult	£1.00 - £4.00
child (5-14 yrs)	£1.00 - £3.00
pup tent (outside 18/07-27/08)	free - £1.90
dog (limited breeds and numbers)	free - £2.00

Tel: 01726 843425. Fax: 01726 843358. E-mail: enquiries@seaviewinternational.com. **Reservations:** Advised for July/Aug. Min 7 nights, w/e - w/e, 28/7-1/9. other times, any length, with £30 deposit and £2 fee. **Open** 1 April - 3 October.

Directions: From St Austell take B3273 towards Mevagissey; 1 mile before Mevagissey village turn right at Gorran and camp sign and continue towards Gorran for 5 miles. Fork right at camp sign and follow signs to park. O.S.GR: SW991412.

Cornwall
Heligan Woods Caravan Park
St Ewe, St Austell PL26 6ER

041

A peaceful park in a mature garden setting, Heligan Woods (formerly Pengrugla) is now owned by Pentewan Sands (opposite) and the Tremayne family. This park comple-ments the Pentewan site with its busy beach life and many activities. Part of Heligan Woods' boundary actually edges the 'Lost Gardens of Heligan' although nothing can be seen. At some time the land used to develop the park must have been part of the Gardens and one can enjoy mature trees and flowering shrubs which have been further landscaped to provide an attractive situation for a number of privately owned holiday homes. These face out over a part of the 'Lost Valley' and are interspersed with touring pitches, with some below on sloping grass and others in a more level situation amongst trees and shrubs. In all, there are 100 good sized touring pitches, 80 with 16A electricity. The many facilities of Pentewan Sands are open to visitors here. There is access to the Pentewan Trail to ride or cycle into Mevagissey or Pentewan.

Facilities: A modern toilet block is heated, fully equipped and well kept, including a unisex room with bath and small size bath. Dishwashing sinks under cover, a laundry room with two washing machines, two dryers, iron and board, but no hand washing sink. Small shop with good takeaway (fish and chip style; Easter, then Whitsun - 14 Sept). Adventure playground. **Off site:** Riding 4 miles, golf 5 miles.

Charges 2002

Per unit incl. 2 adults	£6.30 - £15.95
extra adult	£2.10 - £3.25
extra child (3-15 yrs)	£1.00 - £2.35
extra tent, car or boat	£1.30 - £1.60
dog	£1.00
electricity	£2.25

Tel: 01726 842714. Fax: 01726 844414. E-mail: info@pentewan.co.uk. **Reservations:** Made with deposit (£35-£75, acc. to season); write to Pentewan Sands (no. 025). **Open** 1 April - 31 October.

Directions: From St Austell ring road take B3273 for Mevagissey. After 3.5 miles, pass Pentewan Sands, continue up the hill and turn right following site signs. Park is on left just before reaching Heligan Gardens. O.S.GR: SW999464.

Pentewan Sands Holiday Park

Pentewan, St Austell PL26 6BT

025

Pentewan Sands is a popular, well managed family park with an ideal position right beside a wide sandy private beach. The beach offers safe bathing and is managed by the park. A busy, 32 acre holiday park with lots going on, there are 501 individual touring pitches, 401 with electricity, and 120 caravan holiday homes for hire. The good-sized pitches are on level grass with nothing between them, and are marked and numbered by frontage stones, mostly in rows adjoining access roads. A good sized free heated pool and small children's pool is beside the Clubhouse and bowling centre. The Clubhouse contains two licensed bar lounges upstairs and a further one downstairs opening on to the pool area, open all day and serving a variety of good value food in season. A full entertainment programme, beach activities, watersports and a children's club are organised, and a small water sports centre is on the beach. There is access to the Pentewan Valley Trail, a six mile route for cycling or walking following the old carriageway to Mevagissey with its throngs of tourists (two miles by the main road). The park has been owned by the Tremayne family for 60 years, along with the beach, and there are links with the award winning Lost Gardens of Heligan nearby.

Facilities: The four main toilet blocks serve their purpose, receiving heavy use in peak season but now with individual cleaners. They include two bathrooms and a baby room, plus facilities for disabled people, a well equipped laundry room, and washing up sinks. Motorcaravan service point. Large, self-service shop (from Easter but hours may be limited). Bistro and fast food (Whitsun - mid-Sept). Bars, bar meals. Entertainment programme and children's club. Swimming pool (about 72 x 26 ft, supervised and open Whitsun - mid Sept). Adventure playground. Tennis courts (one full size, one compact). Bicycle hire. Slipway and boat launching service (Whitsun - mid Sept). Freezer service for ice packs, battery charging service. Gas available. Security barrier at entrance. Caravan and boat storage. No jet-skis are permitted and no 4WD vehicles are allowed on the beach. Dogs are not accepted. **Off site:** The sailing club adjoining offers membership to campers, scuba diving, windsurfing courses, etc. Riding or golf 2 miles.

Charges 2002

Per unit incl. 2 adults, awning	£6.65 - £17.65
extra adult	£1.65 - £3.90
child (3-15 yrs)	£1.00 - £2.90
extra small tent, boat or car	£1.30 - £2.05
electricity (10A)	£2.90

Sea front pitch plus 10-20%. **Tel:** 01726 843485. Fax: 01726 844142. E-mail: info@pentewan.co.uk.
Reservations: Made Sat - Sat or Wed - Wed with deposit (£35-£75, acc. to season), £4 booking fee and compulsory cancellation insurance (£3-£6). **Open** Easter/1 April - 31 October.

Directions: From St Austell ring road take B3273 for Mevagissey. Park is 3.5 miles, where the road meets the sea. O.S.GR: SX018468.

Cornwall
Croft Farm Holiday Park
046 Luxulyan, Bodmin PL30 5EQ

This secluded park is just one mile from the new Eden Project. Croft Farm was once part of a larger site and you pass some of the residential homes on the way in. Mature trees and shrubs edge most of the site, except for an open top field. A number of mobile homes are on site, some privately owned and some for hire by the site, along with two holiday cottages. In the top field with good views, there are 30 individual pitches with new hedges planted. The original mature area provides a further 27 pitches (with 10A electricity for the majority), 15 with hardstanding and 5 of these fully serviced. This is the first time we have seen recycling complete with a compost unit. The one mile woodland trail is also part of the conservation effort and takes you through the rest of the park's natural areas which are indeed left very natural!

Facilities: The heated toilet block is of older design but has been neatly updated to provide showers with a plastic door instead of a curtain and plenty of room to change, a baby room, an en-suite washbasin and toilet for ladies, and a new heated bathroom. Three dishwashing sinks under cover, one laundry sink with spin dryer. 'Field kitchen' with sinks in the top field. Reception has a daily newspaper ordering service and keeps basic necessities such as milk. Grass area with adventure type play equipment and goal net. Games room with pool table and amusement machines and a very useful room full of tourist information. Eden tickets are sold. **Off site:** Fishing 1 mile. Golf or riding 3 miles. Village pubs under a mile and the Eden project on the doorstep.

Charges 2002

Per unit incl. 2 adults	£7.90 - £10.75
extra adult	£2.00
child (5-15 yrs)	£1.20
electricity	£2.00
awning/hardstanding	£0.50
dog	£0.50

Tel: 01726 850228. Fax: 01726 850492. E-mail: lynpick@globalnet.co.uk. **Reservations:** Made with £20 deposit p/week or £3 p/night for shorter visits. **Open** 21 March - 21 January.

Directions: From A391 Bodmin - St Austell road follow directions for the Eden project. When you come to the entrance of the project continue straight on for approx. 1 mile, and site is on the left side of this road in the direction of Luxulyan. O.S.GR: SX045588.

Cornwall
Penhaven Touring Park
026 Pentewan, St Austell PL26 6DL

Penhaven is a level 13 acre touring park, with the road on one side (this can be a little noisy on busy Saturdays) and a river on the other. There is a bridge from the site giving access to the Pentewan Valley Trail, a two mile walk or cycle ride to Pentewan village and beach along this quiet, traffic-free track, with links to Mevagissey via Heligan. The park comprises three fields with 105 numbered grassy pitches which are of a good size, 80 with 10A electricity, 5 with hardstanding and 4 fully serviced. The North field is used for rallies and has a refurbished 'portacabin' style toilet unit. The south field is used for ball games, caravan storage and as a tent area for 35 tents on a 28 day licence (no tarmac road and no lighting). The Middle field has all the main facilities which include a heated swimming pool (unsupervised) with a paved sunbathing surround and loungers. Heligan Gardens are nearby, the Eden Project is 4 miles and the beach is only 1 mile. A busy park, but away from the hectic coastal sites, Penhaven will probably appeal to people who don't want bars and evening entertainment.

Facilities: The toilet block is fully equipped and heated, with three family shower rooms (key on request with deposit) with one unit for use by disabled visitors also. Dishwashing sinks under cover. Well equipped laundry with washing lines provided. Motorcaravan services. Shop. In high season a van on site sells takeaway snacks. Outdoor pool (mid May - early Sept). Small play area. Bicycle hire. **Off site:** Restaurant in the nearby village of London Apprentice .Buses pass the gate for St Austell and Mevagissey. Fishing near, boat launching 1 mile, golf 3 miles, riding 8 miles.

Charges 2002

Per pitch	£3.00 - £9.50
adult	£2.40 - £4.50
child (5-15 yrs)	£2.10
extra car, boat on trailer	£2.50
electricity	£2.20
dog	£1.00

Plus various special offers. **Tel:** 01726 843687. Fax: 01726 843870. E-mail: enquiries@penhaventouring. co.uk. **Reservations:** Made for min. 3 days with £20 deposit per week. **Open** 28 March - 31 October.

Directions: From St Austell on A390, take B3273 to Mevagissey and park is on left, 1 mile from London Apprentice before the village of Pentewan. O.S.GR: SX008481.

Carlyon Bay Caravan & Camping Park

029 Bethesda, Carlyon Bay, St Austell PL25 3RE

Tranquil open meadows edged by mature woodland, well cared for by the Taylor family, provide a beautiful holiday setting with a busy Blue Flag beach five minutes walk from the top gate at this park. The original farm buildings have been converted and added to, providing an attractive centre to the park, also home for the owners. There is a certain individuality of design which is very pleasing, particularly in the impressively tiled toilet blocks which are of excellent quality and design. The 180 pitches in five areas are spacious and allow for a family meadow, a dog free meadow, and an area for couples, etc. All are on flat, terraced or gently sloping grass with flowers and shrubs in some areas. The 104 pitches with electricity (5/10A) are marked. There is even a 'discreet' area, well screened and hidden, for naturists. The only official naturist beach in Cornwall, Polgaver Bay, at the far end of Carlyon Bay can be reached by walking over the cliff tops (and is now charged for). The attractive kidney shaped, heated pool (Easter-Sept) with children's paddling pool, is walled and paved for sunbathing. It is part of the central, covered area used for entertainment. Socially the park provides entertainment in high season for families and children but those who wish for more can choose between the Cornish Leisure World complex on the beach, with its pool, bars and discos, or the social club near the entrance to the park which welcomes campers. The coastal footpath passes near. All Cornwall's attractions are within touring distance. Buses to St Austell and Fowey run from the park entrance.

Facilities: Three modern toilet blocks provide a mix of facilities from vanity style washbasins to en-suite toilets and basins, comfortable, roomy, pre-set showers with divider, shelf, etc, facilities for hair-care and make up and thoughtful provision for babies - almost 'home from home'! Dishwashing sinks under cover at all blocks. Fully equipped laundry room (hot water metered). TV lounge, crazy golf, table tennis and pool table. Swimming pool. Two children's play areas, one adventure type. Modern reception with a good little shop and takeaway (May-mid Sept). Eden Project tickets available. **Off site:** Golf course near the park entrance.

Charges 2002

Per unit incl. 2 persons and car	£8.00 - £17.00
extra adult	£3.00 - £3.50
child (3-17 yrs)	£1.50 - £2.50
awning or small tent	free - £1.00
dog	£1.00 - £1.50
electricity	£2.00
serviced pitch	£3.00

Motorcaravan less £1.00, hiker/tent less £2.00 per night. **Tel:** 01726 812735. Fax: 01726 815496. E-mail: jeffst@globalnet.co.uk. **Reservations:** Made with £30 deposit and £2 fee (min. 6 nights 19/7-17/8). **Open** April - October.

Directions: From Plymouth direction on A390, pass Lostwithiel and 1 mile after village of St Blazey, turn left at roundabout beside Britannia Inn. After 400 yds turn right on a concrete road and right again at site sign. O.S.GR: SX053526.

Cornwall

Powderham Castle Tourist Park

028 Lanlivery, nr Lostwithiel PL30 5BU

This is a most pleasant, peaceful touring park with plenty of sheltered green space and a natural, uncommercialised atmosphere. This has been enhanced by careful planting of trees and shrubs to form a series of linked paddocks with a small unfenced stream running through. The nearest beach at Par is some 4 miles. The park has 38 private caravan holiday homes in a separate field and 75 numbered touring pitches spread round the perimeter of the paddocks, each with 10-15 pitches. All have electricity connections (5/10A) and 7 have hardstanding (awning groundsheets must be lifted alternate days). There are 'adults only' sections for tents and touring caravans. A large, well equipped children's activity play area with a super range of adventure type equipment on grass is in one of the hedged paddocks with a fenced paddling pool. Indoor tennis courts (Bodmin) and a swimming pool are near. The village pub is within walking distance and there are several good local restaurants. The Eden Project is very close.

Facilities: The single central toilet block is good but is quite a walk from some pitches. Hot showers are on payment, with curtained cubicles in the ladies' and a family washroom with shower, basin, WC, etc. Separate dishwashing area with five sinks. Fully equipped laundry room. Motorcaravan service point. Gas supplies. Play area. Torch useful. **Off site:** Fresh water fishing 1.5 miles or sea fishing 3 miles, bicycle hire 4 miles, riding 2 miles, golf 1.5 miles.

Charges 2002

Per unit	£3.70 - £5.40
adult	£1.70 - £2.80
child (3-16 yrs)	£0.60 - £1.40
electricity	£1.75
awnings (without groundsheet)	free
extra small tent, car	free
hiker or cyclist	£2.40 - £4.25

No single sex groups (excl. bona fide organisations). No credit cards. **Tel:** 01208 872277. Fax: 01208 872277. **Reservations:** Made with £20 deposit. **Open** Easter/1 April - 31 October.

Directions: Park approach road leads off A390 road 1.5 miles southwest of Lostwithiel. Follow white or brown camping signs. No other approach roads are advised. O.S.GR: SX083592.

Cornwall

The Colliford Tavern Campsite

030 Colliford Lake, St Neot, Liskeard PL14 6PZ

Colliford Tavern must be unique, quietly situated high on Bodmin Moor near Colliford Lake but hidden and protected by tall pines. The project has been developed over the last ten years by the Edwards family with much care and attention and offers a family run free house with excellent, home cooked food and ale in an old world atmosphere complete with 90 year old well and en-suite accommodation. There is a bar, dining room, a family room with outside terrace, garden, water wheel and a good fenced play area with Wendy House. Open to campers and caravanners, some original suggestions for food which can be quite special or simpler bar-type food are worth trying. The camping area is quiet and simple and has been kept very natural with short grass (helped by the rabbits) and sheltered from the moor by tall pines. The main field provides 40 fairly level pitches with 19 electric hook-ups (16A) and 6 hardstandings backing on to the pine trees. The smaller, lower area is nearer to all the facilities. Reception is in the Tavern building. The site gate is closed at night but there is a 24 hour bell. Ideally situated for Colliford Lake and the Moor with its rich history, flora and fauna, be it for walking, fly fishing (permits available) or birdwatching, the park is also suitable for excursions to the north or south coast.

Facilities: The cheerful, pine-fitted toilet block is well equipped, heated and carefully maintained with a baby room, unit for disabled people (no shower), laundry sink and two washing up sinks. Service wash and tumble dry available Monday to Friday. Restaurant and bar. Some occasional family entertainment. Tickets available for the Eden Project (20-30 minutes by car). Barbecues permitted with prior permission.

Charges 2002

Per unit incl. 1 adult	£6.00 - £7.00
Per unit incl. 2 adults	£8.00 - £10.00
extra person (over 4 yrs)	£2.00 - £3.00
electricity	£3.00
dog	£0.50

Tel: 01208 821335. Fax: 01208 821335. E-mail: info@colliford-tavern.co.uk. **Reservations:** Advised for high season and made with £10 deposit, plus £5 for electric hook-up. **Open** Easter - end September.

Directions: Approaching on the A30 travelling south, pass the Jamaica Inn on the right and site is signed a further 1-1.5 miles on the left. Follow for 0.5 miles and site is signed beside Colliford Lake Park. O.S.GR: SX168730.

Trererthern Touring Park

Padstow PL28 8LE

043

Trererthern is a traditional park of wide open fields, although there have been attempts to divide it up with hedging that is gradually developing in places despite the rabbits and the elements. There is room for 300 units but only 100 are taken so there is plenty of open space and the views across Bodmin Moor and the estuary are marvellous. The grass is neatly cut and the pitches mostly level, although there is a gentle slope in parts. Electricity (10A) is available on 67 pitches, there are 10 water points and 9 hardstanding places for motorcaravans, 7 of these with electricity plus an emptying point (the site can accommodate 32-34 ft motorhomes). The 'Kernow' pitches have private facilities. The owners live on site and, along with site wardens, ensure a well run and orderly park. Padstow itself is a mile away either by public footpath through the fields (20-30 minutes) downhill or for bicycles by the road. Rick Stein has now opened a bistro alongside his restaurant so you may just get a reservation!

Facilities: Two sanitary blocks are simple but clean and tidy, with two washbasins in cabins in the smaller block. A toilet with washbasin and ramped access is provided at the back of the main toilet block at the far side of the park. A unique feature is the four individual en-suite washrooms for use with the 'Kernow' pitches (three more planned). These have a key and are for private use, with a pass key for the shower room (see below for cost). The small block which also houses the private units is locked at night so if you need the loo in the night it could be a little walk! Dishwashing sinks. Laundry facilities with two washing machines, spin dryer, tumble dryer and iron. Reception/shop for gas and basic supplies. Children's play area. **Off site:** Bus service passes site. Nearest beach is at Padstow, others are within 5 miles. Access to the Camel Trail cycle route. Riding or fishing 2 miles, golf 5 miles.

Charges 2002

Per unit	£3.40 - £4.40
adult	£2.30 - £3.30
child (under 15 yrs)	£1.20 - £1.50
awning or extra tent	£1.40
dog	£0.50
electricity	£2.20
'Kernow' pitch incl. electricity	£4.60 - £5.80

No credit cards. **Tel:** 01841 532061. Fax: 01841 532061. E-mail: camping.trererthern@btinternet.com. **Reservations:** Made with deposit (£15 p/week). **Open** Easter/1 April - 2 October.

Directions: Park is signed from the A389, SSW of Padstow. Follow unmade approach road, then turn into park. O.S.GR: SW912739.

Trewince Farm Holiday Park

St Issey, Wadebridge PL27 7RL

050

This well established and popular park four miles from Padstow has been developed around a dairy farm with magnificent countryside views. Careful attention has been made to the development of the park, maintaining trees and adding flowering shrubs and plants. There are 35 caravan holiday homes discreetly terraced, some privately owned, some to let. Two touring areas on higher ground provide both hardstanding and level grass pitches with a sheltered tent area. Over half of the 120 touring pitches have electricity hook-ups (10A). The park's main feature is an excellent sheltered, walled and heated swimming pool with paddling pool, and paved sunbathing area. Farm rides and pasty suppers in the barn are organised in the high season.

Facilities: Two fully equipped, well maintained toilet blocks include washbasins in cabins, hair care rooms, dishwashing under cover and laundry rooms. Also children's room with bath (20p) and facilities for disabled visitors. Well stocked shop (all season) by reception. Fish and chip van calls twice weekly, a butcher once a week. Swimming pool. Play area. Games room. Crazy golf. **Off site:** Pubs and restaurants in nearby village of St Issey. Camel Trail nearby for walking or cycling (goes to Padstow).

Charges 2002

Per unit incl. 2 persons	£6.50 - £11.00
extra adult	£3.00
child 3-15 yrs	£1.50 - £2.50
electricity	£1.75
hardstanding, drainage and electricity	£2.25
dog	£1.00

Tel: 01208 812830. Fax: 01208 812835. **Reservations:** Made with £20 p/week deposit (non-refundable); balance on arrival. **Open** 23 March - 31 October.

Directions: From Wadebridge follow A39 towards St Columb and pick up the A389 for Padstow. Site signed on left in 2 miles. Follow for short distance to park entrance on right. O.S. GR: SW937715.

Lakefield Caravan Park

036 Lower Pendavey Farm, Camelford PL32 9TX

Lakefield is a small touring park with a BHS and RDA approved equestrian centre. It was previously a working farm and with only 40 pitches, it is no wonder that the owners, Maureen and Dennis Perring, know all the campers. The well-spaced pitches with 24 electric hook-ups (16A) are on level grass in sight of the small lake (fenced) and its feathered inhabitants. The white-washed shop/reception, converted from one of the old barns and including a fascinating picture gallery, is open all day and all season which impressed us for such a small site. It incorporates a tea room offering cream teas, cakes and sandwiches. A dozen picnic tables are dotted about the site, with some play equipment on grass. Children will love the small animals and 'Wabbit World' is fascinating. Watch out for Sally the pigmy goat. The BHS approved riding school, very much part of the site, offers lessons and hacks with qualified supervision and instruction and over 30 horses, from miniature Shetlands to thoroughbreds. You can actually arrange a riding holiday and even bring your own horse. All abilities are catered for with a very large indoor centre, outdoor sand ménage, show jumping paddock, beginners cross country course and pony rides. This is the Riding for the Disabled (RDA) Centre for north Cornwall. Pony days and activity days are organised. Tintagel, Boscastle, Bodmin Moor and the many beaches and coves of the north Cornwall coast wait to be explored. Cornwall's first wind farm watches over the site.

Facilities: The toilet block is clean and bright. Washing machine and dryer in the ladies' and a dishwashing sink and a laundry sink outside but under cover. No facilities for disabled visitors. Shop and tea room. Gas supplies. Torches may be useful. **Off site:** Fishing (sea 4 miles, coarse 5 miles), golf 2 miles.

Charges 2002

Per unit incl. 2 adults	£6.00 - £10.00
extra adult or child (5 yrs and over)	£0.50
electricity	£2.00

No credit cards. **Tel:** 01840 213279. Fax: 01840 213279. E-mail: lakefield@pendavey.fsnet.co.uk. **Reservations:** Made with £20 deposit per week. **Open** 1 April - 31 October.

Directions: Follow B3266 north from Camelford. Park access is directly from this road on the left just before the turning for Tintagel, clearly signed. O.S.GR: SX097852.

LAKEFIELD

Caravan Park & Equestrian Centre,
Lower Pendavey Farm, Camelford, Cornwall, PL32 9TX.
Tele/Fax 01840 213279 Email : lakefield@pendavey.fsnet.co.uk

Situated in beautiful North Cornwall, a quiet secluded touring site with a small lake and valley views. Toilet block, electric hook-ups and a small shop. Pets corner.
Dogs welcome. Close to sandy surfing beaches, Tintagel, Boscastle and Bodmin Moor.
Also on site a BHS/RDA approved equestrian centre offering lessons and hacks.
All standards very welcome even complete beginners.
Facilities include indoor school, sand school, farm rides and good off-road riding.

Visit our web site www.lakefieldcaravanpark.co.uk

Cornwall
Polruan Holidays Camping & Caravanning
Polruan-by-Fowey PL23 1QH

019

Polruan is a rural site in an elevated position not far from Fowey in an area of Outstanding Natural Beauty 200 metres from the Coastal path. With 40 touring pitches and 11 holiday homes to let, this is a very pleasant little site. The holiday homes are arranged in a neat circle, with a central area for some tourers, including 7 pitches with gravel hardstanding and electricity, one fully serviced. The remaining touring pitches are in an adjacent field with 8 electricity hook-ups, which is part level for motorcaravans and part on a gentle slope for tents. There are marvellous sea views, but it could be a little exposed when the wind blows off the sea. A raised picnic area gives more views across the estuary to Fowey. This is a nice little park in a popular tourist area, within walking distance (down-hill all the way, and vice-versa!) of the village, where there are various hostelries and a passenger ferry to Fowey. A member of the Countryside Discovery group.

Facilities: The small sanitary block of older design has been added to, providing modern controllable showers and includes a laundry sink plus a washing machine - in the ladies'. New dishwashing sinks. Motorcaravan service facilities. Range of recycling bins. Reception (with a small terrace) doubles as a small shop for basics and gas, with drinks machine and provides a freezer for ice packs, tourist information and bus timetables (for Looe, etc). Sloping field area for children's play with swings. **Off site:** Riding or bicycle hire 3 miles, fishing 0.5 miles, golf 10 miles.

Charges 2002

Per unit incl. 1 or 2 persons	£6.75 - £10.25
extra person	£1.75
electricity	£2.00

No credit cards. **Tel:** 01726 870263. Fax: 01726 870263. E-mail: polholiday@aol.com. **Reservations:** Advised for July/Aug. and made with £30 deposit. **Open** Easter - October.

Directions: From main A390 at East Taphouse take B3359 towards Looe. After 5 miles fork right signed Bodinnick and ferry. Watch for signs for Polruan and site to left. Follow these carefully along narrow Cornish lanes to site on right just before village. O.S.GR: SX133509.

Cornwall
Trelay Farmpark
Pelynt, Looe PL13 2JX

040

Situated a little back from the coast, just over three miles from Looe and Polperro in a rural situation, this is a real gem of a park. Neat, tidy and quiet, there is no farm adjacent. On your right as you drive in, and quite attractively arranged amongst herbaceous shrubs, are caravan holiday homes (13 privately owned, some let by the park). The touring area is behind and slightly above, on level to gently sloping, neatly cut grass. An oval hard-core road connects the good sized, numbered pitches that border the site and back onto hedges, the majority with rural views. There are 23 pitches with electricity hook-ups, with a further 30 pitches for tents, etc. Outside the main season the central area is kept free for ball games. You will receive a good welcome from the enthusiastic owners, Heather and Graham Veale and their family, who live in the chalet bungalow near the entrance where the small reception is located.

Facilities: The excellent chalet-type toilet block is purpose built, heated, well equipped and maintained. There are some semi-private washbasins. For disabled visitors an en-suite unit (with ramp) is accessed by key from reception and includes a baby bath. Two dishwashing sinks and a laundry sink. Washing machine and dryer. Gas supplies. Free use of fridge/freezer. Tourist information including map sales and loan. **Off site:** Village with pub and shops within 0.5 miles. 'Coastal Hoppa' bus from the gate on Thursdays. The Eden Project is 10 miles west.

Charges 2002

Per unit incl. 2 persons	£7.00 - £8.50
extra persons (under 5 yrs)	£1.00
over 5 yrs	£2.00
electricity	£1.60
dog	£0.50

No credit cards. **Tel:** 01503 220900. Fax: 01503 220900. **Reservations:** Advised for July/Aug. **Open** 1 April - end October.

Directions: From A390 Lostwithiel road take B3359 south at Middle or East Taphouse towards Looe and Polperro. Site is signed 0.5 miles past Pelynt on the left. From Looe take A387 towards Polperro and after 2 miles turn right onto B3359 towards Pelynt. Site is signed 1 mile on right. O.S.GR: SX210545.

Killigarth Manor Caravan Park

Polperro, Looe PL13 2JQ

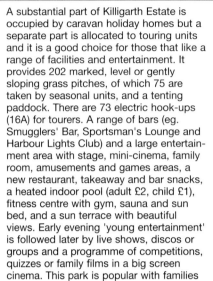

A substantial part of Killigarth Estate is occupied by caravan holiday homes but a separate part is allocated to touring units and it is a good choice for those that like a range of facilities and entertainment. It provides 202 marked, level or gently sloping grass pitches, of which 75 are taken by seasonal units, and a tenting paddock. There are 73 electric hook-ups (16A) for tourers. A range of bars (eg. Smugglers' Bar, Sportsman's Lounge and Harbour Lights Club) and a large entertainment area with stage, mini-cinema, family room, amusements and games areas, a new restaurant, takeaway and bar snacks, a heated indoor pool (adult £2, child £1), fitness centre with gym, sauna and sun bed, and a sun terrace with beautiful views. Early evening 'young entertainment' is followed later by live shows, discos or groups and a programme of competitions, quizzes or family films in a big screen cinema. This park is popular with families with children of all ages and there is much to do in the area.

Facilities: One large, spacious and fully equipped toilet block is supplemented by a small 'portacabin' unit with toilet facilities for peak season. Dishwashing facilities under cover. Facilities for disabled visitors are in the main block. Well equipped laundry with sinks. Well stocked mini-market (all season). Bars and restaurant. Indoor pool. Fitness centre. New indoor play area for under-fives and other play areas. Tennis court (£3/hour). Bicycle hire. Skittle alley, croquet, draughts, badminton and crazy golf. Bus service in high season. **Off site:** Fishing and boat launching approx. 1 mile.

Charges 2002

Per pitch	£2.60 - £5.70
adult	£3.10 - £3.60
child (3-16 yrs)	£1.60 - £1.90
electricity	£2.00

Pup tents not permitted to share a pitch with another unit. Special offers available. **Tel:** 01503 272216. **Fax:** 01503 272065. **E-mail:** killigarthmanor@ breathe.com. **Reservations:** Made (Sat. - Sat. in main season) with £30 deposit. **Open** 4 April - 25 October.

Directions: From Looe take A387 towards Polperro. After 3.5 miles, fork left immediately past a bus shelter and phone box at sign to Killigarth. Site is 0.25 miles. O.S.GR: SX213519.

Polborder House Caravan & Camping Park

Bucklawren Road, St Martins by Looe PL13 1QR

Polborder House may appeal to those who prefer a quiet, well kept little family site to the larger ones with many on-site activities. With good countryside views, up to 31 touring units can be accommodated on well tended grass. Pitches are marked with hedging between pairs of pitches to give privacy and there are 28 electrical connections (10A). A number of hardstandings and 10 serviced pitches have been added recently. The owners live on the park. Polborder is well situated with Seaton only 2 miles, Looe 2.5 and the nearest beach a 20-25 minutes walk from a gate in the corner of the park. A 'Hopper' bus calls at site from last week in June to first in September on Tuesdays and Thursdays. This is a good area for walking with links to the coastal path through Duchy woodland.

Facilities: The sanitary block (key entry) is well kept, of ample size and provides hot showers, a baby room, fully equipped laundry room, and three covered sinks outside for dishwashing. En-suite toilet unit for disabled visitors has a ramped approach. Rubbish is recycled. Motorcaravan service facilities. Shop (all season) for gas and basics, including off licence and some camping accessories. Toddler's play area. **Off site:** Fishing, golf and boat launching within 2 miles, riding 8 miles. Restaurant 500 m.

Charges 2002

Per unit incl. 2 persons	£6.50 - £9.50
extra person	£1.50 - £2.00
child (4-16 yrs)	£1.00
awning or child's tent	£1.00
dog	£0.75
electricity	£1.85

Less 10% for senior citizens for booked stays over 5 nights. **Tel:** 01503 240265. **Fax:** 01503 240700. **E-mail:** rlf.polborder@virgin.net. **Reservations:** Any period, £20 deposit (non-refundable). **Open** 29 March - 2 November.

Directions: Park is under a mile south of the B3253. Turn off 2 miles east of Looe and follow signs to park and Monkey Sanctuary at junctions; care is needed with narrow road. O.S.GR: SX283555.

Whitsand Bay Holiday Park

Millbrook, Torpoint PL10 1JZ

035

Whitsand Bay is a self contained family holiday park that caters well for children. It must also be one of the most unusual places to stay and is, in fact, a designated ancient monument in an 'area of outstanding natural beauty'. The site has been converted from a coastal gun battery built in 1890 to protect Plymouth and the views are magnificent across to the city and the Tamar Estuary with Dartmoor in the background, over the sea towards the Rame peninsula, Whitsand Bay and west to the Lizard, Looe, and Bodmin Moor. Covering 27 acres, some wild and natural you can explore the original gun emplacements and enjoy the views or venture into the dark, damp underground tunnels and earthworks. It is obvious that the solidly constructed clubhouse, laundry and chapel are part of the original fortifications. In fact the laundry was part of the Quartermaster's store. The Battery Club provides a cosy bar alongside a larger bar and dance/disco area with entertainment in high season. The approach along the cliff top road is deceptive as the earthworks hide what is, in essence a self contained village including holiday caravans and older style chalets. The 120 marked grass touring pitches (60 with 16A electricity), connected by tarmac roads, vary in size, are terraced and enjoy mainly landward views. Several are taken by seasonal lets.

Facilities: The two toilet blocks are acceptable, each block having a dishwashing sink under cover. Laundry room. Well stocked shop. Café open all day in season, with takeaway. Barbecue area. Bars with entertainment in high season and big screen films. Indoor, heated pool and paddling pool, sauna, sun bed and new mini-gym. Adventure play area, multisport court, amusement arcade and table tennis. 'Kids Club'. **Off site:** A steep 200 ft. cliff path provides access to Whitsand Bay (unsuitable for small children or the infirm). Fishing 0.5 miles, boat slipway 2 miles, golf 2 miles. Riding 5 miles.

Charges 2002

Per unit incl. adults, children (max 6)	£8.00 - £18.00
electricity	£2.00
dog	£1.00
awning	free

Woodland mini-pitches for cyclists or walkers less 50%. Club membership incl. **Tel:** 01752 822597. **Fax:** 01752 823444. E-mail: rob@whitsandbayholidays.co.uk. **Reservations:** Made with £10 deposit p/week. **Open** March - December.

Directions: Take the Torpoint ferry and on disembarking follow A374 Liskeard road for 3 miles. At village of Antony fork left for Millbrook (B3274) and continue for 2 miles to T-junction. Turn left for Whitsand Bay, then almost immediately right following narrow road overlooking the bay for a further 2 miles. Park is hidden on the left - watch for sign. O.S.GR: SX417506.

Dolbeare Caravan & Camping Park

St Ive Road, Landrake, Saltash PL12 5AF

044

Now under new ownership, this small, but well kept park is in a rural setting, but very easily accessible from the main A38. The park consists of a large rectangular field of neatly cut grass edged with trees and sloping slightly at the top, connected by a gravel road. Caravans and motorcaravans go around the edge, with some terraced pitches with hardstanding, and tents tend to go in the central area where there is also play equipment and water and refuse points. All 60 pitches are numbered and of comfortable size, 51 with electricity (16A). An extra field doubles as a rally and games field and part is set aside for a dog walk area. Leaflets are provided on 'Where to Eat', 'Where to Walk', and 'Suggestions for what to do'. Dog kennels nearby can provide day care from £3.50, but the drawback is that there could be some noise depending on season and wind direction. A very usefully situated park said to be 20 minutes from everywhere - Plymouth, beaches, National Trust properties, Dartmoor and Bodmin Moor, etc.

Facilities: The well kept heated toilet block to one side of the field provides pre-set showers with curtain and seat, plus two outside, but covered washing up sinks. Laundry next to reception provides a sink (H&C), washing machine, dryer, iron and board. Reception doubles as a small shop for basics including gas (limited hours out of main season). Good supply of tourist information and maps in a caravan near the caravan storage area. Park has arranged discounts at the St Mellion Golf and Country Club for golf and leisure facilities. Site barrier (card system with £5 deposit, £1 fee). **Off site:** Fishing 3 miles, golf 5.5 miles.

Charges 2002

Per unit incl. 2 adults and car	£8.50 - £9.50
extra adult	£2.00
child (5-16 yrs)	£1.00
electricity	£1.50 - £2.00
awning	£1.00
small tent per person	£3.00 - £3.50

No credit cards. **Tel:** 01752 851332. E-mail: dolbeare@btopenworld. com. **Reservations:** Made with £10 deposit. **Open** all year.

Directions: After crossing the Tamar Bridge into Cornwall, continue on A38 for a further 4 miles. In Landrake village turn right following signs and site is 0.75 miles on the right. O.S.GR: SX366616.

Wooda Farm Park

038 Poughill, Bude EX23 9HJ

Wooda Farm is spacious and well organised, with some nice touches. A quality, family run park, it is part of a working farm, under two miles from the sandy, surfing beaches of Bude. In peaceful farmland with plenty of open spaces (and some up and down walking), there are marvellous views of sea and countryside. The 200 pitches, spread over four meadows, are on level or gently sloping grass. There are 160 with electricity connections (10A), 30 plus with hardstanding and 21 grass, hedged 'premium' pitches (electricity, water, waste water) linked by tarmac roads. A late arrivals area has electricity. Beside the shop and reception at the entrance are 55 holiday letting units. There is a small farm museum and friendly farm animals - children (and adults) are welcome to assist at feeding time! Tractor and trailer rides, pony riding and trekking, archery and clay pigeon shooting with tuition are provided according to season and demand, likewise barn dances, plus a woodland walk (where the pixies can be found) and an orchard walk. There is much to do in the area - sandy beaches with coastal walks, and Tintagel with King Arthur's Castle and Clovelly nearby. A member of the Best of British group.

Facilities: Three well maintained solid toilet blocks, one heated, include a unit suitable for disabled people, and a baby room with small bath. Three new excellent en-suite family bathrooms are in one block with two more family rooms with shower and bath in the top block (coded access). Washing up sinks under cover. Two fully equipped laundry rooms. New motorcravan service point. Self-service shop with off-licence (8.30 - 8.30 in main season). Attractive courtyard bar with bar meals and a pleasant restaurant, Linney's Larder, with home cooking (closed Mon. and Sat. outside main season). Children's play area in separate field on grass, with plenty of room for ball games, 9 hole 'fun' golf course (clubs provided). Games room with TV, table tennis and pool. Coarse fishing in 1.5 acre lake (permits from reception, £1.50 per half day, £2.50 per day). Certain breeds of dogs are not accepted. Caravan storage.
Off site: Local village inn is five minutes walk. Leisure Centre and Splash Pool in Bude.

Charges 2002

Per unit incl. 2 adults	£7.50 - £12.00
extra adult	£1.50 - £3.00
child (3-15 yrs)	£1.00 - £1.50
awning or pup tent	£1.00 - £1.50
'premier' pitch incl. electricity	£3.50 - £5.00
incl. satellite TV point	£4.50 - £6.00
dog	£1.00 - £2.00

Tel: 01288 352069. Fax: 01288 355258. E-mail: enquiries@wooda.co.uk. **Reservations:** Made with £20 p/week deposit. **Open** 1 April - October.

Directions: Park is north of Bude at Poughill; turn off A39 on north side of Stratton on minor road for Coombe Valley, following camp signs at junctions. O.S.GR: SS225080.

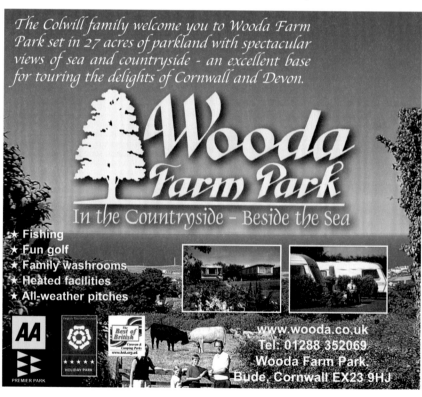

Budemeadows Touring Holiday Park

Poundstock, Bude EX23 0NA

037

Budemeadows is an attractive, family run touring park located south of Bude. It is maturing well with growing hedging and trees and, although close to the A39 through road, offers a good, quiet option being only about a mile from the sandy surfing beaches at Widemouth Bay and 3 miles from Bude with all its amenities. It has been thoughtfully planned and provides large, separated (low hedging or fencing) pitches, some slightly sloping but with panoramic rural views, others more sheltered and nearer the facilities. Some 146 units of any type are taken and there is plenty of room for these numbers with 80 electrical connections (10A) and 26 hardstandings, some with all-weather wooden decking for winter use. An attractive feature is the centrally situated, fenced pool area with a comfortably heated pool and toddlers pool (also heated), patio and grass sunbathing area, and gazebos. A mobile 'Catch a Snack' van calls on certain evenings in high season and the site now has an attractive bar open in the main season and according to demand at other times. The owners live on site.

Facilities: The pine clad toilet block can be heated and has good controllable showers, six private cabins for ladies with basin and WC, one for men. A second similar block provides full facilities for disabled visitors. There are also three family shower units, a family bathroom, baby bath and changing room, dishwashing sinks and a laundry room with tourist information. Motorcaravan service point. Gas supplies. Shop (Spr. B.H. - mid Sept). Bar (peak season). Swimming pool (Spr. B.H. - 2 Sept.) Large adventure playground. TV and games room with pool table and board games. Thoughtfully provided are picnic tables, brick built barbecues, a large scale outdoor chess set, large 'Connect-4', table tennis and skittles. Caravan storage. **Off site:** Boat launching in Bude, lake fishing 5 miles, riding 3 miles, golf 4 miles.

Charges 2002

Per adult	£3.00 - £6.00
child (3-14 yrs)	£1.50 - £3.00
dog	£1.00 - £1.50
electricity	£2.00 - £2.50

Pitch and awning included. **Tel:** 01288 361646. Fax: 01288 361646. E-mail: wendyjo@globalnet.co.uk. **Reservations:** Made with deposit (£5 p/night or £35 p/week). **Open** all year.

Directions: Park entrance is from a lay-by to the east off the A39 just north of a turning to Widemouth Bay. O.S.GR: SS216017.

Lobb Fields Caravan & Camping Park

Saunton Road, Braunton EX33 1EB

114

Braunton village, Saunton Sands, the famous Tarka Trail for cycling, Baggy Point for walking, the biosphere at Braunton Burrows (one of only 13 similar special reserves in the country), Marwood Gardens, and wind surfing and water skiing on the Taw estuary are just some of the many attractions within a short distance of Lobb Fields. If you just want to sit and relax, then the pitches at the park offer views of the Taw estuary and Saunton, as well as magnificent sunsets. Lobb Fields has two camping areas providing 180 pitches on gently sloping grass, with a few hardstandings. Twelve pitches are reserved for seasonal caravans, and 61 have a 16A electricity connection. A third field is open for campers for 28 days only in high season. The pitches are all numbered and grass roadways leading to the amenities are marked. A small children's play area with wooden adventure equipment is located in the lower field. Managers, Robert and Diana Gleed, ably assisted by Bruce and Maureen Reeves, offer their guests a friendly welcome and are pleased to give information about the area. Lobbs Fields may be close to many holiday activities, but it is also a peaceful retreat for those wanting a quiet holiday.

Facilities: Two sanitary blocks (one in each field) include all the usual facilities including a baby room (lower block only), laundry and dishwashing facilities. The lower block can be heated. No facilities for visitors with disabilities. Hair dryers and irons available from reception (£5 returnable deposit). Adventure play area. **Off site:** Nearest shops less than a mile.

Charges 2002

Per unit incl. 2 persons	£7.00 - £13.00
adults over 50 yrs	£6.50 - £13.00
small camper or tent incl. 2 persons	£6.00 - £10.50
extra adult	free - £1.00
child (5-14 yrs)	free - £0.50
extra child's tent or awning	£1.00
electricity	£2.50
dog	£1.00

Tel: 01271 812090. Fax: 01271 812090. E-mail: lobbfields@compuserve.com. **Reservations:** £10 deposit for each week, non refundable - minimum stay 3 nights during B.Hs. **Open** 28 March - 26 October.

Directions: Take A361 Barnstaple to Braunton road, then B3231 (signposted Croyde) to Braunton. Park is 1 mile from Braunton on the right - take care through Braunton as roads are quite narrow and busy. O.S.GR: SS474371.

Hidden Valley Touring & Camping Park

West Down, Ilfracombe EX34 8NU

The owners Martin and Dawn Fletcher run this aptly named award-winning, family park to high standards. In a sheltered valley setting between Barnstaple and Ilfracombe beside a small stream and lake (with ducks), it is most attractive and is also convenient for several resorts, beaches and the surrounding countryside. The original part of the park offers some 74 level pitches of good size on three sheltered terraces. All have hardstanding, electricity hook-ups (16A) and free TV connections (leads for hire), with a water point between each pitch. Kingfisher Meadow, a little way from the main facilities and reached by a tarmac road, provides a further 60 pitches entirely on grass (so suitable for campers with tents), all with electricity, water, waste water and TV hook-ups. Two good play areas have wooden equipment and safe surfaces (one near a fast flowing stream). There is a lounge bar and a good value, family restaurant serving home cooked meals in attractive surroundings. Essentially this is a park for those seeking good quality facilities in very attractive, natural surroundings, without too many man-made distractions - apart from some slight traffic noise during day time. It provides a relaxed setting with woodland walks direct from the site.

Facilities: Two modern toilet blocks (one heated), are tiled and have non-slip floors. One for each area, they provide some washbasins in cubicles, some en-suite with toilets in the Kingfisher Meadow block, baby changing room, laundry facilities including washing machine, dryer and iron, and dishwashing sinks under cover, plus complete facilities for people with disabilities. There are supplementary clean 'portacabin' style facilities in the original area which are due to be replaced. Motorcaravan service facilities. Shop, bar and takeaway. Good restaurant open to the public (weekends only out of season). Gas supplies. Games room. Play areas. Up to two dogs are accepted (otherwise by prior arrangement). Caravan storage. **Off site:** Fishing or golf 2 miles, bicycle hire 4 miles, riding 5 miles.

Charges 2002

Per unit incl. 2 persons	£5.00 - £13.00
as above for over 50s	£4.00 - £13.00
extra adult	£1.50 - £2.00
child 5-15 yrs	£1.00 - £1.50
dog	free - £1.00
electricity	£2.00 - £3.25
TV hook up (leads £15 deposit)	£0.50

Tel: 01271 813837. Fax: 01271 814041. E-mail: relax@hiddenvalleypark.com. **Reservations:** Accepted with £25 deposit. **Open** all year.

Directions: Park is on A361 Barnstaple - Ilfracombe road, 3.5 miles after Braunton. O.S.GR: SS499408.

Step out **Hidden Valley** of this world...

to find out more about our award winning park call us on

01271 813837

or visit our website at

www.hiddenvalleypark.com

1996-2002 PREMIER PARK

West Down Nr. Ilfracombe North Devon EX34 8NU

Golden Coast Holiday Village, Woolacombe

This is the third park in the Woolacombe Bay group (see nos. 107 and 073 on page 42. It is a large complex combining caravan holiday homes, chalets, apartments and a touring section, blending in with the steep contours of the area and the views are exceptional. Some 220 pitches for touring units and 22 for tents are marked and numbered on grass, served by tarmac roads. All have electricity connections (16A).

Sanitary facilities are provided in an unusual unisex building. Fully tiled, in addition to the normal WCs, washbasins and showers, it provides five individual bathrooms with bath, shower and washbasin - all free.

Entertainment is staged all season. The restaurant with waiter service offers a good choice of menu and there are takeaway facilities. A traditional pub, run by the park, is on the public road adjacent to the park. A free, open-top bus operates in high season between the park and the village.

Woolacombe Bay Holiday Village

Sandy Lane, Woolacombe EX34 7AH

107

Woolacombe Bay, and its sister site Golden Coast nearby, are well known holiday parks providing a range of holiday accommodation from caravan holiday homes to chalets and apartments, with many on site amenities including pools, restaurants and bars, and providing a wide range of entertainment. A camping section at the Woolacombe Bay park caters for tents and trailer tents only, so touring visitors can enjoy all the activities and entertainment of both parks. Partly terraced out of the hillside and partly on the hill top with some existing pine trees but with many more trees planted for landscaping, the site has magnificent views out across the bay. Marked and numbered pitches have been provided on grass for 146 tents, 94 with electricity (10/16A). All should be level, having been terraced where necessary and they are connected by gravel roads. Some up and down walking is needed for the toilet block. A courtesy bus service runs between the two parks, the third park in the group (Twitchen Parc) and the beach during the high main season, although there is a footpath to the beach from the site. All three parks have varied entertainment programmes and children's clubs and Woolacombe Bay also boasts a health spa and beauty suite.

Facilities: A super central toilet block has excellent facilities, including en-suite shower and washrooms and separate toilets; also included is a sauna and steam room - unusual but nice. Separate dishwashing and laundry rooms. Unit for disabled visitors. Supermarket. Bars, restaurant and entertainment. Indoor (heated) and outdoor pools with flumes and slides. Sauna and gym. Tennis courts. Dogs are welcome at Woolacombe Bay but not at Golden Coast. **Off site:** Fishing or riding 1 mile.

Charges 2002

Per tent incl. 2 persons	£8.00 - £25.00
child (5-15 yrs)	£2.00 - £6.25
dog	£1.50

Tel: 01271 870343. Fax: 01271 870089. E-mail: goodtimes@woolacombe.com. **Reservations:** Advised for peak season; contact park. **Open** 11 May - 21 September (camping).

Directions: Take A361 Barnstaple - Ilfracombe road through Braunton. Turn left at Mullacott Cross roundabout towards Woolacombe then right towards Mortehoe. Now follow the camping signs by turning left and park is on the left. O.S.GR: SS463445.

See advertisements opposite and on inside cover pages

Twitchen Parc

Mortehoe, Woolacombe EX34 7ES

073

Set in the grounds of an attractive Edwardian country house, Twitchen Parc is now under the same ownership as Woolacombe Bay. Its main concern lies in holiday caravans and flats, although it also provides marked pitches for tourers at the top of the park, with some views over the rolling hills to the sea. With a newly developed touring field, they include 155 pitches with 16A electricity, many with tarmac hardstanding, mostly arranged around oval access roads in hedged areas. Further non-electric pitches are behind in two open, unmarked fields which are sloping (blocks are thoughtfully provided, stored in neat wooden boxes next to water points). A smart, modern entertainment complex incorporates a licensed club and family lounge with snacks, a restaurant, teenage disco room, cartoon lounge, outdoor pool and smart indoor pool complex. All the facilities of the Golden Coast and Woolacombe Bay Parcs are free to visitors at Twitchen, with a courtesy bus running regularly between the three parks and to the beach.

Facilities: There are two sanitary blocks, the larger one of an unusual older design with different levels and rather narrow corridors. Dishwashing and laundry facilities at each block plus a good modern launderette at the central complex. Shop and takeaway. Club, bars, restaurant and entertainment for adults and children, day and evening. Outdoor pool (heated mid-May - mid-Sept). Attractive indoor pool with sauna, paddling pool, fountain and a viewing area. Putting green. Games rooms for table tennis, pool, snooker and arcade games. Good adventure play area. American motorhomes are accepted (up to 30 ft).

Charges 2002

Caravan/motorhome incl. electricity	£11.00 - £35.00
mid season per week only (27/5-3/6)	£125.00
high season per week only (15/7-26/8)	£225.00
tent pitch incl. 2 persons	£8.00 - £25.00
child (5-15 yrs)	£2.00 - £6.25
dog	£1.50

Special offers available. **Tel:** 01271 870343. Fax: 01271 870089. E-mail: goodtimes@woolacombe-bay.com. **Reservations:** Made with deposit (£2 per pitch per night). **Open** 1 April/Easter - end October.

Directions: From Barnstaple take A361 towards Ilfracombe and through Braunton. Turn left at Mullacott Cross roundabout towards Woolacombe and then right towards Mortehoe. Park is on the left before village. O.S.GR: SS466456.

Easewell Farm Holiday Park

Mortehoe, Woolacombe EX34 7EH

072

Near to the sandy beaches of Woolacombe, Easewell Farm is a family run site, run with families in mind. This is a traditional touring park which during the day is a hive of activity, but the nights are quiet and peaceful. The largest of the camping fields is sloping with superb views across the headland to the sea. Two smaller fields are terraced and one area has hardstandings. Together they provide 250 pitches, 90 with electricity connections (15A) and 20 also with TV and water connections. The shop is well stocked (gas available), there is a takeaway and restaurant and an attractive bar with patio overlooking a small duck pond. The park has its own very well maintained 9 hole golf course which is popular and has reduced fees for campers. One of the huge redundant farm buildings has been put to excellent use - divided into three areas, it provides table tennis and pool, a skittle alley and two lanes of flat green bowling with changing rooms. Walks to the local village and along the coastal path are easy from the site and a bus to Ilfracombe and Barnstaple stops 100 yds. from the entrance.

Facilities: The central toilet block is regularly upgraded and can be heated. Two washbasins in the ladies have hoses for hair washing, controllable showers (no dividers). Small area with baby bath facilities. Dishwashing sinks under cover. Laundry. These facilities are arranged around the farmhouse area and include a very well equipped unit for disabled people with everything in one large room including a hairdryer. Motorcaravan service point. Shop. Bar. Golf. Small heated indoor swimming pool is well used, as are games and TV rooms. Fenced play area with bark base. Indoor skittle alley, bowls, and table tennis. In high season only one dog per pitch is allowed. **Off site:** Fishing or riding 1 mile, bicycle hire 3 miles. Tarka Trail for walking and riding. Boat trips to Lundy Island.

Charges 2002

Per caravan incl. 2 persons	£9.00 - £13.00
tent or motorcaravan incl. 2 persons	£8.00 - £11.00
extra person incl. children	£1.50
electricity	£2.50
'supersite' incl. electricity	£4.00
awning or pup tent	free

Tel: 01271 870225. Fax: 01271 870225. **Reservations:** Made with £20 deposit per week booked. **Open** Easter - 30 September.

Directions: From Barnstaple, take A361 Ilfracombe road through Braunton. Turn left at Mullacott Cross roundabout on B3343 to Woolacombe, turning right after 2-3 miles to Mortehoe. Park is on right before village. O.S.GR: SS465455.

Napps Touring Holiday Park

Old Coast Road, Berrynarbor, Ilfracombe EX34 9SW

112

Set in an idyllic location in North Devon, this popular, family-run site offers peace and quiet on site, with plenty to see and do off site. A path just outside the gates leads down to a private beach with safe bathing; although it's only 200 yards to the gate, there are 200 steps down to the beach so it isn't suitable for wheelchair users. Combe Martin and Ilfracombe beaches are also close by. The local pub (just 300 yards down the lane) offers snacks, a beer garden, restaurant, and entertainment. Pitches, most with views of Watermouth Bay, are terraced and spacious, 23 are serviced with electricity, water tap and waste point, and the majority of the others have a 10A hook-up. An outdoor heated swimming pool with shallow section for children is unsupervised, but there is a terrace with table and chairs for non-swimmers to watch or enjoy a light meal from the snack bar. In high season, a ceramics club is organised for older children; they choose a piece of pottery and paint it themselves, then it's glazed and fired for them. Light entertainment is organised during the high season and there are also pony rides around the site.

Facilities: The modern toilet block includes open plan washbasins. Laundry. Dishwashing. Adventure play area still being developed. Licensed shop, gas supplies. Heated outdoor pool with paddling pool and small toddlers' slide. Tennis. Ceramic studio. Games room. Bar with light entertainment during high season. Pony rides. **Off site:** Beach 200 yards downhill, pub 300 yards.

Charges 2002

Per caravan/trailer tent incl. 2 persons	£5.00 - £13.00
tent or motorcaravan incl. 2 persons	£5.00 - £11.00
extra person over 5 yrs	£1.50
awning or extra pup tent	free - £2.00
electricity (10A)	£2.00
dog	free - £2.00

Payment is accepted in Euros. **Tel:** 01271 882557. Fax: 01271 882557. E-mail: info@napps.fsnet.co.uk. **Reservations:** Made with £30 deposit per week or part of week for each booking (non-refundable). **Open** Easter - end-November.

Directions: Leave M5 at junction 27, take the A361 to South Molton and then A399 to Combe Martin. The site is 1.5 miles west of Combe Martin on the A399 (signed). O.S.GR: SS561474.

Stowford Farm Meadows

Combe Martin, Ilfracombe EX34 0PW

Stowford Farm is set in 500 acres of the rolling North Devon countryside, all of which is available for recreation and walking, yet within easy reach of five local beaches. The touring park and its facilities have been developed in the fields and farm buildings surrounding the attractive old farmhouse and provide a village like centre with a comfortable spacious feel. The family are constantly looking to improve the facilities. There are 570 pitches for all units on four slightly sloping meadows separated by Devon hedges of beech and ash. Unseparated, the numbered, marked pitches are accessed by tarmac or hard-core roads, most have electricity (10A) and there are well placed water points. A new field providing 130 extra pitches with electricity has its own heated toilet block. The original stables have become the Old Stable Bars and entertainment in high season includes barn dances, discos and other musical evenings. Children will be entertained by the indoor pool and under cover mini-zoo where they can handle many sorts of animals (on payment). In low season some facilities may only open for limited hours. Stowford provides plenty to keep families occupied without leaving the park. It is a friendly family, countryside base for exploring the North Devon coast and Exmoor.

Facilities: The four identi[cal]... own personal cleaners a[nd]... providing good, functiona[l]... each block also has laun[...] cover dishwashing sinks [...] floor heating includes fa[...] Extra, good facilities for the disabled. family washrooms are beside reception. Well stocked shop (with holiday goods, gas and camping accessories) and a good value takeaway with a restaurant area. Bars and entertainment in season. Swimming pool (22 x 10 m; heated Easter - Oct) at a small charge (90p). Riding stables on site. 18-hole pitch and putt golf course. Games room (pool tables, table tennis and amusement machines) and snooker room. Crazy golf. Bicycle hire. 'Kiddies kar' track (all charged for). Large children's play area. Games and activities organised in high season. Dogs welcome in one section (max. 2 per pitch). Summer parking and winter caravan storage. Caravan workshop and repair centre. **Off site:** Fishing and boat launching 4 miles.

Charges 2002

Per unit and car incl. 2 persons	£4.80 - £11.40
extra person (over 5 yrs)	free - £2.00
awning with groundsheet	£2.00 - £2.50
extra car or small tent	£2.00
dog	£0.60 - £1.00
electricity	£1.50 - £2.00

Reduced fees for over-50s in low and mid seasons. **Tel:** 01271 882476. Fax: 01271 883053. E-mail: enquiries@stowford.co.uk. **Reservations:** Any length, deposit £2 per night, £12 per week, £20 per fortnight. Balance due 28 days before arrival. **Open** Easter - end October.

Directions: From Barnstaple take A39 towards Lynton. After 1 mile turn left on B3230. Turn right at garage on A3123 and park is 1.5 miles on the right. O.S.GR: SS560427.

reenacres Touring Caravan Park

Bratton Fleming, Barnstaple EX31 4SG

A neat, compact, rural park on the edge of Exmoor, Greenacres is managed and run alongside, but separately from, the working farm owned by the family. Drive through the farm access to the park (clearly signed) - you will need to go back and call at the house to book in. No tents are taken. The site has 30 good sized, well drained pitches with connecting gravel paths to the road - in theory you can get to your unit without stepping on the grass; 20 electric hook-ups (16A). The top area is level, the lower part next to the beech woods is semi-terraced to provide six hardstandings and some hedged places. There are marvellous views outside the beech hedge that shelters the site. To the west of Exmoor, the park is very suitable for the coast at Ilfracombe and Combe Martin, or for exploring the moor. The family has opened up a woodland walk across the fields to a secluded valley picnic area beside a stream to take advantage of the marvellous views and surroundings.

Facilities: The toilet block, kept very clean and tidy, is in the centre of the horseshoe layout with showers (1M, 1F) on payment (20p) and an en-suite room for disabled visitors. Laundry room, with sink, spin dryer, iron and board, and dishwashing room. Washing lines provided. Gas supplies. Tourist information hut. An area for children with net and swings is separated by a Devon bank from the 2 acre dog field.

Charges 2002

Per unit incl. 2 persons	£4.50 - £7.50
extra person	£0.75 - £1.25
child (under 7 yrs)	free
awning	free - £1.50
dog	free
electricity	£1.50

No credit cards. **Tel:** 01598 763334. **Reservations:** Made with £5 deposit. **Open** Easter1 April - 31 October.

Directions: From North Devon link road (M5, exit 27) turn north at South Molton onto A399. Continue for 9 miles, past turning for Exmoor Steam Centre and on to Stowford Cross. Turn left towards Exmoor Zoological Park and Greenacres is on the left. O.S.GR: SS663404.

Devon

Minnows Camping & Caravan Park

075 Sampford Peverell EX16 7EN

Minnows is an attractive, neat small park with views across the Devon countryside, separated from the Grand Western canal by hedging. Easily accessible from the M5, it is suitable as an ideal touring centre for Devon and Somerset, for cycling or walking, or simply for breaking a long journey. Open for nine months of the year, it provides 45 level pitches all with 16A electricity. Of these, 36 are all weather (grass and gravel), including 2 fully serviced for motorcaravans. A further 3.5 acres have been added to the park providing space for more and larger pitches, a playground and a large field for ball games, etc. The village of Sampford Peverell, with pub and general store, is only a half mile walk to the towpath, with Tiverton 7.5 miles. In fact, there are 12 miles of level walking on the towpath or one can take a trip on a horse-drawn barge. The site is also on the Sustran cycle route (route 3). Tiverton Parkway station (BR) is 1 mile and buses run from the village to Tiverton. Coarse fishing permits for the canal are available from reception. Part of the Caravan Club's 'managed under contract' scheme, non-members are also very welcome.

Facilities: The heated toilet block is clean and comfortable with all modern facilities and constant hot water. Facilities for disabled visitors, a baby bath on request. Covered dishwashing sinks and one for laundry, plus a spin dryer and washing machine. Motorcaravan service point. Gas supplies. Newspaper delivery can be arranged. Excellent tourist information. Play area. All year caravan storage. Site gates closed 9 pm. and locked 11 pm. - 7.30 am. **Off site:** Bicycle hire 5 minutes walk away. Golf driving range near, full course 4 miles; riding 6 miles.

Charges 2002

Per unit	£4.00 - £5.00
small tent and car	£2.00
adult	£2.75 - £3.75
child (5-16 yrs)	£1.10 - £1.20
dog	free
electricity	£1.50 - £2.25
serviced pitch plus	£1.00

Awning free with breathable groundsheets on grass. Credit cards accepted for £10 or more. **Tel:** 01884 821770. Fax: 01884 821770. **Reservations:** Made with £10 deposit. **Open** 8 March - 12 November.

Directions: From M5 junction 27 take A361 signed Tiverton. After about 600 yds leave on the first exit signed Sampford Peverell. After about 200 yds turn right at roundabout and cross bridge over A361 to a second roundabout. Go straight ahead and park is immediately ahead. From North Devon on A361 go to M5 junction 27 and return back up the A361 as above. O.S.GR: ST042148.

Springfield Holiday Park

105 Tedburn Road, Tedburn St Mary, Exeter EX6 6EW

Quietly situated to explore both Dartmoor and Exmoor, yet easily accessible, Springfield has room for 88 units on its 9 acres, mainly on level, grass terraces with views across the Devon countryside. Sixty pitches have 10A electricity. There are 32 seasonal units and 24 caravan holiday homes which are to be found at the lower part of the park. The reception cum shop is on the right as you drop down into the park and gravel access roads radiate out from here along the terraces and link up at the bottom. Here there is a family 'terrace bar' with a grass terrace making the most of the rural views. Good value meals are served to eat in or takeaway, even cream teas and the odd musical evening. A small play area with wooden equipment is located in the sports field which becomes the overflow camping area when required. Martin and Eileen Johnson, the owners, are keen to help everyone enjoy their stay and can provide plenty of local information on Dartmoor walks and where to find the best fishing lakes, etc. A new bridge on the A30 provides much easier access to the site and to Dartmoor.

Facilities: The two toilet blocks are of older design with pre-set showers (20p external meter), a family bathroom and baby changing facilities. Washing up and laundry sinks (H&C), three washing machines and two dryers. Facilities could be stretched in high season. Well stocked licensed shop featuring local produce. Gas supplies. Terraced bar with bar meals or takeaway (open Easter, then May - Sept evenings and Sunday lunch). Small heated swimming pool, naturally sheltered (unsupervised). Children's play area and games room with skittle alley. **Off site:** Fishing 6 miles, bicycle hire 8 miles, riding 10 miles, golf 2 miles.

Charges 2002

Per caravan, trailer tent, motorhome	£8.00 - £10.00
family tent (acc to season and size)	£7.50 - £9.00
walker or cyclist (1 person and tent)	£5.00 - £6.00
extra person (over 3 yrs)	£1.50
full or half awning, pup tent	£1.00
dog	£1.00
electricity	£1.80

Tel: 01647 24242. Fax: 01647 24131. E-mail: springhol@aol.com. **Reservations:** Made with deposit (£25 per unit per week or £5 per night with electricity, £2 per night without). **Open** 15 March - 15 November.

Directions: From M5 junction 31 take A30 towards Okehampton. Take third exit from the A30 (Woodleigh junction) and follow signs over bridge to park. O.S.GR: SX788936.

Yeatheridge Farm Caravan Park

106 East Worlington, Crediton EX17 4TN

Yeatheridge is a friendly, family park with riding, fishing lakes, and indoor pools. Based on a 200 acre farm, 9 acres have been developed over many years into an attractive touring park. With splendid views of the local hills and Dartmoor away to the south, and Exmoor easily accessible to the north, you can explore three woodland walks ranging from 1 to 2.5 miles and the banks of the River Dalch. There are two deep coarse fishing lakes (bring your own rod), the top one offering family fishing and the lower one for serious fishing (age 14 or over and free of charge). Riding is available on site (best to bring your own hat) with hour-long and park rides available. The ponies and goats are also popular with adults and children alike. The touring area is very neat and tidy with a spacious feel to it as units are sited around the perimeter or back onto hedges, leaving open central areas. The 85 numbered, grass pitches are flat, gently sloping or on terraces and are sufficiently large. Eighty of them have electricity (10A). Seasonal tourers take up 25 pitches and there are four caravan holiday homes. The owners, Geoff and Liz, are constantly upgrading the park (this year they opened their new reception and amenity building) and they try very hard to make everyone feel at home.

Facilities: A new purpose built toilet block provides family rooms, washbasins in cubicles, showers and facilities for babies. En-suite room for disabled visitors. Dishwashing (hot water 10p) and laundry. Shop. Bar and snack bar with opening hours varying acc. to season. Unsupervised indoor swimming pools, toddlers pool and water slide open daily, 10 am - 8 pm. Fenced play area with a fort for under 10's (with parental supervision) and football field. TV room. Pool table, table tennis and skittles. Fishing. Riding.

Charges 2002

Per unit incl. 2 persons	£6.50 - £9.00
extra person over 4 yrs	free - £1.80
awning or pup tent	free - £1.80
extra car	£0.50 - £1.00
dog (first two)	£0.50 - £1.00
extra dog	£2.00
electricity	£2.00

Tel: 01884 860330. E-mail: yeatheridge@talk21.com. **Reservations:** Advised for Bank and school holidays and made with £35 deposit; contact park. **Open** 22 March - 29 September.

Directions: Park is off the B3042 Witheridge - Chawleigh (not in East Worlington). From M5 take exit 27 onto A361 to Tiverton. Turn left onto A396 for 0.5 miles then right on B3137 almost to Witheridge, then left on B3042 for 3 miles to site, well-signed down concrete roadway on left. O.S.GR: SS771112.

Devon

Clifford Bridge Park

077 Clifford, Drewsteignton EX6 6QE

Set in five acres of outstanding natural beauty, this riverside touring park provides peace and tranquillity within the Dartmoor National Park. It is three miles from the nearest village with any facilities in a wooded valley on the banks of the River Teign. It can only be approached on narrow lanes (single track for the last mile), but is a good base with plenty to do for those who like country pursuits 'away from it all'. Fingle Bridge is 3.5 miles and Castle Drogo (National Trust) 5 miles. The site is licensed for 24 touring caravans or motorcaravans and 40 tents. Pitches are of a good size on a flat grassy meadow, mainly around the perimeter with some backing onto the river. Plenty of grassy space is left free for recreation and there is a free swimming pool. There are 2 hardstandings and 25 electrical connections (6A). First class walks are possible from the site and game fishing is available on permit (from reception).

Facilities: The toilet block, near the entrance to the park, is not large or modern but is satisfactory and kept clean, with rather small washbasins and showers. Hand and hair dryers. Adjacent 'portacabin' style unit provides extra facilities in high season. Dishwashing sinks are outside, under cover. The farm outbuildings house a shop (Spr. B.H - 1/9), gas supplies, games room with pool table, amusement machine and tourist information, and a small fully equipped laundry room. Freezer service. Swimming pool (54 x 24 ft. open and heated Spr. B.H - 1/9). **Off site:** riding or golf 6 miles, bicycle hire 3 miles.

Charges 2002

Per unit incl. 2 persons	£8.75 - £12.95
small motorcaravan	£7.65 - £11.10
backpacker or cyclist	£2.95 - £4.50
extra person	£2.50 - £3.50
child 8-16 yrs	£1.50 - £2.50
child 4-7 yrs	£0.95 - £1.75
dog	£0.50
electricity	£1.80

Tel: 01647 24226. Fax: 01647 24116. E-mail: info@clifford-bridge.co.uk. **Reservations:** Advised for school holidays and made for any length with £30 deposit. **Open** Easter - 30 September.

Directions: To avoid much single-track road approach via the A30, turning off 11 miles west of Exeter to Cheriton Bishop. Turn left there (at Old Thatch Inn) and follow for 2 miles to crossroads where right for Clifford Bridge, 1 mile of single track, over crossroads and bridge and left to park. O.S.GR: SX782897.

Devon

Dartmoor View Holiday Park

078 Whiddon Down, Okehampton EX20 2QL

With easy access from the A30 road, this peaceful, neat and well kept park has matured into a very comfortable place to stay. It is bordered by tall trees and hedges and internal trees and shrubs have grown providing areas to pitch with well tended flower beds around. There are 72 flat, grassy touring pitches (13 hardstandings) of which 52 have electricity (10/16A) and 14 have water and waste water. About 30 mobile homes occupy the outside edge pitches. Reception is near the entrance, together with a family bar with entertainment some evenings in season. Children have good quality play equipment and there is a small heated outdoor swimming pool with a children's pool, fenced with paved surrounds and a small 9 hole putting green. The site is situated on the northern edge of Dartmoor National Park.

Facilities: The heated sanitary facilities are well maintained and equipped with three unisex cabins, one with toilet. Baby bath. Drive over motorcaravan service point. Laundry and campers' kitchen. Licensed shop. Family bar (1/4-1/10). TV and games rooms. Swimming pool (10 x 5 m; 1/6-15/9). Play area. Table tennis (charged). Putting green. No kite flying is permitted. Caravan storage. **Off site:** Fishing or riding 5 miles, golf 3 miles.

Charges 2002

Per unit incl. 2 persons	£7.50 - £9.75
small one person tent	£6.00 - £7.50
extra person	£2.00
child (3-11 yrs)	£1.50
dog, awning or pup tent	£1.00
electricity	£2.25
all service pitch	£2.00

Spring or autumn special prices. **Tel:** 01647 231545. Fax: 01647 231654. E-mail: info@dartmoorview. co.uk. **Reservations:** Any length, with deposit of £25 p/week or £4 p/night. **Open** March - November.

Directions: On A30 dual-carriageway at the Merrymeet roundabout, take the Whiddon Down road. Park is 0.5 miles on the right. O.S.GR: SX685928.

Harford Bridge has an interesting history - originally the Wheal Union tin mine until 1850, then used as a farm campsite from 1930 and taken over by the Royal Engineers in 1939. It is now a quiet, rural, mature park inside the Dartmoor National Park. It is bounded by the River Tavy on one side and the lane from the main road to the village of Peter Tavy on the other, with Harford Bridge, a classic granite moorland bridge, at the corner. With 16.5 acres, the park provides 120 touring pitches well spaced on a level grassy meadow with some shade from mature trees and others recently planted; 40 pitches have electrical hook-ups and 6 have 'multi-services'. Out of season or by booking in advance you may get one of the delightful spots bordering the river (these are without hook-up facilities). Some holiday caravans and chalets are neatly landscaped in their own area. At the entrance to the park a central grassy area is left free for games, which is also used by the town band, village fete, etc. It is overlooked by reception which also stocks drinks, ice cream, postcards, stamps. etc. but not groceries. While the river (unfenced) will inevitably mesmerise the youngsters and the ducks and chickens attract their interest, a super central adventure play area on a hilly tree knoll will claim them. Two restored Wickstead stainless steel slides, a 45 year old carnival carousel roundabout and tunnels are just part of a well presented, safe, good provision. With its own and the local history, plus its situation, this is a super place to stay.

Facilities: The single toilet block is older in style but has been refurbished and is well kept, properly maintained, and fully equipped. Facilities include a baby bathroom, good launderette and drying room. Freezer pack facility. Games room with additional campers' information, table tennis and separate TV room. Children's play area. Resurfaced tennis court (free). Two communal barbecue areas. Fly fishing (by licence, £3 p/day, £10 p/week). **Off site:** Bicycle hire, riding and golf, all within 2.5 miles.

Charges 2002

Per unit incl. 2 persons	£6.50 - £10.50
extra adult	£2.20 - £2.70
child	£1.10 - £1.60
electricity	£1.00
awning	£1.00
dog	£1.00

Less 10% for stays over 7 days (not electricity or fishing). **Tel:** 01822 810349. Fax: 01822 810028. E-mail: enquiry@harfordbridge.co.uk. **Reservations:** Made for any length with first night's fees. **Open** Late March - early November.

Directions: Two miles north of Tavistock, off A386 Tavistock - Okehampton road, take the road to Peter Tavy. O.S.GR: SX504768.

HARFORD BRIDGE HOLIDAY PARK

Peter Tavy, Tavistock, Devon PL19 9LS
Tel: 01822 810349   Tel: 01822 810028
Email: enquiry@harfordbridge.co.uk
Website: www.harfordbridge.co.uk

* Level sheltered park set in Dartmoor beside the River Tavy, with beautiful views of Cox Tor.
* Riverside camping and other level spacious pitches - Open end Mar to Nov
* Self-catering luxury caravan holiday homes - Open all year.
* Children s play area, tennis and table tennis, fly-fishing, dog exercise field.
* Nearby pony-trekking and golf.   * Bellamy Gold and Rose Award.

Just 2 miles from Tavistock off A386 Okehampton Road, take Peter Tavy turn.

Higher Longford Caravan Park

080 Moorshop, Tavistock PL19 9LQ

Situated within the Dartmoor National Park boundaries, this small park has views up to the higher slopes of the moor. The site has been reorganised and landscaped to provide a neat, sheltered field with 40 level pitches arranged on each side of a circular access road, three smaller touring areas for 12 units in total and a seasonal camping field for a further 40. Facilities include 62 electrical hook-ups, several multi-serviced pitches and an area of hardstanding for motorhomes in poor weather. Privately owned residential caravans and two chalets are in a separate, adjacent area and some attractive converted cottages form a courtyard area with the farmhouse, reception and bar. Within the 14th century farmhouse is a small licensed shop with gas and some fresh farm produce. It adjoins a pleasant, cosy bar and restaurant with open fire and TV, where takeaway or full meals are offered and a spacious extension, useful in poor weather. Higher Longford is an ideal centre for touring Dartmoor, either by car, on foot, or astride a local pony (riding stables nearby). Plymouth and the cross-channel ferries are a 30 minute drive, Tavistock is 3 miles, with a good market and Goose Fair in October.

Facilities: The main toilet block provides roomy showers and smallish washbasins, including one en-suite cabin for ladies. A new toilet block development includes washbasins in cabins. Full laundry facilities. Covered and indoor dishwashing sinks. Motorcaravan services. Ice block swap service. Shop, bar and restaurant with takeaway (all 31/3-31/10). Pool/snooker table. Caravan storage. **Off site:** Game or coarse fishing 3 miles, Tavistock golf course 1 mile, bicycle hire or riding 3 miles.

Charges 2002

Per unit incl. 1 person	£7.00 - £9.00
2 persons	£8.00 - £10.00
extra adult	£2.00 - £2.50
child	£1.00 - £1.50
electricity	£2.00

Less 50p per/night for booked stays over 7 nights. **Tel:** 01822 613360. Fax: 01822 618722. E-mail: stay@higherlongford.co.uk. **Reservations:** Made with £10 deposit. **Open** all year.

Directions: Park is clearly signed from B3357 Princetown road, 2 miles from Tavistock. O.S.GR: SX520747.

Riverside Caravan Park

081 Longbridge Road, Marshmills, Plymouth PL6 8LD

Riverside is well placed for those visiting Plymouth, the maritime capital of the southwest, to use the car ferries or en-route to Cornwall. It is also ideally situated for touring Dartmoor and south Devon. Although under 4 miles from the city centre, its location on the banks of the River Plym in a wooded valley is a quiet one - in fact riverside walks can take you up to Dartmoor. Attractive shrubs and trees, flower beds, well kept grass and tarmac roads give a neat, park-like appearance. Over 220 units of any type are taken on flat, numbered pitches, including 170 with 10A electrical connections and 60 'winterised' (ie. with hardstanding). There is a separate area for tents and a large, hard area is retained for late arrivals and large American motorhomes. An added advantage is that the site is security patrolled at night.

Facilities: The two sanitary blocks, one subdivided into two, are of different construction and have been modernised and decorated somewhat haphazardly. Some washbasins in private cabins with toilets for ladies in one block. Indoor dishwashing sinks. Laundry facilities with irons on loan. A shop at the entrance open to all (Spr. B.H. - mid-Sept). Lounge bar (fully open from July with nightly entertainment), restaurant with takeaway (5-10 pm), games and TV rooms. Play area. Heated swimming pool (60 x 30 ft), with children's paddling pool, open Spr. B.H. - mid-Sept. Fishing on site. **Off site:** Bicycle hire 3 miles, boat slipway 2 miles, tennis and dry ski slope 1 mile.

Charges 2002

Per adult	£2.75 - £3.75
child (3-10 yrs)	£1.25 - £1.50
pitch	£3.00 - £4.00
electricity	£2.00 - £2.50

Special breaks for the over-50s. No single sex groups. **Tel:** 01752 344122. Fax: 01752 344122. E-mail: info@riversidecaravanpark.com. **Reservations:** Made with £15 deposit p/week or part. **Open** all year.

Directions: From Exeter on A38 dual-carriageway take Marsh Mill exit (first signed to Plymouth city centre). Follow good camp site signs to third exit, turning left after a few yards. O.S.GR: SX518576.

Old Cotmore Farm

Stokenham, Kingsbridge TQ7 2LR

104

A charming and secluded park, two miles from Start Point, Old Cotmore Farm is now the farmhouse, two cottages and a small touring site. The only livestock to be seen now are a few chickens and ducks, and maybe some horses. The site provides 30 pitches, all with electric hook-up, on neatly cut grass, partly in a garden type situation to one side of the driveway with some pitches sloping, and partly on a level, smallish field with children's play equipment in the centre. Pitches here tend to be used for families with children, with those on the other side of the drive kept for adults only. There is a fenced pond area near the entrance. Reception is past the pitches towards the farmhouse and adjoining the toilet block which has been converted from original farm buildings. A separate field with a 28 day licence has water points, two extra sinks (H&C) and two toilets, but it may put pressure on the main block when in use. The site is in an area of Outstanding Natural Coastal Beauty, with Slapton Sands, Salcombe and Kingsbridge near and Dartmouth just a little further. It is an ideal area for walking, boating, diving, windsurfing and safe bathing.

Facilities: The ladies' and men's sections of the toilet block provide modern facilities with a degree of individuality. A separate en-suite unit provides for disabled visitors and also includes a baby bath and changing table. Utility room with dishwashing sinks and a laundry sink, three washing machines and two dryers, plus tourist information. Reception stocks gas and basic necessities - baguettes can be ordered. Table tennis. **Off site:** Riding 4 miles, golf 8 miles. Two pubs are within one mile either way.

Charges 2002

Per unit incl. 2 persons	£8.00 - £11.50
extra adult	£3.50 - £4.50
child 3-15 yrs	£0.65 - £1.25
dog (max. 2)	£1.00
extra car or boat	£1.00
electricity	£2.00

Tel: 01548 580240. Fax: 01548 580875. E-mail: graham.bowsher@btinternet.com. **Reservations:** Made with deposit (£3 per day); contact park. **Open** 14 March - 31 October.

Directions: From Kingsbridge on A379 Dartmouth road, go through Frogmore and Chillington to Carehouse Cross mini-roundabout at Stokenham. Turn right towards Beesands and follow camp signs for 1 mile. Site entrance is on right just past the post box. Roads are a little narrow in places. O.S.GR: SX804417.

Moor View Touring Park

California Cross, Modbury PL21 0SG

082

Moor View has a gently sloping position with terraced, individual, fairly level grass pitches with marvellous views across to the Dartmoor Tors. It provides 68 pitches of varying size, connected by hard core roads. All have 10A electricity, 33 are on hardstanding, with water and drainage on 13. Bushes and shrubs on the lower terraces are growing well, giving the park a more mature feel. A two acre field provides space for children or for the odd rally. The amenities have been designed in one block near the entrance, not too far from the furthest pitches. The block includes reception and a shop stocking fresh local produce and some camping accessories. Burgh Island and Bigbury Bay are nearby, Dartmoor is within striking distance. This is a park in a lovely corner of Devon, with enthusiastic new owners, Edward and Liz Corwood. A member of the Countryside Discovery group.

Facilities: Traditional style, heated toilet facilities have access from a courtyard area and are kept clean, providing all necessary facilities including a laundry room and sink, and covered dishwashing sinks. Shop. Takeaway in season (to order, 6.30-7.30 pm). Games room with pool table and table tennis. TV room. **Off site:** Golf 5 miles, riding and fishing 6 miles. A local country pub is within walking distance, the small town of Modbury is 3 miles.

Charges 2002

Per adult	£3.75 - £5.50
child (5-16 yrs)	£1.00
electricity	£1.50
serviced pitch incl. water and drainage	£1.00
all weather serviced pitch	£2.00
hardstanding pitch	£1.00

Tel: 01548 821485. E-mail: info@moorviewtouring park.co.uk. **Reservations:** Made with £10 deposit. **Open** 15 March - 15 November.

Directions: On the A38 from Exeter, pass exit for A385 (Totnes) and continue for a further 2 miles. Just past Woodpecker Inn leave the A38 at Wrangaton Cross, signed Ermington, Modbury and Yealmpton. Turn left and follow straight on at crossroads (Kitterford Cross) signed Modbury, Loddiswell, Kingsbridge for 3 miles to California Cross. Leave garage on left and follow towards Modbury (B3207). Park is 0.5 miles on left. O.S.GR: SX705533.

Slapton Sands Camping & Caravanning Club Site

Middle Grounds, Slapton, Kingsbridge TQ7 2QW

083

Slapton is a charming village with tiny lanes and cottages, a shop and two historic pubs, one dominated by the ruined tower of an old monastery. The village (unsuitable for camping traffic) is about half a mile inland from the shingle beach of Slapton Sands and the fresh water Ley which is administered as a nature reserve by the Field Studies Council. The Camping and Caravanning Club site is situated on the road which leads from the Sands, on a well kept meadow overlooking the bay - the sea views are panoramic from most areas of the site, with shelter provided by some large bushes and the surrounding hedge. There are 126 grass pitches, some with a slight slope, and electrical connections (16A) are available for 46 (including 10 with hardstanding). Motorcaravans, trailer tents and tents are accepted without problems but the planners will only permit 8 caravan pitches which are kept for club members. This area was used for rehearsals for the WW2 Normandy landings, when the whole population was evacuated - there are memorials, including a tank in the village of Torcross. The quaint port of Dartmouth is 7 miles, Kingsbridge 8 miles and a variety of beaches and coves around the beautiful South Hams coastline are within easy reach.

Facilities: The modern toilet block is central, can be heated and is kept very clean, with washbasins in private cabins. Useful parent and child room and separate unit for disabled visitors (with key). Dishwashing facilities, laundry sinks, washing machine and dryer (and outside lines). Motorcaravan service point. Reception has a small library, gas and freezer for ice blocks. Small play area. **Off site:** Riding 0.5 miles. The Field Studies Centre arranges guided walks and short study courses on a wide variety of interests and can issue fishing permits for the Ley (perch and pike, of legendary size, in the summer months). Beach fishing is also popular.

Charges 2002

Per adult	£3.75 - £5.30
child (6-18 yrs)	£1.65
non-member pitch fee	£4.30
electricity	£1.65 - £2.40

Tel: 01548 580538. **Reservations:** Necessary and made with deposit; contact site. **Open** March - October.

Directions: From A38 Exeter - Plymouth road, take A384 to Totnes. Just before town, turn right on A381 to Kingsbridge, then A379 through Stokenham and Torcross to Slapton Sands. Half way along the beach road turn left to Slapton village and site is 200 yds on right. Note: Avoid the very narrow Five Mile Lane from the A381 which is signed Slapton (just after a filling station) 6 miles from Kingsbridge. O.S.GR: SX825450.

Galmpton Park

Greenway Road, Galmpton, Brixham TQ5 0EP

085

Within a few miles of the lively amenities of Torbay, Galmpton Park lies peacefully just outside the village of Galmpton, overlooking the beautiful Dart estuary just upstream of Dartmouth and Kingswear. Some 120 pitches, 60 marked for caravans, are arranged on a wide sweep of grassy, terraced meadow, each pitch with its own wonderful view of the river. Situated on the hillside, some parts have quite a slope, but there are flatter areas (the owners will advise and assist). There are 90 electrical connections (10A) and 20 pitches are fully serviced. There is a separate tent field. Galmpton is a quiet and simple park (with the gates closed 11.15 pm - 7.30 am) in a most picturesque setting, within easy reach of all the attractions of South Devon. A member of the Countryside Discovery group.

Facilities: A central, substantial looking toilet block provides clean facilities including three washbasins in private cabins, a very attractive under 5's bathroom (key available), baby unit and hair care areas. Dishwashing room also with a washing machine, dryer, iron and ironing board. Reception/shop selling a wide range of basics including gas. Good adventure play equipment. Dogs (max. 2 per unit) are accepted at the owner's discretion and not mid-July and Aug. Motorhomes over 21 ft. are not accepted. **Off site:** Local pub is 5 minutes walk.

Charges 2002

Per unit incl. 2 persons and awning	£7.00 - £11.00
de-luxe pitch plus	£1.50 - £2.00
extra adult	£2.50
child 5-16 yrs	£1.20
electricity	£1.90
dog (off peak only)	£0.50

Various discounts available. **Tel:** 01803 842066. Fax: 01803 844458. E-mail: galmptontouringpark@hotmail.com. **Reservations:** Made with £20 deposit p/week booked. **Open** Easter - 30 September.

Directions: Take A380 Paignton ring road towards Brixham until junction with the Paignton - Brixham coast road. Turn right towards Brixham, then second right into Manor Vale Road. Continue through the village, past the school and site is 500 yds on the right. O.S.GR: SX885558.

Woodlands Leisure Park

Blackawton, Totnes TQ9 7DQ

Woodlands is a surprise, a nice one - from the road you have no idea of just what is hidden away deep in the Devon countryside. To achieve this, there has been sympathetic development of farm and woodland to provide a leisure centre, open to the public and with a range of activities and entertainment appealing to all ages, plus a touring caravan park. Children (and many energetic parents too!) will be kept amused for hours by a variety of imaginative adventure play equipment or amazing water toboggan runs and 'Arctic Coasters' hidden amongst the trees and many farm animals, birds and boats. Those more peacefully inclined can follow woodland walks around the attractive ponds. A Falconry Centre gives opportunities to watch displays (or for the birds to watch you!) There is plenty of play equipment for younger children too, including an indoor play barn with a circus theme. Opened for the millennium, the 'Empire of the Sea Dragon', a two million pounds indoor play centre, has provided marvellous wet weather facilities - the biggest indoor venture in the UK. With a two night stay, campers on the touring park are admitted free of charge to the leisure park. The camping and caravan site overlooks the woodland and the leisure park, taking 320 units on three sloping, grassy fields, one original, the other two newly developed. Two of these have been fully terraced to provide groups of four to eight flat, very spacious pitches (90% with 10A electrical connections and a shared water tap, drain and rubbish bin). The newest field has 120 pitches (with electricity) designed with a more open feel to provide space for larger groups or rallies. A popular park, early reservation is advisable.

Facilities: Three modern, heated toilet blocks are well maintained and kept very clean. One block includes private bathrooms (coin-operated, 20p) and seven family shower cubicles. Two blocks have a well equipped laundry room, dishwashing area and a freezer for ice packs. Baby changing facilities. The leisure park café, with terrace, provides good value meals and cream teas with entertainment (music, Morris men, etc.) at busy times and a takeaway service for campers. Opening hours of the café and adjoining gift shop (with gas and a few basic food supplies) vary according to season and demand. TV and games room. Dogs are accepted on the campsite but not in the leisure park (kennels available). Caravan storage. **Off site:** The charming town of Dartmouth and the South Hams beaches are near. Fishing 3 miles, golf 0.5 miles, riding 5 miles.

Charges 2002

Per unit incl. 2 persons	£7.50 - £14.50
extra person over 2 yrs	£3.75
awning or extra small pup tent	£2.50
large tent or trailer tent (120 sq ft plus)	£2.50
extra car, boat or trailer	£1.00
dog (contact site first)	£2.50
electricity	£2.50

Free entry to leisure park for stays 2 nights or more. **Tel:** 01803 712598. Fax: 01803 712680. E-mail: fun@woodlandspark.com. **Reservations:** Accepted for min. 3 nights with £35 deposit, except July/Aug. when min. 7 days and £50 deposit. Balance in full 21 days before arrival. **Open** 1 April - 4 November.

Directions: From A38 at Buckfastleigh, take A384 to Totnes. Before the town centre turn right on A381 Kingsbridge road. After Halwell turn left at Totnes Cross garage, on A3122 to Dartmouth. Park is on right after 2.5 miles. O.S.GR: SX813521.

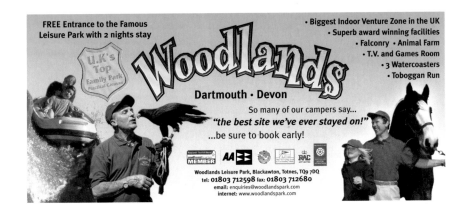

Situated to the south of central Paignton, with a short, signed walk to the sea and some views of Torbay, this Hoburne-owned park's major interest is a complex of 516 holiday homes (182 to let) which totally dominate the higher of the two touring sites. However, there are 157 touring pitches (no tents) in two sections, each with its own resident wardens. One, probably the quieter of the two, is on flat grass by the entrance. The other is on higher ground, through the holiday homes at the top of the park with the sites large shop and café (with bakery) close by. It is on a gentle slope with some views. Pitches are of reasonable size, though with some variation, and all have 10A electricity. For those who like entertainment, the central club complex is the parks best feature, with a good sized heated outdoor pool (80 x 40 ft.) and a super indoor pool with views across the bay, complete with flume, sauna and steam room. The clubhouse has a large club lounge with dance floor, a separate bar/restaurant (with views of Torbay). Entertainment is organised for adults and children from Spr. B.H. to end Sept. and at Easter.

Facilities: Three toilet blocks, two of modern design in lower touring field, third block is of older design at the top touring field. Large launderette. Dishwashing area. Recycling bins. Chemical disposal. Motorcaravan service point. Well stocked shop. Gas available. Club room. Restaurant/bar. Takeaway. Café. Heated outdoor pool. Indoor pool with flume and fountain, sauna and steam room (all free). Mini two lane bowling alley. Pool and snooker tables. Amusement arcade. TV room showing cartoons. Crazy golf. Adventure playground. Indoor soft adventure play area. Daily children's entertainment in high season at the Sammy Seahorse Club. Reception is busy but efficient. Up to 30 American motorhomes accepted (30ft. max). No dogs or pets are accepted.

Charges 2002

Per unit incl. up to 6 persons	£10.00 - £23.00

Tel: 01803 558010. Fax: 01803 696286. E-mail: enquiries@hoburne.co.uk. **Reservations:** Advised for high season. Made for 1-6 nights with payment in full, for 7 nights or over with £50 deposit p/week. Min. 7 days in high season. **Open** 14 February - 25 October.

Directions: Park is signed from the outer Paignton ring road. Look for left turn into Goodrington Road, then left into Grange Road. O.S.GR: SX890585.

Beverley Park Holiday Centre

Goodrington Road, Paignton TQ4 7JE

087

Beverley Park is a quality holiday centre, attractively landscaped and with views over Torbay. With pools, a large dance hall, bars and entertainment, all is run in an efficient and orderly manner. The holiday caravan park has 195 caravan holiday homes and 23 lodges, mainly around the central complex. There are 189 touring pitches in the lower areas of the park, all reasonably sheltered, some with views across the bay and some on slightly sloping ground. All pitches can take awnings and have 16A electricity (15 m. cable), 38 have hardstanding, 21 are fully serviced. Tents are accepted and a limited number of tent pitches have electrical connections. The park has a long season and reservations are essential for caravans. Entertainment is organised at Easter and from early May in the Starlight Cabaret bar. There are indoor and outdoor pools, each one heated and supervised. The Oasis fitness centre provides a steam room, jacuzzi, sun bed and an excellent fitness room. The park is in the heart of residential Torbay, with views across the bay to Brixham and Torquay, and sandy beaches less than a mile away. This popular park has lots to offer and is well maintained and run. A member of the Best of British group.

Facilities: Toilet blocks are adjacent to the pitches. These are good (some of the toilet cubicles are a little cramped) and although they can receive heavy use and need regular attention, they are well maintained and heated. Showers and washbasins have free hot water, baths are on payment. Unit for disabled visitors and facilities for babies. Laundry. Gas supplies. Motorcaravan service point. Large general shop, restaurant, bars and takeaway service (all Easter, then 4/5-26/10). Swimming pools. Fitness centre. Tennis court. Crazy golf. Children's playground. Nature trail. Amusement centre with pool, table tennis and amusement machines. Children's soft play area. Dogs are not accepted. **Off site:** A regular minibus service runs to Paignton (timetable at reception) or normal services from outside the park. Fishing, bicycle hire, riding and golf all within 2 miles.

Charges 2002

Per pitch incl. 2 persons, electricity	£9.30 - £20.50
incl. mains services and awning	£10.00 - £25.50
tent pitch incl. 2 persons	£7.30 - £18.50
extra adult	£4.00
child 4-14 yrs	£3.00

Max. 6 persons per reservation. **Tel:** 01803 843887. Fax: 01803 845427. E-mail: info@beverley-holidays.co.uk. **Reservations:** Made with £25 deposit (7, 14 or 21 days 17/7-3/9, min. 2 nights all other times); balance payable more than 28 days before arrival. **Open** 16 February - 30 November.

Directions: Park is south of Paignton in Goodrington Road between A379 coast road and B3203 ring road and is well signed on both. O.S.GR: SX882584.

ENGLISH RIVIERA

LUXURY TOURING PARK
WITH SUPERB SEA VIEWS
EVERY MODERN FACILITY FOR TOURERS

- Indoor & Outdoor Heated Swimming Pools
- Live Entertainment
- Cabaret & Dancing
- Sports Facilities
- Children's Activities
- Restaurants
- Leisure Club
- Close to many attractions (Inc Paignton Zoo & Water Park)
- Beautiful Parkland & Nature Trail

Call **01803 843887**

For a free colour brochure
Or write to Beverley Holidays, Dept AR, Goodrington Road, Paignton, Devon TQ4 7JE
Email: info@beverley-holidays.co.uk

www.beverley-holidays.co.uk

Widdicombe Farm Tourist Park

The Ring Road, Compton, Paignton TQ3 1ST

Widdicombe Farm is only three miles from Torquay and with easy access from the A380, is well situated for the Torbay area. There are 200 numbered pitches, 180 with electricity connections (10A) of which 130 have hardstandings. Surrounded by farmland, the pitches are on terraces with open views across the countryside. Many trees and shrubs have been planted and there are tarmac access roads. There may be some background traffic noise but it is not too intrusive. Touring areas are separated into sections for families, couples, tent campers, etc. A large comfortable bar offers family entertainment and opposite the bar are three gas barbecues for hire (£2 per session). The site has a relaxed, friendly feel.

Facilities: There are three older style toilet blocks - the original heated block near reception is fully equipped and includes facilities for disabled people, a baby room, dishwashing area and laundry room. Shop and 'Poppy' restaurant that provides evening meals, breakfasts, cream teas and takeaway (both Easter - mid Oct). Family bar. Games room with video games and pool tables. Play area and recreation field for ball games. Certain breeds of dog are not accepted. Caravan storage. **Off site:** Fishing, bicycle hire, riding and golf, all within 2 miles.

Charges 2002

Per unit incl. 2 persons	£6.00 - £11.00
extra adult	£2.50
child (3-16 yrs)	£1.50
under 3 yrs	£0.50
awning or extra car	£1.50
dog	£1.00 - £1.50
electricity	£1.80

Bargain breaks available. **Tel:** 01803 558325. Fax: 01803 559526. E-mail: enq@torquaytouring.co.uk. **Reservations:** Advised for July/Aug. (min. 4 days) and made with deposit (£20 per week) and fee (£2). **Open** 15 March - 31 October.

Directions: From Newton Abbot take A380 south for approx. 5 miles; site is well signed off this road. O.S.GR: SX874641.

Ashburton Caravan Park

Waterleat, Ashburton TQ13 7HU

For tents and motorcaravans only, the four acres of Ashburton Park nestle in a hidden valley below Dartmoor, bordered by mature woodland. The Ashburn, a shallow stream with rocky pools, evenly divides and screens two acres of holiday homes from the two acre camping area. Sheltered and south facing, the park is a tranquil retreat, although for the energetic a half mile steep uphill walk brings you to the moor or by 1.5 miles of Devon lanes to Ashburton village. There are 35 level or gently sloping pitches, 8 with electricity connections (16A), on either side of a tarmac road that culminates in a small field area. Each visitor receives a copy of the 'Dartmoor Visitor', the information paper supplied by the Dartmoor National Park authorities - the campsite is actually within the boundaries of the Park. There are limited bus services to Newton Abbot, Exeter or Plymouth. Torches would be useful. A well maintained, tranquil small park for nature lovers.

Facilities: First class, purpose built toilet block provides washbasins in cabins for ladies and a toilet and washbasin for disabled visitors (baby bath, etc. available). Washing machine and dryer, plus free spin dryer and iron. Reception/information centre provides gas, a freezer pack service, tourist information, maps and walks and a daily weather report. Dogs (limited breeds only) are welcomed if exercised off the park. **Off site:** Shops, banks, post office, a small heated swimming pool and pubs, etc. are in Ashburton, a pleasant walk away by the river. Bicycle hire 1 mile, riding and golf 3 miles.

Charges 2002

Per unit incl. 1 person	£4.00 - £6.00
Per unit incl. 2 persons	£7.50 - £10.00
extra person (over 1 yr)	£1.50 - £2.25
dog	£0.70
electricity	£1.80

No credit cards. **Tel:** 01364 652552. Fax: 01364 652552. E-mail: info@ashburtondevon.freeserve. co.uk. **Reservations:** Made for min. 3 nights with £15 deposit. **Open** Easter - mid July.

Directions: In the centre of Ashburton turn northwest into North Street. As built-up area thins out bear right before bridge following signs for 'Waterleat' (tent symbol) for approx. 1.5 miles. Park is on the left. O.S.GR: SX752721.

The River Dart Country Park

Holne Park, Ashburton TQ13 7NP

With its mature park and woodland, once part of a Victorian estate, this interesting and unusual park could appeal to many, particularly those with children. On the edge of Dartmoor, in the beautiful Dart valley, the park and its activities is open to the general public on payment. It features a variety of unusual adventure play equipment (eg. a giant spider's web) arranged amongst and below the trees, 'Lilliput Land' for toddlers, Jungle Fun, and woodland streams and a lake with raft for swimming and inflatables, fly fishing and marked nature and forest trails - all free to campers except fishing. It can become busy at weekends and school holidays. Supervised courses in caving, canoeing, mountain biking, climbing or sea cliff exploring are arranged, even 'Xtreme Sports' - high adrenaline, active sports such as abseiling or simulated parachute jumps - are also offered (contact the park for dates and details). The camping and caravanning area is in the more open parkland overlooking the woods and is mainly on a slight slope with some shade from mature trees. There are 170 individual pitches of very reasonable size, marked by lines on the grass, some slightly sloping, with 105 electrical connections (10/16A) and 12 hardstandings The entire estate is kept very clean and tidy.

Facilities: Two wooden toilet blocks, the newer one quite smart, the older one a little tired. Both can be heated and provide washbasins in cubicles, baby changing facilities, laundry and dishwashing, and a freezer between them. The newer block includes a separate unit for disabled visitors (access by key), family bathroom and drying room. Motorcaravan service point. Shop (all season). Restaurant, adjoining snack bar with takeaway. Bar, large TV and games room with pool and amusement machines. Indoor climbing wall (some of these open all year - contact park for details of activities on offer). Small, heated swimming pool (April-Oct). Tennis courts. Max. two dogs per pitch. American motorhomes are only accepted in dry periods (no hardstandings). **Off site:** Bicycle hire or riding 4 miles, golf 6 miles.

Charges 2002

Per unit incl. 2 persons	£9.50 - £14.00
extra adult	£4.75 - £6.95
child 3-14 yrs	£3.95 - £5.75
electricity	£2.00
dog (max. 2)	£1.50

Tel: 01364 652511. Fax: 01364 652020. E-mail: enquiries@riverdart.co.uk. **Reservations:** Advised for high season and made with £10 deposit per pitch (additional high season deposit £30 for 7 nights or less, £40 for longer). Balance due 21 days before arrival. All deposits non-returnable. **Open** 1 April - end October.

Directions: Signed from the A38 at Peartree junction, park is about 1 mile west of Ashburton, on the road to Two Bridges. Disregard advisory signs stating 'no caravans' as access to the park is prior to narrow bridge. O.S.GR: SX734701.

Dornafield

Two Mile Oak, Newton Abbot TQ12 6DD

088

The entrance to Dornafield leads into the charming old courtyard of a 14th Century farmhouse giving a mellow feeling that is complemented by the warm welcome from the Dewhirst family. The reception, shop, tourist information/ecology room have been sympathetically converted from the farm outbuildings, with the games room from the old milking parlour, complete with stalls. Once booked in, you may continue down the lane (in spring time overlooked by a tree covered bank and alive with wild flowers) to the Buttermeadow, a tranquil valley providing 75 individual, numbered pitches on flat grass, separated by grassy ridges and in some places, wild rose hedges. You will pass the walled Orchard area, secluded and cosy for tents. Or take the road up the hill and reach Blackrock Copse, the development of large luxury pitches with all facilities including a chemical disposal point for each pitch and TV connections, very cleverly concealed and 61 with hardstanding. All electricity points are 10A. Whilst having been carefully designed, the environment has been kept natural. Both Buttermeadow and Blackrock have super woodland adventure play areas, well maintained and complete with Wendy houses. Dornafield is also a member of the Caravan Club's 'managed under contract' scheme, with both members and non-members made welcome. Dornafield's rural situation is delightful and, being away from the coast and without any evening activities, it is a haven for those seeking a quiet, restful holiday. A park that is well worth consideration.

Facilities: Perhaps the finest features of the park are the toilet blocks. The original one in Buttermeadow is good, heated, with some washbasins in cubicles and comfortable roomy showers, but the new block up the hill could be said to be 'state of the art' with under-floor heating and a heat recovery system. It is stylish yet warm providing everything for your comfort including a large clock! Both blocks have facilities for disabled visitors and babies, laundry rooms and covered washing up areas. They are bright, cheerful and spotlessly clean. Shop, Gas supplies. All year caravan storage. All-weather hard tennis court. Games room with table tennis. Play areas. **Off site:** The local inn is within half a mile. Fishing 2.5 miles, golf 1 mile.

Charges 2002

Per unit incl. 2 adults and electricity	£10.75 - £14.50
incl. mains services and awning	£11.75 - £18.00
extra adult	£3.50 - £4.50
child (5-16 yrs)	£1.10 - £1.20
dog	£1.00

Tel: 01803 812732. Fax: 01803 812032. E-mail: enquiries@dornafield.com. **Reservations:** Any length, £10 p/week in low season, £25 p/week high season. **Open** 17 March - 3 November.

Directions: Park is northwest of A381 Newton Abbot - Totnes road. Leave A381 at Two Mile Oak Inn, opposite garage, and turn left at crossroads after about half a mile. Entrance is on the right. O.S.GR: SX848683.

Ross Park

Park Hill Farm, Ipplepen, Newton Abbot TQ12 5TT

Ross Park has to be seen to appreciate the amazing floral displays with their dramatic colours that are a feature of the park. These are complemented by the use of a wide variety of shrubs which form hedging for most of the 110 pitches to provide your own special plot, very much as on the continent. Many pitches have wonderful views over the surrounding countryside and for those who prefer the more open style, one small area has been left unhedged. The owners, Mark and Helen Lowe, continue to strive to provide quality facilities and maintain standards, and this is reflected in the awards they have won. There are nice personal touches, as seen in the utility room with the beautiful photographs of the country-side and suggestions for visits cross-referenced to a map. Also giving an individual touch is the impressive, heated conservatory with yet more named exotic and colourful plants. Seating is provided here as it is directly linked to the New Barn which provides a comfortable lounge, a mezzanine bar with bar snacks and a restaurant. The touring area is divided into bays or groups by hedging and shrubs and provides 110 pitches all with electricity (10/16A). Some 82 of these have a hardened surface, some made larger with an increased gravel area. Herbs for a barbecue can be found beside the tourist information chalet. An orchard area alive with daffodils in the spring and a conserva-tion area with information on wild flowers and butterflies, and with extended views, completes these environmentally consid-ered amenities. Barn dances with barbecue are organised on Sundays in high season. A well cared for park worthy of consideration.

Facilities: The main toilet facilities next to the New Barn open from under a veranda style roof, colourful with hanging baskets. They comprise six well equipped, heated en-suite units, one with baby changing facilities, one suitable for disabled people. At the rear are further separate shower, washbasin and toilet facilities. Below the New Barn is a new, heated block with toilets, washbasins in cabins and a hair-care centre. Fully equipped laundry room and utility room providing dishwashing sinks, a freezer and battery charging facilities. Dog shower. Motorcaravan service point. Recycling bins. Comfortable reception cum shop. Gas supplies. Bar, bar snacks and restaurant with a la carte menu (all April - end Oct, plus Christmas and New Year). Games room, table tennis, full sized snooker table and billiards room. 7-acre park area for recreation with bowling and croquet greens and large well equipped adventure playground for older children. Caravan storage. **Off site:** Dainton Park 18 hole golf course is adjacent. Fishing 3 miles, riding 1 mile.

Charges 2002

Per unit incl. 2 persons	£7.70 - £13.00
extra adult	£3.25 - £4.25
child (4-16 yrs)	£1.50
electricity	£1.70 - £2.20

Christmas packages available. No credit cards. **Tel:** 01803 812983. Fax: 01803 812983. E-mail: enquiries @rossparkcaravanpark.co.uk. **Reservations:** Made with £20 deposit. **Open** all year except Jan. and first two weeks of Feb.

Directions: From A381 Newton Abbot - Totnes road, park is signed towards Woodland at Park Hill crossroads and Jet filling station. O.S.GR: SX845671.

Devon

Parker's Farm Holiday Park
Higher Mead Farm, Ashburton, Newton Abbot TQ13 7LJ

096

Well situated with fine views towards Dartmoor, Parker's Farm is a modern touring site on a working farm. Close inspection reveals a unique chance to experience Devon country life at first hand, with pigs, sheep, goats, calves and rabbits, etc. in pens to feed and touch or the milking to get involved with. In addition the Parker family have added a family bar which provides entertainment during the season (quiz night, bingo, guitar player) and fills the gap created by the closure of the local pub. Farm walks are tremendously popular and take place four evenings a week in high season, on request at other times. The 100 touring pitches, with electricity (12A), are set directly above the farm buildings on terraces giving broad, flat groups of pitches, all with good views across the valley (to the A38 which may give some road noise). Hardstandings are available. Young trees and hedges are maturing nicely on the lower terraces. Parker's Farm will suit those who don't seek the sophisticated amenities of more developed parks and a warm welcome awaits - in the words of one camper, 'You come here and feel you belong'.

Facilities: Two modern and clean shower and toilet blocks provide good facilities with a family shower room and baby bathroom, plus an en-suite room for disabled visitors, dishwashing and laundry. Small shop (Whitsun-mid Sept). Restaurant, comfortable bar with family room (Whitsun-mid Sept.) and entertainment. Games room with table tennis and pool, an indoor play and TV area, a large outdoor play area, with trampolines around the park, and made-safe farm implements and tractors. Caravan storage. Rallies welcome. American motorhomes accepted by prior arrangement. **Off site:** Bicycle hire 5 miles, golf 4 miles, riding 5 miles.

Charges 2002

Per unit incl. 2 persons	£6.50 - £10.00
extra person over 3 yrs	£1.30
pup tent or awning	£1.30
electricity	£1.80
dog	£0.70

Tel: 01364 652598. Fax: 01364 654004. E-mail: parkersfarm@btconnect.com. **Reservations:** Made with £10 deposit. **Open** Easter - 31 October.

Directions: From Exeter on A38, 26 miles from Plymouth, turn left at Alston Cross signed 'Woodland Denbury'. Site is 400 yards. O.S.GR: SX757702.

Lemonford Caravan Park

098 Bickington, Newton Abbot TQ12 6JR

Lemonford is a well run, neat and tidy site for all ages and families on the southern edge of the National Park, some three miles from both Ashburton and Newton Abbot. It has the look and atmosphere of the 'cultivated' caravan park, close to the main road, yet set in a sheltered, peaceful dip bordered by the pretty River Lemon. Well mown grass and smart, trimmed hedges create the tranquil, attractive atmosphere the owners work hard to maintain. There are 85 pitches (35 used as seasonal pitches) on level grass and grouped in four areas according to whether they are to be used by families, couples or individuals. Most pitches have 10A electricity, about 45 have hardstanding. The park is well located for excursions and two good pubs are within walking distance, one along the banks of the river.

Facilities: Two modern toilet blocks, one new, can be heated and provide some private cabins, a ladies' bathroom (£1 payment) and a family bathroom. The new block has facilities for disabled visitors. Dishwashing area under cover. Laundry facilities. Shop. Gas supplies. Freezer service. Play area. Putting green. No commercial vehicles are accepted. **Off site:** Fishing 4 miles, riding and bicycle hire 3 miles, golf 2 miles. Leisure pool in Newton Abbot.

Charges 2002

Per unit incl. 2 persons	£6.00 - £9.50
extra person	£1.50
child (3-15 yrs)	£1.10
awning	£1.00
electricity	£1.80
dog	£0.80

Special low season offers. No credit cards. **Tel:** 01626 821242. Fax: 01626 821242. E-mail: mark@lemonford.co.uk. **Reservations:** Advised for July/Aug. and made with £15 deposit (min. 3 nights July/Aug). **Open** 23 March - 31 October.

Directions: Travelling from Exeter, turn off A38 Plymouth road at A382 (Drumbridges) exit signed Newton Abbot, Bovey Tracey, Mortonhampstead. At roundabout take third exit to Bickington. Continue for 1 mile to Toby Jug Inn in the village and park is on left at the bottom of the hill. From Plymouth, take A383 (Goodstone) exit, cross A38 and take first left to Bickington to site on right. O.S.GR: SX793723.

Holmans Wood Caravan & Camping Park

094 Chudleigh TQ13 0DZ

Close to the main A38 Exeter - Plymouth road, with easy access, this attractive, neat park makes a sheltered base for touring south Devon and Dartmoor. The hedged park is arranged on well kept grass surrounding a shallow depression, the floor of which makes a safe, grassy play area for children. Many attractive trees are growing and the park is decorated with flowers. In two main areas and accessed by tarmac roads, there 115 level pitches (including a number of seasonal pitches) and 14 mobile homes. There are 109 pitches with electrical hook-ups (10A) and 70 with hardstanding, electricity, TV aerial hook up, water and drainage. Grassy areas are provided for tents. Adventure play equipment is provided for children, with badminton and tennis nets and an extra meadow for recreation. There may be some traffic noise on pitches to the west of the park. This is a pleasant, well run park and with no other on-site amenities would suit couples or families who prefer a peaceful stay.

Facilities: The single, good quality toilet block includes facilities for babies and disabled visitors, a dishwashing room and a laundry room. Children's play area. Caravan storage. **Off site:** Pub/restaurant nearby in Chudleigh village. The beach or Dartmoor are 7 miles and Haldon Forest for walks is 2 miles. Sunday market at Exeter Racecourse (2 miles). Fishing 1 mile, golf or riding 4 miles.

Charges guide

Per unit incl. 2 persons	£6.59 - £8.95
de-luxe pitch	£7.95 - £10.65
extra adult	£1.65 - £2.20
child (4-14 yrs)	£1.39 - £1.69
awning or child's tent	£1.69
porch awning	£0.95
dog	£0.90
extra car or boat	£1.10
electricity	£2.00

Tel: 01626 853785. Fax: 01626 854707. **Reservations:** Any length, £30 deposit per week. **Open** Mid March - end October.

Directions: From Exeter on A38 Plymouth road, 0.5 miles after the racecourse and just after a garage, take Chudleigh exit (signed). Park is immediately on the left. From Plymouth turn off A38 for Chudleigh/Teign Valley, then right for Chudleigh. Continue through the town and park is 1 mile. O.S.GR: SX882811.

This extensive 130 acre park on the edge of Dartmoor, now under new ownership, was purpose built as a modern touring park cum leisure complex providing entertainment. Approached by a long, sweeping drive, with views up to the moor, there are wooden lodges and a range of privately owned mobile homes on well landscaped, undulating ground, some edging the lake. The touring pitches are in more natural areas edging the woodland with some terracing on the higher parts and nosey squirrels abounding. Pitches in the area around the central complex may well be affected by noise from the bars, etc. - for a quieter place, ask for a pitch further away. The pitches are of varying size, all with hardstanding, electric point (10A) and water. A separate, part wooded field is retained for tents and there is a special area for dog owners. Also open to the public, the park offers extensive leisure activities including a 9-hole pitch and putt course, two fishing lakes, fitness track, tennis courts, and track for children and walks in the woodland around the park with pony riding at a centre 100 m. from the entrance. The modern, attractively designed central complex provides three bars around a pool terrace, two with entertainment and one with a restaurant. There is a lively, free organised entertainment programme over a long season (out of season only one bar is open). A fitness suite with qualified instructors also provides a beauty treatment room. The indoor (open all year) and outdoor pools (with slide) are supervised in high season but are also easily observed from the bar areas and terrace. The Lakeside Bar, open in high season and for adults only, overlooks the fishing lake.

Facilities: Five modern toilet blocks are set around the park (one block is heated). They include family shower rooms, bathrooms for ladies, suitable toilet/washrooms for disabled people and dishwashing sinks outside, under cover. These facilities can come under pressure at peak times. Fully equipped launderette. Motorcaravan service points. Supermarket (Easter-Oct, limited opening early and late season). Gas supplies. Bars and restaurant. Swimming pools. Fitness centre (small additional charge, open all year). Fishing. Two tennis courts. Play area. Caravan storage all year. A torch would be useful. **Off site:** Riding centre adjacent. Bicycle hire 6 miles, golf 3 miles.

Charges 2002

Per unit incl. 2 persons, electricity	£10.00 - £18.50
tent incl. 2 persons (no electricity)	£8.00 - £14.00
extra person (from 3 yrs)	£1.50 - £3.00
water and drainage (hardstanding only)	free
awning	free
pup tent	£1.00 - £2.00
dog (max. 2)	£1.00 - £2.00
extra car	£1.00 - £2.00

Special theme weekends - details from park. Bookings from young groups not accepted. **Tel:** 01626 853833. Fax: 01626 854031. **Reservations:** Made with 25% deposit, balance 28 days before arrival. **Open** all year.

Directions: Park is signed on the A38 Exeter - Plymouth dual-carriageway; take exit for Chudleigh Knighton, Kingsteignton, Teign Valley. O.S.GR: SX850778.

Cofton Country Holidays

Starcross, Dawlish EX6 8RP

097

About 1.5 miles from a sandy beach at Dawlish Warren this popular, family site takes over 400 touring units on a variety of fields and meadows with beautiful country views. Although not individually marked, there is never a feeling of overcrowding. The smaller, more mature fields, including a pleasant old orchard for tents only, are well terraced. While there are terraces on most of the slopes of the larger, more open fields, there are still some quite steep gradients to climb. There are some 300 electrical connections (10A) and a few hardstandings. One area has 62 park-owned, holiday homes. A well designed, central complex overlooking the pool and decorated with flowers and hanging baskets, houses reception, a shop and off-licence and a bar lounge, the 'Cofton Swan', where bar meals are usually available (all Easter - 30 Sept). A family room and bar are on the first floor of this building and there is an outdoor terrace and some light entertainment in season. The adjacent supervised kidney-shaped heated pool with paddling pool and slide, has lots of grassy space for sunbathing. Coarse fishing is possible in three lakes on the park and there is a woodland trail towards Dawlish Warren.

Facilities: Toilet facilities comprise five blocks, one on each side of the road dividing the park for the touring pitches and the third near the holiday home area. The newest, at the top of the larger fields are first rate, one with a laundry room and facilities for disabled visitors and babies. Hair dryers. Dishwashing facilities under cover. In addition three 'portacabin' style units with basic toilet facilities are provided for the peak season. Two launderettes. Gas available. Ice pack hire service. Bar lounge. Shop. Fish and chip shop - breakfast possible. Swimming pool (overall length 100 ft. open Spr. B.H. - mid Sept). Games room (busy in high season). Adventure playground in the woods overlooking the pools and two other well equipped play areas. Pony rides in high season. Coarse fishing (from £16.50 per rod for 7 days, discount for senior citizens outside July). Winter caravan storage. **Off** site: Golf 3 miles. Beach 1.5 miles. Woodland walks/pub 0.5 miles.

Charges 2002

Per unit incl. 2 persons	£7.00 - £12.00
extra adult	£1.30 - £2.60
child (2-13 yrs)	£1.10 - £2.40
awning or child's tent	£1.30 - £2.60
boat, dog or extra car	£1.10 - £2.40
electricity	£2.00

Small low season discount for senior citizens. **Tel:** 01626 890111. Fax: 01626 891572. E-mail: info@ coftonholidays.co.uk. **Reservations:** Made for min. 3 nights, 4 nights in peak season with £20 deposit. **Open** Easter - 27 October.

Directions: Access to the park is off the A379 road 3 miles north of Dawlish, just after Cockwood harbour village. O.S.GR: SX965797.

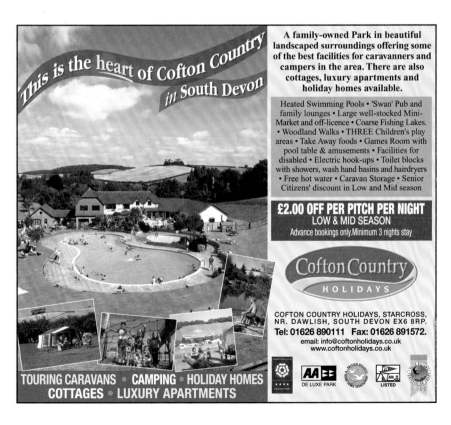

A family-owned Park in beautiful landscaped surroundings offering some of the best facilities for caravanners and campers in the area. There are also cottages, luxury apartments and holiday homes available.

Heated Swimming Pools • 'Swan' Pub and family lounges • Large well-stocked Mini-Market and off-licence • Coarse Fishing Lakes. • Woodland Walks • THREE Children's play areas • Take Away foods • Games Room with pool table & amusements • Facilities for disabled • Electric hook-ups • Toilet blocks with showers, wash hand basins and hairdryers • Free hot water • Caravan Storage • Senior Citizens' discount in Low and Mid season

£2.00 OFF PER PITCH PER NIGHT
LOW & MID SEASON
Advance bookings only. Minimum 3 nights stay

Cofton Country HOLIDAYS

COFTON COUNTRY HOLIDAYS, STARCROSS, NR. DAWLISH, SOUTH DEVON EX6 8RP.
Tel: 01626 890111 Fax: 01626 891572.
email: info@coftonholidays.co.uk
www.coftonholidays.co.uk

AA DE LUXE PARK   LISTED

TOURING CARAVANS • CAMPING • HOLIDAY HOMES
COTTAGES • LUXURY APARTMENTS

This is the heart of Cofton Country in South Devon

Lady's Mile Touring & Camping Park
Dawlish EX7 0LX

101

Lady's Mile is a popular, large family touring park that caters well for children. It has extensive grassy fields (with some trees for shade), in addition to the main, landscaped camping area which is arranged in broad terraces. There are 486 pitches, mostly marked by lines but with nothing between them, and 450 with electrical connections (10A). It is a 20 minute walk to a good sandy beach at Dawlish Warren but the park also has a good sized, free outdoor swimming pool with 200 ft. plus slide, a children's pool and a paved surround (May-Oct), plus a super heated indoor pool (20 x 10 m.) with 100 ft. flume and separate paddling pool (both with lifeguards). A large and attractive bar complex with a family area overlooking the indoor pool provides food and entertainment. Below is a spacious games room including pool tables and video games, and a new separate disco and bar. A sloping recreation field is ideal for kite flying and the large fenced children's adventure playground has a safe, sand surface. A nine hole golf course is on site (free but with small charge for hire of clubs) and a multi-sports pitch. In spite of its size, the park is popular over a long season, with reservation necessary.

Facilities: There are four toilet blocks of various ages and styles, but of a good standard, well spaced around the main areas of the park with an additional shower block. This should be an adequate provision overall. Facilities for disabled people and four family bathrooms (50p). Dishwashing sinks are under cover with free hot water. Two launderettes. Mini-market and fish and chip takeaway (both Easter - mid Sept). Bars. Indoor and outdoor pools. Good adventure play area. Games room. Golf (9 hole). Ball area with nets. Tarmac area at reception for late arrivals. Winter caravan storage. **Off site:** Riding and bicycle hire 1 mile, fishing 3 miles.

Charges 2002

Per unit incl. 2 adults	£8.50 - £15.00
2-man tent (no car)	£7.00 - £12.50
extra child's tent	£1.50 - £3.00
extra person over 2 yrs	£1.50 - £3.00
extra car or boat	£1.00 - £2.50
dog	£1.00 - £2.50
electricity	£2.50

Low season special offers. Low season discount for OAPs. **Tel:** 01626 863411. Fax: 01626 888689. E-mail: info@ladysmile.co.uk. **Reservations:** Made for Sat to Sat only in peak seasons, with £15 deposit. **Open** 13 March - 31 October.

Directions: Park is 1 mile north of Dawlish with access off the A379 (Exeter - Teignmouth) road. O.S.GR: SX969778.

Coast View Holiday Park
Torquay Road, Shaldon, Teignmouth TQ14 0BG

108

On the coast road between Teignmouth and Torquay with magnificent views over Lyme Bay, this family run park has a section of caravan holiday homes and chalets. However, the touring area of 100 pitches is quite separate. On terraced grass, some pitches are part sloping. There are 28 electricity connections (16A). At present, due to recent reconstruction of the park, there is little or no shelter but as the site is terraced into the hillside, there is adequate protection from the prevailing southwest winds. To the right of the park entrance is an attractive indoor pool and an entertainment area comprising a clubroom with bar (bar meals and snacks), takeaway, TV room and games room. All these facilities are open all season. Entertainment is organised each night and also activities in the mornings for children. The park is convenient for the beach (1.5 miles) and the coastal footpath is adjacent. Torbay is 5 miles. A bus service stops at the gates. Good for holidaymakers of all ages, this park offers superb views with excellent facilities.

Facilities: The new toilet block is spacious with free hot showers and open washbasins, and includes a baby room. Separate dishwashing and laundry facilities. Licensed shop for basic provisions. Indoor pool and children's pool. Clubroom with bar, takeaway and games room (arcade games, table tennis and pool). Adventure playground and indoor soft play area. Crazy golf. **Off site:** Fishing or golf 1 mile, riding 3 miles.

Charges 2002

Per caravan incl. up to 8 persons	£7.00 - £16.00
camper or tent incl. up to 8 persons	£7.00 - £14.00
tent incl. 2 persons	£6.00 - £8.00
electricity	£1.75
dog	free - £3.00

Tel: 01626 872392. Fax: 01626 872719. **Reservations:** Contact park. **Open** 22 March - 27 October.

Directions: From A380 Exeter - Newton Abbot road, take A381 to Teignmouth. On entering town turn right over Shaldon Bridge on B3199 for Torquay. Park is on right in approx. 1.5 miles. O.S.GR: SX932714.

Warren Road, Dawlish Warren, Dawlish EX7 0PQ

First impressions of this extensive family run park are perhaps somewhat formal. However, this is quickly dispelled by the friendly reception staff, abundant flowers and the way the pitches have been laid out on the slightly sloping ground. There are 250 pitches, ranging in size, each with electricity (10A), with at least another 60 hook-ups available for tent campers. Tarmac roads thread through the site giving easy access to all areas, each pitch being marked and numbered. Visitors to Peppermint Park can use the full facilities at the adjacent sister site (Golden Sands), which include a large indoor pool. Peppermint Park's own pool complex includes a water slide in the larger pool. Nightly entertainment is staged in the Peppermint Club in high season and at Golden Sands at other times. This site's 'jewel in the crown' is the walking distance (700 yds) to the large, safe beaches of Dawlish Warren and its associated pleasure complex - ideal for families. For others, there is the adjacent coastal footpath or the city of Exeter (7 miles) with its cathedral, museums and historic Quay complex. A passenger ferry operates from Starcross (2 miles) across the estuary to Exmouth during high season. Dawlish Warren nature reserve is adjacent and includes an 18 hole links golf course.

Facilities: The two modern sanitary blocks are kept in spotless condition and can be heated. Two units (WC, washbasin and shower) are provided for disabled visitors. Fully equipped mother and baby room. Laundry (washing machines, dryers and free irons) and dishwashing. Shop with gas. Restaurant, bar and takeaway in high season (1/7-30/8). Entertainment. Swimming pool (26/5-30/8). Children's playground on a hill. Field for ball games. Small coarse fishing lake (£2.50 for adult day ticket).

Charges 2002

Per unit incl. 2 persons	£6.00 - £11.50
tent incl. 2 persons and car	£6.00 - £10.00
extra adult	£1.20 - £2.50
child (2-13 yrs)	£1.00 - £2.40
electricity	£2.00
dog	£1.00 - £2.40

Tel: 01626 863436. Fax: 01626 866482. E-mail: info@peppermintpark.co.uk. **Reservations:** Made with £15 deposit (Sat. - Sat. only 24 July - 28 Aug). **Open** 15 April - 28 October.

Directions: Leave M5 at junction 30 and take A379 Dawlish road. After passing through Starcross (7 miles) turn left to Dawlish Warren just before Dawlish. Continue for 1.5 miles down hill and park is on left in 300 yards. O.S.GR: SX978788.

Set in the Blackdown Hills (designated an area of outstanding natural beauty), Forest Glade is owned and run by the Wellard family, deep in mid-Devon away from the hectic life on the coast. A sheltered site set amongst woodland with extensive walking without using your car, there are 80 touring pitches, 70 of which have 16A electricity connections and 24 hardstanding. The pitches are all level, mostly backing onto the forest, and there is also a rally field. This is a small heated, covered pool with a paddling pool and a patio area outside. The surrounding forest makes this a dog lover's paradise (dogs are accepted). Touring caravans must book in advance and the easiest route for them will be explained then (phone bookings accepted). Although set in the country, the beaches of East Devon are a fairly easy drive away. A member of the Best of British group.

Facilities: There is one main toilet block, heated in cold weather, with some washbasins in cubicles, and washing up sinks. Separate room with WC, low level washbasin and shower for disabled visitors. Laundry with washing machines and dryers, ironing facilities and a stool to sit on. Extra facilities of 'portacabin' style with toilets, washbasins and showers are at the swimming pool, but these are only available when the pool is open (Easter, then early May - late Sept, plus Oct half term). Motorcaravan service facilities. The shop (all season) is quite well stocked including gas and locally made bread and pastries with a takeaway (open evenings except Sunday). Adventure playground. Games room with table tennis, video games and two pool tables. All weather tennis court. Sauna. Caravan storage. **Off site:** Fishing or riding 1.5 miles, golf 6 miles, bicycle hire 5 miles.

Charges 2002

Per unit incl. 2 adults and electricity	£8.10 - £13.60
incl. mains services and awning	£9.10 - £14.60
student (10 yrs-end of study)	£2.00
child (5-9 yrs)	£1.00
backpacker or cyclist	£2.50
dog	£0.50

Tel: 01404 841381. Fax: 01404 841593. E-mail: enquiries@forest-glade.co.uk **Reservations:** Any length with deposit of £4 p/day or £20 p/wk, (£15 for B.H. w/ends). Essential for B.H.'s and school holidays. **Open** 23 March - 28 October.

Directions: Park is 5.5 miles from M5 exit 28. Take A373 for 3 miles, turning left at camp sign towards Sheldon. Park is on left after approx. 2.5 miles. This access is not suitable for touring caravans owing to a steep hill - phone the park for alternative route details. O.S.GR: ST101073.

Webbers Farm Caravan & Camping Park

Castle Lane, Woodbury, Exeter EX5 1EA

110

Set in a lovely location in East Devon, this family run park has developed over 20 years to one that can boast spacious, modern facilities, yet still retain its relaxed, rural atmosphere. The 115 marked, grass pitches are large, with the majority level and a few gently sloping. Some of the higher pitches have marvellous views across the Exe river valley. There are 100 electricity connections (10/16A). The park is surrounded by fields and visitors can watch the wildlife and grazing sheep from a fenced walk around the park perimeter. Within the park is a 'pets paddock' with a friendly donkey, Shetland pony and goats. A short drive takes you to the two miles of glorious sand at Exmouth or the delightful pebble beach at Budleigh Salterton. Woodbury Common for excellent heathland walks is just over a mile away, whilst for a little city life, Exeter is also nearby. A member of the Countryside Discovery group.

Facilities: There are three modern toilet blocks, the newest (completed in 2002) a light and airy building with 4 family shower rooms, a bathroom (£1) and a unit for disabled visitors (WC, shower and washbasin). Dishwashing and laundry facilities. Unusual in terms of number, are seven chemical disposal points, located at each water point (and adequately separated). Small shop at reception for essentials. Ice pack service. Gas supplies. Play area and games field. All year caravan storage. **Off site:** Woodbury village within walking distance with excellent pub/restaurant, post office, etc. Exeter 6 miles. Fishing or golf (Woodbury Park Golf Club) 1 mile. Riding 4 miles. Bicycle hire or boat launching 5 miles.

Charges 2002

Per pitch incl. 2 persons	£8.00 - £12.00
extra person (over 5 yrs)	£2.80
awning or extra tent	£1.50
electricity	£2.30
dog	free

Tel: 01395 232276. Fax: 01395 233389. E-mail: reception@webbersfarm.co.uk. **Reservations:** Essential for peak periods and made with £20 deposit. **Open** Easter - 29 September.

Directions: Leave M5 at junction 30 and follow A376 Exmouth road. At second roundabout take B3179 (Budleigh Salterton and Woodbury). In village centre follow brown signs to park on right. O.S.GR: SY017874.

Salcombe Regis Camping & Caravan Park

Salcombe Regis, Sidmouth EX10 0JH

111

0n the edge of Salcombe Regis village, 1.5 miles from Sidmouth and less than a mile from the sea. Salcombe Regis Park covers 16 acres of land. It is surrounded by farmland with views of the combe and the sea beyond. The focal point of the main camping area is a large 'village green' where the play area and pitch and putt are located. The reception and pitches are arranged around the green, all connected by a tarmac road. The 110 pitches are level, have their own water supply and 16A electricity hook-ups. Next to the reception is a small animal area with two goats, ducks and chickens. A 25 minute walk across fields takes you to a small secluded beach, although the walk there is fairly steep - we were told there are 129 steps that take you down to the beach! There are many footpaths and coastal walks nearby, protected by the National Trust and with views of Sidmouth and Weston Mouth. Sidmouth town, originally a small fishing town but now a seaside resort, is host to the annual International Folk Festival, where for one week in summer the town is filled with folk artists from all over the world.

Facilities: The traditional style toilet block is kept spotlessly clean by the resident wardens and includes a bathroom for families and disabled visitors. Licensed shop at reception selling basic supplies and local produce. Dishwashing area under cover. Laundry room with washing machines, dryers and ironing board. Play area. Pitch and putt. Caravan storage. **Off site:** Sidmouth 1.5 miles.

Charges 2002

Per pitch incl. 2 adults	£10.05
extra adult	£2.85
electricity	£2.35
awning	£1.90
dog	free

Tel: 01395 514303. Fax: 01395 514303. E-mail: info@salcombe-regis.co.uk. **Reservations:** Made with £20 p/week deposit. Book 7 nights, get 1 free. **Open** Easter - 28 October.

Directions: Park is well signed on the A3052 Exeter - Lyme Regis road. From the east, take first left after Donkey Sanctuary. From the west proceed up the hill out of Sidford. Do not take first road signed Salcombe Regis, but take the next right at top of hill. Follow road round to site on left after golf range. O.S.GR: SY149892.

Oakdown is an award winning, exceptionally well kept and environmentally conscious park. It is always neat and tidy and we continue to note developments, under the special care and guidance of Mr and Mrs Franks and their son Alastair. They provide one of the most comfortable, well equipped and attractively laid out family parks we know, complete with welcoming staff who help pitch your unit (and live on site). The park has a spacious, uncrowded feel with large pitches semi-screened in small bays or groves and edged with trees. A marvellous range of trees (all 70 types are named) provides variety and home for wildlife. A circular concrete road links 120 pitches, all with 16A electricity, 29 with water, waste water and drainage and 89 with hardstanding. Tourist information is displayed in the toilet block, together with the interesting history of the park - it was within the boundaries of a secret wartime radar station which accounts for the very solid construction of the block. The latest development provides a 9-hole pitch and putt course, two lakes, wild flower areas and more trees (opening 2003). A trail leads through this area and the fields to the nearby Donkey Sanctuary and one can walk further to the beach and sea (2 miles, steep in parts). There are, in fact, over 143 varieties of wild flower (some named) to be seen and 45 varieties of wild bird. A family of Lesser Spotted woodpeckers have caused interest, skylarks and goldfinches are regular visitors and buzzards wheel overhead. Badgers and foxes visit (after 10.30 pm) and trees and bushes are chosen to encourage butterflies and more birds. It is the attention to all things natural that makes this park rather special. The 'reed bed' development is progressing well. Adjoining the touring park is Oak Grove, with 46 holiday homes, some for hire. A member of the Best of British group.

Facilities: The central toilet block with piped music provides good, fully equipped, heated sanitary facilities, all well maintained. One private cabin for ladies. Two unisex family bathrooms (bath, shower, toilet, washbasin and coin operated entry) also double as useful units for disabled people. Dishwashing sinks. Laundry facilities plus free use of a freezer and a microwave. Motorcaravan service point. Recycling point (glass, paper, cans). Fax service. TV room. Well equipped, grass based play area with adventure style equipment and play castle. No cycling, skateboarding or kite flying is permitted. Certain breeds of dog are not accepted. Site has closed circuit TV. Secure, alarmed caravan storage. **Off site:** Riding 6 miles, golf 2 miles.

Charges 2002

Per unit incl. 2 persons, electricity	£8.10 - £12.15
incl. mains services and awning	£11.90 - £16.10
extra person (5 yrs and over)	£1.75
dog	£1.00
electricity	£2.30

Less 70p for senior citizens in low season. **Tel:** 01297 680387. Fax: 01297 680541. E-mail: oakdown@btinternet.com. **Reservations:** Made with £20 p/w deposit, min. 3 days at B.H's. and 3/4 Aug. (Sidmouth Folk Festival). **Open** 22 March - 3 November.

Directions: Turn south off the A3052 (Exeter - Lyme Regis) road between Sidford and Colyford, 2.5 miles east of the A375 junction and park is on left. O.S.GR: SY167902.

Somerset

Quantock Orchard Caravan Park

Crowcombe, Taunton TA4 4AW

135

The old adage 'small is beautiful' certainly fits Quantock Orchard, nestling at the foot of the Quantocks in quiet countryside, yet close to many of the attractions of the area. Crowcombe Station on the West Somerset Steam Railway is only a short walk. Attractively developed, mature apple trees, recently planted trees, shrubs and pretty flower beds with a nice use of heathers, make a very pleasant environment and the clock tower on the sanitary block adds interest. With access from gravel roads, there are 55 touring pitches, part separated by shrubs and hedging, and 20 for tents. Of various sizes, 52 have 10A electrical hook ups, 20 with hardstanding, 4 have TV hook-up and 2 are fully serviced (one large with patio and TV). A leisure suite provides a sauna, steam room, jacuzzi, spa, mini-gym and conservatory rest area (this facility is open to the public; visitor membership optional with a range of tariffs to suit all; children must be accompanied). It is complemented by an outdoor heated pool, which is walled with paved surrounds. Four purpose built barbecues and picnic tables are set in the central grass area and rarer breeds of duck waddle around the park.

Facilities: The central, heated sanitary block has some nice touches and is very well maintained. Some washbasins in cubicles for ladies, excellent family bathroom (recently refurbished) and separate mother and baby room. Good dishwashing provision, microwave, and laundry facilities. Motorcaravan service point. Well stocked licensed shop includes camping accessories. Mountain bike hire (some with buggies for children). Fish and chip van visits (twice weekly in summer). Swimming pool (40 x 20 ft. and open May - Sept). Leisure suite. Games room, Sky TV. Fenced safe-based play area. Only 'air-flo' style groundsheets are permitted on grass pitches. Caravan storage Oct. - March. **Off site:** The Carew Arms serving meals is within walking distance in the mellow village of Crowcombe. The Brendon and Exmoor hills, Minehead, Dunster Castle and Taunton are within 10-15 miles.

Charges 2002

Per unit incl. 2 adults	£7.50 - £11.50
extra adult	£3.00
child (3-4 yrs)	£0.95
child (5-15 yrs)	£1.95
child's pup tent with caravan	£1.20
electricity	£2.00 - £2.20
backpacker or cyclist	£3.75 - £4.95

Tel: 01984 618618. E-mail: qocp@flaxpool.freeserve. co.uk. **Reservations:** Made with £10 per week deposit, per booking (non-returnable). **Open** all year.

Directions: Park is west off A358 road (Taunton - Minehead), about 1 mile south of Crowcombe village. O.S.GR: ST140363.

Hoburne Blue Anchor

138 Blue Anchor Bay, Minehead TA24 6JT

Although mainly a holiday park, with almost 300 caravan holiday homes, Blue Anchor nevertheless offers good facilities for 103 touring units. Trailer tents are accepted but not other tents (other than pup tents with a touring booking). Virtually in a separate touring area, the level pitches all have hardstanding and 16A electricity. A feature of the park is a good sized, irregularly shaped indoor swimming pool with an area for small children, complete with a mushroom shaped fountain. With views of the sea from the pool, it is heated and supervised. Although not actually within the park itself, there are both restaurants and takeaway food facilities within easy walking distance. The park's situation, directly across the small road from the beach, is unusual and gives some beautiful views across the Bristol Channel to South Wales. Dunster Castle, Exmoor, the Quantocks and Minehead are close and the West Somerset Steam Railway runs along one side of the park. Part of the Hoburne Group.

Facilities: Toilet facilities provide large, free hot showers (with push-button), dishwashing and laundry sinks under cover, and a fully equipped launderette in a single, modern block serving just the touring area. Excellent, attractive children's play area in the copse. Crazy golf. Small supermarket/shop with coffee shop (open 8 am - 9 pm in high season, less at other times). American motorhomes are accepted (max. 36 ft). Dogs are not accepted. **Off site:** Riding 5 miles, golf 4.5 miles.

Charges 2002

Per unit incl. up to 6 persons,
electricity and awning £8.00 - £16.00

Weekend breaks available. **Tel:** 01643 821360. Fax: 01643 821572. E-mail: enquiries@hoburne.co.uk. **Reservations:** For stays of 1-6 days, payment required in full at time of booking; for 7 nights or more £50 deposit. Min. bookings at B.H's. **Open** 1 March - 31 October.

Directions: From M5 junction 25, take A358 signed Minehead. After approx. 12 miles turn left onto A39 at Williton. After 4 miles turn right onto B3191 at Carhampton signed Blue Anchor. Park is 1.5 miles on right. O.S.GR: ST025434.

Halse Farm Touring Caravan & Camping Park

136 Winsford, Minehead TA24 7JL

A truly rural park with beautiful, moorland views, you may be lucky here and glimpse red deer across the valley or be able to see Exmoor ponies and foals graze outside the main gate on one of the highest points on Exmoor. Two open, neatly cut fields that are level at the top, back onto traditional hedging and sloping gently to the middle and bottom where wild flowers predominate. One field provides electricity points (10A) and is used for motorcaravans and caravans, the other is for tents. There is no reception - you leave your unit by the toilet block and walk down to the farm kitchen to book in. The pretty village of Winsford is 1 mile (footpath from farm) with a post office, shop, pub and restaurant. Mrs Brown has encapsulated maps available (at a small cost) detailing six walks of varying distances, starting and finishing at the farm. Also available is a list of the wild birds, flowers, etc. to be found on the site. A member of the Countryside Discovery group.

Facilities: The central toilet block is of good quality and heated. Well equipped and maintained, it includes a toilet, washbasin and shower for visitors with disabilities, washing machine, dryer and iron, and tourist information. Gas is available at the farm Play equipment. **Off site:** Fishing 4 miles, bicycle hire 5 miles, riding 2 miles. Tarr Steps and Barle Valley 3 miles. Winsford Village 1 mile.

Charges 2003

Per unit incl. 2 adults	£7.50 - £9.50
1 person tent and car	£3.25 - £4.25
extra adult	£3.75 - £4.75
child 0-5 yrs	£0.50
child 5-16 yrs	£1.00 - £1.50
electricity	£1.70 - £1.90
awning	£1.00

Less 10% for 7 days paid in advance 10 days before arrival. No credit cards. **Tel:** 01643 851259. Fax: 01643 851592. E-mail: enquiries@halsefarm.co.uk. **Reservations:** Advised for July/Aug. and made with £10 deposit. **Open** 25 March - 29 October.

Directions: Turn off A396 Tiverton - Minehead road for Winsford (site signed). In Winsford village turn left in front of the Royal Oak (not over ford) and keep on uphill for 1 mile (go slowly round the sharp bend at the bottom). Cross cattle grid onto moor and turn immediately left to farm. Caravans should avoid Dulverton - keep to the A396 from Bridgetown (signed). O.S.GR: SS898342.

Exe Valley Caravan Site

159 Bridgetown, Dulverton TA22 9JR

Occupying a prime position in a wooded valley alongside the River Exe, Exe Valley Caravan Site is ideally situated for visiting the Doone Valley, Tarr Steps, Dulverton and many other beautiful venues in the area. Fly fishing along the River Exe is possible from the site or at Wimbleball Reservoir just over four miles away. Travellers find this part of Somerset is a haven for walkers, cycling, horse riding, pony trekking, or as a place to just sit and relax. Owned and managed by Linda Chatwin and her husband Keith, this is a four acre 'adult only' campsite with 30 large pitches (mostly grass but some hardstandings at the top end), all of which have a 16A electricity connection. The reception is part of a small shop that stocks basic provisions. Part of the old mill, complete with water wheel and some of its workings, has been tastefully adapted as a holiday apartment, making Exe Valley ideal for visitors with friends or relatives without their own camping accommodation.

Facilities: The refurbished toilet block houses the usual facilities and an en-suite room for visitors with disabilities (quite short steep ramp to enter). Excellent laundry not only provides domestic washing and drying machines, it also sports a microwave (free) and a cupboard for dirty or wet shoes and hanging space for wet outdoor gear. Small shop with basic provisions. Gas supplies. Free fly fishing. This is an 'adult only' park (over 18 yrs).

Charges 2002

Per unit incl. 1 adult	£7.00
incl. 2 adults	£9.00 - £10.00
extra adult	£2.00
electricity	£2.00
TV cable	£0.50
awning	£1.00

Tel: 01643 851432. **Reservations:** Made for any length with £5 deposit. **Open** 1 March - 30 October.

Directions: Bridgetown is roughly midway between Dunster and Tiverton on the A396. As you enter Bridgetown from Tiverton, look for site sign and turn left in minor road; the site is 100 yards on the right. O.S.GR: SS923332.

Burrowhayes Farm Caravan & Camping Site

137 West Luccombe, Porlock, Minehead TA24 8HT

This delightful park with riding stables on site, is on the edge of Exmoor. The stone packhorse bridge over Horner Water beside the farm entrance sets the tone of the park, which the Dascombe family have created over the last thirty years having previously farmed the land. The farm buildings have been converted into riding stables with escorted rides available (from 7/4). Touring and tent pitches are on partly sloping field with marvellous views or a flatter location in the clearing by the river, while 20 caravan holiday homes are in a separate area. Electrical hook-ups are available (10A). With walking, birdwatching, plenty of wild life to observe, pretty Exmoor villages and Lorna Doone country nearby there is much to do. Children can ride, play in the stream or explore the woods at the top of the site. Limited trout fishing is available in Horner Water (NT permit) alongside the park.

Facilities: Toilet facilities, in the reception and stable block area, are well maintained and equipped with a laundry room, baby changing unit, and indoor washing up. A second older block is only open in high season. Well stocked shop doubles with reception (from 22/3; 08.30-18.00 in the main season). **Off site:** Minehead 5 miles. Local pub 20 minutes walk. Bicycle hire or golf 5 miles.

Charges 2002

Per unit incl. 1 or 2 persons	£6.00 - £8.50
extra person	£2.00 - £2.50
child (3-15 yrs)	£1.00 - £1.50
1 man tent	£4.00 - £5.00
awning	£0.75 - £1.00
electricity	£2.00

Tel: 01643 862463. E-mail; info@burrowhayes.co.uk. **Reservations:** Made with £10 deposit per pitch. **Open** 15 March - 31 October.

Directions: From A39, 5 miles west of Minehead, take first left past Allerford to Horner and West Luccombe. Site is on right after 400 yards. O.S.GR: SS897460.

Waterrow Touring Park

152 Wiveliscombe, Taunton TA4 2AZ

Beside the River Tone in a pretty part of South Somerset, Tony and Anne Taylor have enthusiastically developed Waterrow into a charming, landscaped touring park for adults only. Nestling in a little sheltered valley, it is very peaceful and convenient for an overnight stop (just over 30 minutes from M5 jct 25) or as a base for exploring nearby Exmoor and the Brendon Hills. There are 45 touring pitches, 32 of which are on level hardstandings, including 4 with full services. The remainder are on flat or gently sloping grass with little shade as yet but with bushes and trees planned. All have electrical connections (16A), spring and mains water are available and TV aerial points have been installed (your own lead is required, sometimes quite long). A small area has been set aside for tent campers. Converted barns have been put to good use, providing local tourist information, a small library, nature and conservation notes and diary and a visual record of the park's development. Further down the park, below the touring area, wide steps lead to a private nature reserve where you can find the recently constructed Otter Holt, go fly fishing for wild brown trout, take a riverside walk or just relax and watch the birds. This adults only site is open all year.

Facilities: Well fitted out and clean 'portacabin' style sanitary units, one each for men and ladies, can be heated. Showers are fairly small. Dishwashing, laundry facilities and drying room are behind. Limited provisions are available in reception and you may order jacket potatoes before lunchtime for the evening for just 60p. The Taylors will 'dog sit' for you if you are visiting somewhere your pet is not allowed (£5 per day). Water colour and drawing holidays and photography workshops are arranged at certain times of the year. Caravan storage with 'store and stay' system. **Off site:** Bicycle hire 10 miles. Coarse fishing 5 miles. The Rock Inn is a short walk and provides good value meals and real ales. Wiveliscombe and its shops 3 miles.

Charges 2002

Per unit incl. 2 persons (adults only, 18 years and over)	£8.00 - £11.00
extra adult	£4.00
electricity	£2.50
TV connection	£1.00
awning	£1.00
full services, plus	£5.00
dog	£0.50

Rallies by arrangement. **Tel:** 01984 623464. Fax: 01984 624280. E-mail: taylor@waterrowpark.u-net.com. **Reservations:** Advised for B.Hs. and high season and made with £10 deposit. **Open** all year.

Directions: From M5 exit 25 take A358 (signed Minehead) round Taunton for 4 miles, then at Staplegrove onto the B3227 for 11.5 miles to Wiveliscombe where straight over at lights to Waterrow (still on B3227). Park is on left shortly after the Rock Inn. O.S.GR: ST053251.

Home Farm Holiday Park & Country Club

148 Edithmead, Burnham-on-Sea TA9 4HD

Home Farm is impressive - neatly and attractively laid out covering 44 acres, well organised and professionally run. The 600 level pitches (including privately owned holiday homes) laid out on level mown grass are all clearly marked, accessed by tarmac roadways and divided into various sections, for example an area for those with pets or a tenting area. Including 183 pitches with hardstanding, there are 20 serviced pitches for motorcaravans with water and grey water drainage. Electrical connections (16A) are available everywhere (fewer in the tenting area) with plenty of water points in all the sections, but one central refuse area. A large, modern pool with paved surrounds and a paddling section is neatly walled and overlooked by a pool-side terraced café and takeaway. The club house (with free membership) is a feature of the site providing carvery meals, a range of entertainment, a function room, wide screen TV, an attractive conservatory and outside barbecue area. In all, it is an excellent provision and Burnham-on-Sea is only a mile away - there is a footpath from the site crossing the railway line. With Berrow Sands and Brean Down there is over seven miles of beach to choose from!

Facilities: Five toilet blocks are heated and well situated for all parts of the park. Hot showers in the newest block are family size minus dividers, and there are also some bathrooms (key with £5 deposit). Baby changing room. Dishwashing facilities under cover and a well equipped laundry room. Facilities for disabled visitors. Dog shower! Shop with general groceries, camping accessories and camping gaz. Bar. Restaurants, takeaway (open B.Hs. weekends and high season). Swimming pool. Well equipped children's play area and club for 4-10 yr olds (scholl holidays). Fishing and boating lakes (paddle and bumper boats to hire). BMX and go-karting tracks. Five-a-side football pitch.

Charges 2002

Per pitch incl. 2 persons, electricity	£7.00 - £16.50
extra person over 10 yrs	£2.50 - £4.50
child 4-9 yrs	£1.50 - £3.00
extra car or small tent	£2.50 - £4.00
dog	£1.00 - £2.00
hardstanding	£2.00 - £3.00

Club membership free. Security barrier card £2 (£1 refundable). Special breaks available. **Tel:** 01278 788888. Fax: 01278 780113. E-mail: office@ homefarmholidaypark.co.uk. **Reservations:** Contact park for details. **Open** all year.

Directions: Home Farm is 400 yards from M5 junction 22 and the A38. It is signed from the B3140 into Burnham-on-Sea. O.S.GR: ST327493.

Slimeridge Farm Touring Park

153 Links Road, Uphill, Weston-super-Mare BS23 4XY

This attractive small touring site is next to the beach in Uphill village at the southern end of Weston Bay. There are 56 pitches (24 taken on seasonal lets), on level grass with electricity (16A) available, separated from the beach by stone walling. The view across the bay is quite something, with Brean Down and Steep Holm Island standing out. However it is worth noting that, because of its close proximity to the beach, the site could be affected by the tide in extreme adverse winter weather conditions. A circular tarmac road connects the marked and numbered pitches which are allocated by the wardens. There are five hardstandings for motorhomes. Weston-super-Mare with all its leisure activities and entertainment is 2 miles, Cheddar Gorge, Wooky Hole and Glastonbury are within easy driving distance. The park is under the same ownership as no. 148, Home Farm Holiday Park, a much larger site at Burnham-on-Sea with a wide range of facilities and entertainment. Slimeridge guests are entitled to free membership of Home Farm Country Club and free use of its pool.

Facilities: A modern toilet block with electronic code entry system is well equipped and includes en-suite shower facilities that are also provided for handicapped visitors. Laundry room and washing up sinks. Chemical disposal unit also used for waste water. **Off site:** Post office, general stores and pubs within close walking distance. Golf (note: golfers have right of way to cross the park as the golf course is split by the site).

Charges 2002

Per unit incl. 2 adults, electricity	£5.50 - £12.50
extra adult	£1.50 - £3.00
child (4-9 yrs)	£1.00 - £2.50
extra car or small tent	£2.00
dog	£0.50 - £1.00

Min. stay 2 nights at B.H's. No credit cards. **Tel:** 01934 424272. Fax: 01934 641641. E-mail: homefarmholidaypark@compuserve.com. **Reservations:** Made with deposit of £5 p/night; no refunds given. **Open** 1 March - 30 October.

Directions: Site is south of Weston-super-Mare. From A370 follow sign for Uphill village and sands. O.S.GR: ST312585.

Northam Farm Touring Caravan Park

157 Brean Sands, Burnham-on-Sea TA8 2SE

Brean has been a popular holiday destination for decades and many large campsites have evolved. Northam Farm is one of them; it is a large family park with exemplary facilities. Four hundred of the 850 pitches are seasonal and are separated from the four tourist fields. Visitors are always shown to their pitch and sited - jockey wheels must be placed on a concrete marker on grass pitches or by the arrow on the brick hardstandings. Pitches are large so you won't feel cramped. There are two play areas for youngsters, a sports field with mobiliser swing, football, bicycle track, and cricket pitch for teenagers, and fishing on the lake for adults. The owners and staff are always available to help visitors enjoy their stay. About 500 yards down the road is The Seagull, which is also owned by Northam Farm. Here you'll find an excellent restaurant, bar, and nightly live entertainment, even during the low season. An open top bus stops at the park entrance, or visitors can book a free ride on the bus to Cheddar, famous for its gorge and caves. Alternatively, just down the road is Brean Leisure Park with its swimming complex, funfair, golf and much more.

Facilities: Three good toilet blocks are well maintained and within reasonable distance of all the pitches. They provide ample toilets, washbasins (mostly open plan), large showers (20p pull cord operation), bathrooms (£2), baby room, hair washing and drying, and slatted bench seats. Rooms for visitors with disabilities (opened by key). Dishwashing. Dog shower. Licensed shop well stocked with food and holiday gear. Snack bar/takeaway. Free entry to live entertainment at The Seagull. Games room. Two children's play areas. Sports field. Fishing lake. One field does not take dogs.

Charges 2002

Per unit incl. 2 persons	£4.25
extra adult	£1.00 - £1.25
child	£0.50 - £1.00
hardstanding	£1.00 - £1.50
lakeside pitch plus	£0.25 - £1.00

Dog and awning free. **Tel:** 01278 751244. **Fax:** 01278 751150. **E-mail:** enquiries@northamfarm.demon. co.uk. **Reservations:** Made with deposit to cover two night's fees. **Open** March - October.

Directions: Leave M5 motorway at junction 22 and follow the signs to Burnham-on-Sea, Berrow and then Brean. Continue through Brean and Northam Farm is on the right, half a mile past Brean Leisure Park. O.S.GR: ST297535.

Warren Farm Touring Park

158 Warren Road, Brean Sands, Burnham-on-Sea TA8 2RB

Warren Farm is a popular venue for family campers who want the beach, fun and entertainment. The park is divided into several fields, with touring and seasonal pitches kept well apart; Sunnyside, part of Warren Farm, is about 200 yards further down the road and has its own warden. Access roads are wide and all the 565 pitches are grassy and level, the majority having 16A electric hook-ups. There are no hardstandings so motorhomes may have difficulties in extremely wet weather. Play equipment for children, each piece on a rubberised surface, is located in a line through the centre of the camping fields - ranch-style wooden fences break up the fields and couples usually park around the perimeter overlooking fields and views of the Mendip Hills. A fabulous Play Barn incorporates an indoor play centre, bowling alley, bouncy castle, ball pit, large-screen television, and electronic games. Warren Farm's Beachcomber Inn offers a variety of facilities including a bar, restaurant, Pirate's Cove for youngsters, and cabaret room for live entertainment. With its on-site fishing, direct access to the beach, sports field and walks, this is a holiday park that caters for everyone.

Facilities: Several toilet blocks of varying size (one is 'portacabin' style) comprise WCs, showers (20p) and mostly communal washbasins. Facilities vary depending on which block you are using. Showers are quite small and not partitioned in three blocks, only the newest building in field 5 having larger and partitioned ones. Facilities for disabled visitors are in the new block in field 5. Three laundries with washing machines, dryers, spin dryer, sinks, and ironing boards. Supermarket, snack bar and takeaway (opening times vary). Chinese take-away at Sunnyside. Fish bar. Beachcomber Inn. Play equipment for toddlers. Play Barn, sports field. Fishing lake. One 'no dogs' field. **Off site:** Burnham-on-Sea, Weston-super-Mare, Cheddar, Wells and Glastonbury are all close by.

Charges 2002

Per unit incl. 2 persons	£5.50 - £10.50
extra person over 3 yrs	£1.00
electricity	£2.00

Tel: 01278 751227. **Fax:** 01278 751033. **E-mail:** enquiries@warren-farm.co.uk. **Reservations:** Made with deposit equal to two night's stay. **Open** 28 March - 13 October.

Directions: Leave M5 at junction 22 and follow the B3140 to Burnham-on-Sea, then to Berrow and Brean. Continue through Brean and Warren Farm is on the right about 1.5 miles past Brean Leisure Park. O.S.GR: ST297565.

The Fairways International Touring Park

Bath Road, Bawdrip, Bridgwater TA7 8PP

156

Fairways, a level 5.5 acre park set in rural Somerset, is owned and run by the Walker family. Gravel roads lead to the unmarked pitches that have been developed on well-drained grass - Clive Walker ensures that units are pitched sensibly. There is an ongoing programme of tree planting to shield the winter storage section of the park. The central toilet block has won awards annually since 1994, although its age is beginning to show through. Families with young children are directed to pitches close to the play area, also in the centre of the park. Adjacent to the shop is a games room to keep older children occupied. The reception is in the licensed shop that's stocked with a good selection of provisions (including Somerset cider) and camping products. Several barbecues and picnic tables are sited on the grass opposite the reception. Being located so close to the M5, Fairways is ideal for stopovers as well as sightseeing and, if you visit in November, you will be able to see the famous Bridgwater Carnival.

Facilities: A central toilet block houses both washbasins in cubicles and open plan, showers (push-button control) and baby bath/shower room. Two rooms for disabled visitors, one with toilet and washbasin and a second with shower, both with grab handles. A wheelchair is provided for visitors to use if required. Shop with gas. Freezer (free of charge). Central play area. Games room with pool table, table football, skittles, television and electronic games. **Off site:** Beaches at Burnham-on-Sea 8 miles; walking in the Quantock Hills within 10 miles; Cheddar Gorge and Wookey Hole; cycle routes and footpaths are within a mile of the park.

Charges 2002

Per unit incl. 2 persons	£8.00 - £10.00
extra adult	£2.00
child (3-13 yrs)	£1.00
awning	£1.00 - £2.00
electricity (10A)	£2.00 - £2.50
dog	£0.50

Tel: 01278 685569. Fax: 01278 685569. E-mail: fairwaysint@btinternet.com. **Reservations:** Any length with deposit. **Open** 1 March - mid-November.

Directions: From M5, junction 23, take A39 in the direction of Glastonbury. Turn left just before Texaco garage on B3141 towards Woolavington and site is about 50 yards on the right. O.S.GR: ST348402.

Broadway House Caravan & Camping Park

Cheddar BS27 3DB

141

An interesting and well maintained park offering a range of facilities on continental lines, Broadway has been developed by the Moore family over a period of 30 years. On a gently sloping area at the foot of the Mendips near Cheddar Gorge, the park takes 200 touring units of all types. From the entrance, after a neat caravan holiday home area, a series of touring areas graduates upwards, culminating in a tent and overflow rally field. The central access avenue is lined by trees with the groups of pitches on either side separated by ranch style fencing or hedging. All pitches have electricity (16A) and 30 have water and drainage. This park aims to cater for the normal active family - single sex groups are actively discouraged. There is a secluded, walled, heated pool and children's pool with grass sunbathing area and shade from silver birches. The range of activities organised from the park includes abseiling, canoeing, hill-walking, archery, shooting, caving, mountain biking, windsurfing and dry skiing. Two animal enclosures house a variety of interesting animals and Sonny the parrot is a character with a history! A nature trail leads from the park. This is really a park to be experienced - there is always something to see and do from the moment you turn in the gates and everything is well signed.

Facilities: The large, purpose built, tiled toilet block at the start of the touring area has a good provision of showers, plus eight private cabins. Behind are 10 family shower units with shower, bidet and washbasin, two of which are 'disabled friendly'. Extra facilities with bathroom (coin operated) and a unit for disabled visitors are near reception, with a 'portacabin' type unit (no showers) in the top tent field. Baby room, coin operated hairdryers, dishwashing sinks and a well equipped launderette. Motorcaravan service point. Shop with wide range of goods. Bar and café with extensive, reasonably priced menu at peak periods. Swimming pool (60 x 25 ft; open Easter - Sept; unsupervised). Adventure playground, football field, indoor table tennis, barbecue area, target golf, boules pitch, skateboard ramp, croquet. Games/amusements room, family room and large screen TV and tourist information room. Electronic barrier security. Dogs (not dangerous breeds) are accepted. **Off site:** Fishing 0.5 and 5 miles.

Charges 2002

Per adult	£3.00 - £4.00
child (3-14 yrs)	£1.00 - £2.00
caravan or tent and car	free - £7.00
motorcaravan	free - £3.00
premier pitch (incl. 3 services) plus	£2.50
electricity	£1.50
awning, pup tent or extra car	free - £1.00
dog	£1.00

Special discounts for longer stays and for O.A.P.s. Min. charge £3.50. Credit cards accepted with 5% surcharge. **Tel:** 01934 742610. Fax: 01934 744950. E-mail: enquiries@broadwayhouse.uk.com. **Reservations:** Advisable in high season, with £5 deposit per night. **Open** 1 March - 30 November.

Directions: Park entrance is on the A371 towards Axbridge, about 1 mile northwest of Cheddar. O.S.GR: ST449547.

Bucklegrove Caravan & Camping Park

Wells Road, Rodney Stoke, Cheddar BS27 3UZ

Bucklegrove is set right in the heart of Somerset on the southern slopes of the Mendip Hills and close to the tourist attractions of Cheddar Gorge, Wookey Hole, and Wells. The 125 touring pitches are split between two fields joined by a woodland walk. The top slightly undulating field is more suitable for tents and caravans, while the lower field with some short hardstandings is a little more level and would be suitable for caravans and smaller motorhomes. The children's play area (for the under 14s) includes a fort, swings and obstacle course, and during the high season there's a children's craft workshop (4-14 yrs) and organised treasure hunts. Campers also have a games room and a heated indoor swimming pool. Adjoining the pool is a licensed bar with terrace providing simple bar menus and low-key entertainment mainly during high season or depending on the number of campers on site.

Facilities: Two bright and cheerful toilet blocks house all the usual amenities. The larger, heated block near reception also provides bathrooms (50p) with baby changing facilities, and a room for visitors with disabilities. Large laundry room. Well stocked shop. Indoor swimming pool with terrace bar. Games room with pool table, video and electronic games. Children's play area. **Off site:** Wookey Hole 2 miles, Wells Cathedral 4 miles, Weston-Super-Mare 12 miles, Cheddar about 7 miles. A bus to Wells and Cheddar stops at the park entrance.

Charges 2002

Per unit incl. 2 persons	£5.00 - £11.50
extra adult	£2.00
child (4-14 yrs)	£1.00 - £1.50
awning or pup tent	£1.00 - £1.50
electricity (10A)	£2.00 - £2.20
dog (off peak only)	£1.00

Tel: 01749 870261. Fax: 01749 870101. E-mail: info@bucklegrove.co.uk. **Reservations:** Special offers are available at certain times of the year if booking in advance. **Open** 1 March - 4 January.

Directions: Take A371 Wells to Cheddar road. Park is on right about 1 mile past Westbury village. Take care as the road between Wells and Cheddar is rather narrow through some of the villages. O.S.GR: ST491495.

Mendip Heights Camping & Caravan Park

Priddy, Wells BA5 3BP

Historic Priddy is the highest village in the Mendips and is famed for its annual Sheep Fair in August. Nearby are extensive Roman lead-workings, Bronze Age burial mounds, the Priddy Circle and access to Swildons Hole, one of the popular cave systems in the Mendips. Under new ownership for the 2003 season, this well kept, family run park is half a mile from the village with tranquil views across the Mendip fields, characterised by dry stone walling. It has a simple charm with field margins left natural to encourage wildlife and nest boxes in the mature trees edging the three fields which comprise the site. These provide space for 90 units on mostly level short grass with 21 electric hook-ups (9 at 10A, 12 at 16A) and 8 with hardstanding. The only marked pitches are those with electric hook-up, so visitors can site themselves where they like. A range of activities can be arranged covering canoeing, abseiling, archery, caving, mountain biking and others, with equipment provided. The park is also on the Padstow-Bristol Sustran Route 3. Other than all that activity, places like Cheddar Gorge, Wookey Hole, Glastonbury with the Tor, Wells, Bath and Weston-super-Mare are all within a 20 mile radius. A member of the Countryside Discovery group.

Facilities: The toilet block, although of older design, is bright, cheerful and heated, with coin operated showers and a baby changing area. Dishwashing and laundry facilities. The reception/shop doubles as the village shop and is therefore open all season selling groceries, Calor gas, etc. with an off licence and tourist information. Wendy house, swings and table tennis for children. Torches useful. **Off site:** Two traditional village pubs with very different characters stand by the village green within walking distance (0.5 miles). Fishing 6 miles, riding 2 miles.

Charges 2002

Per adult	£3.30 - £4.95
child (4-16 yrs)	£1.30
electricity	£1.80
dog	£1.00
pup tent or gazebo (peak season)	£1.00

Tel: 01749 870241. Fax: 01749 870368. E-mail: enquiries@mendipheights.co.uk. **Reservations:** Made with £10 deposit (min. 3 nights for electricity at B.Hs.). **Open** 1 March - mid November.

Directions: From M5 exit 21 (Weston-super-Mare) take A371 to Banwell. Turn left on A368, right on B3134 and right on B3135. After 2 miles turn left at camp sign. From M4 westbound exit 18, A46 to Bath, then A4 towards Bristol. Take A39 for Wells and right at Green Ore traffic lights on B3135; after 5 miles turn left at camp sign. From Shepton Mallet, follow A37 north to junction of B3135 and turn left. Continue on B3135 to traffic lights at Green Ore. Straight on and after 5 miles turn left at camp sign. O.S.GR: ST522518.

Bath Chew Valley Caravan Park

Ham Lane, Bishop Sutton BS39 5TZ

151

A small and secluded garden site for adults only, Chew Valley is run with much tender love and care by Ray and Val Belton. The result is that caravans are sited on neat lawns amongst colourful beds of flowers and the car is tucked away on the car park, providing a tranquil and restful atmosphere. Ray will place your caravan for you, levelling it if necessary. Ground-sheets are not permitted in order to protect the grass. Neat hardstandings are on 14 pitches and, again to protect the grass, motorcaravans must always use them. This park will particularly appeal to garden lovers and has actually been featured on BBC TV's Gardeners' World. A very nice touch is the small nursery 'Gone to Pot' where Val (the garden expert) does all her growing and where those staying on site can purchase some of the plants found on the park. Tourist information and a small library with coffee available are next to reception. Chew Valley lake is a walk of about half a mile with trout fishing available and Blagdon lake is popular for bird-watching. There are several circular walks in the area - visitors may borrow the route plans and a walking stick from reception. Bristol and Bath are within an easy distance and Cheddar Gorge or Longleat make excellent days out. A Best of British group member.

Facilities: The heated toilet block is attractively wallpapered giving a 'home from home' feel, with washbasins in cubicles and all the other fittings which make life comfortable. Two separate en-suite units. Useful utility room for dish or hand washing with a spin drier, together with a washing machine and tumble drier for service washes only. Motorcaravan service point. **Off site:** The village is only 100 yds up the road with a useful general store, newsagent, two pubs and a post office. Supermarkets are within 15 minutes drive. Golf 1 mile, riding 8 miles.

Charges 2003
Per pitch incl. 2 persons, electricity, awning, pets and TV hook-up £16.00
No credit cards. **Tel:** 01275 332127. Fax: 01275 332664. E-mail: enquiries@bathchewvalley.co.uk. **Reservations:** Advisable for B.Hs. **Open** all year.

Directions: From Bath direction on A368 turn right opposite the Red Lion pub in Bishop Sutton. Road appears a little narrow but continue past a small track to the left (50 yds) for a further 50 yds. Park entrance appears on your left with neat, clear entrance. O.S.GR: ST584599.

Baltic Wharf Caravan Club Site

Cumberland Road, Bristol BS1 6XG

144

This excellent, city centre site is operated by the Caravan Club. A gem of a site in Bristol's re-developed dockland, it is well laid out and maintained with access via a lockable gate to the Baltic Wharf dockside. It is screened from the road by a high wall with a boatyard on one side and residential apartments on the other, and is well designed with a good use of trees. The view across the dock towards Clifton village and Bristol is unique and you can even glimpse the suspension bridge (effectively lit at night). The 58 pitches are accessed by a circular tarmac road - the central nine are on grass (not used in the winter), the rest are on stone chippings and ideal for all year round use (steel pegs are provided). All are supplied with 16A electricity. It is a 30 minute walk to the city centre, a daily ferry runs throughout the year or there is a regular bus service. An extra ferry runs from the SS Great Britain to Templemeads. TV reception is poor but a booster is available. This is a very popular site so advance booking is necessary.

Facilities: The toilet block is heated for winter use and provides good clean facilities including control-lable showers and washbasins in cubicles. Good facilities are provided for disabled visitors, plus toilets for the walking disabled and showers in the main block. Dishwashing under cover. Fully equipped laundry room. Motorcaravan service point. Tourist information room. Dogs are welcome but there is no dog walk. Wardens live on the site. Arrive by 8 pm. **Off site:** Bus service every 30 minutes, 7.30 am.- 6 pm, excl. Sundays.

Charges 2002
Per pitch (non-member)	£7.00 - £8.00
adult	£3.75 - £4.75
child (5-15 yrs)	£1.20
electricity	£1.50 - £2.25

Tel: 0117 926 8030. Fax: 0117 921 0457. **Reservations:** Always advised, essential in high seasons, and made with £5 deposit; contact the Wardens with SAE for confirmation. **Open** all year.

Directions: Easiest access is to follow signs for the 'Historic Harbour' and SS Great Britain. The site is just west of the SS Great Britain, on the right behind a high wall - look carefully for the club sign (no brown signs to follow). O.S.GR: ST572718.

Somerset
Greenacres Camping

Barrow Lane, North Wootton, Shepton Mallet BA4 4HL

149

Greenacres is a rural site in Somerset countryside for tents, trailer tents and motorcaravans only. Hidden away below the Mendips and almost at the start of the 'Levels', it is a simple green site - a true haven of peace and quiet. The grass is neatly trimmed over the 4.5 acres and hedged with mature trees, though there is a view of Glastonbury Tor in one direction and of Barrow Hill in the other. All of the 39 pitches are around the perimeter of the park, leaving a central area safe for children to play. At the narrower neck end, 5 pitches have electricity hook-ups (16A) and are ideal for those without children or birdwatchers. Wild life abounds. A speciality of the park is the 'Turf Rider' that tows the cart used to give children an evening ride. There are many nearby attractions should you tire of the peace and quiet, such as Wookey Hole, Cheddar Caves and Gorge, Longleat, the beautiful small city of Wells (with leisure centre), Clarks Village, etc. You can cycle into both Wells and Glastonbury.

Facilities: The central wooden toilet block is simple but perfectly acceptable and kept clean. Hot showers are accessed directly from the outside. Two dishwashing sinks, two laundry sinks (H&C) and a spin dryer, with an iron, board and hairdryer available from the park office. A selection of play equipment, a badminton net and a caravan to use as a play house. The park office is across the lane (gate is usually keep shut), at the owner's bungalow. Here too are fridges and freezers for campers' use (free), a library, tourist information and bicycle hire. Batteries may be charged or borrowed. Dogs are not accepted. **Off site:** In North Wootton itself, a walk of under a mile, is a large pub/restaurant and a vineyard. Fishing and riding available nearby.

Charges 2002

Per adult	£4.90
child (4-16 yrs)	£1.50

No credit cards. **Tel:** 01749 890497. E-mail: harvie. greenacres@talk21.com. **Reservations:** Made with £2 deposit. **Open** March - October incl. & Carnival Fortnight in Nov.

Directions: From A39 Glastonbury - Wells road turn east at Brownes Garden Centre and follow camping signs. From A361 Glastonbury - Shepton Mallet road follow camp signs from Pilton or Steanbow. O.S.GR: ST553416.

Somerset
Batcombe Vale Campsite

Batcombe Vale, Shepton Mallet BA4 6BW

154

Set in a secluded valley with fields gently rising around it, contented cows grazing with watchful buzzards cruising the thermals above and views across the distant hills, this is just a very special place. Home to Donald and Mary Sage, Batcombe Vale House is a mellow, attractive building covered with wisteria, to one side of the valley overlooking the lakes and the 'wild' landscape. Trees and shrubs have been skilfully placed to enhance the natural environment providing a range of colour and shape. Designated an 'area of outstanding natural beauty', there are 120 acres around the valley where you are welcome to wander and picnic in the fields - a haven for wild flowers, birds and butterflies. For those who fish, two of the lakes have carp and tench up to 18 lbs but you must have a current licence. As you descend slowly down the narrow entrance drive you see the 30 pitches, attractively set and terraced where necessary, in an oval with the lakes below. The grass is left natural around the 32 pitches (20 have 10A electricity) and paths mown where needed. If you tire of the views and the fishing there is a range of circular walks from the site or you can potter about in one of the four small rowing boats (free gentle exercise). There are many places to visit nearby, from Glastonbury with the Tor, to Cheddar Gorge and the Caves.

Facilities: The small rustic toilet block covered in honeysuckle meets all needs, including a freezer and dishwashing sinks. Groundsheet awnings must be lifted daily. Coarse fishing (up to 20 lbs) adults £3 p/day (child £1.50) or £2 p/day times length of stay. Caravan storage. One dog per pitch is welcome (no dangerous breeds). **Off site:** Bruton (for shops, etc.) is 2 miles. Launderettes at Shepton or Frome.

Charges 2002

Per unit incl. 2 adults	£10.00
extra adult	£3.50
child (8-18 yrs)	£2.50
child's (4-8 yrs)	£1.00
full awning	£1.00
electricity	£1.50
dog	£1.00

No commercial vehicles or motorcycle 'packs' - family groups only. **Tel:** 01749 830246. E-mail: DonaldSage@ compuserve.com. **Reservations:** Only essential for B.Hs. and school holidays; made with £5 deposit and £1 fee (min. 2 nights). **Open** Easter - September.

Directions: Bruton is south of Shepton Mallet and Frome but north of Wincanton where the A359 intersects the B3081. Site is 2 miles north of Bruton and signed in the town. The road is narrow in places but an easier way for caravans is clearly signed. O.S.GR: ST681379.

The Old Oaks Touring Park

Wick Farm, Wick, Glastonbury BA6 8JS

The Old Oaks, an 'adults only' park from 2002, is tucked below and hidden from the 'Tor', in a lovely secluded setting with views across to the Mendips. It has been developed over the last ten years on a working farm. There are 40 extra large pitches in a series of paddocks, most with 10A electricity, 18 with hardstanding and 4 fully serviced (including sewage). Mainly backing on to hedges, they are attractively arranged and interspersed with shrubs and flowers in a circular development or terraced with increasing views. A quiet orchard area or a separated hedged paddock for camping and a larger field with chemical disposal facilities complete the provision. Mature trees and hedging combine with the mellow farm buildings to give a sense of timelessness, tranquillity and peace. An interesting development features reed beds to deal with waste water, a traditional method, which is now coming into its own again. Whether you fish or not, the pond which is well stocked with carp, roach and tench is worth a visit not only for its view of the Tor, but also to see the ducks and the chickens on your way. There is parking for disabled visitors within 25 yards of the pond. In an area steeped in history and legend, this is a very well equipped and maintained park which should meet the needs of the discerning camper or caravanner. A member of the Best of British group.

Facilities: The heated toilet block, converted from the old stables, is of excellent quality and well equipped. Neatly paved outside, it has digital security locks (a public footpath from the Tor passes through the farm). Some washbasins are in cubicles. Two en-suite rooms (shower, toilet and basin) and a bathroom (50p). Disabled visitors have two rooms, one with a toilet and basin, the other with a shower, toilet and basin, both with level access. Fully equipped laundry room. Dishwashing under cover. Motorcaravan service facilities. Two recycling points. Freezer for ice packs (free). Useful dog wash. Shop for basics and locally baked bread in the main season and an off licence (limited hours). Bicycle hire (together with hire of helmets and panniers). Fishing (£2 per half day, £3.50 per day). Adults only accepted (18 yrs and over). **Off site:** Riding 5 miles and golf 6 miles. Market day is Tuesday.

Charges 2002

Per pitch	£3.00 - £4.00
adult	£2.50 - £3.50
awning with breathing groundsheet	£0.75 - £1.00
dog	£0.50 - £0.75
electricity	£1.75
all service pitch (free to disabled badge holders)	£1.00 - £2.00

Tel: 01458 831437. Fax: 01458 833238. E-mail: info@theoldoaks.co.uk. **Reservations:** Advised for high season and made with £15 deposit. **Open** 1 April - 31 October.

Directions: Park is north off A361 Shepton Mallet - Glastonbury road, 2 miles from Glastonbury. Take unclassified road signed Wick for approx. 1 mile and the park is on the left. O.S.GR: ST521394.

The Isle of Avalon Touring Caravan Park

Godney Road, Glastonbury BA6 9AF

This modern park, owned by Mike and Sharon Webb, has a friendly atmosphere and is only a short walk from the centre of Glastonbury. Developed on flat, grassy ground, the park has been landscaped, part with trees and shrubs, part open, to provide 70 individual pitches. Well spaced and connected by hard roads, they have hardstanding with adjacent grass for awning and electrical points (5/10A). A further 50 tent spaces are on the adjoining field, the top corner being left clear as a play area. Water and refuse points are well distributed around and attractively surrounded by trees and shrubs. All visitors are personally seen to their pitches. A well stocked shop with some camping accessories and reception with gas and tourist information is at the entrance. The nearby town of Street boasts 'Clarks Village' comprising a range of factory outlets including shoes!

Facilities: The single, excellent, tiled toilet block is comfortable and spacious, and can be heated. Some washbasins in cubicles for women and excellent units for disabled visitors (plus ramps to the shop and reception). Large laundry room and dishwashing area. Motorcaravan disposal point. Shop. Bicycle hire. Dogs are accepted but by prior arrangement only on tent pitches. American motorhomes are welcome. Winter caravan storage. **Off site:** Glastonbury centre, with shops, restaurants and cafés, and the Abbey 10 minutes walk. Indoor and outdoor swimming pools at Street. Riding or golf 2 miles, fishing 200 yds.

Charges 2002

Per unit	£5.00 - £6.00
adult	£2.00
child (3-14 yrs)	£1.50
awning	£1.50
pup tent	£1.75
electricity	£2.00
dog	£1.00

No credit cards. **Tel:** 01458 833618. Fax: 01458 833618. **Reservations:** Any length with £10 deposit. **Open** all year.

Directions: Park is on west side of the town bypass (A39), just off B3151 (Wedmore Road) with good signs from the bypass. O.S.GR: ST495397.

Southfork Caravan Park
Parrett Works, Martock TA12 6AE

142

Don't be put off by the address which is historic - it was once a 17th century flax mill. Mr and Mrs Metcalfe own and run this excellent, modern, well drained site just outside the lovely village of Martock. With 30 touring pitches on grass with a gravel access road (21 with 10A electrical hook-ups), it is an orderly, quiet park on two acres of flat, tree lined meadow near the River Parrett. All the expected facilities are close to the entrance and as the owners live on the premises, the park is open all year. Most things are available, including an NCC approved caravan repair centre. Despite the rural setting, the A303 trunk road is just ten minutes away. This area of South Somerset contains so much of interest, including gardens, historic houses and sites, the Fleet Air Arm Museum, Haynes Motor Museum and Cricket St Thomas Wildlife Park. Information about access to many cycle routes and numerous walks, including the Parrett Trail, is available from reception.

Facilities: The heated well maintained toilet block is fully equipped. Laundry room and dishwashing sink. Shop and limited off licence with gas supplies and comprehensive camping and caravan spares and accessories (open all year except Christmas and New Year). Children's play area. **Off site:** Fishing available (and licences) on the River Parrett a few yards from the park. Golf 3 miles. Pubs with good food in South Petherton and Martock, less than 2 miles away in each direction.

Charges 2002

Per unit incl. 2 persons	£7.00 - £9.00
extra person	£1.00
child (under 5 yrs)	free
awning	£0.50 - £1.00
dog	£0.50
electricity	£1.80 - £2.30

Tel: 01935 825661. Fax: 01935 825122. E-mail: southfork.caravans@virgin.net. **Reservations:** Advisable for B.Hs. and peak season and made with £10 deposit. **Open** all year.

Directions: From A303 between Ilchester and Ilminster take signs for South Petherton or Martock; park is mid-way on the road between the two villages (follow signs). O.S.GR: ST447187.

Long Hazel International Caravan & Camping Park
High Street, Sparkford, Yeovil BA22 7JH

150

Pamela and Alan Walton, who live at this neat, small site, are really enthusiastic about their park in the Somerset village of Sparkford and will make you most welcome. With neat, level grass, attractive beech hedging, silver birches and many newly planted trees, the park has a comfortable feel. It provides 76 touring pitches for all types of units, 50 with electrical hook-ups (16A). There are 30 pitches with hardstanding, some up to 40 feet long, and the entrance has been widened for easier access. There is a post office/shop in the village selling bread baked on the premises and the Sparkford Inn provides good food. Sparkford is also home to the famous Haynes Motor Museum, a must for those interested in the history of the world's motor industry, and the Fleet Air Arm Museum is nearby at Yeovilton (3 miles). You will also find several National Trust properties and gardens in the area and the park is the midway site for the Leland Trail. Details of safe cycle routes and walks are available at reception. The park edges the A303 bypass; although it is well hedged, there could be road noise at times in some areas.

Facilities: The well equipped heated toilet block is kept immaculate. Well planned en-suite facilities for visitors with disabilities. Motorcaravan discharge point. Gas available from reception. Central recreation area providing play equipment, badminton net, bowls green and a 9-hole putting green. The long hardstanding pitches are large enough for American style motorhomes. **Off site:** Spar mini-market 400 yards. Riding or fishing 8 miles, golf 5 miles.

Charges 2003

Per unit incl. 2 persons, electricity	£11.00 - £13.00
extra person (over 4 yrs)	£2.00
awning	£2.00
extra vehicle	£1.00 - £2.00
extra single tent	£5.00
dog	£1.00

No credit cards. **Tel:** 01963 440002. Fax: 01963 440002. E-mail: longhazelpark@hotmail.com. **Reservations:** Contact park. **Open** 1 March - 31 December.

Directions: From Yeovil direction on A303 take road into village of Sparkford and park is signed on the left 100 yds before the Inn. O.S.GR: ST604263.

Brokerswood Country Park

Brokerswood, Westbury BA13 4EH

163

This countryside campsite is located in an 80 acre country park, with ancient broadleaf woodland, plenty of marked walks, a woodland railway which also runs 'Santa Specials' (bookings taken from 1 Aug). The gift shop has a special Christmas theme from the end of October. The park also has an indoor soft play area for the very small, plus adventure and play trails amongst its many activities for the family. Most are free for campers, except for the train. Fishing in the lake is available, ask at reception. Cycling in the park is forbidden. The campsite has 65 pitches arranged around an open meadow area, served by a circular gravel roadway, with low level site lighting. There are 25 hardstanding pitches, and 30 electric hook-ups (10A). The site is newly laid-out, and will take time to mature and, in the interest of environmental conservation, it has its own biological waste management system. There are also recycling bins for glass, paper and metal cans. American RVs and other large units should use the coach entrance (please phone the site before arrival).

Facilities: A recently constructed, well insulated and heated, timber clad building provides the usual facilities including large, controllable hot showers, a fully equipped suite for disabled people with ramped approach and alarm. There are also covered dishwashing sinks, but there is no laundry Motorcaravan service facility. Gas available. Milk, bread, newspapers to order from reception/shop. The licensed Broadleaf Café serves meals and refreshments throughout the day, evening meals need to be pre-booked. **Off site:** The 'Kicking Donkey' pub offers excellent meals (800 yds). Riding 400 yds. Golf 3 miles. Nearest shops are at Dilton Marsh and Westbury. Longleat House 6 miles. Bath 12 miles.

Charges 2002
Per unit incl. 2 adults and 2 children	£8.00 - £15.00
extra adult	£3.00
extra child	£1.50
electricity	£1.75 - £2.25
dog	£1.00

Tel: 01373 822238. Fax: 01373 858474. E-mail: woodland.park@virgin.net. **Reservations:** Made with £10 non-refundable deposit. **Open** all year.

Directions: From Trowbridge take A361 south for 2 miles, turning left (east) at Southwick, and follow signs to Country Park. O.S.GR: ST830520.

Longleat Caravan Club Site

Warminster BA12 7NL

169

What a magnificent situation in which to find a caravan park, amidst all the wonders of the Longleat Estate including the Elizabethan House, Safari Park, the collection of mazes (including the world's largest), not to mention Doctor Who and the Daleks and the Adventure castle! These are just some of the attractions to be found here to suit all ages amidst a beautiful rural parkland setting. Visitors can roam the woodlands (leaflets are available on a range of walks) and enjoy the views, watch the wildlife and marvel at the azaleas, bluebells, etc. according to the season or listen to the occupants of the Safari Park. The site itself, well managed by Caravan Club wardens, is situated in 10 acres of lightly wooded, level grassland within walking distance of the house and gardens. There are be 98 hardstanding pitches around the perimeter of the park and 66 central grass pitches, all with 16A electricity connections. Water points and re-cycling bins are neatly walled with low night lighting. A separate wooden chalet houses tourist information but the wardens will help you to get the best out of your stay at Longleat. Tents are not accepted (except trailer tents).

Facilities: Two new heated toilet blocks will provide washbasins in cubicles, controllable showers and a vanity section with shelf, mirrors and hairdryers. There will be a baby/toddler room, facilities for disabled visitors, a laundry and a covered dishwashing area. The former toilet block is to be transformed into a games room. Motorcaravan service point. Children's play area. Office is manned 9 am - 6 pm and stocks basic food items, papers can be ordered and gas is available. Paperback exchange library. Fresh fruit and vegetable van drives around the site and a fish and chip van calls.

Charges 2002
Per pitch (non-member)	£6.00 - £8.00
adult	£2.75 - £4.50
child (5-16 yrs)	£1.10 - £1.20
electricity	£1.50 - £2.25

Tel: 01985 844663. Fax: 01985 844964. **Reservations:** Advisable for B.Hs. and school holidays and made with £5 deposit. **Open** 31 March - 30 October.

Directions: The main entrance to Longleat which caravans must use is signed from the A362 Frome - Warminster road near to where it joins the A36 Warminster bypass. Turn into the estate and follow the Longleat House route through the toll booths for 2 miles then follow caravan club signs for 1 mile. There are shorter ways to leave the site. O.S.GR: ST806434.

Piccadilly Caravan Site

166 Folly Lane West, Lacock, Chippenham SN15 2LP

Piccadilly is set in open countryside close to several attractions in northern Wessex, notably Longleat, Bath, Salisbury Plain, Stourhead, and Lacock itself. It is a small, quiet family owned park that is kept neat and tidy. Landscaped shrubs and trees are maturing, giving the impression of three separate areas. There are 40 well spaced, clearly marked pitches, 11 of which have hardstanding. Electrical connections (10A) are available on 34 pitches. A bus service runs from Lacock village to Chippenham.

Facilities: The one toilet block is well maintained and equipped, should be adequate in size for peak periods and can be heated in cool weather. Dishwashing area. Laundry room with baby changing facilities. Ice pack service. Small, bark-based playground and a large, grass play area. Limited gas supplies. Papers can be ordered. **Off site:** Fishing 1 mile, bicycle hire 6 miles, riding 4 miles, golf 3 miles.

Charges 2002

Per unit incl. 2 persons	£9.00
extra person over 5 yrs	£1.00
electricity	£1.50

No credit cards. **Tel:** 01249 730260. **Reservations:** Any length; deposit of 1 nights fee. **Open** Easter/1 April - October.

Directions: Park is signed west off A350 Chippenham - Melksham road (turning to Gastard with caravan symbol) by Lacock village. 300 yds. to park. O.S.GR: ST911682.

Plough Lane Caravan Site

168 Plough Lane, Kington Langley, Chippenham SN15 5PS

Opening for its first season in '98 and catering for adults only, this is a good example of a well designed, quality, modern touring site. The 50 pitches (45 for touring units) are half hardstanding, half grass and all have electricity (16A). Eight pitches are fully serviced. Access roads are gravel and the borders are stocked with newly planted shrubs and trees. The site entrance has an alarm and barrier system for security (£5 deposit for card). This site is an ideal base for visiting Bath, Westonbirt Arboretum, Abbey House and Gardens at Malmesbury, Castle Combe and the many attractive villages of north Wiltshire and south Gloucestershire.

Facilities: The sanitary building is heated, spacious, light and airy, and has all the usual facilities including some washbasins in cubicles, with a hairdressing area for ladies. Separate en-suite room for disabled visitors with ramp access. Dishwashing sinks under cover. Fully equipped laundry with two further dishwashing sinks. This park is for adults only (over 18 yrs). **Off site:** Local facilities include a supermarket, two public houses, and two garages - both stocking Calor and Camping Gaz. Golf 1 mile.

Charges 2002

Per unit incl. 2 adults and electricity	£11.00
extra adult (max. 2 extra)	£3.00

No credit cards. **Tel:** 01249 750795. **Fax:** 01249 750795. **E-mail:** ploughlane@lineone.net. **Reservations:** Made with £10 deposit. **Open** mid-March - mid-October.

Directions: From M4 junction 17 turn south on A350 for 2 miles, then left at traffic lights where site is signed. From Chippenham head north on A350 (towards M4), approaching traffic lights (signed for site and Kington Langley) you need the right hand lane. O.S.GR: ST915765.

Photo: Salisbury Catthedral, STB

Camping & Caravanning Club Site Devizes
Spout Lane, Seend, Melksham SN12 6RN

170

First opened in 1998, this newly constructed site occupies a level field with gravel roads and centrally located facilities. It is also adjacent to the Kennet and Avon Canal (opened in 1810, and recently extensively restored), and the towpath now provides a traffic-free route passing the Caen Hill flight of 29 locks into Devizes (4 miles). In the other direction the towpath runs towards Melksham (also 4 miles). There are 50 hardstanding and 45 grass pitches, 77 with electricity (16A). The site is central for visiting many places of interest including the stone circles at Stonehenge and Avebury. The Vale of Pewsey cycle route can be accessed from the canal towpath to the east of Devizes, and runs for 41 miles between Great Bedwyn and Corsham.

Facilities: The modern, heated toilet block provides spacious hot showers, washbasins in cubicles, laundry, dishwashing room, and a mother and baby room. Facilities for disabled visitors are in a suite (with alarm system) by reception. Motorcaravan services are in the late arrivals parking area. Small playground with rubber safety base. Reception stocks basic foods and drinks, snacks and gas, fishing licences, cycle passes for the canal towpath.

Charges 2002

Per adult	£5.00 - £5.50
child	£1.70
pitch fee (non-members)	£4.50
electricity	£1.75 - £2.50

Tel: 01380 828839. **Reservations:** Advised for B.Hs. and peak season; contact site. **Open** all year.

Directions: From Devizes take A361 westbound, and 0.5 miles before Seend village, take A365 towards Melksham. Cross the canal bridge, take next left by 'Three Magpies' and the site entrance is on your right. Approaching from the M4 junction 17, use A350 to Melksham and A365 to the site. O.S.GR: ST951619.

Greenhill Farm Camping & Caravan Park
New Road, Landford, Salisbury SP5 2AZ

164

Located on the northern edge of the New Forest, this is an attractive, uncommer-cialised, hide-away site set around two small lakes. One is reserved solely for the wildlife which includes kingfishers, ducks, etc., the second is reserved for coarse fishing. The 100 level pitches are generally on grass (35 hardstandings), all with 10A electric hook-ups, and are attractively spread around the 14 acre site. An area for tents is in a separate hill top meadow with views over the nearby forest. There are also separate areas set aside for families, pet owners or adults only.

Facilities: Four portacabin units of varying ages around the site provide basic facilities and can be heated. Showers are free, but a token is issued with a refundable deposit. No facilities for disabled persons. Coarse fishing lake (£3 per rod per day). Torches useful. **Off site:** Golf 3 miles.

Charges 2002

Per unit incl. 3 persons, awning, electricity	£10.00
tent incl. 3 persons and electricity	£8.00
extra person	£1.00

Tel: 02380 811506. Fax: 01794 324117. **Reservations:** Advised for B.Hs. **Open** all year.

Directions: From M27 exit 2 take A36 towards Salisbury for about 6 miles. Pass through West Wellow and after B.P. garage on left, take next left into New Road, and continue for under 1 mile to site entrance on left. O.S.GR: SU266183.

Coombe Touring Park
Coombe Nurseries, Race Plain, Netherhampton, Salisbury SP2 8PN

165

A true touring park with outstanding views over the Chalke Valley, Coombe is adjacent to Salisbury racecourse. There are 100 spacious pitches all on level, well mown grass, 50 with electric hook-ups (10A). The tent pitches are generally around the outer perimeter. Many pitches are individual and sheltered by hedging, with picnic tables provided on many. Reception also has a small shop, there are supermarkets in Salisbury (4.5 miles), and pubs in Netherhampton and Coombe Bissett (2 miles) both serving meals.

Facilities: A well built centrally heated unit provides ample WCs, spacious showers, washbasins in cubicles for ladies. Family room (with bath) has facili-ties for disabled persons, babies and toddlers. Dishwashing room. Laundry with washing machines, dryers and ironing. Small shop (Easter-Sept). Swings, slide and seesaw and grass play area. Gas available. **Off site:** Golf 400 yards.

Charges 2002

Per unit incl. 2 persons	£10.00
extra adult	£2.50
child (3-17 yrs)	£1.00 - £1.50
electricity	£1.50
dog	£0.20

No credit cards. **Tel:** 01722 328451. **Reservations:** Advisable for B.Hs and July/August. **Open** all year.

Directions: From A36 two miles west of Salisbury (just east of Wilton roundabout), turn south on A3094 towards Netherhampton. After 0.5 miles on sharp left bend, turn right to Stratford Tony and Racecourse. At top of hill and turn left (signed) on narrow lane behind racecourse. O.S.GR: SU098282.

Alderbury Caravan & Camping Park

167 Southampton Road, Whaddon, Salisbury SP5 3HB

Under new ownership, this small village touring park is convenient for visiting Salisbury and the New Forest. At the southern end of Alderbury/Whaddon village, it is on level ground with a gravel access road to the 39 numbered pitches; 26 have access to electricity (16A). The park has some mature trees for shade, as well as younger trees, shrubs and flowers. More recently seven hardstandings, extra chemical disposal and waste water points, site lighting, more shrubs and trees have been added. The village shop and post office, a pub serving meals, public phone and a bus stop are within easy level walking distance of the entrance. There are hourly bus services to Salisbury, Southampton and Romsey. The country lanes around the area are good for cycling and walking. Salisbury Museum, the Cathedral and its Close are all well worth a visit. There is some road noise, most noticeable at the far end of the park.

Facilities: The central toilet block is practical, clean and well maintained. It provides hot showers in cubicles with curtain, a separate unit for disabled visitors, and a dishwashing sink also in a separate room. **Off site:** Fishing 1 mile, bicycle hire 3 miles, riding 2 miles, golf 5 miles.

Charges 2002

Per unit incl. 2 adults	£10.50
extra adult	£2.50
child (under 14 yrs)	£1.50
awning	£2.00
electricity	£2.50

No credit cards. **Tel:** 01722 710125. E-mail: alderbury@aol.com. **Reservations:** Contact park for details. **Open** all year.

Directions: From Salisbury take A36 towards Southampton and, after 3 miles (at far end of the dual carriageway section), turn left at sign to Alderbury and Whaddon, then right, over bridge, and left for park entrance. From Southampton on A36 towards Salisbury, continue past the A27 (Romsey) junction and over Pepperbox Hill. At end of a downhill straight, left onto slip road marked Alderbury, park is signed. O.S.GR: SU198263.

Monkton Wyld Farm Caravan Park

173 Monkton Wyld Farm, Charmouth DT6 6DB

Opened in 1991 by Simon and Joanna Kewley, Monkton Wyld is maturing nicely. Planting of flowering shrubs and trees continues (hydrangea and lavender) making an attractive, peaceful park, and a woodland walk has been created in 80 acres of the beautiful countryside surrounding the park. An abundance of mature trees around the perimeter provides shade and plenty of space between the 60 pitches gives a feeling of spaciousness. Most pitches have 16A electricity and around 35 have hardstanding. On site facilities are limited but an area at the top of the park has been turned into a play area, with a good space for ball games, a climbing frame, trampoline, etc. A separate site has been developed next to the existing park for the Camping and Caravanning Club (open to non-members), managed by resident wardens. Bread, milk, groceries and papers may be obtained from here in the main season (09.00-19.00 hrs).

Facilities: The modern, well maintained toilet block has a fully equipped family room with baby changing facilities and that can also be accessed by wheelchairs. Individual showers with folding screen are very spacious. Small laundry with washing machine and dryer. Washing up is under cover. Gas supplies. Play area. Caravan storage. Gate locked at 11 pm. **Off site:** Fishing or riding 2 miles, bicycle hire, golf and boat launching 3 miles. Shops and local pubs are within a mile's walking distance and Charmouth and Lyme Regis are only 3 miles (buses leave from just along the road to both towns).

Charges 2002

Per unit incl. 2 adults	£7.00 - £12.00
extra adult	£2.00
child (5-16 yrs)	£1.00 - £1.50
electricity	£2.00
dog	free - £0.75
pup tent	free - £1.00

No extra charge for awnings, 2nd car, boats or visitors. No credit cards. **Tel:** 01297 34525. Fax: 01297 33594. E-mail: holidays@monktonwyld.co.uk. **Reservations:** Made with deposit of £5 per night booked. **Open** 30 March - 28 October.

Directions: Park is signed on A35 between Charmouth and Axminster, approx. 1.5 miles west of Charmouth. Turn right at Greenway Head (B3165 signed Marshwood) and park is 600 yds on the left past the Club site. Don't go to Monkton Wyld hamlet - the road is very steep. O.S.GR: SY329966.

Newlands Caravan Park

Charmouth DT6 6RB

181

This family owned park, run with care, occupies a prominent position beside the road into Charmouth village with marvellous views southwards to the hills across the valley. The terrain is terraced in two fields to provide over 200 well spaced places for touring units, some for seasonal units and over 80 for caravan holiday homes (some for hire). The mainly sloping, tent field also has super views towards the sea and Lyme Regis. Electricity (10A) is provided on 160 pitches and 30 have hardstanding, water and waste water. Five 'Millennium' pitches have a washing machine and dryer for individual use. Other accommodation includes smart pine lodges, apartments and motel rooms. All the facilities are located in a modern building to one side of the wide tarmac entrance. The club bar opens each evening and lunch times to suit. Family entertainment includes a children's club during school holidays with Dino Dan the dinosaur. There is an indoor pool and an adjacent outdoor pool and paddling pool which are walled, paved and sheltered. A super large play area in the field below the tent field is open dawn to dusk - try the maypole swing and bobsleigh ride! A comfortable site for families with some evening and family activities, the beach and village are an easy walk.

Facilities: The lower toilet block is modern and light with roomy showers, and has an adjoining covered washing up area and small laundry room. The other block is traditional in design with rather psychedelic tiles, but it is heated, clean, neat and tidy. Laundry room adjoining, plus dishwashing sinks (under cover). Well stocked shop (March-Nov). Licensed club bar (limited hours Nov-March). Restaurant (open evenings 6-9 pm. March-Nov plus Xmas/New Year) including takeaway. Outdoor heated pool (supervised in high season; the entrance is key coded). Indoor pool and jacuzzi (small charge, open all year, limited hours Nov-March). Nine-pin bowling alley for hire at £5 per half hour. Play area. **Off site:** Fishing 1 mile, riding 3 miles, golf 2 miles. Charmouth is known for its fossil finds and its connection with Jane Austen.

Charges 2002

Per pitch (max. 6 persons)	£9.00 - £18.00
serviced pitch	£16.00 - £26.00
extra child's pup tent	£4.00
awning	free
dog (max. 2)	£1.00
electricity	£2.00

Only one van or tent per pitch. **Tel:** 01297 560259. Fax: 01297 560787. E-mail: enq@newlandsholidays. co.uk. **Reservations:** Made with £30 deposit per week. **Open** all year.

Directions: Approaching from Bridport leave the A35 at first sign for Charmouth at start of the bypass and site almost directly on your left. O.S.GR: SY373935.

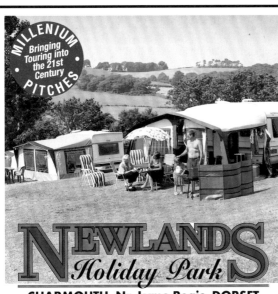

Gezinscamping in het prachtige, landelijke Dorset - op korte afstand van Charmouth en het strand.

Caravan- en tentplaatsen op terrassen met elektriciteit aanwezig.

Binnen- en buitenzwembaden.

Uitgebreide faciliteiten incl. Restaurant, Club en Bowlingbaan.

Châlets, vakantiehuizen & appartementen aanwezig.

Gehele jaar geopend.

CHARMOUTH, Nr. Lyme Regis, DORSET

Gratis kleurenbrochure:

CHEQUES

Camping Cheque

ACCEPTED

Newlands Caravan Park, Charmouth, Dorset DT6 6RB

Tel: **01297 560259** Fax: **01297 560787**

www.newlandsholidays.co.uk

E-mail: enq@newlandsholidays.co.uk

Wood Farm Caravan Park

176 Axminster Road, Charmouth DT6 6BT

Wood Farm is an excellent, family run park, maintained to high standards and with an indoor swimming pool. Situated on the western side of Charmouth beside the A35 (some road noise may be expected) and only a mile or two from Lyme Regis and its beaches, it is part of the Caravan Club's 'managed under contract' scheme (non-members are also very welcome). On sloping, well landscaped ground, it has open views across the countryside. There are 200 pitches for touring units of which 180 are neat, level all-weather pitches with hardstanding, electricity (10A) and TV connections, and provision for awnings. These are divided by neat, box-like leylandii hedging which has almost become a feature of the park. Water and waste water hook-ups are also available. One grassy terraced field takes about 25 tents and there are 80 caravan holiday homes in their own areas. A member of the Best of British group.

Facilities: Four good, modern toilet blocks can be heated and include some washbasins in curtained cubicles for ladies. The excellent lower block provides wash cubicles, and en-suite facilities for disabled people. One block has a baby care unit and laundry sinks with a spin dryer. Separate laundry room. Covered dishwashing sinks at each block. Motorcaravan service point. Shop by reception. Fish and chip van opens 2-4 times a week (acc. to season). Good heated indoor pool (27 x 54 ft; £1.50 per session, under 3s free. Recreation hall with snooker room and family games area with table tennis, TV, 'soft play' and table football. Outdoor tennis court. Play field. Two coarse fishing ponds (carp, rudd, roach, tench, perch) adjacent - day and weekly tickets (rod licence required, also available from park). **Off site:** Golf 1 mile, beaches and shops 1 and 2 miles.

Charges 2002

Per unit incl. 2 adults and electricity	£11.50-£16.50
incl. mains services and awning	£13.00 - £18.00
extra adult	£3.50 - £4.75
child (5-16 yrs)	£1.10 - £1.20
dog	£1.00

Special senior citizens low season discounts. **Tel:** 01297 560697. Fax: 01297 561243. E-mail: holidays @woodfarm.co.uk. **Reservations:** Made with £30 deposit (non-returnable), min. 5 nights in high season, 3 nights other times. **Open** 22 March - 3 November.

Directions: Park is 0.5 miles west of Charmouth village with access near roundabout at junction of A35 with A3052 (Lyme Regis) road. O.S.GR: SY356940.

Golden Cap Holiday Park

174 Seatown, Chideock, nr Bridport, Dorset

Golden Cap, named after the adjacent high cliff (the highest in southern England) which overlooks Lyme Bay, is only 150 metres from a shingle beach at Seatown and is surrounded by National Trust countryside and the Heritage Coastline. The park is arranged over several fields on the valley floor, sloping gently down towards the sea. It is in two main areas, having once been two parks, each separated into fields with marvellous views around and providing 108 touring pitches. All have electricity and 28 also have hardstanding with drainaway and gravel awning area. An extra sloping tent field is used for peak season (torch useful), although it is a five minute walk from here to the toilet blocks and shop. There are 212 caravan holiday homes in their own areas. The most attractive indoor swimming pool at Highlands End (under the same ownership) is three miles away and open for campers on payment. Beaches are nearby, sea fishing, boat launching, riding or fossil hunting are possible in the area, plus good walks including access to the coastal path. A well run park and a member of the Best of British group.

Facilities: The main toilet block is modern and of very good quality, with spacious shower cubicles (some with toilet and washbasin), good facilities for visitors with disabilities (Radar key) and a baby care room. Two other smaller blocks around the park. Laundry room. Motorcaravan service point. Useful and well stocked shop (8 am - 6 pm, or 9 pm in high season). Takeaway service each evening in peak season. Gas supplies. Small play area. Fishing lake. Tourist information rooms. American motorhomes are not accepted. **Off site:** Pub with food service close.

Charges 2002

Per unit incl. 2 persons, electricity	£10.25 - £14.75
incl. mains services and awning	£11.75 - £16.25
extra adult	£2.75 - £3.00
child (4-17 yrs)	£1.25 - £1.50
dog	£1.25 - £1.50

Tel: 01308 422139. Fax: 01308 425672. E-mail: holidays@wdlh.co.uk. **Reservations:** Essential in high season and made with £20 deposit (min. 4 days in high season). For information or booking contact: West Dorset Leisure Holidays, Eype, Bridport, Dorset DT6 6AR. **Open** 20 March - 1 November.

Directions: Turn off A35 road at Chideock, (a bigger village with shops and restaurants) 3 miles west of Bridport, at sign to Seatown opposite church. Park is less than 1 mile down narrow lane. O.S.GR: SY423919.

Highlands End Farm Holiday Park

Eype, nr Bridport, Dorset DT6 6AR

175

On slightly sloping ground with superb open views, both coastal and inland, Highlands End is quietly situated on the Dorset Heritage Coastline. With access to the coastal path, a path in front of the park runs along the cliff top and then leads down to a shingle beach a little further along. It is a good quality park with 180 caravan holiday homes, mostly privately owned, and 195 touring pitches in two areas nearest to the sea - one has to travel through the holiday homes to reach them. All have electricity (10A) and 45 also offer water, drainage, hardstanding and a gravel awning area. A further area is used for tents in high season. A modern, attractive building houses a lounge bar, good value restaurant with takeaway facility, family room and games room with some musical evenings in high season. The park's amenities also include an excellent, air-conditioned indoor heated pool, a gym room, sun beds, steam room and sauna, and a tennis court (all charged). The owners have a long time interest in the fire brigade and an historic fire engine (1936 Leyland Pump Escape) along with memorabilia make an interesting display in the bar. The park was used to film scenes for Nick Berry's TV series based on nearby West Bay harbour. A well run park and a member of the Best of British group.

Facilities: The two toilet blocks near the touring sections are excellent, well maintained and can be heated. They provide washbasins (some in cubicles with toilets), large, comfortable, showers, covered dishwashing sinks and a dishwashing room. En-suite facilities for disabled visitors and a baby care room. Laundry room. Motorcaravan service point. Well stocked shop (opening times vary with the season), including gas supplies. Bar and restaurant/takeaway (Spr. B.H.- late Sept). Tennis. Swimming pool with attendant (20 x 9 m. and charged £2 per session, £1 for children), sunbed and gym. Games room. Pitch and putt. Two adventure play areas. Large sloping field for ball games. **Off site:** Golf or fishing 2 miles.

Charges 2002

Per unit incl. 2 persons, electricity	£10.25 - £14.75
incl. mains services and awning	£11.75 - £16.25
extra adult	£2.75 - £3.00
child (4-17 yrs)	£1.25 - £1.50
dog	£1.25 - £1.50

Tel: 01308 422139. Fax: 01308 425672. E-mail: holidays@wdlh.co.uk. **Reservations:** Essential in high season and made with £20 deposit (min. 4 days in high season). Contact West Dorset Leisure Holidays, Eype, nr. Bridport, Dorset DT6 6AR. **Open** 20 March - 1 November.

Directions: Follow Bridport bypass on A35 around the town and park is signed to south (Eype turning), down narrow lane. O.S.GR: SY452914.

West Dorset Leisure Holidays

Highlands End and Golden Cap Holiday Parks

★ A choice of two select family parks on the West Dorset Heritage coastline
★ Indoor heated swimming pool
★ Caravan holiday homes for hire and for sale
★ Excellent facilities for tourers and tents

Set in the exceptionally beautiful countryside of West Dorset, both our parks are ideally situated for a quiet stay or as a centre for touring. Quiet beaches, places of interest, countryside walks with panoramic views and welcoming country inns make West Dorset a place to come back to year after year.

For a free colour brochure from Martin and Vanessa Cox

Tel: 01308 422139
Fax: 01308 425672
Email: holidays@wdlh.co.uk

Eype, Bridport, Dorset DT6 6AR

www.wdlh.co.uk

Freshwater Beach Holiday Park

Burton Bradstock, Bridport DT6 4PT

178

Family run parks for families with direct access to a beach are rare in Britain and this one has the added advantage of being in beautiful coastal countryside in West Dorset. It is an ideal situation to explore the 'Hidden County' and the resort of Weymouth (17 miles) and is next to the sea and a beach of fine pebbles, sheltered from the wind by pebble banks. The River Bride edges the park and joins the sea here. Approached by a fairly steep access road, the park itself is on level, open ground. The 500 plus touring pitches, over 300 with 10A electricity, are on an open, undulating grass field connected by tarmac or hard-core roads. Caravan pitches (10 x 11 m.) are marked, evenly spaced in lines. Some tent pitches are in the main field, with others well spaced on a newly terraced grass field. In separate areas there are 270 caravan holiday homes, with 40 for hire. This lively holiday park has an extensive range of facilities which include a n outdoor pool, a good value licensed restaurant and three bars with an evening entertainment programme in season. Daytime entertainment caters for all ages - don't miss the donkey derby! Footpaths lead to the thatched village of Burton Bradstock or West Bay. The overall impression is of a large, busy holiday park with a friendly reception and happy atmosphere.

Facilities: Toilet facilities are in two refurbished blocks, plus another with washbasins and toilets only, all with free hot water. A 'portacabin' style unit serves the tent field. In all, it is a good provision for a busy beach park. The main blocks have facilities for disabled people (Radar key), and a baby care room (key system). Laundry and dishwashing sinks cope well at peak times. Launderette. Bars with entertainment and licensed restaurant (weekends only in late season; closed Mondays all season). Good value supermarket and takeaway. Heated and supervised outdoor swimming pool and children's pool (15/5-30/10) with swimming and diving lessons available. Snooker room. Pool table. Adventure play area. Pony trekking (own stables on site). **Off site:** Golf course adjacent, fishing possible from Chesil Bank. Abbotsbury Sub-Tropical Gardens and Swannery 7 miles.

Charges 2002

Per unit incl. up to 6 persons	£10.00 - £24.00
extra person	£2.00
electricity	£2.00
walkers or cyclists (2 persons)	£7.50 - £15.00
dog	£2.50

Single sex groups not admitted. **Tel:** 01308 897317. Fax: 01308 897336. E-mail: enquiries@freshwaterbeach.co.uk. **Reservations:** Made for min. 1 week with £20 deposit p/week, plus £1 fee. Short break reservations available - ring for details. **Open** 16 March - 10 November.

Directions: Park is immediately west of the village of Burton Bradstock, on the Weymouth - Bridport coast road (B3157). O.S.GR: SY980898.

Binghams Farm Touring Caravan Park

Melplash, Bridport DT6 3TT

Binghams is a small, purpose built park, for adults only. In a pleasant, rural situation two miles from the market town of Bridport, with views seaward towards West Bay and inland across Beaminster Downs and Pilsdon Hill, it is open all year. The park provides an area of individual pitches with 10A electricity and over 40 hardstandings, nicely landscaped with shrubs and trees growing between the pitches, plus an open sloping field overlooking the valley with 20 electrical hook-ups. The entrance to the park is neatly tarmaced and resident ducks and chickens provide interest. A cottage has been converted into two flats to let. A path is provided to the river which links with the main footpaths for Bridport (20 minutes) or local hostelries. A limited bus service runs on the main road. The Brit Valley is an unspoilt area of West Dorset with an ancient heritage and coastal West Bay is only a couple of miles.

Facilities: The original farm buildings have been sympathetically converted to provide reception, a good heated toilet block and the other amenities. The toilet block, with under floor heating for winter use, provides well fitted, tiled, curtained showers, hairdryers, a separate, fully equipped room for the less able with ramped access and a laundry room. Dishwashing under cover. Upstairs lounge bar serving bar food in high season (closed Tues/Wed). Games room with table tennis, books, chess and pool table. Gas available. Winter caravan storage. Gates closed 23.00-08.00 hrs. This is an 'adults only' park. **Off site:** Sea fishing and golf 3 miles.

Charges 2002

Per pitch incl. 2 persons, awning	£8.00 - £13.00
extra adult	£4.00
dog	£1.50
electricity	£2.20

Tel: 01308 488234. Fax: 01308 488234. E-mail: binghamsfarm@hotmail.com. **Reservations:** Made with £25 non-returnable deposit per week or part. **Open** all year.

Directions: At main roundabout on A35 road, on east side of Bridport, take A3066 towards Beaminster. Watch for site entrance after approx. 2 miles on the left. O.S.GR: SY482963.

Bagwell Farm Touring Park

Chickerell, Weymouth DT3 4EA

A pleasant, large, family park, Bagwell Farm is situated between Weymouth and Abbotsbury, close to Chesil Beach. In a valley, yet with an open aspect, there are 396 numbered touring pitches, with 44 taken up by seasonal units. With 134 electricity connections (10A) and some serviced pitches, some pitches are on terraces with views of the Chesil Bank and the sea. In addition there is a traditional camping field with a campers' shelter and a barbecue and a rally field with electric hook-ups. An attractive bar has been converted from farm buildings and a grill with a patio overlooking the pets corner (also open to the public). Only 4 miles from Weymouth, the 'blue flag' beaches and other attractions of the resort are easily accessible. This is a useful site, open all year.

Facilities: Fully equipped, traditional style toilet blocks are centrally situated with showers on payment and 2 unisex bathrooms on payment. 'Portacabin' style toilets in the camping field for high season. Dishwashing up sinks and laundry with 2 washing machines and dryer. Motorcaravan service point. Mini-market with off licence opposite reception. Fast food takeaway, bar and grill. All facilities open Easter - end Sept. Games room. Play area and pets corner. **Off site:** Riding and golf 3 miles. Weymouth beach 5 miles. Abbotsbury with Swannery and Tropical Gardens 4 miles. Two pubs are within walking distance, one in the direction of the marvellous walk from the site to the sea.

Charges 2002

Per unit incl. 2 adults and 2 children	£6.50 - £11.50
extra adult	£2.50
child (5-16 yrs)	1.00
electricity	2.20
serviced pitch	2.20
awning, extra car or boat	£1.50 - £2.00

Tel: 01305 782575. **Reservations:** Made with deposit (£30 p/week for each unit), balance in advance or on arrival. **Open** all year.

Directions: Follow B3157 from Weymouth in direction of Bridport. Park is 2 miles after passing Chickerell village. The entrance is on the brow of a hill - care is needed. O.S.GR: SY627816.

East Fleet Farm Touring Park

Chickerell, Weymouth DT3 4DW

East Fleet Farm has a marvellous situation on part level, part gently sloping meadows leading to the shores of the Fleet, with views across the famous Chesil Bank to the sea beyond. The Fleet is a lagoon renowned for its wildlife and popular with bird watchers. The park itself has been developed within the confines of a 300-acre organic working dairy and arable farm and is maturing nicely as bushes and trees grow. The 270 pitches are a comfortable size so there is no feeling of crowding. Of these, 160 are level and marked with 10A electric hook-ups, 25 also having hardstanding. The bar, converted from the barn, features the original beams and brick work with a terrace complete with views over the Fleet (open high season and B.Hs.) providing bar meals. The busy resort of Weymouth with its safe bathing beaches and many watersports facilities is only three miles away (bicycle hire and boat launching possible). There is a bus service from the top of the lane (approx. half a mile) and Abbotsbury Swannery and Gardens are nearby.

Facilities: The central toilet block is built in natural stone and provides adequate rather than luxurious facilities with coin-operated showers (one heated). Dishwashing under cover (H&C). Fully equipped laundry room with a self-contained unit for disabled people off it and two family shower rooms. Extra new toilets and a family bathroom are beside the bar. Reception plus shop with basic groceries, bread, papers and gas, etc. opens longer in high season (bar and shop Easter - end Sept). Games room with pool table. Play area but, remember, elsewhere this is a working farm. **Off site:** Riding or golf 2 miles.

Charges 2002

Per unit incl. 2 persons	£5.50 - £11.00
extra adult	£0.50 - £3.00
child (5-16 years)	£0.25 - £0.50
awning	free - £2.00
dog	£0.25 - £1.00
electricity (10A)	£2.00 - £2.50

Senior citizen discount in June (10%). Families welcome. **Tel:** 01305 785768. E-mail: enquiries@ eastfleet.co.uk. **Reservations:** Write with £20 deposit. **Open** 15 March - 31 October.

Directions: Park is signed from B3157 Weymouth - Bridport road, approx. 3 miles west of Weymouth. The narrow approach road is by the army camp on the southern side of the B3157. O.S.GR: SY639798.

East Fleet Farm

Touring Park

Chickerell, Weymouth,
Dorset. DT3 4DW

www.eastfleet.co.uk
Tel: (01305) 785768

Peaceful & spacious park on the shores of the Fleet, overlooking Chesil Bank & the sea on Dorsets Jurassic Coast.
✆ tel: for a brochure - Season pitches now available

Caravans, Tents & Motor Caravans
Electric Hook-ups • Children's Play Area
Superclean Toilet, Laundry & Shower Block
Well Stocked Shop
'Old Barn' Family Bar & Restaurant
Open Mid-March to Mid-January

Southern Tourist Board

East Dorset, Hampshire, Isle of Wight, South Wiltshire, Oxfordshire, Berkshire and Buckinghamshire

Southern Tourist Board
40 Chamberlayne Road, Eastleigh, Hampshire SO50 5JH
Tel: 023 8062 5400 Fax: 023 8062 0010
E-mail: info@southerntb.co.uk
Internet: http://www.visitsouthernengland.com

From 2003 Southern Tourist Board and the South East Tourist Board are to amalgamate. At the time of going to press both offices remain open.

The Southern Tourist Board covers three distinctive areas:

The South Coast comprises Weymouth with its safe sandy beach and the Isle of Portland joined to the mainland by the unique Chesil beach, and Swanage with the famous Studland beach and Purbeck hills. The cosmopolitan resort of Bournemouth, with its seven miles of golden sand, and the New Forest renowned for its trees and ponies, with its famous yachting havens of Lymington and Buckler's Hard.

The Isle of Wight is just a short ferry trip across the Solent and offers a wealth of activities for all ages with a mild and sunny climate. Portsmouth, the flagship of Maritime England, is now the home of the 'Mary Rose' and several other historic ships, also Southampton, with its maritime connections including the 'Titanic' and the International Boat Show.

Rural Southern England comprises green rolling hills and scenic wooded valleys covering North and West Wiltshire, parts of Dorset, Hampshire, Kennet and Avon Canal country and the New Forest and the Test Valley. Worthy of mention is the beautiful medieval city of Salisbury with its inspirational Cathedral and Close, and Winchester, ancient capital of the Kingdom of Wessex.

Photo: Kennet & Avon Canal, Southern TB

Thames and Chilterns, dominated by the River Thames, its tributaries and the Chiltern Hills offers a mix of internationally famous cities and sporting events, royal pomp and traditional English village life. Buckinghamshire inspired John Betjeman and John Milton finished 'Paradise Lost' in his cottage at Chalfont St Giles. Benjamin Disraeli, the 19th Century Prime Minister came from near High Wycombe and the scenic village of Great Missenden was home to the great children's story teller Roald Dahl. Oxford is the city of dreaming spires. The golden stone university buildings have shaped a graceful and timeless city which no visitor forgets. The Oxfordshire Cotswolds has picturesque villages, the regal splendour of Blenheim Palace and market towns such as Chipping Norton. Berkshire is within 50 miles of London and is well known for its racing connections, and Royal connections at Windsor and Eton.

Photo: HMS Victory, Southern TB

Sandyholme Holiday Park

201 Moreton Road, Owermoigne, Dorchester DT2 8HZ

A peaceful haven in Thomas Hardy country, Sandyholme provides 44 holiday homes (privately owned or to hire) and 40 numbered pitches for touring units on level, short grass fields with one corner lightly wooded. The next door field, owned by the local farmer and operated on a 28 day licence, can be used for tents or rallies. The Holme Club (free membership) is a pleasant provision, open every evening at B.Hs. during April and May, then mid-July to mid Sept. It has a cosy bar and patio, and a good bar meal menu. An unusual feature is a rather special duck pond with an amazing variety of ducks from all over the world with a pleasant walk and seats around the edge (an electric fence keeps the foxes at bay!) There are walks and cycling direct from the site or in Puddletown and Wareham Forests, or along the coastal path. Lulworth Cove, Durdle Door and Weymouth, with its sandy beach, are all near at hand.

Facilities: The modern, fully equipped new toilet block includes some washbasins in cubicles, controllable showers and is bright and well maintained. En-suite facilities for disabled visitors doubles as a family room with baby changing facilities. Fully equipped laundry room. Room for dishwashing. Shop/reception stocks all basic necessities including papers and gas. Bar and bar meals. Good, fenced, safe-based adventure play area. Games room with pool table and amusement machines. **Off site:** Fishing is available on an adjacent farm, bicycle hire or golf 5 miles, riding 6 miles.

Charges 2002

Per pitch incl. 2 persons	£7.50 - £12.50
extra adult	£2.00
child (2-17 yrs)	£1.25
electricity	£2.00
dog	£1.50

Tel: 01305 852677. Fax: 01305 854677.
Reservations: Made with £20 non-refundable deposit; include SAE for receipt. **Open** Easter/1 April - 31 October.

Directions: On A352 Dorchester - Wareham road going west, watch for short dual carriageway section before Weymouth - Osmington roundabout. Turn north through Owermoigne village and park is on the left (clearly signed) after approx. 400 yards. O.S.GR: SY768863.

Durdle Door Holiday Park

217 Lulworth Cove, Wareham BH20 5PU

Durdle Door has a unique situation overlooking the Purbeck coastline with views of Portland Bill. There is public access to Lulworth Cove by the coastal path and private access to Durdle Door beach. Part of the Lulworth estate which includes Lulworth Castle, the Children's Farm and the Heritage Centre at Lulworth Cove, it is well managed. The park is situated partly on gently sloping grassland, and partly in woodland areas. The majority of the 425 pitches are occupied by caravan holiday homes (privately owned or 30 to let) leaving 178 for touring units, 45 with 6-16A electricity. The open touring fields are interspersed between the rows of holiday homes. Some have views of the sea, others of the rolling Dorset countryside. The woodland area is better for smaller units. All areas have communal barbecues. Lulworth Castle is open to the public, hosting events including horse shows, country fair, international floral design show and jousting exibitions (Mon. - Fri. in Aug) and there are walks on

Lulworth Ranges.

Facilities: Two older, traditional type toilet blocks are fully equipped. One modern block at the edge of the wooded area includes some washbasins in cubicles and baby changing mat. Fully equipped laundry room and dishwashing sinks. Well stocked shop including tenting accessories, off licence and gas. Attractive bar with food menu open all day (also open to the public). TV. Play area, adventure trail and toddlers' play room for under 4's. Children's entertainment provided at various times. Mountain bike hire. **Off site:** Bovington Tank Museum and Monkey World nearby. Sports centre and indoor pool at Wareham. Equestrian centre nearby.

Charges 2002

Per pitch	£10.00 - £15.00
extra tent	£5.00 - £7.00
electricity	£2.00
dog (max. 2)	£2.50

Tel: 01929 400200. Fax: 01929 400260.
Reservations: Made with 50% deposit, balance payable 21 days before arrival. **Open** 1 March - 31 October.

Directions: From Wool follow B3071 for West Lulworth. Continue past the Castle Inn and turn right at T-junction by the War memorial. Continue up hill and park entrance is on the brow of the hill on the left. O.S.GR: SY812809.

Wareham Forest Tourist Park

North Trigon, Wareham BH20 7NZ

A peacefully located, spacious park in an unspoilt corner of Dorset, this site becomes very busy in high season. Developed to high standards by the present owners, it provides formal pitching, with or without hardstanding, for caravans or natural pitches for tents in pine wood or open field. Drainage appears satisfactory. The setting in Wareham Forest is attractive offering space for 200 units, 102 with hardstanding and all with electrical connections. There are also 8 luxury pitches on hardstanding with water, drainage, TV aerial, dustbin and light (available 1/3-31/10 only). There are forest walks and the park is well situated to explore the Dorset coast and Thomas Hardy country. In high season a bus service to and from Wareham leaves the site six times daily (mornings and teatime).

Facilities: Two well maintained, spacious toilet blocks are of a good standard with some washbasins in cubicles for ladies, plus adjustable showers on payment. The block used in the winter months is centrally heated. Facilities for disabled people. Well equipped laundry rooms and deep sinks for washing up. Motorcaravan service point. Small licensed shop with gas (limited hours). Cafeteria for breakfasts, etc. (main season). Games room with video amusement machines next door. Open-air, heated swimming pool (60 x 20 ft). Large adventure play area. Entrance closed 11 pm. - 7 am. Resident wardens on site. Caravan storage facilities. **Off site:** Fishing 5 miles, bicycle hire or golf 3 miles, riding 8 miles.

Charges 2003

Per pitch: standard	£4.50 - £6.50
premium	£6.75 - £8.50
serviced	£8.75 - £10.50
adult	£1.50 - £3.00
child 2-14 yrs	£1.00 - £2.00
dog	£0.60 - £1.50
electricity	£2.00 - £2.25
extra tent, awning, boat	£0.60 - £2.20

Couples and families only. **Tel:** 01929 551393. Fax: 01929 551393. E-mail: holiday@wareham-forest.co.uk. **Reservations:** Made with £25 non-returnable deposit and £2 admin. fee, balance 28 days before arrival. **Open** all year.

Directions: Park is north of Wareham between Wareham and Bere Regis, located off the A35 road. O.S.GR: SY899903.

Wareham Forest Tourist Park

OPEN ALL YEAR
For further details and free coloured brochure write or phone: Tel/Fax: (01929) 551393.
Peter & Pam Savage, Wareham Forest Tourist Park, North Trigon, Wareham, Dorset BH20 7NZ.
www.wareham-forest.co.uk email holiday@wareham-forest.co.uk. Credit cards accepted

Rowlands Wait Touring Park

Rye Hill, Bere Regis BH20 7LP

205

Bernard and Linda Hammick have worked hard to make Rowlands Wait into a most attractive park catering for all types of humans and units! The top of the park, edged by mature woods (full of bluebells in spring) is a haven for tents (and squirrels) with marvellous views and providing 30 places in three descending fields. The rest of the park is a little more formal, and nearer to the central toilet block, but most pitches back on to hedging or trees and they are generally level. Many walks are possible from the park with information provided on wildlife. A warm welcome awaits, particularly for those new to camping and caravanning, and a reader reports the park as 'very friendly and relaxed, with few rules'. The park takes bookings for groups or rallies all year. A member of the Countryside Discovery group.

Facilities: The purpose built toilet block is well equipped, including free hot showers. Laundry room. Covered dishwashing area. Recycling bins. Shop (high season) providing milk, papers and basic essentials and a freezer for ice packs. Play area for little ones with miniature assault course and castle is well placed near reception. Games room with pool table, table tennis and table football behind the sanitary block. Crazy golf. Bicycle hire. Torch useful. **Off site:** The village, a 10 minute walk, has shops, two pubs, etc. plus a bus service for Dorchester and Poole. Fishing 5 miles, golf 3 miles, riding 9 miles.

Charges 2002

Per unit incl. 2 persons	£7.00 - £10.00
extra adult	£1.60 - £2.10
child (under 16)	£0.90
awning, pup tent	free - £1.00
electricity (10A)	£2.00
dog	free - £0.60
extra car, boat or trailer	free - £1.00

Tel: 01929 472727. Fax: 01929 472727. E-mail: ar@rowlandswait.co.uk. **Reservations:** Made with £15 deposit per week. **Open** 16 March - 31 October, and winter by arrangement.

Directions: Park is south of Bere Regis, just off the road to Wool, well signed from the A35/A31 roundabout. O.S.GR: SY842933.

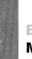

Manor Farm Caravan Park

1 Manor Farm Cottage, East Stoke, Wareham BH20 6AW

204

Near to the Purbeck hills, this is a small, rural park beside, but not part of, a working farm. David and Gillian Topp own and carefully run this simple park which is set in a hedged, level field, semi-broken up by evergreens. It provides 50 level, well spaced pitches, 30 for touring units, with 43 electrical connections (16A), on neatly cut grass. An ice pack service and gas exchange are provided and there is a sturdy children's play unit. East Stoke village has a pub, Wool is 2 miles with a pub and shops. Wareham and Swanage are near.

Facilities: The timber-clad toilet block (key system) is at the top of the field and is adequate inside providing all necessary facilities and kept very clean. Showers are metered (20p). A toilet for disabled people is in the men's room. Sink for washing up and one for laundry with a spin dryer (all 20p). Small shop for basics open July/August, 8.30-10.00 and 16.30-19.00. Caravan storage. Dogs are accepted at the discretion of the owner. **Off site:** Fishing, bicycle hire, boat launching, riding all 3 miles, golf 4 miles.

Charges 2002

Per unit incl. 2 persons	£8.00
extra adult	£1.50
child (3-13 yrs)	£1.40
dog	£1.25
electricity	£2.30

No groups, singles, motorcycles or rallies. No credit cards. **Tel:** 01929 462870. E-mail: info@manorfarmcp.co.uk. **Reservations:** Made with £20 deposit. **Open** Easter - 30 September.

Directions: Off A352 Wareham - Wool road, turn into lane by church, over manned level crossing and park is 0.5 miles on right. Or from B3070 turn right signed East Stoke, then next right signed Manor Farm and site is on left. O.S.GR: SY872867.

The Inside Park

Touring Caravan & Camping Park, Blandford Forum DT11 9AD

The Inside Park is set in the grounds of an 18th century country house that burned down in 1941. Family owned and carefully managed alongside a dairy and arable farm, it is a must for those interested in local history or arboriculture and is a haven for wildlife and birds. The reception/toilet block and games room block are respectively the coach house and stables of the old house. The nine acre camping field, a little distant, lies in a sheltered, gently sloping dry valley containing superb tree specimens - notably cedars, with walnuts in one part - and a dog graveyard dating back to the early 1700s under a large Cedar of Lebanon. In total there are 125 spacious pitches, 90 with electricity (10A) and some in wooded glades. The six acres adjoining are the old pleasure gardens of the house where campers can walk and exercise dogs in the former garden, now mostly overgrown and providing what must be one of the largest children's campsite adventure-lands in the UK. No vehicle access to the park is allowed after 10.30 pm. (separate late arrivals area and car park). The market town of Blandford with its leisure and swimming centre (temporary membership for Inside Park guests) is two miles and the area is excellent for walking and cycling (test your fitness on a five mile mountain bike course). Extensive walking routes are marked through the farm and woodland, with a guide showing points of interest available in the shop and farm tours are organised.

Facilities: The toilet block provides some wash-basins in cubicles, comfortably sized showers with non-slip floors and a room for disabled visitors or mothers and babies. Dishwashing sinks. Laundry room in the same block. Recycling bins. Shop with basics, gas and camping provisions (limited opening out of main season). Mobile fish and chips twice weekly. Spacious games room with pool tables, table tennis, etc. and a tourist information section. Safe based children's adventure play area. Day kennelling facilities for dogs. Winter caravan storage. **Off site:** Fishing and riding 2 miles, golf 3 miles.

Charges 2002

Per pitch	£3.00 - £4.80
adult	£2.50 - £3.00
child (5-16 years)	free - £1.10
dog	£0.60 - £0.90
electricity	£2.25
tent light	free - £1.00

Tel: 01258 453719. Fax: 01258 459921. E-mail: inspark@aol.com. **Reservations:** Essential for B.H's and high season; made with £10 deposit (min. 4 nights 14/7-2/9). **Open** Easter - 31 October.

Directions: Park is about 2 miles southwest of Blandford and is signed from roundabout junction of A354 and A350 roads. If approaching from the Shaftesbury direction, do not go into Blandford but follow the bypass to the last roundabout and follow camp signs. O.S.GR: ST864045.

Merley Court Touring Park

Merley, Wimborne BH21 3AA

Merley Court celebrates its 20th anniversary during 2003 and is a credit to the Wright family. All aspects of this well planned, attractively landscaped park are constantly maintained to the highest of standards. The historic walled garden dating back to the 18th century with its many floral attributes, provides ideal surroundings for a pleasant stroll or a family picnic. There are also opportunities to play croquet, crazy golf, boule, volleyball or basketball. Tarmac roads connect 160 touring pitches (all with 16A electricity) on neat lawns or one of the many hardstandings. This provision includes 11 neat all-service pitches with water, waste disposal and satellite TV. The entire park is interspersed with a variety of shrubs, plants and the odd ornamental urn. Some attractive tent pitches are to be found in a small wooded valley. A well-furnished club complex provides a lounge bar where meals are available, snack bar, takeaway, large games room with pool tables and a family room leading onto a spacious sheltered patio. This in turn leads to the paved walled swimming pool area. There are woodland walks (including dog walks) directly from the site connecting to the disused railway line where nature has returned with an abundance of wild flowers which in turn leads to Delph woods with designated nature trails. A member of the Best of British group.

Facilities: Three heated, well designed toilet blocks are of good quality, two with pre-set well equipped showers. The main block is to be tastefully refurbished for 2003. Separate facilities for disabled visitors and for babies. Excellent dishwashing and laundry facilities. Motorcaravan service point. Shop with caravan accessories and gas. Café and takeaway. Bar with food (limited hours in low and mid season). Outdoor pool (30 x 20 ft) with children's section open mid May - Sept. Tennis court. Table tennis. Children's play areas. Games room with pool tables. Tourist information. Conference/meeting venue available in the Orangery within the Leisure Garden. Dogs are not accepted in high season (14/7-31/8). Barrier card £5 deposit. **Off site:** Fishing, riding and golf all within 5 miles. The park is only 5 miles from from Poole, and 8 from Bournemouth. The Tower Park leisue and entertainment centre is nearby, Kingston Lacy House, Knoll Gardens, Brownsea Island and the Moors Valley Country Park are also near.

Charges 2002

Per standard pitch incl. 2 persons and electricity	£10.00 - £15.00
all service pitch and awning	£14.00 - £19.00
extra adult	£3.00
child (3-13 years)	£2.00
dog (outside 14/7-31/8)	£1.00

No extra pup tent as well as awning. **Tel:** 01202 881488. Fax: 01202 881484. E-mail: holidays@merley-court.co.uk. **Reservations:** Made with deposit (£35 p/w). **Open** all year excl. 8 Jan - 28 Feb.

Directions: Site clearly signed at the junction of A31 and A349 roads (roundabout) on the Wimborne bypass. O.S.GR: ST008984.

Whitemead Caravan Park

East Burton Road, Wool BH20 6HG

The Church family continue to make improvements to this attractive little park which is within walking distance of the village of Wool, between Dorchester and Wareham. Very natural and with open views over the Frome Valley water meadows, it provides 95 numbered pitches on flat grass sloping gently north and is orchard-like in parts. The pitches are well spaced and mostly back onto hedges or fences. There are 75 electrical connections for tourers (10A) and no caravan holiday homes. The park is 4.5 miles from the nearest beach at Lulworth and is handily placed for many attractions in this part of Dorset (train services and limited bus service close). There may be some rail noise.

Facilities: The traditional but comfortably sized toilet block includes a baby room, dishwashing and laundry sinks, washing machine, and tumble dryer. Smart reception cum shop (limited hours) with licence, gas supplies and information room/library. Takeaway with breakfasts at weekends (low season Tuesday, Friday and Sunday, otherwise all 15/03-31/10). Games room with pool table and darts. Playground. Caravan storage. **Off site:** The Ship Inn is 300 m. Riding or golf 3 miles.

Charges 2002

Per unit	£4.30 - £8.50
person over 5 yrs	£1.10
awning	£0.50 - £1.50
extra car, boat	free - £2.00
dog	£0.50 - £1.00
electricity	£2.00

No credit cards. **Tel:** 01929 462241. Fax: 01929 462241. E-mail: whitemeadcp@aol.com. **Reservations:** Made with £15 deposit, min. 3 nights at B.Hs. **Open** 15 March - 31 October.

Directions: Turn off main A352 on eastern edge of Wool, just north of level crossing, onto East Burton road. Site is 300 m. on right. O.S.GR: SY841871.

Ulwell Cottage Caravan Park

Ulwell, Swanage BH19 3DG

Nestling under the Purbeck Hills in this unique corner of Dorset on the edge of Swanage, Ulwell Cottage is a family run holiday park with indoor pool and wide range of facilities. A good proportion of the park is taken by caravan holiday homes (140), but an attractive, undulating area accessed by tarmac roads is given over to 77 numbered touring pitches. There are 68 electricity hook-ups (16A) and 18 hardstandings, 8 of which are serviced. The mixture of level and sloping pitches, interspersed with trees and shrubs, is quite pretty. The colourful entrance area is home to the Village Inn with a courtyard adjoining the heated, supervised indoor pool complex (both open all year and open to the public) and modern reception. The hill above the touring area, Nine Barrow Down, is a Site of Special Scientific Interest for butterflies overlooking Round Down. It is possible to walk to Corfe Castle this way. With Brownsea Island, Studland Bay, Corfe village and the Swanage Railway, Ulwell Cottage makes a marvellous centre for holidays.

Facilities: The toilet block serving the touring section is modern and cheerful with bright yellow doors, and can be heated. It is supplemented by an older block in the holiday home section. Both well equipped, a laundry room and baby washing sinks are in the lower block. Dishwashing under cover. Well stocked shop with gas available (Easter - mid Sept). Bar snacks and restaurant meals with a family room. Indoor pool. Amusement arcade with video games. Playing fields and play areas with a long slide and boat. **Off site:** Bicycle hire or riding 2 miles, fishing 1 mile, golf 1 mile.

Charges 2002

Per unit incl. up to 6 persons	£12.00 - £25.00
with electricity	£12.00 - £27.00
fully serviced with hardstanding	£13.50 - £28.50
extra tent, car or boat	£1.50

Less £2 for two persons only, less £1 for three persons. **Tel:** 01929 422823. Fax: 01929 421500. E-mail: enq@ulwellcottagepark.co.uk. **Reservations:** Made with 25% deposit or minimum £20; balance 2 weeks prior to holiday. **Open** 1 March - 7 January.

Directions: From A351 Wareham - Swanage road, turn on B3351 Studland road just before Corfe Castle, follow signs to right for Swanage and drop down to Ulwell. O.S.GR: SZ019809.

Wilksworth Farm Caravan Park

Cranborne Road, Wimborne BH21 4HW

206

Wilksworth Farm is a spacious, quiet park with a heated outdoor pool, and is well suited for families. It has a lovely rural situation just outside Wimborne and around 10 miles from the beaches between Poole and Bournemouth. With its duck pond at the entrance, it is well designed on good quality ground with fairly level grass and some views. It takes 65 caravans (awning groundsheets up in daytime) and 25 tents mainly on grass but with some hardstandings. All pitches have electrical connections, 10 also with water and drainage. There are some 77 privately owned and self contained caravan holiday homes. Facilities are in converted farm barns or designed to be in keeping with the listed buildings. Local attractions include the Tower Park entertainment centre 6 miles, Kingston Lacy (National Trust) 3 miles and Wimborne town centre (with its Minster) 1 mile.

Facilities: The good quality, central toilet block has been completely refurbished with under-floor heating throughout, and is well maintained. Family bathroom and facilities for disabled visitors, a shower/bath for children and baby changing point. Covered dishwashing sinks outside. Laundry room. Reception and shop (basics only, limited hours, Easter - 30 Sept). Gas supplies. Freezer for ice packs. Attractive coffee shop with full menu and takeaway service (weekends and B.H's. only outside the main season). Heated 40 x 20 ft. swimming pool (unsupervised, but fenced and gated, open May - Sept) with small children's pool. Football ground. Excellent adventure play area. BMX track, golf practice net and two tennis courts, one full and one short size. Games room with table tennis, pool, some games machines. Security barrier. Winter caravan storage. **Off site:** Golf, fishing and riding 3 miles.

Charges 2002

Per pitch incl. 2 adults	£8.00 - £14.00
extra adult	£2.00
child (3-16 yrs)	free - £1.00
dog	£1.00
electricity	£2.00
full services	£1.00

No credit cards. **Tel:** 01202 885467. Fax: 01202 885467. **Reservations:** Advised for July/Aug. and B.Hs. Made with payment in full at booking or £20 per week deposit; balance more than 28 days beforehand (min. 5 days at B.Hs). **Open** 1 March - 30 October.

Directions: Park is 1 mile north of Wimborne, west off the B3078 road to Cranborne. O.S.GR: SU010019.

Pear Tree Touring Park

Organford Road, Holton Heath, Poole BH16 6LA

211

Pear Tree is obviously the pride and joy of its owners, Mr and Mrs Broome, and this clearly shows. It is a neat, well cared for park catering for families and couples only. Set in 7.5 acres, with mature trees and views across to Wareham Forest, the 125 good sized, neatly mown grass pitches are separated into areas by high hedges and shrubs. There are 120 pitches with 10A electricity, 50 with full services (water, waste water and electricity) of which 26 have hardstanding. Only breathable groundsheets are permitted for awnings. The tent area is a lovely secluded spot with many mature trees. Reception and a small shop supplying milk, bread, gas and other basics is at the park entrance where the gates (with key) are closed at 9 pm. (no late arrivals area, so book in before 9 pm) and tourist information. A large, hedged, separate children's play field is at the top of the park with swings, climbing frame, trampolines and ball games area. A bus service stops outside for Wareham (2.5 miles) or Poole (8 miles).

Facilities: The main heated toilet block (opened by key) provides hot water throughout, with a baby changing unit and two WCs for disabled visitors. A separate small block is near the tent area. All is kept spotlessly clean. Motorcaravan service point. Shop (basics only). Fish and chip van calls three times weekly in high season. Children's play area. Dogs are only accepted outside July/Aug. Security key deposit £10 (refundable). All year caravan or boat storage. **Off site:** The Clay Pipe Inn is just 500 m. Coarse fishing lake 500 m. (day tickets from reception). Bicycle hire. Riding 5 miles, golf 2 miles.

Charges 2002

Per unit incl. 2 persons	£8.00 - £12.00
extra adult	£3.00
child (3-13 years)	£1.50
extra tent	£3.00
dog (not July/Aug)	£2.50
extra car or boat	£3.50
electricity	£2.00 - £2.20

Tel: 01202 622434. Fax: 01202 631985. E-mail: info@visitpeartree.co.uk. **Reservations:** Made with £25 deposit (min. 4 nights in high season). **Open** Easter - 6 October.

Directions: Park is just west off A351 (Wareham - Poole) road at Holton Heath near Sandford Park. O.S.GR: SY940915.

Sandford Caravan Park

Holton Heath, Poole BH16 6JZ

210

Sandford Park is a large, well run park with many first-class amenities near the popular coastal areas of Dorset. It has a large permanent section with 248 static holiday homes and lodges. However, the touring section is in an attractive secluded area and can accommodate around 500 units of any type, mainly on distinctive individual pitches, on level grass with mature evergreen hedging, or in a more open style area broken up by shrubs all with 10A electrical connections. Early booking is advisable. Sandford is a large, very busy holiday park with a wide range of entertainment. The clubhouse (free membership) is spacious with dance floor, bar and seating area, and caters for different tastes and age groups. There is also a large air-conditioned ballroom for entertainment and dancing. Both are open over a long season. There is a variety of bars, restaurants (book in busy periods) and simple hot meals, breakfasts and takeaway elsewhere in peak season. The heated outdoor swimming pool (25 m. long, open May-Sept. and supervised) and a very large play pool with a sandy beach, ideal for children, are attractively situated with a snack bar, terraced area and go-kart track. There is also an impressive, heated and supervised indoor pool.

Facilities: The main toilet block in the touring area provides facilities for disabled visitors and a baby room. It is supplemented by the former main block and subsidiary 'portacabin' style units in the touring and static areas (one a bath block). Could be under pressure at peak times. Large launderette. Ladies' hairdresser. Bars, restaurants. TV lounges. Outdoor swimming pool (May-Sept) and indoor pool. Large supermarket and other shops, including well stocked camping accessory shop (all open peak season only). Soft indoor play area for children (April - Oct and Christmas, supervised). Children's playground, two tennis courts, mountain bike hire, table tennis, two short mat bowling greens (outdoor) and a large crazy golf course. Riding lessons available at stables on site. Dogs or pets are only permitted in the touring section in low or mid season (phone site to advise).

Charges 2002

Per unit incl. club membership	£12.50 - £22.50
electricity	£2.95
serviced pitch	£4.75
boat and trailer	£2.50
dog (1 only, after 2 Sept)	£5.00

Tel: 0870 0667793. Fax: 01202 625678. E-mail: touring@weststarholidays.co.uk. **Reservations:** Early booking advisable (min. 3 days). **Open** February - January.

Directions: Park is just west off A351 (Wareham - Poole) road at Holton Heath. O.S.GR: SY940913.

Beacon Hill Touring Park

Blandford Road North, Poole BH16 6AB

218

Beacon Hill is located in a marvellous, natural environment of partly wooded heathland, with certain areas designated habitation for protected species such as sand lizards and the Dartford Warbler, but there is also easy access to main routes. Wildlife ponds encourage dragonflies and other species but fishing is also possible. Conservation is obviously important in such a special area but one can ramble at will over the 30 acres, with the hilltop walk a must. Grassy open spaces provide 170 touring pitches for all units, 120 with 16A electricity, on sandy grass which is sometimes uneven. The undulating nature of land and the trees allows for discrete areas to be allocated for varying needs, e.g. for young families near to the play area, families with teenagers close to the bar/games room, those with dogs near the dog walking area, and for young people further away. The park provides a wide range of facilities including an open air swimming pool and a tennis court, with something for everyone and is well situated for beaches, Poole harbour and ferries for France or the Channel Islands.

Facilities: Two fully equipped toilet blocks include facilities for disabled people. Laundry facilities and washing up sinks. Well stocked shop at reception. Coffee bar and takeaway (main season). Bar (on demand outside the main season). Heated swimming pool. All weather tennis court. Adventure play areas including a hideaway. Games room with pool tables and amusement machines. **Off site:** Brownsea Island, Studland beach with Sandbanks ferry and the Purbecks near. Poole harbour and ferries 3 miles.

Charges 2002

Per standard pitch	£3.00 - £8.00
2-man tent or small motorcaravan	£2.50 - £6.00
adult	£3.00 - £4.50
child (under 16 yrs)	£2.00
awning or pup tent	£1.00 - £2.00
electricity	£2.00
dog	£1.00

Tel: 01202 631631. Fax: 01202 625749. **Reservations:** Made with £20 non-refundable deposit per pitch; balance 21 days before arrival. **Open** Easter/16 April - end September.

Directions: Park is approx. 3 miles north of Poole, 400 yards north of the junction of the A35 and A350 towards Blandford. O.S.GR: SY977945.

Woolsbridge Manor Farm Caravan Park

215 Three Legged Cross, Wimborne BH21 6RA

Adjacent to the Moors Valley Country Park, this family run site is conveniently close to the holiday resort and beaches of Bournemouth and Poole, and the ancient market town of Wimborne Minster. The seven acre camping meadow has 60 large level pitches, arranged on either side of a central tarmac roadway. There are 45 electric hook-ups (10A) and a modern, centrally located sanitary unit. A nice touch here is the bicycle racks outside. Reception has a well stocked shop and a good selection of tourist information, again there are cycle racks outside. American RVs are accepted, but advance booking is appreciated. The site is part of a working beef cattle farm, so parents should be aware of moving farm machinery and tractors. A cycleway/footpath crosses the fields to the Country Park - very safe for children - where amenities include coarse fishing, golf, steam railway, bicycle hire, a tea room and a country shop.

Facilities: The neat, white, modern sanitary building is well maintained and has ample facilities. Two newly built family rooms each with shower, WC, basin, handrails and ramped access provide for disabled people, babies and toddlers. Washing machine, dryer and ironing facilities. Covered dishwashing sinks. Playground. Shop. Gas available. Recycling of aluminium cans. Torches useful. Fishing. Caravan storage. **Off site:** Old Barn Farm inn and restaurant 400 yds. Riding 1.5 miles.

Charges 2002

Per unit incl. 2 adults and 2 children under 4 yrs	£7.00 - £12.00
extra adult	£2.50
extra child (under 16 yrs)	£1.50
tent	£2.00
awning or extra car	£1.00
electricity	£2.50
dog	£0.75

Tel: 01202 826369. Fax: 01202 813172. E-mail: woolsbridge@btconnect.com. **Reservations:** Advised for B.Hs and July/Aug. Made with deposit of 50% of total fees. **Open** Easter - 31 October.

Directions: From Ringwood take A31 southwest towards the large Ashley Heath roundabout, avoid underpass and take left hand slip road up to roundabout, and turn 'right' on unclassified road signed Three Legged Cross, Ashley Heath, Horton and Moors Valley Country Park. Follow signs to Country Park (2 miles), pass the park entrance on right, continue for another 400 yards to campsite entrance (well signed on right). O.S.GR: SZ 099052.

Harrow Wood Farm Caravan Park

216 Poplar Lane, Bransgore, Christchurch BH23 8JE

A spacious, attractive and quiet country site is on the south-western edge of the New Forest. Of the 70 pitches for caravans and motorcaravans, 62 are on concrete/gravel hardstandings with good areas of level, well mown grass around each pitch, and all have electric hook-ups (10A). A further 8 pitches are on grass. Ten pitches are generally occupied by seasonal units and a small tent field takes about 14 units. The site is mostly fairly open with views to the surrounding forest and farmland. There are no facilities or entertainment on site for children and in the main this site is very popular with couples, retired people and those looking for a taste of the real country. In the village you can visit MacPennys Woodland Walks and Nurseries, and at neighbouring Burley village with its antiques and gift shops, the Forest Leisure Cycling shop can provide bicycle hire and details of several way-marked cycle routes around the forest.

Facilities: The main heated toilet building is neat and very well equipped, with excellent large pre-set showers, including one family sized shower per sex. Outside the building, under cover, is a dishwashing sink for tenters. Adjacent laundry room with washing machine, dryer and spin dryer, ironing and sink. Two smaller units at the ends of the field provide WCs and washbasins only. Gas supplies. Coarse fishing lake for campers only is free of charge. Dogs are not accepted. **Off site:** Bransgore village (10 minute walk) has most services, including a choice of pubs serving meals, Spar mini-market, a bakery, fish and chip shop. Christchurch with its Priory Church and larger shops is 4 miles, Bournemouth and its beaches 10 miles, or Highcliffe 6 miles. Golf 4 miles. Riding 5 miles. Bicycle hire 5 miles.

Charges 2002

Per unit incl. all persons	£9.75 - £14.00
awning	£1.50 - £2.50
electricity	£2.50

Tel: 01425 672487. Fax: 01425 672487. E-mail: harrowwood@caravan-sites.co.uk. **Reservations:** Advisable for B.Hs and peak times. Made with £15 deposit. **Open** 1 March - 6 January.

Directions: From M27 exit 1 take A337 to Lyndhurst, then A35 towards Christchurch. After 11 miles, just before the 'Cat and Fiddle' pub, turn right (northwest) towards Bransgore. On entering the village, pass the church on right, and a pub on left, then almost immediately turn right into Poplar Lane (site signed), continue up lane to site entrance (250 yds). O.S.GR: SZ193978.

Mount Pleasant Touring Park

214

Matchams Lane, Hurn, Christchurch BH23 6AW

Mount Pleasant is a surprisingly pretty, rural park for its situation near Bournemouth, however it is on the edge of the New Forest. It is a neat tidy park with 170 numbered pitches on mostly level, sandy grass with circular connecting tarmac roads. Neatly fenced and interspersed with pine trees, rhododendron bushes and newly planted evergreens, there are 95 pitches for touring units, 86 of them marked and with 10A electricity, with a separate, more open and sloping area for tents. A card operated security barrier is at the entrance. Bournemouth is around 10 minutes by car (depending on the traffic). The nearest bus service is 2 miles. Due to its situation between Bournemouth airport and the A338 dual-carriageway there may be road or aircraft noise. Despite this, it is a very popular, well run park.

Facilities: Two good, purpose built modern toilet blocks can be heated and provide some washbasins in cubicles, a toddler room and a separate, en-suite unit for disabled visitors. Laundry room. Can recycling unit. Good basic shop with information area. Cabin café for breakfasts cto, (open main season and on demand). Adventure play area. American motorhomes accepted. Security barrier in operation. **Off site:** Fishing or golf 2 miles. Riding or boat launching facilities 4 miles. Dry ski centre within 0.5 miles with bars and restaurants.

Charges 2002

Per unit incl. up to 2 persons	£7.00 - £13.00
small tent	£6.00 - £10.00
extra person (over 4 yrs)	£2.00 - £2.00
dog	£1.00 - £1.50
electricity	£2.00

Tel: 01202 475474. Fax: 0870 460 1701. E-mail: enq@mount-pleasant-cc.co.uk. **Reservations:** Made with £30 deposit (non-refundable). **Open** 1 March - 31 October (phone for winter stays).

Directions: From A338 Ringwood-Bournemouth road, take B3073 in direction of Hurn airport. Follow camp signs at first mini roundabout onto Matchams Lane. O.S.GR: SZ129987.

Grove Farm Meadow Holiday Park

213

Meadowbank Holidays, Stour Way, Christchurch BH23 2PQ

This is a quiet, traditional park with caravan holiday homes and a small provision for touring caravans. The grassed flood bank which separates the River Stour from this park provides an attractive walkway. The river bank has been kept natural and is well populated by a range of ducks and a resident swan family and early in the season they parade their young through the park. It is also popular with bird watchers. There are just under 200 caravan holiday homes (118 privately owned, 77 for hire), regularly sited in rows. For touring units 41 level grass pitches, all with 15A electricity, are clearly numbered, backing on to fencing or hedging and accessed by tarmac roads. Some are fully serviced (with hardstanding, shingle base for awnings and chemical disposal point), the other grass pitches sharing service points. The impressive modern reception has a good collection of tourist information. The Littledown Centre, said to be the south coast's premier leisure facility is nearby. Bournemouth is 10 minutes by car, Christchurch 5.

Facilities: The toilet block is nicely tiled with a bathroom for each sex (50p), a separate toilet and washbasin with ramped access for disabled visitors, and a baby changing room. Dishwashing sinks, together with spin dryer, iron and board and washing lines provided, with a launderette near reception. Games room with pool table and video games. Adventure play area beside the river bank. Good, well stocked shop providing for most needs, 8-8 in high season but limited hours in early March and late Oct. Fishing is possible on the park, permits from reception. No dogs or other pets are accepted. **Off site:** Boat launching 4 miles, public 18 hole golf course (pay as you go) nearby. St Catherine's nature reserve.

Charges 2002

Per unit, incl. electricity and awning	£11.00 - £25.00
'luxury' pitch incl. electricity	£10.00 - £21.00
large pitch	£8.50 - £18.00
standard pitch (no awnings)	£6.00 - £14.00
extra person (over 5 yrs)	£1.00 - £2.00
extra car or boat	£1.00 - £2.00

Tel: 01202 483597. Fax: 01202 483878. E-mail: enquiries@meadowbank-hols.demon.co.uk. **Reservations:** Made for Sat-Sat or Sun-Sun in high season, min. 3 nights at other times, with £30 deposit. Contact Meadowbank Holidays at above address. **Open** 1 March - 31 October.

Directions: From A388 Ringwood - Bournemouth road take B3073 for Christchurch. Turn right at the first roundabout and Stour Way is the third road on the right. O.S.GR: SZ136946.

Shamba Holiday Park

Ringwood Road, St Leonards, Ringwood BH24 2SB

The Gray family have been gradually upgrading Shamba over the last few years and it is developing into a comfortable, friendly park with good sized, well drained pitches (150 in total, all with 10A electricity). Most of the amenities are good and as the owners have a young family themselves, they seem to be aware of their needs and cater for them. The Grays live on site and have managed to create a relaxed, pleasant atmosphere. A cosy bar offers bar snacks and a takeaway service, with a small family room and a pool table. Bournemouth with its beaches is 8 miles, Ringwood 2.5 miles and the Moors Valley Country Park 1 mile. The site is near the A31 so there could be some road noise. The access road is rather rough, but persevere and you will find a pleasant site.

Facilities: The showers are in a separate heated block. The rest of the provision is adequate if a little dated, although it is kept clean and includes a small toilet and washbasin for children, and a belfast sink for a baby bath. Covered dishwashing sinks. Laundry sink, two washing machines and two dryers. Improvements to these facilities are planned. Well stocked shop. Bar with bar snacks and takeaway. Large play area and a games room with video games and table football. Small heated outdoor pool. **Off site:** Riding stables and a fishing lake 500 yds.

Charges 2002

Per pitch incl. 2 persons	£9.00 - £13.50
extra person	£2.50 - £3.00
electricity	£2.00
dog	£1.00 - £2.00

Tel: 01202 873302. Fax: 01202 873302. E-mail: holidays@shamba.co.uk. **Reservations:** Made with non-returnable deposit of £25. **Open** 1 March - 31 October.

Directions: Site is signed directly off the A31 Ringwood - Wimborne Road, 400 yds. down a small lane. Approaching from the east, after passing Little Chef, you will need to go round the next roundabout back on yourself, then immediately left down lane. O.S.GR: SU104026.

A 7 acre Holiday Park set in wooded surroundings some 8 miles from Bournemouth and ideally situated for the New Forest. This family Park is secluded and caters for discerning holidaymakers

- Large, level, well drained Pitches
- Licensed Clubhouse
- Shop and Off Licence
- Take Away Food Bar / Bar Meals
- Electricity Hook-ups
- Launderette
- Games Room
- Children s Playground
- Pre-bookable Pitches
- Horse Riding, Fishing & Sailing nearby
- Plus Winter Storage

HEATED SWIMMING POOL

(01202) 873302

For a relaxing holiday, come to Shamba Holiday Park. Telephone now for our brochure and booking form.
Shamba Holiday Park, 230 Ringwood Road, St. Leonards, Ringwood, Hants BH24 2SB

Red Shoot Camping Park

Linwood, Ringwood BH24 3QT

Red Shoot is set on three acres of open, slightly sloping grassland, in the heart of the New Forest. A rural retreat with panoramic views of the surrounding countryside and forest, it is very popular in high season. There are around 130 good sized pitches, 45 with electrical hook-ups (16A), served by a circular gravel road. The adjacent Red Shoot Inn (under separate ownership) serves hot or cold meals and brews its own real ales - Forest Gold and Tom's Tipple. There are ample opportunities for walking, cycling and naturalist pursuits, and nearby Ringwood has a market on Wednesday. Local attractions include watersports at the New Forest Water Park near Ringwood, a Doll Museum in Fordingbridge, cider making in Burley, and Breamore House just north of Fordingbridge.

Facilities: The sanitary facilities are fairly modern, well maintained and practical, but not luxurious. Dishwashing under cover. Laundry plus baby bath facility. Good unit for disabled visitors. Very well stocked shop. Fenced adventure style playground. Mountain bike and tandem hire. No site lighting so a torch would be useful. Only breathable groundsheets are permitted.

Charges 2002

Per adult	£3.90
child under 14 yrs	£1.00 - £2.30
car, motorcycle	£1.10
electricity	£2.30
dog	£0.70

VAT not included. Less 20% in low seasons (min. 3 nights). **Tel:** 01425 473789. Fax: 01425 471558. E-mail: enquiries@redshoot-campingpark.com. **Reservations:** Advised for w/ends, B.Hs and peak season (school holidays) and made with £15 deposit per week or part week. **Open** 1 March - 31 October.

Directions: From A338 about 1.75 miles north of Ringwood, turn east (signed Linwood and Moyles Court). Follow signs, over a staggered crossroads, and continue straight on for another 1.75 miles to Red Shoot Inn. O.S.GR: SU188095.

Ashurst Caravan & Camping Site

The Forestry Commission, Lyndhurst Road, Ashurst SO4 2AA

230

An attractive Forestry Commission site on the fringe of the New Forest, Ashurst is set in a mixture of oak woodland and grass heathland which is open to the grazing animals of the Forest. Smaller than the Hollands Wood site (23 acres), it provides 280 pitches, 180 of which have been gravelled to provide semi-hardstanding; otherwise you pitch where you like, applying the 20 ft. rule on ground that can be uneven. There are no electricity connections. Some noise must be expected from the adjacent railway line - the station is just five minutes walk away. Reception is run by the very helpful site managers. There is a late arrivals area and separate car-parking area for those arriving or returning after the gate has closed (22.30 hrs).

Facilities: The single central toilet block has been refurbished and provides everything necessary, including hairdryers, a well equipped unit for visitors with disabilities (key required) and a good laundry room. It could be under pressure when the site is full in the main season. No barbecues in dry weather. Dogs are not accepted. A torch is useful. **Off site:** A local garage sells gas. Nearby pub accessible by footpath across an adjacent field. Shops and local buses within a five minute walk. Guided forest walks are organised during the main season.

Charges 2002

Per unit incl. up to 4 persons	£6.40 - £12.20
extra person (over 5 yrs)	£1.00
extra car, gazebo or pup tent	£3.80

Less 20% all year for disabled guests and outside 7/7-28/8 for senior citizens. **Tel:** 0131 3146505. Fax: 0131 3340849. E-mail: fe.holidays@forestry.gov.uk. **Reservations:** Necessary for B.Hs and peak times (min. 2 nights or 3 nights at B.Hs) with £30 deposit. Contact (at all times): Forest Holidays, Forestry Commission, 231 Corstorphine Road, Edinburgh EH12 7AT. **Open** March - September.

Directions: Site is 2 miles east of Lyndhurst, set back from the A35 Southampton - Bournemouth road, 5 miles southwest of Southampton. O.S.GR: SU334099.

Hollands Wood Caravan & Camping Site

The Forestry Commission, Lyndhurst Road, Brockenhurst SO43 7QH

231

Hollands Wood is a large, spacious (168 acres) site in a secluded, natural woodland setting (mainly oak). In the heart of the New Forest, there is an abundance of wildlife, including the famous New Forest ponies. The site is arranged informally with 600 level unmarked pitches but it is stipulated that there must be at least 20 feet between each unit. There are no electrical connections and possible traffic noise from the A337 which runs alongside one boundary. One area of the site is designated a dog free zone. The site has no shop, but it is only about half a mile from Brockenhurst village where there are shops for supplies and gas, etc, plus trains and buses. Barbecues are not permitted in dry weather. The site can get very busy and we include the smaller Ashurst site as an alternative.

Facilities: Two large utilitarian toilet blocks (and a third smaller, older one) are full equipped if somewhat basic. Facilities for disabled people and baby changing surfaces. Two laundry rooms with washing machines and dryers. These facilities are under pressure at peak times. Motorcaravan service point. Night security with the barrier closed 22.30 - 07.30 hrs (overnight area). Torches essential.

Charges 2002

Per unit incl. up to 4 persons	£7.20 - £14.30
extra person (over 5 yrs)	£1.20
extra car, gazebo or pup tent	£4.20

Less 20% all year for disabled guests and outside 7/7-28/8 for senior citizens. **Tel:** 0131 3146505. Fax: 0131 3340849. E-mail: fe.holidays@forestry.gov.uk. **Reservations:** Necessary for B.Hs and peak times (min. 3 nights with £30 deposit). Contact (at all times): Forest Holidays, Forestry Commission, 231 Corstorphine Road, Edinburgh EH12 7AT. **Open** March - September.

Directions: Site entrance is on east side of A337 Lyndhurst - Lymington road, half a mile north of Brockenhurst. O.S.GR: SU303038.

Photo: New Forest ponies, STB

Sandy Balls Holiday Centre

Godshill, Fordingbridge SP6 2JY

229

Sandy Balls must be one of the oldest 'camp sites' in the UK, celebrating its 75th anniversary in 1995. Ernest Westlake, grandfather of the present owners and an educationalist and idealist, bought the ancient woodland overlooking the Avon Valley in 1919 to save it from the axe and today, while the majestic oaks, beeches, Scots pine and larch have matured, new facilities have been designed to be in sympathy with the setting. Sandy Balls is now an award winning park, high above the sweep of the Avon River and protected as a nature reserve. There is much to discover in the history of the park, such as how it came to get its name, the significance of the organisation founded by Ernest Westlake ('The Order of Woodcraft Chivalry') and his commitment to life-long learning. Perhaps visit Good Friday Hill and try to absorb the atmosphere and some of the thinking behind the development of Sandy Balls to what it is today, deserving of the entry that it has maintained in these guides for over 30 years. It continues to be a very well run and progressive park set within 120 acres and with a wide range of leisure facilities developed around a 'village' centre.

Open all year, it covers an extensive area in a series of fields with terrain of different types: light woodland with 206 caravan and chalet holiday homes (many for rent), and some tent areas with unmarked pitches, touring units for the most part on open meadows, and some general parts including woodland not used for camping. They include 256 all service pitches for touring units with electricity (10-16A), water, drainaway and TV connection (site satellite dish), on concrete or gravel with gravel hardstanding for awnings (steel pegs can be provided if required). In winter only 50 pitches are available.

The central area with the park's facilities is pleasantly laid out and designed to blend with the forest surroundings. It includes a large indoor pool and a solar heated outdoor pool both with lifeguards and free at all times (high season sessions are timed according to demand). Valencio's pizzeria has a bar/grill for eating in or takeaway. The park won a 'Good Lighting Award' from the British Astronomical Association for the design of its lighting that enables visitors to better appreciate the night sky. Sandy Balls provides all-round family entertainment, including a woodland leisure trail where wild animals and birds can be observed in their natural surroundings, as well as the New Forest on your doorstep. An ideal park for families and couples.

Facilities: There are three modern toilet blocks with under-floor heating and one of 'portacabin' type that remains as overflow in the tent field (28 day). One block has a bath in each section (M&F) and all have washbasins in cubicles. The blocks are spacious and airy and should be adequate for peak season, with 'Northfield' having been added to provide extra, good quality facilities. Toilets for disabled visitors and baby changing facilities are provided in at least two blocks. Excellent launderette plus washing machines in all the toilet blocks. Motorcaravan service point and recycling stations - look for the green coloured sheds. Supermarket with own bakery. Takeaway. Restaurants, bars and family room. Wide screen TV and entertainment (every evening in high season). Indoor pool (66 x 30 ft). Outdoor pool (25/5-30/8). Well equipped fitness gym, jacuzzi spa bath, steam room, toning tables, sauna and solarium and dance studios. Games room with pool and table tennis. Adventure playground and play areas including soft ball area. Clay-modelling tuition and story telling for children. River fishing on permit. Riding stables. Bicycle hire. Petanque, archery, orienteering and hot air balloon rides. Tourist information. Dogs are only allowed on certain fields.

Charges 2002

Per serviced pitch w/ends and high season		£17.00
mid-week		£12.75
non-serviced pitch w/ends and high season		£15.00
mid-week		£11.25
mid and high seasons only: adult		£1.50 - £3.50
young adult (12-17 yrs)		£1.25 - £2.00
child (3-11 yrs)		£0.75 - £1.50
additional car/motorcycle		£0.50
dog		£0.50 - £1.25

Tel: 01425 653042. Fax: 01425 653067. E-mail: post@sandy-balls.co.uk. **Reservations:** Made with deposit and compulsory cancellation insurance. **Open** all year.

Directions: Park is northwest off B3078 (Fordingbridge - Cadnam) just west of Godshill village, and about 1.5 miles east of Fordingbridge. O.S.GR: SU168147.

Hampshire
Hill Cottage Farm Caravan Park
Sandleheath Road, Alderholt, Fordingbridge SP6 3EG

First opened in 2000, this is a newly constructed, modern site set in 47 acres of beautiful countryside on the Dorset and Hampshire border. The 32 pitches, all on hardstandings with electric hook-ups (16A) are arranged around a circular gravel roadway. Secluded and sheltered, they have views across the surrounding countryside. A field alongside the camping area is used for tents and rallies, and has space for ball games and a small children's playground. Also on site are a tennis court and a lake for coarse fishing, and there are many woodland walks in the area. Overall this site is more suitable for adults and small children - it is not really designed for active teenagers.

Facilities: A large modern barn-style building provides excellent heated facilities, including covered dishwashing sinks, a laundry room with washing machines and dryers, plus facilities for disabled people and babies - in all, a very generous provision. The first floor has a games room with a full size snooker table, two pool tables and a darts board, plus a separate function room. Motorcaravan services. Playground. **Off site:** The village centre with pub, church, Post Office and store is a 20 minute woodland walk. Local attractions include Rockbourne Roman Villa, Cranborne Chase, The Dolls Museum at Fordingbridge, Salisbury, and Ringwood with its Wednesday market.

Charges 2002

Per unit incl. 2 adults and electricity	£10.00 - £12.00
extra adult	£3.00
child	£1.50
awning or child's pup tent	£1.00
dog	£1.00

Tel: 01425 650513. Fax: 01425 652339.
Reservations: Made with minimum £20 deposit. Advised for B.Hs and peak season. **Open** all year.

Directions: From Fordingbridge take B3078 westwards for 2 miles to Alderholt. On entering the village, at left hand bend, turn right towards Sandleheath (site signed) and site entrance is about 300 yards on the left. O.S.GR: SU 120130.

Lytton Lawn Touring Park

228 Lymore Lane, Milford on Sea SO41 0TX

Lytton Lawn is the touring arm of Shorefield Country Park, a holiday home park and leisure centre. Situated 2.5 miles from Shorefield itself, campers and caravanners staying at Lytton Lawn are entitled to free membership of the Leisure Club there. The comprehensive facilities at Shorefield are of a very good standard and are mostly free (extra charges are made for certain activities). They comprise a very attractive indoor pool (20 m. heated), solarium, sauna, spa bath and steam room, dance studios and two tennis courts, open all year with fully trained attendants. There are outdoor pools, crazy golf, restaurant facilities including a bistro (Easter - 2 Nov) and a range of activity and entertainment programmes, fitness classes and treatments, all well managed and organised. Lytton Lawn provides 136 marked pitches, including 53 'premier' pitches (hardstanding, 16A electricity, pitch light, water and waste water outlet) in a hedged area of natural grass. This section, with its heated toilet block, is open for a longer season. The rest of the pitches, all with electricity (tenters note), are in the adjoining, but separate, gently sloping field, edged with mature trees and hedges and with a further toilet block. The New Forest, Isle of Wight, Bournemouth, Southampton and the beach at Milford on Sea are near.

Facilities: Two purpose built, modern toilet blocks are tiled and well fitted. Dishwashing, washing machine and dryer in each block. Baby changing facilities in one block and facilities for disabled visitors (Radar key). Simple shop (Easter - end Oct), with a supermarket and takeaway (main season) at Shorefield. Small fenced children's play area and hedged field with goal posts. Only one dog per pitch is accepted. **Off site:** Village pub 10 minutes walk. Golf, riding, coarse fishing (all within 3 miles), sailing, windsurfing and boat launching facilities (1.5 miles).

Charges 2002

Per 'premier' pitch incl. all persons, electricity, water, drainage and TV connection	£8.00 - £26.00
standard pitch incl. electricity	£7.00 - £24.00
pup tent or awning free, both together	£2.50
dog (1 only)	£2.50

Less 40% Mon - Thurs in certain periods. Min. weekly charge at busy times. **Tel:** 01590 648331. Fax: 01590 645610. E-mail: holidays@shorefield. co.uk. **Reservations:** Made with deposit and cancellation insurance - contact Shorefield Holidays Ltd, Shorefield Road, Milford on Sea, nr. Lymington, Hampshire SO41 0LH. **Open** all year except 4 Jan - 9 Feb.

Directions: From M27 follow signs for Lyndhurst and Lymington on A337. Continue towards New Milton and Lytton Lawn is signed at Everton; Shorefield is signed at Downton. O.S.GR: SZ293937.

Oakdene Forest Park

227 St Leonards, Ringwood BH24 2RZ

Set in 55 acres of park and woodland, with direct access to the Avon Forest and near the New Forest, Oakdene provides caravan holiday homes to let or over 200 pitches for all types of unit. These include 'premier' pitches with hardstanding, electric hook-up (10A), water, drainage and pitch light (no tents on these pitches), and some grass pitches with or without electricity mostly in the Meadow area. The Leisure and Country Club (free membership) provides a bar, buffet and a range of entertainment. Super new additions are an indoor pool with a flume, sauna, spa bath and gym and a walled outdoor pool with paddling pool. Oakdene is under the same ownership as Shorefield Country Park at Milford on Sea and massive investment is being carried out. The second phase (to start November 2002) covers a new reception, coffee shop, offices, restaurant, ballroom, supermarket and bars. The aim is to provide the quality, standard and range of facilities and entertainment found at Shorefield and Lytton Lawn (no. 228).

Facilities: The new fully equipped, purpose built toilet block includes some washbasins in cabins, but 'portacabin' style facilities remain for the Meadow area. Launderette and dishwashing sinks. Shop. Indoor and outdoor pools. Gym. Table tennis and pool table Crazy golf, compact bowling. Amusement arcade. Play area. Free Squirrel's Kids Club. Bicycle hire. **Off site:** Forest Pines Riding Centre (10% reduction). Forest walks.

Charges 2002

Per pitch incl. electricity and water	£8.00 - £26.00
standard pitch incl. electricity	£7.00 - £24.00

Lower prices are for mid-week. Min. stays at B.Hs. **Tel:** 01590 648331. Fax: 01590 645610. E-mail: holidays@shorefield.co.uk. **Reservations:** All bookings are handled by Shorefield Country Parks, Shorefield Road, Milford on Sea, nr. Lymington, Hampshire SO41 0LH. Tel: (01590) 648331. Fax: (01590) 645610. **Open** all year except January.

Directions: Park access leads off the main A31 westbound carriageway about 2.5 miles west of Ringwood. O.S.GR: SU101016.

South Coast
and New Forest

With three high quality destinations to choose from, Shorefield Holidays offers you the best of both worlds in touring locations.

All three of our touring parks are set in parkland in the beautiful New Forest / South Coast area.

Both Oakdene Forest Park and Forest Edge Touring Park at St Leonards near Ringwood offer easy access to the Avon Forest, while Lytton Lawn Touring Park at Milford on Sea is just over a mile from the beach.

There are comprehensive facilities including entertainment and Free Leisure Club membership.

For full details ask for our brochure or browse on-line.

For further details telephone:

01590 648331

RALLIES WELCOME AT ALL SITES

SHOREFIELD
HOLIDAYS LIMITED

Lytton Lawn Touring Park
Lymore Lane, Milford on Sea, Hants SO41 0TX
Oakdene Forest Park
St. Leonards, Ringwood, Hants BH24 2RZ
Forest Edge Touring Park
St. Leonards, Ringwood, Hants BH24 2SD

e-mail: holidays@shorefield.co.uk   **www.shorefield.co.uk**   Ref. AR

Hoburne Bashley

Sway Road, New Milton BH25 5QR

Hoburne Bashley is an attractive, well run park with many holiday homes (380, including some for hire), but it also has a very sizeable tourist section and can take 300 touring units. However, tents, trailer tents and pup tents are not accepted. Spread over three flat meadows the 300 numbered touring pitches are large, divided by young hedging or low fencing as seen on French sites, a nice development with 20 serviced pitches and 22 for two cars. They are mixed grass and hardstanding with electricity (13A). Set in pleasant park-like surroundings not far from beaches, Bournemouth and the New Forest, the site has a good clubhouse with excellent facilities. This overlooks an 18 m. circular outdoor pool and 18 m. paddling pool, a sensible size and fun with its geysers, clown and beach effect. An impressive indoor pool complex houses a flume, sauna, solarium, spa bath and steam room, all well supervised by the lifeguards. The club facilities are comprehensive, with a ballroom, large lounges and bars, and a wide range of entertainment from cabaret, talent shows, bingo, competitions and quizzes to discos. The Hungry Woodcutter provides simple hot food and takeaway all day. A popular park with lots going on, Bashley is part of the Hoburne group.

Facilities: Three well constructed toilet blocks, one central to each area, are fully tiled with modern fittings in cheerful yellow and blue with washbasins in cabins. They have push-button, pre-set showers (no dividers, but shower heads are set fairly low). Baby changing facilities. Covered washing-up sinks. Launderette. Clubhouse with bars, restaurant and takeaway. TV room. Video arcade and games room with two full-size snooker tables, plus two pool tables, table tennis and darts spread among other rooms. Children's club - sports and games for the teens and Sammy the Seahorse club for under 12s. Shop (mid-May - end Sept). Indoor pool. Outdoor pool (heated mid-May - mid-Sept). Crazy golf. Golf course (9 hole, par 3). Tennis courts (3). Adventure play area. Soft ball play area. Only one dog or pet permitted per unit. Groundsheets must be lifted daily. American motorhomes accepted. **Off site:** Fishing or riding 1 mile. Mudeford beach 8 miles.

Charges 2002

Per unit incl. all persons, electricity	£10.00 - £28.50
multi-service pitch	£12.00 - £30.00
2 car pitch	£12.00 - £29.00
pet (1 only)	£2.00

Weekend breaks available. **Tel:** 01425 612340. Fax: 01425 632732. E-mail: enquiries@hoburne.co.uk. **Reservations:** Necessary for peak season and made for any length: £50 p/w deposit, balance 3 weeks before arrival. **Open** 28 March - 2 January.

Directions: Park is on the B3055 about 400 yards east of the crossroads with the B3058 in Bashley village. O.S.GR: SZ246969.

Hoburne
HOLIDAY PARKS

days to
remember...

...in Hampshire, Dorset, Devon, Cornwall, Somerset and the Cotswolds

For a **FREE** colour brochure please visit:
www.hoburne.com or call: 01425 277661

Chichester Camping & Caravanning Club Site

Main Road, Southbourne PO10 8JH

This small, neat park is just to the west of Chichester and north of Bosham harbour. Formerly an orchard, it is rectangular in shape with 60 pitches on flat, well mown lawns on either side of gravel roads. All pitches have 16A electricity, 42 with level hardstanding. Although the A27 bypass takes most of the through traffic, the site is by the main A259 road so there may be some traffic noise in some parts (not busy at night). Opposite the park are orchards through which paths lead to the seashore. Unfortunately there is no overnight area for late arrivals; the gates are shut between 11 pm. and 7 am. with no parking outside. Nearby are Bignor Roman villa, Apuldram Roses and the Weald and Downland open-air museum.

Facilities: The well designed, brick built toilet block is of first class quality. Fully tiled and heated in cool weather, with facilities for people with disabilities (access by key). Washing machines and dryers. Gas supplies. No ball games permitted on the park. Dogs can be walked in the lane opposite the entrance. **Off site:** Shops, restaurants and pubs within easy walking distance in the nearby village and the park is on a main bus route. Chichester has a leisure centre and market day is Wednesday. Excellent caravan shop nearby. Fishing or golf 5 miles, riding 6 miles.

Charges 2002

Per adult	£5.00 - £5.50
child (6-18 yrs)	£1.70
non-member pitch fee	£4.50
electricity	£1.75 - £2.50

Tel: 01243 373202. **Reservations:** Necessary and made with deposit (min. 2 nights); contact site. **Open** 2 February - 25 November.

Directions: Park is on main A259 Chichester - Havant road at Southbourne, 750 yards west of Chichester Caravans. O.S.GR: SU774056.

Photo: Isle of Wight, Southern TB

Isle of Wight

Isle of Wight Tourism, Westridge Centre, Blading Road, Ryde, Isle of Wight PO33 1QS
Tel: 01983 813818 Fax: 01983 823031

Internet: www.iwight.com

The island is a popular destination with a certain old world charm, combining coast and countryside activities and scenery with a mild, sunny climate and a network of footpaths and bridleways. It has a wide range of tourist attractions and sports facilities. Ferry companies offer mid-week discount packages for touring caravan owners. We found that most of the park owners are knowledgeable about deals and we suggest you contact the parks and let them arrange the most economical crossing.

A new museum has opened in Sandown - Dinosaur Isle. The first purpose built museum for dinosaurs in Britain, it is located on the east coast at Sandown. The striking exterior of the building has been modelled on a pterodactyl. An introductory exhibition deals with the geology and fossils of the island, which is one of the most fruitful regions for dinosaur excavation in Europe, running back 120 million years.

Red Funnel Ferries

As the original cross-Solent operator, Red Funnel celebrated 135 years of running a ferry service between Southampton and Cowes with the introduction of three super modern car ferries. The new ships have been fitted out to a very high standard and we were very impressed with the on-board facilities which include a shop, bar, restaurant, seating areas and sun deck. Each vessel is able to carry up to 140 cars and there are 19 sailings a day in high season. The crossing time is 55 minutes.

Thorness Bay Holiday Park

252 Thorness Bay, Cowes PO31 8NJ

Spread over a large area of rural down and woodland that slopes down to the beach at Thorness Bay, this is a site for both touring units and a holiday homes park. The touring site has 90 marked pitches all with electricity (10A) and divided by ranch style rails, plus an open tent area. The whole area is on open grassland with commanding views of the Solent. There is an older style heated outdoor pool located on the touring field which has flexible opening dates and times dependent on weather and demand. A small adventure playground on bark is also provided. The main activity centre is located in the holiday home area, a short walk from the touring site. The jewels in the crown are the superb indoor fun pool and the Cruisers Bay Beach Club. A full programme of family entertainment and organised activities is offered throughout the main season, including cabarets, wrestling, aerobics, archery, fun fitness, swimming lessons, 5 a-side football, riding (stables on site), discos, bingo, quizzes etc. Sparky's Krew Club for younger children offers a craft corner, colouring and drawing, story time, parties, magic and much more.

Facilities: Several new portacabin buildings (heated) provide well equipped showers, WCs and open washbasins, a separate unit contains a suite for disabled persons. Whilst they are basically container units, and not visually appealing, the facilities they provide are first class. Two older units (not heated), one at the top of the site by the tent area, and one alongside the new facilities, supplement these when required. Dishwashing sinks. Comprehensive launderette in the main complex, plus a good shop, cash machine, pub/diner, cafeteria which also serves breakfasts, takeaways, and games room. Indoor fun pool (with lifeguards). Entertainment programme. Large adventure playground. Multi-sports court. Riding. **Off site:** The beach is easily accessed from the main entertainment complex. Newport and Carisbrooke Castle 4 miles, Yarmouth 7 miles. Golf 4 miles.

Charges 2002

Per pitch incl. up to 6 persons	£8.00 - £19.50
extra person over 6 yrs	free - £1.00
electricity	£3.00
dog	free - £3.00

Tel: 01983 523109. Fax: 01983 822213.
Reservations: Essential for B.Hs. and peak season. Made with deposit of £5 per pitch per night for less than 7 nights, or £35 per pitch per week. **Open** 28 March - 25 October.

Directions: Thorness Bay is southwest of Cowes. From East Cowes ferry terminal follow signs to Newport. From centre follow A3054 towards Yarmouth. Continue for about 2.5 miles to crossroads, turning right (north) to Thorness Bay. After approx. 2 miles, on a sharp right hand bend, turn left where site is signed. After 400 yards entrance on right leads to mobile home site, continue straight on for touring site reception. O.S.GR: SZ448928.

Waverley Park Holiday Centre

253 Old Road, East Cowes PO32 6AW

This pleasant small family owned and run site is set in the grounds of an old country house with magnificent views over the Solent and just five minutes from the Cowes ferry terminal. The 45 touring pitches are in short rows, back to back on sloping grassland, whilst tents are pitched on the lower land nearer to the promenade and sea. To one side of the site is an area housing 75 private and rental holiday homes. Motorcaravans will need some levelling blocks, and there are only 28 electric hook-ups (10A) at present. The newly rebuilt sanitary unit is at the top of the site, and at the bottom of the site a gate leads onto the promenade which provides good walks, and the pebble beach which is popular with sailors, windsurfers, etc. The site is an ideal vantage point for Cowes Week, and has good views of the ocean liners sailing in and out of Southampton.

Facilities: A high quality, recently rebuilt sanitary unit provides the usual facilities, including some spacious cubicles with washbasins en-suite. Washing machine, dryer, spin dryer and ironing. Dishwashing room. Good suite for disabled people. Basic chemical disposal point in the static area. Small well stocked shop. Heated outdoor pool and paddling pool. Club with restaurant and bar serving good value meals, plus a good variety of family entertainment in season (all Whitsun - early Sept). Small adventure style playground. Games room. 9-hole putting green. Boats accepted by prior arrangement - public slipway nearby. **Off site:** Public slipway. Cowes with its shops and services within walking distance. Bus stop outside the site entrance.

Charges 2002

Per adult	£3.00 - £5.50
child (5-13 yrs)	£1.20 - £2.75
electricity	£2.20
dog	£0.50 - £1.20

Min. fee in high season £11, excl. electricity. **Tel:** 01983 293452. Fax: 01983 200494. E-mail: waverley_park@hotmail.com. **Reservations:** Essential for B.Hs, peak season and Cowes Week (1st week August). Made with deposit of 25% of total fees. **Open** 29 March - 30 September.

Directions: Immediately after leaving the Southampton to Cowes ferry, take first left, then right into Old Road, and park entrance is 300 yds on left. O.S.GR: SZ505958.

The Orchards Holiday Caravan Park

Newbridge, Yarmouth, Isle of Wight PO41 0TS

In a village situation in the quieter western part of the island, The Orchards is a busy and lively family holiday park combining 63 holiday caravans (in a separate area) with a neat touring area. Run personally by the proprietor, it provides a pleasant, comfortable base from which to explore, about four miles from the beaches and from Yarmouth. A pool complex provides a medium size, heated swimming pool and children's pool (late May - early Sept) with a grass sunbathing area, supplemented by a supervised irregularly shaped indoor pool with spa pool (on payment, open all year), attractively glass walled with terrace and café bar for relaxing - a nice addition. About 175 marked pitches are arranged on gently sloping meadow, broken up by apple trees, mature hedges and fences. All have electricity and 84 have hardstanding, including 12 with water hook up and drain. The large reception provides useful tourist information. A meeting room (up to 50 persons) is suitable for small rallies. Golfing and walking holidays are arranged. Part of the Caravan Club's 'managed under contract' scheme, non-members are also very welcome, the park is also a member of the Best of British group.

Facilities: Sanitary facilities are provided by three blocks of varying age and size which together should be an ample provision. A few washbasins are in private cabins. Baths on payment. The latest block, a smart mobile unit, provides en-suite facilities (shower, WC and basin). Facilities for disabled visitors (a hardstanding pitch close by can be reserved). Full laundry facilities. Motorcaravan service point. Ice pack and battery charging services. Gas supplies. Well stocked shop and takeaway service (mid-March - Oct, limited opening at quiet times). Indoor and outdoor pools. Football pitch. Multi-court. Exercise stations. Pool, table tennis, TV and amusements rooms (no evening entertainment on site). Coarse fishing on site (no closed season). **Off site:** Bicycle hire, boat launching 4 miles, riding 1 mile. Membership is available for the village social club and a small discount at Freshwater golf course (4 miles) - ask at reception.

Charges 2002

Per unit incl. 2 adults and electricity	£11.45 - £14.40
incl. mains services and awning	£14.60 - £17.65
extra adult	£3.35 - £5.15
child	£1.50 - £3.25
pup tent	£1.50
dog	£0.75 - £1.35

No pitch fee for hikers or cyclists. Packages incl. ferry travel available - ring park for best deal. **Tel:** 01983 531331. Fax: 01983 531666. E-mail: info@orchards-holiday-park.co.uk. **Reservations:** Made for min. 5 days with £30 p/wk deposit. **Open** all year except 3 Jan - 15 Feb.

Directions: Park is in Newbridge village, signed north from B3401 (Yarmouth - Newport) road. O.S.GR: SZ412878.

Heathfield Farm Camping

Heathfield Road, Freshwater PO40 9SH

Heathfield is a pleasant contrast to many of the other sites on the Isle of Wight, in that it is a 'no frills' sort of place, very popular with tenters, cyclists and small camper vans. Despite its name, it is no longer a working farm. A large, open meadow provides 60 large, level pitches, 30 with electricity (10A), and a very large open area for non-electric pitches. A play field for ball games also has two picnic tables and two barbecues provided. There is no shop as you are only eight minutes walk from the centre of Freshwater. The site overlooks Colwell Bay and across the Solent towards Milford-on-Sea and Hurst Castle. It is ideal for visiting attractions on the western side of the island including Totland and Freshwater Bays, The Needles and Old Battery, Compton Down, and Mottistone Manor Garden. The Military road which runs from Freshwater Bay to St Catherine's Point gives spectacular coastal views.

Facilities: The main sanitary unit is housed in a modern, ingeniously customised, 'portacabin' type unit including one washbasin cubicle for ladies and a baby room. Showers are slightly different in that they have two pushbutton controls, one for pre-mixed hot water, the other for cold only (provided at the special request of some of the regular customers). A second similar unit has WCs and washbasins in cubicles, plus facilities for disabled visitors. Laundry and dishwashing sinks. Recycling bins. Motorcaravan service point. Gaz and ice pack service. Children's play field. No commercial vehicles are accepted. Gate locked 22.30-07.00 hrs.

Charges 2002

Per adult	£3.50 - £4.00
child (3-15 yrs)	£1.50 - £2.00
extra car	£0.50
dog	£1.00
electricity	£1.75

Min pitch fee July/Aug £7.50. One night booking supplement £2.00-4.00 No credit cards. **Tel:** 01983 756756. Fax: 01983 756756. **Reservations:** Advisable for B.Hs and peak season; made with £15 deposit. **Open** 1 May - 30 September.

Directions: From A3054 north of Totland and Colwell turn into Heathfield Road where site is signed. Site entrance is on right after a short distance. O.S.GR: SZ334878.

Appuldurcombe Caravan & Camping Park

Wroxall, nr Ventnor, Isle of Wight PO38 3EP

Quietly situated in a village and once part of the grounds of Appuldurcombe House, this park is under new ownership. Set a little back from the sea - Ventnor beach 2.5 miles and Shanklin 3 - there are distant views and good walks nearby. It has a good, sheltered, heated swimming pool and an attractive bar and lounge, with dance floor, beside the pool, where there is limited entertainment in the school holidays. The park is therefore quite lively - there are also 40 holiday caravans for hire in the attractive, old walled garden and two 8-bed flats. The 100 marked touring pitches, 48 with electricity (10A), are arranged on either side of gravel access roads on a slightly sloping grassy meadow. A further field with a pond is available for recreation, with goal posts, and a little stream flows past the reception block. The park can be peaceful and quiet in early and late season, whilst being busily active in high season.

Facilities: Two small toilet units serve the site. The older one, now very dated, is behind reception and to one side of the touring field. The other unit, more recently refurbished, is close to the pool in the old walled garden with facilities for disabled visitors. Small shop in school holiday periods, otherwise limited. Bar. Swimming pool (60 x 25 ft; Spr. BH.-end Aug). **Off site:** Fishing, bicycle hire, riding, golf and boat launching facilities within 3 miles.

Charges 2002

Per adult	£3.50 - £5.50
child (3-13 yrs)	£2.50
pitch	£1.00 - £2.25
dog	£0.50
electricity	£2.50

Tel: 01983 852597. Fax: 01983 856225. E-mail: appuldurcombe@freeuk.com. **Reservations:** Made with £10 non-refundable deposit per week booked. **Open** 1 April - 31 October.

Directions: From Newport take A3020 Sandown road, turning right to Shanklin. Follow through Godshill to Whiteley Bank roundabout and turn right for Wroxall. Continue for 1 mile past Donkey Sanctuary and site is to right in village - watch for sign. The entrance to the site access lane is off a narrow road on a blind bend and the access lane itself is too narrow for two units to pass (unguarded stream on one side and corners with jutting out walls). O.S.GR: SZ548803.

Southland Camping Park
Newchurch, Sandown, Isle of Wight PO36 0LZ

247

Southland has been developed in the grounds of a former nursery and it has matured nicely with many attractive shrubs and trees. In the peaceful country setting of the Arreton valley, it is a sheltered and well run park with 120 large, level pitches backing on to and separated by hedging. Comfortable and spacious, all have electricity (10/16A) and some water points. Two acres of land have been acquired recently and a nature area is being developed overlooking the countryside at the back of the site (no dogs). Nearby Arreton and Newchurch have craft shops and in August there is the National Garlic Festival. Sandown and Shanklin are 3 miles, the beach at Lake, 2.5 miles. A member of the Countryside Discovery group.

Facilities: The excellent toilet block is well maintained - the ladies' is modern, with washbasins in spacious cubicles, low level washbasins for children, three en-suite basin and shower cubicles, and a hairdressing area. Bathroom (on payment), baby room, a good unit for disabled people, and two family shower rooms also suitable for disabled visitors. Laundry and dishwashing sinks. Motorcaravan service point. Shop. Fenced children's play area. Only raised barbecues are permitted. More than one dog per pitch by prior arrangement only.
Off site: Fishing 0.5 miles, riding 2 miles, bicycle hire or golf 3 miles. Main bus route stops at the top of the road, two pubs are within walking distance and there is access to walks and bridleways.

Charges 2003

Per adult	£4.75 - £6.80
child (3-15 yrs)	£1.75 - £3.50
dog	£1.10

Packages incl. ferry travel available. Special low season offers. **Tel:** 01983 865385. Fax: 01983 867663. E-mail: info@southland.co.uk.
Reservations: Made for any length with £30 deposit per pitch, per week (or part week). **Open** Easter - end September.

Directions: Park is signed from A3055/6 Newport-Sandown road, southeast of Arreton. O.S.GR: SZ557847.

Whitecliff Bay Holiday Park
Hillway, Whitecliff Bay, Bembridge PO35 5PL

251

Whitecliff Bay is a very large complex divided by a lane, with a holiday home and chalet park on the right hand side, and a touring site on the left hand side. The large touring site is on a sloping hillside with commanding views over the surrounding countryside. The 429 pitches are spread over three fields, the top and second fields are terraced, but field three (the only one in which dogs are permitted, in low season only) is quite level. Half of the pitches have electric hook-ups (10A), and there are around 44 gravel hardstandings, 12 in the top field, the remainder in lowest field. There are only 13 individual hedged multi-serviced pitches available, so book early. Three toilet blocks serve the site and are situated to one side. On the opposite side of the lane, in the holiday home and chalet park, you will find all the main entertainment and leisure facilities. These include The Culver Club with its bar, dance floor, stage and a full programme of evening entertainment, cabarets and shows in season. On the cliff above the beach is the pub and restaurant, a heated outdoor pool with a large paved surround and indoor facilities including a funpool with jacuzzi, a sauna and sunbed, small gym, a soft playzone (under 8 yrs), and a snack bar.

Facilities: Three sanitary units, one on the lower part of the site. The other two are fairly close together, not far from reception and both of these have been refitted to a good standard, and provide showers (on payment), and a suite (with shower) for disabled people. A second suite is at the lower block with a similar facility to serve as a baby/family room (this block due for refurbishment for 2003). Laundry with ironing facility. Small mini-market with reception. Motorcaravan service point. Playground. At the holiday home park: Launderette, hairdresser and second larger shop. The Culver Club with bar and evening entertainment. Several snack bars, takeaways. Swimming pool (18 x 18 m, Whitsun - end Aug). Indoor funpool with jacuzzi, a sauna and sunbed, small gym, a soft playzone (under 8 yrs), and a snack-bar. Both pools are supervised. Most facilities open March - Oct. Dogs only accepted in lower field outside 20/7 - 31/8. **Off site:** Close to the outdoor pool a very steep path which leads down to a sandy beach. Normal bus service weekdays, site runs a courtesy mini-bus at weekends to Bembridge and Sandown. Golf 5 miles. Bicycle hire 4 miles. Riding 2 miles.

Charges 2002

Per pitch incl. 2 persons	£7.20 - £12.60
incl. electricity	£9.70 - £15.60
incl. full services	£12.00 - £18.60
extra adult	£3.10 - £4.80
child (5-13 yrs)	£2.10 - £3.20
dog (excl. 20/7-31/8)	£1.00

Tel: 01983 872671. Fax: 01983 872941. E-mail: holiday@whitecliff-bay.com. **Reservations:** Made with deposit of £40 per week (£80 if special offer package). **Open** 22 March - 26 October.

Directions: Bembridge is at the eastern end of the island. From the A3055 between Ryde and Sandown, turn east at Brading on B3395 for approx. 2 miles passing the Airfield and Propeller Club, fork right (site signed). Follow signs to site, first entry on right is static area, touring entrance is on left shortly after. O.S.GR: SZ635865.

Lincoln Farm Park

High Street, Standlake, Witney OX8 7RH

From its immaculately tended grounds and quality facilities, to the efficient and friendly staff, this park is a credit to its owner. Situated in a small, quiet village, It Is well set back and screened by mature trees, with wide gravel roads, hedged enclosures, attractive brick pathways and good lighting. All 90 numbered, level touring pitches are generously sized and have electrical connections (10/16A), 75 with gravel hardstanding and adjacent grass for awnings, and 22 are fully serviced (fresh and waste water, electricity and satellite TV). Although only a relatively small site its leisure facilities are quite outstanding. One indoor swimming pool is always appreciated, but two (30' x 15' and 40' x 20') plus a toddlers' pool, spa pools, saunas, steam room, sun bed and a fitness suite really offer something rather special. Charges for all of these are modest, and outside of the open sessions everything can be hired privately by the hour. Oxford and the Cotswolds are conveniently close. A member of the Best of British group.

Facilities: The two heated toilet blocks are of notable design and quality, well maintained and exceptionally clean, with showers (sensibly sized and designed), and washbasins in cubicles. A well equipped, separate unit for disabled people is adjacent to a specially reserved pitch with direct access. Two family bathrooms (incorporating baby bath and changing facilities). Each block also contains a laundry room, dishwashing sinks under cover (more throughout the site), freezers, fridges and microwaves. Motorcaravan service point. Shop (basic supplies). Information kiosk. Outdoor chess/draughts, putting green and sizeable adventure play area (bark chipping and rubber base). Indoor swimming pools. Up to two dogs are welcome with allocated walks. **Off site:** Fishing (lake and river) 300 yds - 5 miles, riding centre and water sports nearby.

Charges 2002

Per unit incl. 2 persons and electricity	£9.70 - £16.45
incl. mains services and awning	£14.95 - £21.70
extra adult	£2.25
child (5-14 yrs)	£1.50
dog	£0.75

Low season offers. **Tel:** 01865 300239. Fax: 01865 300127. **Reservations:** Made with £15 non-returnable deposit. **Open** 1 February - 18 November.

Directions: Take A415 Witney - Abingdon road and turn into Standlake High Street by garage; park is 300 yds on the right. O.S.GR: SP396029.

Barnstones Caravan and Camping Park

Great Bourton, Banbury OX17 1QU

Three miles from Banbury and open all year round, this small, neat park provides an excellent point from which to explore the Cotswolds, Oxford and Stratford-upon-Avon. The 49 level pitches all have gravel hardstanding with a grass area for awnings (no groundsheets are allowed) and 10A electricity; 20 of these are fully serviced. Shrubs, flowers and an oval tarmac road convey a tidy impression throughout and the low level lighting is subtle but effective. A rally field is near the main road, so some traffic noise is to be expected. New arrivals should report to the warden's caravan at the park entrance. The church in Great Bourton (250 m) has a most unusual lych gate and there is a canal-side walk to Banbury (3 miles).

Facilities: The newly upgraded toilet block is small, but it can be heated and is quite adequate for the number of people it serves. It has adjustable, unisex showers and a separate dishwashing and laundry room. Small, fenced play area for children (grass and bark chipping base) adjacent to the entrance road. Gas is available. **Off site:** Nearest shop 1 mile. supermarket 3 miles, pub 150 yds. Fishing, bicycle hire, golf and riding, all within 3 miles.

Charges 2002

Per unit incl. 2 persons	£6.00
extra person over 12	£1.50
child (5-12 yrs)	£1.00
1 man tent	£4.50
awning	£0.50 - £1.00
electricity	£1.50

OAPs less 50p per night. No credit cards.**Tel:** 01295 750289. **Reservations:** Contact park. **Open** all year.

Directions: From M40 take exit 11 for Banbury. Turn off following signs for Chipping Norton, straight on at two small roundabouts. At third roundabout turn right on A423 signed Southam and in 2.5 miles turn right signed Great Bourton, Site entrance is 100 yds on right. O.S.GR: SP455454.

Cotswold View Caravan & Camping Site

258 Enstone Road, Charlbury OX7 3JH

On the edge of the Cotswolds and surrounded by fine views, this well-run family site offers a warm welcome. It successfully combines a working farm, touring site and self catering country cottages. Wide gravel or tarmac roads ensure easy access to the 125 pitches (all with 10A electricity) in the 10-acre touring area. Part of this area has been carefully developed more recently to a high standard and will naturally take some time to mature. The small reception also serves as a licensed shop selling freshly baked bread, home-made cakes and eggs from their own hens. Farmhouse breakfasts (ordered the night before) are served in the farmhouse itself with B&B also offered. The farm's animals (sheep, hens, pigs, rabbits, ducks, goats, ponies and a donkey) add great interest to one's stay. Well defined and maintained trails around the enclosures enable the animals to be safely observed, whilst additional trails and woodland plantations provide more walking opportunities, particularly for dogs which can be allowed off the lead. Convenient for touring the Cotswolds, there is also a good train service for day trips to London.

Facilities: Two well maintained toilet blocks provide excellent facilities including washbasins in cubicles, showers with ample changing space, two family rooms, baths (50p), hairdryers, central heating and even soft piped music! Both blocks have good units for disabled people. Baby changing facilities, laundry room, freezers for ice packs and dishwashing sinks under cover. Motorcaravan service point. Shop. Children have a two sheltered grass areas in which to play and a games room with table tennis, pool table and football table. Hard tennis court. Outdoor chess. Bicycle hire. Skittle alley is for hire. American motorhomes accepted. New barrier system (£5 deposit). **Off site:** Fishing 1 mile, riding 10 miles, golf 7 miles.

Charges 2002

Per unit incl. 2 persons	£8.00 - £11.00
extra adult	£1.75
child (5-16 yrs)	£1.00
electricity	£2.00
dog	free

Tel: 01608 810314. Fax: 01608 811891. E-mail: bookings@cotswoldview.f9.co.uk. **Reservations:** Advisable for B.Hs and peak season. **Open** Easter - 31 October.

Directions: From A44 Oxford - Stratford-on-Avon road, take B4022 to Charlbury, just south of Enstone. Park is 2 miles on left. O.S.GR: SP365210.

Wysdom Touring Park

262 The Bungalow, Burford School, Burford OX18 4JG

You'll have to go a long way before you find anything else remotely like this site! The land is owned by Burford School and the enterprising caretaker and his wife, caravanners themselves, suggested that they create this wonderful place to raise money for the school (hence cheques payable to Burford School). It is really like putting your caravan or motorcaravan (tents are not accepted) into their own private garden. The 25 pitches (6 seasonal) are separated by hedges, all have electricity (16A) and a picnic table and some have their own tap. When we visited, the site was a true riot of colour. This is a lovely location for exploring the Cotswolds - Burford calls itself the 'Gateway to the Cotswolds'. The turn into the site off the school drive is narrow and the site is not therefore considered suitable for large motorhomes. It is also best to avoid school pick-up and drop-off when the drive can be congested.

Facilities: The small sanitary building offers all you need although with only one shower per sex, whilst it meets statistical requirements there may be a queue at times. **Off site:** Burford is yards away with its famous shop lined hill full of antique shops, old coaching inns and all those 'interesting' shops it is so much fun rooting about in. Burford Golf Club next door you can walk from your caravan to the first tee.

Charges 2003

Per unit incl. 2 persons and electricity	£7.00 - £9.00
extra person	£1.50
dog (in excess of one)	£0.50

No credit cards. **Tel:** 01993 823207. **Reservations:** Contact park. **Open** all year.

Directions: From roundabout on A40 at Burford, take A361 and site is a few yards on the right signed Burford School. Once in school drive watch for narrow entrance to site on right in about 100 yards. O.S.GR: SP249117.

Bo Peep Caravan Park

Aynho Road, Adderbury, Banbury OX17 3NP

261

Set amongst 85 acres of farmland and woodland, there is an air of spacious informality about this peaceful, friendly park and it blends perfectly with the views surrounding it. Part of the Caravan Club's 'managed under contact' scheme, non-members are also very welcome. All of the 114 numbered pitches are large, have 16A electricity and, with the exception of eight that slope gently, are otherwise quite level. Gravel roads connect the various areas, such as Poppy Field, The Paddocks and The Warren, with reasonable shelter provided by hedges and trees. Pitches are mostly grassy and set around the perimeters, leaving central areas free for a liberal sprinkling of picnic tables. A separate 4 acre field is reserved for tents and 18 seasonal units occupy the hardstandings and some other pitches. Children are welcome but there is no play area. A network of circular walks around the site, including the pleasant river walk, has wide, well-kept paths, even bench seats and waste bins are provided. Dogs are also welcome on these walks. A 15 acre field can be used for recreation and a lake is planned, plus the reclaiming of farmland to redevelop as woodland and more walks, a clear indication that owners Andrew and Margaret Hodge seek to improve an unusual site even further.

Facilities: The original toilet block has been supplemented by a larger, purpose-built unit, all clean and heated. Ample showers with changing space, hairdryers. Dishwashing sinks under cover. Laundry rooms. Motorcaravan service point. Low level lighting. Small shop with off licence, gas and basic supplies. Information centre (with maps, leaflets, sample menus from local pubs, etc). Fishing (apply to office). Caravan storage. Caravan cleaning area. **Off site:** Golf course next door. Banbury is just 3 miles, the famous Blenheim Palace 6. Great day trips to Stratford upon Avon, Warwick and its castle and even Silverstone can be entertained from this base.

Charges 2002

Per adult	£4.00
child (over 5 yrs)	£2.00
pitch (non member)	£5.00
electricity	£1.50
tent camper per adult	£4.00
tent camper per child	£1.20

No credit cards. **Tel:** 01295 810605. Fax: 01295 810605. E-mail: warden@bo-peep.co.uk. **Reservations:** Advised and made with £10 deposit. **Open** 16 March - 1 November.

Directions: Adderbury village is on the A4260 Banbury - Oxford road. At traffic lights in Adderbury turn on B4100 signed Aynho; park is clearly signed, 0.5 miles on the right (0.5 mile drive). O.S.GR: SP482353.

Highclere Farm Country Touring Park

Newbarn Lane, Seer Green, Beaconsfield HP9 2QZ

275

Only 25 miles from London and 10 miles from Legoland and Windsor, this is a peaceful park that backs onto fields and woodland. Developed around a working chicken farm, there are also sheep, horses and a pot-bellied pig to provide that country feel. There are 60 level grass pitches, most with 10A electricity and gravel hardstanding, the rest being reserved for tents. Converted chicken houses also form the basis for the excellent en-suite bed and breakfast facilities. The atmosphere is friendly, but informal, with reception doubling as a small shop that can supply all types and sizes of fresh laid eggs. A fenced children's play area plus a footpath are at the top of the park. A bus service to Uxbridge passes the site, London is 35 minutes by train, whilst Windsor Castle and Thorpe Park are also within easy reach. A member of the Countryside Discovery group.

Facilities: The heated sanitary facilities, fully equipped, have been converted from a chicken house with large showers (20p), all is very clean and cosy. A unit with toilet and washbasin is provided for disabled people. Laundry room including washing up and laundry sinks. Shop. Children's play area. **Off site:** Fishing 8 miles, bicycle hire 3 miles, riding or golf within 1 mile.

Charges 2002

Per unit	£10.00 - £13.00
tent	£8.00 - £10.50
extra pup tent	£1.00
electricity	£2.00
awning, dog or extra car	free

Tel: 01494 874505. Fax: 01494 875238. **Reservations:** Contact park. **Open** all year except February.

Directions: From M40 take exit 2, then follow A40 towards London. Take first left for Seer Green, then follow site signs. O.S.GR: SU977927.

Hurley Riverside Park

Hurley, Maidenhead SL6 5NE

On the banks of the river Thames, not far from Henley-on-Thames, you will find the picturesque village of Hurley where some buildings date back to 1086. Just outside the village is Hurley Riverside Park. You can enjoy walks along the banks of the Thames. Nearby Windsor has its famous castle or for younger members of the family, it is the home of Legoland. Alternatively, you can just relax in the peaceful settings of the site. The touring area is flat and separated into smaller fields, With pitches arranged around the outside edges of each field, the centre left free, the park has a spacious feel. All pitches have 10A electricity with some fully serviced pitches. A very popular park, there is also a large rally field.

Facilities: Three spacious toilet blocks (raised on legs) include good showers and facilities for disabled visitors. Laundry, dishwashing. Motorcaravan service point. Shop. Re-cycling point. Rally field. **Off site:** golf and riding 3 miles. Bicycle hire 4 miles. Pubs and restaurants in the village.

Charges 2002

Per unit incl. 2 persons	£7.00 - £13.00
extra adult	£1.50
child 5-15 yrs	free - £1.50
electricity	£2.00
multi-services	£3.00

Tel: 01628 823501. Fax: 01628 825533. E-mail: info@hurleyriversidepark.co.uk. **Reservations:** Made for min. 2 nights (3 nights at B.Hs.); contact park. **Open** 1 March - 31 October.

Directions: From M4 exit 8/9 take A404M and after 3 miles take A413 signed Henley. Go down steep hill and Hurley village is signed on the right - ignore this turning and take next right (site signed from here). O.S.GR: SU825838.

Wellington Country Park

Riseley, Reading RG7 1SP

Wellington Country Park is open to all on payment of an entry fee (entry for campers included in pitch fee) and many visit it for a day out. It contains a boating and fishing lake, a large adventure playground and other activities for children, nature trails, deer park, fitness course, crazy golf, narrow-gauge railway and animal farm. The campsite is situated in a wood within the 350 acre park. It has 73 pitches, 18 with hardstanding and 56 with electricity (10A). There are several individual pitches and some small groups all within woodland clearings which gives a rustic, casual feel to this site. It is a very pleasant setting and we found it quite nostalgic, the site being of the more traditional style of camping found frequently some 20 years ago. Once the Country Park closes at 5.30 pm. all is very quiet. Access is through a locked gate (deposit for key) and you must make arrangements if you plan to arrive after 5.30 pm. However, there is a late arrivals field at the entrance (but no sanitation).

Facilities: The toilet facilities were completely refitted over the last two seasons. This work has brought the standards up greatly, with comfortable facilities including washbasins in cubicles and well equipped showers with good dry areas. Dishwashing sinks, and ample laundry. Small shop stocks basics (from 1/5; no gas) with limited hours. Fishing. Family events. Torch useful. **Off site:** Riding nearby. Legoland and Windsor are 30 minutes drive.

Charges 2002

Per unit incl. up to 2 adults and 2 children	£8.00 - £15.00
extra adult	£1.50
child	£1.00
dog	free
electricity	£1.75

Fee includes fishing permit for ONE person. **Tel:** 01189 326444. Fax: 01189 326445. E-mail: info@wellington-country-park.co.uk. **Reservations:** Made with £15 non-returnable deposit (min 2 nights June, July or Aug. or 3 nights at B.Hs). **Open** 22 February - 5 November.

Directions: Park is signed at Riseley, off A32/A33 road between Reading and Basingstoke, and from M4. It is 4 miles south of M4 exit 11 and 7 miles north of M3 exit 5. O.S.GR: SU727628.

South East England Tourist Board

East Sussex, West Sussex, Surrey and Kent

South East England Tourist Board
The Old Brew House, Warwick Park,
Tunbridge Wells, Kent TN2 5TU
Tel: 01892 540766 Fax: 01892 511008
E-mail: enquiries@seetb.org.uk
Internet: http://www.southeastengland.uk.com

From 2003 Southern Tourist Board and the South East Tourist Board are to amalgamate. At the time of going to press both offices remain open.

Picture yourself soaking up the sun on a secluded beach, strolling through golden downland or enjoying a lively city break in the distinctive and beautiful counties of Kent, East and West Sussex and Surrey.

For visitors enjoying history and heritage, there's a feast of interesting places to see. Step back in time to the ages of Chaucer, Kipling and Churchill; discover 1066 Country where the Normans invaded and changed the history of England; or track down the secret coastal history of smugglers and pirates.

Many religious buildings offer much to interest the secular visitor. Historic Canterbury Cathedral, mother church of the church of England, Rochester, the second oldest see in England, Chichester which combines Norman architecture with the work of 20th century artists such as John Piper within, and Guildford Cathedral, consecrated in 1961 and refreshingly light with clean design lines.

The South East has long been a favourite with great garden makers. The temperate climate and ideal growing conditions have produced world-famous gardens to delight every taste from the romantic gardens built around the ruins at Scotney Castle to the unique, late 20th century Denmans Gardens.

Many of the rich and famous have also chosen to make their home in South East England. Sir Winston Churchill and his family lived at Chartwell in Kent from 1922 until his death and Dickens readers will enjoy visits to Broadstairs where 'Bleak House' (now a museum) was his holiday home and Rochester, the scene of many of his novels.

Families need never be short of things to do. Choose from hundreds of great days out including the award winning, child-friendly Fishers Farm Park near Billingshurst

and Buckleys Yesterdays World where you can step back in time to experience the sights and sounds and even smells of a bygone age.

If cosmopolitan, lively cities are more to your taste, look no further than the City by the Sea, Brighton, with the exotic Royal Pavilion and famous piers, whilst historic Canterbury and Arundel offer beautiful cathedrals and are full of character and culture. For entertainment, pre-London runs with all-star casts can be seen at Brighton's Theatre Royal and the Chichester Festival Theatre. There is Glyndebourne Festival Opera and many larger venues play host to major pop and orchestral concerts, opera and ballet. Famously, Leeds Castle stages open-air orchestral concerts each summer.

When looking for the perfect gift to take home, antiques hunters will enjoy Petworth, Tenterden or Westerham. For a more modern shopping experience try Bluewater near Datford, the largest retail park in Europe, or hunt for bargains at the McArthur Glen Designer Outlet in Ashford or De Bradelei Wharf in Dover.

The region, though, is definitely not all hustle and bustle - there are wide open spaces and hundreds of footpaths and scenic viewpoints for walker and cyclist to appreciate. The North and South Downs in particular provide not too demanding, but rewarding walking. Over 250 miles of coastline offers everything from traditional bucket-and-spade family seaside holidays to romantic breaks.

The South East offers endless holiday ideas to suit every budget with the chance to sample excellent cuisine from fresh local seafood to village pubs serving traditional ale made from local hops. There is a wealth of theatres and outdoor venues providing live music, festivals and full dramatic productions, and London's West End is just a stone's throw away.

Chertsey Camping & Caravanning Club Site

281 Bridge Road, Chertsey KT16 8JX

This is an old-established site (1926), a flagship for the Club, which is splendidly located on the banks of the River Thames, only a few minutes walk from the shops and amenities of Chertsey. In the summer, lovely flower displays greet you as you drive in. There are 200 pitches (for all types of unit), 94 with 16A electricity and 33 with hardstanding. They are either in open, field-like areas, beside the river creek or in little nooks and corners, which avoids the regularity of some sites. Squirrels, rabbits and ducks abound and mature trees and plants create a pretty site with views across the water and towards Chertsey bridge, although unfortunately there is some road noise and, depending on flight paths, aircraft noise. A good tourist information area is by reception, suitable for disabled people. Rail stations for London are at Chertsey or Weybridge. Fishing is possible and canoeing can be arranged (Chertsey is the main base of the Club's canoe section). The river can flood but the site has a well established warning system and will not allow camping near the river when floods are expected.

Facilities: The main toilet block is centrally situated next to the recreation hall (with table tennis). The other is at the site entrance in the same building as reception and the shop. Well equipped, there are washbasins in cabins, hairdryers, laundry and dishwashing rooms. Separate facilities for wheelchair users are approached via a ramp. There is an area for hanging clothes out. Motorcaravan service point. Well stocked shop for essentials and gas (8-11 am. and 4-6 pm). Children's play area on bark. Fishing (adults £1.10, children 55p per day, NRA licence needed). Short dog walk areas. Caravan storage. Torches are necessary.

Charges 2002

Per adult	£5.00 - £5.80
child (6-18 yrs)	£1.70
non member pitch fee	£4.50
electricity	£1.75 - £2.50

Tel: 01932 562405. **Reservations:** Necessary and made with deposit; contact site. **Open** all year.

Directions: Suggested: from M25 use junction 11. Turn left at roundabout on A317 towards Shepperton and continue to second set of traffic lights. Turn right then almost immediately left watching for green Club camp sign just before Chertsey bridge; the opening is narrow. O.S.GR: TQ052667.

Horsley Camping & Caravanning Club Site

282 Ockham Road North, East Horsley KT24 6PE

London and all the sights are only 40 minutes away by train, yet Horsley is a delightful, quiet unspoilt site with a good duck and goose population on its part lily covered lake (unfenced). It provides 135 pitches, of which 70 have 10/16A electrical connections and 42 are all weather pitches (most with electricity). Seventeen pitches are around the bank of the lake, the rest further back in three hedged, grass fields with mostly level ground but with some slope in places. There is a range of mature trees and a woodland dog walk area (may be muddy). The soil is clay based so rain tends to settle - sluice gates remove extra water from the lake area when the rain is heavy. A recreation hall with table tennis (bats to hire) is sometimes used for bingo. Basic provisions, gas and books are kept in reception and resident wardens will make you comfortable. Guildford and the R.H.S. gardens at Wisley are close by.

Facilities: Two purpose built, heated toilet blocks with good design and fittings, with some washbasins in cabins, a Belfast sink and parent and child room with vanity style basin, toilet and wide surface area. Washing up sinks, laundry room and new drying areas. Well designed facilities for disabled people. Papers and milk can be ordered the day before at reception. Play area. Fishing is possible from May (£3.10 per day, NRA licence required). **Off site:** Shops and the station are 1 mile, pubs 1.5 - 2 miles. Golf 1.5 miles, riding 2 miles.

Charges 2002

Per adult	£3.90 - £5.50
child (6-18 yrs)	£1.70
non member pitch fee	£4.50
electricity	£1.75 - £2.50

Tel: 01483 283273. **Reservations:** Necessary and made with deposit; contact site. **Open** March - October.

Directions: From M25 junction 10, in the direction of Guildford, after 0.5 miles take first left B2039 to Ockham and East Horsley, continuing through Ockham towards East Horsley. After 2 miles start to watch for brown site sign - not easy to see - and site is on right in 2.5 miles. O.S.GR: TQ083552.

White Rose Touring Park

Mill Lane, Wick, Littlehampton BN17 7PH

289

Situated about midway between the imposing castle at Arundel and the beaches of Littlehampton, White Rose makes an excellent base from which to enjoy the many attractions of this popular district. Watersports centres, race courses, beaches, historical and cultural interests, downland walks and the resorts of Bognor and Brighton are within easy reach. There are 124 pitches for tourists, 88 with electricity (10/16A). The flat grassy meadow is surrounded by trees and divided into two areas. The first part has individually hedged pitches, as on the continent, on either side of concrete access roads, with electricity hook-ups and shared water/waste water connections. The second area includes 14 'super' pitches (each having electricity, fresh and waste water and sewage connections, TV aerial socket and night light), further full sized pitches with no electricity, plus a few special pitches for small tents and small motorcaravans. A busy road runs along one side of the park and road noise could be disturbing in the early mornings during the week to a few pitches.

Facilities: The central toilet block is heated and fully equipped, with two rooms for disabled people, one with shower, the other with WC and basin (key from reception). Reception has a few basic supplies and gas. Central play area for children. Trailed boats by prior arrangement only. **Off site:** Supermarket 400 yds. Fishing, boat launching, bicycle hire, riding and golf within 2 miles.

Charges 2002

Per unit incl. up to 3 people and electricity	£14.00
full service pitch	£16.00
pitch with no services	£12.00
extra person over 3 yrs	£2.00

Reductions for 1 week or 1 month outside 10 July - 31 Aug. **Tel:** 01903 716176. Fax: 01903 732671. E-mail: snowdondavid@hotmail.com. **Reservations:** Made with deposit of 1 nights fee p/week reserved. **Open** all year excl. 14 Jan - 15 March.

Directions: Take A284 Littlehampton road from A27 just to the east of Arundel station (ignore campsite behind the pub at this junction) and park is signed along on the left. O.S.GR: TQ026041.

Raylands Caravan Park

Jackrells Lane, Southwater RH13 7DH

288

A pleasant, reasonably priced park (owned by Roundstone Caravans at Southwater), deep in the heart of the Sussex countryside, Raylands is well maintained and thoughtfully landscaped. The 65 caravan holiday homes occupy an area of their own and touring units use marked, numbered pitches on gently sloping grass meadows separated into smaller areas by trees and hard access roads. Electricity (15A) is available to 50 of the 65 pitches. The park manager seems to have engendered a friendly atmosphere and is willing to advise on the very numerous attractions the locality has to offer. London and Brighton are easily reached by rail from nearby Horsham and the region abounds with places of historical, cultural and sporting interests. The clubhouse (weekends only in low season) has snacks and good value full meals at weekends (to early Sept) with a special bar/dining room for non-smokers. There is some road noise from the A24.

Facilities: The single toilet block is centrally situated with hot showers on payment. Separate en-suite facilities for disabled visitors. Laundry room. Bar, restaurant. Large field for children's ball games. Children's games room with pool, table tennis, video games and TV. Adult's games room has pool, darts and a small library. Tennis court. **Off site:** Supermarket and other shops are under 2 miles. Swimming pool 3 miles. Fishing, bicycle hire riding and golf, all 2 miles.

Charges guide

Per unit incl. 2 persons	£10.00
extra person	£0.50
hiker or cyclist tent, 1-2 persons	£7.00 - £8.50
electricity	£1.50

Tel: 01403 731822. Fax: 01403 732828. **Reservations:** Essential for B.Hs, advisable for peak season, with £10 deposit. **Open** 1 March - 31 October.

Directions: Leave A24 Worthing - London road for Southwater and follow signs for approx. 2 miles on narrow lanes to park. O.S.GR: TQ170265.

THE LOW COST LOW SEASON SOLUTION

Looking for the best sites in The UK?
Looking for low season value?
Looking for flexibility?

Camping Cheque©

imefitt Park - Windermere

Pentewan Sands - Cornwall

Eagle Point Camping - Cork, Ireland

Camping Cheque offers a choice of 330 of Europe's finest sites, including Britain and Ireland, all at an incredible fixed price of just **£8.50** per night for pitch, 2 adults and the electric hook-up. That's a saving of up to **50%** off normal site tariffs.

European Guide to Camping & Caravanning in Low Season

330 campsites in 17 countries

For a full colour guide

Phone 0906 22 44 800

www.campingcheque.co.uk

Travelling to Ireland?

IRISH FERRIES

Phone today for great ferry prices

Honeybridge Park

Honeybridge Lane, Dial Post, nr Horsham RH13 8NX

294

Honeybridge's owners, Jeff and Val Burrows, continue to develop this 15 acre park which now has around 140 pitches, 40 with gravel hardstanding and 118 with electric hook-ups (16A). They include a large number of seasonal caravans. Some pitches are individually hedged places, others are on slightly sloping grass, well spaced and in single rows. The reception building houses a small shop, and the park provides a discount voucher pack for local attractions. A large wooden, adventure-style playground is provided for children on an area of grass well away from the pitches, and simple family entertainment is organised on special occasions. A recently added games room has darts, table tennis and free use of many board games. A TV is to be installed and the room provides extensive tourist information. This site is ideally situated for visiting the South Downs with its many attractive villages.

Facilities: The toilet unit can be heated in cool weather and provides all modern facilities including some washbasins in cubicles. It can come under pressure in peak season. Unit for disabled persons. Dishwashing and laundry sinks, washing machine and dryer. Motorcaravan service point. Play area. Games room. Security barrier (card access, £10 deposit) is locked 11 pm - 7 am. **Off site:** Pub and tea shop in Dial Post. Billingshurst and Horsham are both 8 miles. Fishing 1 mile, golf or riding 10 miles.

Charges 2002

Per adult	£2.50
child (5-14 yrs)	£1.00
pitch	£4.00
backpacker 2-man tent (incl. pitch fee)	£8.50
electricity	£2.00
dog	free

Senior citizen discounts. **Tel:** 01403 710923. Fax: 01403 710923. E-mail: enquiries@honeybridgepark. co.uk. **Reservations:** Made with £10 p/night deposit (June-Aug); contact park. **Open** all year.

Directions: Two miles south of the junction of A24 and A272 at Dial Post, turn east by Old Barn Nurseries. Follow signs to site (0.5 miles approx). O.S.GR: TQ150190.

HONEYBRIDGE PARK

Honeybridge Lane, Dial Post, Horsham, West Sussex RH13 8NX
Tel/Fax: 01403 710923 Email: enquiries@honeybridgepark.co.uk Website: www.honeybridgepark.co.uk

Spacious 15 acre park adjacent to woodlands.

✳ Level hardstanding & grass pitches ✳ EHU's
✳ Heated amenity block ✳ Free hot showers
✳ Disabled facilities ✳ Shop ✳ Telephone ✳ Gas
✳ Launderette ✳ Washing-up facilities ✳ Childrens Play Area
✳ Seasonal Pitches ✳ Storage facilities ✳ Dogs welcome
✳ Open all year

Follow brown international signs from A24 Horsham-Worthing trunk road by Old Barn Nursery

---

Washington Caravan & Camping Park

Old London Road, Washington RH20 4AJ

295

Washington is an unusual campsite with superb equestrian facilities and a bias towards tenting families. It provides only 21 hardstanding pitches for caravans or motorcaravans, and a large gently sloping grassy field with enough space for 80 tents. The 23 electric hook-ups (16A) are on slot meters (50p). Security is good, but unobtrusive. There is some road noise from the A24. The latest development is an equestrian centre adjacent to the campsite, including an Olympic standard floodlit arena, a small children's pony arena and stabling facilities. There are excellent riding opportunities on the bridle paths of the South Downs Way. Local attractions (all with free admission, check opening times) include Highdown Chalk Gardens at Worthing, Nutbourne Vineyard near Pulborough, and Steyning Museum.

Facilities: A heated chalet style building houses sanitary facilities of an excellent standard, including spacious shower rooms (on payment) and indoor dishwashing and laundry facilities. No on-site shop but eggs, bread, butter and milk can be obtained from the reception office. Drinks machine and freezer. **Off site:** Eating out options include the local pub and a nearby restaurant.

Charges 2002

Per caravan or motorcaravan incl. 2 persons	£10.00
extra person	£3.00
electricity (metered)	£0.50
Per tent pitch	£2.50
person	£3.00
car or motorcycle	£1.50

Weekly terms acc. to time of year. **Tel:** 01903 892869. Fax: 01903 893252. E-mail: washcamp@ amserve.com. **Reservations:** Contact site for details. **Open** all year.

Directions: Site entrance is just east of the junction of A24 and A283 at Washington, 6 miles north of Worthing. O.S.GR: TQ125130.

Horam Manor Touring Park

Horam, Heathfield TN21 0YD

In the heart of the Sussex countryside, this rural touring park is part of (but under separate management from) Horam Manor which has a farm museum, nature trail and the well known Merrydown Winery. The 90 pitches, 54 with electricity, are on two open meadows joined by a tarmac/gravel access road. The field nearer reception has an undulating surface, the second field is flatter but slopes - levelling blocks are needed for motorcaravans. Pitches are of generous size, those with electricity being numbered and marked. Both areas are ringed with a variety of mainly tall trees. The whole park, back from the main Eastbourne to Tunbridge Wells road, is a haven of peace and tranquillity. The site has no shop but the village is close. Two inns are within walking distance and the Barn cafe at the Farm Centre serves drinks and snacks (10 am - 5 pm). The Craft Centre to the side of the site has some interesting exhibits, farm machinery and riding stables. The nature trail (with free access for campers) has walks ranging from 30 to 90 minutes in length (written guide available). A member of the Countryside Discovery group.

Facilities: The modern, well built toilet block (unheated) is fully equipped and is said to be cleaned four times daily. Family room (access by key from reception) with shower, washbasin and toilet, suitable also for disabled visitors. Laundry and washing up sinks. Washing machine. Gas available. Fishing is possible in 10 lakes on the estate (adults £3). Up to two dogs per unit are accepted. **Off site:** Supermarkets in Heathfield (3 miles). Tennis (small fee) 200 yds. Bicycle hire and golf within 1 mile.

Charges 2002

Per unit incl. 2 adults and 2 children under 18	£12.50
extra adult	£3.50
extra child	£1.15
electricity	£1.95
extended awning	£2.50
dog (max 2)	free

No credit cards. **Tel:** 01435 813662. E-mail: horam.manor@virgin.net. **Reservations:** Contact park. **Open** 1 March - 31 October.

Directions: Entry to the park is signed at the recreation ground at southern edge of Horam village. O.S.GR: TQ577169.

HORAM MANOR

Touring Park

Horam, Nr Heathfield
East Sussex TN21 0YD

Tel: 01435 813662

In the beautiful Weald of Sussex, an area of outstanding natural beauty

◆90 Pitches
◆Free hot water & showers
◆Gently sloping site
◆Electric hook-ups
◆Mother & toddler shower room

◆Nature trails
◆Riding
◆Fishing
◆Merrydown Winery
◆Farm Museum

◆Ashdown Forest
◆Historic Houses
◆Motor Museum
◆Drusillas Zoo
◆Cuckoo Trail
and many other attractions nearby

◆Brighton
◆Hastings
◆Lewes
◆Tunbridge Wells
◆Eastbourne
all within 15 miles

Crazy Lane Tourist Caravan Park

Crazy Lane, Sedlescombe, Battle TN33 0QT

Formerly known as Whydown Farm, this peaceful, traditional style, two acre park has just 36 pitches arranged on grassy terraces, all with electric hook-ups (5/10A) and 4 with hardstanding. It may be best to phone to make sure space is available before travelling long distances. Set in the heart of '1066 country' with its historical links, other local attractions include the very pretty village of Sedlescombe, two steam railways, an organic vineyard, Rye with its quaint cobbled streets and of course Battle itself. This is an ideal park for couples.

Facilities: The tiny but well maintained sanitary unit has recently been refurbished. It includes controllable hot showers (on payment), laundry facilities with washing machine and dryer, dishwashing sinks and a suite for disabled visitors. Shop at reception.

Charges 2002

Per unit incl. 2 adults	£10.00 - £13.00
extra person over 12 yrs	£1.50
awning or extra car	£1.00
electricity	£2.00

Tel: 01424 870147. Fax: 01424 870147. E-mail: info@crazylane.co.uk. **Reservations:** Contact site for details. **Open** March - October.

Directions: From A21, 100 yards south of junction with B2244 (to Sedlescombe) turn into Crazy Lane, where site is signed. O.S.GR: TQ782170.

Sheepcote Valley Caravan Club Site

East Brighton Park, Brighton BN2 5TS

293

Brighton is without doubt the South of England's most popular seaside resort and the Caravan Club's Sheepcote Valley Site is a first class base from which to enjoy the many and diverse attractions both in the town and this area of the south coast. The site occupies a quiet situation in an almost fully enclosed valley in the South Downs, a mile north of the town's interesting Marina which has a superstore and good variety of shops and restaurants. A wide tarmac road winds its way through the site from reception, with pitches on either side, leading to terraces with grass pitches on the lower slopes of the valley. With a total of 249 pitches, 169 have electricity connections (16A), 82 have hardstanding and 13 have water, drainage and TV sockets. Two grass terraces are for tents and these have hard parking near - low fence prevents cars being taken onto the camping areas. Although there are a number of trees, many are young so do not yet provide shade. Flower beds add to the attractiveness of the site. The site fully lives up to the high standards expected from the Caravan Club and provides a first class venue both for a quiet holiday and as a base from which to explore this interesting and historic town and delightful Sussex downland countryside either by car or on foot.

Facilities: Two well built, brick, heated sanitary blocks have excellent facilities including all washbasins in private cabins. In the main season a 'portacabin' type building provides additional services near the tent places. Well equipped room for wheel chair users, another one for walking disabled and two baby and toddler wash rooms. Laundry facilities. Motorcaravan service point. Gas available. Children's play area with safety base. **Off site:** Brighton is only two miles away with a bus service from the entry road. Extensive recreation grounds adjacent.

Charges 2002

Per pitch (non member)	£7.00 - £8.00
extra adult	£3.75 - £4.75
child (5-16 yrs)	£1.10 - £1.20
electricity	£1.50 - £2.25

Tel: 01273 626546. Fax: 01273 682600.
Reservations: Advised for high season with £5 deposit. **Open** all year.

Directions: Site is in eastern part of Brighton and well signed from A259 coast road opposite the Marina through to site entrance. O.S.GR: TQ341043.

Bay View Caravan & Camping Park

Old Martello Road, Pevensey Bay BN24 6DX

292

The Adams family have developed this friendly beach-side park with care over the last few years, a fact which is obvious as soon as you arrive and see the tidy state of everything. There are 3.5 acres of mainly flat grass with gravel access roads and a low bank on three sides giving some shelter if it is windy. Careful use of fencing adds to the attractiveness, whilst also keeping the rabbits off the flowers. The 79 pitches (80 sq.m, 60 with 10/16A electricity and 10 with hardstanding) are neatly marked out by numbered posts, while five caravan holiday homes for hire are at the back of the park. A large overflow field opposite the entrance with small 'portacabin' style sanitary facilities is used in the peak season. At other times this space may be used for games. Apart from all the attractions of Sussex, you may swim, fish, windsurf, sail or just enjoy the view from this very pleasant park. A newly developed cycle/walking path leads into Pevensey Bay and Eastbourne. A marina complex is under construction nearby.

Facilities: The central toilet facilities are housed in a very well maintained 'portacabin' style building which is heated when necessary. Showers on payment (20p). Laundry room with washing machine, dryer, spin dryer, iron and board, plus tourist information. Motorcaravan service point. Well stocked, good value shop (open long hours as the owners live next to it). Gas available. Popular, well made and fenced play area with bark surface and adventure equipment (10 years and under). Winter caravan storage. **Off site:** Golf 2 miles.

Charges 2002

Per unit incl. 1 or 2 persons	£9.85 - £13.45
2 person tent	£9.20 - £10.15
extra adult	£2.35
child (2-16 yrs)	£1.65
awning	£1.75
dog	£0.60
extra tent	£2.70

Couples and families only. No commercial vehicles, large vans or pick-ups. No credit cards. **Tel:** 01323 768688. Fax: 01323 769637. E-mail: holidays@bay-view.co.uk. **Reservations:** Made with deposit (£25). **Open** 4 April - 5 October.

Directions: Park is about 1 mile west of Pevensey Bay and 2 miles east of Eastbourne, off the A259 Pevensey Bay road. O.S.GR: TQ648028.

THE CARAVAN CLUB

You're welcome at our Sites!

Pandy Club Site, Abergavenny, Monmouthshire

We're pleased to welcome non-members* on many of our 200 Club Sites across the UK and Ireland.

Discover sites in outstanding locations...in National Parks, close to quiet beaches or more lively seaside resorts, in Country Parks, near heritage attractions and historic cities. Whichever you choose, you'll enjoy high standards, excellent facilities, a warm welcome and great value too!

✂ -

FOR YOUR **FREE** 2003 SITES BROCHURE

Call us free on
0800 521161
quoting ref ARG4

www.caravanclub.co.uk

All Caravan Club members will automatically receive this brochure.
* Tourer and motor caravanners, trailer tenters and tent campers

Return coupon (or write) to: **The Caravan Club, Dept DC, FREEPOST WD3000, EAST GRINSTEAD, RH19 1BR**

Mr, Mrs, Miss, Ms	Initials	Surname
Address		
		Post Code
Tel. No.		ARG4

Tanner Farm Touring Caravan & Camping Park

Goudhurst Road, Marden TN12 9ND

Developed as part of a family working farm, Tanner Farm is recognised as a top class quality park. This is the heart of the Weald of Kent with orchards, hop gardens, lovely countryside and delightful small villages. The owners are much concerned with conserving the natural beauty of the environment and visitors are welcome to walk around the farm and see the Shire horses at work. The park extends over 15 acres, most of which is level and part a gentle slope. The grass meadowland has been semi-landscaped by planting saplings, etc. which units back onto (the owners don't wish to regiment pitches into rows). Places are numbered but not marked, allowing plenty of space between units which, with large open areas, gives a pleasant, comfortable atmosphere. There are 100 pitches, all with 16A electricity, 13 with hardstanding, 4 with water tap and 1 with waste water point also. The farm drive links the park with the B2079 and a group of refurbished oast houses (listed heritage buildings) with a duck pond in front, along with rare pigs, pygmy goats, lambs, etc. make a focal point. The friendly management will advise on local attractions, shops and pubs. There are many National Trust attractions in the area (Sissinghurst, Scotney Castle, Bodiam Castle) The park is a member of the Caravan Club's 'managed under contract' scheme although non-members are also very welcome.

Facilities: Two heated, well cared for sanitary units include some washbasins in private cubicles in both units. Purpose built facilities for disabled visitors. A bathroom (£1 token) and baby facilities have been added in the newer block (this block is not opened Nov - Easter). Small launderette. Dishwashing sinks. Motorcaravan service point. Small shop/reception (opening hours and stock limited in winter) and reception. Gas supplies. Small children's play area. Fishing on site (on payment). Torches may be useful. Caravan storage all year. **Off site:** Riding and golf within 6 miles, leisure centres and sailing facilities near and good shopping facilities at Maidstone and Tunbridge Wells.

Charges 2002

Per adult	£2.75 - £3.75
child	£1.10 - £1.20
pitch	£3.00 - £4.00
2 man tent plus car (all incl.)	£9.00 - £9.50
2 man tent plus bicycles	£6.50 - £7.00
electricity	£1.50 - £2.25
all service pitch (extra charge)	£2.00

Only one car per pitch permitted. **Tel:** 01622 832399. Fax: 01622 832472. E-mail: enquiries@ tannerfarmpark.co.uk. **Reservations:** Essential for high season and B.Hs, recommended for other times. Made with deposit (£5 for 1-3 nights; £10 over 3 nights and B.Hs). A popular park, early reservation is advised. **Open** all year.

Directions: Park is 2.5 miles south of Marden on B2079 towards Goudhurst. O.S.GR: TQ732417.

TANNER FARM
TOURING CARAVAN & CAMPING
PARK
Goudhurst Road, Marden, Kent TN12 9ND
Tel: 01622 832399 Fax: 01622 832472
e-mail: enquiries@tannerfarmpark.co.uk www.tannerfarmpark.co.uk

Attractively landscaped, peaceful Touring Park set in the centre of 150 acre idyllic Weald family farm.
Spotless facilities. Central for a wealth of attractions, including our own Shire Horses.
★ Open All Year ★ 100 Electric Touring Pitches ★ Centrally Heated Toilet Blocks ★ Free showers
★ Dogs Welcome on Leads ★ Children's Play Area ★ Shop/Gas Supplies
★ Launderette ★ Hard Standings ★ Disabled Facilities

Broadhembury Caravan & Camping Park

Steeds Lane, Kingsnorth, Ashford TN26 1NQ

In quiet countryside just outside Ashford, near to Folkestone and the ferries, this well landscaped, sheltered park takes 65 touring units of any type, plus 25 caravan holiday homes (5 for hire). All pitches are on level, neatly cut grass backing onto hedges, 50 have electrical connections (10A), 4 are fully serviced and have 16A electricity, 8 have double hardstanding plus a grass area for an awning. The park is friendly and popular and often becomes full in the main season, with a good proportion of continental visitors, so reservation is advisable. Security arrangements are excellent - the gates are closed at 11 pm. in high season with coded entry. For those who would like a trip to France, the new International Railway Terminal is at Ashford (Paris in 2 hours) - take your passport. A member of the Best of British group.

Facilities: The single small well equipped toilet block is kept very clean, and can be heated in cool weather. Alongside is a new campers' kitchen, fully enclosed with dishwashing sinks, plus a microwave, fridge and freezer, all free of charge. Small laundry room. Motorcaravan service point. Well stocked shop and comprehensive tourist information. TV and pool room, games room with table tennis. Two children's playgrounds (grass or wood-chip bases) and a play field away from the touring area. Dog exercise field - up to two dogs per pitch are accepted. **Off site:** Fishing 500 m, bicycle hire or riding 2 miles and golf 1 mile.

Charges 2002

Per unit incl. 2 persons	£10.00 - £14.00
extra adult	£2.20
child (5-16 yrs)	£1.80
electricity	£2.20
'super' pitch supplement	£6.00

Less 10% outside July/Aug. for bookings of 7 nights or more. **Tel:** 01233 620859. Fax: 01233 620859. E-mail: enquiries@broadhembury.co.uk. **Reservations:** Essential for B.Hs and peak season and made with £5 per night deposit (min. 3 nights at Easter or Spr. B.H). Balance 21 days before arrival for B.Hs, on arrival at other times. **Open** all year.

Directions: From M20 junction 10 take A2070. After 2 miles follow sign for Kingsnorth. Turn left at second crossroads in Kingsnorth village. O.S.GR: TR010382.

Black Horse Farm Caravan Club Site

309 385 Canterbury Road, Densole, Folkestone CT18 7BG

This neat, tidy and attractive six-acre park, owned by the Caravan Club, is situated amidst farming country in the village of Densole on the Downs just 4 miles north of Folkestone, 8 northeast of Dover and 11 south of Canterbury. This makes it ideal for a night stop travelling to or from the continent via the Channel ports or the Tunnel, or as a base for visiting the many attractions of this part of southeast England. Accessed directly from the A260, the tarmac entrance road leads past reception towards the top field which has gravel hardstanding pitches with a grass area for awnings (possibly some road noise), past hedging to the smaller middle area with 8 hardstandings, then to the large bottom field which has been redeveloped to give 104 large pitches, all with electricity (16A). A late arrivals area and pitches for 'one-nighters' are now located in the top field. Opposite the entrance is a general store and newsagent and within 100 m, a pub and filling station.

Facilities: The carefully thought out and well constructed toilet blocks, one below reception and the other at the far end of the site, have washbasins in private cabins with curtains, good sized shower compartments, a baby room and facilities for disabled visitors, laundry and washing-up facilities, all well heated in cool weather. Motorcaravan service point. Gas supplies. Caravan storage. **Off site:** Riding 1 mile, golf or fishing 5 miles.

Charges 2002

Per pitch (non-member)	£6.00 - £8.00
adult	£3.50 - £4.50
child (5-17 yrs)	£1.10 - £1.20
electricity	£1.50 - £2.25

Tel: 01303 892665. **Reservations:** Advised at all times - contact the Warden. **Open** all year.

Directions: Directly by the A260 Folkestone - Canterbury road, 2 miles north of junction with A20. Follow signs for Canterbury. O.S.GR: TR211418.

Hawthorn Farm Caravan & Camping Site

310 Martin Mill, Dover CT15 5LA

Hawthorn Farm is a large, relaxed park close to Dover. Set in 27 acres, it is an extensive park taking 224 touring units of any type on several large meadows which could accommodate far more, plus 157 privately owned caravan holiday homes in their own areas. Campers not requiring electricity choose their own spot, most staying near the two toilet blocks leaving the farthest fields to those liking solitude. There are 120 pitches with electricity (10/16A), 46 of which are large pitches separated by hedges, the remainder in glades either side of tarmac roads. A well run, relaxed park with plenty of room, mature hedging and trees make an attractive environment. Being only 4 miles from Dover docks, it is a very useful park for those using the ferries and is popular with continental visitors. Close to the sea at St Margaret's Bay, it is a fairly quiet situation apart from some rail noise (no trains 23.30 - 05.30). Member of the Best of British group.

Facilities: The heated toilet blocks are well equipped and of good quality, including a WC for disabled visitors and a baby room. Dishwashing and laundry sinks. Launderette. Motorcaravan services. Breakfast and other snacks are served at the shop (closed 31/10) and a pub is nearby. Gates close at 8 pm. - cards available. A torch would be useful. Caravan storage. **Off site:** Riding 0.5 miles, golf 3 miles, bicycle hire, fishing and boat launching 4 miles.

Charges 2003

Per unit incl. 2 persons and electricity	£9.50 - £14.50
extra adult	£2.50 - £3.00
child (5-16 yrs)	£1.50 - £2.00
hikers and bikers (2 man tent) less	£2.00
dog	£1.00

Less 10% for 4 nights booked (and paid for on arrival). **Tel:** 01304 852658. Fax: 01304 853417. E-mail: keat@martex.co.uk. **Reservations:** Made with deposit (£5 per night, max. £20). **Open** 1 March - 31 October.

Directions: Park is north of the A258 road (Dover - Deal), with signs to park and Martin Mill where you turn off about 4 miles from Dover. O.S.GR: TR341464.

Quex Caravan Park

Park Road, Birchington CT7 0BL

Although there are a fair number of privately owned holiday homes at Quex, they do not intrude on the touring area which is in a sheltered glade under tall trees. There are 60 touring pitches with 48 electric hook-ups (16A). This park does not accept tents. Local attractions include Quex House and gardens, the model village and motor museum at Ramsgate, whilst in the seaside resort of Margate you can walk through 1,000 years of history at the Caves, or visit the Hollywood Bowl. Reception can provide you with a map of the local area. A member of the Best of British group.

Facilities: The well equipped central sanitary unit is in a heated chalet style building with all the usual facilities. Dishwashing sinks under cover. Laundry room with sink, washing machine and dryer. Well stocked shop. More than one dog per pitch is accepted by prior arrangement only. **Off site:** Supermarkets close by. Fishing, golf or riding 3 miles.

Charges 2003

Per unit incl. 2 adults and electricity	£9.50 - £12.00
de-luxe pitch	£12.00 - £14.50
extra adult	£2.50 - £3.00
child 5-16 yrs	£1.50 - £2.00
dog	£1.00

Less 10% for 4 nights booked (and paid for on arrival). **Tel:** 01843 841273. Fax: 01843 841273. E-mail: info@keatfarm.co.uk. **Reservations:** Contact site for details. **Open** 7 March - 7 November.

Directions: From roundabout at junction of A28 and A299, take A28 east towards Birchington and Margate. At Birchington carry straight on at roundabout by church, then take next right, then right again, and left at mini roundabout. Site is on right in half a mile (well signed). O.S.GR: TR320685.

Photo: Traditional Kent Oast Houses, STB

Yew Tree Park
Stone Street, Petham CT4 5PL

306

Yew Tree Park is a small, quiet site located in the heart of the Kent countryside overlooking the Chartham Downs. Just 5 miles south of Canterbury and 8 miles north of the M20, it is ideally placed either to explore the delights of the ancient city or the many attractions of eastern and coastal Kent. Its nearness to the Channel ports also makes it useful for a night stop on the way to, or on return from, the continent. If catching a late evening ferry you may remain on site after 12 noon for a small payment. With some caravan holiday homes, the site also has 45 pitches for tourers and tents. The 20 with electricity (10A) are marked on mainly level grass either side of the entrance road, the remainder unmarked on a rather attractive, sloping area which is left natural with trees and bushes creating cosy little recesses in which to pitch. This neat, tidy, well cared for park that resident proprietors, Derek and Dee Zanders, have created makes an excellent base away from the hurly-burly of life where you can enjoy the rural scenery and also have the opportunity for walking, riding, visiting local places of interest or for cross-Channel excursions.

Facilities: Two brick-built sanitary blocks (one for each sex) can be heated. Washbasins with warm water from a single tap, and four showers (on payment). Extra toilets on the edge of the camping area. Recently added is a toilet/shower room for families or disabled visitors. Laundry and dishwashing sinks, plus a washing machine, dryer and iron. Shop (23/5-31/8). Gas supplies. Swimming pool (60 x 30 ft. open June-Sept). Torches may be useful. Dogs are not accepted. **Off site:** Riding 4 miles, golf 6 miles. Bicycle hire 5 miles. The County cricket ground is 4 miles.

Charges 2002

First two adults	£3.00 - £4.00
extra adult	£2.00 - £3.00
child (2-11 yrs)	£0.75 - £1.10
child (12-16 yrs)	£1.00 - £1.60
caravan or trailer tent	£2.50 - £4.50
motorcaravan or tent	£1.50 - £3.50
small tent	£1.20 - £3.00
electricity (deposit required)	£2.00 - £2.20

Tel: 01227 700306. Fax: 01227 700306. E-mail: info@yewtreepark.com. **Reservations:** Made with deposit of £5 per night. **Open** March - October.

Directions: Park is on B2068 Canterbury - Folkestone road. From south, take exit 11 from the M20. From Canterbury, ignore signs to Petham and Waltham on B2068 and continue towards Folkestone. From either direction, turn into road beside the Chequers Inn, turn left into park and follow road to owners' house/reception. O.S.GR: TR138507.

Canterbury Camping & Caravanning Club Site
Bekesbourne Lane, Canterbury CT3 4AB

307

Situated just off the A257 Sandwich road, about 1.5 miles from the centre of Canterbury, this site is an ideal base for exploring Canterbury and the north Kent coast, as well as being a good stop-over to and from the Dover ferries, and the Folkestone Channel Tunnel terminal. There are 200 pitches, 86 with electric hook-ups (10/16A) and, except at the very height of the season, you are likely to find a pitch, although not necessarily with electricity. Most of the pitches are on well kept grass with hundreds of saplings planted, but there are also 24 pitches with hardstanding. Some pitches do slope so blocks are advised. A good sized overnight area for late arrivals can be reached even when the barriers are down. The site is adjacent to Bekepond nature reserve and within walking distance of Howletts Zoo. Although the busy A257 is close, there is minimal noise from the traffic. Note: power lines cross the site.

Facilities: Two modern toilet blocks, the main one with a laundry room, a room for dishwashing, an outside vegetable preparation area, and recycling bins. Motorcaravan service point. Reception stocks a small range of essential foods, milk and gas. Excellent tourist information room. Children's play area with equipment on bark chippings. **Off site:** Golf adjacent, bicycle hire 2 miles.

Charges 2002

Per adult	£3.75 - £5.30
child (6-18 yrs)	£1.65
non-member pitch fee	£4.30
electricity	£1.65 - £2.40

Tel: 01227 463216. **Reservations:** Necessary and made with deposit; contact site. **Open** all year.

Directions: From A2 take Canterbury exit and follow signs for Sandwich - A257. After passing Howe military barracks turn right into Bekesbourne Lane opposite golf course. O.S.GR: TR172577.

Sandwich Leisure Park

Woodnesborough Road, Sandwich CT13 0AA

313

A pleasant well kept site, with modern facilities, this park is in one of England's historic old Cinque ports and within walking distance of all its attractions, shops and services. From the entrance barrier by reception, you drive through the area of privately owned holiday homes, to reach the main touring field which has 99 pitches, all on grass with electric hook-ups (10A). There are 18 multi-service pitches with electricity, TV, water and waste water drain, nine of which have hardstandings. A second field is being developed for more tourist pitches, and should be ready for the 2003 season. A railway runs along one side of the site and there is a little rail noise at times during the day but it is quiet at night. The site is well lit and all roads are well surfaced. Children will love the large, fenced adventure playground with its tube slides etc. which is on a bark surface, and in the mobile home park area the more adventurous will find the aerial rope-way.

Facilities: Stylish new sanitary building (completed in 2001) provides washbasins in cubicles, controllable hot showers, plus a room which can be heated with some family suites and a full suite for disabled people (radar key). Dishwashing sinks under cover at each end of the building. Laundry in reception building with washing machines, dryers, spin dryer and ironing facility. Adventure playground. Note: skateboarding, rollerblading, skating, scooters and cycling are not permitted on site. **Off site:** Supermarket 5 minutes walk from the site entrance. Sandwich has a market on Thursdays. In and around the town are a folk museum, roman fort, nature reserve, swing bridge, the old gaol, weavers, a sports and leisure centre and further afield is the Dreamland Fun Park. Fishing 3 miles, golf and beach 2 miles.

Charges 2002

Per pitch incl. all persons	£9.00 - £12.50
electricity	£1.70
awning	£1.00
multi-service pitch, plus	£4.70
one man tent	£5.50 - £8.00

Tel: 01304 612681. Fax: 01304 615252. E-mail: info@coastandcountryleisure.com. **Reservations:** Advisable for BHs and peak season. **Open** 1 March - 31 October.

Directions: Sandwich is mid-way between Ramsgate and Deal, with access from the A256. The town's streets are narrow and there is a one-way system in operation. Follow the brown campsite signs from anywhere in the town centre, the site is to the west of town, just after a railway level crossing. O.S.GR: TR 330575.

Pine Lodge Touring Park

Ashford Road, Bearsted, Maidstone ME17 1XH

305

Set in the heart of Kent, near Leeds Castle and central for the historical and scenic attractions of this county, this park is under new ownership. On a slight slope, the rectangular field is surrounded by rolling hills, farmland and trees. A gravel, one-way road circles the site with pitches set against hedges around the perimeter and around a figure of eight in the centre with picnic areas. Trees have been planted for decoration and shade. Of the 100 pitches, 85 have electricity (16A), several have hardstanding and 3 are serviced. It is a useful park near the main London - Folkstone - Dover M20 and access from the A20 road is wide, but there may be background traffic noise. The park is very convenient for events staged at Leeds Castle and is a useful overnight stop between London and the Channel ports.

Facilities: Good sanitary facilities at the entrance to the park include metered showers (token), laundry and washing up facilities, plus a shower and toilet room for disabled visitors. Motorcaravan services. Basic supplies and gas are available from reception plus tourist information. Small children's play area. Dogs are not accepted. **Off site:** Local shops 1 mile (Bearsted) or 3.5 miles (Maidstone). Fishing 3 miles, riding 2 miles, golf 1 mile.

Charges 2002

Per unit incl. 2 adults	£10.00 - £12.00
extra adult	£4.00
child (3-14 yrs)	£1.00
electricity	£2.25
awning or extra tent	£1.00
cyclist or walker (per person)	£6.00 - £8.00

Tel: 01622 730018. Fax: 01622 734498. E-mail: booking@pinelodgetouringpark.co.uk. **Reservations:** Contact park. **Open** all year.

Directions: From M20 junction 8, at A20 roundabout, turn towards Bearsted and Maidstone and park is about 0.5 miles on the left. O.S.GR: TQ808548.

Gate House Wood Touring Park

Ford Lane, Wrotham Heath, Sevenoaks TN15 7SD

This sheltered park, which opened for its first season in '98, has been created in a former quarry where all the pitches are on well drained grass. A spacious paved entrance with a new reception building and well stocked shop, leads on to the park itself. The 60 pitches are level and open with a few small trees, two brick built barbecue units, and 40 electric hook-ups (10A). A children's playground has swings, seesaw and a slide, all set on a safety base, and the entire site is enclosed by grassy banks on three sides, with a wild flower walk around the top. Local attractions include Brands Hatch Circuit, the International Karting Circuit at Buckmore Park, and the nearby Country Park at West Malling.

Facilities: Comprehensive toilet facilities are smart and well maintained, including a well equipped family room, which is also designed for disabled people. The laundry and dishwashing room is at one end of the modern heated building. No dogs or other pets, commercial vehicles or caravans/motorcaravans greater than 25' overall are admitted. **Off site:** Within walking distance are three pubs and a Cantonese restaurant. Trains run to London Victoria from Borough Green (2.5 miles).

Charges 2002

Per unit incl. 2 adults	£8.00 - £10.00
hikers tent (incl. 2 adults)	£6.00 - £7.00
extra adult	£1.50
child (3-12 yrs)	£1.00
awning	£1.00
extra car	£1.00
electricity	£1.70 - £2.20

No credit cards. **Tel:** 01732 843062. **Reservations:** Made with deposit (£5 for 3 days, £10 over 3 days or £10 p/week for longer stays). **Open** 1 April - end October.

Directions: From M26 junction 2a, take A20 eastwards towards Wrotham Heath and Maidstone. Just past junction with A25, and opposite the Royal Oak pub, turn left into Ford Lane, and park is immediately on left. O.S.GR: TQ630580.

London Tourist Board

London Tourist Board

Glen House, Stag Place,

Victoria, London SW1E 5LT

Tel: 0207 932 2000 Fax: 0207 932 0222

Internet: www.londontouristboard.com

London is the largest city in Europe, covering some 610 square miles with a population of nearly seven million. However, the centre is fairly compact and covers the financial district called 'The City', the entertainment and shopping area known as 'The West End' and Westminster, seat of Parliament and home of royalty. London's wealthiest neighbourhoods, such as Knightsbridge, Kensington and Chelsea, lie to the west.

East of the city is the culturally intriguing East End and the ambitious Docklands development and further down-river, historical Greenwich.

For information on West End shows, visit the web site: **www.officiallondontheatre.co.uk**

For more details about London's restaurants visit the web site: **www.eatlondon.net**

For information on shopping visit: **www.shop-london.net.**

Experience the London Eye, phone 0870 5000600 or: **www.ba.londoneye.com.**

The world's highest observation wheel sweeps the London skyline at an incredible 450 feet. Thirty-two high tech capsules carrying up to 25 passengers each, offer unique and breathtaking views of London, day and night.

Photo: BA London Eye, London Tourist Board

London
Crystal Palace Caravan Club Site
Crystal Palace Parade, London SE19 1UF

The Caravan Club's site at Crystal Palace in south London provides easy access to the city centre and all its many attractions. A pleasant and efficiently run site, it is arranged in terraces overlooking the ruins of the old Crystal Palace, its park and National Sports Centre. It is surprisingly quiet given its location (with the possible exception of regular police sirens and over-flying aircraft). In peak season it is even busier than Abbey Wood with many overseas visitors and advance booking is always necessary. However, as most of the pitches are on gravel hardstanding, it is particularly useful for out of season stays. There are places for 84 caravans or motorcaravans, all with electricity connections (16A). Tents are placed on the site's well mown lawns at the top near reception. In summer an overflow area across the approach road (with portacabin style sanitary facilities) takes further tents or small motorcaravans. Reception has plenty of tourist information (travel cards for sale). Many buses stop outside the site, including services to central London. The Crystal Palace park is extensive and provides open spaces for strolls or picnics and plenty of activities for children. The Sports Centre has two swimming pools, tennis and squash courts and gym facilities, with national events in a variety of sports to watch at certain times. The park and the Sports Centre are due for substantial redevelopment and when this begins access will obviously be restricted. An area at the site entrance should be used for arrivals after 10.30 pm.- the pitch areas have a coded security barrier.

Facilities: The single toilet block can be heated in cool weather with curtained washbasins for ladies, washbasin for disabled visitors and a laundry room. The block is kept locked and new arrivals are given a key (without deposit). Washing up sinks and neat rubbish bins are outside, under cover. Motorcaravan service facilities. Gas available. **Off site:** Shops, pubs, etc. 400 yards.

Charges 2002

Per pitch (non-member)	£7.00 - £8.00
adult	£3.75 - £4.75
child (5-16 yrs)	£1.20
electricity	£1.50 - £2.25

Tent campers - apply to site. **Tel:** 020 8778 7155. Fax: 020 8676 0980. **Reservations:** Essential at all times and made with £5 deposit - contact site. **Open** all year.

Directions: On A205 South Circular road travelling east, pass Dulwich College and golf course on right (avoid College Road - width restriction), turn right at traffic lights (Harvester pub on left). Within 400 yards, at traffic lights, turn right into Sydenham Hill. In 350 yds at roundabout turn left (still Sydenham Hill). Site entrance is 1 mile opposite mini-roundabouts (take care on these). Travelling west on A205 South Circular, immediately after passing under Catford railway bridge, keep left onto A212 signed Crystal Palace. After 2.75 miles, site entrance is on left at top of Westwood Hill before two mini-roundabouts. O.S.GR: TQ341724.

Abbey Wood Caravan Club Site

Federation Road, Abbey Wood, London SE2 0LS

Previously run on a lease, the Caravan Club have now been able to buy this strategically situated site and its surrounding woodland. With planning permission agreed, they embarked on an ambitious redevelopment project costing over £2.4 million to totally upgrade the site by May 2002. The first step was to install a new three metre high secure fence around the perimeter of the site linked to close circuit TV cameras. Re-landscaping left in place the mature trees which gave this site its park like atmosphere. Two toilet blocks have been rebuilt and fully equipped and the third block refurbished for campers including a drying room. The development allows for 105 level caravan pitches all with 16A electricity and TV arial connections. Of these, 62 have hardstandings. An additional 42 pitches are provided in high season for motorcaravans and a camping area can accommodate 120 tents (again this may increase in high season). With a new reception, accommodation for wardens and a late arrivals area, this is a very good, safe provision for a site with easy access to central London. A train service runs every 15 minutes from Abbey Wood station (5 minutes walk) to either Charing Cross or Cannon Street.

Facilities: Three modern, fully equipped toilet blocks, two with under-floor heating, one to be designed to be open all year, include washbasins in cubicles, a shower room for disabled persons, baby/toddler washroom, laundry equipment and dishwashing sinks. Motorcaravan service point. Gas available. Bread, milk and cold drinks available from reception in high season. Play area. Good travel and information centre (08.30-11.00 hrs) can provide tickets for travel and tourist attractions. **Off site:** Golf 4 miles. Sports centre at Crook Log, 1 mile.

Charges 2002

Per pitch (non-member)	£7.00 - £8.00
adult	£3.75 - £4.75
child (5-16 yrs)	£1.20
electricity	£2.25 - £1.50

Tent campers - apply to site. **Tel:** 010 8311 1465. Fax: 010 8311 7708. **Reservations:** Essential for Easter, Spring B.H. July/Aug with £5 deposit. **Open** all year.

Directions: From east on M2/A2 or from central London: on A2 turn off at A221 junction (third exit off the A2) into Danson Road (signed Bexleyheath, Welling and Sidcup). Follow sign Bexleyheath to Crook Log (A207 junction); at traffic lights turn right and immediately left into Brampton Road. In 1.5 miles at traffic lights turn left into Bostal Road (A206); in 0.75 miles at traffic lights turn right into Basildon Road (B213). In 300 yds turn right into McLeod Road, in about 0.5 miles at roundabout turn right into Knee Hill; in 100 yds turn right (second right) into Federation Road. Site on left in 50 yds. From M25, north, west or south approach: leave at junction 2 onto A2 (signed London), then as above. Note: route is well signed with International caravan and camping signs. O.S.GR: TQ472785.

Lee Valley Camping & Caravanning Park

Meridian Way, Edmonton, London N9 0AS

323

Possibly one of the only sites in this guide with a multiplex cinema just outside the gate, you are greeted here by a very attractive entrance with flower displays. Spacious level pitches, with hardstanding and electric hook-ups, are well laid out around a large field and there is a tent area just behind two mounds. The grass and gardens are well trimmed and kept very tidy. New for 2002 was a well designed kitchen and eating area for the tent campers and even a covered outside TV area. The site also offers hook-up points for tents. The cinema complex incorporates a restaurant and bar, and from here you can hop on a bus into London. A popular site, very well looked after and kept clean and tidy by site managers, this is a peaceful stop within easy reach of the city.

Facilities: Two modern, heated toilet blocks include spacious showers and two large en-suite units for disabled people. All facilities are accessed by key. Dishwashing. Laundry. Motorcaravan service point. Kitchen. Shop. Play area. Table tennis and badminton. **Off site:** Cinema, restaurant and bar at entrance. Supermarket 0.5 miles. Golf adjacent.

Charges 2002

Per adult	£5.65
child (under 16 yrs)	£2.35
electricity	£2.40

Tel: 0208 8036900. Fax: 0208 8844975. E-mail: leisurecantre@leevalleypark.org.uk. **Reservations: Open**

Directions: From M25 take exit 25 onto A10 signed for the city. Turn left at traffic lights on A1055 signed Freezywater and follow for about 6 miles over three sets of lights and four roundabouts. After final set of lights site is on left (signed with international campsite signs from A10) at the rear of UCI cinema complex. O.S.GR: TQ357940.

Perfectly Placed for the
City of London
and the countryside of Hertfordshire and Essex

Lee Valley Regional Park is a perfect place to stay. All sites have modern facilities, offer value for money and are located in pleasant surroundings with their own leisure attractions.

Lee Valley Caravan Park, Dobbs Weir, Hoddesdon, Herts
Enjoy the peace and tranquillity of this riverside site with good fishing, walking and boating nearby. Get to the West End by train and tube in under an hour.
Tel/Fax: 01992 462090
caravanpark@leevalleypark.org.uk

Lee Valley Campsite, Chingford, London
Situated on the edge of Epping Forest and close to the historic town of Waltham Abbey, this site is easily accessible from the M25

and just 42 minutes from the West End by public transport.
Tel: 020 8529 5689
Fax: 020 8559 4070
scs@leevalleypark.org.uk

Lee Valley Camping and Caravan Park, Edmonton, London
Not only is this peaceful site within easy reach of central London, the site boasts a 18-hole golf course and a 12 screen UCI cinema.
Tel: 020 8803 6900
leisurecentre@leevalleypark.org.uk

For more information, call the Lee Valley Park Information Centre on 01992 702200 or find us on the web at: www.leevalleypark.com

Lee Valley Campsite

Sewardstone Road, Chingford, London E4 7RA

325

This site provides an excellent base from which to visit London, having both easy access to the M25 and excellent public transport links into the centre of London. Close to Epping Forest in the heart of the Lee Valley, this site is on a hillside overlooking the King George reservoir in a very pleasant and relaxed setting. Like its sister sites, it is very popular with foreign tourers. With capacity for 200 units of all types the site is mostly level, with several bush sheltered avenues and plenty of trees throughout. There are 20 pitches with tarmac hardstanding and 100 with electricity (10A). Current redevelopment work will include a kitchen area for tent campers. Just outside the gate is the bus stop (special rates for campers available at reception). Alternatively you can park at South Woodford or Chingford stations and use the train for London visits. Staff are very pleasant and helpful.

Facilities: There are three blocks offering good facilities, all totally refurbished this year. Good en-suite room for disabled visitors, dishwashing, laundry. Motorcaravan service point. Well stocked shop. Gas available. Children's playground. **Off site:** Waltham Abbey 3 miles, shops 1 mile. Fishing 2 miles.

Charges 2002

Per adult	£5.60
child (under 16 yrs)	£2.45
electricity	£2.25

Tel: 020 8529 5689. Fax: 020 8559 4070. E-mail: info@leevalleypark.org.uk. **Reservations:** Any length up to 14 days with £5 deposit. **Open** Easter - 27 October.

Directions: From M25 take exit 26 (site signed) on A112 to Chingford and site is on right in 3 miles. From A10 take A110 signed Chingford. After passing between reservoirs, at next traffic lights turn left on A112. Site on left after 1 mile (just over brow of hill). O.S. GR: TQ378970.

Lee Valley Caravan Park

Essex Road, Dobbs Weir, Hoddesdon EN11 0AS

321

Right on the banks of the River Lee, this site offers a large open touring field which is very level. Pitches are well spaced around the outer edge of the field, with a tent area in the centre, with an additional small tent field on the river bank for the keen angler. Of the 100 touring pitches, 36 have 10A electricity. Although the site has very few trees, those that are there give some shade and the perimeter trees are tall enough to keep out any noise from the nearby industrial area. The managers work hard to keep the site clean and tidy and they have planted some very attractive tubs and pots around the site. Just outside the site and across the road is the Weir with a large picnic area and even a pub - at weekends and holiday times this spot can get very busy.

Facilities: The large toilet block is old but has been refurbished to provide clean and tidy facilities (all key access). Excellent en-suite disabled room. Dishwashing, laundry, drying area. Motorcaravan service point. Shop with camping accessories and sweets. Play area. Fishing. **Off site:** Hoddesdon 1.5 miles, supermarket 1 mile. Swimming pool 2 miles. Pub and restaurant 100 yards.

Charges 2002

Per adult	£5.44
child (3-16 yrs)	£2.20
electricity	£2.25

Min charge (not backpackers). Checking out time 5 pm. **Tel:** 01992 462090. Fax: 01992 462090. E-mail: info@leevalleypark.org.uk. **Reservations:** Made with £5 deposit - write to park for reservation form. (For information contact PO Box 88, Enfield, Middlesex. tel: 01992 700766). **Open** March - 31 October.

Directions: Take exit 25 from M25 and then north on A10 for 4 miles; take the Hoddesdon exit, turn left at second roundabout following signs for Dobbs Weir and park is on the right within 1 mile. O.S.GR: TL383082.

East of England Tourist Board

Essex, Suffolk, Norfolk, Cambridgeshire, Hertfordshire and Bedfordshire

Toppesfield Hall, Hadleigh, Suffolk IP7 5DN
Tel: 01473 822922 Fax: 01473 823063
E-mail: eastofenglandtouristboard@compuserve.com
Internet: http://www.eastofenglandtouristboard.com

Step into the East of England and you step into a subtly different world. It is England as you like it - the perfect mix of soft and gentle countryside, ancient cities, charming towns, storybook villages, bird-reserved beaches and old-fashioned seaside fun. Somehow this welcoming region has missed the relentless march of time - so take your time and let the pleasures quietly unfold for you.

The East of England is ideal for short breaks, and especially for cycling and walking holidays - it is here that you can truly 'get away from it all'.

In **Bedfordshire** and **Hertfordshire** you can visit the peaceful canals, go antique hunting, or see Old Warden Park - where you can find the Shuttleworth Collection of historic aircraft, a Swiss Garden and a Falconry Centre. Or visit some of the country's greatest stately homes - Knebworth House, Woburn Abbey, and Hatfield House.

In Cambridgeshire there is, of course, the fascinating university city of Cambridge, with King's College Chapel, the Botanical Garden and the varied museums. Not far from Cambridge is Oliver Cromwell Country, the ancient cathedral cities of Ely and Peterborough, or the Georgian town of Wisbech where you can visit the 'hidden' garden of Peckover House. The flat Fenland is a network of canals and rivers, ideal for narrowboat trips, and for something completely different there is the Imperial War Museum at Duxford, Europe's premier aviation museum.

Essex is the home of charming villages, unspoilt coastline and a rich maritime history - so close to London. The landscape has been immortalised by the artist John Constable, while towns such as Saffron Walden, Finchingfield and Coggeshall are 'pretty as a picture'. There are fabulous gardens, such as the Gardens of Easton Lodge, Beth Chatto's Garden and the gardens of stately homes such as Hyde Hall, Audley End and Marks Hall.

Photo: Sandringham, East of England Tourist Board

Norfolk has miles of beautiful coastline where you can enjoy seaside fun or nature trails, or visit the ancient ports such as Kings Lynn. The man-made waterways of The Broads, are ideal for exploring by boat. Or take a stately tour of Holkham Hall, Houghton Hall, Blickling Hall, Oxburgh Hall, and of course, the Queen's country retreat, Sandringham - with special exhibitions to celebrate the Queen's Golden Jubilee.

Suffolk is where you'll find space, peace and picturesque villages set in gently rolling countryside. Lavenham, Long Melford and Kersey are medieval remnants of a more wealthy time, while the larger towns of Bury St Edmunds and Ipswich have a rich heritage with lots to explore. And if you fancy a flutter, head for Newmarket, the horse racing capital since the 17th century.

Essex
Fen Farm Caravan & Camping Site
329 East Mersea, Colchester CO5 8UA

Tents were first pitched at Fen Farm in 1924 and since then the park has 'grown rather than developed' - something of which owners Raph and Wenda Lord are proud. The site now has over 80 caravan holiday homes and three areas for touring units. These are 'Heron Bay', the sea front field, 'Mulberry Orchards' with the odd fruit tree and the new, very spacious 'Travers Field'. Although Travers Field is large and very open, once the trees and bushes have become established, it will look very appealing and it also offers sea views. It provides 45 pitches, all with electricity connections. The site provides facilities for launching boats from the seashore and it is popular with water skiers. Places to visit nearby include West Mersea with its sailing regatta in August and Colchester.

Facilities: Travers Field pitches are served by a 'portacabin' style sanitary unit at present. The main facilities in the Heron Bay area are clean, tidy and well cared for, although the building is quite old. They include facilities for disabled visitors. Recycling. Play area. Basic supplies provided by a visiting van from the local shop, daily in high season, weekends in low season. Gas supplies. Caravan and boat storage. **Off site:** Village shop and post office 1.5 miles, also 'pick your own' fruit farm and tea room.

Charges 2002

Per unit	£11.00 - £13.00
electricity	£1.50
awning	£1.50
extra car	£2.00
boat	£1.50

No credit cards. **Tel:** 01206 383275. Fax: 01206 386316. E-mail: fenfarm@talk21.com. **Reservations:** Not normally necessary, but contact park. **Open** 1 March - 31 October.

Directions: From Colchester, take the B1025 to Mersea Island. After crossing the causeway bridge, take left fork to East Mersea and follow road for 2.75 miles to 'Duck and Pheasant' pub. Site entrance is next right. O.S.GR: TM058144.

Suffolk
Moat Barn Touring Caravan Park
333 Dallinghoo Road, Bredfield, Woodbridge IP13 6BD

Mike Allen opened this small, new touring park in April 2000. Family run, it provides just 25 level pitches, all with electricity hook-ups (10A). As yet, the hedges have not matured, but the pitches are spacious and the park provides a tranquil environment making it a very pleasant place to use as a base. Walkers and cyclists will enjoy this location - the park is on the Suffolk Heritage Cycle Route, and also the Hull - Harwich National Cycle Route. Moat Barn also offers bed and breakfast.

Facilities: The well equipped sanitary block can be heated. A separate unit houses a dishwashing sink. Laundry and shop planned. Motorcaravan service point. Bicycle hire.

Charges 2003

Per unit incl. 2 adults	£10.00
extra person or car	£1.00
electricity	£2.00

Tel: 01473 737 520. **Reservations:** Advised, especially for B.Hs and made with £10 deposit. **Open** 1 March - 15 January.

Directions: From Ipswich on A12 to Lowestoft, after Hasketon roundabout take first left signed Bredfield. At village pump turn right and follow road past public house and church. Continue through S-bends and, after 200 yards, site entrance is on left, just after farm buildings. From Lowestoft, take right turn to Bredfield just before Hasketon roundabout, then as above. O.S.GR: TM 270537.

Low House Touring Caravan Centre

331 Foxhall, Ipswich IP10 0AU

Set in 3.5 acres, this beautiful garden site has 30 pitches and an abundance of trees, shrubs and flowers. In two sections, you drive through one field (the rally field) to reach the more secluded, sheltered garden area. We understand from the owner that there are 90 different varieties of trees on site, and an ornamental tree walk can be followed around the edge of the park. All the pitches have electrical connections (most 16A, but some 10A) and they back onto trees that provide plenty of shade and the opportunity to observe a range of wildlife. The rally field has a more open aspect, but is still well sheltered and tranquil. The park now has a warden and reception is in a mobile home (with rather steep steps). A good bus service to Ipswich stops just outside the site. Low House lies between Felixstowe (8 miles) and Ipswich (5 miles) and would be a useful stopover for the Felixstowe port or Harwich. Note: tents are only accepted subject to space.

Facilities: The modern, heated sanitary block is spotlessly clean with hot showers (50p). There are chemical disposal facilities, but no dishwashing sinks. No on-site provisions but a supermarket is 2 miles (towards Ipswich). Frozen goods can be stored. Calor gas is available. Small children's adventure play area. Pets area with rabbits and ornamental fowl. Picnic area. A torch would be useful. **Off site:** Pub in Bucklesham village (1.5 miles) and other good pubs nearby. Golf 2 miles.

Charges 2002

Per unit incl. 2 adults and children	£7.50
extra adult	£2.00
child (5-15 yrs)	£1.00
awning	free
electricity	£1.50 - £2.20

No commercial vehicles. No credit cards. **Tel:** 01473 659437. Fax: 01473 659880. E-mail: john.e.booth@ talk21.com. **Reservations:** Advanced booking advised - phone any time. **Open** all year.

Directions: Turn off A14 (was A45) Ipswich ring road (south) via slip road onto A1156 (signed Ipswich East). Follow road over bridge which crosses over the A45 and almost immediately turn right (no sign). After 0.5 miles turn right again (signed Bucklesham) and site is on left after 400 yards. O.S.GR: TM225423.

Polstead Touring Park

334 Holt Road, Polstead, Colchester CO6 5BZ

This lovely 30-pitch touring park in the Suffolk countryside (in the heart of 'Constable Country') is within easy reach of many places of interest. These include Flatford Mill, the scene for Constable's famous painting, Sudbury, the birthplace of Gainsborough, and Long Melford with its Hall and the location for many scenes in the TV series 'Lovejoy'. If your interest is in more ancient times, then Britain's oldest town, Colchester, offers plenty of history. The park offers really good facilities, its 30 level pitches all having electricity (10A), most with gravel hardstanding. Water and waste point are adequate and placed at regular intervals. The site may go 'adult only' for 2003 - phone to check.

Facilities: The toilet block offers tiled walls and floors, and large spacious showers. The enclosed dishwashing area will also provide a washing machine and dryer. Facilities for disabled visitors are provided in both men and ladies' rooms (showers large enough for wheelchair access). Shop for basics. Barbecue and picnic benches. Rally field. **Off site:** Fishing and golf nearby. Pub serving food, 3 minutes walk.

Charges 2002

Per unit incl. 2 persons	£7.50 - £9.00
extra adult	£1.50
child (2-16 yrs)	£1.00
electricity	£1.50
awning	£1.00

No credit cards. **Tel:** 01787 211969. Fax: 01787 211969. **Reservations:** Contact site. **Open** 1 March - 31 October.

Directions: From the A1071 Hadleigh - Sudbury road, just past the 'Brewers Arms' public house, turn left just before a water tower towards Polstead; park is 250 yards on the right. O.S.GR: TL985403.

Little Lakeland Caravan Park

Wortwell, Harleston IP20 0EL

348

This peaceful hideaway with its own fishing lake, is tucked behind the houses and gardens that border the village main street. It is a traditional, mature little site with 58 pitches and a number of caravan holiday homes and long stay units, but there should always be around 22 places for tourers. The pitches are mostly individual with mature hedges and trees separating them. Fishing in the lake is free for campers. Places to visit nearby include The Cider Place at Ilketshall St Lawrence, The Otter Trust at Earsham, and there are numerous local way-marked walks around Wortwell and nearby Harleston which also has a market every Wednesday. A member of the Countryside Discovery group.

Facilities: A modern, heated toilet block provides washbasins all in cubicles for ladies, and one for men. Fully equipped laundry. Separate en-suite room for disabled visitors also has facilities for baby changing. A further unit (also heated) by reception provides a shower, WC and basin per sex and is used mostly in the colder months. Recycling bins. Reception stocks gas and some basic essentials. Small children's play area, and library of paperback books in the summer house. Fishing (max. 4 rods per unit). **Off site:** Riding 6 miles, golf 4 miles.

Charges 2003

Per unit incl. 2 adults	£8.50 - £10.60
extra adult	£2.20
child (4-16 yrs)	£1.10
electricity (10A max)	£1.80

No credit cards. **Tel:** 01986 788646. Fax: 01986 788646. E-mail: information@littlelakeland.co.uk. **Reservations:** Advisable for B.Hs and peak season; made with £20 deposit or full fee if less. **Open** 15 March - 31 October.

Directions: Approaching from Diss, leave A143 at roundabout signed Wortwell. Continue to village, pass 'The Bell' public house then a garage on the right, after which turn right at first bungalow (Little Lakeland Lodge) watching carefully for signs. Site is down lane, 250 yards on right. O.S.GR: TM270850.

The Grange Touring Park

Ormesby St Margaret, Great Yarmouth, Norwich NR29 3QG

349

The appealing overall appearance of this family touring site is that of a garden, with many hanging baskets, flower beds, bluebells and daffodils under the trees in spring, and all carefully tended by the resident wardens. The 70 level grassy pitches are arranged around tarmac access roads, 62 with electricity (5A). Next to the campsite is The Grange itself - a free house offering a wide range of meals, beers and real ale, plus children's play equipment (open all year). The site owner also has a holiday campsite at Hemsby (4 miles) with its own wide sandy beach, which guests at The Grange are welcome to use. Local attractions include Caister Castle and Motor Museum, Norfolk Rare Breed Centre, Yarmouth greyhound stadium and ten pin bowling. There is traffic noise from the adjacent main road.

Facilities: A modern stylish toilet building is exceptionally well appointed, and spotlessly clean, housing all the usual facilities including a baby changing room in the ladies'. Laundry room with washing machine and dryer. Washing lines are provided at the rear of the building. Gas supplies. Children's swings. Mobile shop calls daily in high season. Dogs are accepted but there is no exercise area. **Off site:** Fishing 4 miles, golf 3 miles

Charges 2002

Per unit incl. up to 4 persons	£7.00 - £11.50
extra adult	£2.00
awning	£3.00
electricity	£2.00
extra car or boat	£2.00
first dog free, extra dog by arrangement	free - £2.00

No credit cards. **Tel:** 01493 730306. Fax: 01493 730188. E-mail: info@grangetouring.co.uk. **Reservations:** Advisable for B.Hs (min. 3 nights), school holidays and peak season and made with deposit (£10 for under 7 days or £25 per week). **Open** 20 March - 1 October.

Directions: Site is north of Great Yarmouth and east of Ormesby St Margaret, just south of the roundabout where the B1159 road joins the A149. O.S.GR: TG515140.

Liffens Holiday Park
Burgh Castle, Great Yarmouth NR31 9QB

351

This popular well established family holiday park is in a semi-rural location, but within easy reach of Great Yarmouth. On site is an area with 109 privately owned caravan holiday homes, plus 35 site owned units for rent. A separate open, grassy area provides around 150 touring pitches, some slightly sloping, with only 100 having electrical hook-ups (16A), plus 2 fully serviced pitches. A large restaurant/bar providing club style entertainment in season and a takeaway service (noon-7 pm) overlooks a heated outdoor swimming pool. Campers can also use the indoor pool and other facilities at Liffens Welcome Holiday Centre close by. The excellent children's playground and a fenced, hard-surfaced multi-court for ball games are far enough from the pitches to preserve peace and quiet. The site also operates a post office/shop which is adjacent to the site, and a regular bus service runs from here to Great Yarmouth. The remains of a Roman fortress border the site.

Facilities: Two sanitary units of differing ages provide clean but fairly standard facilities with a unit for disabled persons, a baby room, and dishwashing sinks. The laundry is located in a separate older unit. Restaurant, bar and takeaway. Swimming pool (60 x 30 ft; open 29/5-10/9) with new water slide. Children's playground. Crazy golf. Bicycle hire planned. Multi-court. Torches advised. **Off site:** Golf 2 miles, fishing 400 yards.

Charges 2002

Per unit incl. 4 persons	£10.00 - £15.00
extra person	free - £2.00
service pitch plus	£3.50
awning	free - £2.00
extra pup tent	£3.00 - £5.00
electricity	£3.00
dog (1 only)	free - £1.50

Special offer breaks available. **Tel:** 01493 780357. Fax: 01493 782383. **Reservations:** Essential for high season and made with £20 p/week deposit. **Open** 2 April - 30 October.

Directions: From junction of A12 and A143 at roundabout south of Great Yarmouth take Burgh Road westwards, straight over at next roundabout, then second left into Butt lane. Site is on right. Avoid width restricted road closer to Great Yarmouth. O.S.GR: TM490050.

Norfolk
Two Mills Touring Park
Yarmouth Road, North Walsham NR28 9NA

Two Mills is a quiet site for adults only. Graham and Hilary offer a very warm welcome to all visitors with a cup of tea or coffee on your arrival. Set in the bowl of a former quarry, the park is real sun trap, both secluded and sheltered, with bird song to be heard at all times of the day. The park is neatly maintained with natural areas, varied trees, wild flowers and birds. It is a good centre from which to explore the north Norfolk coast, the Broads or for visiting Norwich and a footpath from the park joins the Weavers Way. There are 54 level, marked pitches for tourers, 33 all weather gravel, including six 'panorama' pitches (hardstanding, patio area, water and waste water drainage) and 21 on grass. All are generously sized and have electricity (10/16A). A small, secluded area is reserved for tents (no plastic groundsheets). A member of the Best of British group.

Facilities: The central, heated toilet block is neat and well maintained with some washbasins in cabins, excellent en-suite facilities for disabled people, laundry and dishwashing rooms. Small shop. Community room with TV and tea and coffee facilities. Ice service. Fish and chip van calls Thursday evenings. Dogs are accepted by arrangement only with kennels provided. Only adults are accepted. **Off site:** Hotel/pub across the road. Town 20 minutes walk. Fishing, golf or riding 5 miles, bicycle hire 1.5 miles and the coast is 5 miles.

Charges 2002

Per unit incl. 2 adults	£8.00 - £11.00
'Panorama' pitch per week	£91.00 - £115.50
extra person	£2.50
dog	£0.50
electricity	£2.00

Senior citizen discounts. **Tel:** 01692 405829. Fax: 01692 405829. E-mail: enquiries@twomills.co.uk. **Reservations:** Made with £10 deposit (£30 for B.Hs); balance payable on arrival. **Open** all year except 2 Jan - 1 March.

Directions: From the A149 Stalham - North Walsham road, watch for caravan sign 1.5 miles before North Walsham (also signed White Horse Common). The road runs parallel to the A149 and site is on right after 1.25 miles. From North Walsham take Old Yarrmouth road past hospital, and park is on left after 1 mile. O.S.GR: TG292287.

Norfolk
Little Haven Caravan & Camping Park
The Street, Erpingham, Norwich NR11 7QD

Within easy reach of the coast and the Broads, this is an attractive and peaceful little site has excellent facilities. Only adults and accompanied children over 14 years are accepted. The 24 grassy pitches, all with electricity (16A), are arranged around the outside of a gravel access road, with a central lawn and decorative pergola, a neat little garden and a seating area. There is no shop, but two pubs serving food and traditional ales are within walking distance. An ideal base for cycling, walking, horse riding, or just relaxing, the Weavers Way footpath is within half a mile of the site, whilst riding stables and a craft centre are at nearby Alby. Also close by is magnificent Blickling Hall with its superb state rooms, gardens and park, or a short drive takes you to the historic market town of Aylsham.

Facilities: The well maintained toilet unit is heated and provides modern facilities including spacious hot showers and two covered dishwashing and laundry sinks. Gas available. Site is unsuitable for American motorhomes. An 'adults only' park.

Charges 2002

Per unit incl. 2 adults	£8.00 - £10.00
extra adult	£3.00
extra car	£2.00
extra small tent	£0.50
dog	free
electricity	£2.00

Single person discount £1.50. Less 10% in low season for senior citizens Mon - Thurs. No credit cards. **Tel:** 01263 768959. Fax: 01263 768959. E-mail: pat@haven30.fsnet.co.uk. **Reservations:** Advisable for B.Hs and peak season and made without deposit. **Open** 1 March - 31 October.

Directions: From A140 Cromer - Norwich road, going south towards Aylsham and 3 miles south of Roughton, past the Horseshoes pub and Alby crafts, take first turning right signed Erpingham 2 miles. Site is 175 yards on right. O.S.GR: TG190320.

Kelling Heath Holiday Park

Weybourne, Holt, Sheringham NR25 7HW

343

Set in 250 acres of heath land overlooking the north Norfolk coast. this spacious holiday park offers freedom and relaxation (which is why most of us like camping). Kelling Heath has 300 touring pitches in four different zones. Pitching is good on quite firm, level grass (no hardstanding) with electricity connections for 250 (16A). Together with 384 caravan holiday homes (36 to let, the rest privately owned), they blend easily into the part-wooded, part-open heath. A wide range of on-site facilities provides activities for all ages. 'The Forge' comprises an entertainment bar, an adult only bar and a family room, with a range of entertainment and amusements all season. 'Fitness Express' offers an indoor pool, spa pool, sauna, steam rooms and gym. An adventure playground with assault course is near. The central reception area has been attractively paved to provide a 'village store' and an open air bandstand where one can sit and enjoy the atmosphere. The park's natural environment allows for woodland walks, a nature trail and cycling trails, and a small lake for free fishing (permit holders only). Other facilities include two hard tennis courts, a small outdoor, heated fun pool (main season only), sports field, play areas (some rather hidden from the pitches). Kelling Heath's own halt on the North Norfolk Steam Railway gives access to shopping in Holt or the beach at Sheringham.

Facilities: Three toilet blocks serve the touring pitches, the most modern of which is heated with a conservatory that provides covered access all year to disabled people, baby room and dishwashing and laundry sinks. All blocks have a few washbasins in private cubicles, baby baths and, in season, a nappy disposal service. Washing machines and tumble dryers, with irons to hire. Shop. Gas supplies. Bar, restaurant and takeaway. Indoor leisure centre with pool (19 x 9 m), gym, etc. with fully trained staff (membership on either daily or weekly basis). Outdoor pool. Adventure play area. Tennis. Fishing. Bicycle hire. Entertainment programme. Torches are useful. **Off site:** The Norfolk coast, Felbrigg Hall, the Walsingham Shrine and the Norfolk Broads National Park are nearby.

Charges 2002

Per unit	£10.75 - £15.45
pitch with electricity	£12.75 - £17.45
extra persons (under 16 yrs)	free - £1.95
extra car or pup tent	£2.00
dog (max 2)	£1.50

Min 7 day stay in high season. No single sex groups. **Tel:** 01263 588181. Fax: 01263 588599. E-mail: info@kellingheath.co.uk. **Reservations:** Necessary for July/Aug. on a weekly basis with £30 deposit. **Open** 19 March - 16 December.

Directions: On the A148 road from Holt to Cromer, after High Kelling, turn left just before Bodham village (international sign) signed Weybourne. Follow road for about 1 mile to park O.S.GR: TG117418.

The Old Brick Kilns Caravan & Camping Park

Little Barney Lane, Barney, Fakenham NR21 0NL

340

This tranquil, family run park is a credit to the owners Alan and Pam Greenhalgh. Its development on the site of old brick kilns has resulted in land on varying levels. This provides areas of level, well drained pitches (eg. the Dell, the Orchard) which include some hardstanding. There are 60 pitches in total, all with electricity (10/16A). Banks around the park and a wide range of trees and shrubs provide shelter and are home for a variety of wildlife. There are garden areas, including a butterfly garden, and a central conservation pond is the central feature. Drinking water is supplied by a 285 ft. bore and excellent, roofed service areas provide water and waste disposal. Amenities include a large, comfortable bar and à la carte restaurant, open selected evenings and weekends. A friendly, helpful atmosphere prevails and as the park is 8 miles from the coast, it is ideally situated to explore north Norfolk. A member of the Best of British group.

Facilities: A very smart, heated building provides very good, clean toilet facilities with washbasins in curtained cubicles, and hand and hair dryers. Baby room. Facilities for disabled people (unisex; Radar key). Laundry room. Motorcaravan service point. Good shop with gas supplies and gas barbecues for hire. Bar/restaurant with patio area outside with barbecue. TV room, information centre. Table tennis, giant chess and a mini library. Bicycle hire. Fenced children's play area with bark surface. Fishing. Winter caravan storage. B&B also available. **Off site:** Riding 6 miles, golf 5 or 8 miles

Charges 2002

Per pitch incl. 2 persons	£10.00 - £14.00
extra adult	£2.00
child (4-15 yrs)	£1.00 - £1.50
child (0-3 yrs)	£0.50 - 0.75
dog (max 2)	free

Tel: 01328 878305. Fax: 01328 878948. E-mail: enquire@old-brick-kilns.co.uk. **Reservations:** Advised and made with £15 deposit (non-refundable). **Open** all year excl. 7 Jan - 20 Feb.

Directions: From Fakenham take A148 Cromer road. After 6 miles, at Thurston, fork right on B1354 Melton Constable road. In 300 yds, turn right, signed Barney, and then first left along a narrow country lane with passing places, for 0.75 miles. O.S.GR: TG004332.

Norfolk
Woodhill Park

350 Cromer Road, East Runton, Cromer NR27 9PX

Woodhill is a seaside site with good views and a traditional atmosphere. It is situated on the cliff top, in a large gently sloping open grassy field, with 300 marked touring pitches. Of these, 175 have electricity (16A) and many have wonderful views over the surrounding countryside. A small number of holiday homes which are located nearer to the cliff edge unfortunately have the best sea views, although perhaps at times a little bracing! Although the site is fenced there is access to the cliff top path, a possible hazard for small children. Nearby attractions include 'Karttrax' at Cromer (go-karting), boat trips to see the seals off Blakeney Point, the Shire Horse Centre at West Runton, the North Norfolk Steam Railway, and at Sheringham you can find 'The Splash' fun pool complex with wave machine.

Facilities: The three sanitary units (the newest part of the reception building) are fully equipped but could be a little short of showers at peak times. Laundry with washing machines and dryer (iron available from reception). Fully equipped unit for disabled persons. Well stocked mini-market plus gas exchange. Adventure playground and plenty of space for ball games. Crazy golf. 9 hole golf course adjacent to the site. **Off site:** Bicycle hire, golf or riding 2 miles. Fishing 1 mile.

Charges 2002

Per standard small pitch	£4.55 - £6.10
pitch with electricity	£8.10 - £9.45
multi-service pitch	£10.70 - £12.25
adult	£1.50
child (4-16 yrs)	£0.80
dog	£1.00

Tel: 01263 512242. Fax: 01263 515326. E-mail: info@woodhill-park.com. **Reservations:** Accepted for min. 3 nights with £15 p/week non returnable booking fee. **Open** 19 March - 31 October.

Directions: Site is beside the A149 coast road between East and West Runton. O.S.GR: TG190420.

The Garden Caravan Site

346 Barmer Hall, Syderstone, Kings Lynn PE31 8SR

An imaginative touring site in an enclosed, south facing, walled garden, this newly developed site has 30 spacious marked pitches, all on gently sloping grass in the most attractive setting behind the Hall itself. There are 30 electrical connections (16A), each with a TV hook-up as reception is variable, possibly due to the high wall and woodland surrounding the site. However, this does mean that the site is peaceful and a little sun-trap, a haven from the busy world outside. Attractive mature trees, shrubs and climbers provide shade at various times of the day. Reception is housed in a small kiosk (not always manned, so pitch yourself and pay later). Barmer Hall is not far from Sandringham, and there are plenty of peaceful lanes to explore on your bicycle or take a woodland walk from the little door in the wall at the rear of the site. Maybe visit Norfolk Lavender, Langham Glass or the Thursford Collection of steam engines, mechanical organs and Wurlitzer fame. The north Norfolk coast and beaches, numerous golf courses and bird sanctuaries are all within easy reach.

Facilities: Toilet facilities are in a new building (heated when necessary) including extremely spacious hot showers and free hot water throughout. Dishwashing sinks are under cover at one end of the building. There is no shop, but gas, ices, soft drinks and free range fresh eggs are usually available. **Off site:** Bicycle hire 4 miles, riding 6 miles, golf 10 miles.

Charges 2002

Per adult	£3.50 - £5.00
child under 16 yrs	£2.00
electricity	£2.00
TV aerial hook-up	£1.00

No credit cards. **Tel:** 01485 578220. Fax: 01485 578178. E-mail: nigel@mason96.fsnet.co.uk. **Reservations:** Advised for B.Hs and peak season. **Open** 1 March - 1 November.

Directions: Approx. 4 miles west of Fakenham turn off A148, taking B1454 northwards and turning to Barmer Hall after a further 4 miles, where site is signed - the road is marked 'unsuitable for motor vehicles' but ignore this and follow past and behind the Hall and farm buildings. O.S.GR: TF810330.

Gatton Waters Lakeside Touring Site

344 Hillington, nr Sandringham, Kings Lynn PE31 6BJ

Developed around two fishing lakes (formerly stone quarries), Gatton Waters has a open aspect. Fishermen will delight in pitching at the lakeside, while other pitches are available away from the water at this adult only park. The 60 level caravan pitches (all with electricity) and 30 tent pitches provide quiet and very pleasant surroundings. Quite a number are occupied by seasonal caravans. However, there is room for those looking either to fish (day tickets available) or for a quiet base to visit Sandringham or the north Norfolk coast. Everything is kept as natural as possible and skylarks, pheasants, ospreys and leverets are to be seen, in addition to the many types of ducks, etc. on the lakes. In general the site retains a natural look but the grass is well trimmed and cared for. The owners are still adamant that their best ever decision was only to take adults - this also seems popular with their visitors as pre-booking is a must at all times. Only people over 18 years are accepted.

Facilities: Three modern, heated toilet blocks provide good clean facilities including dishwashing. Extra facilities are near reception. The bar with its open fire is very welcoming and with the attraction of real ales and good food (booking required). Caravan storage. Torches are necessary. **Off site:** Riding or golf 8 miles. Within easy reach are Sandringham (2.2 miles) and the north Norfolk Coast (8 miles).

Charges 2002

Per unit incl. 2 persons:

caravan or trailer tent	£5.00 - £9.00
tent	£4.00 - £9.00
extra person	£1.00
electricity	£1.75 - £2.00

No credit cards. **Tel:** 01485 600643. E-mail: gatton. waters@virgin.net. **Reservations:** Essential and made for min. 3 days at B.Hs. **Open** Easter - 1 October.

Directions: From Kings Lynn follow A148 Cromer road. Site is on left just after West Newton turn, but before Sandringham turn and Hillington village. O.S.GR: TF705255.

Searles Holiday Centre

352 South Beach, Hunstanton PE36 5BB

This park at the top of the north Norfolk coast offers everything you need for that seaside family holiday. Although now a major caravan holiday home park, for more than fifty years there has also been a touring park on this site. It has spacious pitches separated by hedges, either fully serviced, with electricity or not, all set in seven different areas of the park. Being such a large site security is very important both for safety and peace of mind for the visitors and site owners, with 24 hour CCTV and guards patrolling the site. Hunstanton seaside resort is under a mile away, offering all the usual expected ice creams and buckets and spades. The royal Norfolk house of Sandringham with its gardens and parts of the house open to the public is within easy reach. For the bird watcher a trip further round the coast will bring you to some excellent spots for some interesting species. The site offers all sorts of entertainment both day and night with bars and restaurants, swimming pools indoor and out, golf and fishing.

Facilities: Three large toilet blocks offer clean and tidy facilities with background music adding that little extra. Washbasins are in cubicles. En-suite disabled rooms in all blocks. Baby room. Laundry. Dishwashing facilities on the side of each block. Indoor and outdoor swimming pools. Gym. Tennis. Golf (9 hole course, driving range and putting course). Fishing lake. Bicycle hire. **Off site:** Nearest beach 200 yards.

Charges 2002

Per pitch	£9.00 - £21.00
pitch with electricity	£10.00 - £24.00
fully serviced pitch	£12.00 - £27.00
awning	£2.30
dog	£1.50

Tel: 01485 534211. Fax: 01485 533815. E-mail: bookings@searles.co.uk. **Reservations:** Max. permitted stay 2 weeks. Only propriety makes of tourers and campers are accepted. Large caravans or tents by arrangement. Contact site for details. **Open** March - October.

Directions: On the A149 from Kings Lynn take Hunstanton exit at roundabout. At next roundabout take second exit then immediate left into site. O.S.GR: TF670401.

Breckland Meadows Touring Park

347 Lynn Road, Swaffham PE37 7PT

Within walking distance of the historic market town of Swaffham, this is a pleasant little park with enthusiastic owners that would make a good base to explore Norfolk and the local area. The 45 pitches are on fairly level, neat grass, all with electricity (16A), some with hardstanding. There may be some road noise at times but newly planted trees should reduce this as they mature. Adjacent to the site is the Swaefas Way, a seven mile circular walk which links to the better known Peddars Way. Local attractions include Cockley Cley Medieval Iceni Village and Saxon Church, Castle Acre Priory, Oxburgh Hall and the Thursford Collection of steam engines, mechanical organs and Wurlitzer fame. Swaffham (half a mile) has a popular Saturday market.

Facilities: The toilet block has been completely refurbished and is neat, clean and heated when necessary. It provides all the usual facilities, a separate toilet and washbasin unit for disabled visitors, and outside covered washing-up facilities. Gas is available. **Off site:** Fishing 5 miles, riding 4 miles, golf 2 miles.

Charges 2002

Per unit incl. 2 adults	£6.00 - £8.00
extra adult	£2.00
child (5-15 yrs)	£0.50
tent from	£6.00
awning	£1.00
electricity	£2.00

Tel: 01760 721246. Fax: 01760 725994. E-mail: info@brecklandmeadows.co.uk. **Reservations:** Essential for B.Hs and advised for peak season; made with non-refundable £10 deposit. **Open** all year, but reservation essential Nov - Feb.

Directions: Park is just west of Swaffham on the old A47, approx. 1 mile from town centre. O.S.GR: TF809094.

Norfolk
The Dower House Touring Park
339 Thetford Forest, East Harling NR16 2SE

Set in 20 acres of Britain's largest woodland forest on the Suffolk and Norfolk borders, The Dower House provides quiet woodland walks and cycle ways, with an abundance of wildlife. Owners David and Karen Bushell have worked hard to upgrade the facilities without compromising the park's natural features. In three fields with electricity available (10A), there are pitches for 100 units, some of these separated by fences with climbing bushes. Most pitches are level but in some areas blocks may be necessary because of tree roots. A fourth field provides 60 pitches for tents. Six pitches for visitors with mobility problems are linked by a path to the main facilities. The Dower House, as well as being the home of the owners, houses a pleasant bar that also serves bar food (weekends only in low season) and a takeaway. A pleasant patio area is used for occasional entertainment at weekends. A torch is necessary as there is no site lighting.

Facilities: Two toilet blocks - a small, refurbished one near the entrance, and a larger one with a baby room. A separate building houses the showers (5 for each sex and 20p) and a unit for disabled people. Dishwashing room, including a lower sink for children or disabled people. Laundry room with washing machine and dryer. Separate licensed shop doubling as reception and open daily in the season, on request at other times. Gas supplies. Information room. TV and quiet rooms (no games machines). A smallish swimming pool (only 1.1 m. deep, late May - early Sept), with a paddling pool alongside, is near the house. Caravan storage. **Off site:** Fishing nearby (1.5 miles). Snetterton motor racing circuit and Sunday market (2-3 miles).

Charges 2002

Per unit incl. 2 persons	£9.25 - £12.75
extra adult	£0.75 - £2.00
child	£0.50 - £1.00
hikers or cyclists (2 persons)	£7.25 - £10.75
electricity	£2.50

Tel: 01953 717314. Fax: 01953 717843. E-mail: info@dowerhouse.co.uk. **Reservations:** Accepted by phone; deposit of £10 required for electricity. **Open** 15 March - 29 September.

Directions: From A11 (Thetford - Norwich) road, 7 miles from Thetford, turn right on the B111 towards East Harling. Turn right at the church and right at T junction; park is on right. From the A1066 Thetford-Diss road take left fork signed East Harling. Ignore signs for Forestry Commission site and park is next on left. Follow long drive (unmade road) for approx. mile - keep speed down. O.S.GR: TL969853.

Cambridgeshire
Yarwell Mill Caravan Park
359 Yarwell, nr Wansford, Peterborough PE8 6PS

This very popular site offers good, spacious riverside or lakeside pitches in a peaceful countryside setting in the Nene valley. Just 6 miles from the town of Stamford and 7 miles from the city of Peterborough, there are some pretty, stone built villages in the area to explore or you could just enjoy the tranquillity of the site. Fishing is permitted on the river or lake. If watersports appeal then not far from the site is Europe's largest man-made lake at Rutland Water where windsurfing, sailing and other water based activities take place. Walking is also popular with many riverside and woodland walks from the site. All site roads are tarmac and the 140 pitches are level and well spaced with electricity available.

Facilities: The single toilet block offers good clean facilities, with showers for 20p. Vanity style washbasins for ladies. Laundry room. Dishwashing facilities. Good unit for disabled visitors. Gas supplies. Fishing (£3 per rod, per day). Boat launching. Large rally area. Caravan storage. **Off site:** The nearby villages of Yarwell, Wansford and Nassington provide shops, pubs and restaurants. Several golf courses in the area. Watersports facilities within 7 miles. Nene valley railway 2 miles.

Charges 2002

Per unit	£9.00 - £10.00
electricity	£1.90
awning	£1.50
dog	£1.00
boat	£10.00

Tel: 01780 782344. **Reservations:** Advised - contact site. **Open** 1 March - 31 October.

Directions: From A1 heading north take A47 exit, signed Leicester. At roundabout take second exit, signed Wandsford. Turn right at crossroads then almost immediately left fork (down hill) to Yarwell. Go through village. Just before old railway bridge turn left up hill to site at top on right. O.S.GR: TL071974.

Highfield Farm Touring Park

Long Road, Comberton, Cambridge CB3 7DG

Situated five miles from Cambridge, this eight acre park is set in a delightfully quiet touring location. Family run and very well kept, the welcome is always warm and the facilities of superior quality. Grass and hedges are extremely well cared for - a visitor from over the North Sea described the owner, Brian Chapman, as 'a professor of grass' which gives you some idea of what to expect. Divided into five enclosures by hedges and conifers, there are also shady glades for those who wish to retreat even further; plus one enclosure is reserved for those without children. Offering 60 numbered pitches for caravans or motorcaravans, and 60 for tents, pitching is around the outer edges. As a result, the park never looks crowded even when fully booked (which is frequently the case). All pitches have 10A electricity, 50 have gravel hardstanding, and most are level. A good dog walk is provided, which can be extended to a pleasant 1.5 mile walk, with seats, around the farm perimeter. A member of the Best of British group.

Facilities: Three heated toilet blocks provide more than adequate coverage and good facilities. The original block provides controllable showers on payment, and an additional set of unisex showers. The other two blocks have some washbasins in cubicles, all outstandingly clean and well maintained. Baby room but no dedicated provision for disabled visitors, although one block has extra wide doors and easy access. Laundry room. Small but very visible children's play area. Good shop. Motorcaravan service point. Excellent tourist information room. Bicycle hire. Gates closed midnight to 7.30 am. **Off site:** Fishing 3.5 miles, golf 2 miles. Cambridge 5 miles, Comberton village 0.5 miles.

Charges 2002

Per unit incl. 2 persons	£7.75
motorcyclist tent	£6.75
hiker/cyclist tent	£6.50
extra adult	£2.00
child (5-16 yrs)	£1.50
awning/pup tent	£1.00
electricity	£1.75

No credit cards. **Tel:** 01223 262308. Fax: 01223 262308. E-mail: enquiries@highfieldfarmtouringpark. co.uk. **Reservations:** Made for any length with £10 deposit and 50p fee. **Open** 23 March - 31 October.

Directions: From M11 take exit 12, the A603 towards Sandy. After 0.5 miles turn right on B1046 to Comberton. Turn right just before village signed Maddingly (also caravan sign). Site on right at top of hill. O.S.GR: TL391571.

Ferry Meadows Caravan Club Site

358 Ham Lane Farm, Ham Lane, Peterborough PE2 5UU

Only 3 miles from Peterborough and closer still to the East of England Showground, Ferry Meadows occupies 30 acres of the much larger Nene Country Park. The meadows, lakes and woodlands provide ample opportunities to sample the numerous facilities on offer, more of which later. Open all year, the site provides 254 pitches in total, 160 grass pitches on one side of the park and 94 gravel hardstandings on the newer side, just across the road. Privacy, shade and character are assured by the abundance of trees, bushes and shrubs that are part of the park as a whole. All pitches have electricity (16A) and tents are accepted on the grass section of the site. Families with children may prefer the grass section, from where they can keep a watchful eye on the well-equipped children's play area. Returning to the Country Park, it covers over 500 acres within which are miles of walks and cycle ways, horse routes, lakes for coarse fishing, sailing and windsurfing, a wetland nature reserve, archery field, two golf courses and a miniature railway. Well laid out for the disabled visitor, free wheelchair hire is available on request. Also passing within nostalgic earshot and yielding the occasional tempting aroma of bygone eras is the Nene Valley Steam Railway, complete with Thomas the Tank Engine. Other attractions include Spalding Flower Festival and Burghley Park.

Facilities: Two modern, heated toilet blocks are of the usual good standard, with curtained washbasins and en-suite facilities for disabled visitors. Each section has dishwashing sinks under cover, as well as a laundry room. Motorcaravan service point. The office stocks basic provisions (nearest shops 1.5 miles). Tourist information room with ideas on where to go. Children's play area.

Charges 2002

Per pitch (non-member)	£6.00 - £8.00
adult	£3.50 - £4.50
child	£1.10 - £1.20
electricity	£1.50 - £2.25

Tel: 01733 233526. **Fax:** 01733 361342.
Reservations: Essential for B.Hs, July/Aug and all w/ends. **Open** all year.

Directions: From A1 south, do not turn onto A1139, but turn left at next junction (signed Showground, Chesterton, Alwalton). At T-junction turn left on A605, continue straight at three roundabouts, following signs for Nene Park to site in Ham Lane. O.S.GR: TL151975.

Old Manor Caravan Park

355 Church Road, Grafham, Huntingdon PE28 0BB

This small, attractive park, situated near Grafham Water, is now under the ownership of David and Christine Howes, who plan to upgrade and improve the site, but without compromising its natural charm or background. The old white cottage was once owned by Oliver Cromwell's family and the grounds formed part of the garden. Even today the horse pond and part of the moat still remain. A tarmac road serves the numbered pitches, most with 10A electrical connections. There are now 7 all-weather pitches available. Privacy and shade is provided by varied and plentiful trees and hedges throughout the six acre, level grounds and the neat park is carefully maintained. Sailing, fishing, bicycle hire, nature trails and bird watching can be found at nearby Grafham Water - a large reservoir.

Facilities: The single, toilet block is thoughtfully planned and exceptionally clean. Parent and baby room. Dishwashing and laundry rooms, plus a free freezer for ice blocks and food storage. Basic provisions are available from reception (1/3-31/10), with the nearest shops being at West Perry or Buckden (5 and 3 miles respectively). Small playground. Large, heated outdoor pool (small extra charge; unsupervised). **Off site:** Cambridge, the Imperial War Museum at Duxford, Woburn Abbey and the Shuttleworth Collection at Old Warden are nearby.

Charges 2002

Per unit incl. 2 adults	£11.00 - £13.00
extra person	£3.00 - £3.50
child (5-15 yrs)	£1.50 - £1.75
dog (max 2)	£1.00
electricity	£2.00 - £3.00

Tel: 01480 810264. **Fax:** 01480 819099. **E-mail:** camping@old-manor.co.uk. **Reservations:** Made with £10 non-returnable deposit (min 3 nights at B.Hs). **Open** all year (reduced facilities Nov.-Feb.)

Directions: Leave A1 at Buckden roundabout and follow B661 towards Grafham Water for about half a mile. Turn right towards the village of Grafham following camping signs. From A14 at Ellington, turn off and follow camping signs. O.S.GR: TL160680.

Heart of England Tourist Board

Lincolnshire, Derbyshire, Nottinghamshire, Staffordshire, Leicestershire, Northamptonshire, West Midlands, Warwickshire, Gloucestershire, Worcestershire, Shropshire and Herefordshire

Heart of England Tourist Board
Larkhill Road, Worcester WR5 2EZ
Tel: 01905 761100 Fax: 01905 763450
or Premier House, 15 Wheeler Gate, Nottingham NG1 2NA
Tel: (0115) 959 8383 Fax: (0115) 959 8686
Internet: www.visitbritain.com/heart-of-england

This central area of England, bordering Wales on the west, Lincolnshire on the east and with Birmingham at its heart covers:

Derbyshire

The Peak District is ideal for leisure and activity holidays, with spectacular crags, dales and moorland. There are ample opportunities for walking, cycling or the more daring challenges of rock climbing, gliding or hang-gliding.

Staffordshire

Stunning countryside and moor-lands, combine with Britain's number one theme park, Alton Towers. Stoke on Trent, the birthplace of British ceramics, is where Josiah Wedgwood, Sir Henry Doulton and Josiah Spode worked their magic transforming base clay to objects of beauty. Visitor centres and factory shops tell their story.

Nottinghamshire

Nottingham Castle above the city presides over a modern vibrant city and nearby Sherwood Forest is still alive with tales of Robin Hood and his merry men.

Leicestershire

Home to the pork pie of Melton Mowbury fame and Stilton cheese.

Rutland

England's smallest county, just 20 miles across. Rutland Water is a Mecca for watersports.

Northamptonshire

Known as the county of 'spires and squires', Kings and Queens of England used to hunt in Rockingham Forest but today its royal connection is centred on Althorp the resting place of Diana, Princess of Wales. It is also home to Silverstone, Britain's Formula 1 Grand Prix circuit.

Lincolnshire

From the gently rolling landscape of the Lincolnshire Wolds and dramatic open land-scape of the Fens, to the cathedral and antique shops in Lincoln, traditional seaside resorts and the network of tranquil waterways. There is a huge variety in the setting of vast skies and unforgettable sunsets.

Warwickshire

Shakespeare Country, birthplace of the world's greatest playwright and home of the Earls of Warwick. Warwick castle must be the finest medieval castle in England.

Birmingham

One of the UK's most important cities and a leading international centre.

Worcestershire

Ranks as one of England's most attractive counties. Home to Malvern Water, Worcestershire Sauce and the Morgan sports car.

Shropshire and Herefordshire

Where England meets Wales and a mix of heritage and history brought to life in Ellis Peters' Brother Cadfeal series, the medieval 'whodunits' based on Shrewsbury. Herefordshire is the home of cider and timber framed buildings are a feature.

Gloucestershire

From the Cotswold hills and villages, the Forest of Dean, the Wye valley to Regency Cheltenham with its world standard festivals of literature, jazz and famous for its horse racing not to mention the art of chasing a Double Gloucestershire cheese down a hill!

Tallington Lakes Caravan & Camping

Barholm Road, Tallington, Stamford PE9 4RJ

376

This large, 160-acre site spreads around a series of lakes that provides for many watersport activities including water-ski (slalom and jump courses), jet-ski, sailing (sailboards and dinghies), and angling. The touring campsite has recently been brought up to date and now has around 120 pitches, of which 106 have electric hook-ups (10A), and 11 are on hard-standings. Major roads are tarmac, with gravel roads around the pitches, but the small hedges and shrubs separating the pitches are new and will need time to mature. The complex also has a good number of permanent holiday homes. Local places of interest are Stamford Museum, Burghley House, Sacrewell Farm and Country Centre and the Nene Valley Railway.

Facilities: The heated sanitary unit, newly built in 2000, includes facilities for babies, small children and disabled visitors, plus a room with dishwashing sinks. Additional WCs and showers (also used by the water skiers). Laundry. Excellent motorcaravan service point has facilities for chemical disposal, fresh and waste water, and a drive-over drain. Bar and restaurant. Watersports. Fishing. Dry-ski slope, snowboard centre and tennis. Small, well fenced, children's adventure style playground (age 5-12 yrs). Key-card for toilet unit and barrier (£10 refundable deposit).

Charges 2002

Per adult	£1.50
pitch	£6.00
electricity	£1.50
awning or pup tent	£1.50
dog (max 2 per unit)	£1.00

Tel: 01778 347000. Fax: 01778 346213. E-mail: info@tallington.com. **Reservations:** Accepted with full payment. **Open** 1 March - 31 January.

Directions: From A16, midway between Stamford and Market Deeping, just east of the railway crossing at Tallington, turn north into Barholm Road and site entrance is on the right (site is signed). O.S.GR: TF085090.

Foreman's Bridge Caravan Park

Sutton St James, Spalding PE12 0HU

375

Foreman's Bridge is an extremely pleasant and compact park that makes an excellent base from which to explore the Fens, including Spalding, famous for its annual flower festival. Fishing and cycling are popular pastimes in the area, indeed bicycle hire and fishing licences are both available from the site, with fishing possible in the river that runs just past the entrance. Arranged around a large, level and grassy meadow are 40 pitches, 32 with electricity (10A) and 20 with gravel hardstanding. Fruit trees, flower beds, hanging baskets and planted troughs provide bursts of vibrant colour.

Facilities: The modern, brick built toilet unit is spacious and kept very clean, providing really large individual shower rooms with seats and washbasins (showers on payment). Dishwashing room. Laundry room with washing machine, dryer and ironing. Recycling of glass, aluminium and paper. Motorcaravan service points. Basic provisions and gas are kept. Fishing. Bicycle hire. Site barrier (£5 deposit for card). Winter caravan storage. **Off site:** Nearest shop 2 miles. Riding 8 miles, golf 5 miles.

Charges 2002

Per unit incl. 2 adults	£6.00
small 1 person tent	£4.50
extra adult	£2.00
child	£1.00
awning	£1.00
dog	£0.50
electricity	£2.00

No credit cards. **Tel:** 01945 440346. Fax: 01945 440346. E-mail: foremans.bridge@btinternet.com. **Reservations:** Advisable for Flower Festival, B.Hs (min. 3 nights), and peak season; made with £10 deposit. **Open** 1 March - 30 November.

Directions: From A17 Spalding - Kings Lynn road turn south on B1390 at Long Sutton towards Sutton St James for approx. 2 miles. Site entrance is on the left immediately after the bridge. O.S.GR: TF410198.

Low Farm Touring Park

Spring Lane, Folkingham, Sleaford NG34 0SJ

377

This quiet secluded park is a lovely spot to either just relax or to tour the Lincolnshire countryside. Jane and Nigel Stevens are working hard to make this site a pleasant place to stay and have a really well laid out park offering good quality facilities which are very clean and tidy. The site is in countryside and offers some good views of Lincolnshire, and about 200 yards from the site is the village of Folkingham with good eating and drinking houses and shops. There are some pleasant walks around the village. The site offers 36 touring pitches, 27 of which have electric hook-ups.

Facilities: Controllable free showers. Washing up and laundry. Bar at weekends in high season. **Off site:** For larger shops and other interesting places, Sleaford, Bourne and Lincoln are within easy reach.

Charges 2002

Per unit	£6.50 - £7.50
electricity	£1.50 - £2.00
awning	£0.50

No credit cards. **Tel:** 01529 497322. **Reservations:** Contact site. **Open** Easter - October.

Directions: Site is on the main A15 Lincoln - Peterborough road, 2 miles from the roundabout junction with the A52. From this roundabout follow the A15 towards Peterborough and Folkingham is about 1.5 miles. Go through the village and down the hill. At the bottom, at campsite sign, take the road opposite to your right and site is at end of lane. O.S.GR: TF070333.

Pilgrims Way Caravan & Camping Park

Church Green Road, Fishtoft, Boston PE21 0QY

370

In a rural setting, this delightful, family run park is two miles from Boston and its famous church tower. There are 22 individual pitches all with access to electricity (10A) and including 6 with hardstanding. The park's facilities are housed in a good quality conversion at one end of what was once a workshop. Local attractions include the 'Boston stump', the Pilgrim Fathers Memorial and Maud Foster Windmill, all in and around the town. Further afield is Heckington village and its unique eight sailed windmill (6 miles) and the Aviation Heritage Centre (12 miles). Boston market days are on Wednesdays and Saturdays and the town also has a fine marina, two sport and leisure centres (one with swimming pools), a ten-pin bowling alley and a tennis centre.

Facilities: Heated in low season, the sanitary facilities are thoughtfully planned and exceptionally clean and well maintained. Entry is by keypad and all of the usual facilities include dishwashing and laundry sinks, plus an excellent unit for disabled persons. Washing machine and dryer. Gas supplies. Ground-sheets, kite flying and ball games are not allowed. Site is not really suitable for American motorhomes. Dogs are accepted only by prior arrangement. **Off site:** Mini-market within 1 mile. Golf, fishing, bicycle hire and riding within 2 miles.

Charges 2002

Per unit incl. 2 persons	£8.00
electricity	£2.00
extra person or car	£1.00

No credit cards. **Tel:** 01205 366646. Fax: 01205 366646. E-mail: maria@pilgrims-way.co.uk. **Reservations:** Advised for B.Hs and peak season. **Open** 1 April/Easter - 30 September.

Directions: From A52, 1 mile east of junction with A16, turn south by the 'Ball House' public house, continuing past the Boston Bowl towards Fishtoft, where the site is on your left. O.S.GR: TF360420.

Skegness Sands Touring Site

Winthorpe Avenue, Skegness PE25 1QZ

373

This very well organised touring site is actually part of a much larger holiday home park, but it has its own entrance and, indeed, its own, more intimate character. It is a modern, well appointed site adjacent to the promenade and beach. There are 85 pitches, all level and with electricity (16A). Most are grass but there are now 40 gravel hardstandings, 4 of which are fully serviced. Site lighting is good throughout and there are regular security patrols. The gate to the promenade is kept locked at all times, campers getting a key. Local attractions include Funcoast World, Fantasy Island, Hardys Animal Farm, a seal sanctuary. The site is a member of the Caravan Club's 'managed under contract' scheme, members and non-members are all made very welcome.

Facilities: The good heated sanitary unit includes washbasins in curtained cubicles plus three family bathrooms and a well equipped room for disabled people. Two dishwashing sinks outside under cover. Laundry room. Gas supplies. Hairdressing salon. Indoor heated pool (end May - 30 Sept; adult £2, child £1.50) in the static area of the site. Small playground. Entry gates locked 6 pm - 8 am. **Off site:** Well stocked shop/post office 200 m. Bus service to Skegness and Ingoldmells 200 m. Golf near.

Charges 2002

Per adult	£2.85 - £4.75
child (5-16 yrs)	£1.20
pitch	£6.00 - £11.00
electricity (higher in winter)	£1.50 - £2.25

Tel: 01754 761484. Fax: 01754 767594. **Reservations:** Advised for B.Hs, school holidays and peak season. **Open** all year.

Directions: Park is north of Skegness. Turn off A52 opposite 'Garden City' pub into Winthorpe Avenue. When this gate closed use Roman Bank entrance just past Garden City pub. O.S.GR: TF570640.

Cherry Tree Site

365 Huttoft Road, Sutton on Sea LN12 2RU

Cherry Tree is a good example of a small, good value touring park. The grass is neatly trimmed and well drained, and is divided by evergreen hedging to site your unit against. Some hedges are well grown, the rest recently planted. Connected by a one-way circular gravel road, there are 60 good sized pitches all with 10A electricity. Buses stop outside hourly, and a shop and pub are within 10 minutes walk. It is also possible to walk to the sea via the road. Mablethorpe beach is known for its sand yacht racing and Skegness, with all its popular attractions is just down the road. A very warm welcome awaits from Geoff and Margaret Murray.

Facilities: The brick built toilet block can be heated and is immaculately kept, providing controllable hot showers (20p) and a new en-suite unit for disabled visitors. Combined dishwashing and laundry room with washing machine, spin dryer and tumble dryer. Neat reception. Well fenced children's play area on grass. Gas available. **Off site:** Tennis and bowls nearby, fishing 1.5 miles, golf 1 mile, riding 4 miles.

Charges 2002

Per pitch	£1.50 - £3.50
child (3-16 yrs)	£1.00
awning or extra pup tent	£0.75
electricity	£1.75

Min. stay 3 nights at B.Hs. No credit cards. **Tel:** 01507 441626. E-mail: murray.cherrytree@virgin. net. **Reservations:** Made with £20 deposit (non-returnable). **Open** 2 March - 28 October.

Directions: Park is 1.5 miles south of Sutton-on-Sea on A52 coast road to Skegness, with the entrance leading off a lay-by on the left. O.S.GR: TF518828.

Lakeside Park

367 North Somercotes, Louth LN11 7RB

With a splendid water feature at the entrance, good tarmac access roads and well tended grounds, first impressions here are most rewarding. Set in 47 acres of pine forest, this park is continually seeking to improve and develop the service it offers. The majority is occupied by 300 privately owned holiday homes, all proudly maintained, with the touring section in a separate 15 acre field, but furthest from the leisure areas and activities. Although rather open, a programme of long term landscaping has commenced, intended to impart more character to this area. There are about 150 level, grass based touring pitches, all with 16A electricity, and 66 hardstanding 'super' pitches. The heated indoor 'Tropicana' complex with pool, jacuzzi and sauna is an outstanding facility and well worth the small charge. The pool is well maintained and supervised at all times. An impressive, new development, with family, cabaret room and stylish bar is the Waterfront Club, providing a varied entertainment programme all season. Staff are friendly and helpful. The nearest beach, at Mablethorpe, is 15 minutes by car, and Grimsby, Alford and Louth are also accessible. No tents are accepted.

Facilities: The original heated toilet facilities have been augmented by another newer block so the provision should be adequate (although showers are rather slow to drain and cleaning can be variable). Indoor dishwashing. Launderettes. Motorcaravan service facilities. Licensed shop (from April). Bar and restaurant (daily 12-2 and 6-11 except Sunday). Takeaway (1/5-30/9). Indoor Tropicana complex (adult £2.20, child £1.50). Play areas. Amusement arcade. Games room. Seven acre fishing lake. Tennis. Nine hole golf course (£5 per day). Gas available. Caravan storage. Security barrier (£10 deposit for card) and night patrols. Max. two dogs accepted. **Off site:** Riding 4 miles.

Charges 2002

Per unit incl. up to 5 persons, awning and electricity	£8.00 - £22.00
'super' pitch plus	£3.00
extra person	£5.00
extra car	£2.00
dog (max 2)	£1.50

Min. 3 night stays at B.Hs. **Tel:** 01507 358315. Fax: 01507 358135. E-mail: lakeside@donamott.com. **Reservations:** Advised for B.Hs and main summer season with deposit (£5 per night booked). **Open** March - end November.

Directions: Park is on A1031 road, 7 miles north of Mablethorpe towards Cleethorpes. O.S.GR: TF430960.

Bainland Country Park

369

Horncastle Road, Woodhall Spa LN10 6UX

A family park with many amenities, Bainland has 170 spacious, level pitches in hedged bays, linked by circular roadways, forming circles and islands. Of these, 51 are 'super' pitches with hardstanding for car and caravan, honeycombed for awnings, individual water, drainage and chemical disposal, electricity and TV aerial hook-ups. The remainder of the pitches are either on gravel hardstanding or level grass, all with 16A electricity. The friendly reception is housed in a pleasant Swiss-style building adjacent to the shop. Also here are the heated indoor pool and jacuzzi, overlooked by the bistro and spacious bar area. These also overlook the golf course and outdoor bowls area. An adventure play area has been created in a large hollow with a sand base. For adults there is the 18 hole, par 3 golf course, and a tennis club with a year round floodlit tennis dome with 3-4 courts including badminton (the dome comes off in the summer). Barbecues, jazz, country and western evenings are organised. Bainland is 1.5 miles from Woodhall Spa, with its old fashioned charm and Dambusters associations, yet deep in the heart of the Lincolnshire Wolds, surrounded by mature trees and with access to woods for walks. A member of the Best of British group.

Facilities: Four solid toilet blocks including two new ones are heated and equipped for all basic necessities. They include a baby care centre, unisex shower room for families, hair care room, family bathroom, fully equipped unit for disabled people. Laundry room. Enclosed dishwashing and separate hand washing sinks. Motorcaravan service points. Licensed shop (Feb-Dec). Bistro (all year) and bar, both also open to the public. Indoor pool (under 16s must be accompanied by an adult). Golf. Tennis and badminton. Play areas, trampoline. Crazy golf, croquet. TV and games room and soft play area. The great range of leisure activities, including the pool, are individually booked and paid for at reception. Winter caravan storage. **Off site:** Fishing 3 miles, riding 6 miles.

Charges 2002

Per unit incl. electricity and awning	£9.50 - £15.00
serviced pitch	£11.50 - £18.00
pup tent	free - £3.00

Special rate for firework display (min. 2 nights, 5/6 Nov). Discounts for senior citizens. **Tel:** 01526 352903. Fax: 01526 353730. E-mail: bookings@ bainland.com. **Reservations:** Advised and made for any length. Deposit at B.Hs. only (one night's fee). **Open** all year (in winter, 'super' pitches only).

Directions: Entrance to park is off B1191 Horn-castle road just outside Woodhall Spa by derestriction sign. O.S.GR: TF214637.

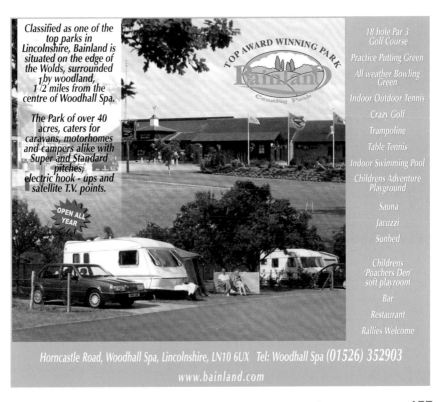

Classified as one of the top parks in Lincolnshire, Bainland is situated on the edge of the Wolds, surrounded by woodland, 1 1/2 miles from the centre of Woodhall Spa.

The Park of over 40 acres, caters for caravans, motorhomes and campers alike with Super and Standard pitches, electric hook-ups and satellite T.V. points.

OPEN ALL YEAR

TOP AWARD WINNING PARK

Bainland Country Park

18 hole Par 3 Golf Course

Practice Putting Green

All weather Bowling Green

Indoor/Outdoor Tennis

Crazy Golf

Trampoline

Table Tennis

Indoor Swimming Pool

Childrens Adventure Playground

Sauna

Jacuzzi

Sunbed

Childrens 'Poachers Den' soft playroom

Bar

Restaurant

Rallies Welcome

Horncastle Road, Woodhall Spa, Lincolnshire, LN10 6UX Tel: Woodhall Spa (01526) 352903

www.bainland.com

Walesby Woodlands Caravan Park

366 Walesby, Market Rasen LN8 3UN

Surrounded by mature Forestry Commission woodland, this family owned, small touring park is therefore mainly very peaceful (if the wind is in a certain direction trains may be heard in the distance). The new owners, Paul and Christine Burrows will make you welcome. About 1.5 miles away is the small town of Market Rasen, but further afield and within easy driving distance, are Lincoln, the east coast including Skegness and, of course, the Lincolnshire Wolds. There are 64 well spaced pitches, 60 with 10A electricity, marked out on a single, mainly flat, grassy field divided by a central gravel road and with a double row of trees providing useful visual screening. The Viking Way passes through Walesby and there are many other shorter walks in the forest and surrounding area.

Facilities: The single toilet block (with a deposit charged for the key) is spacious and ample for the site. It has toilet facilities for disabled people and outside, covered, dishwashing sinks. Laundry room. Small shop with information section (all season). Battery charging. Gas supplies. Children's play area. No kite flying - overhead wires. Winter caravan storage. **Off site:** Market Rasen racecourse is 2 miles. Fishing 3 miles, riding 2 miles, golf 1.5 miles.

Charges guide

Per unit incl. 2 persons	£8.00
extra person	£1.25
child (2-12 yrs)	£1.00
awning or child's pup tent	£1.25
electricity	£2.00

Tel: 01673 843285. E-mail: walesbywoodlands@ talk21.com. **Reservations:** Any length, with deposit. **Open** 1 March - 31 October.

Directions: Park is northeast of and signed from the main approach roads to Market Rasen. O.S.GR: TF117907.

Orchard Park Touring Park

395 Marnham Road, Tuxford NG22 0PY

This well established family run site has been created in an old fruit orchard in a quiet location. It has 65 pitches, including 28 with hardstanding, 20 of which were occupied by seasonal units at the time of our visit. All pitches have access to electricity (10A). Reception is at the owner's house and at the far end of the park is a children's play area with swings and slide, a grassy area for ball games and a nature walk with wild flowers, birds and butterflies. Local attractions include Tuxford Windmill, Sundown Adventureland children's theme park, Laxton Medieval village and Victorian Times, with its working horse-drawn carriage driving centre, at nearby Kirton.

Facilities: The specially designed toilet unit (with piped music) has the usual facilities including a well equipped room for disabled persons. Laundry with washing machines, dryer and sinks. Two dishwashing sinks outside. Small shop with basic essentials and gas; more services (some open to 10 pm) are in the village (0.5 miles). Children's play area. New entrance barrier (£5 deposit for key).

Charges 2002

Per unit incl. 2 adults	£7.50 - £8.00
extra adult	£1.00
child (4-15 yrs)	£0.50
electricity	£1.50
extra motorcycle or car	£1.00
awning or child's pup tent	£1.00

Tel: 01777 870228. Fax: 01777 870320. E-mail: info@orchardcaravanpark.co.uk. **Reservations:** Advised for B.Hs (min. 3 nights) and peak season with £10 deposit. **Open** March - October.

Directions: From the A1 turn onto A6075 towards Lincoln, continue through village to the eastern outskirts, turning right towards High Marnham. Site is on right 0.5 miles after railway bridge (well signed in village). O.S.GR: SK750710.

Riverside Caravan Park

Central Avenue, Worksop S80 1ER

392

A town centre touring park, adjacent to the County cricket ground, this excellent site is attractive and surprisingly peaceful. Riverside is within easy walking distance of the town centre pedestrian precinct and shops, and the Chesterfield Canal runs close to its northern side offering delightful tow-path walks or fishing (children would need to be watched). For those who cannot resist the thwack of leather on willow, this site is ideal. Of the 60 marked level pitches, 50 are on gravel hardstanding, some separated by trees and low rails, and all have electric hook-ups (10A). There is excellent site lighting. This is also a good base for exploring Creswell Craggs, Clumber Park, the Dukeries Cycle Trail, and Rufford Mill Craft Centre and Country Park.

Facilities: The modern sanitary unit near reception can be heated and has all the usual facilities, although showers are on payment (20p). There is no laundry, but a launderette is close by in the town. **Off site:** Activities available locally include squash, flat or crown green bowling, bicycle hire and campers are also very welcome at the cricket ground clubhouse. Worksop provides well for golfers with three courses in the area. One of the town's most interesting buildings, the medieval Priory Gatehouse, is open free of charge. Market days are Wednesday, Friday and Saturday.

Charges 2002

Per adult	£3.50 - £4.00
electricity	£2.00
child (5-16 yrs)	£1.50
awning	£1.00

No credit cards. **Tel:** 01909 474118. **Reservations:** Advised for B.Hs, peak season and weekends, with £5 deposit. **Open** all year.

Directions: Easiest approach is from roundabout west of the town (A57) - third roundabout from the A1, junction of A57/A60. Turn into Newcastle Avenue, then left into Stubbing Lane, right into Central Avenue, left into Cricket Ground, follow through to camping site (well signed). O.S.GR: SK580790.

Smeaton's Lakes Touring Caravan Park

Great North Road, South Muskham, Newark-on-Trent NG23 6ED

394

This 82-acre site is really ideal for fishermen, with three fishing lakes (coarse, carp and pike) and river fishing on the Trent. Smeaton's Lakes is a new site with tarmac access roads and a modern building near the entrance housing reception and the sanitary facilities (quite a walk from some of the pitches). Ground maintenance is good and there are now 130 pitches on grass, 48 with hardstanding (more to come) and 76 with electricity connections (16A). This site is probably the best choice for visiting events at nearby Newark Showground, or Newark town (1 mile) with its castle and various weekly markets. The park is only two minutes from DMG Newark Antique Fairs and Arthur Swallow's Swinderby Antique Fairs. It is also well placed for visiting Southwell Cathedral, Lincoln with its castle and cathedral or Nottingham with its Lace Hall, Castle or Caves and, for people who like to look at motorhomes, Brownhills is nearby.

Facilities: Toilet facilities (with keypad access) are heated and include a good unit for disabled people, but no laundry room. Laundry and dishwashing sinks are outside. At busy times these facilities could be stretched. Reception keeps gas, soft drinks, dairy produce, etc. and newspapers can be ordered. On site concessions for lake and river fishing. Security cameras and night-time height barrier (about 6 ft). **Off site:** Bus stop is at the end of the entry lane and buses run into Newark every hour until 10 pm.

Charges 2002

Per unit incl. 2 adults	£8.50 - £9.50
extra adult	£1.00 - £1.50
child (over 5 yrs)	£0.75 - £1.00
electricity	£2.00 - £2.50

No credit cards. **Tel:** 01636 605088. Fax: 01636 704076. **Reservations:** Essential for electric hook-ups. **Open** all year.

Directions: Site lies on A6065 west of the town, south of junction of A616 towards Ollerton (well signed). O.S.GR: SK792558.

Shardaroba Caravan Park

391 Silverhill Lane, Teversal, Sutton-in-Ashfield NG17 3JJ

In a peaceful village location, and yet surprising close to the motorway network, this attractive, six acre campsite has 100 pitches in total and takes around 25 seasonal and 75 touring units. Many of the spacious touring pitches are on hardstandings, arranged in well spaced rows surrounded by areas of grass and flower beds. All have electric hook-ups (10A), and 20 are multi-serviced (electricity, water and waste water). Picnic tables are provided around the site, and the facilities are housed in modern buildings grouped to one side of the site near the entrance. Adjacent to the site is a recently developed country park, with footpaths, cycle and bridleways, and hundreds of newly planted trees - an ideal place for a picnic. If you walk to the top of the hill you will reach the highest point in Nottinghamshire and on a clear day you can see five counties. The nearby Carnarvon Arms pub is a short walk away and serves good value meals. A bakery, chip shop and general stores are about 1 mile, and more comprehensive facilities including a swimming and fitness complex are in Mansfield (4 miles). There is an hourly bus service from the pub into the town.

Facilities: Excellent, well equipped, heated sanitary unit includes spacious showers, a family room with facilities for disabled people, and a utility room. Separate laundry has washing machines and dryers, plus dishwashing sinks. The latest addition for 2002 is an extra building (also heated) with three full suites (WC, basin, shower) per sex, with more dishwashing sinks under cover to the rear. Drive over motorcaravan service point. Calor gas. Shop with basic essentials. Children's playground. Bicycle hire. Tourist information chalet. **Off site:** Nearby attractions include Teversal Visitor Centre, Hardwick Hall, The Hardwick Inn (good restaurant), Crich Tramway Museum, Newstead Abbey, and the Pleasley Trails. Golf 800 yds. Riding 200 yds. Fishing 1 mile.

Charges 2002

Per adult	£4.00
child (3-14 yrs)	£2.00
facilities and electricity	£2.00
facilities only	£1.00
awning	£1.00

Tel: 01623 551838. Fax: 01623 552174. E-mail: stay@shardaroba.co.uk. **Reservations:** Advisable for B.Hs and July/August. Made with £10 non-refundable deposit. **Open** all year.

Directions: Teversal is central in a triangle formed by M1 jcn. 28 and jcn. 29, and Mansfield. Site is signed off B6014 at western end of the village, turning north by the Carnarvon Arms, into Silverhill Lane and site entrance is 300 yds on left. O.S.GR: SK485625.

Darwin Forest Country Park

382 Darley Moor, Two Dales, Matlock DE4 5LN

Between Matlock and Bakewell, this park, as its name implies, is set amongst 44 acres of mixed woodland close to the Peak District National Park. A large proportion of the park is given over to pine lodges for holiday letting and it is still expanding, but it also provides 50 touring pitches. All with hardstanding and electric hook-up (16A), they are clearly defined with hedging or open fencing in level grass bays amongst the woodland which is home to a variety of birds and wildlife. The pleasant Forester's Inn provides meals and a beer garden. The indoor swimming pool has a railed off section for children, spectator area and terrace, with good changing and shower facilities (see charges below). This is a useful park from which to explore the picturesque towns and villages of the Peak District. The Peak District Steam Railway currently operates a two mile section from Darley Dale to Matlock Riverside.

Facilities: The timberclad toilet block is tiled and well equipped, although WC cubicles are rather small. Washbasins in cabins, free hairdryers, a full unit for disabled people, laundry room and covered washing up area. Small shop for basics and Calor gas. Inn. Heated indoor pool (40 x 20 ft) - charges: adult £1.00 - £2.50, child (4-14 yrs) 50p - £1.50. Children's adventure play area on bark. Games room with snooker and pool tables. Tennis court, short-tennis. Minigolf. Soft playroom. **Off site:** Fishing 2 miles, bicycle hire 8 miles, riding 2 miles, golf 4 miles. Chatsworth House 4 miles, Alton Towers 40 minutes.

Charges 2002

Per unit incl. all persons: Fri. and Sat. nights	£12.00
other nights	£10.00 - £12.00
awning	£2.00
electricity	£2.00 - £2.50

Tel: 01629 732428. Fax: 01629 735015. E-mail: admin@darwinforest.co.uk. **Reservations:** Advised and made with deposit. **Open** March - October.

Directions: Park is best approached via the A632 Chesterfield - Matlock road. North of Matlock take B5057 signed Darley Dale and park is on the right before descending into the village of Two Dales. O.S.GR: SK287633.

Rivendale Caravan & Leisure Park

Buxton Road, Alsop-en-le-Dale, Ashbourne DE6 1QU

When we first visited this new park in the Peak National Park at the invitation of the owners we were immediately struck by the size of the project they had taken on. Now five years later, they are very near to achieving their goal of being one of the premier sites in the Peaks National Park. The reception, shop, bar and restaurant are now up and running (including an excellent breakfast). Located in an old quarry, the park provides 100 pitches with hardstanding, 80 of which have 16A electrical hook ups. Set out in small groups with names such as 'Little Delving' or 'Crickhollow', each pitch is separated from its neighbour and some have a grass area. Up to 40 tents and other units can be taken on a separate grassy area (metal tent pegs advised but drainage good). The touring park will eventually take up about 11 acres of the total land space of 37. An environmental pond has been completed (fenced for safety) and tress and plants around the site are maturing to add character. Take a walk in the meadow area to appreciate the wild flowers and the views. The park is situated almost on The Tissington Trail offering walking and off road cycling and with the Peak National Park on hand and towns such Ashbourne, Bakewell and even Buxton nearby, there is lots to do and see here. The A515 is a busy road and some traffic noise is to be expected early and late.

Facilities: The sanitary facilities are first rate with under-floor heating, some washbasins in cubicles for ladies, and an excellent en-suite room for disabled visitors. Laundry room. Glass and paper recycling binc. Bar (evenings) and café (mornings, lunch times and evenings, both with limited opening in low season). Special events and games in main season. Shop (all essentials). **Off site:** Riding 3 miles, fishing 5 miles, bicycle hire 2.5 miles.

Charges 2002

Per pitch incl. 2 adults	£7.60 - £9.80
extra person (over 3 yrs)	£1.00
electricity	£2.20
pitch with water connection plus	£2.70
tent pitch on field	£6.80
extra car	£1.00
awning	£1.50
dog	£0.75

Tel: 01332 843000. Fax: 01332 842311. E-mail: rivendale@fsmail.net. **Reservations:** Made with £10 deposit. **Open** all year excl. February.

Directions: Park is about 6.5 miles north of Ashbourne on the A515 road to Buxton (14 miles south of Buxton). Pass right turns to Alsop station and village and site is clearly signed to the right a little further on. Care should be taken as this is a very fast section of the A515. O.S.GR: SK161566.

Beautiful surroundings in the Peak District National Park. Open all year except February. Ideal for cycling, walking, outdoor and adventure sports. Convenient for Chatsworth, Alton Towers & Dove Dale. Holiday homes for sale.

www.Rivendalecaravanpark.co.uk Tel: +44 (0)1335 310311 or 310441

Highfields Holiday Caravan Park

380 Fenny Bentley, Ashbourne DE6 1LE

Highfields is set on high, flat ground in the Peak District National Park with marvellous views. Run by the Redfern family, it takes 50 touring units and 50 seasonal vans in open, hedged fields accessed by tarmac roads. There is an area for tents, another for vans with concrete slabs for jockey wheels and an area for adults only. There are 8 hardstandings and 89 electrical connections (16A), with 55 privately owned caravan holiday homes in separate fields. An indoor, heated swimming pool is open all season (with restricted opening times if the park is not very full), with a small charge. Although not supervised at all times, the pool is monitored from reception by closed circuit TV. A room, complete with in-built barbecue, table and chairs, is available for hire. People frequently venture off the site to enjoy the Peak District - Dovedale and Ilam are only a mile or two's distance by footpath and the Tissington Trail with access to the High Peak Trail passes by the park.

Facilities: The main toilet block is kept locked (deposit for key) and is well maintained. Hot water is metered for laundry and dishwashing, and to the showers. Baby bath. A smaller block is in the far static field and further sanitary facilities are provided adjacent to the rally room. All blocks are heated when necessary. Shop for basics and gas. Good children's playground with new rubber base. Bicycle hire. Swimming pool (90p per session). American motorhomes accepted. Winter caravan storage. Torches are useful. **Off site:** Pub and restaurant close. Fishing 3 miles, golf 5 miles, riding 2 miles, boat launching 5 miles.

Charges 2002

Per unit incl. 2 persons	£10.00
extra adult	£3.00
child (under 17 yrs)	£1.00
electricity	£2.50
awning	£1.00
dog	£1.00

Tel: 0870 741 8000. Fax: 0870 741 2000. **Reservations:** Made with payment of one night's fee; min. stay at B.Hs - 3 nights. **Open** 1 March - 31 October.

Directions: Park is west off A515 Buxton - Ashbourne road, just north of Fenny Bentley village and just south of old railway bridge (take care at sharp turn to site road when approaching from Ashbourne). O.S.GR: SK170510.

Lime Tree Park

384 Dukes Drive, Buxton SK17 9RP

A select park with high quality, modern facilities, Lime Tree is in a convenient, edge of town location that makes a very good base for touring the Peak District. There are 99 pitches including some for seasonal and rental units. The 64 for tourists with 10A electricity (hardstandings available) and an area for tents are on the two upper terraces which have the best views and are slightly more exposed. Below are areas set aside for late arrivals and the caravan holiday homes (most privately owned, some for rent). On site is a small shop for gas and basics, and a recently extended children's playground. Buxton town centre is a comfortable stroll away. A member of the Best of British group.

Facilities: A modern toilet building serves the caravan and motorcaravan area, complete with patio and pergola frontage, whilst the refitted original unit serves the tent area. Both units can be heated and have top quality fittings, including washbasins (some in cubicles), a baby room with the very latest design of baby bath, and a family room with facilities for disabled people. Dishwashing sinks are outside under cover. Laundry room with washing machine and dryer. Motorcaravan service area. Shop. Children's play area. Games/TV room. **Off site:** The nearest pub serving food is just around the corner. Fishing, bicycle hire, riding and golf, all within 5 miles. Alton Towers is 22 miles.

Charges 2002

Per unit incl. 2 adults	£8.50 - £11.00
extra adult	£1.50
extra child (5-15 yrs)	£0.75
hiker, cyclist or m/cyclist	£3.75 - £4.50
electricity	£2.00
dog	£0.75

Tel: 01298 22988. Fax: 01298 22988. **Reservations:** Made with £10 deposit. **Open** 1 March - 31 October.

Directions: From Buxton take A515 Ashbourne road south. After the hospital on the outskirts of town, turn sharp left into Dukes Drive, go under railway viaduct and site is on the right. O.S.GR: SK069725.

Longnor Woods Caravan and Camping Park

398 Longnor, Buxton SK17 0NG

A secluded rural location, deep in the heart of the Peak District, Lognor Wood is an ideal environment for a relaxing break from the outside world. Actually located in Staffordshire, it is a good base for walking, red deer and bird watching (barn owls) and serious cycling - the area is very hilly. There are 47 pitches, of which 12 are taken by holiday homes, the remaining 33 touring pitches are level, some on small terraces, all with 16A electric hook-ups. Fourteen are multi-serviced with electricity, water, waste water and TV connections. Some are on hardstandings. The tenting area is at the top of the site with wonderful views over the National Park, but you may have a problem with tent pegs as the topsoil can be rather thin in places. Sight-seeing opportunities include Dovedale and the Manifold Valley, Arbor Low Stone Circle, and Flash, at 1,580 ft. is the highest village in England. Reception has a brochure with the history of the old market town of Longnor, which includes several places worth visiting. This is an adult only park (over 18 yrs).

Facilities: The single heated building has been recently refurbished, and includes cubicles with a toilet and washbasin, spacious showers (on payment), and has dishwashing sinks under cover. Laundry with washing machine, dryer, spinner and also a microwave cooker (donations to charity). Reception is licensed and stocks basic requirements. Gas supplies. Putting green, croquet, boules court. Dogs accepted, max. 2 per unit. Site is not suitable for American RVs. **Off site:** Markets in Buxton (Tues/Sat), Leek (Wed). Fishing 5 miles, golf 8 miles, riding 8 miles.

Charges 2002

Per unit	£6.00
person	£1.50
electricity	£1.50
awning (with groundsheet)	£1.50

No credit cards. **Tel:** 01298 83648. E-mail: leek@ rwedd.fsbusiness. co.uk. **Reservations:** Advisable for weekends, B.Hs and peak season. Made with £10 deposit. **Open** Easter - 31 October.

Directions: Longnor village is on the B5053, about 6 miles south of Buxton. Site is west of village (where it is signed) on a minor road (1 mile). Also signed from the A53 between Leek and Buxton, turning opposite the 'Winking Man' public house. O.S.GR: SK072640.

Glencote Caravan Park

397 Station Road, Cheddleton, Leek ST13 7EE

At the entrance to the Churnet Valley, three miles south of the market town, Glencote is a pleasant, family run park of six acres. It has 68 numbered pitches set on flat grass, 50 with patio style hardstandings, with tarmac access roads. There are 30 pitches for touring units and all have electrical connections (10A) and a dedicated water supply. Pretty flower-beds and trees make a very pleasant environment. An attractive, sunken children's play area, on grass and bark with an abundance of shrubs and flowers, sits alongside the small (fenced) coarse fishing pool, together with a barbecue area with a tented cover. Attractions nearby include a renovated Flint Mill powered by two giant water wheels and Cheddleton railway centre. The Churnet Valley, an Area of Outstanding Natural Beauty is good for walking, the Staffordshire Way is also near. For the more energetic, canoeing and hang gliding opportunities are close. Alton Towers is 10 miles (you may leave your unit on site after 3 pm. for an additional £2 charge).

Facilities: The toilet block is centrally situated and can be heated. Facilities include one private cabin for ladies, a small laundry room, and two dish-washing sinks under cover. Gas supplies. Max. 2 dogs per unit. **Off site:** In the village of Cheddleton, 0.5 miles away, is a small supermarket and a post office. A variety of inns are within easy walking distance - the Boat Inn beside the canal is very good value. Riding 10 miles, bicycle hire 5 miles, golf 4 miles.

Charges 2002

Per unit incl. 2 persons	£10.00
extra adult	£2.00
child (under 16 yrs)	£1.50
pup tent or extra car	£1.00
electricity	£1.80

For each 7 nights booked, one night free (except electricity).Min. stay of 3 nights at B.Hs. **Tel:** 01538 360745. Fax: 01538 361788. **Reservations:** Advised for peak season and made with deposit of £18 (2 nights) or £25 (over 2 nights). **Open** Easter - end October

Directions: Park is signed off A520 Leek - Stone road, 3.5 miles south of Leek on northern edge of Cheddleton Village. O.S.GR: SJ982524.

Silvertrees Caravan Park

396 Stafford Brook Road, Penkridge Bank, Rugeley WS15 2TX

Silvertrees, as its name suggests, is in a beautiful wooded setting with many silver birches on the edge of Cannock Chase, but it only takes caravans and motorhomes. In the evenings the deer roam down the little valley in which the site is situated and there is evidence of much more animal and bird life - the park is actually designated a Site of Special Scientific Interest (SSSI). Of the older style, it comprises three paddock areas with 80 mobile homes (most privately owned), plus 40 touring pitches on sloping grass. Double paving stones for the main wheels mark each pitch - chocks would be useful. All pitches have 10A electrical connections. The park is set in 20 acres of woodland adjoining the natural heathland of the chase so there is plenty to do. The owners live on site. There is a little library and useful tourist information in the games room. A member of the Countryside Discovery group. Note: tents are not accepted.

Facilities: The small toilet block can be heated and provides two showers each for men and women (20p) with shared changing area, laundry and dishwashing sink, and a washing machine and dryer. It could be under pressure at B.Hs. Small, unheated fun pool (3 ft deep, open May - Sept) in the valley bottom. Good tennis court, adventure play area, ball field. Games room with table tennis, video games, TV and an unusual ceiling. Gas supplies. Barbecues must be raised off the ground. Only certain breeds of dog are accepted. **Off site:** Fishing 1 mile, riding 6 miles, golf 3 miles. Supermarket 2 miles. Bus service outside park. Pub with food within walking distance. Alton Towers is nearby.

Charges 2002
Per pitch incl. 2 persons, electricity	£9.00 - £11.00
extra person	£1.20
awning	£2.00

Credit cards accepted (+3%). **Tel:** 01889 582185. Fax: 01889 582185. E-mail: enquiries@silvertrees caravanpark.co.uk. **Reservations:** Made with £20 deposit and essential at B.Hs. (when min. 3 nights). **Open** April - October.

Directions: Park is 2 miles from Rugeley just off the Penkridge - Rugeley road. It is signed from Rugeley off the A51. O.S.GR: SK014173.

Bosworth Water Trust

390 Far Coton Lane, Market Bosworth, Nuneaton CV13 6PD

Essentially designed for the watersport enthusiast, the camping area at Bosworth has 80 pitches on mostly level grass with electricity (6/10A) available to 45 and hardstanding for 6. This RYA recognised centre offers a range of watersports - dinghy and board sailing, canoeing, rowing and fishing (swimming is not advised in the lake). Tuition is available for all watersports activities - lifejackets and wet suits can be hired - and there is a 'Kids Club' every Saturday (call site for brochure). On arrival you will need £2 to operate the Centre's entrance barrier. Local attractions include Snibston Discovery Park, Twycross Zoo, Mallory Park motor racing circuit, steam trains and the battlefields.

Facilities: The good quality, heated toilet facilities in the main building are designed more for the watersports users, with communal showers and changing area, however a new, substantial log cabin unit was built in 2002 to provide facilities for the touring pitches. It can be heated and includes 3 showers per sex, vanity style washbasins. Dishwashing facilities under cover will be installed for 2003. Reception serves a good range of snacks, soft drinks, ices, etc. Gas available. Fishing and lake fees: 50% discount for campers. Torches advised. **Off site:** Riding 1 mile, golf 0.5 miles.

Charges 2002
Per unit incl. all persons	£8.00
electricity	£2.00
awning	£1.00
pup tent	£2.00
extra car	£1.00

No credit cards. **Tel:** 01455 291876. Fax: 01455 291876. E-mail: ingo@bosworthwatertrust.co.uk. **Reservations:** Advised for B.Hs, school holidays and peak season. **Open** all year.

Directions: Site is off B585 about 1 mile west of Market Bosworth. O.S.GR: SK370020.

Somers Wood Caravan & Camping Park

Somers Road, Meriden CV7 7PL

Somers Wood is a useful site near the NEC, open all year for adults only. It is attractively located and edged by pine woods, with views of the adjacent 18 hole golf course (including driving range) and coarse fishing lake, both being available for visitors to use. Log buildings that blend comfortably into their surroundings provide reception, with the owners' home at the entrance and separate sanitary facilities. An oval, gravel road provides access to the 48 large pitches, all on hardstanding with 10A electricity connections. This is a very useful park for those visiting the NEC. For certain shows, such as the Boat, Caravan and Leisure Show in February, it can be busy, although at other times it is quiet and peaceful. Only adults are accepted.

Facilities: The central, heated sanitary block is fully equipped. Two dishwashing sinks are on the veranda area. Laundry service at reception. Rally field available. **Off site:** Local shops and restaurant less than 1 mile and visitors also welcome to use the bar and restaurant at the golf club.

Charges 2002

Per pitch incl. 2 persons and electricity	£15.00
over 50s pitch fee (excl. exhibitions)	£13.00
extra adult	£3.00

No credit cards. **Tel:** 01676 522978. Fax: 01676 522978. E-mail: info@somerswood.com. **Reservations:** Advised for B.Hs and certain NEC exhibitions; made with deposit of £5 per night booked. **Open** all year.

Directions: From M42 junction 6 (NEC) take A45 towards Coventry. Almost immediately, on left-hand side, take A452 signed Leamington. Turn right at roundabout on A452 then turn left into Hampton Lane at the next roundabout, signed Stonebridge Golf Centre and site is signed with golf and fishing centres on the left. O.S.GR: SP228819.

Riverside Caravan Park

Tiddington Road, Tiddington, Stratford-upon-Avon CV37 7AB

On the bank of the River Avon, this spacious site has about 250 pitches in total, and about 100 privately owned mobile homes. The 150 touring pitches are on level grass, with 100 electric hook-ups (16A), and some have TV aerial sockets. There is a small shop and cafe on site, which serves breakfasts and takeaways in addition to stocking a good selection of basic supplies. A clubhouse that incorporates a bar, restaurant, children's playground, games room and TV room is on the adjacent Rayford Park which is under the same management. There is a possible flood risk during periods of inclement weather. A courtesy river launch runs to Stratford.

Facilities: The main toilet unit has been re-fitted to modern standards, and is bright and comfortable with heating. Utility room with dishwashing and laundry sinks, washing machines and dryers. Facilities for disabled guests planned for 2003. Slipway and fishing on-site. Gas supplies. **Off site:** Tiddington village has a PO/stores, pub with meals, restaurants, etc. Golf 2 miles.

Charges 2002

Per caravan or motorcaravan incl. 4 persons	£9.50
tent or trailer tent	£5.00 - £9.00
extra person	£1.00
electricity	£2.50
dog	£1.00

Tel: 01789 292312. Fax: 01789 415330. E-mail: info@stratfordcaravans.co.uk. **Reservations:** Advisable for weekends, BHs, and peak season and made with £10 deposit. **Open** 1 April - 31 October.

Directions: From Stratford take B4086 towards Wellesbourne. Site entrance is on left, after one mile, just before Tiddington village (ignore entrance to Rayford Park). O.S.GR: SP219559.

Island Meadow Caravan Park

The Mill House, Aston Cantlow B95 6JP

This peaceful, traditional, family run site is in a rural location, surrounded by the River Alne and its mill race. A good base for walking, cycling and birdwatching, it has 80 pitches in total, with 56 holiday homes (4 for rent) located around the perimeter. The 24 touring pitches are on the spacious, central grassy area of the site, all have 10A electric hook-ups. Only environ- mentally friendly groundsheets are permitted. The millpond and its weir offer good coarse fishing. Note: The site is on an island with obvious hazards for small children. There is a good playground in the village centre (five minutes walk via footpath across Mill Meadow).

Facilities: Two heated sanitary units - the original with adequate WCs and washbasins for men, the more modern unit for women, with a separate shower unit for men, and a suite for disabled people on one end. Dishwashing sink. Washing machine and iron. Small shop. Gas supplies. Fishing. **Off site:** Golf 3 miles, riding 2 miles, bicycle hire 6 miles.

Charges 2002

Per unit incl. 2 persons	£11.50
extra person	£0.50 - £1.00
electricity	£2.50

Gazebos only by prior arrangement. No credit cards. **Tel:** 01789 488276. Fax: 01789 488273. E-mail: holiday@islandmeadowcaravanpark.co.uk. **Reservations:** Advised for B.Hs (3 nights minimum), and July/August. **Open** 1 March - 31 October.

Directions: Site is well signed from the A46 mid- way between Alcester and Stratford-upon-Avon, and also from the A3400 at Wootton Wawen. O.S.GR: SP136598.

Clent Hills Camping & Caravanning Club Site

404 Fieldhouse Lane, Romsley, Halesowen B62 0NH

Conveniently close to Birmingham and only a couple of miles or so off the M5/M42 intersection, this site is a real surprise in terms of being quiet and peaceful and very pretty with good views. Its only disadvantage is that it is on sloping ground, but the present, very helpful wardens are happy to assist in pitching anyone who has a problem in getting level (mainly motorcaravanners); in fact, there are some level pitches and these are all earmarked for motorcaravans. The 115 pitches are all of a good size, 74 with electrical connections (10/16A) and 17 with hardstanding. The modern reception building with excellent tourist information, arrivals area and larger car parking area are at the entrance. Generally this is a well run and attractive site, very usefully situated.

Facilities: The central sanitary toilet block can be heated and provides the latest facilities, including washbasins in cabins, hairdryers, baby room and a toilet and shower for disabled people. It was spotless when last visited. Washing machine, dryer and ironing facilities. Small children's play area with rubber safety surface. Gas supplies. Caravan storage. **Off site:** Fishing 3 miles, riding 1 mile.

Charges 2002

Per adult	£3.75 - £5.30
child (6-18 yrs)	£1.65
non-member pitch fee	£4.30
electricity	£1.65 - £2.40

Tel: 01562 710015. **Reservations:** Necessary and made with deposit; contact site. **Open** March - October.

Directions: From M5 junction 4 take A491, branch right to Romsley on B4551 and watch for site signs in Romsley village by shops. Site is on left. O.S.GR: SO955795.

Fernwood Caravan Park

438 Lyneal, Ellesmere SY12 0QF

Fernwood is set in a lovely area known as the Shropshire 'Lake District' - the mere at Ellesmere is the largest of nine meres - and the picturesque Shropshire Union Canal is only a few minutes walk. The park itself is a real oasis of calm and rural tranquillity with its floral landscaping, the setting and the attention to detail, all of a very high standard with planted and natural vegetation blending harmoniously. In addition to 165 caravan holiday homes, used normally only by their owners, the park takes 60 caravans, motorcaravans or trailer tents (but not other tents) in several well cut, grassy enclosures (plus 27 seasonal long stay). Some are in light woodland, others in more open, but still relatively sheltered situations. All 60 pitches have electricity. One area is set aside for adults only. Siting is carried out by management - there is always generous spacing, even when the site is full.

Facilities: The refurbished toilet block for tourers can be heated and includes a unit for disabled people, but no dishwashing sinks. Motorcaravan service points. Well tiled laundry room near the shop and adjacent are WCs for ladies and men. Small shop doubling as reception (open from 1 April, sometimes limited hours). Coarse fishing lake. Forty acres of woodland for walking. Children's play area on grass.

Charges 2002

Per unit incl. electricity	£11.00 - £15.00
awning	free - £1.75
extra car	free - £1.00

Tel: 01948 710221. Fax: 01948 710324. E-mail: fernwood@caravanpark37.fsnet.co.uk. **Reservations:** Necessary for peak season and B.Hs (min. 3 nights) with deposit of £5 per night. **Open** 1 March - 30 November.

Directions: Park is just northeast of Lyneal village, signed southwest off the B5063 Ellesmere - Wem road, about 1.5 miles from junction of the B5063 with the A495. O.S.GR: SJ453338.

FERNWOOD — CARAVAN PARK

LYNEAL NR. ELLESMERE SHROPSHIRE SY12 0QF

- ● ESTABLISHED FAMILY-RUN PARK
- ● PEACEFUL WOODLAND SETTING
- ● TOURERS WELCOME
- ● ALL PITCHES HAVE ELECTRICAL HOOK-UPS
- ● PICTURESQUE LAKE
- ● CHILDRENS PLAY AREA
- ● SHOP
- ● LAUNDRY

www.ranch.co.uk/fernwood.htm
TEL: (01948) 710221

Severn Gorge Park

Bridgnorth Road, Tweedale, Telford TF7 4JB

This six acre touring park, in a woodland setting, has 51 pitches, all with electricity hook ups (10/16A), and 40 with hardstanding (including a few seasonal tourers). A development of park homes has been constructed on one side of the park and a new tent area was opened for 2002. There could be some road noise from the A442 which runs down one boundary. A barrier is locked at 11.45 pm, but parking and a late arrivals area is outside. The main local attraction has to be the Ironbridge Museums, featuring the Blists Mill Victorian Town, where you can discover and enjoy a working Victorian town. Hawkstone Park, with its walks and follies, is very popular and the Cosford Aerospace Museum is essential visiting for those interested in aviation.

Facilities: The sanitary buildings can be heated and have been upgraded to provide comprehensive facilities including facilities for disabled visitors and a baby room, plus a dishwashing conservatory leading to an ample laundry (8 am - 9 pm). Motorcaravan service points. Small, limited shop (8.30 am - 5.30 pm daily). Gas supplies. Small play area. Kite flying is discouraged because of nearby overhead cables. **Off site:** Two pubs within walking distance, one with a tempting menu. Golf 1 mile, riding 3 miles.

Charges 2002

Per unit	£3.70 - £4.40
adult	£2.70 - £3.25
child (5-15 yrs)	£1.10 - £1.35
awning	£1.10
dog (max 2)	£1.10
electricity	£2.45 - £2.75

Tel: 01952 684789. Fax: 01952 684789. E-mail: info@severngorgepark.co.uk. **Reservations:** Contact park for details. **Open** all year.

Directions: From M54 junction 4 follow signs (A442) onto the A442 signed Kidderminster. Take slip road signed Bridgnorth to Brockton roundabout, turn right and pick up park signs. O.S.GR: SJ704052.

Westbrook Park

Little Hereford, Ludlow SY8 4AU

A beautifully kept, traditional, quiet touring campsite in a 'working' cider apple orchard, Westbrook Park is bordered on one side by the River Teme and within walking distance of the village and pub. The 52 level pitches with 6A electric hook-ups, are mostly on well mown grass, but there are several hardstandings. Five are also multi-serviced with electricity, water and waste water, and satellite TV hook-ups are available to all pitches (leads for rent). A footpath along the river bank in one direction leads to the Temeside Inn which serves hot meals. Local attractions include Burford House Gardens, Croft Castle, and the market towns of Tenbury Wells, Leominster, Ludlow.

Facilities: A modern timber clad sanitary block provides spacious hot showers (20p for 5 mins), washbasins in curtained cubicles. Washing machine, dryer and dishwashing sinks. Limited facilities for disabled people (WC and basin) - the current steps need to be replaced with a ramp. Playground. Fishing (£3 per day). Gas available. Caravan storage. Gazebos and bicycles are not permitted. **Off site:** Golf 3 miles. Riding and bicycle hire 5 miles.

Charges 2002

Per unit incl. 2 adults	£8.00 - £12.00
extra person	£0.50 - £1.00
electricity	£1.75
dog	£0.50

Min. B.H. stay 3 nights. **Tel:** 01584 711280. Fax: 01584 711460. **Reservations:** Advised for B.Hs (min. 3 nights) and made with £10 deposit. **Open** all year.

Directions: From A49 mid-way between Ludlow and Leominster, turn east at Woofferton on A456 signed Tenbury Wells, Kidderminster. In 2 miles turn right just before bridge over river. Turn left after 150 yds, to site on left. O.S.GR: SU547679.

The Green Caravan Park

Wentnor, Bishop's Castle SY9 5EF

Remotely situated in a pleasant valley, in a designated 'area of outstanding natural beauty', and sandwiched between the Stipperstones and The Long Mynd, the Green would make an ideal base for some serious walking or cycling. The 15 acre site is very natural, and is divided into several fields. There are 140 pitches, taking 40 seasonal units, and around 20 holiday homes, with approximately 80 pitches for tourists. The main field has some hardstandings, but there are only 28 electric hook-ups (16A). The East Onny is a small, shallow river which runs through the site, much enjoyed by the youngsters, who can spend many hours catching minnows.

Facilities: One main sanitary block, rather austere in appearance, but providing fairly modern facilities with spacious showers (on payment), dishwashing and laundry facilities, but no dedicated unit for disabled people. Well stocked shop with reception. Playground. **Off site:** Fishing 3 miles.

Charges 2002

Per unit incl. 2 persons	£7.00
extra adult	£2.00
child (3-14 yrs)	£1.25
dog	£0.50

Tel: 01588 650605. E-mail: info@greencaravanpark. co.uk. **Reservations:** Made with £10 deposit for min 3 or 4 days for B.Hs. **Open** Easter - 31 October.

Directions: From Shrewsbury take A488 south for 21 miles. At Lydham Heath turn east on A489, then turn north on minor road (signed Wentnor and site). Follow signs for 3 miles to site just after 'The Inn on the Green'. O.S.GR: SO378933.

Beaconsfield Farm Caravan Park

441 Battlefield, Shrewsbury SY4 4AA

Just north of the historic market town, a neat stone entrance and a tarmac drive of half a mile through open fields lead to this purpose-designed park for adults only. Neatly laid out in a rural situation, with a well stocked trout fishing lake and a small coarse pool forming the main feature, the ground has been levelled and grassed to provide 60 well spaced pitches, 25 'deluxe' hardstanding pitches with 16A electricity connections (with 10A hook-ups to the other pitches). The park is well lit with a circular tarmac access road. A large timber chalet-style building with a tiled Canadian maple roof provides reception and a coffee shop that is open during reception hours. A recent addition is the bowling green - use is free and woods may be hired by those without such essential caravanning kit. Limousins and pedigree Suffolk sheep graze in neighbouring fields and a 'park and ride' scheme operates nearby for those interested in Shrewsbury and its medieval past, bought to life by the Brother Cadfael novels. This is a top class park, maturing by the year. It is now 'adults only' (21 yrs) all year round. A member of the Best of British and the Countryside Discovery groups.

Facilities: Heated toilet facilities (£2 key deposit) are of excellent quality, with curtained, roomy, pre-set showers and free hairdryers. Dishwashing room, plus with washing machine, dryer, free irons and boards. Motorcaravan service point. Indoor heated swimming pool, available all year, with daily open sessions (£2.50 per person) and to hire privately at other times. Bowling green. Small library. Bicycle hire. Security barrier in operation. Only two dogs per unit are accepted. An 'adult only' park. **Off site:** Golf 2 miles. Riding 7 miles.

Charges 2002

Per grass pitch incl. unit, 2 persons	£8.00 - £10.50
hardstanding pitch£10.50	£12.50
extra adult	£4.00
electricity	£2.50
awning	£1.50
dog (max 2)	£0.75

No credit cards. Last arrivals 7 pm. (8 pm. Fridays). **Tel:** 01939 210370. Fax: 01939 210349. E-mail: mail@beaconsfield-farm.co.uk. **Reservations:** Advised for weekends, B.Hs and July/Aug. and made with £20 deposit. **Open** all year.

Directions: Site is north of Shrewsbury and off the A49 Whitchurch road just before the village of Hadnall. Turn opposite the New Inn at brown camping sign towards Astley and park entrance is 400 m. on right. O.S.GR: SJ523196.

Stanmore Hall Touring Park

Stourbridge Road, Bridgnorth WV15 6DT

This good quality park is situated in the former grounds of Stanmore Hall, where the site's huge lily pond, fine mature trees and beautifully manicured lawns give a mark of quality. Open views take precedence over maximising the number of units per square metre, with the result that all pitches are generously sized. In addition, caravans can be orientated in any direction, thus breaking the feeling of regimentation. There are 135 pitches, 130 with 16A electricity, 30 of which are hardstanding 'super pitches' with TV connections. A few standard hard-standing pitches are available, but most are on grass. Some pitches are reserved for adult only use (over 21). Reception is located within the shop. The adjacent conservatory and patio overlook the lake, which accommodates everything from humbler ducks to the resident peacocks who strut proudly around their domain. But there's something else too; this is a peaceful site with personality. Little wonder it needs advance booking and people keep returning to enjoy its atmosphere. Open all year round, there are even groups who spend Christmas and New Year at Stanmore Hall. The Severn Valley is full of interest - Bridgnorth nearby, the Clee Hills and Ironbridge Gorge Museum are just a few suggestions. The site is a member of the Caravan Club's 'managed under contract scheme' but non-members are also very welcome.

Facilities: Access to the centrally heated sanitary block is by key. Facilities are excellent and provide washbasins in cubicles and a room for disabled people (which includes equipment for baby care) demonstrating thoughtful design. Full laundry facilities. Motorcaravan service points. Licensed shop (open all year) is well stocked, including caravan accessories and repair items. Limited, bark based children's play area. Dogs are limited to two per unit. **Off site:** Fishing at Bridgnorth (1.5 miles), golf 2 miles.

Charges 2002

Per pitch	£4.00 - £4.75
adult	£4.00 - £4.75
child (5-15 yrs)	£1.65
full services	£2.50 - £3.00
electricity	£2.00 - £2.75
awning or pup tent	£1.25
dog (max. 2)	£1.00

Tel: 01746 761761. Fax: 01746 768069. E-mail: stanmore@morris-leisure.co.uk. **Reservations:** Advisable and made with £10 deposit. **Open** all year.

Directions: Site is 1.5 miles from Bridgnorth on the A458 (signed Stourbridge). O.S.GR: SO742923.

Oxon Hall Touring Park

Welshpool Road, Shrewsbury SY3 5FB

Oxon Hall is a purpose-built park, well situated for visiting Shrewsbury. It is under the same ownership as Stanmore Hall (no. 440) and has been developed from a green field site by an experienced park operator to a very high standard. The site has matured well and the trees and shrubs now provide some shade and shelter. Of the 120 pitches, half are all weather, full service pitches (fresh and waste water facilities, TV hook-up), the others being either grass or with hardstanding. An area is set aside as an 'adult only' section. All pitches have 16A electricity. Some extra long hardstandings are provided for American motorhomes. Entry to the park is controlled by electronic barriers. Virtually adjacent to the park is the Oxon 'park and ride' which makes a trip into Shrewsbury some 2 miles away very simple. The famous Ironbridge Gorge Museum and the mysteries of the Welsh Borders are all easy day trips from this excellent base.

Facilities: Toilet facilities here are first rate with washbasins in cubicles, ample showers, baby room, facilities for disabled visitors, dishwashing room and laundry, all situated at the entrance in a centrally heated building which also houses reception and the shop - perhaps a hike from some of the pitches. Motorcaravan service point. Up to two dogs are welcome per pitch. **Off site:** Golf, riding and fishing nearby.

Charges 2002

Per standard grass pitch	£4.00 - £4.75
adult	£4.00 - £4.75
child (5-15 yrs)	£1.65
awning or pup tent	£1.25
electricity	£2.00 - £2.75
'super pitch' plus	£2.50 - £3.00
dog (max 2)	£1.00

Tel: 01743 340868. Fax: 01743 340869. E-mail: oxon@morris-leisure.co.uk. **Reservations:** Made with £10 deposit. **Open** all year.

Directions: From junction of A5 and A458, west of Shrewsbury, follow signs for Oxon 'park and ride'. Park is signed just 0.5 miles from junction. O.S.GR: SJ455138.

Poston Mill Caravan Park

430 Peterchurch, Golden Valley HR2 0SF

Poston Mill Park is a pleasant, neat park in farmland a mile from Peterchurch in the heart of the Golden Valley. It offers 82 touring pitches set on level grass, including some very pleasant pitches near the River Dore, with mature trees and conifers around the perimeter. All pitches have electricity, water and TV connections (leads to hire), and 35 have waste water and sewage outlets. The park covers 33 acres and also has 80 caravan holiday homes. An attractive walk along one side of the park, edging the River Dore (fishing available), follows the line of the old Golden Valley railway and there is a footpath from the site over the fields. Next to the park is 'The Mill' restaurant for lunches, evening meals and takeaway. The restaurant also has a TV room and sells bread and milk. A member of the Best of British group.

Facilities: There is one central sanitary block with a smaller block near the holiday home area. Of reasonably modern construction and fully equipped, they include a unit for disabled people (toilet and basin only) and a baby changing room. Motor-caravan service point. Small, well equipped laundry room housing a campers' fridge and a freezer for ice packs. Gas supplies. Large children's play area. Pitch and putt. Tennis court. Petanque and croquet. Bicycle hire. Golf driving range. Football pitch. Games room with snooker and darts. Winter caravan storage. **Off site:** Peterchurch village is 1 mile. Riding 3 miles.

Charges 2002

Per unit incl. 2 adults and electricity	£10.00 - £14.00
incl. mains services and awning	£11.50 - £15.50
extra person	£1.00
child (3-10 yrs)	£0.50
dog	£0.50

Min. charge at B.Hs. 5 nights. **Tel:** 01981 550225. Fax: 01981 550885. E-mail: enquiries@poston-mill.co.uk. **Reservations:** Made with £10 deposit, min. 5 nights for B.Hs **Open** all year.

Directions: Park is 1 mile southeast of Peterchurch on the B4348 road. O.S.GR: SO356371.

Penlan Caravan Park

435 Apostles Lane, Brilley, Hay-on-Wye HR3 6JW

This is a tiny site with a big view, just 500 yards from the Welsh border. From the pitches you have a panoramic view of the Malvern Hills, Brecon Beacons and the Black Mountains, and on a really clear day you can even see the Cotswolds (about 60 miles). Indeed, it would be hard to find a more peaceful and unspoiled location - a real hideaway site on a National Trust land and run by the tenant farmer. The 12 pitches are arranged around the upper edge of a well mown south facing grass meadow, with 10 electric hook-ups (10A). Levelling blocks and a torch would be useful. Access is via narrow lanes, unsuitable for large units.

Facilities: A neat little wooden chalet (built 1997) houses the heated sanitary facilities. These include the usual WCs, a vanity style washbasin and well equipped shower per sex. **Off site:** Golf 5 miles.

Charges 2002

Per caravan or family tent	£8.00
1 or 2 person tent	£6.00
electricity	£2.00
awning	£1.00 - £2.00

No credit cards. **Tel:** 01497 831485. Fax: 01497 831485. **Reservations:** Essential and made with £10 deposit. **Open** Easter - 31 October.

Directions: From Leominster take A44 to Kington. Follow A44 towards Wales, passing two round-abouts on Kington bypass. After 0.75 miles turn left (signed Kington town centre, Hergest, Brilley). After 0.5 miles second left (signed Brilley, Hergest). After 4 miles look out for NT sign on left, and turn sharp left (Apostles Lane) signedBollingham. Site is 0.5 miles on a left hand bend. O.S.GR: SO275518.

Pearl Lake Leisure Park

434 Shobdon, Leominster HR6 9NQ

Principally, this is a large holiday home park spread over 80 acres, with some 150 units arranged around an attractive 15 acre lake. However, it does have a very small touring site with just 15 pitches, a modern sanitary unit, located at the park entrance adjacent to the road. Most of the pitches are on gravel hardstandings and are fully serviced, with electricity (10A), water and waste water connections. A variety of activities includes fishing (15 acre lake), golf and a bowling green. Places to visit include The Black and White Village Trail, Lingen Gardens and the churches of Wigmore Abbey Parish.

Facilities: The sanitary unit provides hot showers (25p) - we found them not easily controllable. Club with bar/restaurant (weekends only in low season). Fishing. 9-hole golf course. Bowling green. Play field and playground. **Off site:** Shobdon Village has a shop and pub. Riding 1 mile. Bicycle hire 2 miles.

Charges 2002

Per unit incl. 2 persons, electricity	£10.00 - £14.00
child	£0.50

Min. charge at B.Hs. 3 nights. **Tel:** 01568 708326. Fax: 01568 708408. E-mail: enquiries@pearl-lake.freeserve.co.uk. **Reservations:** Made with £20 deposit. **Open** 1 March - 30 November.

Directions: From Leominster take A44 southwest, after 4.5 miles at crossroads turn right (north) on A4110, and after 5 miles at Mortimers Cross turn left (west) on B4362 for 2.5 miles. Site is at western end of village on right. O.S.GR: SO390630.

Doward Park Camp Site

Great Doward, Symonds Yat West HR9 6BP

Created around 1997 in a disused quarry, this is a very pleasant, peaceful little site, partially terraced, and in a sheltered location. The access roads and the physical proportions of the site make it suitable only for tents, trailer tents and camper vans. A site that is popular with couples and young families, but has nothing to offer teenagers. The 40 pitches are mostly on grass, with a few hardstandings, and there are 14 electric hook-ups (16A). Visit King Arthur's Caves, and Seven Sisters Rocks. Walk to Symonds Yat Rock and cross the River Wye on the suspension bridge. In nearby Symonds Yat West you'll find The Amazing Hedge puzzle, and The Splendour of the Orient with gardens, waterfalls, tea-rooms and gift shop. Further afield is Goodrich Castle.

Facilities: A neat timber clad building provides the usual facilities including controllable hot showers, dishwashing sinks and a fridge/freezer for campers use. The owner also runs an on-site café which serves cream teas, home-made cakes, sandwiches, soft drinks and ices. Torches are advisable. Groups or canoe clubs not accepted. Note: This site is totally unsuitable for large units, double axle caravans, and American RVs. **Off site:** A good variety of Inns can be found at both Symonds Yat West and East all offering meals. Shops and services in Monmouth 4 miles.

Charges 2002

Per adult	£4.50
child (3-14 yrs)	£2.50
pup tent or gazebo	£3.00
electricity	£2.50
dog	£0.50

No credit cards. **Tel:** 01600 890438. E-mail: enquiries@doward-park.co.uk. **Reservations:** Advised for B.Hs. (min. 3 nights) and made with £10 deposit and S.A.E. **Open** Easter - 31 October.

Directions: From A40 between Ross-on-Wye and Monmouth, take turning for Symonds Yat West, and follow signs for Doward Park and Biblins. You will then turn into a fairly narrow lane for about 1 mile (passing places), and site entrance is on right, on a sharp left hand bend. O.S.GR: SO543164.

The Millpond Touring Caravans & Camping

Little Tarrington, nr Hereford HR1 4JA

This peaceful little site with its own fishing lake is set in 30 acres of countryside. Opened for the first time in 1997, it only has 30 large pitches on open grassland, all with electricity hook-ups (8A). The large fishing lake (unfenced) is well stocked with a good mix of coarse fish, has facilities for disabled fishermen and offers reduced rates for campers. The large acreage surrounding the campsite has a mix of well-established trees that have been supplemented with many new plantings, and well-mowed paths encourage you to wander and enjoy the great variety of trees, wild flowers, birds and the peaceful surroundings. Site lighting is minimal (local authority regulations) so a torch might be useful, but it is an ideal site for amateur astronomers. A railway track is at the rear of the site, so there may be a little noise at times. The site is just 7 miles from Hereford with its cathedral, the fascinating Mappa Mundi and chained library, 7 miles from Ledbury and close to the Black & White Village Trail.

Facilities: A new building houses heated sanitary facilities and dishwashing sinks, a unit for disabled persons and a 'common room' with a good supply of tourist information. Note: The site is not really suitable for American motorhomes. **Off site:** The local pub is only a 10 minute walk, but there is no shop in the village.

Charges 2002

Per caravan, motorcaravan or trailer tent	
incl. 2 adults and awning	£8.00 - £9.00
large tent incl. 2 persons	£9.00 - £11.00
small tent incl. 2 persons	£7.00 - £9.00
extra person from	£1.50
electricity	£2.00

Tel: 01432 890243. Fax: 01432 890243. E-mail: enquiries@millpond.co.uk. **Reservations:** Made with full payment for 1-3 days, £21 deposit for 1-6 nights, or £26 per week. Advised for B.Hs and peak season **Open** 1 March - 31 October.

Directions: Little Tarrington is midway between Hereford and Ledbury. The site is just north of A438 on eastern edge of Tarrington village (signed). O.S.GR: SO627409.

Luck's All Caravan & Camping Park
Mordiford, Hereford HR1 4LP

Set in around 9.5 acres on the bank of the river Wye, Luck's All has 80 large, well spaced and level touring pitches, of which 55 have electricity (10/16A). The river is open to the site but lifebelts and safety messages are in evidence. Canoes are available for hire - or bring your own - and fishing permits may be obtained from the local tackle shop. A small, unfenced playground and a large grassy area for games are provided for children. The site shop has basic supplies and gas, plus home-made cakes - a mini-market is within 1.5 miles. Amongst the local places worthy of a visit are the Cider Museum and King Offa Distillery in Hereford, Belmont Abbey and Queenswood Country Park. The park is also a good base for touring the Wye Valley. A member of the Countryside Discovery group.

Facilities: The main sanitary facilities, housed in a new building, provide showers (20p) and a separate unit for disabled visitors with ramped entrance, WC, washbasin, shower and hand-dryer. Dishwashing sinks. A smaller, older unit near the entrance to the park provides extra facilities for peak periods and a fully equipped laundry room. Shop (basics only). Fishing. Canoeing. Winter caravan storage. **Off site:** Golf 5 miles, bicycle hire 9 miles.

Charges 2002

Per unit incl. 2 adults	£7.50 - £8.00
extra person (over 5 yrs)	£1.50
awning	£1.00 - £1.25
pup tent on same pitch	£3.00
electricity	£1.75
dog	£0.75
small 2 man tent	£6.50 - £7.00

Tel: 01432 870213. **Reservations:** Essential for B.Hs. and peak season and made with £15 deposit. **Open** Easter/1 April - 31 October.

Directions: Between Mordiford and Fownhope, 5 miles southeast of Hereford on B4224, the park is well signed. O.S.GR: SO571355.

Broadmeadow Caravan & Camping Park
Broadmeadow, Ross-on-Wye HR9 7BH

This modern, spacious park, with open views and its own fishing lake, is convenient for the town of Ross-on-Wye. The approach to the site is unusual, but persevere and you will find one of the best laid out, immaculately maintained sites with the very highest quality facilities. Recently constructed, level and with good lighting, it offers 150 large pitches on open grass, and is especially good for tents. Each set of four pitches has a service post with water, drain, electricity points (16A) and lighting, and is within view of the clock-tower on one of the sanitary buildings. The town centre is within easy walking distance. Although the A40 relief road is at the eastern end of the site, the traffic noise should not be too intrusive (but tenters be aware). This is a good base for touring Herefordshire, the Wye Valley or the Forest of Dean.

Facilities: Two superb modern sanitary buildings are fully equipped, including hairdryers, baby rooms, family bathrooms each with WC, basin and bath, and a comprehensive unit for disabled visitors with alarm and handrails. A dishwashing room and a laundry with sinks, washing machine, dryer, iron (tokens from reception), are at each building. New entrance barrier and keypad entry system on this and all external doors. Small fenced playground. Well fenced fishing lake (coarse fishing £5.50 per day). **Off site:** Bicycle hire in town, riding 8 miles, golf 3 miles. Supermarket 200 m.

Charges 2002

Per pitch	£6.00 - £7.50
adult	£2.50
child (4-14 yrs)	£2.00
electricity	£2.50
dog	£1.00
awning or pup tent	£1.75

Tel: 01989 768076. Fax: 01989 566030. E-mail: BMCP4811@aol.com. **Reservations:** Made with £10 deposit. **Open** Easter/1 April - 30 September.

Directions: From A40 relief road turn into Ross at roundabout, take first right into industrial estate, then right in 0.5 miles, before Safeway supermarket, where site is signed. O.S.GR: SO610240.

Kingsgreen Caravan Park

Kingsgreen, Berrow, Malvern WR13 6AQ

419

A friendly, comfortable, farm site with views of the Malvern Hills, Kingsgreen is situated in an attractive rural location. An ideal site for adults who like the quiet life, there are no amusements for children. The surrounding countryside is ideal for walking or cycling, and the small, fenced fishing lake on the site is well stocked (£3 per day). There are 45 level, grass and gravel pitches, all with electricity (16A), plus an additional area for tents. Some old orchard trees provide a little shade in parts. The site is 7 miles from the market town of Ledbury with its half timbered buildings and within easy driving distance of Malvern, the Three Counties show-ground, Cotswolds, Forest of Dean or Tewkesbury with its 12th century Abbey.

Facilities: Modern toilet facilities (key on deposit) provide hot showers (25p token from reception) and a separate unit for disabled people (WC and washbasin). Dishwashing sinks under cover. Laundry room with washing machine, dryer, sink and iron and board (all metered). Gas and barbecue fuels are stocked and a milkman calls daily with milk, eggs, bread, soft drinks, etc. **Off site:** Nearest shop and pub 1.5 miles. Bicycle hire 2 miles, riding 3 miles, golf 5 miles.

Charges 2002

Per unit incl. 2 adults	£6.00
extra person (over 2 yrs)	£1.00
electricity	£1.50
awning	£1.00
dog	£1.00

No credit cards. VAT not included. **Tel:** 01531 650272. Fax: 01531 650272. **Reservations:** Essential for peak season and B.Hs. **Open** 1 March - 31 October.

Directions: From M50 junction 2, take A417 towards Gloucester, then first left, where site is signed, also signed the Malverns, back over the motorway. Site is 2 miles from the M50. O.S.GR: SO767338.

The Boyce Caravan Park

Stanford Bishop, Bringsty, nr Worcester WR6 5UB

420

The Boyce is a very peaceful park on rolling downland, with distant views of the Malvern Hills. Within its 17 acres are 20 touring pitches and 150 permanent caravan holiday homes. The relatively new landscaping and screening is maturing and electrical connections (10A) are available throughout. There is a fenced and gated playground for smaller children, plus plenty of open space for ball games (no cycling on the park). The adjacent disused railway line is now the dog walk (dogs accepted by arrangement, no dangerous breeds). Coarse fishing is available across a meadow, and the area is rich in wildlife. Nearby Shortwood Farm has Jacob sheep, cider making, sheep shearing and a farm trail. The new reception building offers good tourist information including maps of local walks. Bromyard with its shops and restaurants is 4 miles, and the cathedral cities of Hereford and Worcester are within easy driving distance.

Facilities: The modern toilet unit, built to serve the touring section, can be heated and provides controllable hot showers (10p for 4 mins), and a hairdressing area. Utility room housing dishwashing and laundry sinks, a washing machine, dryer, iron, and a freezer for campers' use. Gas available. **Off site:** Local pub 500 yards serving meals including breakfast. Riding 5 miles and several golf courses in the area.

Charges 2002

Per unit incl. 2 adults	£7.50
extra person (over 5 yrs)	£1.00
1 person tent	£4.00
awning/pup tent	£1.50
electricity	£1.50
extra car	£1.00

No tent pitches at B.H. weekends. No credit cards. **Tel:** 01886 884248. Fax: 01886 884187. **Reservations:** Made with deposit of one night's fee; contact park. **Open** 1 March - 31 October.

Directions: From A44 (Worcester - Leominster), turn on B4220 1 mile east of Bromyard. After 1.5 miles, turn opposite 'Herefordshire House' inn (signed Linley Green), site is 400 yards and signed. O.S.GR: SO698527.

Riverside Caravan Park

Little Clevelode, Malvern WR13 6PE

A traditional, older style site, Riverside at Little Clevelode is set in the picturesque Severn Valley four miles east of Great Malvern, and close to the Malvern Hills. The main touring site is located on high ground above the river near the site entrance, and has around 70 pitches, with a good many seasonal units, but there is usually space for tourists. There are two children's playgrounds and an area for football and ball games and a tennis hard-court. The lower level of the site near the river has an area for holiday homes and a new clubhouse/bar, games room with pool table, electronic machines and TV, the well stocked shop plus a further older sanitary unit and a small laundry. No dogs, washing lines, children's cycles, roller skates, skateboards, or scooters are permitted on site.

Facilities: The recently refurbished toilet block which serves the touring site provides controllable hot showers, vanity style washbasins and a small dishwash room. Whilst not luxurious these basic facilities are adequate and kept clean. Clubhouse/bar (open weekends only low season, daily at other times). Shop (09.00-09.30 and 17.30-18.00 weekdays plus 14.00-15.00 at weekends). **Off site:** Riding 3 miles. Golf 4 miles.

Charges 2002

Per unit incl. 2 persons	£7.00
extra person (over 4 yrs)	£2.00
hiker or cyclist	£5.00
awning	£1.00
electricity	£2.00
water hook-up	£0.50

No credit cards. **Tel:** 01684 310475. Fax: 01684 310475. **Reservations:** Advised for B.Hs (min. 3 nights) and school holidays and made with one nights pitch fee. **Open** Easter - 1 November.

Directions: Little Clevelode is due east of Great Malvern on the B4424. From Great Malvern take B4211 east for 2 miles, turning north on B4424 for about 0.5 mile to site entrance. From Worcester (north) take A449 south and fork left on B4424 for 2 miles to site entrance. O.S.GR: SO83046.

Ranch Caravan Park

Honeybourne, Evesham WR11 7PR

The Vale of Evesham is noted for being a sheltered area growing fruit and other produce from early spring through to late autumn. Ranch lies not far from both Evesham and Broadway in quiet rural surroundings of 50 acres and is also only half an hour's drive from Stratford-on-Avon. A free swimming pool with a slide is open and heated June - Sept. The park takes 120 touring units - caravans, motorcaravans or trailer tents but not other tents - on flat, partly undulating, hedged meadows with well mown grass and a spacious feel. Pitches are not marked but the staff position units. There are around 100 electrical connections (10A) and 20 hardstandings including 8 fully serviced pitches (electricity, TV, water and sewer connections). There are 169 caravan holiday homes in their own section.

Facilities: Two well appointed, modern sanitary blocks have hot showers on payment. Comfortable clubhouse (weekends only in early and late season) offers a range of good value meals. Entertainment is arranged at B.H. weekends and Saturdays in school holidays. Swimming pool (55 x 30 ft; June - Sept). Small games room with TV (incl. Sky), video machines and pool table. Playground. Tents are not accepted. **Off site:** Fishing 2 miles, bicycle hire 4 miles, and riding stables close.

Charges 2002

Per unit incl. 2 adults and electricity	£11.00 - £16.00
extra person (over 5 yrs)	free - £2.00
multi-services	£2.50
awning	free - £1.75
dog	free - £1.75

Tel: 01386 830744. Fax: 01386 833503. **Reservations:** Advised for peak weeks and B.Hs. Made with £5 p/night deposit and essential for B.Hs. (when min. 3 days). **Open** 1 March - 30 November.

Directions: From A46 Evesham take B4035 towards Chipping Campden. After Badsey and Bretforton follow signs for Honeybourne down unclassified road (Ryknild Street). Park is through village on left by station. O.S.GR: SP112444.

Lickhill Manor Caravan Park
Lower Lickhill Road, Stourport-on-Severn DY13 8RL

421

A well managed touring or holiday site within easy walking distance (15 minutes) of the town centre via a footpath along the River Severn which lies a short distance below the site. There are opportunities for fishing and boating. The touring field has 90 marked, level, grassy pitches accessed via gravel roadways, all with electricity (10/16A). The 124 holiday homes, well screened from the touring area amongst tree lined avenues, are not visually intrusive, and there is a separate rally field (with 50 hook-ups). There is an extended children's playground and the site has recently created wildlife ponds and planted over 1,000 native trees and shrubs. With its new sanitary block, roads and landscaping and friendly welcoming staff, this park promises to mature into one of the best in the area. Stourport is a lively bustling town with some splendid public parks, amusements and sports facilities. Kidderminster, the Forestry Commission Visitor Centre at Bewdley, the Severn Valley Railway and West Midland Safari Park are a short drive from the site.

Facilities: A second sanitary building was added in '98 to serve the touring pitches and complement the older unit at the other end of the park. This heated building provides sparkling modern facilities including a comprehensively equipped suite for disabled guests which also double as a family washroom with facilities for baby changing. Excellent drive over motorcaravan service point. Recycling bins. Gas supplies. Children's playground. **Off site:** Riding 1 mile, bicycle hire 3 miles. Six golf courses within 5 miles. A small parade of shops and the nearest pub are 10 minutes walk.

Charges 2002

Per unit incl. 4 persons	£7.00 - £11.00
extra person, car, trailer or boat	£1.00
electricity	£2.00
2 person tent	£7.50
awning	£1.50
dog	£0.50

Weekly rates available. Senior citizen discounts. **Tel:** 01299 871041. Fax: 01299 824998. E-mail: enquiries@lickhillmanor.co.uk. **Reservations:** Advised for B.Hs. and peak season. **Open** all year.

Directions: From centre of Stourport take B4195 northwest towards Bewdley. After 1 mile turn left at crossroads (traffic lights), into Lickhill Road North where site is signed. O.S.GR: SO790730

Moreton-in-Marsh Caravan Club Site
Bourton Road, Moreton-in-Marsh GL56 0BT

413

This excellent, busy, but rural, tree-surrounded site in the heart of the Cotswolds offers everything one would hope for from a caravanning holiday. Only 250 yards from the town, there is plenty of choice for food and pubs. The site has 182 pitches, all with electricity (16A), 120 with hardstanding and most offering TV sockets. Milk, bread, papers and ice-cream are available from reception. A large play field provides a climbing frame with bark base and space for football, volleyball, boules and crazy golf. Kite flying is not allowed because of low power cables. Moreton-in-Marsh is famous for its Tuesday street market and is always a busy town, being only a few miles from the pretty villages of Bourton-on-the-Water and Stow-on-the-Wold, just two of the many interesting Cotswold villages worthy of a visit in this lovely area of England. Tents are not accepted.

Facilities: The two toilet blocks offer very good facilities with spacious showers, washbasins in cabins, with facilities in each block for the walking disabled (4 inch step). Excellent en-suite room for disabled visitors in another building and a large laundry. Play field.

Charges 2002

Per pitch (non-member)	£6.00 - £8.00
adult	£3.50 - £4.50
child (5-16 yrs)	£1.10 - £1.20
electricity	£1.50 - £2.25
extra car, boat or trailer	£1.00

Tel: 01608 650519. **Reservations:** Contact site. **Open** all year.

Directions: From Evesham on A44, site on left after Bourton-on-the-Hill village, 150 yards before town sign. From Moreton-in-Marsh take A44 towards Evesham and site is on right, 150 yards past the Wellington museum. O.S.GR: SP200323.

Winchcombe Camping & Caravanning Club Site

Brooklands Farm, Alderton, nr Tewkesbury GL20 8NX

414

This is a popular, quiet site in a rural location, close to the Cotswold attractions. Some pitches surround a small coarse fishing lake, with others in a more recently developed area with open views over the surrounding countryside. In total there are 80 pitches, 53 with electric hook-ups (10A) and 42 with gravel hardstandings. The reception building flanks a small gravel courtyard car park and late arrivals area approached from a tarmac drive. Places to visit include Gloucester Docks and the National Waterways Museum, whilst south of Gloucester are Owlpen Manor near Uley, and the Painswick Rococo Garden. The Wildfowl and Wetlands Trust at Slimbridge, first opened in 1946 by Sir Peter Scott is also well worth a visit. Much closer to the site is the GWR (Gloucester Warwickshire Railway) at Toddington or Winchcombe.

Facilities: The main, heated sanitary unit, kept very clean and tidy by the wardens, is well equipped. Dishwashing sinks are under cover. To the rear of the site is a small, 'portacabin' style sanitary unit (also heated). Well equipped unit for disabled people. Laundry with washing machine and dryer. Gas supplies. On Saturdays between 5-6 pm. a fish and chip van calls. Large games room with a bowling alley, table tennis and a pool table. Small outdoor children's play area. **Off site:** Several pubs and restaurants in the area.

Charges 2002

Per adult	£3.90 - £5.50
child	£1.70
non-member pitch fee	£4.50
electricity	£1.75 - £2.50

Tel: 01242 620259. **Reservations:** Contact site. **Open** 16 March - 15 January.

Directions: From M5 exit 9, take A46 Evesham road for 3 miles to Toddington roundabout, then take B4077 towards Stow-on-the-Wold, for a further 3 miles to the site entrance. Ignore signs for Alderton village. O.S.GR: SP 007324.

Tewkesbury Caravan Club Site

Gander Lane, Tewkesbury GL20 5PG

411

There are two important reasons why the Caravan Club site at Tewkesbury is so popular: firstly, it is within five minutes walk of the town centre and is overlooked by the Norman Abbey, the focal point of the town and secondly, it is a good base for exploring the eastern end of the Cotswolds as well as some of the country's most delightful towns. Gloucester, Cheltenham, Stow-on-the-Wold, Bourton-on-the-Water, Chipping Norton and Broadway are just a few that immediately spring to mind. The Malvern hills are also within driving distance. Covering nine acres, the site has 170 pitches reached by tarmac roads. All are on grass, but some slope so blocks are essential, and all have electric hook-ups (16A). The entrance to the site is locked at night but there is a late arrivals area just outside. A popular site and one of the largest sites operated by the Caravan Club with friendly and helpful wardens.

Facilities: There are three toilet blocks, all built and maintained to the Club's high standards and they can be heated. The one in the reception building is without showers. One block has facilities for disabled visitors and two have laundry rooms. Motorcaravan service facilities. Reception sells basic supplies and gas. **Off site:** Food shops, restaurants, pubs, etc. are all within easy walking distance. Fishing 400 yds, riding 5 miles, golf 1 mile.

Charges 2002

Per pitch (non-member)	£6.00 - £8.00
adult	£3.50 - £4.50
child (5-17 yrs)	£1.10 - £1.20
awning	free
electricity	£1.50 - £2.25

Tel: 01684 294035. **Reservations:** Accepted and are essential all B.Hs. and June-Aug. **Open** April - October.

Directions: From all directions follow signs for town centre and head for the Abbey which is easily distinguished. Turn by the Abbey into Gander Lane, follow down passing two car parks to site at end of the lane. O.S.GR: SO894324.

Croft Farm Water and Leisure Park

Bredon's Hardwick, Tewkesbury GL20 7EE

415

Croft Farm is an AALA licensed Watersports Centre with Royal Yachting Association approved tuition available for windsurfing, sailing, kayaking and canoeing. The lakeside campsite has around 96 level pitches, with 80 electric hook-ups (10A), but there are many seasonal units, leaving around 36 pitches for tourists, plus some tent pitches. There are some gravel hardstandings but very little shade or shelter. 'Gym & Tonic' is a fully equipped gymnasium with qualified instructors, sun bed and sauna. Sports massage, aromatherapy and beauty treatments available by appointment. The 'Playzone' has a soft play area, play structure, bouncy castle, table football and a Playstation. In school holidays supervised activities the 'Playzone Pirates' are run on weekday mornings, and afternoon 'Funtimes' for parents and children. Campers can use their own non-powered boats on the lake with reduced launch fees. Places of interest nearby include Bredon Barn, pottery and church, Beckford Silk Mill, and Tewkesbury Abbey. The Black Bear Inn in Tewkesbury claims to be the oldest in Gloucestershire. Climb Bredon Hill (2 miles) for a panoramic view of the Severn and Avon Valleys.

Facilities: A new building (open in summer months) on the far side of the lake, has excellent modern facilities with spacious hot showers, plus some dishwashing sinks outside to the rear. A heated unit at the back of the gymnasium in the main building (near the reception/watersports shop) is always open and best for cooler months, this provides further WCs, washbasins and showers, laundry and includes facilities for disabled persons. Cafe/bar (open Fri-Sun low season and daily at other times), gym, and the indoor 'Playzone' for children under 10 years. River fishing. Gas available. **Off site:** The Cross Keys Inn opposite the site entrance serves meals. Supermarkets in Tewkesbury 1.5 miles. Golf 3 miles. Riding 8 miles.

Charges 2002

Per unit incl. 2 persons and awning	£8.00
extra person (over 3 yrs)	£2.50
extra pup tent	£1.00
2-man tent	£7.00
electricity	£2.00
dog	£0.50

Discount 10% for 8 nights or more (excl. July, August and B.Hs). **Tel:** 01684 772321. Fax: 01684 773379. E-mail: enquiries@croftfarmleisure.co.uk. **Reservations:** Essential for weekends. B.Hs. and July/Aug. Made with £10 deposit. **Open** all year, excl. Jan and Feb.

Directions: Bredons Hardwick is mid-way between Tewkesbury and Bredon on B4080. Site is well signed at western end of village, site entrance opposite 'Cross Keys Inn'. From M5 jcn.9 take A438 toward Tewkesbury, at first traffic lights turn right into Shannon Way. Turn right at next lights, cross M-way bridge, and turn left (housing estate), and cross second M-way bridge. At T-junction turn right on B4080, site entrance is immediately on your left. O.S.GR: SO915350.

Forestry Commission - Christchurch Caravan & Campsite

Bracelands Drive, Christchurch, Coleford GL16 7NN

416

With 280 unmarked pitches, this 20 acre site is on an undulating, open grassy area in the heart of the Forest of Dean. There are around 60 seasonal units, seven hardstandings, and 95 pitches have electric hook-ups (16A). The reception also houses a well stocked licensed shop, and has a good selection of tourist information, including a leaflet about the local forest trails (55p). Tenters will appreciate the large pavilion in the centre of the site, a large common room with a wood burning stove (logs supplied), tables and chairs, an ideal retreat if the weather proves inclement. Symonds Yat Rock is within walking distance of the site, with spectacular views over the Wye Valley. Also nearby are the Clearwell Caves, and ancient iron mines.

Facilities: Four sanitary units, two fairly modern with spacious well equipped showers, some vanity style basins with dividers, plus two much older units with WCs and washbasins only. The central block has a laundry with washing machines and dryers, a room with dishwashing sinks, and facilities for disabled people and baby changing. Shaded adventure playground on a bark surface. Dogs are not accepted. **Off site:** Shops and other services in Coleford - 1.5 miles. Dean Forest Railway 6 miles. Ross-on-Wye 8 miles. Fishing 1 mile. Swimming 1 mile. Golf 2 miles. Bicycle hire 3 miles. Riding 10 miles.

Charges 2002

Per unit incl. 2 persons	£6.20 - £11.50
extra adult	£3.00
child (5-14 yrs)	£1.80
electricity	£2.30 - £2.60

Less 20% all year for disabled guests and outside 26/7-31/8 for senior citizens. **Reservations:** Necessary for B.H.s and peak times (min 2 nights with £30 deposit). Contact site Tel: (01594) 833376, or Forestry Commission, 231 Corstorphine Road, Edinburgh EH12 7AT. Tel: (0131) 314 6505. **Open** 21 March - 4 November.

Directions: From Monmouth take A4136 east for approx. 5 miles turning north at crossroads at Pike House Inn (site signed), site entrance on left after 0.5 miles. From centre of Coleford take road towards Monmouth, turning right to Symonds Yat and Berry Hill (site signed). O.S.GR: SO575129.

Tudor Caravan and Camping Park

Shepherds Patch, Slimbridge GL2 7BP

417

This traditional style campsite is adjacent to the Gloucester - Sharpness Canal, and behind the Tudor Arms public house. It has 75 pitches, all with electric hook-ups (16A), and is divided into two separate fields, the old orchard for long stay or adults only units, with some concrete wheel track hardstands, and a more open grassy meadow for family touring units. The Wildfowl and Wetlands Centre at Slimbridge, founded in 1946 by artist and naturalist Sir Peter Scott, has an incredible variety of different species which visit each year. This site is an obvious choice if you are at all interested in ornithology, being only 800 yards from the Centre. Other attractions include Berkeley Castle, Frampton with its half timbered buildings, Stroud is famous for alternative medicine, homeopaths, reflexologists, herbalists, acupuncturists, chiropractors and cranial masseurs.

Facilities: The toilet building located to one side of the orchard, provides all the usual facilities including push-button hot showers and it can be heated in cool weather. Dishwashing sinks outside under cover. No facilities for disabled persons. Gas available. Some site lighting but a torch would be useful. Gate locked 22.30 - 07.00. **Off site:** Meals at the Tudor Arms public house. Shop and cafe in boatyard opposite the site (Easter-Sept), also serves breakfasts. Fishing adjacent. Towpath walks.

Charges 2002

Per unit incl. 2 persons	£8.00
extra adult	£1.00
child (under 12 yrs)	£0.50
awning	£1.00 - £1.50
electricity	£2.00
1-man tent	£5.00
dog	£0.50

Supplement for B.Hs and school holidays 50p. No credit cards. **Tel:** 01453 890483. **Reservations:** Advisable for B.Hs and July/Aug. **Open** all year.

Directions: From A38 by the junction with A4135 (Dursley), turn west, signed Slimbridge Wild Fowl Trust. Continue for 1.5 miles turning left into car park of the Tudor Arms. Site entrance is at rear of car park. O.S.GR: SO728040.

Celebrating the Queen's Golden Jubilee at Whitemead Caravan Park, Dorset

Hoburne Cotswold

Broadway Lane, South Cerney, Cirencester GL7 5UQ

410

Since this park is adjacent to the Cotswold Water Park, those staying will have easy access to the varied watersports there which include sailboarding and water skiing. On the park itself there is a lake with pedaloes and canoes for hire. Its wide range of other amenities include an outdoor heated swimming pool and an impressive, large indoor leisure complex. There are 340 well marked touring pitches for any type of unit, all with hardstanding (only fairly level) and a grass surround for awning or tent; 40 are serviced 'super' pitches. Of good size but with nothing between them, all have electricity (some need long leads). There are also 150 holiday units, mainly for letting. The large clubhouse has a big general lounge with giant TV screen, entertainment at times, food service (or food bar in lounge), big games room and a lounge bar which overlooks the outdoor pool and lake with a patio. Part of the Hoburne group.

Facilities: Six toilet blocks, all quite small, but clean and well maintained with pre-set showers. Baby changing facilities. Basic facilities for disabled visitors are in toilet block 4 and at the clubhouse. The site has heavy weekend trade. Launderette. Supermarket. Indoor leisure complex including pool with flume, spa bath, sauna, steam room (all free) and sun bed (charged). Outdoor pool (open Whitsun - early September; 44 x 22 ft). Clubhouse with bar, food and entertainment. Football field. Tennis courts. Good quality adventure playground with bark base. Crazy golf. Fishing lake (permits from reception). No dogs or pets are accepted.

Charges 2002

Touring pitch incl. electricity	£10.50 - £24.50
pup tent	£3.00

Weekly rates and weekend breaks available. **Tel:** 01285 860216. Fax: 01285 862106. E-mail: enquiries@hoburne.co.uk. **Reservations:** Bookings of 1-6 nights payable in full at time of reservation; caravans with £50 deposit for 1 week. Min. 4 nights booking at B.Hs. **Open** March - 31 October.

Directions: Three miles from Cirencester on A419, turn west towards Cotswold Water Park at new roundabout on bypass onto B4696. Take second right and follow signs. O.S.GR: SU055957.

Yorkshire Tourist Board

North, South, East and West Yorkshire

Yorkshire Tourist Board
312 Tadcaster Road, York YO24 1GS
Tel: (01904) 707961 Fax: (01904) 701414
24 hour brochure hotline: (01904) 707070
E-mail: info@ytb.org.uk
Internet: http://www.yorkshirevisitor.com

Variety is the spice of life in Yorkshire, a region of scenic contrasts with an historic past and a wealth of new attractions, which makes an ideal destination for visitors at any time of the year. Rural charm and scenic softness, rugged castles, stately homes and ancient churches are packed into a compact area with excellent transport communications, making the region a favourite spot for short breaks.

For many people, the scenic grandeur of the Yorkshire Dales National Park - 680 square miles of unspoilt countryside, rivers, caves, castles and unforgettable views - is a major attraction. This is the landscape made famous world-wide in the books and TV programmes featuring Dales Vet, James Herriot.

The great city of York, with its unparalleled wealth of ancient sites, continues to be a powerful magnet for visitors: more than 2 million visit the Minster each year. Other top attractions are the National Railway Museum and the Jorvik Viking Centre, and the fascinating Castle Museum.

Kingston Upon Hull is a maritime city with powerful links to Britain's proud seafaring tradition, and north of here is the lovely market town of Beverley, with its Georgian Houses in the shadow of the Minster.

The North York Moors National Park has miles of open moorland with picturesque villages nestling in hollows. The North Yorkshire Moors Railway, starting at Pickering, is one of many steam railways in the region.

On the coast, traditional family resorts like Scarborough, Bridlington and Cleethorpes have added many new attractions in recent times, and offer the holidaymaker a wide range of activities, from the relaxed to the energetic. And of course, don't forget the fascinating fishing port of Whitby, once home to Captain James Cook, and the charming smaller resorts including Filey and the "smuggler's village" of Robin Hood's Bay. For anyone interested in experiencing the coastal wildlife, a visit to the RSPB nature reserve at Bempton Cliffs is a must.

The towns and cities of West Yorkshire make interesting destinations, with their powerful blend of heritage combined with the spirit of renovation and renewal. Leeds shows the way with the recent opening of the Royal Armouries and the only branch of Harvey Nichols outside of London. Salts Mill, Saltaire is home to the largest collection of work by Bradford born artist David Hockney, as well as floors of excitingly eclectic shopping opportunities. Nearby is the Bronte village of Haworth, high on the Pennine moors.

South Yorkshire was made famous on the big screen, with hits such as The Full Monty and Brassed Off, so why not pay it a visit? As well as the busy market town of Doncaster and the vibrant city of Sheffield, the area has country parks, nature reserves and woodlands, and fascinating places of historical interest including Conisborough Castle and Brodsworth Hall. One of the region's most highly praised new attractions, the science adventure centre Magna is also here.

Calderdale district offers an intriguing cocktail of bustling towns and vast swathes of open moorland. In nearby Kirklees is Holmfirth, the setting for TV's "Last of the Summer Wine", one of many film and television locations in Yorkshire.

A memento of your time in Yorkshire is a must and there are many locally made craft products for you to choose from. Whitby Jet became fashionable after Queen Victoria was so taken by it and still remains a popular semi-precious stone to this day. Sheffield was once provider of most of the country's cutlery and is still regarded as home to some of the best crafted in the country. For those with a sweet tooth, try Harrogate toffee or Pontefract Cakes or, for something a little more permanent, Yorkshire is home to an array of craft shops. One thing is for sure, whatever you are looking for, there will be something to suit every taste.

Nostell Priory Holiday Home Park

Nostell, Wakefield WF4 1QD

470

A tranquil, secluded woodland park within the estate of Nostell Priory, this site provides 60 touring pitches, all with electrical connections (5A), in a grassy, flat and sheltered area edged with mature trees. There is a hardstanding area suitable for motorcaravans, plus 80 caravan holiday homes in a separate area (5 for hire). Amenities are designed to blend into the environment in rustic wood, including the sanitary block. Nostell Priory itself with its collection of Chippendale furniture and attractive gardens is well worth a visit. The Dales, York and the Peak District are all an easy drive away. A fishing lake is within the grounds, with golf and watersports locally (details in reception). The park is very well cared for and the natural environment is encouraged so there is an abundance of birds and wildlife. A rally field is adjacent to the site. Buses pass the end of the drive (half a mile long).

Facilties: The toilet block although older in style, has been refurbished throughout to include some washbasins in cubicles. Accessed by key, it includes a separate room for dishwashing. Laundry with two washing machines and a dryer (opening times on the door). Motorcaravan services. Milk and papers can be ordered at reception, the nearest shops are 2 miles. New play area (no ball games on site). Up to two dogs accepted. **Off site:** Golf 5 miles, boat launching 8 miles.

Charges 2002

Per unit incl. 2 persons	£8.50
extra person (over 5 yrs)	£1.00
awning (no pup tents)	£1.25
electricity	£1.50
dog (max 2)	£1.00

Less 10% for 7 night bookings. Less 10% for senior citizens. No single sex groups or units over 21'6" overall length. **Tel:** 01924 863938. Fax: 01924 862226. **Reservations:** Advised made with £5 deposit and 50p booking fee (min. 2 nights). **Open** 1 March - 31 October.

Directions: Park entrance is off A638 Wakefield - Doncaster road, 5 miles southeast of Wakefield. Follow drive for 0.5 miles keeping the rose nursery on your left. O.S.GR: SE394181.

Bronte Caravan Park

off Halifax Road, Keighley BD21 5QF

479

Bronte Caravan Park is a peaceful haven set in a 50 acre park with wonderful views. It is hard to believe that you are only 1.5 miles from the busy town of Keighley, as only the rolling hillsides with a village on the opposite side are visible. Ten acres of the land are devoted to the owners' own deer herd. A two acre lake is in a lovely setting with its island, weeping willows and several varieties of waterfowl, not to mention the local heron or kingfisher. It is well stocked to provide sport for both coarse and fly fishermen. The hillside has been terraced and a stream tumbles down into the lake. The River Worth runs alongside the site (well fenced). The level pitches have gravel surfaces and 10A electricity (some are a little small). There are also 25 pitches for tents. Three pitching areas cater for all needs - two areas are for adults only, the third for families quite separate with an adjacent play area on bark chippings. The Worth Valley railway of 'The Railway Children' fame running alongside the site is a big attraction and one of its smaller stations is only a short walk. Ingrow station with a railway museum and free parking is half a mile. Haworth and its Bronte heritage (two miles) is a must with the museum, the parsonage where the sisters lived and the moorland walks. Further away at Bradford is the cinema and photography museum and Cliffe castle museum in Keighley is well worth a visit.

Facilties: The well appointed, central toilet block of local stone includes a very large room for families or disabled visitors. Laundry with washing machine, dryer and iron. Dishwashing sinks under cover. This block is quite a walk from the family pitches but two 'portacabin' style blocks nearer to the pitches are well equipped with toilets, washbasins and an outside dishwashing sink. Children's play area. Fishing (1 rod/1 line, adult or child £2.50). Barrier access (key £10 deposit). **Off site:** Supermarkets 1.5 miles.

Charges 2002

Per unit incl. 2 persons	£9.00
tent	£6.00
electricity	£2.00
extra person (over 5 yrs)	£2.00

Tel: 01535 691746. Fax: 01535 691746. **Reservations:** Made with £5 deposit (non-returnable). **Open** 1 April - 31 October.

Directions: Park is south of Keighley off the A629 Keighley - Halifax road, on the right approx. 1.75 miles from Keighley.

Burton Constable Caravan Park

450 The Old Lodges, Sproatley HU11 4LN

This park is in the grounds of the stately home of Burton Constable - consequently the entrance is most impressive. One of the gatehouses acts as reception and the 20 acre campsite is part of the 300 acre park, which was landscaped by Capability Brown in the 18th century. With well trimmed grass and hedges, the campsite has a spacious feel. All 200 pitches have 10A electricity. There is a separate field for tents and a large hardstanding area providing electricity, water and drainage for six motorcaravans. All the pitches overlook two small lakes, one of which is used for fishing (permits at reception), the other for boating (bring your own, but no engines). Privately owned caravan holiday homes are quite separate and do not intrude. For weekly bookings there is a three day family pass to visit the house and its 30 rooms.

Facilties: Two heated toilet blocks - one older and small with unisex showers. The central block is quite new and includes a laundry room with baby changing. Well equipped room for disabled visitors (Radar key). Shop in the mobile home area. Bar with family room and tables outside overlooking the lakes. Good adventure play area. **Off site:** Sproatley 1 mile, Hull 7 miles. Golf 4 miles, riding 3 miles.

Charges 2002

Per unit incl. 2 persons	£8.50 - £10.00
extra person	£1.00
electricity	£2.00
awning	£2.00

Tel: 01964 562508. Fax: 01964 563283. E-mail: bchall@dircon.co.uk. **Reservations:** Contact park. **Open** 1 March - 31 October.

Directions: From south via M62 or Humber Bridge, take A63 into Hull, then follow signs to A165 Bridlington. On eastern outskirts of Hull follow B1238 signed Aldborough. At Sproatley site is signed to left. From north and Beverley, take A1035 toHornsea. At roundabout with A165 (Hull - Bridlington) follow signs to Burton Constable for about 8 miles. Pass the Hall to Sproatley, then follow caravan signs. O.S.GR: TA186357.

Fangfoss Old Station Caravan Park

465 Fangfoss, York YO41 5QB

Fangfoss railway station stands on the old York - Market Weighton line (closed in 1965). The Station House and its platform give this small, simple site character, its rural situation amongst rolling farmland gives it peace and quietness and its owners, a friendly welcome and clean and comfortable facilities. The grassed over track and sidings provide hardstanding and with the adjacent fairly level grass field, give a total of 75 marked pitches, all with 10A electricity and 18 with hardstanding. York is 10 miles (with 'park and ride') and the Yorkshire Wolds 5 miles. There are nearby market towns and a variety of pubs and restaurants within a 6 mile radius.

Facilties: A modern, centrally situated toilet block provides free adjustable hot showers, vanity style washbasins (two in cubicles for ladies). A separate wooden utility block, 'The Wendy House', provides sinks for dishwashing, laundry and food preparation bar (useful for tenters). No washing machine but a laundry room is offered. Reception sells essentials with an off-licence and gas. Some play equipment on grass. Winter caravan storage. **Off site:** Fishing, bicycle hire, riding and golf within 4 miles.

Charges 2002

Per unit incl. 2 persons	£7.50 - £13.00
extra person	£1.00
electricity	£2.00

Tel: 01759 380491. E-mail: fangfoss@pi2000.co.uk. **Reservations:** Made with £20 deposit. **Open** 1 March - 31 October.

Directions: From A1079 York - Hull road, follow site signs at Wilberfoss for 1.5 miles (north). On A166 York - Bridlington road, park is clearly signed at Stamford Bridge, on right just after crossing the river. O.S.GR: SE748527.

Moorside Caravan Park

461 Lords Moor Lane, Strensall, York YO32 5XJ

Strensall is only a few miles from York, and this 'adult only' park will provide a peaceful haven after a day's sightseeing. It will impress you with its pretty fishing lake, masses of flowers and the quiet (except for the odd passing daytime train). There are 57 marked pitches on neat well trimmed grass, most with electricity (5/10A) and 18 with paved hardstanding. The whole park is very well maintained making it a very pleasant environment. The pitches bordering the lake are the most popular. Children under 16 are not accepted.

Facilties: The purpose built toilet block can be heated and houses well kept facilities with wash-basins in cubicles for ladies. One WC is suitable for use by disabled visitors. Laundry room. Dishwashing area. Caravan storage. Coarse fishing (£2 per day). **Off site:** Strensall village under 1 mile. Golf 0.5 miles.

Charges 2002

Per unit incl. 2 persons	£6.50
extra person	£2.00
electricity	£1.50

No credit cards. **Tel:** 01904 491208. **Reservations:** Contact park. **Open** March - end October.

Directions: From A1237 York outer ring road follow signs for Earswick and Strenshall. At Strenshall follow Flaxton road. The park entrance is on the left past signs to Strensall village and York Golf Club. O.S.GR: SE647614.

Goose Wood Caravan Park

464 Sutton-on-the-Forest, York YO61 1ET

A family owned park in a natural woodland setting, Goose Wood provides a quiet, relaxed atmosphere from which to explore York itself or the surrounding Yorkshire Dales, Wolds or Moors. The park has a well kept air and a rural atmosphere, with 95 well spaced and marked pitches on level grass, all with electricity (16A) and 95 with paved hardstanding and patio pitch. No tents are accepted. For children, there is a 'super plus' adventure playground in the trees at one side of the park and, for adults, a small coarse fishing lake and attractive, natural woodland for walking, plus a large scale chess set. The park is popular with families in high season when it can be busy at weekends. A 'park and ride' scheme for York operates from nearby all year, six days a week or there is a local bus every two hours, six days a week. The park is just over a mile from Sutton village and only 7 miles from 'Water World' a new water leisure centre with pool, slides, wave machines, etc. A member of the Best of British group.

Facilties: Newly tiled and heated, the modern toilet block is of excellent quality and well maintained. Bathroom (£1). An additional new unit provides family shower rooms, WC and washbasins in large cubicles and extra dishwashing sinks (coin operated hot water). Full facilities for disabled visitors and a motorcaravan service point are planned. Laundry room. Small shop (with gas). Fishing lake. Large adventure playground. Dogs (max. two per pitch), to be exercised in nearby woodland. No tents are accepted. **Off site:** Riding or golf 1 mile. York 6 miles.

Charges 2002

Per unit incl. 1 or 2 persons and car	£5.00 - £11.50
extra person	£1.50
awning, extra pup tent (1 only), or extra car	£1.50
electricity	£2.50

Tel: 01347 810829. Fax: 01347 811498. E-mail: edward@goosewood.fsbus.co.uk. **Reservations:** Made with £20 deposit (min. 3 nights at B.Hs). **Open** all year excl. 15-31 Jan.

Directions: Park is 6 miles north of York; from the A1237 York outer ring-road take the B1363 for Sutton-on-the-Forest and Stillington, taking the first right after the Haxby and Wigginton junction and follow park signs. O.S.GR: SE595636.

Thorpe Hall Caravan & Camping Site

451 Rudston, Driffield YO25 4JE

This pleasant small touring park is in the grounds of Thorpe Hall, just outside the village of Rudston and 4.5 miles from the sea at Bridlington. Enthusiastically managed by Jayne Chatterton, it is set on flat grass, largely enclosed by the old kitchen garden wall. The 90 pitches are numbered and well spaced with 78 electrical hook-ups (16A) and TV connections. A separate area takes tents and there are no caravan holiday homes. There is always a chance of finding space, though it is best to book for B.Hs and peak weeks. Information sheets on a range of local walks are provided. A member of the Countryside Discovery group.

Facilties: The solid, central toilet block can be heated. Ladies have three washbasins in private cabins and a bath. Well equipped unit for disabled visitors with bath. Launderette. Covered dishwashing sinks. Small shop with gas, essentials and local produce. Games room with pool table, table football and table tennis. TV room. The site's own coarse fishing lake is now open nearby. **Off site:** Bicycle hire, golf and boat launching at Bridlington (4.5 miles), riding 2 miles. Footpath to the village with a shop, post office, garage, a pub serving bar meals and a new restaurant, plus a twice weekly bus service to Bridlington.

Charges 2002

Per unit incl. all persons	£6.20 - £12.00
tent field	£5.20 - £10.80
electricity	£2.10

Less 10% on booked stays of 7 days or over. No credit cards. **Tel:** 01262 420393. Fax: 01262 420588. E-mail: caravansite@thorpehall.co.uk. **Reservations:** Made with advance payment (min. 4 nights at Spr. B.H). **Open** 1 March - 31 October.

Directions: Site is by the B1253 road, 4.5 miles from Bridlington, on east side of Rudston. O.S.GR: TA105676.

Yorkshire
Far Grange Park

473 Skipsea, Driffield YO25 8SY

Far Grange is a very well maintained holiday park that will especially appeal to families. A comprehensive leisure centre is located at the park entrance, well away from the touring pitches. The indoor pool, fitness suite, sauna and solarium (with charges) are excellent facilities with lifeguards who are happy to give assistance to swimmers with disabilities if needed. This area also includes bars with shows, cabaret acts and dancing (adults only). A family room provides games and shows for children and discos for teenagers. These rooms are very tastefully decorated and furnished, making a pleasant, relaxing environment. There are also facilities for pool, snooker, darts and a TV room (all requiring children to be accompanied by parents). Bar meals are served in the evenings and Sunday lunches. Outside is an attractive patio area. The 130 touring pitches all have electrical hook-ups (10A) and include 66 'super' pitches (these available for long weekends all winter). This is a large, popular site with many caravan holiday homes and seasonal tourers, but with lots of space and plenty to do whatever the weather. A member of the Best of British group.

Facilties: Tiled toilet blocks are heated in low season and provide some washbasins in cabins, baths and mother and baby rooms, also a bathroom for wheelchair users. These facilities are clean and well maintained. In the central reception area is a well stocked supermarket (with gas), takeaway, amusement arcade and a well appointed laundry. Indoor leisure complex. Bar. Restaurant. The park grounds are extensive with plenty of room for team games, tennis, a fitness trail for young and old, an excellent adventure playground with a skateboard ramp, and a play area for younger children (both with rubber safety bases). Fishing. **Off site:** Adjacent is golf with pitch and putt. Across the road is a country park with fishing and wildfowl lake, visitor centre and a dipping pond for youngsters - an idyllic place to get away for a walk and a picnic.

Charges 2002

Per unit incl. 2 persons, electricity	£11.00 - £16.00
incl. mains services and awning	£15.00 - £19.00
extra person (3 yrs and over)	£1.00
dog, car or small tent	£1.00

Tel: 01262 468293. Fax: 01262 468648. E-mail: enquiries@fargrangepark.co.uk. **Reservations:** Made with £20 per week deposit (min. 7 days B.Hs and high season). **Open** 1 March - 31 October.

Directions: From A165 (Bridlington - Beverley) take B1242 Skipsea road. Park is on the seaward side of this road, about 1.5 miles south of Skipsea. O.S.GR: TA186530.

Yorkshire
Lebberston Touring Park

478 Home Farm, Filey Road, Lebberston, Scarborough YO11 3PE

Lebberston Park is a quiet, spacious touring site, but it takes no tents. It is highly suitable for anyone seeking a quiet relaxing break, such as mature couples or young families. There is no play area and no games room so teenagers may get bored. The only concession to children is a large central area with goal posts. The site itself has a very spacious feel. It is gently sloping and south facing and the views are superb. There are 125 numbered pitches, all with 10A electricity and 6 with hardstanding. The circular access road is tarmac, the grass is well manicured and the entrance is an attractive log cabin, which is also the home of the owners and their young family. The resorts of Filey, Bridlington, Scarborough and Hornsea provide something for everyone, the moors and the Dalby forest are also within a short distance. Because there is such a popular and busy area we feel justified in adding another site to the guide, especially one of such quality.

Facilties: Recently upgraded toilet blocks are of high quality, with large shower cubicles and washbasins in cubicles with curtains. Both blocks have dishwashing sinks and one has a family bathroom (20p). The room for disabled visitors is very good. Laundry with washing machine, dryer, spin dryer, iron and board. A key is supplied for the laundry, bathroom, telephone booth and the disabled room. Reception sells a few supplies plus papers, ice cream and gas. **Off site:** Local pub within walking distance. Each new arrival is given details of parking in Scarborough including a parking disc.

Charges 2002

Per unit incl. 2 persons	£7.50 - £9.50
B.Hs (min 3 or 4 nights)	£12.00
extra adult	£1.00
child (5-14 yrs)	£0.75
extra car	£1.00
awning	£1.50
trailer tent over 8 sq.m. plus	£1.50
electricity	£2.00

Tel: 01723 585723. **Reservations:** Made with £10 non-returnable deposit. **Open** 1 March - 31 October.

Directions: From A64 Malton - Scarborough road turn right at roundabout (MacDonalds, pub and superstore) signed B1261 Filey. Go through Cayton, Killerby and in 4.5 miles site is signed on right. O.S.GR: TA082823.

Cayton Village Caravan Park

455 D23, Mill Lane, Cayton Bay, Scarborough YO11 3NN

Cayton Village Caravan Park is just three miles from the hustle and bustle of Scarborough, yet it is a peaceful, attractive haven. Originally just a flat field with caravans around the perimeter, four years of hard work, a lot of time and even more expense has produced a park which is very pleasing to the eye and of which the owner, Carol, can be justly proud. The entrance is a mass of flowers. The late arrivals area here has electrical hook-ups, very handy as the gates are locked at night and anyone leaving early is also expected to use it so as not to disturb others. The 200 pitches, of which 160 are for touring units, are numbered and everyone is taken to their pitch. There are 170 with electricity, 30 'super' pitches and 8 with hardstanding. A short walk across a field takes you to Cayton Village which has a popular pub providing excellent meals, a shop/post office and a church, and Cayton Bay is half a mile. The North York Moors are a short distance away, as is the Forestry Commission's Dalby Forest Drive with its scenic drive, mountain bike trails and way-marked walks. The steam railway at Pickering is a big attraction.

Facilties: Three toilet blocks (key code locks) can be heated and have very high quality tiling and fittings. Some showers are pre-set, others controllable. Two family shower rooms, family bathroom and baby changing facilities. Reception and shop, both open 8.30 am. to 8 pm. The shop's comprehensive range includes gas and caravan spares. Adventure playground with safety surface. Superb dog walk (an enormous well mown field, floodlit at night). Caravan storage. **Off site:** Fishing and bicycle hire 0.5 miles, riding 4 miles, golf 3 miles. Regular bus service from the village to Scarborough or Filey.

Charges 2002

Per unit incl. 4 persons	£9.50 - £14.50
extra person (over 3 yrs)	£1.00
awning	£2.00
dog	£1.00

Special offers available. **Tel:** 01723 583171. E-mail: info@caytontouring. co.uk. **Reservations:** Are advised and made for min. 3 nights (4 at B.Hs) with £20 deposit. **Open** Easter - 1 October.

Directions: From A64 Malton - Scarborough road turn right at roundabout (with MacDonald's and pub) signed B1261 Filey. Follow signs for Cayton, in Cayton Village take second left after Blacksmiths Arms down Mill Lane (at brown caravan site sign) and park is 200 yds. From roundabout to park is 2.25 miles. From A165 turn inland at Cayton Bay traffic lights and park is 0.5 miles on right. O.S.GR: TA057837.

Jasmine Park

474 Cross Lane, Snainton, Scarborough YO13 9BE

This is an area of North Yorkshire that is very popular so although we have other parks nearby, we feel there is room for another. Jasmine is a very attractive, quiet, well manicured park with owners who go to much trouble to produce masses of plants to give a very colourful entrance. Set in the Vale of Pickering, the park is level, well drained and protected by a coniferous hedge. The 106 pitches (54 for touring units) are on grass, with electricity connections (10A) for all caravans and some tents. There is no play equipment for children, although a field is provided for football, etc. Masses of tourist information is provided in a log cabin and the owners are only too happy to advise. The market town of Pickering and the seaside town of Scarborough are both 8 miles. Many local attractions are within easy reach, including Castle Howard, Dalby Forest, Sledmere House, Nunington Hall, Goathland (the setting for ITV's 'Heartbeat') and the North York Moors Railway. Some privately owned log cabins and seasonal tourers are also on the site. This is a quiet, peaceful park for a restful holiday. A member of the Countryside Discovery group.

Facilties: The toilet block is kept very clean and includes a large room for families or disabled visitors containing a bath, shower, WC and washbasin (access by key). Laundry room with dishwashing sinks, washing machine, dryer and iron (hot water metered). Motorcaravan service point. Licensed shop selling essentials and gas. Dogs are welcome but there is no dog walk. **Off site:** Riding 2 miles. Golf driving range 2 miles. Fishing 5 miles.

Charges 2002

Per unit incl. 2 persons	£7.50 - £9.50
extra adult	£1.00
child (5-14 yrs)	£0.75
awning or tent over 150 sq ft	£1.50
extra car	£1.00
electricity	£2.00

Min. stay at Easter 4 nights, other B.Hs 3 nights. **Tel:** 01723 859240. Fax: 01723 859240. E-mail: info@jasminepark.co.uk. **Reservations:** Made with £10 deposit and S.A.E. **Open** 1 March - 31 December.

Directions: Snainton is on the A170 Pickering - Scarborough road and park is signed at eastern end of the village. Follow Brakers Lane to park on left in 1 mile. O.S.GR: SE928813.

Yorkshire
Flower of May Holiday Park
452 Lebberston Cliff, Scarborough YO11 3NU

Flower of May is a large, family owned park for both touring caravans and caravan holiday homes situated on the cliff tops, 4.5 miles from Scarborough and 2.5 miles from Filey. There is a cliff walk to the beach but it is only suitable for the reasonably active - there is an easier walk down from a car park one mile away. The entrance to the park is very colourful and the reception office is light and airy. The range of leisure facilities grouped around reception, includes an indoor pool with areas for both adults and children, a water flume and a jacuzzi. In the same building are two squash courts, 10 pin bowling, table tennis and amusement machines. The leisure centre is also open to the public (concessionary rates for campers) but in high season is only available to local regulars and the caravanners and campers on the park. The park is licensed for 300 touring units and 184 caravan holiday homes (45 to hire, the remainder privately owned). The touring pitches are pretty level, arranged in wide avenues mainly on grass and divided by shrubs. There are 210 with electricity (5A), including 45 'star' pitches with water and drainage also. Riverside Meadows at Ripon and Rosedale Country Caravan Park near Pickering are under the same ownership.

Facilties: The three toilet blocks, all refurbished in a light and colourful style, are fully tiled with washbasins in both cabins and vanity style, plus baby rooms and facilities for disabled visitors. Well stocked and licensed shop (closes end Sept) near the leisure centre, as is the laundry room. Two modern bar lounges, one for families and one for adults only, with discos in season, a games room with TV, large adventure playground with safety base, and a café plus takeaway fish and chips. The Plough Inn near the park entrance offers a good bar meal. Pay and play golf course (£5 a round). Indoor swimming pool. Dog exercise area, but numbers and breeds are limited (one per pitch) and not allowed at all at B.Hs and the six week summer holiday. **Off site:** Fishing, boat slipway or riding 2 miles, bicycle hire 4 miles.

Charges 2002

Per unit incl. up to 4 persons	£8.50 - £13.00
child (under 3 yrs)	free
awning	£2.00
electricity	£2.50
dog (see above)	£1.00

10% discount on pitch fee for weekly bookings. No credit cards. **Tel:** 01723 584311. Fax: 01723 581361. **Reservations:** Made with £20 deposit per week and £1 booking fee (Sat.-Sat. only for Spr. B.H. and 13/7-31/8). **Open** Easter - 31 October.

Directions: Park is signed from roundabout at junction of A165 and B1261 from where it is 600 yds. O.S.GR: TA088836.

Yorkshire
Rosedale Caravan & Camping Park
477 Rosedale Abbey, Pickering YO18 8SA

In a beautiful location below Rosedale Moor and on the edge of a popular village, this is a campsite that is highly suitable for walkers. The surrounding hillsides are a maze of public footpaths and these and nearby Cropton Forest can all be reached without using your car. The site itself has a wide entrance on the edge of the village and as it is within the National Park, the buildings are in the local stone and in keeping with the area. The site is reasonably level, with 200 pitches, a few with hardstanding and with 28 electricity connections (10A). One field is for tents only, there are some caravan holiday homes (private) and seasonal touring pitches in their own areas, with the remainder for touring caravans and motorcaravans. The majority have superb views of the surrounding hills. There is a glass blower at the village blacksmith. In summer the Dales bus runs through the village, connecting several of the popular villages. The 13 mile Rosedale circuit follows the route of the old iron-ore railway, giving magnificent views and reminders of bygone industries.

Facilties: The toilet blocks are due to be refurbished, together with laundry and dishwashing sinks. Reception provides maps and a small selection of camping accessories, plus gas supplies. Games room with pool and video games. Large play area with space for ball games. Entrance barrier controlled by card (£5 deposit). **Off site:** The village has a general store with daily papers, a post office, bakery, pubs and a restaurant. A 9 hole golf course, set on a picturesque hillside is 500 yards. The Ryedale Folk Museum at Hutton-le-Hole is 3.5 miles.

Charges 2002

Per unit incl. up to 4 persons	£8.50 - £13.00
2-man tent	£4.50 - £6.50
awning	£2.00
extra person (over 3 yrs)	£2.00 - £5.00
dog	£1.00
electricity	£2.50

10% discount on pitch fee for weekly bookings. No credit cards. **Tel:** 01751 417272. Fax: 01751 417272. E-mail: rosedale@flowerofmay.com. **Reservations:** Contact site. **Open** 31 March - 31 October.

Directions: Rosedale is signed from the A170, 2 miles west of Pickering. Site is in the village of Rosedale Abbey, 8 miles north of the A170. O.S.GR: SE725958.

YORKSHIRE SAND, SEA & SUN

To make the most of your holiday, including indoor heated swimming pool, jacuzzi, 10 pin bowling, superb squash courts, games room with pool and snooker.

■ Heated Indoor Pool & Jacuzzi ■ 9 Hole Golf Course ■ Supermarket ■ Family Bar & Entertainment ■ Excellent Touring Facilities ■ Seasonal Tourers ■ Luxury Holiday Homes for Sale or Hire ■ Exciting Playground with safety surface
Special terms early and late season – send for details.

Please send for colour brochure from the resident proprietors.

AA WINNER
BEST CAMPSITE NORTHERN ENGLAND

Mr and Mrs J.G. Atkinson,
Dept. F. Flower of May, Lebberston Cliff,
Scarborough YO11 3NU
Telephone 01723 584311

RELAX IN THE COUNTRY

■ Touring Pitches ■ Seasonal Pitches
■ Luxury Caravans for Sale **AA ▶▶▶**
■ Nearby Amenities Include:
Walking • Fishing • HistoricTowns & Villages, Studley Royal & Harlow Carr, Gardens of International Repute

RIVERSIDE MEADOWS COUNTRY CARAVAN PARK
Dept. F., Ure Bank Top, Ripon
HG4 1JD Telephone (01765) 602964

UNWIND IN IDYLLIC SETTINGS

■ Touring Pitches ■ Tent Pitches
■ Seasonal Pitches ■ All main facilities
■ Nearby amenities include: **AA ▶▶▶**
Walking on the Moors • Fishing • Pickering Attractions, York and Helmsley Country Houses, Museums and History

ROSEDALE COUNTRY CARAVAN PARK
Dept. F., Rosedale Abbey, Pickering
Telephone (01751) 417272

E-Mail: deptf@flowerofmay.com   www.flowerofmay.com

Yorkshire
Northcliffe Holiday Park
Bottoms Lane, High Hawsker, Whitby YO22 4LL

Northcliffe is a high quality, family park with splendid sea views, set within the North Yorkshire Moors National Park. As well as touring units, it caters for 170 caravan holiday homes, although they are entirely separate. The modern park is well planned and attractive, the very friendly owners keeping everything neat and tidy. The toilet facilities are especially good. The 30 touring pitches are of a good size, all with electrical hook-up, and 16 fully serviced. These 16 have 16A electricity, the rest have 10A. Many trees and flowering bushes have been planted to provide wind breaks. The park is situated on the Heritage Coast and one can walk the Cleveland Way into Whitby or to Robin Hood's Bay. Available at reception are leaflets on walks and countryside notes (75p) produced by the park. Whitby and Scarborough with their sandy beaches are within easy reach as are the moors. York is about an hour away. A member of the Best of British group.

Facilties: The toilet block is heated in early and late seasons and uses a coded number pad entry system. Some washbasins are in cabins. Good facilities for babies and for disabled visitors. Dishwashing room. Well equipped laundry. Well stocked shop (with gas) incorporating an attractive tea-room with range of reasonably priced food to eat in or takeaway (8 am - 8 pm in high season, mornings and evenings in low season). Two fenced play areas have good quality fittings and safety bases. Grass area for games. Indoor room with pool table and amusement machines. Dogs are not accepted. **Off site:** Bicycle hire 0.5 miles, fishing 4 miles, riding 5 miles, golf 4 or 6 miles.

Charges 2002

Per unit incl. 2 persons, electricity	£10.00 - £14.00
incl. mains services and awning	£12.00 - £16.00
extra adult	£2.00 - £3.00
child (under 16 yrs)	£1.00 - £1.50
backpacker (no car) or cyclist	£3.50 - £4.50

Less 10% if 7 nights booked. **Tel:** 01947 880477. Fax: 01947 880972. E-mail: enquiries@northcliffe-seaview.com. **Reservations:** Made with deposit and fee, min. 2-6 nights acc. to pitch type and season. **Open** 15 March - 31 October.

Directions: Three miles south of Whitby on A171 (Scarborough) road turn left onto the B1447 signed High Hawsker and Robin Hood's Bay. Go through Hawsker village and continue on Robin Hood's Bay road. At top of hill turn left onto private road - go on 0.5 miles towards sea. O.S.GR: NZ936080.

Yorkshire
St Helens in the Park
Wykeham, Scarborough YO13 9QD

St Helens is a high quality touring park with pleasant views, set within 30 acres of parkland. The 250 mainly level pitches have a spacious feel and the 52 pitches with hardstanding are used by seasonal lets in the summer months but are available for tourers in winter. Electrical hook-ups (16A) are available on 240 pitches, also in the late arrivals area. Set on a hillside (hence the views), the park's buildings are built in local stone and all is maintained to a high standard. The Downe Arms, a short stroll away, is known for its good food and it occasionally runs family discos in high season. Scarborough is only 5 miles with its beaches and summer shows and buses pass the site gates.

Facilties: Four heated toilet blocks are well equipped and maintained, two having been extended and refurbished. Some washbasins in cabins and baby baths. The new unit for disabled visitors is of a very high standard. All four blocks have dishwashing sinks under cover. Good laundry room. Well stocked shop also providing snacks and takeaway (1/4-31/10). Adventure playground set on bark is part of a three acre area set aside for children with goal posts and a mountain bike track. Bicycle hire. Small games room with pool table and amusement machines. Caravan storage. **Off site:** Nearby Wykeham Lakes offer fishing (trout and coarse), scuba diving, windsurfing and sailing (in your own boat). Golf or riding 2 miles.

Charges 2002

Per unit incl. 2 persons	£8.50 - £10.60
extra person (over 3 yrs)	£1.00
awning	£1.90
porch awning	£1.50
pup tent	£6.00
dog	£1.00
electricity	£2.30

Tel: 01723 862771. Fax: 01723 862771. E-mail: caravans@wykeham.co.uk. **Reservations:** Made with £20 deposit (min. 4 nights for Spr. and Aug. B.Hs). **Open** all year excl. 15 Jan-13 Feb.

Directions: Park access road leads off the A170 (Pickering - Scarborough) road in Wykeham village 2 miles west of junction with B1262. O.S.GR: SE963835.

Yorkshire

Jacobs Mount Caravan Park

459 Stepney Road, Scarborough YO12 5NL.

Situated just two miles from the centre of Scarborough, yet in the heart of the country, Jacobs Mount is well placed to meet many holiday needs. The sea and the sand are the main attractions, but this is also on the doorstep of the North York moors and the Dalby Forest Drive. The park has 142 pitches, all with 16A electricity. Of these 131 are fully serviced (water, drainage) on well spaced gravel hardstandings. In sunny locations, some pitches have good views. There is a bar with a pleasant lounge (no children), plus a family room and a games/TV room. Bar meals and a quite extensive range of takeaways can be purchased. Footpaths lead into the surrounding woods and buses pass the gates.

Facilities: The heated toilet block is new and of a high standard. It provides washbasins in cubicles with WCs, large shower cubicles (free) and a family bathroom (metered hot water) and baby changing facilities. Separate unisex cubicles contain WC, washbasin and shower. Motorcaravan service point. Small shop in reception for basic needs. Bar with bar meals and takeaway. Two play areas for different ages. Caravan storage. No gazebo style tents allowed. Up to two dogs per pitch are accepted. **Off site:** Scarborough centre and beach 2 miles. Golf, fishing or bicycle hire 2 miles. Riding 5 miles.

Charges 2002

Per unit incl. 4 persons	£8.00 - £12.00
extra person 3 yrs and over	£1.50
awning	£2.00
pup tent beside unit	£7.00
electricity	£2.00
dog (max 2)	£1.00

No single sex parties. **Tel:** 01723 361178. Fax: 01723 361178. E-mail: jacobsmount@yahoo.co.uk. **Reservations:** Made with deposit (3 days charge); min. stay at B.Hs 3 nights. **Open** 1 March - 31 October.

Directions: Site entrance is on the A170 Pickering Scarborough road, about 2 miles west of Scarborough (on the right as you start to drop down into the town). O.S.GR: TA021877.

Yorkshire

Upper Carr Chalet & Touring Park

462 Upper Carr Lane, Malton Road, Pickering YO18 7JP

Being centrally located in the Vale of Pickering, Upper Carr is well placed for the many attractions the area has to offer. The park is surrounded by a high, well trimmed hedge which protects it from the wind and deadens the road noise. There are colourful gardens and a pets corner where children can feed unusual breeds of poultry. Upper Carr's six acres provides 80 level pitches, 75 with 10A electricity and some with hardstanding. Seasonal units use 25 pitches. The picturesque village of Thornton Dale can be reached on foot or by cycle along the Upper Carr nature trail. A member of the Countryside Discovery group.

Facilties: The toilet blocks are a little dated (in 'portacabin' style) with open plan washbasins, but all is kept very clean and well decorated. Showers are charged for. Baby changing facilities. A separate room houses a WC and washbasin for disabled visitors. Dishwashing sinks are outside, but under cover. Laundry room. Motorcaravan service point. Small shop in reception supplies basic needs and gas. Good children's play area. Bicycle hire. Nature trail. **Off site:** Pub 100 yards. Golf (9 hole) or tennis adjacent to park. Fishing 5 miles. Swimming pool 1.5 miles. Bus service passes entrance.

Charges 2002

Per unit incl. 2 persons	£8.00 - £10.50
extra person (over 3 yrs)	£1.00
electricity	£2.00
awning or child's pup tent	£1.50
extra large tent plus	£1.50

Tel: 01751 473115. Fax: 01751 473115. E-mail: harker@uppercarr.demon.co.uk. **Reservations:** Made with £15 deposit - contact park. **Open** 1 March - 31 October.

Directions: Travelling on the Pickering - Malton A169 road, park is on the left hand side about 1.5 miles south of Pickering. O.S.GR: SE804815.

Yorkshire
Spiers House Caravan & Camping Site
457 Cropton Forest, Cropton, Pickering YO18 8ES

The Spiers House site, run by the Forestry Commission, is set in a sunny clearing in the middle of Cropton Forest. It is an ideal location for a cycling or walking holiday without having to move your car. The site buildings, built in local stone, are set around a central courtyard with a pedestrian archway leading to the pitches. The welcoming reception with its cane furniture, also incorporates a well stocked shop. Sloping fields provide for 150 pitches, which include 74 with 10A electricity and 19 with hardstanding. The Moors bus calls at the site every Sunday from 1 May - 1 Sept, and daily in high season (21 July - 1 Sept) making journeys to Rosedale, or beyond, and Pickering possible.

Facilties: The tiled toilet block is spacious, if a little Spartan, with open plan washbasins and roomy, pre-set showers. Unit for disabled campers (WC and washbasin only). Dishwashing sinks under cover with free hot water, laundry room with washing machine, dryer and sinks (hot water charged). Well stocked shop. Large adventure playground and games field set under tall pines. Reception provides leaflets for way-marked walks in the forest and orienteering. Raised barbecues are permitted. **Off site:** Pub with home-brewed beer 1 mile. Riding 5 miles, golf 12 miles.

Charges 2002

Per unit incl. 2 persons	£6.60 - £9.60
extra person (over 5 yrs)	£1.20
child's tent, awning or extra car	£2.50
electricity	£2.00
backpacker	£3.80 - £4.80

Prices are higher at weekends. Less 20% all year for disabled guests and outside 7/7-28/8 for senior citizens. **Tel:** 01751 417591. Fax: 01751 417591. **Reservations:** Necessary for B.Hs and peak times; made for min. 3 nights with £30 deposit. Contact site when open, otherwise Forest Holidays, Forestry Commission, 231 Corstorphine Road, Edinburgh EH12 7AT. **Open** 21 March - 30 September.

Directions: From Pickering take A170 westwards towards Helmsley for about 2 miles. Just after delimited speed sign, take unnumbered road to the right signed Cropton and Rosedale. In about 4 miles site is signed to the right into the forest (do not go into Cropton village). O.S.GR: SE758918.

Yorkshire
Vale of Pickering Caravan Park
460 Carr House Farm, Allerston YO18 7PQ

Vale of Pickering is a level park edged by grassy banks and, although over the years that the site has been developing these have been partly hidden by foliage, trees and attractive flower beds, they do give shelter from the wind. The family owners, who are local farmers, have put a lot of thought into planning their site and it is a well designed, neat and tidy park.There are 120 pitches, of which 75 are for touring units, all with electrical connections (10A), plus further pitches for tents. Buses run from the village to Scarborough and Pickering.

Facilties: The refurbished toilet block is tiled, heated and well maintained, providing some washbasins in cabins, showers (coin-operated 20p) and a bath. Separate toilet and washbasin for visitors with disabilities. Dishwashing sinks (2p for hot water). Launderette. Microwave oven. Motorcaravan service point. Well stocked, licensed shop also stocking a few caravan accessories and gas (open according to demand in low season). Good play area and play field for football, etc. Boules pitch. **Off site:** Local pub at Yedingham, 1.5 miles. Fishing 1 mile, bicycle hire and riding 3 miles, golf 5 miles.

Charges 2002

Per unit incl. 2 adults and 2 children under 12 yrs	£6.75 - £9.75
extra adult	£2.00
child (over 12 yrs)	£1.00
awning	£1.50
electricity	£2.00
small tent or extra car	£2.00
large tent plus	£1.50
hardstanding	£0.50
2 dogs free, extra dog	£1.00

Early and late season discounts for stays over 5 days and for OAPs. No credit cards. **Tel:** 01723 859280. Fax: 01723 850060. E-mail: vopcp@ netscapeonline.co.uk. **Reservations:** Made with £10 deposit (min. 3 nights at B.Hs with £20 deposit). **Open** all year excl. 11 Jan - 28 Feb.

Directions: Park is 1 mile off the main A170 (Scarborough - Helmsley) road at the village of Allerston. O.S.GR: SE879808.

Foxholme Touring Caravan & Camping Park

Harome, Helmsley YO62 5JG

458

Foxholme is an unusual park with only 60 pitches for caravans and a small field for a few tents. Nearly all the pitches are individual ones in clearings in the quite dense coniferous plantation. The trees give much shade and quite a lot of privacy (manoeuvring may be difficult on some of the pitches). All pitches have electricity (6A, a few need long leads) and six places have hardstanding. Some picnic tables are provided. There are 30 pitches for tourers, the remainder being taken by seasonal units. The site is managed by a warden and his wife with reception usually open 9 am. - 9 pm. (6 days). Very basic provisions are kept. The park is set in quiet countryside and would be a good base for touring, being within striking distance of the moors, the coast and York. There are no on site activities but campers may use the indoor pool at the Pheasant Hotel in Harome. There is lighting, but a torch would be useful.

Facilities: The toilet block is of good quality, built in local stone, with all washbasins in private cubicles, a laundry room with washing machine and sinks and a washing up room. Two further small blocks provide WCs only in other parts of the park. Motorcaravan service point. Caravan storage. **Off site:** The nearest shops are at Helmsley and Kirkbymoorside, both about 4 miles away, where there is also bicycle hire. Riding and golf also 4 miles.

Charges 2002

Per unit	£8.50
extra adult	£1.50
child	£1.00
electricity	£2.50
awning	£1.50

No credit cards. **Tel:** 01439 771696. Fax: 01439 771744. **Reservations:** Made for any dates with £10 deposit. **Open** Easter - 31 October.

Directions: Turn south off the A170 between adjoining villages of Beadlam (to west) and Nawton (to east) at sign to Ryedale School, then 1 mile to park on left (passing another park on right). From east ignore first camp sign at turning before Nawton. From west turn right 400 yards east of Helmsley, signed Harome, turn left at church, go through village and follow camp signs. O.S.GR: SE661831.

ALAN ROGERS' GUIDES

Travelling further afield?
Remember the other Alan Rogers'
guides to FRANCE and EUROPE

Available from
all good bookshops or
online at www.alanrogers.com

Yorkshire
Golden Square Caravan & Camping Park
Oswaldkirk, York YO62 5YQ

456

Golden Square is a popular, high quality, family owned touring park. Mr and Mrs Armstrong are local farmers who have worked hard to turn an old quarry into a very attractive caravan park with a number of levelled bays that have superb views over the Vale of Pickering. The 130 pitches are not separated but they do have markers set into the ground and mainly back onto grass banks. In very dry weather the ground can be hard, steel pegs would be needed (even in wet weather the park is well drained). All pitches have electrical connections (10A), 24 have drainage and 6 are 'deluxe' pitches (with waste water, sewage, electricity, water and TV aerial connection). The licensed shop is very well stocked, selling home-made fresh bread and cakes, dairy produce, fresh vegetables and groceries, newspapers, gas and gifts. Visitors may have membership of the Ampleforth College sports centre, with its indoor pool, tennis and gym, etc. The area abounds with footpaths and three well known long distance footpaths are near. Dog owners are well catered for with two or three enormous fields for exercising alongside the park.

Facilties: Two heated well cared for toilet blocks are of excellent quality, with some washbasins in private cabins. Showers are pre-set and metered (token) and a bathroom (token) also houses baby changing facilities. Both ladies' and men's blocks have full facilities for disabled visitors. Dishwashing sinks are under cove. Laundry with washing machines, dryers, a spin dryer and iron and board. Motorcaravan service point. The tourist information room also houses a microwave and an extra iron and board. Shop. Two excellent play areas allow tiny tots to be kept separate from older children. Games field and a barn with table tennis and pool table. Bicycle hire. All year caravan storage. **Off site:** Riding 2 miles, golf 3 miles, fishing 5 miles. Nearby Helmsley and Ampleforth have shops and pubs with food.

Charges 2002

Per unit incl. 2 persons and	
all children up to 10 yrs	£7.00 - £11.50
extra person (10 yrs or over)	£1.50
awning	£1.50 - £1.40
electricity	£2.00
de-luxe pitch, all inclusive	£15.00 - £20.00
hikers and bikers, per person	£3.50 - £4.00

No credit cards. **Tel:** 01439 788269. Fax: 01439 788236. E-mail: barbara@goldensquarecaravanpark.com. **Reservations:** Essential for B.Hs and made with £10 deposit (£20 for B.Hs). **Open** 1 March - 31 October.

Directions: From York take B1363 to Helmsley. At Oswaldkirk Bank Top turn left on B1257 to Helmsley. Take second left turn signed Ampleforth to site. O.S.GR: SE605797.

Yorkshire
Brompton on Swale Caravan & Camping Park
Brompton on Swale, Richmond DL10 7EZ

480

Brompton is a quiet family site in a delightful setting on the banks of the river Swale, only two miles from the ancient market town of Richmond (the Lass of Richmond Hill fame). This caravan park is on level meadows of well cut grass with pitches marked by a slab for the jockey wheel. Of the 214 pitches 100 are allocated to seasonal lets and the remainder to tourers. There are some fully serviced pitches and 177 with electricity (10/16A). The ones alongside the river are ideal for families with older children as they can easily be supervised in their unending efforts to catch tiddlers and crayfish. Both fly and coarse fishing are possible on the river. The town of Richmond can be reached by a riverside walk. Its cobbled market square is dominated by the 100 feet high keep of the Norman castle and is home to the Green Howards museum and a Georgian theatre. The site is on the route of the long distance Coast-to-Coast trail.

Facilties: Both shower blocks are heated and have facilities for disabled visitors and babies. Showers have a curtain divider, and washbasins are open plan, vanity style. One block has two rooms for families or disabled people. Each block has dishwashing sinks. Laundry with washing machines, dryers and an iron. Motorcaravan service point. Licensed shop with reception at the entrance wide range of produce and gas. Fenced play area. Fishing (permits from reception). Security barrier (key for toilets and barrier £5 deposit) and late arrivals area with hook-up. **Off site:** Swimming pool and leisure centre in Richmond.

Charges 2002

Per unit incl. 2 persons	£9.00
awning/gazebo	£2.00
electricity	£2.50
backpacker, cyclist or m/cyclist	£4.00
extra person (12 yrs or over)	£2.00
fully serviced pitch	£16.50
dog (max 2)	£0.50

Tel: 01748 824629. Fax: 01748 826383. **Reservations:** Made with £10 deposit (min 3 nights at B.Hs). **Open** 15 March - 31 October.

Directions: Park is by the B6271 road, 1.5 miles southeast of Richmond. O.S.GR: NZ197004.

Yorkshire
Constable Burton Hall Caravan Park

Constable Burton Hall, Leyburn DL8 5LJ

469

This tranquil park is in beautiful Wensleydale and the emphasis is on peace and quiet, the wardens working to provide a relaxing environment. Being in the grounds of the Hall, it has a spacious, park-like feel to it. On part level, part sloping, well trimmed grass, the 120 pitches (40 for touring units) are of a good size and all have electrical connections (10A). There are 5 pitches for tents. Ideally placed for visiting the Northern Dales, the gardens of the Hall are open to the public, with a collection of maples and terraced gardens developed by Mrs Vida Burton. There is no shop on site but nearby Leyburn will provide all your needs. Opposite the park entrance is the Wyvill Arms for bar meals. Ball games are not permitted on site.

Facilties: Two toilet blocks built of local stone and blending in with the local surroundings, have been refurbished recently, are well tiled and kept immaculately clean, and can be heated. The former deer barn has been adapted for use as a laundry room and extra washrooms with basins for both men and women. Gas supplies. Gates closed 10 pm - 8 am. **Off site:** Fishing, riding or golf within 4 miles.

Charges 2002

Per unit incl. 2 persons	£7.50 - £10.00
extra adult	£2.50
child (5-16 yrs)	£1.00
awning	£1.80
electricity	£2.00

No commercial vehicles. No credit cards. **Tel:** 01677 450428. **Reservations:** Made with deposit (£20 for B.Hs. £5 other times). **Open** late March - 31 October.

Directions: Park is by the A684 between Bedale and Leyburn, 0.5 miles from the village of Constable Burton on the Leyburn side. O.S.GR: SE152907.

Yorkshire
Riverside Meadows Country Caravan Park

Ure Bank Top, Ripon HG4 1JD

476

Riverside Meadows is under the same ownership as Flower of May (no. 452) with owners who have lots of experience in the caravan park world. All the facilities are being upgraded and brought up to their demanding standards. This is a rural park, although the approach to it belies that fact. The short approach from the main road passes a row of houses and a factory, but once they are passed, the park opens up before you and you are once again back in the countryside. There are plenty of caravan holiday homes but they are, on the whole, quite separate from the touring units. The pitches, practically all with electrical hook-ups, are mainly on gently sloping grass with just a few hard-standings. A meadow separates the park from the River Ure, a favourite place for strolling and fishing (licences available). Close to Ripon is the Lightwater Valley theme park, and a little further are Fountains Abbey, Harrogate, Knaresborough, the Yorkshire Dales and Thirsk with its market and the new James Herriot centre. There is lots to see and do on and off the park for both families and couples.

Facilties: The new, tiled toilet block includes a baby room, dishwashing room, a fully fitted shower room for disabled visitors and laundry facilities. New shop, reception, bar with snacks and games room. Well equipped new children's play area. **Off site:** Golf course within a mile. The delightful market town (city) of Ripon with its ancient cathedral is only 15 minutes walk.

Charges 2002

Per unit incl. 4 persons	£7.00 - £11.00
extra person	£2.00
awning or extra car	£2.00
dog (max 2)	£1.00
electricity	£2.00

10% discount on pitch fee for weekly bookings. No credit cards. **Tel:** 01765 602964. Fax: 01765 604045. E-mail: riverside@flowerofmay.com. **Reservations:** Made for min. 3 nights with £20 per week deposit. **Open** Easter - 31 October.

Directions: At the most northern roundabout on the Ripon bypass (A61), turn onto the A6108 signed Ripon, Masham and Leyburn. Go straight on at mini-roundabout and park is signed on right. O.S.GR: SE317727.

See advertisement on page 187

Yorkshire
Street Head Caravan Park
Newbiggin, Bishopdale, Leyburn DL8 3TE

468

Street Head is a no frills, simple site next door to the local hostelry and with marvellous views. There are 50 privately owned holiday homes arranged over two areas, while a separate, fairly level, hedged field with a circular gravel road provides 25 pitches for touring units. Each has hardstanding and 10A electricity. A further separate sloping field is for tents. Thoralby village (400 yards) has a general store and West Burton (1.5 miles) is very pretty with a pub and shops. Bar snacks are served next door at the Street Head Inn. Aysgarth Falls are only 1.5 miles and there are local markets at Hawes and Leyburn.

Facilties: Sanitary facilities provide metered hot showers (20p), free hot water to washbasins, but metered for washing up sinks. Washing machine and dryer. Basic essentials and gas are available from reception (only open for two hours morning and afternoon in the main season, less in low season). Caravan storage. **Off site:** Bicycle hire 0.5 miles, fishing 4 miles.

Charges 2002

Per unit	£9.00
hikers tent	£8.00
awning	£2.00
electricity	£2.00

No credit cards. **Tel:** 01969 663472. **Reservations:** Advised at B.Hs; contact site. **Open** 1 March - end October.

Directions: From A684 travelling west (just after Swinithwaite) take B6160 signed Kettlewell, continue to Newbiggin past turning to West Burton and park is on right. O.S.GR: SD998862.

Yorkshire
Woodhouse Farm Caravan & Camping Park
Winksley, Ripon HG4 3PG

466

This secluded family park on a former working farm, is only 6 miles from Ripon and about 4 miles from the World Heritage site of Fountains Abbey. It is a very rural park with a spacious feel and various pitching areas tucked away in woodland areas or around the edges of hedged fields with the centres left clear for children. There are hard roads and most of the 160 pitches have 16A electricity. There are 56 acres in total, 17.5 devoted to the site and 20 acres of woodland for walks, etc. The 2.5 acre fishing lake is a big attraction and provides a pleasant area for picnics or walks. The Yorkshire Dales of Nidderdale, Wharfedale, Wensleydale and Swaledale are all within easy reach and there are many villages with attractive country inns. The small historic city of Ripon has a beautiful cathedral. Woodhouse Farm has a quiet, secluded location from which many excursions can be made. As in most parts of the Dales, the peace is occasionally disturbed by passing jets, but happily not very often.

Facilties: The clean, functional toilet block nearer the pitches has been upgraded includes heating and roomy showers (20p) and some washbasins in cabins. Covered dishwashing sinks. Two bathrooms and facilities for disabled visitors are planned. Extra facilities are in the farm buildings along with a well equipped laundry, reception and shop. Motorcaravan services. New restaurant. Games room, table tennis, pool table and TV. Play equipment around the park. Fishing (day tickets from reception). Caravan storage. **Off site:** Riding 3 miles, golf 6 miles.

Charges 2002

Per caravan and car or motorcaravan incl. 2 persons	£8.50
tent incl. car and 2 persons	£7.50 - £8.00
cyclist or hiker with tent	£4.50
extra person (over 5 yrs)	£1.00
awning, pup tent	£2.00
electricity hook-up (B.Hs only)	£1.00

Tel: 01765 658309. E-mail: woodhouse.farm@talk21.com. **Reservations:** Contact park. **Open** 1 March - 31 October.

Directions: From Ripon take Fountains Abbey - Pateley Bridge road (B6265). After approx. 3.5 miles turn right to Grantley and then follow campsite signs for further 1-2 miles. O.S.GR: SE241715.

Woodhouse Farm & Country Park

¥ 56 Acres —Fishing — Children s Play Area

¥ Laundry — Licenced Shop — Indoor Games Room

¥ New toilet block and Restaurant

¥ Mountain Bike Hire — Plus All Usual Facilities

www.woodhousewinksley.com

Winksley, Ripon, N. Yorkshire HG4 3PG

email woodhouse.farm@talk21.com

Tel: 01765 658309

Yorkshire
Wood Nook Caravan Park
Skirethorns, Threshfield, Skipton BD23 5NU

Wood Nook is a family run park in the heart of Wharfedale, part of the Yorkshire Dales National Park. The access road is narrow for a short distance, but you will find it is well worth this slight rural inconvenience as the site includes six acres of woodland with quite rare flora and wildlife. Reception is in the farmhouse, as is the small shop. The gently sloping fields have gravel roads and provide 25 pitches with gravel hardstanding. All have electricity (10A, long leads may be required) and there are water and chemical disposal points. There is also room for 24 tents and the park has some caravan holiday homes to let. The Thompson family are very friendly, trying always to have time for a chat, although Wood Nook is still a working farm producing beef cattle. The park itself adjoins the fells, with direct access from the top of the site. A visit to the nearby village of Grassington is a must, with its cobbled main street and quaint gift shops. All in all, this is a peaceful park from which to explore the Yorkshire Dales.

Facilties: Farm buildings have been converted to provide modern, neat sanitary facilities which can be heated, are well maintained and kept very clean (opened by key). Washbasins in cubicles for ladies. Roomy showers (in another building) are coin operated. Fully equipped laundry with clothes lines. Dishwashing sinks under cover. Motorcaravan service points. Licensed shop for basics and a range of gifts (from Easter). Gas supplies. Small, attractive play area on top of a small hill. American motorhomes are taken by prior arrangement. **Off site:** Fishing or bicycle hire 2 miles, riding 3 miles, golf 9 miles. Good range of bar food available locally. Leisure centre with pool nearby.

Charges 2002

Per adult	£2.50
child (5-15 yrs)	£1.00
young adult (16-17 yrs) as part of family unit	£1.50
caravan or motorcaravan incl. electricity	£7.00
tent and car	£5.00
hiker/cyclist	£4.00
awning	£1.00

Tel: 01756 752412. Fax: 01756 752412. E-mail: enquiries@woodnook.net. **Reservations:** Necessary for high season and B.Hs with £10 deposit. **Open** 1 March - 31 October.

Directions: From Skipton take B6265 to Thresh-field, then B6160. After 50 yds turn left into Skirethorns Lane and follow signs for 600 yds, up narrow lane then 300 yds. O.S.GR: SD974641.

Yorkshire
Knight Stainforth Hall Caravan & Camping Park
Little Stainforth, Settle BD24 0DP

This traditional park is located in the heart of the Yorkshire Dales, the whole area a paradise for hill-walking, fishing and pot-holing and with outstanding scenery. The camping area is on slightly sloping grass, sheltered by mature woodland in a very attractive setting. There are 100 touring pitches, 50 with electricity (10A) and 10 with hardstanding. A separate area houses 60 privately owned caravan holiday homes. Buildings near the farmhouse provide reception, a games/TV room and a shop (for basics). A gate leads from the bottom of the camping field giving access to the river bank where the Ribble bubbles over small waterfalls and rocks and whirls around deep pools where, we are told, campers do swim in warm weather. This is not fenced and children should be supervised, although it is a super location for a family picnic. Fishing permits and licences are available from reception and one can fish for trout (or salmon when available). Settle is only two miles away, as is Giggleswick and its well known school. Train buffs will want to travel on the Settle - Carlisle railway over the famous Ribblehead Viaduct. The magic of the Dales National Park is on the doorstep and just off the A65 to the west of Settle at Felzor is the Dales Falconry and Conservation Centre.

Facilties: Toilet facilities, in a converted stone barn, are very basic but there is heating and a good supply of hot water, plus three curtained cubicles with washbasins for ladies. A new block is planned. Dishwashing sinks. Laundry room with washing machine and dryers. Shop. Games/TV room. Children's playground. Fishing. Bicycle hire. Security barrier at entrance (£10 deposit). **Off site:** Riding or golf 3 miles.

Charges 2002

Per unit incl. 2 adults	£8.75
extra adult	£2.50
extra child (5-16 yrs)	£1.50
backpacker	£3.90
extra vehicle	£1.00
electricity	£1.75

Weekly rate: 7 nights for the price of 6. **Tel:** 01729 822200. Fax: 01729 823387. E-mail: info@knightstainforth.co.uk. **Reservations:** Write or phone for details. **Open** 1 March - 31 October.

Directions: From Settle town centre, drive west towards Giggleswick. Ignore turning marked Stainforth and Horton, and after 200 yards turn right into Stackhouse Lane (signed Knight Stainforth). After 2 miles turn right at crossroads. O.S.GR: SD815671.

Ripley Caravan Park
where the country and enjoyment comes naturally...

This luxury touring caravan park in the beautiful North Yorkshire countryside is within easy reach of Ripley Castle and village and only ten minutes north of Harrogate. First class facilities include indoor heated swimming pool, sauna, games room, nursery playroom, children's playground and play area. There is a shop, laundry, telephone, electric hook-up points and amenities for the disabled.

Special offers on minimum seven nights stay in low season.

For further information: -
Peter & Valerie House,
Ripley Caravan Park
Ripley, Harrogate, HG3 3AU
Tel: (01423) 770050   *Dogs permitted*

 SILVER

Yorkshire
Rudding Caravan Park
Follifoot, Harrogate HG3 1JH

471

The extensive part wooded, part open grounds of Rudding Park are very attractive, peaceful and well laid out. One camping area is sloping but terraces provide level pitches and further pitches are in the very sheltered old walled garden. All 141 touring pitches have electricity (10/16A) and 17 'super pitches' are fully serviced. Some pitches are let on a seasonal basis and a separate area contains 90 owner occupied caravan holiday homes and pine chalets. On the outer edge of the park is an 18 hole golf course and driving range, together with the 'The Deer House', a bar and restaurant open twice daily during B.Hs and school holidays, otherwise only at weekends. Tennis, markets, pubs and restaurants are within a few miles, and the majestic City of York is less than an hour away. This is an attractive park with something for all the family.

Facilties: Two tiled toilet blocks are of a good standard, centrally heated and well maintained. Some washbasins in cabins, a baby room and bathroom. Fully equipped laundry room at each block. Disabled people have well appointed facilities. Motorcaravan service point. Large, well stocked shop (all season, sometimes limited hours). Gas supplies. Restaurant and bar. Heated outdoor swimming and paddling pools with sunbathing areas (Spr. B.H.- early Sept), supervised at all times (extra charge). Adventure playground. Football pitch, games room and minigolf. Golf. **Off site:** Buses pass the gate hourly to Harrogate and Knaresborough. Fishing 2 miles, riding 1 mile.

Charges 2002

Per pitch	£10.00 - £14.50
awning	£2.00
electricity	£2.50
'supersite' incl. awning, electricity	£17.00 - £23.00
tent per adult	£3.50 - £5.00
child (under 16 yrs)	£1.25 - £3.00

Tel: 01423 870439. Fax: 01423 870859. E-mail: holiday-park@ruddingpark.com. **Reservations:** Made with full advance payment (essential for B.H. w/ends). **Open** 14 March - 2 November.

Directions: Park is 3 miles south of Harrogate clearly signed between the A658 and A661 roads. O.S.GR: SE333528.

RUDDING
HOLIDAY PARK

FOLLIFOOT, HARROGATE,
NORTH YORKSHIRE HG3 1JH

TEL: 01423 870439
FAX: 01423 870859

e-mail - holidaypark@ruddingpark.com
www.ruddingpark.com

Relax at Britain's AA
Campsite of the Year - 2001   **AA**

• Deer House family pub
• Children's adventure playground
• Heated outdoor swimming pool & paddling pool
• 18 hole pay & play golf course plus floodlit driving range
• Pets welcome • Games room • Launderette
• Free showers • Park lighting • Shop

Ripley Caravan Park

463 Ripley, Harrogate HG3 3AU

Peter and Valerie House are the resident owners of Ripley Park, an 18 acre grass caravan park with an indoor heated pool. Accommodating 130 units on fairly level grass, undulating in parts, there are 130 electricity connections (10A) and 20 hardstandings. Connected by a circular gravel road, some pitches are marked, others carefully spaced (allowing the grass to recover). Recent developments include electricity hook-ups, water points and refuse areas for tents and 2,000 trees have been planted. The trees are developing well to provide individual areas and shelter. A small pond (lake) with ducks provides an attractive feature. The park is situated at the gateway to the Yorkshire Dales National Park and almost midway between the spa town of Harrogate and historic Knaresborough. The village of Ripley, dominated by its castle, is within walking distance.

Facilties: The central, attractively designed toilet block provides washbasins in curtained cubicles, a baby bath and a separate unit with a shower for disabled people. It can be heated and has been extended to provide extra, smart facilities. Small laundry. Dishwashing sinks under cover. Motorcaravan service point. Recycling bins. Shop (with gas). Games room with TV. Nursery playroom. Adventure play equipment and football area. Heated indoor pool (50p per person) and sauna. Up to two dogs per unit are welcome unless by prior arrangement. Winter caravan storage. **Off site:** Fishing, riding or golf 3 miles. Bus service 150 yds.

Charges 2002

Per unit incl. 2 adults	£6.95 - £8.50
extra adult	£2.00
child (5-18 yrs)	£1.00
small tent incl. 2 persons, no vehicle	£5.00
awning	£1.50
porch awning, child's pup tent or extra car	£1.00
electricity	£1.95
water and drainage	£2.00
max. per family unit (2 adults, 2 children)	£11.50

Tel: 01423 770050. Fax: 01423 770050.
Reservations: Made with £10 deposit, min. 3 nights at B.Hs. **Open** Easter - 31 October.

Directions: About 4 miles north of Harrogate, site access is 150 yds. down the B6165 Knaresborough road from its roundabout junction with the A61. O.S.GR: SE291601.

Howgill Lodge Caravan & Camping Park

475 Barden, Skipton BD23 6DJ

Howgill Lodge is a traditional family site, set in the heart of the Dales. Arranged on a sloping hillside, the terraced pitches have fantastic views. It is a small park catering for the needs of walkers, tourers and the people who like to just relax. The whole area is a haven for both experienced walkers or the casual rambler, without having to move your car. All the pitches at the upper part of the park are on hardstanding and have electricity connections (10A), the lower ones are mainly on grass (30 in total). Picnic tables and chairs are provided. Reception also houses a small shop which sells most of the basics including fresh foods. Part of the farmhouse has been tastefully converted into a licensed restaurant, open six days a week (noon - 6 pm) in season, weekends only in winter. Pretty villages abound in the area, all with attractive inns and nearby Embsay has the Dales Railway with steam trains. This very pleasant park, with clean facilities, has a very relaxing feel to it. A member of the Countryside Discovery group.

Facilties: Heated toilet facilities are at the entrance, close to reception, with dishwashing sinks outside, under cover. Showers are large and adjustable (on payment). Fully equipped laundry room with washing machine, dryer and iron and four unisex showers also here. Outdoor washing lines are provided. Two small blocks housing WCs are lower down the site for the convenience of tent campers. Shop. Licensed restaurant. No children's play area. Fishing licences are available from reception. B&B is offered. **Off site:** Skipton, an agricultural market town, is only 8 miles and the well known Bolton Abbey, with its beautiful riverside walks is only 3 miles.

Charges 2002

Per unit incl. 2 persons	£9.50 - £12.00
tent or motorcaravan	£9.50 - £12.00
awning	£1.50
hiker	£3.50

Tel: 01756 720655. Fax: 01756 720623. E-mail: info@howgill-lodge.co.uk. **Reservations:** Made with £15 deposit. **Open** 1 April - 31 October.

Directions: Turn off A59 Skipton - Harrogate road at roundabout onto B6160 Bolton Abbey, Burnsall road. Three miles past Bolton Abbey at Barden Towers, bear right signed Appletreewick.

North West Tourist Board

Cheshire, Lancashire, Merseyside, Greater Manchester and the High Peaks of Derbyshire

North West Tourist Board
Swan House, Swan Meadow Road,
Wigan Pier, Wigan WN3 5BB
Tel: (01942) 821222 Fax: (01942) 820002
Internet: http://www.visitnorthwest.com

The North West Tourist Board includes the counties of Cheshire, Greater Manchester, Lancashire and Merseyside, and the High Peak District of Derbyshire.

The north of England expresses itself in a scale and sternness not found in the south of the country, with some magnificent scenery. However, the area suffers from the legacy of the cotton industry and the effects of the Industrial Revolution.

Merseyside with Manchester and Liverpool was at the heart of the cotton business, expanded rapidly and then experienced economic decline. Now Greater Manchester is England's second largest urban area, boasting a very vibrant night life and, with Liverpool, brings together one of the most innovative music and arts scenes in Britain. Liverpool's once thriving docks are now clustered with museums and each pub, restaurant and corner claim a Beatles connection.

Cheshire has distinctive timber framed houses best seen in Chester, which is also a Roman city well worth visiting. Again much of the region was, and is still, industrial; cotton mills can be visited at Style.

The most well known resorts are Lancashire's Blackpool and Morecambe, still with a fairly strong working class flavour developed from the past. Brash and cheerful Blackpool with its three piers and dominated by the Tower, still attracts many visitors who go, not only to visit the Pleasure Beach with its 140 rides, but to see the famous 'illuminations' in September and October. Morecambe is more family orientated.

The Peak District National Park wedged between industrial giants like Manchester, Sheffield, Nottingham and Stoke on Trent, serves as a play-ground to 17 million urban neighbours and receives over 26 million visitors a year.

Photo: Blackpool; North West Tourist Board

For latest information visit www.**alanrogers**.com

Chester Southerly Caravan Park

523 Balderton Lane, Marlston-cum-Lache, Chester CH4 9LF

This is a well managed friendly campsite within three miles of the city of Chester. It is easily accessible from the Chester Southerly bypass and convenient to the new ferry terminal at Mostyn. It enjoys a quiet countryside environment and the 90 pitches mostly on hardstanding for touring outfits are spaciously spread in bays around this mature site. Pitches are marked, numbered and level with 10A electricity connections. To the left of the card operated security barrier stands reception which incorporates a small shop selling basic food items. Chester is one of England's most historic cities and this site makes a convenient base for spending time discovering its famous rows, walls, gates and towers. There are many other touring possibilities from here such as the North Wales Coast, the Dee valley, Cheshire Plain, etc.

Facilties: A single toilet block (key system), whilst not ultra modern is brightly decorated, kept clean and can be heated. Open style washbasins; facilities for people with disabilities (washbasin and WC), laundry room with sinks, washing machine and dryer and dishwashing area. Motorcaravan service point. Shop. Adventure type play area. **Off site:** City centre 3 miles.

Charges 2002

Per unit incl. 2 persons	£10.00
electricity	£2.00

Tel: 01244 671308. Fax: 01244 659804.
Reservations: Contact site.

Directions: Park is on Dodleston - Kinnerton turn off from A483 and is signed from the junction of A55 and A483 roads. O.S.GR: SJ385624.

Abbey Farm Caravan Park

528 Dark Lane, Ormskirk L40 5TX

This quiet, well equipped, family park beside the Abbey ruins has views over open farmland. It is an ideal base for a longer stay with plenty of interest in the local area, including Ormskirk parish church, unusual for having both a tower and a spire. Market days are on Thursday and Saturday. The park is divided into small paddocks, one of which is for 44 privately owned seasonal units, one for tents, the others for touring units, plus a rally field for special events. The 60 touring pitches, all with electricity (10 or 16A), are on neatly mown level grass, separated by small shrubs and colourful flower borders. Some mature trees provide shade in parts. Amenities include a farm walk and a small, free lending library with a good stock of tourist information. The site organises two events annually - a barbecue in early June and a Bonfire Night in November. Wigan Pier, the British Commercial Vehicle Museum, Aintree for the Grand National, the annual Beatles Festival or Southport Flower Show and Martin Mere Nature reserve are some of the attractions within easy reach. A member of the Countryside Discovery group.

Facilties: The main toilet block is modern, heated and spotless, providing controllable hot showers, hand and hair dryers, plus a dual purpose family bathroom, that includes facilities for disabled people. A second smaller unit has individual shower/WC/washbasin cubicles. Dishwashing sinks are under cover at both units and a laundry room has washing machine, dryer, spinner, ironing board and airing cupboard. A little well stocked shop shares space with reception, with a butcher calling twice weekly. Children have an indoor games room with table tennis and football games machine, whilst outside is a small adventure playground and a large field for ball games. Fishing lake on site for exclusive use of customers (£2 per rod, per day).

Charges 2002

Per unit incl. 2 adults standard pitch	£8.75 -	£10.25
serviced pitch	£11.75 -	£13.25
extra adult		£2.00
child (5-15 yrs)		£1.20
electricity	£1.50 -	£2.00

Less 10% for 7 nights booked on or before arrival.
Tel: 01695 572686. Fax: 01695 572686. E-mail: abbeyfarm@yahoo.com. **Reservations:** Essential for high season or B.Hs. Min charge 3 nights for B.Hs. + £10 deposit. **Open** all year.

Directions: From M6 junction 27 take A5209 (Parbold) road. After 5 miles turn left (just before garage) onto B5240, and then first right into Hob Cross Lane, following signs to site. O.S.GR: SD433099.

Willowbank Touring Park

Coastal Road, Ainsdale, Southport PR8 3ST

Well situated for the Sefton coast and Southport, Willowbank is a fairly new park still under some development. The touring park is on the edge of sand dunes amongst mature, wind swept trees. Entrance is controlled by a barrier, with a pass-key issued at the excellent reception building which doubles as a sales office for the substantial static development that is underway at the same site. The owner/operators, Mike and Janet, are very well supported on the touring side by Norman and Christine Roberts who have considerable experience in managing touring parks and have encouraged the development of the touring pitches. Already there are 40 gravel hardstanding pitches, with more planned. Eventually the park will have 99 pitches, but presently only 54 are developed, all with 16A electricity. The park does not accept motorhomes longer than 27 feet. There could be a little noise at times from the nearby main road. This is a young park, being enthusiastically developed.

Facilties: The purpose built, heated toilet block is of a high standard including an excellent bathroom for disabled visitors, although the showers are rather compact. Baby room. Small dishwashing room. Laundry with washing machine and dryer. **Off site:** Beaches and sand dunes are everywhere. Martin Mere, the town of Southport and the hallowed Royal Birkdale are just down the road.

Charges 2002

Per unit incl. 2 adults, standard pitch	£8.50 - £11.50
hardstanding	£1.00
extra adult	£2.10
child (5-16 yrs)	£1.60
dog (max 2)	£0.50
backpacker or cyclist	£3.50

Less 5% for stays over 7 days or more. **Tel:** 01704 571566. Fax: 01704 571566. E-mail: mail@willowbankcp.co.uk. **Reservations:** Made with £5 deposit and £1 fee. **Open** all year excl. 11 Jan - 28 Feb.

Directions: Park is 4 miles south of Southport. From A565 in Ainsdale turn into Coastal by traffic lights 1.5 miles south of the town centre. O.S.GR: SD308108.

Pipers Height Caravan & Camping Park

Peel Road, Peel, Blackpool FY4 5JT

Only 4 miles south of Blackpool, this well-run, value-for-money, family park is a useful alternative to the larger holiday sites nearer to town, and is also convenient for visiting Lytham St Anne's with its attractive gardens. There are 140 pitches with electricity (10A) on concrete hardstandings and a further grassy area for tents. Unlike many sites in this area, there are only 28 holiday homes at Pipers Height. Due to its rather flat and exposed location it can be windy at times, even with two grassy dividing banks topped with small trees and shrubs, and there are no dividing hedges between the pitches. The large club room/lounge with bar and restaurant is open evenings in peak season and weekends at other times, providing disco or cabaret entertainment during peak season. Family groups are encouraged at this well-run park.

Facilties: The modern sanitary unit, which can be heated, provides a separate unit for disabled visitors. A refundable deposit (£4) is payable for the amenity building key which includes a barrier card for entry. Dishwashing sinks. Laundry with washing machine and dryer. Club room, bar and restaurant. Small shop stocking basic supplies and gas (open mid-peak season). Games room with pool table and TV. Commercial vehicles are not accepted. **Off site:** Hourly bus service to Blackpool. Riding 1 mile, golf 3 miles.

Charges 2002

Per unit incl. up to 4 adults	£8.00 - £13.00
extra adult	£2.00
child (3-12 yrs)	£1.00
extra car	£2.00
awning	£1.75
electricity	£1.75

Reduced rates for low season. No credit cards. **Tel:** 01253 763767. **Reservations:** Essential for B.Hs, peak season and the illuminations (Sept/Oct) and made with £10 deposit. **Open** 1 March - 30 November.

Directions: From M6 junction 32 take M55 towards Blackpool. Leave at junction 4, taking first left off roundabout, straight on at second roundabout, then right at traffic lights into Peel Road, where site is signed. O.S.GR: SD355327.

Marton Mere Holiday Village

Mythop Road, Blackpool FY4 4NX

533

If Blackpool is your holiday destination and your family are looking for lots to do then this may well be a suitable park. At the time of our visit quite a lot of redevelopment work was being undertaken, including a new purpose built reception for the touring area. Although mainly used for static caravan holiday homes, there are 310 touring pitches with hardstanding, of which 58 are fully serviced. All have electric hook ups, some 10A and some 16A. A few trees give a small amount of shade, but as with a lot of coastal sites, it can be a little windy. During the day buses depart every 30 minutes from the main reception area to Blackpool. On site there is plenty of entertainment including three licensed bars, discos and the Rainbow room where children are entertained. For small children under twelve, there is also the Bradley Bear Club with face painting, disco dancing, games and competitions. In the autumn months (Sept - Nov) there is, of course, the Blackpool illuminations which are a must for young and old alike. Other places to visit include the historic towns of Lytham and St Annes, the world of Coronation Street and many fantastic golf courses.

Facilties: Three toilet blocks, with key pad entry system have piped music playing and although of older design are clean and well kept with large pre-set showers and hairdryers. Each block has dishwashing sinks under cover, a suite for disabled people, baby room, family bathroom and launderette. Well stocked supermarket with all day bakery, bars, fast food outlets and restaurants. New outdoor splash pool and heated indoor pool with flume, jacuzzi and sauna. Amusement arcades, multi sports court, crazy golf and bowling. Two children's clubs with full entertainment schedule. Dogs are not accepted in high season.

Charges 2002

Per person (over 3 yrs)	£2.00
basic pitch	£4.00 - £8.00
with electricity	£8.00 - £12.00
serviced pitch	£13.00 - £17.00
dog (not in high season)	£1.50

Tel: 01253 767544. Fax: 01253 791544.
Reservations: Made with £25 deposit; contact site for details. **Open** 21 March - 31 October.

Directions: From M55 junction 4, turn right at roundabout taking A583 towards Blackpool. Pass the windmill, then right at the traffic lights by the Clifton Arms into Mythop Road. Park is on the left O.S.GR: SD344351.

Kneps Farm Holiday Park

River Road, Stanah, Thornton-Cleveleys FY5 5LR

530

A well established park with top class modern facilities, Kneps Farm is still operated by the family who opened it in 1967. It is adjacent to Wyre Country Park and makes an excellent base from which to explore the area. A card operated barrier system flanks the reception building which also houses a well stocked shop. The 70 marked and numbered touring pitches are generally on hardstandings with electricity (10A) available to most, and all are accessed from tarmac roads. There are also some grassy pitches and a separate area with 80 caravan holiday homes (most privately owned). A path leads through a gate at the back of the site into the country park. Just down the lane is a public slip-way and the Wyreside Ecology Centre. A list and map are provided of local services and amenities, including pubs, restaurants, takeaway, etc. Other local attractions include Marsh Mill Village with a restored windmill, the Freeport Shopping and Leisure village at nearby Fleetwood (discount shopping), and several bird-watching sites around the estuary and country park.

Facilties: The excellent, large, centrally heated sanitary building is warm and inviting with ten individual family bathrooms, each providing a WC, basin and bath/shower. Separate toilet facilities with electric hand-wash units for men and women. Well equipped room for disabled visitors. Dishwashing sinks. Combined baby care/first aid room. Laundry room with washing machines, dryers, spin dryer and ironing facility. Shop. Small, fenced children's playground. Up to two dogs are accepted per unit. **Off site:** Fishing 0.5 miles, golf 2.5 miles.

Charges 2002

Per unit incl. 2 adults and 2 children	£14.00 - £16.00
adult couple	£11.00 - £12.50
senior citizen couple	£10.00 - £11.50
extra adult	£2.75 - £3.25
extra child	£1.50 - £1.75
electricity	£2.00 - £2.50

Tel: 01253 823632. Fax: 01253 863967. E-mail: enquiries@knepsfarm.co.uk. **Reservations:** Essential for B.Hs. and peak season and illuminations and made with £10 deposit. **Open** 1 March - 15 November.

Directions: From M55 junction 3, take A585 towards Fleetwood. Turn right at traffic lights by Shell station (for Thornton-Cleveleys), straight across next traffic lights, then right at the next roundabout by River Wyre Hotel. After one mile (past school) turn right at mini-roundabout into Stanah Road, continue across second mini-roundabout and eventually into River Road with site entrance ahead of you. O.S.GR: SD350430.

Holgates Caravan Park

Middlebarrow Plain Cove Road, Silverdale, Carnforth LA5 0SH

This attractive, very high quality park is in an outstanding craggy, part-wooded, hillside location with fine views over Morecambe Bay. It takes 70 touring units, with 339 privately owned caravan holiday homes and 11 to rent located in woodland away from the tourist pitches. With just 5 grassy pitches for tents, the remaining 65 large touring pitches, all with electricity (16A), free TV connection, individual drainage and water points are on gravel hardstandings. The main complex, with reception and the entrance barrier, recently redeveloped, provides a well stocked supermarket, boutique, lounge bar, restaurant with good value meals and a terrace with views over the bay. There is also an indoor leisure centre. Children have a choice of two adventure playgrounds and plenty of space for ball games. Also on site is a small but challenging golf course. Everything is completed to the highest standards.

Facilties: Two modern, heated toilet buildings, built from local stone, are fully equipped with top quality fittings and including some private cubicles with WC and washbasin. Dishwashing sinks are at each block. Excellent separate provision for disabled visitors with a reserved pitch and parking bay adjacent. Launderette. Shop. Bar and restaurant. Indoor pool (17 x 17 m; with lifeguard) with spa pool, steam room and sauna (all free to campers, no unaccompanied under 10s). Children's playgrounds. Games room with pool table and video games. Golf course (£1 per person). Gas supplies. Facilities are limited mid-week in January and early February. Admission restrictions include no unaccompanied under 18's or single sex groups, no dangerous breeds of dog or commercial vehicles. **Off site:** Riding, cycling, walking and fishing all within 7 miles. Morecambe or Lancaster are just 12 miles and Kendal 15 miles.

Charges 2002

Per unit incl. 2 adults and 2 children	£10.00 - £20.50
extra adult	£4.50
extra child (5-17 yrs)	£2.50
awning/pup tent	£2.00
electricity	£2.50

Minimum stays apply for all B.H. weekends. **Tel:** 01524 701508. Fax: 01524 701580. E-mail: caravan@ holgates.co.uk. **Reservations:** Essential for B.Hs and peak season; made with £15 deposit for 1 or 2 nights, £25 for longer. **Open** all year excl. 3 Nov - 21 Dec.

Directions: From traffic lights in centre of Carnforth take road to Silverdale under low bridge (12' 9"). After 1 mile turn left signed Silverdale and after 2.5 miles over a level crossing carry on and then turn right at T junction. Follow the Holgates signs from here watching for left fork followed by right fork (narrow roads). O.S.GR: SD460755.

Photo: North West Tourist Board

Cumbria Tourist Board

Cumbria Tourist Board
Ashleigh, Holly Road, Windermere LA23 2AQ
Main brochure line: 08075 133059 Fax: (015394) 44041
E-mail: infol@golakes.co.uk

Internet: http://www.gocumbria.co.uk

From the tallest mountain in England to the deepest lake, from the country's steepest roads to the world's biggest liar – Cumbria has a lot to offer and it is no surprise so many visitors return year after year. The heart of the county is the Lake District National Park, well known for the dramatic scenery of mountains and lakes which inspired the lake poets including William Wordsworth and formed the setting for Beatrix Potter's many characters.

Each valley and lake has its own character and charm from powerboats on Windermere to sailing boats on Derwentwater, from the rolling hills east of Coniston Water to the rugged drama of Ulls-water's surrounding mountains. While the Lake District is well known, there are also many quiet, undiscovered areas including the wild moors of the north Pennines and the peaceful green Eden Valley.

Photo: Mountains, North West TB

from Ennerdale and Eskdale to the sandstone cliffs of St Bees Head, part of a designated Heritage Coast. The Georgian town of Whitehaven was once Britain's third largest port and is now undergoing its renaissance and developing as a major new tourism centre.

The southern coast of Cumbria – the Lake District Peninsulas – were recent winners of the English Holiday Destination of the Year largely due to its spectacular scenery and the mildest climate in the North. This corner of the county has its fun side too with Ulverston not only being home to the world's only Laurel and Hardy Museum but also the birthplace of Quakerism and pole vaulting.

Photo: Steamboat, North West TB

In the north, the city of Carlisle still bears the marks of a turbulent history. Tullie House Museum & Art Gallery highlights that violent past from the Romans and the Border Reivers to the present day.

The contrasts of Cumbria are best seen in the west where the Lakeland fells drop down to a long and varied coastline. There are many undiscovered and quiet corners

Compact and accessible, Cumbria is a region which can offer something for every taste with many undiscovered and quiet corners waiting to be explored. It is no surprise that National Geographic Traveller Magazine listed the county as one of 50 places in the world which had to be seen in a lifetime.

Walls Caravan & Camping Park

553 Ravenglass CA18 1SR

Once part of the large Pennington Estate in western Cumbria, Walls is a small, neat park set in five acres of woodland amongst a variety of mature trees. It has space for 25 touring units on hardstanding pitches with a grass verge for awnings (plus 25 seasonal units). A circular gravel road provides access and all pitches have electrical hook-ups (10A). A small grass area at the top and back of the park provides an attractive spot for ten tents overlooking the fields. A central courtyard complex includes the owners' home, reception and the facilities. All is maintained by Keith and Stephanie Bridges, who provide a warm welcome and, having used the site since it was first developed, now own it. It is a useful site for all sorts of walking - estuary, river or fell - or to explore the Cumbrian coast with its Roman connections, the western Lake District or to enjoy the Ravenglass and Eskdale Miniature Railway. Some rail noise was heard during the day but this stops at about 10.30 pm. giving an undisturbed night sleep.

Facilities: The toilet block provides all the usual amenities, is well kept and has a fully equipped laundry room and dishwashing facilities. Motor-caravan service point. Shop (only a few basic necessities plus gas). **Off site:** Fishing and bicycle hire 3 miles, boat launching 1.5 miles, golf 6 miles. The small village of Ravenglass, a single, cottage lined street, is within walking distance, has a pub and holds a Charter Fair in June. Daily bus service runs from Whitehaven to Barrow calling at Ravenglass, or trains from the local station to Carlisle and Barrow.

Charges 2002

Per unit incl. 2 adults	£9.00
medium tent (2 persons)	£8.00
small tent (1 person)	£4.00
extra person	£1.00
child (under 16 yrs)	free
awning	£1.00
electricity	£1.75

No credit cards. **Tel:** 01229 717250. E-mail: wallscaravanpark@ravenglass98.freeserve.co.uk. **Reservations:** Contact park. **Open** 1 March - 31 October.

Directions: Park is just off A595 (between Egremont and Millom) on road into village of Ravenglass. O.S.GR: SD096965.

Skelwith Fold Caravan Park

552 Ambleside LA22 0HX

Skelwith Fold has been developed in the extensive grounds of a country estate taking advantage of the wealth of mature trees and shrubs. The 300 privately owned caravan holiday homes and 150 touring pitches are absorbed into this unspoilt natural environment, sharing it with red squirrels and other wildlife in several discrete areas branching off the central, mile long main driveway. Touring pitches (no tents) are on gravel hardstanding and metal pegs will be necessary for awnings. Electricity hook-ups (10A) and basic amenities are available in all areas. Youngsters and indeed their parents will find endless pleasure exploring over 90 acres of wild woodland and, if early risers, it is possible to see deer, foxes, etc. taking their breakfast in the almost hidden tarn deep in the woods. This is a fascinating site where you feel at home with nature at any time of the year, but it is particularly beautiful in the spring with wild daffodils, bluebells and later rhododendrons and azaleas. Note: Only caravans, motorcaravans and trailer tents taken.

Facilities: Eight toilet blocks, well situated to serve all areas, have the usual facilities including laundry, drying and ironing rooms. Some blocks have facilities for disabled visitors. Well stocked, licensed self-service shop, together with a store for gas, battery charging and caravan spares and accessories. Adventure play area. Family recreation area with picnic tables and goal posts in the Lower Glade. **Off site:** Ambleside village 1.5 miles. Pubs within walking distance.

Charges 2002

Per pitch	£11.00 - £13.00
electricity	£2.00
awning	£2.50
pup tent on pitch	£5.00

Discounts for weekly or monthly stays. **Tel:** 01539 432277. Fax: 01539 434344. **Reservations:** Essential for July/Aug and B.Hs. and made for min. 3 days with £10 deposit. **Open** 1 March - 15 November.

Directions: From Ambleside take the A593 in the direction of Coniston. Pass through Clappergate and on the far outskirts watch for the B5286 to Hawkshead on the left. Park is clearly signed approx. 1 mile down this road on the right. O.S.GR: NY358028.

The Larches Caravan Park

551 Mealsgate, Wigton CA7 1LQ

Mealsgate and The Larches lie on the Carlisle - Cockermouth road, a little removed from the hectic centre of the Lake District, yet with easy access to it (and good views towards it) and to other attractions situated near - the Western Borders, Northumberland, etc. It is a quality, family run park which takes 73 touring units of any type and also accommodates 100 privately owned holiday homes. Touring pitches are in different grassy areas with tall, mature trees, shrubs and accompanying wildlife. Some are sloping and irregular, others on marked hardstandings, with electricity (10A), water and waste water connections. A well stocked self-service shop, includes gas, camping accessories and off-licence, with events in the surrounding district each day displayed prominently in the window. A camping kitchen provides a breakfast bar and metered power to a cooker and microwave. On arrival everyone is loaned very comprehensive tourist information brochures. The Elliott family provide a warm welcome at this peaceful, well organised park, which is an ideal haven for couples - only adult visitors are accepted.

Facilities: Toilet facilities, in two purpose designed blocks, are of good quality providing en-suite facilities for both sexes. Washbasins for ladies are in cubicles, those for men are set in flat surfaces. A separate unit for disabled visitors can be heated. Laundry room. Shop. Small indoor heated pool. Table tennis. TV room. Caravan storage. **Off site:** Fishing 8 miles, bicycle hire 7 miles, riding 10 miles, golf 3.5 miles. There are bus routes to Carlisle and Keswick, walks from the park and good restaurants nearby.

Charges 2002

Per unit incl. 2 adults	£8.00 - £10.00
backpacker	£4.00 - £5.00
extra person, awning or car	£1.00
electricity	£2.00

Discounts for senior citizens and bookings over 7 nights. No credit cards. **Tel:** 01697 371379. Fax: 01697 371782. E-mail: info@larchescaravanpark. co.uk. **Reservations:** Made with £1 per night deposit, balance on arrival. **Open** 1 March - 31 October.

Directions: Park entrance is south off A595 (Carlisle - Cockermouth) road just southwest of Mealsgate. O.S.GR: NY206415.

Castlerigg Hall Caravan & Camping Park

566 Keswick CA12 4TE

This well laid out park was started in the late 1950s by the Jackson family, who over the years have developed and improved the site whilst maintaining its character. Good use has been made of the traditional stone buildings to house the reception, shop and café, whilst another building houses a modern amenity block along with a really excellent campers' kitchen. Tarmac roads wend their way around the site to the separate tent area of 110 pitches. Gently sloping with some shelter, these pitches have fine views across Keswick, Derwentwater and the western Fells. The 45 caravan pitches tend to be on terraces, again overlooking the lake. Each terrace has a maximum of seven pitches, all on hardstanding and with 10A electricity and nearly all with a water tap and grey water drain. Places to visit include Keswick (about 20 minutes walk), Derwentwater, Ullswater, Penrith, Carlisle, Hadrian's Wall and Rhegad (the village in the hill). Quite close to the site is Castlerigg stone circle which is believed to be some 4,000 years old, and of course as much walking as you might want. The Jacksons are committed to conservation.

Facilities: The main toilet block (opened in 2000) is beautifully fitted out, fully tiled and heated, with showers, vanity style washbasins (two in cabins) and hair care areas. Within the block is a unit for disabled visitors (key available), baby changing area, fully equipped laundry and dishwashing area, games room and campers' kitchen complete with microwave, toasters, kettle and hot plates. Two other toilet blocks are older in style but newly decorated and clean. Reception houses tourist information, a breakfast café and a well stocked shop (with gas). **Off site:** Hotel/pub for meals adjacent to site. Fishing, golf, riding, bicycle hire and boat launching, all 1.5 miles.

Charges 2002

Per caravan incl. 2 persons	£9.40 - £11.50
motorcaravan	£8.20 - £9.80
extra person	£2.00
awning (strong steel pegs required)	£0.80 - £1.50
electricity	£1.80
tent camper	£3.30 - £3.90
car with tent	£1.30 - £1.70

Tel: 017687 72437. Fax: 017687 72437. **Reservations:** Accepted for caravans or motor-caravans only with £10 deposit. **Open** April - November.

Directions: From Penrith take A66 towards Keswick and Cockermouth. Leave at first sign for Keswick (A591) and follow to junction (A5271). Turn left on A591 signed Windermere and after 1 mile, take small road on right signed Castlerigg and Rakefoot. Park entrance is on right after 400 yards. O.S.GR: NY282227.

Limefitt Park

Windermere LA23 1PA

555

Limefitt Park is owned and run by the Whiteley family, who also own Fallbarrow Park. Centrally situated for the southern Lakes, it is a well managed and popular park with fine views and walks, alongside the beck. With various active pursuits nearby and some evening entertainment, it is designed for families or couples. There are 85 hardstanding pitches for touring caravans or motorcaravans (20 seasonal). Each has electricity (10A), fresh water tap and waste water point. Cars are parked at an angle on hardstanding in front of each pitch. There are 38 fully serviced pitches on grass for tents or tourers and further pitches for any unit on flat or slightly sloping grass with some terracing and shade provided by trees. The ground by the beck has been developed for 45 log cabins (for sale) in addition to some caravan holiday homes (a few for hire). Activities include walking and fishing, and many local facilities, including bicycle hire, can be booked from the park. Away from the camping area is a play field and adventure playground on grass by the river and a small riverside area with picnic tables. American motorhomes, dogs, boats, single persons, groups and rallies are not accepted; to quote, 'in order to preserve Limefitt's unique atmosphere and provide restful nights ... we accept families and couples only.' The park is popular throughout the season so advance reservation is recommended.

Facilities: Sanitary facilities consist of one large, central block for the tenting area and a smaller block for the caravan area, accessed by combination locks. Both are of excellent quality, well equipped with modern fittings. Part of one building is dedicated to three toddlers' rooms with half-size bath and changing facilities. Covered washing up and vegetable preparation areas. Camper's kitchen. Launderette. Motorcaravan service point. Supermarket. Bar (real ales), bar meals and takeaway, all open all season. Weekly entertainment. Gas available. Games room with many machines. Play area. Dogs are not accepted. **Off site:** Riding 3 miles, golf 5 miles.

Charges 2002

Per unit incl. 2 persons, electricity and TV hook up	£8.50 - £14.00
tent	£9.50 - £13.00
extra adult	£2.00 - £3.00
child (2-14 yrs)	£1.00 - £1.25
awning, pup tent, trailer or 2nd car	£2.00 - £3.00
serviced pitch	£3.00

Prices are higher for stays not booked in advance.
Tel: 015394 32300. Fax: 015394 32848.
Reservations: Made with full payment at time of booking; cancellation insurance available. **Open** 22 March - 3 November.

Directions: Limefitt Park lies 2.5 miles north up the A592 from its junction with the A591 north of Windermere. O.S.GR: NY416030.

Sykeside Camping Park

Brotherswater, Patterdale, Penrith CA11 0NZ

556

This small touring site is under new ownership. Set in the northern lakes area (just 400 yards from Brotherswater Lake) and surrounded by fells, it is ideal for active holidays with walking or climbing on high hills. It would also be useful for a touring holiday being a little away from the busiest areas. The park is licensed to take 80 tents which could include 6-8 small motorcaravans, but definitely no caravans, on flat grass in the valley floor. Pitches are not marked and campers arrange themselves. There are 16 electrical connections (5/10A). The stone-built building, an original barn, near the entrance just 200 yards from the field, houses all the facilities. The Brotherswater Inn, 200 yards from the site and overlooking the fells, is open all day including meals and has rooms to let.

Facilities: The toilet block includes hot showers (20p); a little basic but clean and functional - updating is planned. No chemical disposal point although one is planned. Small launderette and dishwashing room. Self-service shop with camping equipment, gas and an ice-pack service, doubles as reception. Cosy, licensed bar and restaurant serving breakfast (8.15-10 am) and evening meals during peak periods (6-9 pm, bar open 5-11 pm). Bunkhouse accommodation. **Off site:** Bicycle hire 3 miles, riding 8 miles, golf 10 miles.

Charges 2002

Per adult	£2.20 - £2.75
child (4-14 yrs)	£1.50
car or motorcycle	£2.20 - £2.75
electricity	£1.60

Tel: 017684 82239. Fax: 017684 82558.
Reservations: Made with £15 deposit (not possible to book electric hook-up). Easter or Spr. B.H. - min. booking, 3 and 4 days respectively. Reservation is essential in peak seasons. **Open** all year.

Directions: On west side of A592 road about 2 miles south of Patterdale, at the southwestern end of Ullswater - entrance is just behind the Brotherswater Inn. (Note: the road is narrow and hilly, and not suitable for touring caravans and large motorhomes). O.S.GR: NY396005.

Fallbarrow Park

Rayrigg Road, Bowness, Windermere LA23 3DL

Fallbarrow Park is most attractively situated alongside Lake Windermere with a lake frontage of about 600 metres - one can stroll among the lawns and gardens near the lake. The park is owned and managed by its founders, the Whiteley family, who are committed to caring for the countryside and raise funds for the District Tourism and Conservation Partnership. The major part of the park is occupied by about 260 seasonal holiday homes, with about 90 for letting, the remainder privately owned. In the 'Lake' area (not actually by the lake, but some pitches have lake views), there are 38 fenced or hedged touring pitches, all with hardstanding, fresh and waste water points, electricity (10/16A) and TV aerial connections. Reception is smart and comfortable, with lots of tourist information. The Boathouse pub has a spacious and comfortable lounge with bar meals and snacks, a separate restaurant section with varied menu and table service, and an attractive outdoor terrace. TV lounge with occasional entertainment and a large games room. The site has a boat park with winter storage and two launching ramps and three jetties can cater for craft up to 18 ft in length. Bowness centre is only a short walk and facilities for pony trekking and numerous visitor attractions are close.

Facilities: Two excellent toilet blocks serve the touring sections (combination locks) with top quality fittings and heating when required, controllable showers, make up and hairdressing areas and a baby washroom. Dishwashing sinks. Very well equipped laundry which also houses a freezer. Motorcaravan service point. Gas is available at the well stocked supermarket. Restaurant. Bar. American motorhomes are accepted by prior arrangement. Pet area. Fishing on site. Dogs are accepted, but only one per booking (exercise area provided). **Off site:** Bicycle hire 1 mile, riding 2 miles, golf 3 miles.

Charges 2002

Per unit inclusive	£14.80 - £20.90
awning	£2.95 - £4.10
boat (max 18 ft)	£10.00
sailboard or canoe	£2.00
second car	£2.60

Tel: 015394 44422. Fax: 015394 88736.
Reservations: Made for 3 nights min. (7 at Spring B.H.). Payment in full at time of booking. Fallbarrow Park is very popular and reservations are essential for June - Sept. and B.Hs. **Open** 8 March - 9 November.

Directions: Park is beside the A592 road just north of Bowness town centre. O.S.GR: SD401971.

Waterfoot Caravan Park

561 Pooley Bridge, Penrith CA11 0JF

Waterfoot is a quiet family park for caravans and motorcaravans only. It is set in 22 acres of partially wooded land, developed in the fifties from a private estate. The 126 private caravan holiday homes are quite separate from the 57 touring pitches. Lake Ullswater is only about 400 yards away and a half mile stroll through bluebell woods brings you to the village of Pooley Bridge. Waterfoot's touring pitches are arranged very informally in a large clearing. Most are level, there are some hardstandings and all have 10A electricity. Several pitches are long enough for American RVs, although there is quite a tight corner leading into the main touring area. There is a bar in a large, imposing mansion, in the past a family home then a golf hotel. Public footpaths lead straight from the park. The regular lake steamer service calls at Pooley Bridge and the market town of Penrith is 5 miles.

Facilities: The heated toilet block includes some washbasins and showers in cubicles which are activated by a button on the wall outside the cubicle giving five minutes showering time. Large, light and airy dishwashing room and fully equipped laundry. Small shop selling basics, gas and newspapers. Bar with strictly enforced, separate family room open weekend evenings in low season and every evening in high season. Large fenced field with play equipment to suit all ages and goal posts for football. **Off site:** Fishing close, boat slipway, riding 1.5 miles, golf 5 miles. Pooley Bridge has a post office/general store, hotels and restaurants. The historic house and gardens of Dalemain are a short walk.

Charges 2002
Per unit incl. all persons
and electricity   £10.00 - £14.50
No credit cards. **Tel:** 017684 86302. Fax: 017684 86728. E-mail: ide@netcomuk.co.uk. **Reservations:** Essential for B.Hs and summer holidays; contact the Warden. **Open** 1 March - 31 October.

Directions: From M6 junction 40, take A66 signed Keswick. After 0.5 miles at roundabout take A592 signed Ullswater and site is on right after 4 miles. O.S.GR: NY460245.

ULLSWATER

Waterfoot Caravan Park, in the grounds of a Georgian Mansion overlooking Ullswater is the ideal location for touring caravans, motor-homes and static caravan holidays.

The Park enjoys a quiet family orientated character even in busier holiday periods, with 24 hour security. Camping is not allowed. Two touring areas with Toilet/Shower Block, Baby Changing and Laundry facilities. Large secure Children's Play Area. Shop and Bar.

Ullswater, the most beautiful lake in the Lake District National Park is within a short walk. Ullswater 'Steamers' cruise the length of the lake, the perfect day out during your stay here.

Touring & Static Caravans in the beautiful Lake District

Waterfoot Park
Ullswater, Pooley Bridge, Penrith, Cumbria CA11 0JF Tel: 017684 86302
E-mail: lde@netcomuk.co.uk www.ukparks.co.uk/waterfoot

Flusco Wood Touring Caravan Park

567 Flusco, Penrith CA11 0BN

Flusco Wood Caravan Park is still being developed but everything is to a very high standard. Set amongst woodland with the touring pitches in bays, this park will meet the needs of those requiring a quiet holiday (with plenty of walks from the site) and also those travelling up or down the M6 looking for a quiet night's rest. The pitches are all on grass, although there is an area near reception with hardstandings for motorcaravans if the weather makes the pitches unsuitable. The area abounds with wildlife including deer and red squirrels, as well as many breeds of birds. For a wet day you are about 2.5 miles from Rheged, the 'village in the hill' and, if the weather improves, a short drive from Ullswater, Keswick, Penrith and Carlisle. Member Countryside Discovery group.

Facilities: A log cabin style building houses very clean, heated facilities including pre-set showers and vanity style washbasins (1 cubicle). Large en-suite shower rooms for families or disabled visitors, one for ladies and one for men. Dishwashing sinks under cover. Laundry, drying room. Second log cabin serves as reception/shop with basic supplies, gas and newspapers. Play equipment. **Off site:** Pub and P.O. stores 2 miles. Fishing 4 miles, riding 5 miles.

Charges 2002
Per unit incl. 2 persons	£7.50 - £9.00
extra adult	£1.75 - £2.00
child (under 14 yrs)	£1.00 - £1.50
serviced pitch	£2.50 - £3.00
dog	£0.50 - £0.75

Tel: 017684 80020. E-mail: fluscowood@btclick.com. **Reservations:** Made with deposit (£20 per week, £5 for single nights). **Open** Easter - end October.

Directions: From M6 take A66 towards Keswick. Go straight on at first roundabout, then third right at top of hill signed Greystoke and Flusco. After 0.5 miles road turns right up hill, site is on left at the top. Site is 4 miles from M6. O.S.GR: NY457293.

Cove Camping Park
562 Ullswater, Watermillock, Penrith CA11 0LS

Cove Camping is a delightful small site, some of the 50 pitches having great views over Lake Ullswater. A separate area behind the camping field holds 38 privately owned caravan holiday homes, plus one for hire. The grass is well trimmed, there are ramps to keep speeds down to 5 mph and the site is well lit. At the top of the park are 17 level pitches with electric hook-ups and 13 with hardstanding suitable for touring caravans and motorcaravans. The rest of the site is quite sloping. Rubbish bins are hidden behind larch lap fencing, as are recycling bins. The park is well situated for walking, boating, fishing and pony trekking activities. The road up from the A592 is narrow, but a self imposed one way system is generally adhered to and the warden will advise on a different way to leave the site.

Facilities: The tiled toilet block is immaculate and heated in cooler months, providing adjustable showers, some washbasins in cabins and, for ladies, a hairdressing area and a baby unit. A foyer contains a freezer (free), coffee machine and tourist information. Laundry. Washing up sinks are in a separate area. Gas supplies. Small, grass based play area. **Off site:** Shop nearby. Fishing 1.5 miles, riding 3 miles, golf 6 miles, bicycle hire 7 miles (will deliver).

Charges 2002

Per person (over 3 yrs)	£1.50 - £2.00
caravan, motorcaravan or large tent	£3.00 - £6.00
pup tent or awning	£1.50 - £2.00
car, boat or motorcycle	£1.50 - £2.00
dog	£0.50

No credit cards. **Tel:** 017684 86549. Fax: 017684 86549. **Reservations:** Made with £10 deposit. **Open** March - 31 October.

Directions: From A66 Penrith - Keswick road, take A592 south (Ullswater). Turn right at Brackenrigg Inn (site signed) and follow road uphill for about 1.5 miles to park on left. This road is narrow so if you have a larger unit, phone the park for advice about an alternative route. O.S.GR: NY431236.

Pennine View Caravan & Camping Park
560 Station Road, Kirkby Stephen CA17 4SZ

Pennine View was opened in 1990 and is built on reclaimed land from a former railway goods yard. Suitable for night halts or longer breaks, it is a super small park, well managed and well maintained. With a very attractive rockery at the entrance, the site is very neat and tidy. Level, pitches with gravel hardstandings are arranged around the perimeter with grass pitches in the centre. Of a good size (some being especially large), are all supplied with electricity hook-ups (16A). One end of the park adjoins the River Eden with steps leading down from the site to huge projecting stone slabs on the river bank (good for sunbathing). There are trout but a licence is needed for fishing.

Facilities: Built of local stone, the modern toilet block (keypad entry) includes wash cubicles and deep sink for a baby bath. Ladies and men have a large en-suite unit for disabled visitors. Good laundry room. Dishwashing sinks under cover. Gas available. **Off site:** A nearby hotel offers bar meals and takeaway pizzas. Kirkby Stephen 1 mile.

Charges 2002

Per adult	£4.00 - £4.30
child (4-15 yrs)	£1.50
pitch	£1.00 - £2.00
electricity	£1.50 - £2.00
cyclist or backpacker	£4.00

Tel: 017683 71717. **Reservations:** Made with £5 deposit; min. 3 days Easter and B.Hs. **Open** 1 March - 31 October.

Directions: Park is on the A685 on the southerly outskirts of Kirkby Stephen (just under a mile from the town centre). Turn left at small site sign opposite the Croglin Castle hotel. Site is 50 yards on the right. O.S.GR: NY772075.

Westmorland Caravan Site
559 Tebay, Orton, Penrith CA10 3SB

For caravans and motorcaravans only, this is the ideal stopover for anyone heading either north or south, near the M6 motorway, but far enough away for the traffic noise not to be too disturbing. There are 77 level pitches on gravel, divided into bays of about six or seven units (41 for touring units, 34 seasonal and 7 for caravan holiday homes). All touring pitches have electricity (10/16A). The bays are backed by grassy banks alive with rabbits and birds - a long list in the office describes the large variety of birds to be seen on the site. There is good site lighting and a late arrivals area.

Facilities: The heated toilet block is kept very clean. Showers are pre-set and coin operated (10p) with all other hot water free. Sinks for laundry and dish-washing. Laundry. Reception sells gas. **Off site:** Shops, restaurants and a bar five minutes walk away at the motorway service area.

Charges 2002

Per unit	£9.45 - £10.50
OAP unit	£8.40 - £9.45
electricity	£2.20 - £2.10
awning	£1.25 - £1.60

No credit cards. **Tel:** 015396 24511. Fax: 015396 24511. **Reservations:** Advised for B.Hs. and July/Aug. **Open** 22 March - 28 October.

Directions: From the M6, just north of junction 38, exit for Tebay Services (site signed). Site is accessible from the services travelling north or south. O.S.GR: NY607060.

Wild Rose Park

557 Ormside, Appleby-in-Westmorland CA16 6EJ

Set in the Eden Valley within easy reach of the Lake District and the Yorkshire Dales, Wild Rose is a well known park with an excellent reputation. The entrance is very inviting with its well mown grass, trim borders and colourful flower displays and impressive with a 'state of the art' entrance barrier and intercom system. It is immediately apparent that this is a much loved park, and this is reflected throughout the site in the care and attention to detail. There are three touring areas, two with their own warden to ensure that everything is always spick and span. The top areas have been upgraded to provide neat, level, fully serviced pitches. These are separated by hedges (plus a small fence until the hedge grows) and many have views. The lower touring area on a slightly sloping field caters for both tents and caravans. Next to this are six individual 'super' pitches, fenced or hedged with full services, some including patio, barbecue, picnic table, grass area and satellite TV connections. Privately owned caravan holiday homes occupy their own areas and do not intrude. The final touring field is for 60 tents, gently sloping with an oval roadway linked to the large field or ball game area with its special viewpoint. Wild Rose deserves its excellent reputation, which the owners strive to maintain and improve. Nothing is overlooked from recycling bins, electric dust carts to keep the noise down, 'sac-o-matic' special bags in the dog walk and cycle racks placed around the park. A member of the Best of British group.

Facilities: The three toilet blocks (two heated) are of excellent quality and kept spotlessly clean. Most washbasins are in cubicles, and there are hair-washing basins, baby baths and bottle warmers, full facilities for disabled visitors, and a fully equipped laundry with washing lines and drying rooms. Motorcaravan service point. Exceptionally well stocked shop (with gas). Licensed restaurant with takeaway and conservatory/coffee lounge (all 1/4-5/11), good for Sunday lunches. Outdoor kidney shaped pool with sunbathing area (heated mid-May - mid-Sept and open 10 am-10 pm). Well kept, fenced play area. Indoor playroom for under fives. Games room with table tennis and video games for older children and two TV rooms, one with a cinema style screen. Bicycle hire. BMX track. Half court tennis. Field for ball games. Certain breeds of dog are not accepted. Caravan storage. **Off site:** Fishing, golf or riding within 4 miles.

Charges 2002

Per unit incl. 2 adults and electricity	£7.90 - £13.90
incl. mains services and awning	£14.00 - £25.00
walker or cyclist	£3.50
extra person (over 4 yrs)	£1.60
extra car, toilet or pup tent	£1.90
dog	£0.50

Less 10% for 7 nights or more. Special winter or long-stay rates. **Tel:** 01768 351077. Fax: 01768 352551. E-mail: mail@wildrose.co.uk. **Reservations:** Essential for B.Hs and July/Aug; made with deposit of £5 per night + £2 fee, remainder on arrival. Min. 3 nights at B.Hs. **Open** all year.

Directions: Park is signed south off B6260 road 1.5 miles southwest of Appleby. Follow signs to park, in the direction of Ormside. O.S.GR: NY697165.

The Ashes 'Exclusively Adult' Caravan Park

565 New Hutton, Kendal, Cumbria LA8 0AS

The Ashes is a friendly, small, adult only park in an extremely peaceful setting in the rolling Cumbrian countryside, yet less than three miles from the M6, and only slightly further from Kendal. Thus it is not only a convenient night stop, but also a useful base from which to explore the Lake District and the Yorkshire Dales. A very tidy park, the central grass area is attractively planted with shrubs and bushes, and there is an open vista with little shade. There are 24 hardstanding gravel pitches, all with electricity (10A), with grass for awnings. They are neatly placed around the perimeter, with an oval access road. The whole area slopes gently down from the entrance, with some pitches fairly level and others with a little more slope. No other tents are accepted other than trailer tents.

Facilities: A small, purpose built stone building with a slate roof houses two unisex, heated shower rooms and the washing and toilet facilities. Grab rails and step-free access for disabled visitors. Laundry service. **Off site:** Mr and Mrs Mason have prepared a full information sheet with details of shopping, eating and many other local venues. Fishing 2 miles, golf or riding 3 miles.

Charges 2002

Per unit incl. 2 adults, electricity	£9.50 - £11.50
extra person (over 18's only)	£2.50
awning	£2.00
extra car/trailer	£1.00

No credit cards. **Tel:** 01539 731 833. Fax: 01539 731 833. E-mail: info@ashescaravanpark.co.uk. **Reservations:** Made with minimum £10 deposit. Advised for B.Hs and peak season. **Open** 1 March - 15 November.

Directions: From M6 junction 37 follow the A684 towards Kendal for 2 miles. Just past a farm B&B and a white cottage turn sharp left at crossroads signed New Hutton. Site is on right in 0.75 miles at a left bend. O.S.GR: SD560908.

Northumbria Tourist Board

Northumberland, Durham, Tyne and Wear and Teeside

Northumbria Tourist Board
Aykley Heads, Durham DH1 5UX
Tel: (0191) 375 3000 Fax: (0191) 386 0899
E-mail: enquiries@ntb.org.uk

Internet: http://www.visitnorthumbria.com

Northumbria covers the counties of Northumberland, Durham, Tyne and Wear and the Teeside area. Even before the Victorians invented tourism travellers were drawn to this vast empty area between England's industrial belt and the rugged wilderness of Scotland, bisected by the Pennine Mountains and the start of the Pennine Way. Proud castles, glorious coastline and unspoilt countryside, with a spirit of history and a buzzing modern life - that's Northumbria today.

The Pennine Way was the country's first official long-distance path and still the longest (268 miles), stretching from the Peak National Park to the border. Northumberland borders Scotland and is an ancient rugged area dotted with forts from its passionate past when the Scottish raiding parties ventured south.

The 400 square mile Northumberland National Park stretches south from the now peaceful Cheviot Hills near the border, through the Simonside Hills, to the crags of Whin Sill, where it engulfs part of Hadrian's Wall. When the Romans ruled, this line marked the northern limit of their Empire. The surviving sections of this 73 mile long fortification must be the most impressive legacy of Roman rule. The best part, popular for walking, is along the crest of Whin Sill crags around Housteads fort, the most complete fort on the wall.

The coastline is not to be forgotten, deserted white sandy beaches, majestic castles, including Bamburgh and islands. Lindisfarne known for its links with St Cuthbert and early Christianity and the Farnes, remembered locally through the daring of Grace Darling, now a bird sanctuary.

The small city of Durham has a more historical feel, dominated by England's greatest Norman Cathedral. Surrounded on three sides by the river Wear, with cobbled medieval streets and restricted car access it is a popular with tourists. For hundreds of years Durham was a quasi-regal state called a 'palatinate' with its own currency, arms and courts with the governors and prince bishops living in the castle, divided from the cathedral by Palace Green. Today it is all part of the university, the third oldest after Oxford and Cambridge in England.

The North East was a coal-producing and ship-building area and proud of its heritage but the high-tech industries have moved in, watched over by the 'Angel of the North'.

Photo: Northumbria Tourist Board

Teeside
White Water Caravan Club Park
Tees Barrage (A66), Thornaby, Stockton-on-Tees TS18 2QW

574

Being part of the multi-million pound development at the Tees Barrage, this pleasantly landscaped club site caters for all tastes, especially water sports enthusiasts. The recently opened Tees Barrage has transformed eleven miles of the Tees, providing clean, non-tidal water for many activities. The adjoining White Water Course (Britain's largest purpose-built canoe course) provides facilities for both advanced and beginner canoeists, and hosts major national and international events. Close to the site are wetlands that provide a home for a variety of birds. The site itself provides 117 pitches set in bays and hedged with bushes, all with 16A electricity connections, plus 21 fully serviced pitches (fresh water and waste disposal) on hardstandings. The site is well lit, with a security barrier.

Facilities: The central, heated toilet block is of high quality and includes washbasins in cubicles, baby changing facilities and a well appointed unit for disabled visitors. Washing up sinks. Laundry room Motorcaravan service point. Play area on fine gravel. Club room with a TV and pool table for wet weather. **Off site:** Supermarket six minutes. Hotel near the entrance. Retail and leisure park, just across barrage bridge, with 14-screen cinema, 10-pin bowling, shops and fast food outlets. North Yorkshire Moors and the Hartlepool Historic Quay within 40 minutes drive.

Charges 2002

Per pitch	£6.00
adult	£2.50 - £3.50
child (5-16 yrs)	£1.10
extra car, boat or trailer	£1.00
electricity (31/03- 02/10)	£1.50 - £2.25

Tent campers apply to site. **Tel:** 01642 634880. **Reservations:** Contact site by phone or in writing. Made with £5 deposit. **Open** all year.

Directions: From A1(M1) take A66 for Darlington and follow until you pick up signs for Teeside Retail Park and the Tees Barrage. Cross railway bridge and the Barrage bridge, then first right to site on left in 400 yards. O.S.GR: NZ463194.

Co. Durham
Doe Park Touring Caravan Park
Cotherstone, Barnard Castle DL12 9UQ

571

This is Hannah Hauxwell country and the Dales, less frequented than other upland areas, provide wonderful walking country; indeed part of the Pennine Way runs near this peaceful site. The farm and park are close to where the River Balder joins the Tees at Cotherstone and the ancient oak wood beside the river is an SSSI (Site of Special Scientific Interest) for its insects and flowers, but is also a haven for bird-watchers. The park's reception is in a log cabin at the entrance to the pitch area, although at quiet times you may be directed to the farmhouse, formerly Leadgard Hall. This is a mellow three storey, Grade II listed building with a history of its own. Mr and Mrs Lamb or son Stephen will make you very welcome and personally take you to your pitch. The camping fields have a lovely open aspect with wonderful views and the 70 pitches are spacious with well mown grass, all with 10A electricity, over 20 with hardstanding (no tents are taken). A bus service passes the park from Barnard Castle to Middleton and there is a local leisure centre with swimming pool (4 miles). The village of Cotherstone is 0.5 miles with post office and a restaurant with bar meals, a pleasant walk by road or river bank.

Facilities: There are toilet facilities at the farmhouse, but the two newer blocks are closer to the pitches. Built in local stone, these are good quality, fully tiled facilities, with the newest one heated. There are washbasins in cabins, metered, adjustable showers (20p) and a really well appointed unisex unit for disabled visitors. Dishwashing sinks and a small laundry. Eggs and milk are available from the farmhouse, plus gas supplies and battery charging. Although there is no play area, a large grass area in front of some of the pitches can be used for ball games. River fishing on site. Dogs and pets are accepted by arrangement only. **Off site:** Reservoirs 3 miles, bicycle hire or golf 4 miles, riding 2 miles.

Charges 2002

Per unit incl. 2 persons	£6.50 - £7.50
extra adult	£1.00
child over 6 yrs	£0.80
full awning or extra car	£1.00
electricity	£1.90 - £1.80

No credit cards. **Tel:** 01833 650302. Fax: 01833 650302. **Reservations:** Advised for high season and made with £10 deposit (send SAE); min. 4 days at B.Hs. **Open** 1 March - 31 October.

Directions: Follow B6277 from Barnard Castle in direction of Middleton in Teesdale. The farm is signed on the left just after Cotherstone village (there is no need to go into Barnard Castle). O.S.GR: NZ005204.

Co. Durham
Barnard Castle Camping & Caravanning Club Site
Dockenflatts Lane, Lartington, Barnard Castle DL12 9DG

572

For those readers with tents who wish to visit this area, we have added this new Club site as unfortunately nearby Doe Park does not take tents. Also accepting non-members, the Camping and Caravanning Club site at Barnard Castle was only opened in '96. Originally level farm fields, one side of the site is bordered by mature trees and 11,000 young trees and bushes have been planted so eventually it will become an even more attractive location. Most of the 90 pitches are on grass, with 56 electrical hook-ups (16A) plus 12 hardstanding pitches which have a gravel base with room for both car and caravan and space for an awning on grass. Barnard Castle, an old town with its market cross still standing, is well worth a visit. The Bowes museum in the town is a French style chateau housing one of Britain's finest art collections. Raby Castle, near Staindrop, is an impressive medieval castle, formerly the seat of the powerful Neville family. Durham has a castle and cathedral (both World Heritage Sites). High Force, England's highest waterfall is about 12 miles away, and the forest of Hamsterly about 16 miles. A riding centre is next to the site and a public footpath leads from the site to Barnard Castle, with a network of public footpaths in the area.

Facilities: The centrally located toilet facilities are of good quality and kept spotlessly clean. Washbasins are in cubicles and free, controllable showers are roomy. Dishwashing sinks, a baby room and a large, fully equipped unisex unit for visitors with disabilities. Large laundry with washing machine, dryer, iron and sink, with outside lines provided. Motorcaravan service point. Gas supplies. Central children's play area with rubber safety base. Caravan storage. **Off site:** Fishing 4 miles, golf 2.5 miles. Bus service from end of lane.

Charges 2002

Per adult	£3.90 - £5.50
child (6-18 yrs)	£1.70
non-member pitch fee	£4.50
electricity	£1.75 - £2.50

Tel: 01833 630228. **Reservations:** Necessary and made with deposit; contact site. **Open** March - October.

Directions: Follow B6277 from Barnard Castle (towards Middleton in Teesdale) for 1 mile to Lartington. Turn left at club sign into narrow lane with passing places to site entrance on left (there is no need to go into Barnard Castle). O.S.GR: NZ025168.

Northumberland
Fallowfield Dene Caravan & Camping Park
Acomb, Hexham NE46 4RP

581

Although only 2.5 miles from Hexham, Fallowfield Dene Caravan Park is very secluded, situated in mature woodland at the end of a no-through road. Set in woodland glades, each with a Roman name (Hadrian's Wall is close), are 118 seasonal pitches and 32 touring pitches, all with 16A electricity. The park entrance, with reception and a small shop, is neat, tidy and very colourful. There is no play area or games field, but the surrounding woods are a children's paradise. Fallowfield Dene itself is a network of tracks and there are footpaths from the site entrance. The site is a haven for wildlife with red squirrels, foxes and badgers. Hadrian's Wall is only a mile away, with Roman forts such as Housteads Fort and Chesters, being great attractions. In fact the whole area abounds with well preserved Roman remains. Hexham has its Border History museum, housed in the oldest purpose-built gaol in England, where one can learn about the Border Reivers. Bicycle hire can be arranged with advice on routes for exploring the area. This site has a very friendly atmosphere.

Facilities: Brick built toilet blocks (one for each sex) are central and heated in cool weather. Well tiled and kept very clean, there are washbasins in cabins and free hairdryers. A separate, fully equipped room is provided for disabled people and a laundry room with dishwashing sinks. Motorcaravan service point. Small shop for necessities, including gas. Barrier card £5 deposit. **Off site:** Supermarkets and other shops at Hexham or Corbridge. Good restaurant five minutes walk. Fishing or riding 3 miles, golf 5 miles.

Charges 2002

Per adult	£3.00
child (5-17 yrs)	£1.25
caravan, trailer tent or motorcaravan	£3.00 - £4.00
tent	£2.50 - £3.00
car	£1.25
motorcycle	£1.00
awning	£0.50
dog	£0.50
electricity	£2.00

Tel: 01434 603553. **Fax:** 01434 601252. **Reservations:** Made with deposit (£5 for one night, £10 for two or more); min. 3 nights at B.Hs. **Open** 1 April - 2 January.

Directions: From A69 Newcastle - Carlisle road, take A6079 north signed Bellingham and Rothbury. At village of Acomb, site is signed to right. Follow site signs for approx. 1.5 miles. The last 0.5 miles is single track with passing places. O.S.GR: NY938676.

Percy Wood Caravan Park

Swarland, Morpeth NE65 9JW

576

Percy Wood provides excellent, modern facilities whilst still maintaining the feel of camping in woodland. A lot of thought and effort has gone into developing a park which blends with its natural surroundings. Open for 11 months of the year, there are 60 level touring pitches. All have electrical connections (10A) and 20 also have hardstanding and full services. A grass tent field with 5A electricity has a more open aspect with views, and there are also 60 privately owned holiday homes. On the boundary of the park is an 18 hole golf course, with a bar and restaurant, and membership can be arranged. This is an excellent area for rambling and for nature lovers generally. The park is only 4 miles from Throughton Wood and on the bus route for Alnwick and Rothbury. Druridge Bay Country Park is near (lake visitor centre, good for watersports).

Facilities: The central sanitary block is of wooden construction (heated) and in consequence blends naturally with the woodland surroundings. Very well equipped, it includes dishwashing under cover, a laundry room and a baby room. Motorcaravan service facilities. Basic necessities and gas. Children's play area. Outdoor table tennis. Games room with two pool tables and video games. New tennis court. Dogs are accepted on leads (but not certain breeds). **Off site:** Village store and post office 0.5 miles, local pubs and a restaurant within a mile. Fishing 1.5 miles. Local leisure centre with all-weather bowls.

Charges 2002

Per unit incl. 2 persons, awning and 10A electricity	£9.00 - £11.00
full-service pitch in July/Aug plus	£1.50
camping field incl. 2 persons and 5A electricity	£9.00
extra person (over 5 yrs)	£1.00
dog	£0.50

Tel: 01670 787649. Fax: 01670 787034. E-mail: enquiries@percywood.freeserve.co.uk. **Reservations:** Made with 10% non-refundable deposit (min. £10). **Open** all year except February.

Directions: Park is about 2 miles west of the A1 (only signed northbound), 3 miles from the A697. It is 12 miles north of Morpeth and 7 miles south of Alnwick. Site is signed at the northern end of Longframlington on the A697. O.S.GR: NU160042.

Dunstan Hill Camping & Caravanning Club Site

Dunstan Hill, Dunstan, Alnwick NE66 3TQ

577

Northumberland is not very well blessed with good campsites, so we are pleased to feature Dunstan Hill. Off a quiet lane between Embleton and Craster this is a rural site with a tree belt to shelter it from the north wind and access to the beach by a level footpath through the fields, across the golf course and past the ruins of Dunstanburgh Castle. This is just over a mile by car. With gravel access roads, the peaceful site has 150 level, well spaced pitches, 83 with 16A electricity. Reception is located in a new building and is manned by very helpful wardens and there is a large area for outside parking and late arrivals at the entrance. This is a wonderful area to visit, with its unspoilt beaches and the whole area is steeped in history with Holy Island, the Farne Islands, Bamburgh, Dunstanburgh, Walkworth and Alnwick castles.

Facilities: Very clean and well maintained, the two toilet blocks have some washbasins in cubicles, hairdryers and a washroom for children with deep sinks. Fully equipped suite for disabled visitors in one block, a laundry in the other. Small shop for gas and basic provisions. Bread and milk can be ordered and a mobile shop and the paper man visit. Tourist information room. Small children's play area. Torches are useful. **Off site:** Buses pass the site entrance and there are good eating places near. Fishing 1.5 miles, riding 8 miles. Golf (with 10% discount) 10 miles.

Charges 2002

Per adult	£3.90 - £5.50
child (6-18 yrs)	£1.70
non-member pitch fee	£4.50
electricity	£1.75 - £2.50

Tel: 01665 576310. **Reservations:** Necessary and made with deposit; contact site. **Open** March - October.

Directions: From A1 just north of Alnwick take B1340 or B6347 (further north) for Embleton. Site is signed in Embleton village - avoid signs to Dunstanburgh Castle and follow those for Craster. Site is (south) on the left after approx. 0.5 miles. O.S.GR: NU236214.

Northumberland
Ord House Country Park

580 East Ord, Berwick-upon-Tweed TD15 2NS

Ord House is a 40 acre park for 200 privately owned holiday homes and 75 touring caravan and tent pitches. The whole park has a very well cared for appearance, with well mown grass and colourful arrays of flowering bushes. The touring pitches, all with electricity (10A), are in small sections, from the secluded, walled orchard to the more open areas nearer the toilet blocks. There are 39 hardstanding pitches, each with electricity, water and drainage, 19 in the walled garden separated by flowering shrubs and camomile lawns. At the entrance to the park is an area with a few pitches suitable for wheelchair users and close by is a small sanitary unit with WCs and showers plus a large, unisex, well appointed unit (Radar key). The whole site is 'wheelchair friendly' with good access to the airy reception and the well stocked accessory shop. Ord House itself, an 18th century mansion, has been tastefully converted to provide a bar, lounge bar and family room. Although there are many caravan holiday homes on the park, they are not over-whelming and their presence does mean that other amenities can remain open all season. A member of the Best of British group.

Facilities: The main, modern toilet building is of excellent quality and cleanliness, very well maintained and can be heated. It has two good large family bathrooms (with two showers, a bath, WC and washbasin). Two rooms for disabled visitors. Dishwashing sinks. Large well equipped laundry. Motorcaravan service point. Gas supplies. Bar, bar food and family room (1/3-10/1). Six-hole golf practice area. Bicycle hire. Crazy golf. Table tennis. Draughts. Children's play area. No commercial vehicles are accepted. Dogs are only accepted by prior arrangement. **Off site:** Post office stores 50 yards from the entrance. Leisure centre with a pool is 15 minutes walk. Fishing 1.5 miles, riding 8 miles, golf 2 miles. Sea fishing can be booked in Berwick.

Charges 2002

Per unit incl. up to 4 persons	£9.00 - £13.95
extra person over 6 yrs	£2.50
awning	£2.50
electricity	£2.50
dog	free - £1.50

Extra car, boat and trailer by prior arrangement. 1-man tent less £3.00, 2-man less £2.00. Discounts for longer stays. **Tel:** 01289 305288. Fax: 01289 330832. E-mail: enquiries@ordhouse.co.uk. **Reservations:** Advisable at all times, essential in high seasons (min. 3 nights at B.Hs) - contact park for details. **Open** all year.

Directions: From the A1 Berwick bypass take East Ord exit and follow signs. O.S.GR: NT982515.

Northumberland
Brown Rigg Caravan & Camping Park

578 Bellingham, Hexham NE48 2JY

Bellingham is tucked away amidst heather clad moors in the North Tyne valley, just below the Scottish Borders on the edge of the Northumberland National Park - 'full of history, myth and legend', to quote from the Bellingham town guide. John Mowatt went to school here and has returned with his wife and family to establish Brown Rigg in part of the grounds of his old school. This interesting, developing park provides 70 pitches, 26 with electricity (10/16A), for all types of unit on a level grass field between the moor and the road. Reception, a games room and the sanitary facilities have all been converted from the former wooden school dormitory buildings with a central courtyard area and are rather distinctive. A tea shop and plant sales area have been added. Bellingham is half a mile away and an 18 hole golf course has been opened recently. The Pennine Way passes the entrance and Kielder Water is 9 miles to the west, as is Hadrian's Wall to the south.

Facilities: Ladies' toilet facilities, finished in pine, provide washbasins in cubicles, controllable showers on payment (10p) and a free hairdryer. Baby bath available. The unit for men has been tiled. In total, it is a good provision, cleverly adapted and well maintained and is operated on a key system. Washing machine and dryer, free iron and board. Laundry and dishwashing sinks. Motorcaravan service point. Reception provides tourist information and basic food supplies, gas and battery charging. Games room with pool and table tennis. TV room. Children's play area. **Off site:** Fishing or golf within 1 mile.

Charges 2002

Per unit incl. 2 adults	£8.50 - £10.00
2-man tent	£8.00 - £9.50
1-man tent	£4.50
child's pup tent	£2.00
extra adult	£1.50
child (6-14 yrs)	£1.00
awning	£1.00
dog	free - £0.50
electricity	£1.50 - £2.00

No credit cards. **Tel:** 01434 220175. Fax: 01434 220175. E-mail: enquiries@northumberland caravanparks.com. **Reservations:** Made with £10 deposit for bookings. **Open** Easter - 31 October.

Directions: Park is on the B6320, south of Bellingham. O.S.GR: NY835826

Waren Caravan Park

Waren Mill, Bamburgh, nr Belford NE70 7EE

575

Developed from 100 acres of undulating private heath and woodland, Waren Park is a large, spacious family site with marvellous sea views. A large section of caravan holiday homes (for hire), is separate from a self contained four acre touring area. Enclosed by sheltering banks, this provides 170 reasonably level pitches, 100 with electrical connections (10A). As well as the spacious grounds to wander in, there is much to see nearby from historic castles, the Farne Islands to the Cheviot Hills and miles and miles of sandy beaches.

Facilities: The older toilet facilities are only of fair quality, whilst a good new block provides excellent facilities for disabled visitors, baby mats, bathroom and four self-contained family rooms with shower, WC and washbasin. Laundry room. Dishwashing sinks. Motorcaravan service point. Licensed shop. Bar with terrace serving bar meals (all season). Games room. Solarium. Children's play park and playing fields. Splash pool (Whitsun - Sept). **Off site:** Birdwatching opportunities nearby. Golf or bicycle hire 2 miles, riding 5 miles.

Charges 2002

Per unit incl. 2 persons	£8.50 - £14.00
extra person (over 5 yrs)	£1.50
1-man tent	£6.00 - £10.00
boat or awning	£2.00
dog	£1.00
electricity	£2.50

Less 10% for bookings of 7 days or over. **Tel:** 01668 214366. Fax: 01668 214224. E-mail: enquiries@ warencp.demon.co.uk. **Reservations:** Early reservation advisable for high season. Deposit of one night's charge plus £1 fee. **Open** Easter/1 April - end October.

Directions: Follow B1342 from the A1 to Waren Mill towards Bamburgh. After Budle Bay turn right and follow signs. O.S.GR: NU154342.

WALES

Wales Tourist Board

Brunel House, 2 Fitzalan Road, Cardiff CF24 0UY

Tel: 08701 211251 Fax: 08701 211259

E-mail: info@tourism.wales.gov.uk

Internet: http://www.visitwales.com

Invigorating. Natural. Rejuvenating. Relaxing. Wales can be all of these things. And much more...

Wales is a compact country with an endless variety of landscape and terrain. Its mountains and lakes, rivers and valleys, coast and country can offer you a break from the pressures of everyday living; Wales has all the benefits of a relaxing escape without any of the disadvantages attributed to travelling long distances.

With a population of just under three million, Wales is a small country with plenty of spirit. It is currently experiencing the most exciting period in its recent history, having in the last few years seen the opening of the National Assembly and hosted the European Summit and Rugby World Cup.

Few parts of the world can claim such a varied landscape in such a small land area; only in Wales can you go from mountains as dramatic as those in Snowdonia to beautiful golden beaches in no time at all. Only in Wales is it but a short journey from city centre to undulating countryside, from inland waterfalls and lakes to coastal cliffs and islands.

Add to this one of Europe's richest cultures, a thriving arts scene, the unique lyrical Welsh language and a wealth of history spanning many centuries and an image emerges of a nation which has much to offer.

Wales' capital, Cardiff, is Europe's youngest, and one of its fastest growing, cities. Many exciting projects are giving the city an air of dynamism and newfound confidence. The barrage in Cardiff Bay is complete and projects such as the new building for the National Assembly and the Wales Millennium Centre are under way. Pride of place goes to Wales' new national stadium – the Millennium Stadium – which has a retractable roof and a 72,500 capacity. Located in the heart of the city, it creates a unique atmosphere during sporting and non-sporting events.

Wales' biggest asset is undoubtedly its countryside. Wales has three National Parks, making up almost a quarter of the country's total area. The dramatic towering mountain scenery of Snowdonia National Park in the north contrasts with the boulder-shaped bare hilltops of the Brecon Beacons in the south and the marine-based coastal beauty of the Pembrokeshire Coast in the west.

Wales also has five designated Areas of Outstanding Natural Beauty, namely the Gower Peninsula, the Wye Valley, the Lln Peninsula, the Anglesey Coast and the Clwydian Range.

An outdoor enthusiast's dream as it evidently is, Wales offers much more. There are many tourist attractions, such as the Great Little Trains, museums, theme and wildlife parks, country houses and estates and of course, more castles per square mile than any other country in Europe.

South Wales

Tourism information for South and West Wales may also be obtained from:

Tourism South and West Wales, Charter Court, Enterprise Park, Swansea SA7 9DB

Tel: (01792) 781212 Fax: (01792) 781300 E-mail: marketing@tsww.com

St Pierre Caravan Park

591 Portskewett, nr Chepstow NP6 4TT

Up-market and attractive, St Pierre Caravan Park was created in the early 1990s on fairly level grass with outstanding views over the Severn Estuary with its two magnificent bridges. A wide entrance drive, leads on to the site which is well served by a wide, circular, block paved roadway. The site has 50 pitches, all with electric hook-ups (6A), generally on grass but 10 hardstandings are available. Some hedging divides up the site, providing several small bays of two or three pitches, and there are some individual ones. There is no shop on-site, with the nearest supermarket in Chepstow, 4.5 miles. The site has no children's playground or activities for teenagers.

Facilities: A modern stylish heated building provides large controllable hot showers, dishwashing and laundry facilities with washing machine and dryer. WC and basin unit for disabled people. A small well equipped gymnasium is free for campers use. Boules court. Calor gas available. **Off site:** Sightseeing opportunities include Newport Transporter Bridge, Caerleon Roman Fortress, Tintern Abbey and Caerwent Roman town (admission free). Golf 0.5 miles. Fishing on Rivers Wye and Usk.

Charges 2002

Per unit incl. electricity	£15.00
1-man tent	£8.00
2-man tent	£10.00
large tent	£12.00

Discount (10%) for senior citizens. No credit cards. **Tel:** 01291 425114. **Reservations:** Advisable for B.Hs and peak season. **Open** all year.

Directions: From Chepstow take A48 south for 4 miles to roundabout, and turn left on B4245, and immediately turn left again (signed to site and Portskewett). Site is 250 yds. on left. O.S.GR: ST510895.

Glen Trothy Caravan & Camping Park

589 Mitchel Troy, Monmouth NP25 4BD

Glen Trothy is a pretty park on the banks of the river Trothy and visitors are greeted by an array of colourful flowerbeds and tubs around the entrance and reception area. The owners, Horace and Merle Price, are working hard on their site bringing its facilities up to date. Three fields provide 86 level touring pitches. The first and largest field has a circular gravel road with seasonal pitches arranged on the outer side of the road and touring pitches on the inner side. These have slabs for vehicle wheels and electricity hook-ups. The second field, just past the toilet block, has pitches for tourers and trailer tents, whilst the final field is for tents only (no cars are allowed on this area).

Facilities: The sanitary block is old but is bright and cheerful, and includes facilities for disabled visitors, a laundry and dishwashing. Fishing in the River Trothy (licence required). Dogs are not permitted in tents or the tent area. Only purpose built barbecues are allowed. **Off site:** Shopping and supermarkets at Monmouth. Golf 2 miles. Bicycle hire 2 miles.

Charges 2002

Per unit	£7.50
extra person	£1.50
electricity	£2.00
dog	£2.00

Tel: 01600 712295. **Reservations:** Made for min. 2 nights in July/Aug; contact park. **Open** 1 March - 31 October.

Directions: From the A40 at Monmouth continue on at roundabout, straight over at lights and after 150 metres take left just before tunnel. At T junction turn left following signs for Mitchel Troy. Site is on right just past village sign. O.S.GR: SO496106.

Tredegar House Country Park Caravan Club Site

606 Coedkernen, Newport NP10 8TW

This immaculate Caravan Club site is ideally situated for breaking a journey or for longer stays. It can accommodate 82 caravans, all with 16A electricity and 40 with gravel hardstanding. A further grass area is allocated for 30 tents, with its use limited to families and couples - no single sex groups are accepted. Entry and exit from the park are controlled by a barrier (card required). The site itself is set within the gardens and park of Tredegar House, a 17th century house and country park which is open to the public to discover what life was like 'above and below stairs'. Some road noise may be expected, but otherwise this is an excellent site.

Facilities: The sanitary block is of an excellent standard with a digital lock system. It includes washbasins in cubicles, a bathroom for visitors with disabilities and a baby and toddler bathroom complete with small bath, toilet, washbasin and changing unit. Dishwashing sinks and laundry. Good motorcaravan service point. Calor gas available. **Off site:** Large supermarket near.

Charges 2002

Per pitch (non-member)	£6.00 - £8.00
adult	£3.50 - £4.50
child (5-16 yrs)	£1.10 - £1.20
electricity	£1.50 - £2.25

Tel: 01633 815600. Fax: 01633 816372. E-mail: cc92@gofornet.co.uk. **Reservations:** Advisable for peak season - contact the warden. **Open** all year.

Directions: From M4 take exit 28 or from A48 junction with the M4 follow brown signs for Tredegar House. The caravan park is indicated to the left at the house entrance. O.S.GR: ST299855.

Cwmcarn Forest Drive Campsite

Cwmcarn, Crosskeys, Newport NP1 7FA

593

Set in a narrow, sheltered valley with magnificent wooded slopes (it's hard to believe it was once the site of the Cwmcarn Colliery), this park is not only central for the many attractions of this part of Wales, but there is now also much of the natural environment to enjoy including a small fishing lake. The seven mile forest drive (open daily in season) shares its Visitor Centre with the camp reception and has much to offer - bird watching, badger seeking, the Twmbarlwm ancient hill fort to visit with its magnificent views across the Severn to Somerset, Devon and Gloucestershire. The site has a slightly wild feel, but is stunningly located and has 40 well spaced, flat pitches (30 with 15A electric hook-ups, 3 with concrete hardstanding and with tarmac for the car) spread over three small fields between the Visitor Centre and the small lake (fishing permits available). Wardens are on hand daily and from Easter to September the Visitor Centre and reception are manned 9 am - 5 pm. (6 pm. at weekends), so arrive before then.

Facilities: The single well equipped, heated toilet block (£5 deposit for key) including toilet facilities for disabled visitors, laundry with washing machine, dryer, iron and board, and a kitchen with two washing up sinks, small cooker and fridge (hot water free). Visitor Centre has a coffee shop open 1-5.30 pm. at weekends from Easter. Guided walks and the popular Twrch (15 km) mountain bike route are available. Numeracy trail and environmenteering routes for children. Rallies accommodated. Dogs accepted by prior arrangement. **Off site:** Shops, a leisure centre, pubs and takeaway food are available in the village under a mile away. Riding 2 miles, golf 6 miles.

Charges 2003

Per unit	£7.50 - £8.50
large tent	£6.50 - £7.50
small ridge tent	£5.00 - £6.00
electricity	£2.00

Tel: 01495 272001. E-mail: tic@caerphilly.gov.uk.
Reservations: No stated policy. 14 day max. stay. Contact the Warden. **Open** all year excl. 23 Dec - 2 Jan.

Directions: Cwmcarn Forest Drive is well signed from junction 28 on M4. From the Midlands and the 'Heads of the Valleys' road (A465), take A467 south to Cwmcarn. O.S.GR: ST230935.

Springwater Lakes

Harford, Llanwrda SA19 8DT

588

Set in 20 acres of Welsh countryside, Springwater offers a selection of fishing lakes to keep even the keenest of anglers occupied. However, it is not just anglers who will enjoy this site - it is a lovely base to enjoy the peace and tranquillity of this part of Wales. Springwater offers spacious, flat pitches either on grass or hardstanding, all with electricity hook-ups (16A). Malcolm and Shirley Bexon are very proud of their site and welcome all visitors with a smile. This is not a site for children unless they enjoy fishing (no play areas). If you want to learn about fishing Malcolm will be happy to help.

Facilities: The modern, heated toilet block is very clean and includes facilities for disabled visitors (there is also access to the lakes for wheelchairs). Dishwashing. Baker visits daily. Off site: Spar shop and garage 500 yards, other shops 5 miles. Golf 5 miles. Bicycle hire and riding 2 miles.

Charges 2002

Per unit incl. 2 persons	£10.00
person	£4.00
dog	free
electricity	£2.00

Tel: 01558 650788. **Reservations:** contact site. **Open** March - 31 October.

Directions: From A40 at Llanwrda take A482 to Lampeter. After 6 miles go through village of Pumsaint and site is 1 mile further on the left, just before garage shop. O.S.GR: SN637431.

Pembrey Country Park Caravan Club Site

594 Pembrey, Llanelli SA16 0EJ

This very popular Caravan Club site reopened in June 2002 following major changes and refurbishment to the club's high standards. The extended 12-acre grounds provide 50 large hardstanding pitches and 75 level, grass pitches, all with 16A electricity. Tents are accepted, space permitting (strong pegs may be required). Thoughtful landscaping has included the planting of many species of tree and a circular, one-way tarmac road provides easy access. Sensibly placed service points provide fresh water and waste disposal of all types. Close to reception is a late arrivals area that includes electric hook ups. RAF jets do practice in this area (generally no flying at weekends). However, the real plus for this site is its proximity to the Country Park - access to this is free on foot direct from the site, or the Club has organised a special weekly car pass for £11. Within the 520 acres of parkland are delightful walks, cycle trails, unlimited flora and fauna, bird hides, an equestrian centre, children's play area, toboggan and ski runs, pitch 'n' put, narrow gauge railway and picnic areas, all fronted by Cefn Sidan an eight mile stretch of golden sands backed by sand dunes. The nearest section of beach is a 20 minute walk, whilst car parks place you close to the visitor centre, gift shop and the lifeguard patrolled bathing area. At some distance, naturists frequent the extreme northern end of the beach.

Facilities: The alterations to the toilet block are so extensive it gives the impression of a new building with the interior to the latest design and specification. Well situated for all pitches, there are en-suite facilities for disabled visitors (with key). Fully equipped laundry room. Dishwashing sinks under cover. Motorcaravan service point. Gas available. Local delivery vans visit each morning selling milk, bread and newspapers. New children's play area, giant draughts set and boules pitch. **Off site:** Dogs are restricted on the beach May - Sept.

Charges 2002

Per pitch (non-member)	£6.00 - £8.00
adult	£3.50 - £4.50
child (5-16 yrs)	£1.10 - £1.20
electricity	£1.50 - £2.25

Tel: 01554 834369. **Reservations:** Essential for July/Aug. and B.Hs; contact the Warden. **Open** all year, except 6 Jan. - 30 March.

Directions: Leave M4 at junction 48 onto A4138. After 4 miles turn right onto A484 at roundabout signed Carmarthen. Continue for 7 miles to Pembrey. The Country Park is signed off the A484 in Pembrey village; site entrance is on right 100 yds before park gates. O.S.GR: SN415005.

Rhandirmwyn Camping & Caravanning Club Site

607 Rhandirmwyn, Llandovery SA20 0NT

This is a popular site with those who like a peaceful life with no on-site entertainment, just fresh air and beautiful countryside. The site is only a short drive from the magnificent Llyn Brianne reservoir and close to the Dinas RSPB nature reserve, where a two mile trail runs through oak and alder woodland alongside the River Tywi and the wildlife includes many species of birds including red kites. The site is in a sheltered valley with 95 pitches on level grass, 55 electric hook-ups (16A), and 12 hardstandings. The village is within walking distance although there is a fairly steep hill to negotiate (but the return is much easier), and you can take a short cut through the woodland grove dedicated to John Lloyd, a former Chairman of the Club.

Facilities: The single heated sanitary block is kept very clean and tidy. Some washbasins in cubicles, dishwashing sinks and fully equipped laundry. Drive-over motorcaravan service point. Small children's playground with rubber base. **Off site:** The village has a P.O. and general store, and the Royal Oak Inn serves good value meals.

Charges 2002

Per adult	£3.90 - £5.50
child (6-18 yrs)	£1.70
non-member pitch fee	£4.80
electricity	£1.70 - £2.50

Tel: 01550 760257. **Reservations:** Advised for high season and made with deposit; contact the wardens. **Open** March - October.

Directions: From centre of Llandovery take A485 towards Builth Wells, after a short distance turn left, signed Rhandirmwyn, continue for approx. 7 miles along country lanes. O.S.GR: SN779435.

Abermarlais Caravan Park

596 Llangadog SA19 9NG

Apart from the attractions of south or mid Wales for a stay, this sheltered, family run park could also double as a useful transit stop close to the main holiday route for those travelling to Pembrokeshire. In a natural setting, up to 88 touring units are accommodated in one fairly flat, tapering five-acre grass field edged by mature trees and a stream. Pitches are numbered, and generously spaced around the perimeter or on either side of a central, hedged spine at the wider end, with 42 electrical hook-ups (10A) and some hardstanding. Backpackers have a small, separate area. The park is set in a sheltered valley with a range of wildlife and nine acres of woodland walks. There is also an old walled garden, with some pitches and lawns for softball games, that screens the park, both audibly and visibly, from the A40 road. However, the most sought after pitches are beside the stream, loved by children and a haven for wildlife.

Facilities: The one small toilet block is older in style, but can be heated, is clean, bright, cheerful and adequate with controllable showers. Two external, covered washing-up sinks but no laundry facilities - nearest about 5 miles. Motorcaravan service point. Shop doubling as reception. Gas supplies. Play area with tennis and volleyball nets and play equipment. A torch would be useful. Winter caravan storage. **Off site:** Little Chef restaurant near. Pubs, etc. at Llangadog. Fishing 2 miles.

Charges 2002

Per pitch	£4.50
adult	£1.50
child (over 5 yrs)	£1.00
awning	£0.75
electricity	£1.75
dog	free

No credit cards. **Tel:** 01550 777868. **Reservations:** Any length, with £5 deposit. **Open** 14 March - 14 November.

Directions: Park is on the A40, between the junctions with the A4069 and A482, between Llandovery and Llandeilo. O.S.GR: SN685295.

Afon Lodge Caravan Park

595 Parciau Bach, St Clears SA33 4LG

Formerly known as Parciau Bach Caravan Park, this small park is personally run by new owners. There are some narrow lanes to be negotiated to get here, but it is well worth it to enjoy its quality and peaceful, rural setting. The 26 privately owned caravan holiday homes are hidden in the wooded slopes at the back of the park - a haven for wild flowers and squirrels. The open field for tents is sloping, but now has individual terraced places with dividing shrub hedges (10 pitches) and a lower level, part terraced for 25 caravan pitches, all with electrical hook-ups (16A), 9 with hardstanding, water and TV connections. All are on neatly cut grass with views across the valley. The owner's pine chalet home, sited on the slope between the touring field and the wooded area houses reception, a tourist information room and the sanitary facilities. The park is a haven of tranquillity, even when we visited in peak season. If you tire of the rural atmosphere, Tenby is only 18 miles, with the 7 mile long Pendine Sands 6 miles away or to the north, the Preseli Mountains. Birdwatching opportunities abound. A member of the Countryside Discovery group.

Facilities: Recently extended toilet facilities also include a laundry room and facilities for dishwashing. Children have an adventure play unit and a pets corner. Shop at reception (limited hours, Easter - end Oct). **Off site:** Riding 0.5 miles, fishing 2 miles, golf 5 miles. Bar snacks and evening meals are available at the Parciau Bach Inn (weekends only in low seasons) situated above the site.

Charges 2002

Per unit incl. 4 persons	£7.80 - £10.50
2 person tent	£5.00 - £7.50
awning	£1.00
electricity	£2.00
TV connection	£0.50
dog	£0.50

No credit cards. **Tel:** 01994 230647. E-mail: yvonne@afonlodge.f9. co.uk. **Reservations:** May be advisable for B.Hs. **Open** all year except 9 Jan. - 1 March.

Directions: From St Clears traffic lights, take road to Llanboidy forking right after 100 yds. Follow this road for almost 2 miles and turn right. After less than a mile turn right at small crossroads and park is on left. O.S.GR: SN298184.

Moreton Farm Leisure Park

598 Moreton, Saundersfoot SA69 9EA

Moreton Farm has been developed in a secluded valley, a 10-20 minute walk from Saundersfoot and 4 miles from Tenby. It provides 20 caravan (all with 16A electricity, and including 16 with hardstanding) and 40 tent pitches on two sloping, neatly cut grass fields, with 12 pine holiday lodges and 4 cottages for letting occupying another field. The site is approached under a railway bridge (height 10'9", width across the top 6'6", but with alternative access over the railway line for larger vehicles just possible). There are a few trains during the day, none at night. An attractive lake at the bottom of the valley is home to ducks, geese and chickens (fishing is no longer available) - pride of place must go to 'Missy and her girls'! Pembroke and Carew castles and a variety of visitor attractions are close. This is a quiet family site.

Facilities: The toilet blocks (heated) are light and airy, providing excellent facilities with pre-set hot showers (metered), and a ramp to a unit for disabled visitors with toilet and washbasin, a baby bath, dishwashing sinks and laundry facilities. Fenced, outside clothes drying area. Small shop for basics and gas. Children's playground. No dogs or pets are accepted. **Off site:** Fishing or riding 1 mile, bicycle hire 2 miles, golf 4 miles.

Charges 2002

Per unit incl. 2 persons	£9.00 - £11.00
trailer tent incl. 2 persons	£8.00 - £10.00
tent incl. 2 persons	£6.00 - £8.00
extra adult	£1.00
child (2-17 yrs)	£0.50
awning	£1.50
electricity	£2.50

No credit cards. **Tel:** 01834 812016. Fax: 01834 811890. E-mail: moretonfarm@btconnect.com. **Reservations:** Made with deposit (£20 p/wk caravans, £15 p/wk tents), balance 28 days before arrival. **Open** 1 March - 31 October.

Directions: From A477 Carmarthen - Pembroke road take A478 for Tenby at Kilgelly. Park is signed on left after 1.5 miles. Watch carefully for sign and park is 0.5 miles up poorly made-up road and under bridge. O.S.GR: SN122047.

Tything Barn Naturist Camping

590N West Williamson, Kilgetty SA68 0TN

Described by the owners June and Joe Folder as an estuary-side naturist and nature reserve, this is indeed a naturist site with a main camping field for 20 units. Of the 20 well spaced undulating grass pitches, 16 have electricity (6A). Readers who have ventured to enjoy some of the naturist sites featured in our France guide or Southleigh Manor in Cornwall may be intrigued to visit Tything Barn. Stretching down to the backwaters of the Milford Haven estuary, it is situated in 23 acres of ancient quarries where meadow land and springy turf edge the salt marsh which is covered by spring tides. The main sea water lagoon of two acres is suitable for swimming with access steps, a diving platform and a little beach for toddlers. Fishing is possible on the incoming tide flowing up the gullums (gullies) or messing about on boats either side of the tide and children can enjoy crabbing when the water is out. Parents do need to be responsible for children in this type of environment. It is possible to walk in 10 acres of secluded grounds dissected by inlets and lagoons. For those wishing to explore the aspects of naturism, Tything Barn could be a suitable stepping stone. The site is idyllic if you're seeking an unspoilt, tranquil setting, with Pembrokeshire offering something for everyone, from cathedral to castles, coastal walks, fishing, and boat trips to view grey seals and dolphins.

Facilities: The limited sanitary facilities are used by both sexes, very clean but basic. In high season one may have to wait for one of the unscreened showers or use of the dishwashing sink. Washing machine and dryer. Use of freezer and fridge and cooking possible. The 'Flower House' or 'The Tunnel' is a large polythene rounded greenhouse for relaxing or socialising when the weather is inclement. It is paved, tastefully planted with tropical plants and has a soothing water feature. Small library. Croquet, boule and badminton. Events are never organized they just happen. Two cottages and two log cabins to rent. **Off site:** Local farm shop 2.5 miles. Supermarkets 6 miles. Nearby pubs and restaurants provide good food although transport is required. Tenby, Pembroke and Pembroke Dock approx. 6 miles. Carew Castle with various entertainments and children's activities one mile downstream.

Charges 2002

Per unit	£9.00
extra adult	£1.00
teenager	£2.00
dog	£1.00
electricity	£1.50

Tel: 01646 651452. **Reservations:** Made with deposit (£2 per night, £10 per week). **Open** all year.

Directions: Travel north for 1.5 miles on A4075 from its junction with A477. At brow of hill, left into Lawrenny Road signed West Williamston, Cresswell and Lawrenny. Continue for 1.5 miles then hard left keeping phone box to your right. Site on right in 500 yds. O.S.GR: SO035053.

Freshwater East Caravan Club Site

599 Freshwater East, Lamphey SA71 5LN

This Caravan Club site in the Pembrokeshire Coast National Park is open to non-members (for all units). At the bottom of a hill, it has 126 mainly level pitches bounded by trees and with 16A electrical hook-ups available. Around half of the pitches are on hardstanding. The beach and the Pembroke Coastal Path are about a five minute walk. This is an excellent area for walking with magnificent cliff views and birdwatching. You will find St David's, the smallest cathedral city, well worth a visit. Note: TV aerial connections are available, but you will need your own extension cable.

Facilities: The two heated toilet blocks are modern and clean with washbasins in cubicles, and free hairdryers or sockets for your own. Facilities for disabled visitors. Fully equipped laundry rooms. Waste point for motorcaravans. Small play area. Gas supplies. **Off site:** Shop 0.5 miles. Fishing within 5 miles.

Charges 2002

Per pitch (non-member)	£6.00 - £8.00
adult	£3.50 - £4.50
child (5-16 yrs)	£1.10 - £1.20
electricity	£1.50 - £2.25

Tel: 01646 672341. **Reservations:** Contact the Warden. **Open** 26 March - 1 November.

Directions: From the east on A477, fork left 1.25 miles past Milton onto A4075 Pembroke road. After 2 miles in Pembroke immediately (after railway bridge) turn sharp left at roundabout on A4139 Tenby road. In 1.75 miles in Lamphey turn right onto B4584 signed Freshwater East. In 1.75 miles turn right signed Stackpole and Trewent and after 400 yds at foot of hill, right into lane at Club sign. Do not tow to the beach area. O.S.GR: SS015979.

Gwaun Vale Touring Park

600 Llanychaer, Fishguard SA65 9TA

In a superb rural setting, with wonderful views across the countryside towards the sea, Gwaun Vale provides 29 pitches. On mainly level grass, with one terrace above another, connected by an oval, gravel and tarmac road, 10 pitches have hardstanding and 21 have electricity connections (10A). There are plenty of water points and several picnic tables. A useful little shop doubles as reception with a well presented display of tourist information and variety of books on local walks to buy or borrow. One can also borrow a barbecue, iron and board, or a baby bath. Very convenient for Fishguard and the ferries, day trips to Ireland are possible, as well as windsurfing, boating and fishing trips, and the Pembroke coastal footpath is nearby. A 'must' to see is Wales' answer to the Bayeux Tapestry, a 100 ft. long tapestry on view in Fishguard (the French invaded Britain in 1797 and the tapestry, embroidered by 70 local women, gives a carefully researched account of this invasion and its defeat - full of life and humour).

Facilities: The toilet block, beside reception and to one side of the site has been refurbished and is neat, clean and heated. Cheerful laundry room with laundry sink, washing machine and dryer and two dishwashing sinks. New shop in an attractive landscaped garden. Children's play area in a small sloping fenced field with adventure type equipment and a field for dogs adjoining. **Off site:** A family pub serving bar meals is within easy walking distance. Fishing, bicycle hire and riding 2 miles. Golf 7 miles.

Charges 2002

Per unit incl. 1 or 2 persons	£8.50 - £10.00
incl. 3 or 4 persons	£9.75 - £11.50
incl. 5 or more persons	£11.00 - £13.00
electricity (10A)	£1.50

Awning, dog, extra car no charge. No credit cards. **Tel:** 01348 874698. **Fax:** 01348 874000. **E-mail:** margaret.harries@talk21.com. **Reservations:** Advised for high season and B.Hs. and made with £10 deposit. **Open** 1 April - 31 October.

Directions: Park is on the right, 1.5 miles from Fishguard on the B4313; follow brown camping signs from centre. O.S.GR: SM977356.

Cenarth Falls Holiday Park

Cenarth, Newcastle Emlyn SA38 9JS

601

The Davies family have developed an attractively landscaped, part wooded holiday home park with 80 privately owned units and 7 for hire. However, a neat well cared for, sheltered grassy area at the top of the park provides 30 touring pitches, 29 with sunken grass grid hardstanding and all with electricity (16A). Accessed via a semi-circular tarmac road, they enjoy views across the Teifi valley. A sunken, kidney shaped heated outdoor pool with landscaped surrounds and sun-beds is very pleasant. A recent addition is the Coracles Health and Country Club which provides an indoor pool, sauna and steam rooms and fitness suite, plus a bar, restaurant area and a large function room where live entertainment is organised weekly all season. A footpath leads to the village and the famous Cenarth Falls (with leaping salmon). The National Coracle Centre is well worth a visit. A member of the Best of British group.

Facilities: The excellent, heated sanitary block has easy ramped access, even to the chemical disposal unit. etc. Accessed by key, it uses a 'P.I.R.' system that controls heating, lighting, water and air-freshener on entry - very efficient. Tiled with non-slip floors, both men and ladies have an en-suite family room (doubling as provision for disabled visitors), an additional well equipped shower and also one washbasin in a roomy private cabin. Laundry room with two washing machines, two dryers and ironing facilities (used by the whole park). No laundry sinks, but two dishwashing sinks are under cover. Motorcaravan service point. Shop for essential groceries, newspapers, gas. Outdoor pool (Whitsun - mid-Sept). Coracles Health and Country Club (see above). Play area. Games room with pool table and video game machine. **Off site:** Fishing 0.25 miles, bicycle hire 8 miles, riding 7 miles, golf 10 miles.

Charges 2002

Per unit incl. up to 4 people	£8.00 - £15.00
extra person	£2.00
awning	£2.00
extra pup tent (space permitting)	£2.50
dog	£1.00
electricity (16A)	£2.00

Tel: 01239 710345. Fax: 01239 710344. E-mail: enquiries@cenarth-holipark.co.uk. **Reservations:** Made with 33% deposit; contact park. **Open** all year except 1 Dec. - 10 Jan.

Directions: Follow A484 Cardigan - Newcastle Emlyn road and park is signed before Cenarth village. O.S.GR: SN265421.

Pencelli Castle Caravan and Camping Park

Pencelli, Brecon LD3 7LX

604

Open all year round, this is a quality park with atmosphere and character. Set amidst the Brecon scenery, it offers excellent facilities in peaceful, rural tranquillity. The owners, Liz and Gerwyn Rees, have retained the country charm but have added an all embracing range of spacious, heated, luxury facilities, attractively enhanced by potted plants, etc. There are three touring fields. The 'Orchard' incorporates 15 fully serviced pitches with hardstanding, amongst shrubs, fruit trees and a stone cider mill. The 'Oaks' taking 20 caravans and tents and the 'Meadow' for 40 tents (with boot and bike wash) are bordered by majestic trees and the Monmouthshire and Brecon Canal, where gaily painted barges slip past. All the fields are level with neatly mown grass and tarmac access roads. The historic manor house, that dates back to 1583, is adjacent to arched barns that house an increasing collection of vintage farm machinery. For mountain bikers and walkers, a path leaves the village to reach the top of the Brecon Beacons or there is an easy towpath ramble to Tal-y-Bont where there are pubs, tea rooms and a post office.

Facilities: The toilet block is very well designed and includes some private cubicles, two large fully equipped rooms for families or disabled visitors incorporating double showers, baby changing and bath facilities, all humorously decorated for the young at heart. Laundry. Drying room with lockers (a must as this is walking country). Information and planning room. Indoor dishwashing and food preparation room. Motorcaravan service point (with washbasin, soap and hand dryer). Dogs are not accepted. **Off site:** The Royal Oak inn with meals is 100 m. Buses pass regularly for Brecon, Abergavenny. Golf or bicycle hire 5 miles. Riding 2 miles.

Charges 2002

Per caravan or motorcaravan incl. 2 persons	£10.50
extra adult	£3.50
child (5-13 yrs)	£2.00
awning	£1.50
electricity	£2.50
tent - per adult	£5.50

No credit cards. **Tel:** 01874 665451. Fax: 01874 665452. E-mail: pencelli.castle@virgin.net. **Reservations:** Advised for peak season and B.Hs. **Open** all year.

Directions: From A40 south after Brecon bypass take B4558 at signs for Llanfrynach and later Pencelli (narrow bridge). If travelling north on A40, approach via Tal-y-Bont. Site at south end of Pencelli. O.S.GR: SO096248.

Brynich is a well kept, family run park with a picturesque setting and super views towards the Brecon Beacons, developed over the years by Colin and Maureen Jones to very high standards. Originally farmland near the Brecon bypass, there are now three level, hedged and neatly mown camping fields with tarmac roads and a mixture of hardwood trees and shrubs maturing nicely. These fields provide for 130 touring units of all types with 108 electricity points (10/16A) and hardstanding on many pitches. Recent additions include new style grass or gravel hardstandings, a new motorcaravan service point (with mountain bike wash) and a boules court. In a sloping field leading down to a stream, is an extensive dog walk on one side of the Brynich Brook and an adventure play area, reached by a new bridge on the opposite side. The stream is shallow and an added attraction along with the play equipment. For smaller children there is some play equipment near reception and there is a large recreation field for ball games. A restaurant and takeaway facility are planned for 2003. Being within the Brecon Beacons National Park, this is a good area for hill walking and climbing. A member of the Best of British group.

Facilities: Two modern, heated toilet blocks have well equipped showers, washbasins in cubicles, washing up sinks, and a laundry room. Two fully equipped units for disabled visitors are in one block, one providing left handed toilet facilities, the other right handed (key system) and a baby unit including bath. Fridge, freezer and microwave for visitors' use. Motorcaravan service point. Restaurant and takeaway planned. Reception and well stocked shop (with gas). Children's play areas. **Off site:** Local pub serving 'pub grub' is within walking distance. Access to the towpath of the Brecon and Monmouthshire Canal is 200 yds from the park. Market days in Brecon on Tuesday and Friday. Fishing or bicycle hire 1.5 miles, riding 2 miles, golf 3 miles.

Charges 2002

Per unit incl. 2 persons	£8.50 - £10.00
1 person	£6.50 - £8.00
extra adult	£2.25 - £3.00
child (4-16 yrs)	£1.25 - £1.75
backpacker	£4.00 - £4.50
awning	£1.50 - £1.75
electricity	£2.00 - £2.75
dog	£0.50

Tel: 01874 623325. Fax: 01874 623325. E-mail: brynich@aol.com. **Reservations:** Advisable for hook-ups at B.Hs. and made with £10 deposit. **Open** 28 March - 27 October.

Directions: From the A40 Abergavenny road, at roundabout on the Brecon bypass (A40/A470) take A470 and park is 150 yards on right. O.S.GR: SO069278.

Brynich Caravan Park

Brecon, Powys LD3 7SH
Tel/Fax: **01874 623325**
Email: **brynich@aol.com**
Web address: **www.brynich.co.uk**

DE LUXE   appointed

Family run park with panoramic views of the Brecon Beacons. Well maintained, flat site with closely mown grass and large pitch sizes. Modern shower facilities with free hot water, including disabled and baby rooms – cleanliness a priority. Well-equipped licensed shop, telephone, adventure playground, recreation field and dog exercise field.

Calor Award - Most Improved Park in Wales 1998
AA - Best Campsite in Wales ׀ Practical Caravan Top 100 Parks 2000

Mid Wales

Tourism information for Mid Wales may also be obtained from:
Mid Wales Tourism, Marketing Dept, The Station, Machynlleth SY20 8TG
Tel: 0800 273747 Fax: 01654 703855 E-mail: info@brilliantbreaks.demon.co.uk

Mid Wales
Glan-y-Mor Leisure Park
629 Clarach Bay, Aberystwyth SY23 3DT

Follow the road to Clarach Bay and on the sea-front is Glan-y-Mor, a busy, holiday-style park with an enviable situation. On a wet day you may not wish to go far with the comprehensive leisure centre on site - it is open eight months of the year with reduced entry fee for campers. Although the balance of pitches is very much in favour of caravan holiday homes (3:1) which dominate the open park and bay, there are 60 touring pitches, 45 with electricity (10A) and 4 new 'super' pitches. They are rather pressed together in two small sections on the lower part of the park. In high season, tents, tourers or motorcaravans can opt for space and fine views (but maybe winds) on a ridge of higher ground above the park. The well equipped leisure centre offers a heated pool, jacuzzi, solarium, sauna, steam room and gym. This complex also includes reception, a video and amusement room, 10-pin bowling, bar, buffet bar and dance room (free entertainment nightly, Easter and May-Oct). This is an ideal site for those seeking 'all the bells and whistles'!

Facilities: The heated toilet block is on the lower touring area with dishwashing facilities and laundry room, plus a toilet for disabled people. A 'portacabin' type block (high season only) is on the ridge ground. A suite including shower for disabled people is in a block in the upper site, with further facilities at the leisure centre (RADAR key). Motorcaravan service point. Supermarket. Play area designed with younger children in mind, and a large sports field. Swimming pool. Licensed restaurant and takeaway (from Easter). Freezer pack service and gas supplies. No dogs are accepted on touring pitches during B.H. and school summer holiday periods. **Off site:** Reduced rates are available at local golf courses.

Charges 2002

Per unit incl. 2 persons	£6.00 - £12.00
super pitch	£20.00
child	free
extra person (over 18 yrs)	£2.00
awning	£3.00

Top camping area max. charge £10 plus £2 electricity. Club membership (but not Leisure complex) included. **Tel:** 01970 828900. Fax: 01970 828890. E-mail: glanymor@sunbourne.co.uk.
Reservations: Any length, with £20 deposit; balance 28 days before arrival. **Open** 1 March - 31 October.

Directions: Clarach is signed west from the A487 (Aberystwyth - Machynlleth) in village of Bow Street. Follow signs over crossroads to beach and park. Access for caravans from Aberystwyth on B4572 is difficult. O.S.GR: SN580850.

Mid Wales
Aeron Coast Caravan Park
North Road, Aberaeron SA46 0JF

628

Aeron Coast is a family park with a wide range of recreational facilities, on the west coast of Wales. Although it has a high proportion of caravan holiday homes (150 privately owned), touring units of all types are provided for in two fields separated from the beach and sea by a high bank (although the best beach is on the south side of this traditional fishing village). Pitches are on level grass with all units regularly and well spaced in lines in traditional style. The main attraction of the park is its excellent recreational provision, both in and out of doors. This includes a heated kidney shaped pool plus a toddlers' pool (unsupervised) and a paved, walled area good for sunbathing, tennis court and small half-court for youngsters, football and a sand pit. The indoor leisure area provides an under-5's room with slide, etc, teenagers-only room and a TV room. High season activities are organised nightly free of charge in the large entertainment room.

Facilities: Two modern toilet blocks offer excellent facilities (card operated entry system with £10 deposit) including large family showers. Facilities for disabled people and babies are in one block. Basic motorcaravan service point. Swimming pool (1/6-30/9). Club house and bar (from Easter, 12 -2 and from 7 pm) with family room serving bar meals and takeaway in school holiday periods. Reception keeps a wide range of tourist information. Shop at the petrol station at the entrance. Under-5's room with slide, etc, teenagers-only room with juke box, table tennis, pool and games machines and TV room. Only one dog per unit is accepted. **Off site:** Fishing and boat launching 0.5 miles. A steam railway, craft centre, woollen mills and potteries can be visited locally.

Charges 2003

Per unit incl. 2 persons	£9.00 - £12.50
extra person over 12 yrs	£1.00
child 2-12 yrs	£0.50
electricity	£1.50

Tel: 01545 570349. E-mail: aeroncoastcaravanpark@ aberaeron.freeserve.co.uk. **Reservations:** Made with £20 deposit. **Open** 1 March - 31 October.

Directions: Park is on northern outskirts of Aberaeron village with entrance on the right beside a petrol station - not too easily seen. O.S.GR: SN461633.

Mid Wales
Fforest Fields Caravan & Camping Park
Hundred House, Builth Wells LD1 5RT

632

This secluded 'different' park is set on a family hill farm in the heart of Radnorshire. Truly rural, there are glorious views of the surrounding hills and a distinctly family atmosphere. This is simple country camping and caravanning at its best, without man-made distractions or intrusions - a place to unwind and watch the stars. The facilities include 50 large pitches on level grass on a spacious and peaceful, carefully landscaped field by a stream. Electrical connections (mostly 16A) are available and there are 10 hardstanding pitches, also with electricity. George and Kate, the enthusiastic owners, have opened up much of the farm for moderate or ample woodland and moorland trails which can be enjoyed with much wildlife to see. Indeed wildlife is actively encouraged with nesting boxes for owls, song-birds and bats, by leaving field margins un-mown to encourage small mammals and by yearly tree planting. George and Kate also run a para-gliding school where beginners are welcome.

Facilities: The toilet facilities are acceptable with baby bath, dishwashing and laundry facilities including washing machines and a dryer, and heating in cool weather. Milk, eggs and orange juice are sold in reception and gas, otherwise there are few other on-site facilities, but the village of Hundred House, one mile away, has a pub, village stores and post office. **Off site:** Fishing 3 miles, bicycle hire or golf 5 miles, riding 10 miles.

Charges 2003

Per unit incl. 2 persons	£7.50
extra adult	£2.50
child (4-16 yrs)	£1.50
awning	£1.00
electricity	£1.50

Special low season rates for senior citizens. No credit cards. **Tel:** 01982 570406. Fax: 01982 570444. E-mail: office@fforestfields.co.uk. **Reservations:** Contact park. **Open** Easter - 17 November.

Directions: Park is 4 miles east of Builth Wells near the village of Hundred House on A481. Follow brown signs. O.S.GR: SO098535.

Llwyn Celyn Caravan Park

623 Llwyn Celyn, Adfa, Newtown SY16 3DG

Llwyn Celyn is a truly peaceful site with superb views of the Welsh hills and Montgomery countryside. Although predominantly a holiday home park, the upper field has been levelled and drained to provide 16 touring pitches, all with electrical connections. It is a real country retreat, ideal for quiet walks or cycle rides, yet only 10 miles from Newtown.

Facilities: Modern toilet facilities comprise 4 en-suite units (2 with showers). Laundry and dishwashing. Adventure play area. Garden with water feature and seat. **Off site:** Shops 10 miles.

Charges 2002

Per unit	£8.35
awning	£1.50
electricity	£1.50

Tel: 01938 810720. **Reservations:** Made with 25% deposit. **Open** 1 March - 31 October.

Directions: From the A483 (Newtown - Welshpool) take B4390 to Newmills and, 400 yards after village, turn right on bend just before bridge. At crossroads turn left signed Adfa, go through the village and take next left, site on left. O.S. GR: SJ056008.

Cringoed Caravan Park

624 Cringoed, Llanbrynmair, nr Newtown SY19 7DR

Cringoed is a pleasant, peaceful, small park with a river to one side, hills on the other and trees at either end. There are 50 spacious pitches of which 25 are in a level open touring field. Some of these have hardstanding and all have electricity (16A). Caravan holiday homes are at the far end amongst the trees. This is a relaxing base where you can sit and listen to the river and watch the wildlife, but it is also within easy reach of some of mid-Wales' best scenery and not far from the coast. Paul and Sue Mathers will make you very welcome.

Facilities: The single toilet blaock is neat, modern and quite adequate. Laundry and dishwashing. Adventure play area. Small tourist information room. **Off site:** Shops 1 mile. Fishing 5 miles. Riding 12 miles.

Charges 2002

Per unit incl. 2 persons	£8.00
extra person	£1.50
awning	£1.50
electricity	£2.00
dog	free

Tel: 01650 521237. Fax: 01650 521237.
Reservations: contact site. **Open** 7 March - 7 January.

Directions: From the A470 between Newton and Machynlleth in the village of Llanbrynmair take the B4518 signed Staylittle (caravan signs) after 1 mile just before bridge turn right go over site bridge turn right into site. O.S.GR: SH886014.

ALAN ROGERS' GUIDES

Travelling further afield?
Remember the other Alan Rogers'
guides to FRANCE and EUROPE

Available from all good bookshops or

online at www.alanrogers.com

Mid Wales
Dolswydd Caravan Park

625 Dolswydd, Penybont, Llandrindod Wells LD1 5UB

Dolswydd is on the edge of a pretty, traditional working farm. Peaceful and tranquil, with fine views of the Welsh hills and surrounding area, it has modern facilities and 25 good spacious pitches mainly on hardstandings, all with electrical connections (16A). The park is within walking distance of the local pub which offers good, home cooked food. The Hughes family extend a warm and friendly welcome to their little park, surrounded by hills and wandering sheep, which is ideal as a touring base or for a one night stop, but booking is essential.

Facilities: Modern and clean facilities include lots of hot water, dishwashing, laundry, and WC/washroom for disabled people. Fishing is possible in the river alongside the site. **Off site:** Within walking distance are the local pub, Post Office and garage.

Charges 2002

Per unit with 2 persons	£7.50
extra person	£1.00
child under 16 yrs	£0.50
electricity	£1.50

Tel: 01597 851267. Fax: 01597 851267. E-mail: Hughes@dolswydd.freeserve.co.uk. **Reservations:** Contact site. **Open** Easter - end October.

Directions: Penybont is 1 mile from the junction of the A44 and A483 roads at Crossgates. Take A44 signed Kington. Go through village of Penybont and immediately after crossing the cattle grid, the site entrance is on the right. O.S.GR: SO117639.

Mid Wales
Pen-y-Garth Camping & Caravan Park

636 Bala LL23 7ES

An attractively located touring park in a high valley, Pen-y-Garth has 63 pitches (35 with 10A electrical hook-ups) and two rally fields. Adjacent to the touring area are 54 caravan holiday homes, mainly privately owned (5 for hire). At reception, the well stocked shop has gas and comprehensive tourist information. A good six acre recreation field is opposite the park. Watersports are plentiful in this area with the National White Water Centre 5 miles away and Lake Bala and Lake Vyrnwy close. Portmeirion, Snowdonia, Bodnant Gardens and many of those little railways are easy day trips.

Facilities: The main sanitary block offers free controllable showers. In addition to this block, there are two further men's and ladies' toilets and showers on payment (10p or 20p). All these facilities have been refurbished and redecorated. Dishwashing and food preparation room with further facilities for dishwashing, a free freezer for ice blocks, and a laundry. Shop (Easter - end Sept). Small games room. Recreation field. Dogs are accepted by prior arrangement. **Off site:** Fishing, bicycle hire, riding and golf, all within 3 miles.

Charges 2002

Per unit incl. 2 persons	£7.95 - £9.50
extra person (over 5 yrs)	£1.75
awning	£1.80
extra vehicle	£2.00
electricity	£1.85

Less 25% for one person with small tent. Min. 3 night stay at B.Hs. **Tel:** 01678 520485. Fax: 01678 520401. E-mail: stay@penygarth.co.uk. **Reservations:** Made with 25% deposit (min. 3 nights at B.Hs). **Open** 1 March - 31 October.

Directions: Take B4391 from Bala and in 1 mile turn right uphill at sign. Park is 600 yds on right before road narrows. O.S.GR: SH940349.

Bacheldre Watermill Caravan Park

Churchstoke, Montgomery SY15 6TE

631

A delightful little site, Bacheldre has just 25 pitches arranged around the perimeter of a grass meadow, with 18 electric hook-ups (10A), no site roads or hardstandings, and one lamp on the outside of the toilet block. Ideal for tenters and small units, it is not really suitable for large units and American RVs. The watermill is fully operational, producing high quality organic wheat flour, which can be purchased from reception. The mill is not normally accessible, although guided tours can be arranged. Note: there are obvious hazards for small children - a deep partially fenced millpond, moving waterwheel and the stream.

Facilities: A modern portacabin provides the usual facilities including controllable hot showers, with dishwashing sinks in a separate room. **Off site:** Walking and cycling along Offa's Dyke 800 yards from site. Clun Castle ruins are worth a visit. Steam enthusiasts are well catered for with the Welchpool and Llanfair light railway. Supermarket at Churchstoke 2 miles.

Charges 2002

Per person	£4.00
electrcity	£2.00
dog	£0.50

Minimum charge per night: caravan £10.00; camping £8.00. Discounts for stays of 2 weeks or 4 weeks. No credit cards. **Tel:** 01588 620489. Fax: 01588 620105. E-mail: bacheldremill@onetel.net.uk. **Reservations:** Advisable for B.Hs and peak season and made with 50% deposit. **Open** Easter - 31 October.

Directions: Bacheldre is just off the A489 between Newtown and Churchstoke, about 9 miles east of Newtown and 2 miles west of Churchstoke. Turn into narrow lane (signed Bacheldre Mill), over the bridge and site entrance is almost immediately on your right. O.S.GR: SO243928.

Daisy Bank Touring Caravan Park

Snead, Montgomery SY15 6EB

633

For adults only, this pretty, tranquil park in the Camlad Valley has panoramic views, and is an ideal base for walkers. Attractively landscaped with 'old English' flower beds and many different trees and shrubs, this small park has been carefully developed. The Welsh hills to the north and the Shropshire hills to the south overlook the two fields of 20 pitches each, with a third opening for 2003. The field nearer to the road (perhaps a little noisy) is slightly sloping but there are hardstandings for motorcaravans, while the second field is more level. All pitches have 16A electricity, water and waste water drainage and TV hook up. With many walks in the area, including Offa's Dyke, a series of walk leaflets is available centred on Bishop's Castle three miles away. The owners will site your van for you and there is a late arrivals area with hook-up. A security bar at the entrance has to be lifted for motorcaravans. Although technically in Wales, the park is 500 yards from the Shropshire border, an area rich in history.

Facilities: The well equipped, heated toilet block now incorporates modern, en-suite units (6 with shower, WC and washbasin, 6 with WC and washbasin). Dishwashing sinks at the rear of the block are covered. No laundry facilities (launderette at Churchstoke, 2 miles). Brick built barbecues. Small putting green (free loan of clubs and balls). Gas is stocked. An adult only park. **Off site:** Supermarket 2 miles. Many eating places near. Bicycle hire or fishing 3 miles. Golf or riding 10 miles.

Charges 2002

Per unit incl. 2 adults and all services	£13.00
extra person	£2.00
dog	£0.50

Tel: 01588 620471. Fax: 01588 620471. E-mail: J.Spurgeon@tesco.net. **Reservations:** Contact park. **Open** all year.

Directions: Site is by the A489 road 2 miles east of Churchstoke in the direction of Craven Arms. O.S.GR: SO303929.

Penybont Touring & Camping Park

634 Llangynog Road, Bala LL23 7PH

This is a pretty little park with 95 pitches on level grass for caravans, on either flat or sloping grass for tents. Connected by circular gravel roadways, they are intermingled with trees and tall trees edge the site. Gravel strips are provided for cars and there are 44 electric hook-ups (16A). The park entrance and a stone building housing reception and the shop provide quite a smart image. Penybont has a useful location being the closest park to Bala town, 100 yards from Bala Lake and 3 miles from the Welsh National White Water Centre, with Snowdonia on hand.

Facilities: The sanitary block includes washbasins in cubicles. Separate laundry room and an en-suite unit for disabled visitors, that doubles as a baby room, operated by key (£2 deposit). Outside is a large covered area with fencing and concrete floor for dishwashing sinks, and bins. Motorcaravan service point. Shop. Barbecues for hire. Caravan storage. **Off site:** Fishing 200 yds, boat launching, bicycle hire and golf 800 yds, riding 3 miles.

Charges 2002

Per caravan or trailer/frame tent	
incl. 2 persons	£10.90
motorcaravan	£10.30
ridge tent	£9.790
extra person (over 5 yrs)	£2.45
awning	£1.95 - £2.25
electricity	£1.95

Tel: 01678 520549. Fax: 01678 520006. E-mail: penybont@balalake.fsnet.co.uk. **Reservations:** Made for exact dates for particular pitches, with deposit of £10 per pitch. **Open** 1 April - 31 October.

Directions: Park is 0.5 miles southeast of Bala village on the B4391. Bala is between Dolgellau and Corwen on the A494. O.S.GR: SH931349.

Barcdy Caravan & Camping Park

635 Talsarnau, Harlech LL47 6YG

Barcdy is partly in a sheltered vale, partly on a plateau top and partly in open fields edged by woods, with fells to the rear and marvellous views across the Lleyn peninsula in one direction and towards the Snowdon range in another. The Roberts family opened to their first visitors sixty years ago, and they still welcome them today. The park provides for all tastes with level or sloping grass pitches, either secluded in the valley or enjoying the view from the plateau or the lower field. There are 108 pitches, including 38 for touring caravans and 40 for tents, with or without 10A electricity (50 electricity points), plus 30 caravan holiday homes. The grounds of the farm include 28 acres of open fields and natural oak woods (a haven for children) and further up the hills are the two Tecwyn lakes for fishing or just to relax by and enjoy the views. Harlech beach and the castle are only 4 miles, the Italianate village of Portmeirion is nearby and Snowdonia is on your doorstep. A member of the Countryside Discovery group.

Facilities: Two toilet blocks, the one at the top of the valley opened in high season only, include large, comfortable showers, that open direct to the outside except for one in each male and female sections. Hot water is free to the washbasins and dishwashing sinks, metered to the showers (25p). Shop for essentials including gas (open 8.30-11 am. and 4-7 pm. Spr. B.H, then mid July-end Aug). Dogs are not accepted. **Off site:** Riding 4 miles, golf 4 or 6 miles.

Charges 2003

Per unit incl. 2 persons	£8.50 - £11.50
Per unit incl. 2 adults plus 2 children	£10.50 - £13.50
extra adult	£4.00
child (up to 16 yrs)	£1.00
electricity	£2.50

Tel: 01766 770736. E-mail: anwen@barcdy.idps. co.uk. **Reservations:** Contact park. **Open** Easter - 31 October.

Directions: Park is just off the A496 between villages of Llandecwyn and Talsarnau, 4 miles north of Harlech. O.S.GR: SH622371.

Hendre Mynach Touring Caravan & Camping Park

Llanaber, Barmouth LL42 1YR

637

A neat and tidy family park, colourful flowers and top rate facilities make an instant impression on arrival down the steep entrance to this park (help is available to get out if you are worried). The 220 pitches are allocated in various areas, with substantial tenting areas identified. Thirty gravel hardstandings are available and around the park there are 120 electricity hook-ups (10A) and ample water taps. The quaint old seaside and fishing town of Barmouth is under a mile away, a 15-20 minute walk along the prom. Here you will find 'everything'. The beach is only 100 yards away but a railway line runs between this and the park. It can be crossed at one of two points by pedestrian operated gates which could be a worry for those with young children. Snowdonia National Park and mountain railway, the famous Ffestiniog railway, castles and lakes everywhere provide plenty to see and do - a classic park in a classic area.

Facilities: Two toilet blocks, one modern and one traditional, both offer excellent facilities including spacious showers (20p) and washbasins in cubicles in the new block. Extra showers are provided in mobile units used in peak times. Motorcaravan service point. Well stocked shop incorporating a snack bar and takeaway (Easter - 1 Nov; 08.30-21.00 hrs. in peak season, less at quieter times).

Charges 2002

Per caravan or large motorcaravan	
incl. 2 persons	£8.00 - £14.00
2 adults and up to 3 children	£11.00 - £16.00
electricity	£2.00
standard awning	free
tent or small camper	
incl. 3 or 4 persons	£10.00 - £14.00
extra adult	£3.00
child (2-15 yrs)	£1.00
first dog free, extra dog	£0.50

Less 25% for one person with small tent. Min. 3 night stay at B.Hs. **Tel:** 01341 280262. Fax: 01341 280586. E-mail: mynach@lineone.net. **Reservations:** Made with £20 deposit and £1.50 booking fee. **Open** all year excl. 10 Jan - 28 Feb.

Directions: Park is off the A496 road north of Barmouth in village of Llanaber with entrance down a steep drive. O.S.GR: SH608168.

North Wales

Tourism information for North Wales may also be obtained from:

North Wales Tourism, 77 Conwy Road, Colwyn Bay LL29 7LN

Tel: 01492 531731 Fax: 01492 530059   E-mail: croeso@nwt.co.uk www.nwt.co.uk

Llanystumdwy Camping & Caravanning Club Site

Tyddyn Sianel, Llanystumdwy, Criccieth LL52 0LS

658

Overlooking mountains and sea, Llanystumdwy is one of the earliest Camping and Caravanning Club sites. Well maintained with good facilities, it is on sloping grass. However, the managers are very helpful and know their site and can advise on the most suitable pitch and even have a supply of chocks. There are 60 pitches in total (20 ft. spacing), 45 with 10A electricity connections, spaced over two hedged fields with mainly caravans in the top field with four hardstandings for motorcaravans, and with tents lower down. A little library with a supply of tourist information is next to the small reception. A shop and pub are in the village and a bus leaves each hour from outside the site to Pwllheli or Porthmadog. This is a good base from which to explore the Lleyn peninsula or Snowdonia National Park. Portmeirion with its Italianate village is near.

Facilities: A purpose-built toilet block to one side provides excellent, full facilities for disabled visitors including access ramp, one washbasin each in a cubicle for male and female and extra large sinks. Facilities for babies. Laundry (taps with fitting for disabled people). Gas supplies. **Off site:** Riding or fishing 0.5 miles, golf 2.5 miles.

Charges 2002

Per adult	£3.75 - £5.30
child (6-18 yrs)	£1.65
non-member pitch fee	£4.30
electricity	£1.65 - £2.40

Tel: 01766 522855. **Reservations:** Necessary and made with deposit - contact site. **Open** April - October.

Directions: Follow A497 from Criccieth west and take second right to Llanystumdwy. Site is on the right. O.S.GR: SH469384.

North Wales
Forestry Commission - Beddgelert Caravan & Camp Site
659 Caernarfon Road, Beddgelert LL55 4UU

This well equipped Forestry Commission site is in the heart of Snowdonia. Set in a marvellous, natural, wooded environment on the slopes of Snowdon there is abundant fauna and flora, tumbling streams and always something to watch from the cheeky squirrels to the smallest bird in Britain. Well equipped and well managed, the site provides 280 pitches - tents in a semi-wooded field area and caravans amongst the trees with numbered hardstandings, and 105 places with 10A electricity. Tents may pitch where they like in their areas leaving 6 m. between units or there are 6 new grass pitches with electrical hook-ups for tents. Metal tent pegs may be best (available from the shop). Free maps of the forest walks are provided in reception and orienteering and fishing are possible. A bus service stops at the top of the entrance lane (two hourly for Caernarfon and Porthmadog).

Facilities: Two fully equipped modern sanitary toilet blocks clad in natural wood provide large, free hot showers (with good dry areas). Laundry equipment is in one block. A small unit provides extra washbasins and toilets in peak season and there is a toilet and washbasin for disabled visitors. Motorcaravan service point. Recycling bins. Reception is central, as is a well provisioned shop. Well equipped children's adventure playground. **Off site:** Pub within walking distance (under a mile) and other eating places nearby. Bicycle hire within 500 m. in forest.

Charges 2002

Per unit incl. 2 persons	£6.80 - £10.20
extra adult	£2.50
child 5-14 yrs	£1.50
electricity	£2.20 - £2.40

Less 20% all year for disabled guests and outside 7/7-28/8 for the over 60s. **Tel:** 01766 890288. **Reservations:** Necessary for B.Hs and peak times (min. 3 nights with £30 deposit). Contact (at all times): Forest Holidays, Forestry Commission, 231 Corstorphine Road, Edinburgh EH12 7AT. **Open** all year except 20 Nov.- 20 Dec.

Directions: Site is clearly signed to the left 1 mile north of Beddgelert on A4085 Caernarfon road. O.S.GR: SH578490.

North Wales
Bryn Gloch Caravan & Camping Park
660 Betws Garmon, Caernarfon LL54 7YY

Bryn Gloch is a well kept and family owned touring park in the impressive Snowdonia area - an unusual feature is the mountain railway which passes through the park. Neat and quiet, it takes some 160 units on five flat, wide meadows with some breathtaking views. With tarmac access roads and free areas allowed in the centre for play, 100 pitches have electricity connections (10A). These include 6 all weather pitches, 18 'super' pitches and 6 serviced pitches (shared), all with hardstanding. In addition, there are 12 caravan holiday homes. Fishing is possible on the river bordering the park with a barbecue and picnic area, adventure play area and field for ball games. Tourist information is provided in the complex by reception and the park is very popular with walkers and cyclists. Caernarfon with its famous castle 5 miles.

Facilities: The two main toilet blocks are new and include washbasins in cabins, a family bathroom (hot water £1), baby room and complete facilities for visitors with disabilities (coded access). The far field has a 'portacabin' style unit containing all facilities, for use in peak season. Well equipped laundry and separate drying room. Motorcaravan service point and car wash. Shop (1/3-30/10). TV and games rooms with pool tables and amusement machines. Minigolf. Entrance barrier with coded access. **Off site:** Riding 2.5 miles, bicycle hire or golf 5 miles

Charges 2002

Per unit incl. 2 persons	£10.00
extra adult	£2.00
child (3-16 yrs)	£1.50
awning or pup tent	£1.50
dog	£0.50
electricity	£2.50
'super' pitch incl. electricity	£3.00
serviced pitch	£2.00

Tel: 01286 650216. Fax: 01286 650591. E-mail: eurig@bryngloch.co.uk. **Reservations:** Necessary for B.Hs. (min. 3 nights) with payment in full; other times with deposit of first night's fee. **Open** all year, limited facilities 1 Nov - 1 March.

Directions: From Caernarfon take A4085 signed Beddgelert. Park is just beyond Waunfawr, 4.5 miles southeast of Caernarfon. At Betws Garmon, after crossing river bridge, watch for signs and entrance is opposite St Garmon church. O.S.GR: SH538578.

Home Farm Caravan Park

664 Marianglas, Isle of Anglesey LL73 8PH

A tarmac drive through an open field leads to this neatly laid out quality park, with caravan holiday homes to one side. Nestling below what was once a Celtic hill fort, later decimated as a quarry, the park is edged with mature trees and farmland. A circular, tarmac access road leads to the 61 well spaced and numbered pitches, which include 9 fully serviced with electricity, water and waste water and a further 19 with electricity and water. All these have hardstanding with 16A electricity; other pitches all have 10A supply. On neatly cut grass, some areas are slightly sloping, and there is a separate area for tents. The 'piece de resistance' of this park must be the children's indoor play area, large super adventure play equipment, complete with tunnels, bridges on safe rubber matting, not to mention an outside fenced play area and fields available for sports, football, etc. and walking. Various beaches, sandy or rocky, are within a mile. A member of the Best of British group.

Facilities: Two purpose built toilet blocks, one part of the reception building, are of the same design and can be heated. They include en-suite provision for people with disabilities (with key) and an excellent small bathroom for children with baby bath and curtain for privacy, a laundry room and good washing up facilities. Motorcaravan service point. Reception provides basic essentials, gas and some caravan accessories. Indoor and outdoor children's play areas. TV and a pool table. **Off site:** Fishing or golf 2 miles, riding 8 miles.

Charges 2002

Per unit incl. 2 persons, electricity	£8.50 - £11.50
incl. mains services and awning	£11.50 - £14.50
extra adult	£2.00
child (5-16 yrs)	£1.50
dog	£0.50

Tel: 01248 410614. Fax: 01248 410900. E-mail: enq@homefarm-anglesey.co.uk. **Reservations:** Essential for peak season (min. 3 days at B.Hs) and made with £20 deposit. **Open** April - October.

Directions: From the Britannia Bridge take second exit left signed Benllech and Amlwch on the A5025. Two miles after Benllech keep left at roundabout and park entrance is approx. 300 yards on the left beyond the church. O.S.GR: SH498850.

Bron-Y-Wendon Touring Caravan Park

669 Wern Road, Llanddulas, Colwyn Bay LL22 8HG

Bron-Y-Wendon is right by the sea between Abergele and Colwyn Bay on the beautiful North Wales coast road. This is a quiet park which, by its own admission, is not really geared up for the family unit - there is no children's playground here, although there is a games room with table tennis and a separate TV room. The park is manicured to the highest standards and caters for a large number of seasonal caravans on pitches with gravel bases which are kept very tidy. There are a further 65 grass based, and 20 hardstanding touring pitches, all with electrical hook ups (16A) and tarmac access roads. All pitches have coastal views and the sea and beach are just a short walk away. Colwyn Bay, Conwy, Anglesey, Llandudno, Snowdonia and Chester are all within easy reach, so there is lots to do. Having said how peaceful and quiet everything is (particularly for a seaside park in this area), there is some road noise from the adjacent A55 and during our visit a small train passed on the tracks between the park and the sea (just a few yards) and at night with little else going on it could be just noticeable.

Facilities: Two toilet blocks, both with heating, provide excellent facilities including men's and women's shower rooms separate from the toilets and washbasins. Good facilities for disabled visitors. Laundry with washing machines and dryers. Mobile shop visits daily. Gas supplies on site. **Off site:** Llanddulas village with shops and several good pubs is very near.

Charges 2002

Per pitch	£5.00 -£7.00
person	£2.00
child (2 -12 yrs)	£1.00
awning	£2.00
electricity (16A)	£2.00

Tel: 01492 512903. Fax: 01492 512903. E-mail: bron-y-wendon@northwales-holidays.co.uk. **Reservations:** Made with £5 per night deposit; contact park. **Open** 21 March - 31 October.

Directions: From A55 Chester - Conwy road turn at Llanddulas junction (A547). Turn right opposite Shell garage and park is approx. 400 yards, signed on coast side of the road. O.S.GR: SH903785.

Hunters Hamlet Caravan Park

665 Sirior Goch Farm, Betws-yn-Rhos, Abergele LL22 8PL

This small, family owned park is licensed for all units except tents (trailer tents allowed). On a gently sloping hillside providing beautiful panoramic views, one area provides 15 well spaced pitches with hardstanding and 10A electricity hook-ups, with access from a circular, hard-core road. A more recent area has been developed next to this of a similar design but with 8 fully serviced 'super pitches' (water, waste water, sewage, TV and electricity connections). Shrubs and bushes at various stages of growth enhance both areas. A natural play area incorporating rustic adventure equipment set amongst mature beech trees with a small bubbling stream is a children's paradise. Milk and papers can be ordered and the Hunters will do their best to meet your needs, even to survival rations! The park is well situated to tour Snowdonia and Anglesey and is within easy reach of Llandudno and Rhyl.

Facilities: The tiny heated toilet block has fully tiled facilities including showers en-suite with toilets for both sexes. A covered area to the rear houses laundry and dishwashing (H&C), washing machine and dryer, iron and board, freezer and fridge. Family bathroom (metered) and basic toilet and shower facilities for disabled visitors. Children's play area. All year caravan storage. Max. 2 dogs per pitch. **Off site:** Fishing or golf 2 miles, riding 10 miles.

Charges 2002

Per unit incl. 2 adults, basic pitch	£9.00 - £11.00
'super' pitch (fully incl.)	£16.00 - £19.00
extra person	£2.00
child	£1.00
electricity	£2.00

Less £5 on weekly bookings. Aug. B.H, plus £1.00. **Tel:** 01745 832237. Fax: 01745 832237. E-mail: huntershamlet@aol.com. **Reservations:** Made with £20 deposit; B.H. bookings min. 4 nights. **Open** 21 March - 31 October.

Directions: From Abergele take A548 south for almost 3 miles; turn onto B5381 in direction of Betws-yn-Rhos and park is on left after 0.5 miles. To date there are no local authority caravan signs so watch carefully for the farm after turning - it can be identified by an artistically painted sign with the house and farm name: 'Sirior Goch Farm' and Hunter's Hamlet. O.S.GR: SH929736.

Ty-Ucha Farm Caravan Park

670 Maesmawr Road, Llangollen LL20 7PP

Only a mile from Llangollen, world famous for the Eisteddfod, Ty Ucha has a rather dramatic setting, nestling under its own mountain and with views across the valley to craggy Dinas Bran castle. It is a neat, ordered park, carefully managed by the owners and providing 40 pitches (30 with 10A electrical hook-up) for caravans and motorcaravans only. They are well spaced round a large, grassy field with an open centre for play and a small paddock area. One side slopes gently and is bounded by a stream and wood. A path leads from here for various mountain walks, depending on your energy and ability. Because of overhead cables, kite flying is forbidden; no bike riding either. The paddock area provides for those who prefer to be without the company of children or dogs. Eisteddfod is an international festival of music and dance held for six days starting on the first Tuesday of the first full week in July every year - it is a very busy time for the area. No tents are accepted.

Facilities: The single toilet block, although of 'portacabin' style, is clean and well maintained and can be heated. It includes two metered showers for each sex (a little cramped). Dishwashing sink with cold water outside. No laundry facilities but there is a launderette in Llangollen. Gas supplies. Games room with table tennis. Late arrivals area. Note: tents are not accepted. **Off site:** Hotel 0.5 miles with reasonably priced meals. Fishing 1 mile, golf 0.5 miles.

Charges 2002

Per caravan incl. 2 persons	£7.50
motorcaravan	£7.00
extra person	£1.00
awning (environmental groundsheets)	£0.50 - £1.00
electricity	£2.00

Reductions for OAPs for weekly stays. No credit cards. **Tel:** 01978 860677. **Reservations:** Necessary for B.Hs. and Eisteddfod and made with £10 deposit; 3 days min. at B.Hs. **Open** Easter - October.

Directions: Park is signed off A5 road, 1 mile east of Llangollen (250 yds). O.S.GR: SJ228411.

The Plassey Touring & Leisure Park

667 Eyton, Wrexham LL13 0SP

Set in 247 acres of the Dee Valley, The Plassey offers many activities. It is not just a touring park but is also a leisure and craft centre with a friendly, busy atmosphere and pleasant environment. The Edwardian farm buildings have been tastefully converted to provide a restaurant, coffee shop, health, beauty and hair studio, a small garden centre and 16 different craft and retail units, open all year to the public. Unusually there is also a small brewery on site, producing its own unique Plassey Bitter! The park itself is spacious with pitches around the outer edges of a series of fields forming circles. There are 110 touring pitches with electrical connections (16A), including 30 new serviced pitches (with hardstanding, water, waste water, electricity, lighting), and five areas taking 120 seasonal caravans which will put pressure on the facilities. There is much to do and to look at in a rural setting at the Plassey but it is probably best enjoyed mid-week and avoiding the busy Bank Holidays. Certainly for peace and quiet, you should try and pitch away from reception, the clubhouse and arcade games.

Facilities: The original toilet facilities beside the entrance and under the clubhouse have been refurbished to a good standard. These are supplemented by a good, new heated block in the top field area with individual washbasin cubicles, a room for disabled visitors or families, dishwashing sinks and laundry. Motorcaravan service point. Shop (all season) and gas. Club house with children's room (open March-Oct.). Indoor, heated swimming pool with sunbed and sauna (May - Sept, limited hours mid-week, 80p per hour). Badminton courts including indoor one which can be booked. Adventure playground with equipment for smaller children (note: bicycles, skateboards or footballs are not allowed). Nine hole golf course, fishing pools, wildlife meadow and countryside footpaths. Winter caravan storage.

Charges 2003

Per unit incl. 2 adults, 2 children, electricity	£13.00 - £15.50
serviced pitch	£4.00
extra person	£2.50
awning or pup tent	£2.00
dog	£1.50

Includes club membership, coarse fishing, badminton and table tennis (own racquets and bats required). B.H. supplement £4 per weekend. Discount for weekly bookings. **Tel:** 01978 780277. Fax: 01978 780019. E-mail: enquiries@theplassey. co.uk. **Reservations:** Necessary for weekends, B.Hs and July/Aug. and made with £20 deposit. **Open** 5 March - 7 November.

Directions: Follow brown and cream signs for The Plassey from the A483 Chester - Oswestry bypass onto the B5426 and park is 2.5 miles. Also signed from the A528 Marchwiel - Overton road. O.S.GR: SJ349452.

James' Caravan Park

668 Ruabon, Wrexham LL14 6DW

Open all year, this park has a heated toilet block and attractive, park-like surroundings with mature trees and neat, short grass. However, edged by two main roads it is subject to some road noise. The old farm buildings and owner's collection of original farm machinery, carefully restored and maintained, add interest. The park has over 40 pitches, some level and some on a slope, with informal siting giving either a view or shade. Electricity (6/10A) is available all over, although a long lead may be useful. Tourist information and a free freezer for ice packs are in the foyer of the toilet block. This is a useful park with easy access from the A483 Wrexham - Oswestry road.

Facilities: The heated toilet block offers roomy showers (20p) with a useful rail to help those of advancing age with feet washing. En-suite facilities for visitors with disabilities complete with special 'clos o mat' toilet! Motorcaravan service point. Gas available. **Off site:** The village is a 10 minute walk with a Spar shop, fish and chips, a restaurant, launderette and four pubs. Golf 3 miles.

Charges 2002

Per unit incl. 2 persons	£8.00
extra person	£1.00
awning	£2.00
dog	£0.50

No credit cards. **Tel:** 01978 820148. Fax: 01978 820148. E-mail: ray@carastay.demon.co.uk. **Reservations:** Contact park for details. **Open** all year.

Directions: Park is at junction of A483/A539 Llangollen road and is accessible from the west-bound A539. O.S.GR: SJ302434.

SCOTLAND

Scottish Tourist Board
23 Ravelston Terrace, Edinburgh EH4 3TP
Tel: (0131) 332 2433 Fax: (0131) 315 4545

E-mail: info@visitscotland.com
Internet: http://www.visitscotland.com

We have used the following Regional Tourist Areas to list our parks:

1. **Scottish Lowlands**   2. **Heart of Scotland**
3. **Grampian**   4. **Highlands and Islands**

Scotland provides superb opportunities to enjoy wild and grand scenery. It also offers towns and cities with a rich cultural life and over the centuries has had a disproportionately large impact on the world with many of its philosophers, scientists and inventors being responsible for the ideas on which we base our understanding of the world.

Lowlands

The area we identify as the Scottish Lowlands or Southern Scotland, covers Dumfries and Galloway, the Scottish Borders, Edinburgh and Lothians, Greater Glasgow and the Clyde valley. In Dumfries and Galloway lonely hills roll down to pastures and dark woods which give way to rich farmlands and a sunny south facing coast. The Borders is an area of tranquil villages, bustling textile towns and a wild coastline running north from Berwick-upon-Tweed. There are magnificent historic houses, great Border abbeys, working woollen mills and craft workshops. Sir Walter Scott, the famous Scottish writer, lived at Abbotsford near Melrose and is buried at Dryburgh Abbey. The Lothians, bordered by the sea waters of the Firth of Forth to the unspoiled Pentland Hills, has a beautiful coastline and rich countryside. Edinburgh is dealt with elsewhere as is Glasgow. Paisley is known for the Paisley shawl and Lanark for the enlightened industrialist Robert Owen whose Utopian ideas on workers welfare in his textile mills

Heart of Scotland

Heart of Scotland covering Loch Lomond, Stirling and the Trossachs, Perthshire, Angus, Dundee and the Kingdom of Fife. Here the Lowlands meet the mountains of the north and west and in old days all routes led to Stirling. Because of its strategic position whoever held Stirling Castle controlled the Scottish nation. The Trossachs with their heather-clad hills are the home of Rob Roy the folk hero. Fife boasts two ancient 'capitals'. Dunfermline, the seat of early Celtic kings and the final resting place of Robert the Bruce and St Andrews, the ecclesiastical capital, now a university town and the 'Home of Golf'.

Grampian

Grampian includes the Grampian Highlands, Aberdeen and the North East Coast and is probably best known for Royal Deeside where Prince Albert built Balmoral Castle as a summer home for Queen Victoria and the Malt Whisky Trail. This is a signed route featuring seven whisky distilleries, each with excellent interpretation facilities for visitors.

Highlands and Islands

The Highlands and Islands is one of the last wildernesses in Europe, from the soaring beauty of Glencoe to the to the idyllic charm of the Isles, and from the crashing waves of the northern coastline to the silence of the windswept moors. Home to the Loch Ness Monster and the famous Fort William to Mallaig railway, one of the greatest railway journeys in the world.

The oldest part of Hoddom Castle itself is a 16th century Borders Pele Tower, or fortified Keep. This was extended to form a residence for a Lancashire cotton magnate, became a youth hostel and was then taken over by the army during WW2. Since then parts have been demolished but the original 'Border Keep' still survives, unfortunately in a semi-derelict state. The site's bar and restaurant have been developed in the courtyard area from the coach houses, and the main ladies' toilet block was the stables. The park is landscaped and spacious, well laid out on mainly sloping ground with many mature and beautiful trees, originally part of an arboretum. The drive to the site is just under a mile long, with a one way system. Many of the 120 numbered pitches have good views of the castle and have gravel hardstandings with grass for awnings, most with electrical connections (10A). In front of the castle are flat fields for tents and caravans not needing electricity. Amenities include a comfortable bar lounge with a family room and TV. The park's nine hole golf course is in an attractive setting alongside the Annan river, where fishing is possible for salmon and trout (tickets available). Coarse fishing is also possible elsewhere on the estate. This is a peaceful base from which to explore historic southwest Scotland.

Facilities: The main toilet block can be heated and is very well appointed, with washbasins in cubicles and an en-suite shower unit for disabled visitors. Two further tiled blocks, kept very clean, provide washbasins and WCs only. Each block has dishwashing sinks. Well equipped laundry room at the castle. Motorcaravan service point. Licensed shop at reception (gas available). Bar, restaurant and takeaway (restricted opening outside high season). Games room with pool tables, table tennis and video games. Large, grass play area. Crazy golf. Bicycle hire and mountain bike trail. Fishing. Golf. Guided walks organised in high season. Caravan storage.
Off site: Tennis nearby.

Charges 2002

Per unit incl. up to 4 persons	£6.00 - £11.00
small tent incl. 1 or 2 persons	£5.00 - £8.50
extra person (over 7 yrs)	££1.00 - £2.00
awning	£2.00
electricity	£2.00

Tel: 01576 300251. Fax: 01576 300757. E-mail: hoddomcastle@aol.com. **Reservations:** Necessary for July/Aug and B.Hs. Any length with deductible £5 deposit. **Open** 1 April - 25 October.

Directions: Leave A74M at exit 19 (Ecclefechan) and follow signs to park. Leave A75 at Annan junction (west end of Annan by-pass) and follow signs. O.S.GR: NY155725.

Lowlands
Cressfield Caravan Park

692 Ecclefechan, nr Lockerbie DG11 3DR

Cressfield is just north of the border, close to main routes (A74M/M6) and is an ideal transit park, or for longer stays with the Solway Firth, Dumfries and Galloway tourist features nearby. A purpose designed, modern park, it has been developed to a very high standard in pleasant undulating countryside next to the village of Ecclefechan, and is personally managed by the owner. Open all year, the park provides 153 pitches of which many are taken by holiday homes and seasonal units, leaving around 35 for tourers. The park is landscaped (trees are growing well) and the level pitches, mostly with hardstanding, are connected by tarmac or gravel roads and provided with electric hook-ups (16A). A good rally field is also fully equipped with electrical hook-ups. There is no shop but it is only 400 yards from the village and adjacent to the park is an hotel for a drink or a meal. For the more active seven golf courses are near, opportunities for coarse or game fishing, cycling, walking, birdwatching and historical Solway to explore. Some road noise is possible.

Facilities: The modern, heated toilet block is central (key system) and provides excellent facilities - well equipped showers, washbasins in cubicles and hairdryers (metered). A bath is a welcome addition in the ladies' (20p). A toilet and washbasin, plus a separate shower area are provided for disabled visitors, plus shower seats, in both male and female sections. Excellent laundry room. Washing up area under cover. Motorcaravan service point. Large dog exercise field and dog waste bins. Gas supplies. Well equipped, fenced children's play area, 9 hole putting green and sports field with goal posts (not in wet weather or Nov-March), tennis and badminton nets, netball posts. Giant chess and draughts. Boules. **Off site:** Hotel for meals adjacent. Boat launching 8 miles.

Charges 2002

Per unit incl. 2 adults	£7.00 - £9.00
awning, extra car or small tent	£1.00
extra adult	£2.00
child (under 16 yrs)	£1.00
car and small tent	£7.00 - £8.00
walkers or cyclists with 2-man tent	£5.00
electricity	£2.00 - £2.50

B.Hs. - £2 extra per night, per unit. No credit cards. **Tel:** 01576 300702. Fax: 01576 300702. **Reservations:** Phone bookings accepted. **Open** all year.

Directions: Approaching from north or south on A74(M) take exit 19 for Ecclefechan (10 miles north of Gretna, 5 miles south of Lockerbie) and follow B7076 for half a mile to south side of village; park is signed. O.S.GR: NY196744.

Lowlands
Glenearly Caravan Park

687 Dalbeattie DG5 4NE

Glenearly is a new park (opened in 2000), owned and managed by Mr and Mrs Jardine. Rurally located, it has been tastefully developed from farmland into a touring and mobile home, all year park. There are 39 marked, open pitches, all with 16A electrical connections (and TV), mostly on level grass areas with 4 hardstandings available. Walls and shrubs divide the touring section from the caravan holiday homes, with mature trees around the perimeter. There are attractive views over the hills and forest of Barhill and buzzards, yellow wagtails, woodpeckers and goldfinch are some of the birds that can be seen, along with the park's own donkeys, ponies and sheep. The large games room, converted from an old barn, is excellent - heated and with plenty of chairs and tables for parents to supervise the activities. A super play area suitable for all ages is conveniently situated behind the touring area. A 10 minute stroll brings you into the small town of Dalbeattie. Just 6 miles from the park along the Solway coast is Kippford, a well known sailing centre from which you can walk the Jubilee Path (1 mile) to Rockcliffe. Set in a bay, Rockcliffe has a small sandy beach, an excellent tea room and gift shop.

Facilities: Situated in the centre of the touring area, the toilets and showers are fitted out to a high standard, and there is a unit for disabled visitors or families. Laundry room with washing machines and dryer and an outside drying area. Large games room. Play area. **Off site:** Shops, pubs, restaurants, etc. at Dalbeattie. Bicycle hire at Mabie Forest just 3 miles from Dumfries on the A710.

Charges 2002

Per unit incl. 2 persons	£7.00
extra person (over 5 yrs)	£1.00
awning	£0.50 - £1.00
electricity and TV hook-up	£1.75 - £2.25
animal	free

Tel: 01556 611393. Fax: 01556 612058. **Reservations:** Made with £10 deposit. **Open** all year.

Directions: From Dumfries take A711 towards Dalbeattie. Six miles beyond Beeswing, after passing sign for Edingham Farm, park is signed with entrance on right (beside a bungalow). O.S.GR: NX834626.

Lowlands
Park of Brandedleys
Crocketford, Dumfries DG2 8RG

693

Brandedleys is a first class park providing pitches for some 75 caravans and a limited number of tents, plus 60 self-contained caravan holiday homes in three or four flat and variably sloping fields with tarmac access roads. It has excellent installations and amenities. Caravan pitches are on lawns or terraced hardstandings, many with a pleasant outlook across a loch. There are 80 electrical connections (10A), 21 pitches with water and drainage, plus some 'premier' pitches with TV connections and a picnic bench. A new area for caravans is being developed for 2003. A small, heated outdoor swimming pool is open when the weather is suitable and the heated indoor pool adjacent to the bar/restaurant is open all season with changing room (both pools free) and a sauna. The bar and licensed restaurant with full menu at reasonable prices, are open for lunch and dinner, with a patio area overlooking Auchenreoch Loch. Walks on the open moors or forest and beautiful sandy beaches 12 miles away. A popular, quality park and a member of the Best of British group.

Facilities: The main heated toilet block has been extensively modernised with clean, well appointed shower cubicles with toilet and washbasin (just one for men), in addition to the normal provision. Hairdryers. Bathroom for disabled visitors. Laundry room, baby and hair care room. Covered dishwashing sinks. A second block of equal size and standard is in the lower field, also with laundry and dishwashing facilities. Well stocked shop. Bar and restaurant. Takeaway food to order (18.00-21.30 hrs). Swimming pools. All-weather tennis courts, outdoor badminton court and draught board. Games room with TV. Table tennis, pool table and air-hockey table. Football pitch. Putting course and golf driving net. New play area. **Off site:** Fishing (0.5 miles); golf, riding and pony trekking nearby.

Charges 2002

Per unit incl. 2 persons	£10.00 - £15.00
family unit	£13.00 - £18.00
electricity	£2.00
serviced pitch	£2.00
awning	£2.00
pup tent	£3.00

No single sex groups. **Tel:** 01556 690250. Fax: 01556 690681. E-mail: brandedleys@holgates.com.
Reservations: Advised for peak dates and made with £20 deposit per pitch. **Open** all year.

Directions: Park is 9 miles from Dumfries on the south side of the A75 Dumfries - Stranraer road, just west of the village of Crocketford. O.S.GR: NX830725.

Lowlands
Mossyard Caravan Park
Gatehouse of Fleet, Castle Douglas DG7 2ET

689

Mossyard is a family run park set within a working farm right beside the sea in a sheltered bay. The park and farmhouse appear together suddenly over the horizon and in the distance as you approach, with some breathtaking views across the Solway where the Galloway Hills and the waters of Wigtown Bay meet. On arrival you pass through the farm buildings into the park, which is divided into two sections by stone walling. Around the perimeter are several new wooden chalets and holiday homes and self catering holiday cottages. There are 30 grass pitches (15 for tourers), some flat but most on an elevated sloping area, plus 20 for tents or motorhomes on a level camping field which adjoins the beach but is a little way from the sanitary facilities. Electrical connections (10 A) are available for the caravans and some tent pitches. This is a wonderful park for outdoor activities such as watersports and fishing where small craft can be launched from site. Although some of the beaches and tides around the Solway Coast are dangerous, the one around this bay is very safe.

Facilities: Some of the farm buildings around the main farmhouse have been utilised for the toilet facilities, which are are of traditional design. Showers are coin operated (20p). Dishwashing area covered, with plenty of hot water. Airy laundry room with washing machine, dryer and spin dryer (coin operated). No shop on site but milk can be obtained from the farmhouse. **Off site:** Gatehouse of Fleet with shops, pubs and restaurants, 4 miles.

Charges 2002

Per caravan	£7.00 - £8.00
motorcaravan	£7.00
tent	£6.00 - £8.00
electricity	£1.50

Tel: 01557 840226. E-mail: mossyard@talk21.com.
Reservations: Contact park. **Open** Easter - October.

Directions: Take A75 road from Dumfries towards Stranraer and park is signed to the left, 4 miles west of Gatehouse of Fleet, approx. 1 mile down a single track farm road. O.S.GR: NX547518.

Lowlands
Sandyhills Bay Leisure Park
Sandyhills, Dalbeattie DG5 4NY

Sandyhills Bay Leisure Park is part of the Gillespie Leisure Group that also includes Brighouse Bay (no. 695) and Seaward (690). A small, quiet park beside a sheltered, sandy beach, reception is on the left through a car park used by visitors either walking the hills or enjoying the beach. Beyond is a large flat camping area, above which, divided by a tree lined hedge, are 60 pitches, half taken by mobile homes situated around the perimeter. The 30 touring pitches, 28 with electricity (16A) are in the centre of the all grass flat area. This is an excellent family park, with the beach and children's play area at the site, whilst up the hill next to the park is an 18 hole golf course where you can enjoy a bar meal in the clubhouse and within walking distance at Barend is an approved riding centre suitable for all the family. There is a well stocked shop and a takeaway with table and chairs outside from where you can enjoy the well kept garden and splendid views across the Solway.

Facilities: The sanitary facilities are of traditional design, situated in one central block to the side of the touring area. Laundry room (tokens from reception). Shop and small takeaway. New adventure play area by the beach. Visitors can also use the facilities at Brighouse Bay the largest park in the Gillespie Group. **Off site:** For the energetic, you can take a cliff top walk from Sandhills to Rockcliffe approx. 10 miles, or take a pleasant drive to Rockcliffe and Kippford a well known sailing centre.

Charges 2002

Per unit incl. 2 persons	£7.75 - £11.30
extra adult	£1.65
child (4-15)	£1.05
full awning	£1.75
extra car, small tent, boat	£1.05
porch awning, gazebo	£1.05
electricity	£2.85 - £2.30
dog	£1.05

Tel: 01387 780257. E-mail: info@sandyhills-bay.co. uk. **Reservations:** Made with £25 deposit. **Open** 23 March - 31 October.

Directions: From Dumfries take A710 Solway coast road (approx. 16 miles). Park is on left just after signs for Sandyhills. O.S.GR: NX890549.

Lowlands
Seaward Caravan Park
Dhoon Bay, Kirkcudbright DG6 4TJ

Seaward Caravan Park is little sister to the much larger Brighouse Bay Holiday Park, 3.5 miles away. Set in an idyllic location overlooking the bay, this park is suitable for all units. The terrain is slightly undulating, but most of the numbered pitches are flat and a good size. There are 35 pitches (18 hardstandings) designated for caravans and motorcaravans, a further 14 for tents, and 43 caravan holiday homes for hire. Electric hook-ups (16A) are on 32 of the touring pitches, 12 also serviced with water tap, waste water disposal, and TV socket. Visitors can play golf on the park's nine-hole course (£3 per round) or watch others play while walking the dog around its perimeter. Facilities at the larger Brighouse Bay Holiday Park are available to all campers at discounted rates. This is a quiet park with excellent views ideally suited for that relaxing holiday or for touring the region.

Facilities: The principal, fully equipped toilet block is to the rear of the park. Four rooms with en-suite facilities are also suitable for disabled campers. Well equipped baby room. Laundry and dishwashing room. No motorcaravan service point but the manager can lift a manhole cover to empty waste water tanks. The reception/shop stocks basic provisions, books, gifts, gas, and tourist information. TV/family room. Unsupervised heated outdoor swimming pool with sunbathing area (15/5-15/9). Central play area with bark surface, outdoor chess, rocking horse, table tennis and picnic tables. Excellent games room. Golf. **Off site:** Beach and sea angling nearby, riding or bicycle hire 3.5 miles. Kirkcudbright is 2.5 miles.

Charges 2002

Per unit incl. 2 adults	£8.50 - £11.60
extra adult	£1.65 - £1.70
child (4-15 yrs)	£1.25 - £1.30
awning	£1.75 - £1.80
extra car, porch awning or small tent	£1.05
electricity	£2.30 - £2.85
electricity and TV aerial	£2.95 - £3.30
dog	£1.05

Less 5-10% for bookings (not valid with some other discount schemes). **Tel:** 01557 331079. E-mail: info@seaward-park.co. uk. **Reservations:** Made with deposit of £25 per week booked, balance on arrival. **Open** 1 March - 31 October.

Directions: Follow international camping signs from Kirkcudbright on A711. Proceed with caution when turning right into site entrance as the turn is tight. O.S.GR: NX680510.

Hidden away within 1,200 exclusive acres, on a quiet, unspoilt peninsula, this spacious family park is only some 200 yards through bluebell woods from a lovely sheltered bay. It has exceptional all weather facilities, as well as golf and pony trekking. Over 90% of the 120 touring caravan pitches have electricity (16A), some with hardstanding and some with water, drainage and TV aerial. The three tenting areas are on fairly flat, undulating ground and some pitches have electricity. There are 120 self-contained holiday caravans of which about 30 are let, the rest privately owned. On site leisure facilities include a golf and leisure club with 16.5 m. pool, water features, jacuzzi, steam room, fitness room, games room (all on payment), golf driving range and clubhouse bar and bistro. The 18 hole golf course extends onto the headland with superb views over the Irish Sea to the Isle of Man and Cumbria. Plans for 2003 include a further, 9 hole family golf course. Like the park, these facilities are open all year. The BHS approved pony trekking centre (April - Oct) on the farm offers treks for complete beginners, slow hacks for the nervous or inexperienced or gallops on the beach for the more experienced. A well run park of high standards and a member of the Best of British group.

Facilities: The well maintained main toilet block is large with hot showers. It also has 10 unisex cabins with shower, basin and WC, and 12 with washbasin and WC, a launderette and covered dishwashing sinks. A second, excellent block next to the tent areas has en-suite shower rooms (one for disabled people) and bathroom, separate washing cubicles, showers, baby room, laundry sinks, and covered dishwashing sinks. One section is heated in winter. Motorcaravan service point. Mountain bike hire. Quad bikes, boating pond, 10 pin bowling, playgrounds, putting. Nature trails. Coarse fishing ponds plus sea angling and an all-tide slipway for boating enthusiasts. Licensed supermarket. Takeaway. Gas supplies. Caravan storage.

Charges 2002

Per unit incl. 2 persons	£9.80 - £13.15
extra adult	£2.05 - £2.25
child (4-15 yrs)	£1.30 - £1.55
full awning	£1.85 - £2.05
porch awning, extra car or small pup tent	£1.05
electricity	£2.30 - £2.85
fully serviced pitch	£4.05 - £4.35
trailed craft	£3.10 - £3.30
other craft	£1.55 - £1.65
dog	£1.05

Tel: 01557 870267. Fax: 01557 870319. E-mail: arogers@brighouse-bay.co.uk. **Reservations:** Advance booking is advised and made with £25 deposit. **Open** all year.

Directions: From Kirkcudbright turn south off A755 onto B727 (to Borgue); after 4 miles Brighouse Bay is signed to south. From west take B727 to Borgue and beyond, turning south as above. Or follow Brighouse Bay signs off A75 just east of Gatehouse of Fleet. O.S.GR: NX630455.

Aird Donald Caravan Park

London Road, Stranraer DG9 8RN

Aird Donald makes a good stopping off place when travelling to and from the Irish ferries, but it is also useful for seeing the sights around Stranraer. The tidy park comprises 12 acres surrounded by conifers, flowering trees and shrubs and the 300 yard drive is lit and lined with well trimmed conifers. There are grass areas for caravans or tents and hardstandings with electricity hook-up (these are very handy for hardy winter tourers). A small play area provides for young children, but the local leisure centre is only a walk away and caters for swimming, table tennis, gym, etc, and a theatre that hosts everything from country and western to opera. It also has bar facilities. The area has three world famous gardens to visit, numerous golf courses, fishing, riding and watersports.

Facilities: Two toilet blocks, the new block modern and heated. Kept very clean with excellent, tiled facilities, this one is kept locked with a key deposit of £5. There are two types of shower, an electric one which is metered (20p) and two others which are free (strange, because they are all excellent). Washbasins are in vanity units, ladies having one in a cubicle. Both sexes have hair dryers. A unit for visitors with disabilities has a washbasin and WC. The original block is being renovated but is more basic with free showers and open all the time. Dishwashing sinks and a small laundry with sinks, dryer, twin-tub washing machine, an old fashioned mangle and clothes lines. Motorcaravan service facilities. Play area. Caravan storage.

Charges 2002

Per unit incl. 2 persons	£9.00
extra adult	£1.00
extra child	£0.50
awning	£1.00
electricity	£1.60

No credit cards. **Tel:** 01776 702025. E-mail: aird@mimman.u-net.com. **Reservations:** Contact park. **Open** all year.

Directions: Enter Stranraer on A75 road. Watch for narrow site entrance on left entering town, opposite school. O.S.GR: NX075605.

Culzean Castle Camping & Caravanning Club Site

Maybole KA19 8JJ

This quiet Camping and Caravanning Club site is next door to Culzean Castle (pronounced Kullayne) with its grounds and 17 miles of footpaths and visitors are given a pass to walk in the grounds (when open) as many times as they wish. The 18th century, cliff top castle is built on the site of a former ancient castle and its armoury exhibition is superb. Besides the woodland walks, deer park and aviary, there are three miles of rocky shore, small sandy beaches and stunning views of the Firth of Clyde. A full programme of events is staged at the castle over the season, including special children's weeks, sheep-dog trials, bands, battle re-enactments, ranger walks and craft fairs. The campsite has 90 pitches, some level, others slightly sloping, and 60 have electrical hook-ups (10A). A few level pitches are suitable for motorcaravans and 20 pitches have hardstanding. American style motorhomes (less than 27 ft. only) are advised to make prior arrangements, as large pitches are limited. Should you have your fill of the castle and its grounds, Maybole with shops, etc. is only 4 miles and the area has a wealth of places to visit. Buses pass the gate.

Facilities: The toilet blocks, kept very clean, can be heated and include some washbasins in cubicles, dishwashing sinks and a well equipped laundry with clothes lines. A unit for disabled visitors has a WC, washbasin and shower - an excellent facility. A small shop with very basic provisions opens for short periods morning and evening. Adventure playground. Units over 25 ft long only accepted by prior arrangement. **Off site:** Golf or bicycle hire 4 miles, fishing 8 miles.

Charges 2002

Per adult	£3.90 - £5.50
child (6-18 yrs)	£1.70
non-member pitch fee	£4.50
electricity	£1.75 - £2.50

Tel: 01655 760627. **Reservations:** Advised for high season and made with deposit; contact site. **Open** March - October.

Directions: From Maybole follow signs for Culzean Castle and Country Park, turning in the town on B7023 which runs into the A719. Country Park entrance is clearly signed on right after 3.75 miles; entrance to caravan park is on the right in Country Park drive. O.S.GR: NS247103.

Gibson Park Caravan Club Site

703 High Street, Melrose TD6 9RY

This is an ideal transit park, being so close to the A68, but is also a perfect base for exploring this Southern Scotland area or indeed a trip to Edinburgh, as this is only 35 miles away by car or one of the regular buses which run from the park entrance. This small, three acre park has only 60 touring pitches plus, unusually, an extra 12 tent pitches (summer only) next to the adjacent rugby pitch. All touring pitches have electricity (16A) and TV connections (otherwise it is a bad signal here), 57 have hardstanding and 10 are serviced with water and drainage. A one way system on the tarmac roads is in operation. This is Sir Walter Scott country - visit Abbotsford House, his romantic mansion on the banks of the River Tweed. Melrose's Abbey ruins are believed to be the final resting place of Robert The Bruce and the starting place of St Cuthbert's Way. A new cross border 62 mile trail leads to Northumberland's Lindisfarne.

Facilities: First rate sanitary facilities are in a new building with spacious showers, washbasins in cabins, centrally heated and all fitted out with purpose made faced boarding giving a very pleasing finish. Laundry facilities. Separate room with shower and WC for disabled visitors. Motorcaravan service point. Gas is available. **Off site:** Situated on the edge of the little town of Melrose, a five minute walk, shops, pubs and restaurants are all in easy reach.

Charges 2002

Per pitch (non-members)	£6.00 - £8.00
adult	£3.50 - £4.50
child (5-16 yrs)	£1.10 - £1.20
electricity	£1.50 - £2.25

For tent pitches apply to site. **Tel:** 01896 822969. Fax: 01896 823641. **Reservations:** Made with £5 per night deposit. **Open** all year.

Directions: Turn left off A68 Jedburgh - Lauder road at roundabout about 2.5 miles past Newton St Boswell onto A6091 Galashiels road. In about 3.25 miles at roundabout turn right onto B6374 to Melrose. Site is on right at filling station opposite Melrose Rugby Club, just before entering town centre. O.S.GR: NT545340.

Crossburn Caravan Park

696 Edinburgh Road, Peebles EH45 8ED

A peaceful, friendly small park, suitable as a night stop, Crossburn is on the south side of the A703 road, half a mile north of the town centre. The entrance has a fairly steep slope down to reception and the shop, which sells basic food items (as the town is so close) and a very large selection of caravan and camping accessories. Passing the caravans for sale and the holiday homes you might think that this is not the site for you, but persevere as the touring area is very pleasant, with attractive trees and bushes. Of the 50 pitches, 46 have electricity (16A), 20 have hardstanding and 8 are fully serviced. There is also a sheltered area for tents. The field behind the resident donkey has a nine hole putting green. If you decide to stay longer, the area has many places to visit and things to do. From historic homes, abbeys, woodland walks, fishing, horse riding, golf and canoeing - it's all there. Edinburgh is only 40 minutes drive. Perhaps the night halt may turn into a longer visit.

Facilities: There are two toilet blocks, the smaller one (which can be heated) with fairly basic facilities, the other more modern with washbasins in cubicles, free hairdryers and spacious, controllable free showers. Campers' kitchen (key at reception) with free use of an electric hot plate, kettle and fridge. Shop. Adjacent is a large games room with table tennis and games machines. Good play area is on bark chippings. Mountain bike hire. Riverside dog walk.

Charges 2003

Per unit incl. 2 persons	£9.00 - £10.00
extra person (5 yrs and over)	£1.00
awning	£2.00
hiker or cyclist plus tent	£5.00
electricity	£2.50

Tel: 01721 720501. Fax: 01721 720501. E-mail: enquiries@crossburncaravans.co.uk. **Reservations:** Advised for July/Aug. and made with £14 deposit including £2 fee. **Open** Easter/1 April - end October.

Directions: Park is by the A703 road, about 0.5 miles north of Peebles. O.S.GR: NT248417.

Tantallon Caravan Park

706 Dunbar Road, North Berwick EH39 5NJ

Tantallon is a large park with views over the Firth of Forth and the Bass Rock, which is a popular venue for bird-watchers with its world famous gannet colony. Tantallon and Dirleton Castles are also nearby. Access to the beach is through the golf course and then down the road or via cliff paths. The park has 140 quite large, grass touring pitches in two lower, more sheltered areas (Law Park), with the rest having good views at the top (Bass Park). Many have some degree of slope. There are 75 electrical connections (15A) and 10 pitches also with water and waste water. Each area has its own sanitary facilities, the top block a little way from the end pitches. About 55 caravan holiday homes for sale or hire are in their own areas. This is a mature, well managed park with good facilities.

Facilities: Bass Park has 8 unisex units with shower, washbasin and toilet. The other areas have open washbasins. Two heated units for disabled visitors. Dishwashing sinks. Good launderette with spin dryer and free iron. Motorcaravan service point. Reception combines with a small shop and there is a games room here with pool table and TV. Good children's playground and better than average putting green. Dogs are accepted by prior arrangement. **Off site:** Golf next door, sea fishing, safe sandy beaches in walking distance

Charges 2003

Per unit	£8.00 - £13.00
electricity	£2.00
awning	£2.00
dog	£1.00

Tel: 01620 893348. Fax: 01620 895623. E-mail: tantallon@meadowhead.co.uk. **Reservations:** Advisable in July and August. **Open** 20 March - 31 October.

Directions: Park is beside the A198 just to the east of North Berwick, which lies between Edinburgh and Dunbar. O.S.GR: NT567850.

Mortonhall Caravan Park

699 38 Mortonhall Gate, Frogston Road East, Edinburgh EH16 6TJ

The Mortonhall park makes a good base to see the historic city of Edinburgh and buses to the City leave from the park entrance every ten minutes (parking in Edinburgh is not easy). Although only four miles from the city centre, Mortonhall is in quiet mature parkland, in the grounds of Mortonhall mansion, and easy to find with access off the ring road. There is room for 250 units mostly on numbered pitches on a slight slope with nothing to separate them, but marked by jockey wheel points. Over 170 places have electricity (10A), several with hardstanding, water and drainage as well, and there are many places for tents. The park is very popular but only part is reserved and tourists arriving early may find space. An attractive courtyard development houses a lounge bar and restaurant, open to all, with good value meals in pleasant surroundings.

Facilities: Two modern toilet blocks with outside, but covered dishwashing sinks, but the only cabins are in the third excellent facility at the top of the park, which has eight unisex units incorporating shower, washbasin and WC. The courtyard area provides further standard facilities and 'portacabin' type units are added for the high season to serve the large number of tents. Facilities for disabled visitors. Laundry room with washing machines and dryer. Bar/restaurant. Self-service shop. Games and TV rooms. Table tennis, Play area. Late arrivals area with hook-ups. Torches useful in early and late season. **Off site:** Golf courses and driving range 2 miles. Riding 2 miles. Bicycle hire 4 miles.

Charges 2002

Per unit incl. 2 persons	£9.50 - £13.90
extra person (5 yrs and over)	£1.00
serviced pitch	£4.00
electricity	£2.00
awning	£2.50 - £5.00
dog	£1.00

Tel: 0131 664 1533. Fax: 0131 664 5387. E-mail: mortonhall@meadowhead.co.uk. **Reservations:** Made with 1 night's charge plus £1.50 fee. **Open** 15 March - 7 January.

Directions: Park is well signed south of the city, 5 minutes from A720 city by-pass. Take the Mortonhall exit from the Straiton junction and follow camping signs. Entrance road is alongside the Klondyke Garden Centre. O.S.GR: NT262686.

Edinburgh

The capital, a World Heritage Centre and now the home of the Scottish Parliament, is one of the most beautiful cities in the world dominated by its castle. At the very heart is the Royal Mile where you can stroll through the centuries from Parliament Square, the magnificent 15th century St Giles' Cathedral and down to the Palace of Holyrood-house, the Queens's official Edinburgh residence. At the new Museum of Scotland you can absorb the essence of Scottish architecture and material culture from beam engines to Bonnie Prince Charlie.

Drum Mohr Caravan Park

Levenhall, Musselburgh EH21 8JS

This family owned, attractively laid out touring park is on the east side of Edinburgh. It is a secluded, well kept modern park, conveniently situated for visits to Edinburgh, the Lothian and Borders regions. It has been carefully landscaped and there are many attractive plants, flowers and hedging. There are 120 individual pitches, 40 with hardstanding, for touring units of any type, well spaced out on gently sloping grass in groups of 12 or more, marked with white posts. Most have electric hook-ups and 8 are fully serviced with water and waste water connections. Free space is left for play and recreation. Five new chalets to rent were added in 2002. Musselburgh centre is 1.5 miles, Edinburgh 7, with a frequent bus service to the latter. Managed personally by the owner, Mr Melville, this is a well run park and is a member of the Best of British group.

Facilities: The two toilet blocks are clean, attractive, of ample size and can be heated. Free hot water to washbasins (one cabin for men, two for ladies in each block) and to four external washing-up sinks, but hot water is on payment for the showers (outside the cubicle) and laundry sinks. Laundry facilities in each block. Motorcaravan service point. Well stocked, licensed shop (gas available, bread and papers to order). Children's playground on sand. **Off site:** Golf course adjacent.

Charges 2002

Per unit incl. 2 persons	£9.00 - £12.00
extra person (over 3 yrs)	£1.50 - £2.00
extra pup tent	£2.00
awning	£1.00
electricity	£2.00
service pitch incl. electricity	£6.00
dog	£0.50

Tel: 0131 665 6867. Fax: 0131 653 6859. E-mail: bookings@drummohr.org. **Reservations:** Made for any length with deposit of one night's charge plus £1 fee. **Open** 1 March - 31 October.

Directions: From Edinburgh follow A1 signs for Berwick on Tweed for 6-7 miles. Turn off for Wallyford and follow camp and Mining Museum signs. From south follow A1 taking junction after Tranent village (A199 Musselburgh) and follow signs. O.S.GR: NT371732.

Edinburgh Caravan Club Site

Marine Drive, Edinburgh EH4 5EN

Situated as it is on the northern outskirts and within easy reach of the city of Edinburgh, this large Caravan Club site (open to non-members) provides an ideal base for touring. A bus (numbers 8A and 28A stop just outside the gates) takes you right into the centre of the city and within walking distance of many of its attractions. Enter the site through rather grand gates to find the visitors' car park and reception to the left. There are 150 large flat pitches (103 hardstandings, 12 with water tap and waste water disposal) with electric hook-ups (16A) and TV aerial, and provision for 50 tents in a separate field (hook-ups available) with a covered cooking shelter, and bicycle stands close by. As the bushes planted around the site mature, there will be shade. The nearest hotel/restaurant is about half a mile, Royal Yacht Britannia and many other attractions in the city, Firth of Forth bridge about 2 miles.

Facilities: Two heated, well kept toilet blocks provide washbasins in cubicles, hair and hand dryers, an en-suite room for campers with disabilities, plus a baby and toddler room with child-size facilities. Each block houses a dishwashing/vegetable preparation area, and a laundry. Drying room. There is no shop, but milk, bread, and newspapers can be ordered, or purchase ice cream and exchange gas cylinders at reception. Fenced play area for youngsters, and a dog walk in the only natural wood in Edinburgh (part of the site).

Charges 2002

Per pitch (non-member)	£7.00 - £8.00
adult	£3.75 - £4.75
child (5-16 yrs)	£1.20
electricity	£1.50 - £2.25

Tent campers apply to site. **Tel:** 0131 312 6874. **Reservations:** Made with £5 deposit, balance on arrival. **Open** all year.

Directions: From A720 (signed City Bypass North), turn right at Gogar roundabout onto A8 and follow international camping signs. O.S.GR: NT212768.

Slatebarns Caravan Park

Slatebarns, Roslin EH25 9PU

Slatebarns is a recently developed, well groomed park, perfectly located for that trip to Edinburgh, a nightstop on the way north or for local walks, including the nearby Pentland Hills. It has only 30 pitches, all with electricity hook-ups (10A), some with hardstanding (with grass for awnings) and some on grass (steel awning pegs useful). Buses run from the village (five minutes' walk) regularly into Edinburgh (30 minute journey, 6 miles), although they are less frequent in the evening. Slatebarns is a small park with little on site for children or teenagers. Managed under contract for the Caravan Club, non-members are also very welcome. An ideal base to get away from the bustle after a full day in Edinburgh, or equally attractive as a touring base or country hideaway.

Facilities: Small purpose built toilet block with washbasins in cubicles for ladies and excellent separate provision for those with disabilities. Good launderette. Very practical motorcaravan service point. Gas supplies. **Off site:** Village shops, pubs and hotels.

Charges 2002

Per unit incl. 2 persons from	£12.50
extra adult	£3.50 - £4.00
child	£12.00
electricity	£1.50 - £2.00

No credit cards. **Tel:** 0131 440 2192. **Reservations:** Contact park for details. **Open** Easter - 31 October.

Directions: From Straiton junction on A720 (Edinburgh bypass) go south on A701 signed Bilston, Penicuik. At roundabout in Bilston turn left on B7006 signed Roslin. After 1 mile, in Roslin continue over crossroads signed Rosslyn Chapel. Site entrance is immediately past Chapel. O.S.GR: NT275632.

Lowlands
Strathclyde Country Park Caravan Site
Strathclyde Country Park, 366 Hamilton Road, Motherwell ML1 3ED

The 1,200 acre Country Park is a large green area less than 15 miles from the centre of Glasgow. Well kept and open to all, it provides nature trails, children's adventure play area, sandy beaches and coarse fishing, with an 18 hole golf course 2 miles away. In addition there is a large water sports centre offering sailing, water skiing, windsurfing, canoeing, rowing (all with craft for hire), a water bus, a selection of family 'fun boats' and bicycle hire, plus Scotland's own theme park nearby. The touring site, part of the park, is suitable for both overnight or period stays (max. 14 days) and has 100 numbered pitches for caravans, all with electrical connections (10A). Arranged in semicircular groups on flat grass they are served by made-up access roads and the site is well lit. There is also a camping field which holds 150 units or more for special events. It is close to the motorway so there may be some traffic noise.

Facilities: Four solidly built toilet blocks make a good provision. Enclosed sinks for dishwashing or food preparation, Launderette (irons from reception). Block 4 has facilities for visitors with disabilities. Motorcaravan services. Shop with gas available. Bar and restaurant facilities (100 yds) in the Country Park. Children's play equipment. American motorhomes accepted up to 22 ft. 24 hour security.

Charges 2002

Per caravan pitch incl. 2 persons	£8.50
awning	£2.10
tent pitch (3 or 4 persons)	£7.30
small ridge tent	£3.80
extra adult	£1.10
child	£0.90
electricity	£2.40

No credit cards. **Tel:** 01698 266155. Fax: 01698 252925. E-mail: strathclydepark@northlan.gov.uk. **Reservations:** Made for any period with deposit of one night's fee. **Open** Easter - 18 October.

Directions: Take exit 5 from M74 and follow sign for Strathclyde Country Park. Turn first left for site. O.S.GR: NS720584.

Glasgow

One of the most magnificent 19th century cities in Europe and now known as Scotland's style capital with its art deco brasseries, stylish shops and cultural centres boasting more than 30 art galleries and museums. Worth visiting is the new elegant Gallery of Modern Art in Queen Street and Charles Rennie Mackintosh's finest building - The Glasgow School of Art. Also interesting along the banks of the River Clyde is the restored Carlton Terrace and Glasgow's newest landmark, the Clyde Auditorium, popularly known The 'Armadillo', due to its distinctive shape.

Heart of Scotland
Trossachs Holiday Park
Aberfoyle FK8 3SA

Nestling on the side of a hill, three miles south of Aberfoyle, this is an excellent base for touring this famously beautiful area. Lochs Lomond, Ard, Venachar and others are within easy reach, as are the Queen Elizabeth Forest Park and, of course, the Trossachs. This park specialises in the sale and hire of top class mountain bikes. Very neat and tidy, there are 45 well laid out and marked pitches arranged on terraces with hardstanding. All have electricity and TV connections and most also have water and drainage. There is also a large area for tents. There are trees between the terraces and lovely views across the valley. The adjoining oak and bluebell woods are a haven for wildlife, with wonderful walks. You will receive a warm welcome from Joe and Hazel Norman at this well run, family park. A member of the Best of British group.

Facilities: A modern wooden building houses sanitary facilities providing a satisfactory supply of toilets, showers and washbasins, the ladies' area being rather larger, with two private cabins. Laundry room. Well stocked shop (all season) and bike shop. Games room with TV. Play equipment (on gravel). **Off site:** Nearby are opportunities for golf, boat launching and fishing (3 miles). A passport scheme arranged with a local leisure centre (10 miles, 8 passes) provides facilities for swimming, sauna, solarium, badminton, tennis, windsurfing, etc.

Charges 2002

Per unit incl. 2 persons	£9.00 - £12.00
extra adult	£2.00
child (2-14 yrs)	£1.25
porch awning	£1.50
full awning	£2.00
small pup tent	£3.00
extra car	£1.00
electricity and TV connection, hardstanding	£2.00
all services	£3.00

Tel: 01877 382614. Fax: 01877 382732. E-mail: info@trossachsholidays.co.uk. **Reservations:** Advisable and made for min. 3 days with £15 deposit. **Open** 1 March - 31 October.

Directions: Park is 3 miles south of Aberfoyle on the A81 road, well signed. O.S.GR: NS544976.

Heart of Scotland
Ardgartan Forestry Commission Campsite
Ardgartan, Arrochar G83 7AR

Ardgartan is a rugged Forestry Commission site in the Argyll Forest Park. Splendidly situated with mountains all around and lovely views of Loch Long, there are lots of sightseeing and activity opportunities. At the northern end of the Cowal Peninsula, the site is on a promontory on the shores of Loch Long, with good sea fishing and facilities for launching small boats. The 160 touring pitches are in sections which are well divided by grass giving an uncrowded air. Most with hardstanding and marked by numbered posts, they are accessed from hard surfaced roads and 46 have electrical hook-ups. There are additional grass areas for tents. Walking and climbing, as well as sea and river fishing (permits obtainable locally), are all possible nearby. The site gate is locked 10.30 pm. - 7.30 am.

Facilities: The main toilet block is opposite the reception and shop with two small others (one for each sex) close by for the busiest periods. It is a basic, but clean provision with facilities for disabled visitors and a launderette. These facilities may be quite stretched when the park is busy. Play equipment is provided (bark surfaces). Raised barbecues are allowed. **Off site:** Arrochar village (2 miles) has fuel, general stores and a restaurant.

Charges 2002

Per adult	£3.00 - £4.50
child (5-14 yrs)	£1.20 -£1.90
electricity	£2.20
'select' pitch incl. electricity	£3.40
boat, extra car, trailer or pup tent	£3.00

Less 20% all year for disabled guests and outside 7/7-28/8 for senior citizens. **Tel:** 01301 702293. E-mail: fe.holidays@forestry.gsi. gov.uk. **Reservations:** Necessary for B.Hs and peak times (min. 3 nights with £30 deposit); contact site. Brochure requests: Forest Holidays, Forestry Commission, 231 Corstorphine Road, Edinburgh EH12 7AT. Tel: (0131) 314 6505. **Open** 21 March - 24 October.

Directions: From A82 Glasgow - Crianlarich road take A83 at Tarbet signed Arrochar and Cambletown. Site is 2 miles past Arrochar, the entrance on a bend. O.S.GR: NN275030.

Heart of Scotland
Lomond Woods Holiday Park
Tullichewan, Old Luss Road, Balloch G83 8QP

A series of improvements over the last few years has made this one of the top parks in Scotland. Almost, but not quite, on the banks of Loch Lomond, this landscaped, well planned park is suitable for both transit or longer stays. Formerly known as Tullichewan Holiday Park, it takes 120 touring units, including 30 tents, on well spaced, numbered pitches on flat or gently sloping grass. Most have hardstanding, 106 have electrical connections (10A) and 8 have water and waste water too. Watersport activities and boat trips are possible on Loch Lomond, with a new visitor attraction, 'Lomond Shores' opened nearby. This is a well run park, open all year, with very helpful wardens and reception staff. A member of the Best of British group.

Facilities: The single large heated, well kept toilet block has been totally refitted over the past two winters. It includes some showers with WCs, new baths for ladies, a shower room for disabled visitors and two baby baths. Covered dishwashing sinks. Launderette. Motorcaravan service points. Well stocked shop at reception. Games room with TV, table tennis and pool table. Children's playground. Leisure suite providing a sauna, sun-bed and spa-bath (on payment). Bicycle hire. Caravan storage. American motorhomes accepted with prior notice. **Off site:** Fishing and boat launching 400 yards, riding 4 miles, golf 5 miles. Rail and road connections to Glasgow. Restaurants and bar meals in Balloch (5 mins).

Charges 2002

Per unit incl. 2 persons, electricity	£11.00 - £15.00
incl. mains services and awning	£16.00 - £19.00
extra adult	£2.00
child (3-12 yrs)	£1.00
dog	£0.50
hikers (2 persons, no car)	£6.50 - £9.00

Tel: 01389 755000. Fax: 01389 755563. E-mail: lomondwoods@holiday-parks.co.uk. **Reservations:** Made for any length with deposit of first night's charge and £2 fee. **Open** all year except November.

Directions: Turn off A82 road 17 miles northwest of Glasgow on A811 Stirling road. Site is in Balloch at southern end of Loch Lomond and is well signed. O.S.GR: NS389816.

Blair Castle Caravan Park

Blair Atholl, Pitlochry PH18 5SR

This attractive, well kept park is set in the grounds of Blair Castle, the traditional home of the Dukes of Atholl. The castle is open to the public, its 32 fully furnished rooms showing a picture of Scottish life from the 16th century to the present day, while the beautiful grounds and gardens are free to those staying on site. The caravan park has a wonderful feeling of spaciousness with a large central area left free for children's play or for general use. There is space for 283 touring units with 196 electricity connections (10/16A), 144 hardstandings and 42 fully serviced pitches with water and waste water facilities also. Caravan holiday homes, 85 privately owned and 28 for hire, are in separate areas. The castle grounds provide many walking trails and the village is within walking distance with hotels, shops, a water mill craft centre and folk museum. A quality park, quiet at night and well managed. A member of the Best of British group.

Facilities: The four toilet blocks can be heated and are of excellent quality with very high standards of cleanliness. Large hot showers are free, some also incorporating WC and washbasin, and further cubicles with WC and washbasin. Three blocks have facilities for disabled visitors, one with WC and washbasin, the others with a bath also. Baby changing mats. Dishwashing. Motorcaravan service point. A new central development incorporates reception, a shop, games room, laundry and internet gallery. Gas supplies. American motorhomes are accepted (max. 30 ft or 5 tons). **Off site:** Mountain bike hire, riding, golf and fishing within 1 mile.

Charges 2002

Per unit incl. 2 persons	£8.50 - £11.50
tent (no car)	£6.00 - £9.50
child (5-12 yrs)	£0.50
dog (max 2)	£0.50
electricity	£1.50 - £2.00

Tel: 01796 481263. Fax: 01796 481587. E-mail: mail@blaircastlecaravanpark.co.uk. **Reservations:** Made for any length with deposit of 1 night's charge + £2 booking fee except 15/7-15/8 when min. 3 nights and payment in full. **Open** 1 March - 30 November.

Directions: From A9 just north of Pitlochry take B8079 into Blair Atholl. Park is in grounds of Blair Castle, well signed. O.S.GR: NN868659.

Nether Craig Caravan Park

By Alyth, Blairgowrie PH11 8HN

728

Nether Craig is a family run touring park, attractively designed and beautifully landscaped, with views across the Strathmore valley to the long range of the Sidlaw hills. The 40 large pitches are accessed from a circular, gravel road; 26 have hardstanding (for awnings too) and 10A electrical connections. The majority are level and there are 9 large tent pitches on flat grass. There is a personal welcome for all visitors at the attractive wooden chalet beside the entrance (with a slope for wheelchairs) which doubles as reception and shop providing the necessary essentials, gas and tourist information. A one mile circular woodland walk from the park has picnic benches and a leaflet guide is provided. Otherwise you can just enjoy the peace of the Angus Glens by hill walking, birdwatching, fishing or pony trekking. Alyth with its Arthurian connections is only 4 miles away and Glamis Castle, the childhood home of the Queen Mother, is nearby, as is the beautiful Glenshee and Braemar with its castle.

Facilities: The central, purpose built toilet block is modern, well equipped and maintained, and can be heated. Unit for disabled visitors (entry by key). Separate sinks for dishwashing and clothes are in the laundry room (metered hot water), plus a washing machine, dryer and iron, and a rotary clothes line outside. Shop. Children's play area. Small football field. Caravan storage. **Off site:** Three golf courses are within 4 miles.

Charges 2002

Per unit incl. 2 persons	£10.00 - £11.00
tent incl. 2 persons	£8.00
extra person	£1.00
electricity	£2.00

Tel: 01575 560204. Fax: 01575 560315. E-mail: nethercraig@lineone.net. **Reservations:** Advisable for main season - contact park. **Open** 15 March - 15 December.

Directions: From A926 Blairgowrie - Kirriemuir road, at roundabout south of Alyth join B954 signed Glenisla. Follow caravan signs for 4 miles and turn right onto unclassified road signed Nether Craig. Park is on left after 0.5 miles. O.S.GR: NO265528.

Auchterarder Caravan Park

Nether Coul, Auchterarder PH3 1ET

727

This is a charming small park, purpose designed and landscaped by the owners Stuart and Susie Robertson. In a sheltered position, it is conveniently situated for exploring central Scotland and the Highlands with many leisure activities close at hand (particularly golf) and within walking distance of the village (1 mile). The 21 original pitches, all with electricity (6A) and hardstanding, 12 with drainage, are well spaced around the edge of the elongated, level grass park. Marked pitches with grass frontage back on to raised banks which are planted with trees. Further pitches have been developed to one side of the site, along with a trout fishing pond (exclusively for campers) and a woodland walk. A tarmac area at the entrance for late arrivals (with electricity) ensures that no one is disturbed. Also at the entrance, a modern pine chalet blending with the environment houses reception and a small library. There is easy access from the nearby A9 road which does create some background road noise, although it is peaceful at night.

Facilities: Excellent toilet facilities with key system and piped music include controllable, well equipped hot showers. A toilet for disabled people is provided in both the male and female units. Laundry room with sink and washing machine; an iron can be provided. Dishwashing is under cover. Caravan storage. **Off site:** Golf 1 mile, bicycle hire or riding 6 miles. The historic cities of Perth and Stirling are less than half an hour's drive away.

Charges 2002

Per unit incl. up to 4 adults	£8.00 - £10.00
extra person (over 5 yrs)	£1.00
awning	£1.00
electricity and drainage	£1.50 - £2.50

No credit cards. **Tel:** 01764 663119. Fax: 01764 663119. E-mail: nethercoul@talk21.com. **Reservations:** Advisable July/Aug. and made with deposit of one night's charge and booking fee (£1). Bookings held until 5 pm. on day reserved. **Open** all year.

Directions: Park is between the A9 and A824 roads east of Auchterarder village, only 0.5 miles from the main road. It is reached by turning on to the B8062 (Dunning) road from the A824. O.S.GR: NN964138.

Craigtoun Meadows Holiday Park

Mount Melville, St Andrews KY16 8PQ

729

This attractively laid out, quality park has individual pitches and good facilities, and although outnumbered by caravan holiday homes, the touring section is an important subsidiary. Its facilities are both well designed and comprehensive. With 70 units taken on gently sloping land, caravans go on individual hardstandings with grass alongside for awnings on most pitches. All caravan pitches are large (130 sq.m) and are equipped with electricity (16A), water and drainage. There are 24 larger 'patio pitches' with summer house, barbecue patio, picnic table and chairs, partially screened. Tents are taken on a grassy meadow at one end, also with electricity available. The 157 caravan holiday homes stand round the outer parts of the site; 27 are owned and let by the park. Buses pass the entrance and Craigtoun park with boating pond and miniature railway, etc. is within walking distance. This is a well run park, 2 miles from St Andrews with its golf courses and long, sandy beaches, from where there is a picturesque view of St Andrews and its ruined Abbey and Castle.

Facilities: An excellent, de-luxe, centrally heated sanitary building serves the touring area. All washbasins are in cabins and each toilet has its own basin. Showers are unisex, as are two bathrooms, with hand and hair dryers, facilities for disabled people and babies. Dishwashing room. Launderette. Shop and attractive licensed restaurant (both restricted hours in low seasons), also providing takeaway. Games room. Well equipped playground, play field and 8 acres of woodland. Barbecue area. All weather tennis court. Small information room. Dogs and other pets will not be accepted in 2003. **Off site:** Fishing 5 miles. Golf or bicycle hire 1.5 miles. Riding 6 miles.

Charges 2002

Per unit incl. 3-6 persons, electricity	£15.00 - £21.50
tent incl. 2 persons and electricity	£14.00 - £20.50
backpackers tent (1 person)	£12.00

Tel: 01334 475959. Fax: 01334 476424. E-mail: craigtoun@aol.com. **Reservations:** Advised for main season; any length with full payment at time of booking. **Open** 1 March - 31 October.

Directions: From M90 junction 8 take A91 to St Andrews. Just after sign for Guardbridge (to left, A919), turn right at site sign and sign for Strathkinness. Go through village, over crossroads at end of village, left at next crossroads, then 0.75 miles to park. O.S.GR: NO482151.

Twenty Shilling Wood Caravan Park

Comrie PH6 2JY

731

Everyone gets a warm welcome from the Lowe family when they arrive at Twenty Shilling Wood. Set amongst 10.5 acres of wooded hillside, this unusual park has a few touring pitches for caravans and motorcaravans (no tents), plus a number of owner occupied caravan holiday homes. However, with terracing and landscaping not many of these are visible and flowering trees and shrubs help to hide them. The lowest level is the entrance where there is a late arrivals area and visitor car park. The just 16 level touring pitches are on gravel with grass bays between them. All have electricity hook-ups (10A) and, because of poor TV reception, a free TV aerial hook up with lead provided. You will be escorted to your pitch. There are many walks in the area from strenuous Munros to a gentle stroll to the Devil's Cauldron waterfall.

Facilities: The toilet blocks are of an older design but well kept, and have been refurbished to give some washbasins in cubicles for ladies. Dishwashing area and laundry. No shop but rolls, milk and papers can be ordered at reception. Games room with pool table, table tennis (both free) and lounge area with comfortable seating and well stocked library. Fenced adventure playground for all ages. Automatic entrance barrier; £10 deposit for card. Only two dogs per pitch are accepted. **Off site:** Buses pass the gate. Comrie is 1 mile where most things can be purchased. Golf or fishing within 1 mile, riding or bicycle hire 6 miles. Glen Turret, Scotland's oldest distillery is at Crieff, 7 miles away, Auchingarrich Wildlife centre is 2.5 miles, there are watersports at Loch Earn, 11 miles.

Charges 2002

Per unit incl. 2 adults, electricity and TV hook-up	£13.50 - £14.50
extra person (over 5 yrs)	£1.50
awning (rock pegs required)	£1.00

Tel: 01764 670411. Fax: 01764 670411. E-mail: alowe20@aol.com. **Reservations:** Advised for B.Hs and July/Aug; made with £10 deposit. **Open** 23 March - 23 October.

Directions: Park is on north side of A85 Crieff - Lochearmead road, about 0.75 miles west of B827 junction, 0.5 miles west of Comrie. O.S.GR: NN762222.

Heart of Scotland
Witches Craig Caravan Park
Blairlogie, Stirling FK9 5PX

732

Witches Craig is a neat and tidy park, nestling under the Ochil Hills and the friendly Stephen family take each visitor to their pitch to make sure that they are happy. All 60 pitches have electrical hook-ups (10A) and 14 have hardstanding, 7 of these being large (taking American style motorhomes easily). Reasonably level, the park covers five well maintained acres with the grass beautifully manicured. Seven residential park homes are well kept and surrounded by flowering shrubs. The area has a wealth of historic attractions, starting with the Wallace Monument which practically overlooks the park. Its 220 ft. tower dominates the surrounding area and the climb up its 246 steps gives spectacular views. Stirling is known as the 'Gateway to the Highlands' and its magnificent castle is world renowned. Being by the A91, there is some day-time road noise. Trees have been planted to try to minimise this but the further back onto the park you go, the less the traffic is heard, although the main touring section with the sanitary facilities is at the front.

Facilities: The modern, heated toilet block is well maintained, and includes one cubicle with washbasin and WC each for ladies and men. Showers are on payment. Baby bath and mat. Good unit for disabled campers. Dishwashing sinks. Laundry. Bread, milk, drinks and papers are available daily (supermarket 2.5 miles). Large fenced play area. Field for team games. **Off site:** Riding or bicycle hire 2 miles, fishing 3 miles, golf 1 mile. Buses stop at the park entrance. Within 10 miles there are castles, museums, cathedrals and parks. There are many walks from the site into the Ochil Hills.

Charges 2002

Per unit incl. 2 adults	£10.00 - £11.00
extra adult	£2.00
child (2-13 yrs)	£1.00
extra car	£1.50
awning (no groundsheet) or extra small tent	£2.00
electricity	£2.00
walker with tent (per person)	£4.25 - £5.25

No credit cards. **Tel:** 01786 474947. Fax: 01786 447286. E-mail: witchescraig7545@aol.com. **Reservations:** Made without deposit. **Open** 1 April - 31 October.

Directions: Park is on the A91, 2 miles northeast of Stirling. O.S.GR: NS822968.

Grampian
Huntly Castle Caravan Park
The Meadow, Huntly AB54 4UJ

755

Huntly Caravan Park was opened in '95 and its hard-working owners, Hugh and Debbie Ballantyne, are justly proud of their neat, well landscaped 15 acre site that is managed under contract for the Caravan Club (non-members welcome). The 76 level grass and 41 hardstanding touring pitches are separated and numbered, with everyone shown to their pitch. Arranged in three bays with banks of heathers and flowering shrubs separating them, 66 of the pitches have electric hook-ups (16A) and 15 are fully serviced with water and waste water also. Two bays have central play areas and all three have easy access to a toilet block, as has the camping area. Campers are provided with a covered cooking shelter (with work tops) should the weather turn inclement. The park also has 33 privately owned caravan holiday homes (3 to hire). An Activity Centre near the entrance contains two indoor safe play areas (one for up to 2 yrs old, the other up to 9 yrs). In addition there are snooker and pool tables, table tennis, badminton and short tennis. There is a charge for these facilities which are also open to the public. The area abounds with things to do, from forest trails to walk or cycle, a falconry centre, malt whisky distilleries and an all year Nordic ski track. A member of the Best of British group.

Facilities: The three heated toilet blocks are well designed and maintained, with washbasins (in cubicles for ladies) and large, free showers with lots of changing space. Each block also has a family shower room (even larger), dishwashing sinks with free hot water and a good room for disabled visitors. Well equipped laundry room. No shop on site but milk and papers may be ordered at reception. Activity centre (open weekends and all local school holidays). **Off site:** The town of Huntly is only 10 minutes walk with shops and pubs and castle. Fishing, golf or bicycle hire within 1 mile, riding 5 miles.

Charges 2002

Per unit incl. 2 persons, electricity	£11.30 - £13.50
incl. mains services and awning	£14.55 - £16.75
pup tent	£2.00
extra adult	£2.25
child (5-16 yrs)	£1.10

Tel: 01466 794999. E-mail: enquiries@huntlycastle. co.uk. **Reservations:** Contact park. **Open** 24 March - 29 October.

Directions: Site is well signed from A96 Keith - Aberdeen road. O.S.GR: NJ526402.

Grampian
Aden Country Park Caravan Park
753 Old Deer, Mintlaw AB42 8FQ

Aden Country Park is owned by the local authority and is open to the public offering several attractions for visitors, including an Agricultural Heritage Centre, Wildlife Centre, Nature Trail and restaurant, as well as open and woodland areas with a lake, for walking and recreation. The caravan and camping site is on one side of the park. Beautifully landscaped and well laid out with trees, bushes and hedges, it is kept very neat and tidy. It provides 48 numbered pitches for touring units, with varying degrees of slope (some level) and all with electrical hook-ups (16A), plus an area for tents. There are also 12 caravan holiday homes in a row on the left as you enter. Large dog exercise area. The park is in a most attractive area and one could spend plenty of time enjoying all it has to offer.

Facilities: The modern, fully tiled sanitary toilet block, with good facilities for disabled visitors, was very clean when we visited. It can be heated and provides free, pre-set hot showers, with dressing area, hairdryer for ladies, and a baby bath, but no private cabins. Dishwashing and laundry facilities are together, with washing machines, tumble and spin dryers and an iron - all metered. Small shop (sweets and ice-creams) in the reception area. Restaurant in the Heritage Centre for meals. For children, two games areas and various items of play equipment (with safety surfaces). **Off site:** Mintlaw half a mile for shopping. Fishing 1 mile, riding 2 miles.

Charges 2002

Per unit	£9.50 - £11.00
small tent per person	£3.50 - £4.50
awning	£1.00
electricity	£2.00
OAPs (out of season, per unit)	£5.00

Tel: 01771 623460. **Reservations:** Advisable for weekends; write for details. **Open** Easter - 25 October.

Directions: Approaching Mintlaw from the west on A950 road, park is shortly after sign for Mintlaw station. From the east, go to the western outskirts of the village and entrance is on left - 'Aden Country Park and Farm Heritage Centre'. O.S.GR: NJ985484.

Grampian
Aberlour Gardens Caravan & Camping Park
754 Aberlour-on-Spey AB38 9LD

This pleasant park is within the large walled garden of the Aberlour Estate on Speyside. Mr and Mrs Moss, the owners, have made many improvements to the sheltered, five acre, family run park which provides a very natural setting amidst spruce and Scots pine. Of the 64 level pitches, 35 are for touring units leaving the remainder for holiday homes (1 for rent) and seasonal units. All pitches have electrical connections (10A) and 9 are 'all-weather' pitches. This is an ideal area for walking, birdwatching, salmon fishing and pony trekking or for following the only 'Malt Whisky Trail' in the world, while Aberlour has a fascinating old village shop - a 'time capsule'.

Facilities: The toilet block can be heated and has four large unisex showers on payment and facilities for visitors with disabilities (can be used as family or baby changing room). Laundry facilities. Motorcaravan service point. Small licensed shop stocking basics and with an information area. Children's play area. Caravan storage. **Off site:** Fishing 1 or 5 miles, golf 4 miles, riding 0.5 miles, swimming or bicycle hire 1 mile, bowls 2 miles.

Charges 2002

Per caravan, motorcaravan, trailer tent incl. 2 persons	£7.00 - £10.00
tent	£6.75 - £8.50
backpacker and tent (per person)	£3.50 - £4.50
extra person	£2.00
child (5-16 yrs)	£1.00
electricity	£1.60 - £1.80

Tel: 01340 871586. Fax: 01340 871586. E-mail: abergard@compuserve.com. **Reservations:** Advised for July/Aug; made with deposit (1 nights fee). **Open** 1 April - 31 October.

Directions: Turn off A95 midway between Aberlour and Craigellachie onto unclassified road and site is signed in 500 yds. Vehicles over 10' 6" high should use A941 Dufftown Road (site is signed). O.S.GR: NJ282432.

Spindrift Caravan & Camping Park

Little Kildrummie, Nairn IV12 5QU

766

Mr and Mrs Guillot have put a lot of thought into the landscaping of their park, making it into an absolute gem. It is situated in an elevated position overlooking the distant Monadlaith mountains and a short walk from the River Nairn. The popular seaside resort of Nairn with its shops, restaurants, beach and harbour is some 2 miles away and it is said to take 30 minutes to walk via the riverside path. The park is surrounded by trees and is arranged on three terraces (roads down to the lower pitches have been re-laid and give easy access). The lowest level is used primarily for tents. With 40 pitches altogether, there are 28 electrical connections (16A), all on the highest terrace, although if you have a long cable, reached from the second level too. A part of the top level is set aside for motorcaravans, however there is no dedicated service point. The front porch of the owners house is used as reception and also provides tourist information. It is left open at all times. The river footpath is easily accessible.

Facilities: Two modern well equipped sanitary blocks. Large laundry room with separate dishwashing and laundry sinks. Large table and chairs for campers use in inclement weather. Salmon fishing permits available. **Off site:** Bicycle hire, riding, golf and boat launching within 2 miles. Bus passes the lane end (400 yds). Shops at Nairn.

Charges 2002

Per unit incl. 2 adults and 2 children	£7.50 - £9.50
small tent (2 adults)	£6.50 - £9.00
extra adult	£1.00
child	free - £0.50
awning	free - £1.00
electricity	£2.00

No credit cards. **Tel:** 01667 453992. E-mail: camping@spindriftcaravanpark.freeserve.co.uk. **Reservations:** Advised for July/Aug. with £5 deposit. **Open** 1 April - 31 October.

Directions: From Nairn take B9090 south for 1.5 miles following signs for Spindrift. O.S.GR: NH863537.

Torvean Caravan Park

Glenurquhart Road, Inverness IV3 6JL

769

Torvean is a small and neat, select touring park for caravans and motorhomes only. It is situated on the outskirts of Inverness beside the Caledonian Canal and is within easy reach of the town's amenities which include an ice rink, theatre and leisure sports centre. Excursions to the coast and Highlands, including Loch Ness, are possible in several directions. The pitches on level grass are well spaced and clearly marked with a tarmac access road and street lighting giving a very neat appearance. There are 47 touring pitches (27 with 10A electricity connections, 18 fully serviced with fresh water tap, waste water disposal and electricity).

Facilities: Two toilet blocks are of good quality - ladies have two cubicles with washbasin and toilet and a hair washing cubicle. Controllable hot showers on payment. Suite for disabled people with toilet and shower. Launderette. Motorcaravan service point. Children's play area. Only one dog per unit is accepted. **Off site:** Golf adjacent, bicycle hire or fishing 3 miles.

Charges guide

Per unit incl. 2 adults	£9.00 - £9.50
electricity	£2.00
de-luxe pitch incl. electricity	£11.50 - £12.00
extra adult	£1.50
child (under 16 yrs)	£0.75
awning	£2.00 - £3.00
small dog (1 only)	£1.00

No credit cards. **Tel:** 01463 220582. Fax: 01463 233051. **Reservations:** Necessary for July/Aug. and made with first night's charge and £1 fee. **Open** Easter - end October.

Directions: Park is off the main A82 road on the southwest outskirts of the town by the Tomnahurich Canal Bridge. O.S.GR: NH638438.

Grantown-on-Spey Caravan Park

767 Seafield Avenue, Grantown-on-Spey PH26 3JQ

Gerald and Brenda Naylor take care of this excellent park which is owned by Sandra McKelvie and her son John Fleming, and managed under contract for the Caravan Club (non-members are welcome). Peacefully situated on the outskirts of the town, with views of the mountains in the distance, the park consists of well-tended gravel (raked so that it is perfect for each occupant) and grass pitches. Trees and flowers are a feature of this landscaped location. There are 100 pitches for caravans or motorcaravans, of which 5 offer fresh and waste water facilities and 16 have individual fresh water taps. A further 20 pitches are used for seasonal occupation, and there is space for 50 or more tents. More than 80 pitches have 10A electrical hook-ups. Gerald Naylor escorts visitors to their pitch and will help to site caravans if necessary. Caravan holiday homes are located in a separate area of the park. Grantown is a pleasant touring base for the Cairngorms and for the Malt Whisky Trail. A peaceful park with a warden on site at all times.

Facilities: Two modern blocks provide good, clean toilet facilities, with new private wash-cabins for ladies. Dishwashing sinks are covered behind each block. Laundry room with washing machines, and spin dryers and irons. Motorcaravan service point with drive-over emptying facility and a fresh water tap. No on-site shop because the town is just a short distance, however gas cylinders, ice creams, cold drinks and various camping accessories can be purchased at reception. Games room with table tennis and pool table. Winter caravan storage. **Off site:** Fishing, golf and mountain bike hire within 1 mile, riding 3 miles.

Charges 2002

Per pitch incl. 2 persons, electricity	£11.00 - £13.00
small 2-man tent	£6.00 - £8.00
extra person	£1.00 - £2.00

Tel: 01479 872474. Fax: 01479 873696. E-mail: team@caravanscotland.com. **Reservations:** Advised for peak periods and made with £10 deposit. **Open** 28 March - 31 October.

Directions: Park is signed from the town centre. O.S.GR: NJ028283.

Forestry Commission - Glenmore Caravan and Camp Site

768 Aviemore PH22 1QU

Since July 2000 there have been site managers here who have made tremendous improvements to this park, which had been neglected for a while. The Glenmore Forest site lies close to the sandy shore of Loch Morlich amidst conifer woods and surrounded on three sides by the impressive Cairngorm mountains. It is conveniently situated for a range of activities, including skiing (extensive lift system), orienteering, hill and mountain walking (way-marked walks), fishing (trout and pike) and non-motorized watersports on the Loch. The campsite itself is attractively laid out in a fairly informal style in several adjoining areas connected by narrow part gravel, part tarmac roads, with access to the lochside. One of these areas, the Pinewood Area, is very popular and has 32 hardstandings (some distance from the toilet block). Of the 220 marked pitches on fairly level, firm grass, 137 have electricity (10A).

Facilities: There are two very basic toilet blocks with heating, but only one shower/laundry block some distance from the majority of the pitches and reached by an underpass. Opened by key pad (you are given a number), the heated block has small, basic, free hot showers. Separate unit for visitors with disabilities. Next to the site is a range of amenities including a well stocked shop, a café serving a variety of meals and snacks, and a Forestry Commission visitor centre and souvenir shop. Barbecues are not permitted in dry weather. **Off site:** The Aviemore centre providing a wide range of indoor and outdoor recreations is only 7 miles and there are several golf courses within a range of 15 miles, as well as fishing and boat trips.

Charges 2002

Per unit incl. up to 4 persons	£7.70 - £10.30
extra person (over 5 yrs)	£1.00
'select' pitch	£3.30
electricity	£2.20
extra car, trailer or child's tent	£2.60

Less 20% all year for disabled guests and outside 7/7-28/8 for senior citizens. **Tel:** 01479 861271. E-mail: fe.holidays@forestry-gsi.gov.uk. **Reservations:** Made with £30 deposit (min. 2 days or 3 at B.Hs). Contact site when open, otherwise Forest Holidays, Forestry Commission, 231 Corstorphine Road, Edinburgh EH12 7AT. **Open** all year except 1 Nov - 15 Dec.

Directions: Immediately south of Aviemore on B9152 (not A9 bypass) take B970 then follow sign for Cairngorm and Loch Morlich. Site entrance is on right past the loch. O.S.GR: NH976097.

Pitgrudy Caravan Park

Poles Road, Dornoch IV25 3HY

In a rural situation, Pitgrudy has superb views over the Dornoch Firth and the surrounding Ross-shire hills. There are 40 touring pitches for caravans, motorcaravans or tents, mostly on slightly sloping grass and with electrical connections (10A). A few have hardstanding (unfortunately still on a slope) and six are fully serviced (drinking water, waste water disposal point and electricity). Located at the top of the park are 35 caravan holiday homes, of which 25 are privately owned. The whole park is on immaculately tended grass with tarmac roads. The pleasant little town of Dornoch is less than a mile away with shops, restaurants, plus the cathedral. A member of the Best of British group.

Facilities: Sanitary facilities are provided in a modern, superior 'portacabin' style unit which is very clean and well equipped. Laundry with washing machine, dryer and iron. Dishwashing sinks. Gas supplies. **Off site:** A safe sandy beach is 1 mile and the area is good for walking and golf (there are 7 courses within 15 miles of the park). Fishing 1 mile, bicycle hire or boat launching 3 miles, riding 5 miles.

Charges 2002

Per unit incl. 2 persons	£7.50 - £11.00
extra adult	£1.00
child (under 16 yrs)	£0.50
awning	£1.50
dog (max 2)	£0.50
electricity	£2.00

No credit cards. **Tel:** 01862 821253. Fax: 01862 821382. **Reservations:** Made with deposit (1st night's rent) and £1 fee. Bookings and enquiries to: GNR Sutherland, Caravan Sales, Edderton, Tain, Ross-shire IV19 1JY. **Open** 25 April - 30 September.

Directions: At the war memorial in Dornoch, turn north (park signed) on the B9168. Park is 0.5 miles on the right (45 miles north of Inverness). O.S.GR: NH795911.

Woodend Camping & Caravan Park

Achnairn, Lairg IV27 4DN

Woodend is a delightful, small park overlooking Loch Shin and perfect for hill walkers and backpackers. Peaceful and simple, it is owned and run single-handedly by Mrs Cathie Ross, who provides a wonderfully warm Scottish welcome to visitors. On a hill with open, panoramic views across the Loch to the hills beyond and all around, the large camping field is undulating and gently sloping with some reasonably flat areas. The park is licensed to take 55 units, although few pitches would be suitable for caravans or motorcaravans. Most of the 22 electrical hook-ups (16A) are in a line near the top of the field, close to the large, fenced children's play area which has several items of equipment on grass. There are opportunities for fishing and hill walking. The famous Falls of Shin with a Visitor Centre is an ideal place to see the salmon leap (about 10 miles).

Facilities: The modernised sanitary facilities are kept very clean and are quite satisfactory, with dishwashing on small payment. There are books and magazines to borrow in the dishwashing room. Laundry with two machines and a dryer. Kitchen and eating room for tent campers. Reception and a shop at the house, Sunday papers can be ordered, strawberries are on sale in season and daily milk and bread may be ordered. Fishing licences for the Loch (your catch will be frozen for you). **Off site:** Mountain bikes can be hired in Lairg (5 miles). Several scenic golf courses within 20-30 miles.

Charges 2002

Per unit incl. electricity	£8.00
tent	£7.00

No credit cards. **Tel:** 01549 402248. **Reservations:** Not considered necessary. **Open** 1 April - 30 September.

Directions: Achnairn is near the southern end of Loch Shin. Turn off the A838 single track road at signs for Woodend. From the A9 coming north take the A836 at Bonar Bridge, 11 miles northwest of Tain. O.S.GR: NC558127.

Scourie Caravan & Camping Park

773 Harbour Road, Scourie IV27 4TG

Mr Mackenzie has carefully nurtured this park over many years, developing a number of firm terraces with 60 pitches which gives it an attractive layout - there is nothing regimented here. Perched on the edge of the bay in an elevated position, practically everyone has a view of the sea and a short walk along the shore footpath leads to a small sandy beach. The park has tarmac and gravel access roads, with well drained grass pitches and some hard-core hardstandings with 10A electric hook-ups. A few are on an area which is unfenced from the rocks (young children would need to be supervised here). Reception, alongside the modern toilet block, contains a wealth of tourist information and maps. There are very good facilities for disabled visitors on the park and at the restaurant, although the ramps leading to them are a little steep. Mr Mackenzie claims that this is the only caravan park in the world from where, depending on the season, you can see palm trees, Highland cattle and Great Northern divers from your pitch. Red throated divers have also been seen. Trips to Handa Island (a special protection area for seabird colonies) are available from here and Tarbet. The clear water makes this area ideal for diving.

Facilities: The toilet facilities can be heated. Showers have no divider or seat. Fully equipped laundry and dishwashing sinks. Motorcaravan service point. The 'Anchorage' restaurant at the entrance to the park (used as reception at quiet times) is large and well appointed with meals at reasonable prices cooked to order (1/5-15/9). Boat launching facilities. Fishing permits (brown trout) can be arranged. **Off site:** The village has a well stocked shop with post office, gas is available from the local petrol station and mobile banks visit regularly.

Charges 2002

Per unit incl. 1-2 adults	£9.00
extra adult	£1.50
child (3-16 yrs)	£0.75
hiker and tent	£5.00
extra tent, vehicle or awning	£1.00 - £2.00
electricity	£2.00

No credit cards. **Tel:** 01971 502060. **Reservations:** Not made. **Open** 1 April - 30 September, but phone first to check.

Directions: Park is by Scourie village on A894 road in northwest Sutherland. O.S.GR: NC153446.

Dunroamin Caravan & Camping Park

764 Main Street, Lairg IV27 4AR

Lewis and Margaret Hudson run this small park, close to the centre of Lairg and ideally suited for touring Sutherland and Caithness. Fifty level pitches are reserved for touring caravans, motorcaravans and tents on well-tended grass, and there are ten caravan holiday homes for hire. None of the pitches are marked so the owner directs caravans and motorhomes to the camping area and positions them correctly. Tent campers are able to select their own spot in a field behind the row of holiday homes. There are 15 electrical hook-ups (10/16A) and 8 hardstandings, which are concrete below an inch of grass. A licensed restaurant next to the reception (open 8 am-8 pm) serves breakfasts, snacks and evening meals. Local activities include a weekly ceilidh at the village hall, a multi-sports area, walking, fishing (permits are arranged at park) and watersports on nearby Loch Shin. There are three buses daily to Inverness, and three trains daily further afield (timetable in reception). This is a superb location for exploring the Shin Triangle.

Facilities: Fully equipped central toilet block is clean and tidy with showers (20p for 6 mins). Covered dishwashing sink. No motorcaravan service point although tanks can be drained in a manhole near the entrance. Well equipped laundry. Restaurant. Tourist information, basic camping requisites and gas exchange at reception; the nearest shop is 300 yds. Bicycles and barbecues can be hired. Max. two dogs per unit. **Off site:** Ferrycroft Country Centre is a 20-minute walk.

Charges 2002

Per unit incl. 2 adults	£8.00 - £9.50
backpacker	£5.50 - £6.50
extra person	£1.00
electricity	£2.00
awning	£2.00
dog	£1.00

Less 10% for 7 or more nights. **Tel:** 01549 402447. Fax: 01549 402784. E-mail: dunroamin@hudson38. freeserve.co.uk. **Reservations:** Made with £20 per week deposit, balance 4 weeks prior to arrival. **Open** 1 April - 1 November.

Directions: On A836 (Lairg - Roagart road), park is on the south side of Lairg. Follow international camping signs. O.S.GR: NC586062.

Reraig Caravan Site
776 Balmacara, Kyle of Lochalsh IV40 8DH

This is a small, level park close to Loch Alsh with views over to Skye and a wooded hillside behind (criss-crossed with woodland walks). Set mainly on well cut grass, it is sheltered from the prevailing winds by the hill and provides just 40 numbered pitches, 36 with electrical connections (10A) and some hardstandings. Large tents and trailer tents are not accepted at all. Small tents are permitted at the discretion of the owner, so it would be advisable to telephone first if this affects you. Awnings are not permitted during July and August in order to protect the grass. The ground can be stony so there could be a problem with tent pegs. Reraig makes a good base from which to explore the Isle of Skye and the pretty village of Plockton with its palm trees (remember Hamish Macbeth on TV?) Reservations are not necessary but it may be best to arrive before late afternoon in July and August.

Facilities: The single sanitary block has been extensively refurbished and is kept immaculately clean. Children have their own low basins, controllable hot showers are on payment (10p for 2 minutes). Sinks for clothes and dishwashing. Use of a spin dryer is free. Motorcaravan drainage point. **Off site:** Adjacent to the park is the Balmacara Hotel (with bar), shop (selling gas), sub-post office, off licence and petrol station.

Charges 2002

Per unit incl. 2 persons	£8.30
extra adult	£1.50
electricity	£1.20
awning (May, June, Sept only)	£1.50
backpackers/cyclists per tent	£6.80

Tel: 01599 566215. **Reservations:** Not necessary so not accepted by phone; if considered essential, by letter enclosing cheque/PO for first night's fee (non-returnable). **Open** mid-April - 30 September.

Directions: Take A87 towards Kyle of Lochalsh. Park is signed very soon after sign for Balmacara, on the right just before hotel and petrol station. O.S.GR: NG815272.

Ardmair Point Caravan Park
771 Ardmair Point, Ullapool IV26 2TN

This spectacularly situated park, overlooking the little Loch Kanaird, just round the corner from Loch Broom, has splendid views all round. The 68 touring pitches are arranged mainly on grass around the edge of the bay, in front of the shingle beach. Electrical hook-ups (10A) are available and some gravel hardstandings are on the other side of the access road, just past the second sanitary block. Motorcaravans are not permitted on the grass pitches and must use the hardstandings. Tent pitches, together with cheaper pitches for some tourers are in a large field behind the other sanitary facilities. The park provides rowing and motorboats for hire and arranges fishing trips. Scuba diving is popular at Loch Kanaird because the water is so clear. Seals are regularly seen in the bay and the whole area is full of interest, including visits to Inverewe Gardens and the Isle Martin bird and seal colonies.

Facilities: Two toilet blocks, both with good facilities. One block has wonderful views from the large windows in the launderette and dishwashing rooms, plus large en-suite rooms for disabled people. Motorcaravan service point. Limited shop (no bread and other basics). Children's play area. **Off site:** Ullapool for shopping 6 miles. Golf or bicycle hire 3 miles.

Charges 2002

Per unit incl. 2 persons	£9.00 - £11.00
awning	£2.00
extra adult	£2.00 - £3.00
child (over 5 yrs)	£1.00
extra tent	£1.00 - £2.00
electricity	£2.00

Less for 7 or more nights pre-paid. **Tel:** 01854 612054. Fax: 01854 612757. E-mail: p.fraser@ btinternet.com. **Reservations:** Recommended for July/Aug. (min. 2 nights). **Open** 1 May - late September, depending on the weather.

Directions: Park is off the A835 road, 3 miles north of Ullapool. O.S.GR: NH109983.

Loch Greshornish Camping Site

Arnisort, Edinbane IV51 9PS

774

Mr and Mrs Palmer took over this simple, spacious site with simple facilities in 1999. In a beautiful, peaceful setting with views over the loch to the low hills to the northwest of Skye, it is suitable for long or short stays. There are 30 level grass pitches for motorcaravans and caravans, 28 with 10A electric hook-ups. There are also places for up to 100 tents (but numbers never reach that level). A new building houses reception and a small shop selling basic essentials and now including an off-licence. The owners offer bicycle hire (with safety helmets) and canoe hire, with future plans including a children's play area.

Facilities: The refurbished toilet facilities are light, airy and spotlessly clean. The showers are a little cramped. Dishwashing sink in the ladies' and another in the men's. The only acknowledgement of any clothes washing needs is a tumble dryer in a little cabin outside. Camper's shelter with seating, cooking and eating area. Small shop. Bicycle hire. Canoe hire. **Off site:** The local village has two hotels for drinks and meals; Portree, the nearest town, is 15 miles.

Charges 2002

Per caravan or motorcaravan	£1.50
tent	£0.75
adult	£3.25
child 5-10 yrs	£1.00
child 11-16 yrs	£2.00
electricity	£1.60

Tel: 01470 582230. Fax: 01470 582230. E-mail: info@greshcamp.freeserve.co.uk. **Reservations:** Advised for high season. **Open** Easter - 15 October.

Directions: Site is 15 miles west of Portree on the A850 Dunvegan road by Edinbane. O.S.GR: NG343524.

Staffin Caravan & Camping Site

Staffin IV51 9JX

775

This simple camping site is on the side of a hill just outside Staffin, where the broad sweep of the bay is dotted with working crofts running down to the sea; it is perhaps more suited to backpackers and small tents. A marked walk from the site leads to the seashore and slipway (good for walking dogs but too far to be taking a boat). With 50 pitches, the site is quite sloping but there are 18 reasonably level pitches with irregular hardstanding for caravans and motorcaravans, all with electrical hook-ups (16A). Skye has many activities to offer and for the truly dedicated walker the Cuillins are the big attraction but the hills above Staffin look demanding!

Facilities: The sanitary block includes large, controllable showers. Washing up sinks are unfortunately not under cover and have only cold water. An older block is only opened at very busy times. Large hardstanding area has a motorcaravan service point. Gas available. **Off site:** Fishing or boat launching 1 mile, bicycle hire 5 miles, riding 9 miles. Staffin village is 400 yards and has a large shop (open six days a week), a restaurant and a launderette (useful as the site has no laundry).

Charges 2002

Per unit	£8.00
tent incl. 1 person	£4.00
extra adult	£3.00
child 5-12 yrs	£1.00
child 13-18 yrs	£1.50
electricity	£1.50

No credit cards. **Tel:** 01470 562213. **Reservations:** Maybe necessary for peak periods (made with £10 deposit), but will always try to fit you in. **Open** 1 April - 30 September.

Directions: Site is 15 miles north of Portree on A855 (2 miles of single track at the start), just before Staffin on the right and up a slope. O.S.GR: NG496668.

Faichem Park

778 Ardgarry Farm, Faichem, Invergarry PH35 4HG

Small and unsophisticated, Faichem Park is situated on a hillside in a beautiful setting with glorious views over Ben Tee (2,955 ft) near Loch Ness. The road up to the site has been tarmaced so it is now accessible to all except American motorhomes. For children there is the attraction of helping to feed the animals - sheep and lambs, chickens, many types of ducks and strange marvellous looking types of pheasants (Mr Wilson's hobby), and the pony and the white 'runner' ducks which march like soldiers around the park and farm. There are 30 pitches with plenty of space, including 14 with electrical connections and 10 with level concrete hardstanding. Four barbecues are strategically positioned around the camping area for visitors to use. Dogs are accepted (but care is needed with the livestock) and there is an excellent area above the site for walks. TV reception is good. A flexible system for night-time road illumination allows campers to turn off lights close to their pitch if necessary. There are numerous places to fish in the area, golf in Fort Augustus and Fort William, pony trekking, a pleasure cruiser on Loch Ness (you might see Nessie) and the Great Glen water park (2 miles).

Facilities: A log type cabin houses the toilet facilities which are older in style but very clean (key, £1 deposit). Hot water to the showers is metered but is free to washbasins and dishwashing sinks. Hair and hand dryers. Gas is available and free range eggs are sold at the farm but there is no shop (closest 2 miles towards Fort William). **Off site:** Bicycle hire or boat slipway 2 miles, golf 7 miles. The village is 0.5 miles with a hotel.

Charges 2002

Per unit incl. 2 persons	£7.00 - £7.50
extra adult	£1.00
child	£0.50
electricity	£1.50 -£2.00

No credit cards. **Tel:** 01809 501226. Fax: 01809 501307. E-mail: ardgarry.farm@lineone.net. **Reservations:** Advisable in main season and made with small deposit. **Open** 15 March - 15 October.

Directions: From A82 at Invergarry take A87 (in direction of Kyle of Lochalsh) and continue for 1 mile. Turn right at Faichem sign and bear left up hill, farmhouse and reception is the first entrance on the right, the site is second. From opposite direction on A87, turn left at Faichem sign, take third entrance on left for reception, second left for park. O.S.GR: NH285023.

Resipole Farm Caravan & Camping Park

780 Loch Sunart, Acharacle PH36 4HX

This quiet, open park is marvellously set on the banks of Loch Sunart, 8 miles from Strontian, on the Ardnamurchan peninsula. With views across the water and regularly visited by wild deer, it offers a good base for exploring the whole of this scenic area or, more locally, for fishing, boating (launching from the site's own slipway) and walking in the unspoilt countryside. There are 60 touring pitches here, more than half with hardstanding and electric hook-ups (10/16A), and 4 with all services. Tents are sited by the hedges. Resipole Farm is well located for day trips to Mull via the Lochaline ferry.

Facilities: The central, modern sanitary block can be heated and is kept very clean. Good dishwashing facilities. Excellent provision for disabled visitors. Laundry facilities. Adjoining the farmhouse is a well equipped bar and restaurant offering reasonably priced home made food in the evenings (vegetarians catered for). Caravan storage. Park has its own 9 hole golf course. **Off site:** Riding 5 miles.

Charges 2002

Per caravan incl. 2 persons	£9.50 - £10.00
motorcaravan or tent	£9.00 - £9.50
cyclists (2 persons)	£7.50
extra adult	£3.00
child up to 5 yrs	£0.50
child 6-12 yrs	£1.00
child 13 yrs upwards	£1.50
electricity	£2.00
awning, extra tent	free

Tel: 01967 431235. Fax: 01967 431777. E-mail: info@resipole.co.uk. **Reservations:** Advisable for hook-ups and made for any period with one night's fee. **Open** 1 April - 31 October.

Directions: From A82 Fort William road, take the Corran ferry located 5 miles north of Ballachulish and 8 miles south of Fort William. On leaving ferry, turn south along the A861. Park is on the north bank of Loch Sunart, 8 miles west of Strontian. The road is single track for 8 miles approaching Resipole and care is needed, but it is well worth it. O.S.GR: NM676740.

Invercoe Caravan & Camping Park

779 Invercoe, Glencoe PH49 4HP

On the edge of Loch Leven, surrounded by mountains and forest, Iain and Lynn Brown are continually developing this attractively located park in its magnificent historical setting. It provides 60 pitches for caravans, motorcaravans or tents on level grass with gravel access roads (some hardstandings). You choose your own numbered pitch, those at the loch side being very popular, although the majority of the electrical hook-ups (10A) are to the back of the park. The only rules imposed are necessary for safety because the owners prefer their guests to feel free and enjoy themselves. There is much to do for the active visitor with hill walking, climbing, boating, pony riding and sea loch or fresh water fishing in this area of outstanding natural beauty.

Facilities: The well refurbished toilet block can be heated (shower/wash room locked 10 pm. - 7 am). Dishwashing under cover, excellent laundry facilities with a drying room. Motorcaravan service point comprising multi-drainage point, fresh water, dustbins, and chemical disposal point. Shop (May-end Sept). Play area with swings. Fishing. **Off site:** The village with pub and restaurant is within walking distance. Visitor's Centre at Glencoe 2 miles. Golf 3 miles. Bicycle hire 2 miles.

Charges 2002

Per unit incl. 2 persons	£11.00
extra adult	£1.00
child (over 2 yrs)	£0.50
awning	£1.50
extra car, boat or trailer	£1.00
electricity	£2.00
tent incl. 2 persons, no car	£10.00
single person unit	£8.00

Senior citizens less £1 per person outside July/Aug. **Tel:** 01855 811210. Fax: 01855 811210. E-mail: invercoe@sol.co.uk. **Reservations:** Advised for electricity for peak season; made with £17 deposit and £3 fee. **Open** Easter/1 April - end October.

Directions: Follow A82 Crianlarich - Fort William road to Glencoe village and turn onto the B863; park is 0.5 miles along, well signed. O.S.GR: NN098594.

Camping & Caravanning Club Oban Site

781 Barcaldine, By Connel PA37 1SG

Owned by the Camping and Caravanning Club, this site at Barcaldine, 12 miles north of Oban, is a small, intimate site taking 86 units. Arranged within the old walled garden of Barcaldine House, the walls give it some protection from the wind and make it quite a sun trap. There are 27 level pitches with hardstanding and 52 electrical hook-ups (16A). Being a small site, it has a very cosy feel to it, due no doubt to the friendly welcome new arrivals receive. Through the garden gate, one is immediately in the Barcaldine forest with its miles of forest tracks, absolutely perfect for both dog walking and mountain biking. Unusually for a club site there is lounge bar selling very reasonably priced meals most evenings. This is a very comfortable area, only open until 10.30 pm. (no children after 8 pm) with bar meals served 6-8 pm. The loch across the road is handy for sea fishing and a 20 minute walk takes you to a freshwater lake for fishing. A not too frequent bus passes the gate.

Facilities: The central toilet block can be heated and is kept very clean with free hot showers, hair dryers and plenty of washbasins and WCs. Excellent unit for disabled visitors. Laundry. Motorcaravan service point. Small shop open a few hours each day for basic provisions and gas. Bar serving bar meals. Small play area with effective safety base. **Off site:** Sea Life Centre 2 miles.

Charges 2002

Per adult	£3.15 - £4.80
child (6-18 yrs)	£1.55
non-member pitch fee	£4.30
electricity	£1.65 - £2.40

Tel: 01631 720348. **Reservations:** Necessary for high season and made with deposit; contact site. **Open** April - end October.

Directions: Park entrance is off the A828 road on south side of Loch Creran, 6 miles north of Connel Bridge. O.S.GR: NM966420.

Oban Divers Caravan Park
Glenshellach Road, Oban PA34 4QJ

782

Set most attractively in a four-acre valley, yet close to Oban with all its facilities and local attractions, this park has been thoughtfully developed as an extension to the garden of the owner's family home and his diving business which is run alongside the caravan park. A small stream runs through the park, with several types of young eucalyptus and bamboo growing and fuchsias planted along one side at the entrance. Some 60 tons of stone have been sympathetically used to enhance its general appearance. There are only 45 pitches with 12 hardstandings, 34 electrical connections (10A) and plenty of space. Tents are placed mainly on a higher back terrace. An open fronted room is provided for tenters to rest and eat. The single track road leading to the park has few passing places, so it is only suitable for smaller units. There are three bunk houses for groups to rent, two sleeping up to six people, one up to twelve. Local attractions include the Oban distillery, the island of Kerrera for walking, cruises to lochs and islands, plus many more.

Facilities: Toilet facilities are provided in two chalets, the smaller one near the tent pitches. The main chalet provides comfortable facilities with two of the three ladies' washbasins in cabins. Dishwashing and laundry (with a very popular mangle!) with drying rooms (may be closed in very early or late season). Motorcaravan service point. Small shop at reception with gas. Divers' shop with hot drinks machine. Covered barbecue with seating. Children's play items on gravel (those with children can pitch close by). Definitely no dogs accepted. **Off site:** Fishing 1 mile, bicycle hire 2 miles, riding or golf 3 miles.

Charges 2002

Per unit	£8.00
person	£0.50
electricity	£1.50
awning or extra car	£1.00

Less £1.00 for senior citizens excl. B.Hs and July/Aug. No credit cards. **Tel:** 01631 562755. Fax: 01631 562755. E-mail: info@obandivers.co.uk. **Reservations:** Made with £10 deposit. **Open** mid March - end October.

Directions: From north follow A85 one way system through town to traffic island then take ferry terminal exit (Albany St). By Job Centre turn left and then follow signs to Camping Glenshellach. From south go into town to traffic island, then as above. Site is 2 miles from Oban on single track road with passing places. O.S.GR: NM841277.

North Ledaig Caravan Park
Connel, By Oban PA37 1RT

784

The views over the Sound of Mull here are magnificent and Mr and Mrs Weir have tried to ensure good views by staggering the pitches and not planting many trees. The park provides 240 pitches for caravans, motorcaravans and trailer tents only. Of these, 230 pitches have electricity (10A) and 228 have hardstanding. A dog walk follows the disused railway track that runs through the park. An award winning 30 acre nature reserve with ponds and walks (strictly no dogs) to attract wildlife has been developed on land across the road. Being well organised and run, this is a quiet park which makes a good base for exploring the area, visiting the islands from Oban or simply relaxing on the shores of the loch. Fishing and sailing are possible from the site (there is a slipway for small boats), hill walking or pony trekking are close. Buses pass the gate five or six times a day. A member of the Caravan Club's 'managed under contract' scheme, non-members are also very welcome.

Facilities: The main sanitary block is centrally located - you may have a bit of a walk depending on your pitch but a new, semi-underground block should be built soon. The current amenities are excellent and include full facilities for disabled visitors and for babies (access by key). Washbasins in cabins for ladies (one for men). Well equipped laundry with irons for hire, and dishwashing. Motorcaravan service area. Further, well renovated sanitary facilities are behind the reception block. Well stocked, licensed shop. Play area. Caravan storage. **Off site:** Bicycle hire and golf 6 km.

Charges 2002

Per pitch	£4.00
adult	£4.00
child (5-17 yrs)	£1.20
electricity	£2.25
extra car, trailer or motorcycle	£1.00

Debit cards accepted (not credit cards). **Tel:** 01631 710291. Fax: 01631 710291. **Reservations:** Any length, with £10 deposit incl. £1 non-returnable fee. **Open** 27 March - 31 October.

Directions: Park is about 1 mile north of Connel Bridge, on the A828 Oban - Fort William road, 7 miles from Oban. O.S.GR: NM913456.

Glen Nevis Caravan & Camping Park

Glen Nevis, Fort William PH33 6SX

783

Just outside Fort William in a most attractive and quiet situation with views of Ben Nevis, this spacious park is used by those on active pursuits as well as sightseeing tourists. It comprises eight quite spacious fields, divided between caravans, motorcaravans and tents (steel pegs required). It is licensed for 250 touring caravans but with no special tent limits. The large touring pitches, many with hardstanding, are marked with wooden fence dividers, 200 with electricity (13A) and 100 also have water and drainage. The park becomes full in the peak months but there are vacancies each day. If reception is closed (possible in low season) you site yourself. There are regular security patrols at night in busy periods. The park's own modern restaurant and bar with good value bar meals is a short stroll from the park, open to all. A well managed park with bustling, but pleasing ambience, watched over by Ben Nevis. Around 1,000 acres of the Glen Nevis estate are open to campers to see the wildlife and explore this lovely area.

Facilities: The four modern toilet blocks make a good provision with hot showers on payment (20p), (extra showers in two blocks); and units for visitors with disabilities. An excellent block in Nevis Park (one of the eight camping fields) has some washbasins in cubicles, showers, further facilities for disabled visitors, a second large laundry room and dishwashing sinks. Motorcaravan service point. Self-service shop (Easter - mid Oct), barbecue area and snack bar (May - mid-Sept). Children's play area on bark. **Off site:** Pony trekking, golf and fishing near.

Charges 2002

Per person	£1.20 - £1.70
caravan, motorcaravan or tent	£5.60 - £8.10
small tent	£4.90 - £7.30
backpacker tent (1 person)	£3.20 - £4.80
backpacker tent (2 persons)	£3.90 - £5.80
awning	£1.20 - £1.70
serviced pitch plus	£1.20 - £1.70

Tel: 01397 702191. Fax: 01397 703904. E-mail: camping@glen-nevis.co.uk. **Reservations:** Advised for July/Aug. **Open** 15 March - 31 October.

Directions: Turn off A82 to east at roundabout just north of Fort William following camp sign. O.S.GR: NN124723.

Linnhe Lochside Holidays

785 Corpach, Fort William PH33 7NL

This quiet well run park has a very peaceful situation overlooking Loch Eil, and is beautifully landscaped with wonderful views. There are individual pitches with hardstanding for 65 touring units (12 seasonal) on terraces leading down to the water's edge. They include 32 special ones with electricity connection (16A), water and drainaway, plus 30 with electricity only (10A). A separate area on the lochside takes 15 small tents (no reservation). There are also 64 caravan holiday homes and 11 centrally heated pine chalets for hire. Fishing is free on Loch Eil and you are welcome to fish from the park's private beach or bring your own boat and use the slipway and dinghy park. About 5 miles from Fort William on 'The Road to the Isles', the park is conveniently placed for touring the Western Highlands. Easily accessible are Ben Nevis and the Nevis range (cable car to 2,000 ft.), geological, Jacobite and Commando museums, distillery visits, seal island trips, the Mallaig steam railway and the Caledonian Canal.

Facilities: The toilet facilities are of an excellent standard, are heated in the cooler months and include baths (£1). Dishwashing room. First class laundry and separate outdoor clothing drying room (charged per night). Self-service, licensed shop (end May - end Sept). Gas supplies. Barbecue area. Toddlers' play room and two well equipped children's play areas on safe standing. Up to two dogs per pitch are accepted. Large motorhomes are accepted but it is best to book first. Caravan storage. **Off site:** Bicycle hire 2.5 miles, riding or golf 5 miles.

Charges 2002

Per unit incl. 2 persons, electricity	£11.50 - £13.50
'special' pitch	£12.00 - £14.50
small tent pitch	£8.50 - £10.50
awning, extra tent or car	£1.50
extra person	£1.00
dog (max 2, not on tent pitches)	£0.50

Seasonal rates available. **Tel:** 01397 772376. Fax: 01397 772007. E-mail: holidays@linnhe.demon.co.uk. **Reservations:** Made with £30 deposit for min. 3 nights. **Open** all year except 1 Nov - 19 Dec.

Directions: Park entrance is off A830 Fort William - Mallaig road, 1 mile west of Corpach. O.S.GR: NN072772.

Glendaruel Caravan Park

786 Glendaruel PA22 3AB

Glendaruel is in South Argyll, in the area of Scotland bounded by the Kyles of Bute and Loch Fyne, yet is less than two hours by road from Glasgow and serviced by ferries from Gourock and the Isle of Bute. There is also a service between Tarbert and Portavadie. Set in the peaceful wooded gardens of the former Glendaruel House in a secluded glen surrounded by the Cowal hills, it makes an ideal centre for touring this beautiful area. The park takes 35 units on numbered hardstandings with electricity connections (10A), plus 15 tents, on flat oval meadows bordered by over 50 different varieties of mature trees. In a separate area are 28 privately owned holiday homes. The converted stables of the original house provide an attractive little shop selling basics, local produce, venison, salmon, wines (some Scottish!) and tourist gifts. Glendaruel is a park for families with young children or for older couples to relax and to enjoy the beautiful views across the Sound of Bute from Tighnabruaich or the botanical gardens which flourish in the climate. The owners, Quin and Anne Craig, provide a warm welcome and will advise you where to eat and what to do - they are justifiably proud of their park and its beautiful environment. A member of the Best of British group.

Facilities: The toilet block is ageing but it is kept very neat and tidy and can be heated. Washing machine and dryer. A covered area has picnic tables for use in bad weather and dishwashing sinks. Shop (hours may be limited in low season). Gas available. Games room with pool table, table tennis and video games. Behind the laundry is a children's play centre for under 12s and additional play field. Fishing. Torches advised. **Off site:** Sea fishing and boat slipway 5 miles, adventure centre (assault courses, abseiling and rafting) and sailing school close. Golf 12 miles.

Charges 2002

Per unit incl. 2 persons	£8.50 - £10.50
tent per person, no car	£4.00 - £5.00
extra adult	£1.50 - £2.00
child (4-15 yrs)	£1.00 - £1.50
awning, extra tent, car, trailer or boat	£1.50
electricity	£2.00

Special weekly rates and senior citizen discount outside July/Aug. **Tel:** 01369 820267. Fax: 01369 820367. E-mail: enquiries@glendaruelcaravanpark. co.uk. **Reservations:** Any length, with £10 deposit and £2 fee. **Open** 28 March - 26 October.

Directions: Entrance is off A886 road 13 miles south of Strachur. Alternatively there are two ferry services from Gourock to Dunoon, then on B836 which joins the A886 about 4 miles south of the park - this route not recommended for touring caravans. Note: the park has discount arrangements with Western Ferries so contact the park before making arrangements (allow 7 days for postage of tickets). O.S.GR: NS001865.

NORTHERN IRELAND

For information on all parts of Northern Ireland contact:

Belfast Welcome Centre
Tel: 028 9024 6609 Fax: 028 9031 2424
E-mail: visitorservices@nitb.com

Internet: http://www.discovernorthernireland.com

The natural beauty and variety of the countryside, the historic landscape and the friendly people are what holidaymakers remember best about Northern Ireland. In addition, a wide selection of good quality campsites, uncluttered roads, an abundance of pubs and restaurants and plenty to see and do wherever they go keeps visitors coming back for more.

As Northern Ireland is barely 85 miles from north to south and about 110 miles wide driving is something to be enjoyed. A matter of hours can transport you from the dramatic coastline and the nine Glens of Antrim to the rugged heart of the wild Sperrin Mountains, from the timeless landscape and glittering lakes of Fermanagh to the foothills of the Mourne Mountains sweeping down to Carlingford Lough.

Irish miles: the old granite milestones that still peep out from behind the cow parsley on road verges, especially in County Down, are marked in Irish miles. An Irish mile at 2,240 yards is 480 yards longer than a standard English mile. Distances on road signs, however, are marked in standard miles!

For youngsters and the young-at-heart, action and adventure are never far away. Pan for gold, take a subterranean journey through underground caves, enjoy a literary break or leap from pre-history to the future, then have a go at kayaking, abseiling, archery, horse riding or any one of the numerous sports and activities on offer throughout Northern Ireland. No matter where you pitch your tent, or park your caravan, you will find good company and great 'craic' just around the corner.

Ferry Services

The following ferry services are expected to operate between the UK mainland and Ireland in 2003:

Irish Ferries
For bookings/enquiries: 08705 171717
or e-mail: info@irishferries.co.uk
www.irishferries.ie/index
Holyhead - Dublin
(ferry 3 hrs 15 mins, fastcraft 109 mins)
Pembroke - Rosslare (ferry 3 hrs 45 mins)

P&O Irish Sea
0870 24 24 777 www.poirishsea.com
Cairnryan - Larne (Super ferry 105 mins,
Superstar Express 60 mins - no caravans)
Fleetwood - Larne (ferry 8 hrs)
Liverpool - Dublin (ferry 8 hrs, Super ferry 6 hrs)
Mostyn - Dublin (6 hrs)

Sea Cat Scotland
08705 523 523 www.seacat.co.uk
Troon - Belfast (2 hrs 30 mins)
Heysham - Belfast (4 hrs)
Liverpool - Dublin (4 hrs)

Swansea Cork Ferries
01792 45 61 16 www.swansea-cork.ie
Swansea - Cork (10 hrs)

Stena Line
08705 70 70 70 www.stenaline.co.uk
Fishguard - Rosslare
(Super ferry 3 hrs 30 mins, Lynx 110 mins)
Holyhead - Dun Laoghaire (HSS 99 mins)
Holyhead - Dublin Port
(Super ferry 3 hrs 45 mins)
Stranraer - Belfast
(Super ferry 3 hrs 15 mins, HSS 105 mins)

Norse Merchant Ferries
0870 600 4321
www.norsemerchant.com
Liverpool - Belfast (8 hrs)
Liverpool - Dublin (8 hrs)

Curran Court Caravan Park
Larne BT40 1XB

832

Formerly run by the local borough council, this park is now managed by the Curran Court Hotel (opposite the park). Attractive garden areas add to the charm of this small, neat site which is very conveniently situated for the ferry terminal and only a few minutes walk from the sea. The 29 pitches, all with hardstanding and electricity connections (12A), give reasonable space off the tarmac road and there is a separate tent area of 1.5 acres. Larne market is on Wednesdays. You may consider using this site as a short term base for discovering the area as well as an ideal overnight stop. The warden can usually find room for tourists so reservations are not normally necessary.

Facilities: The toilet block is clean and adequate without being luxurious. Laundry room with dishwashing facilities. Children's play area with good equipment and safety surfaces. Bowls and putting on site. **Off site:** Bicycle hire 1 km. Golf 3 km. Boat launching 500 yds. Many other amenities are very close including a shop (100 yds), the hotel for food and drink, tennis and a leisure centre with swimming pool (300 yds).

Charges 2002

Per caravan or motorcaravan	£10.00
tent	£8.50 - £5.00
electricity	£1.50

Tel: 028 2827 3797. Fax: 028 2826 0096. E-mail: curran.court-hotel@virgin.net. **Reservations:** Not normally considered necessary. **Open** Easter - 30 September.

Directions: Immediately after leaving the ferry terminal, turn right and follow camp signs. Site is just 400 yards on the left.

Carnfunnock Country Park Caravan Site
Coast Road, Drain's Bay, Larne BT40 2QG

831

In a magnificent parkland setting overlooking the sea, what makes this touring site popular is its scenic surroundings and convenient location. It is 3.5 miles north of the market town of Larne on the famed Antrim Coast Road and offers 28 level 'super' pitches, all with hardstanding, water, electricity (15A), drainage, individual pitch lighting and ample space for an awning. The site has a neat appearance with a tarmac road following through to the rear where a number of pitches are placed in a circular position with allocated space for tents. Run by the Borough Council and supervised by a manager, the surrounding Country Park is immaculately kept. The Visitor Centre includes a gift shop and information about local attractions and the restaurant/coffee shop is pleasant and looks towards the sea. Spending time around the parkland, you find a walled time garden with historic sundials, a maze, forest walk, adventure playground, putting green, 9 hole golf course, wildlife garden and miniature railway. There is also a summer events programme.

Facilities: A small building beside the entrance gates houses sanitary toilet facilities (entry by key) which are kept clean, but now starting to show signs of wear. There are shower units, facilities for disabled people and dishwashing. Motorcaravan service point. **Off site:** Fishing and boat launching 400 m.

Charges 2002

Per caravan or motorcaravan	£11.50
serviced hardstanding	£13.00
5-7 nights (incl. electricity)	£59.00 - £80.00
tent	£7.00 - £9.50
awning	£1.50

Tel: 028 2827 0541. Fax: 028 2827 0852. **Reservations:** Advisable for week-ends; peak periods and B.Hs. **Open** Easter - 30 September.

Directions: From ferry terminal in Larne, follow signs for Coast Road and Carnfunnock Country Park; well signed 3.5 miles on A2 coast road.

Drumaheglis Caravan Park

834

36 Glenstall Road, Ballymoney BT53 7QN

A caravan park which continually maintains high standards, Drumaheglis is popular throughout the season. Situated on the banks of the lower River Bann, approximately 4 miles from the town of Ballymoney, it appeals to watersports enthusiasts or makes an ideal base for exploring this scenic corner of Northern Ireland. The marina offers superb facilities for boat launching, water-skiing, cruising, canoeing or fishing, whilst getting out and about can take you to the Giant's Causeway, seaside resorts such as Portrush or Portstewart, the sands of Whitepark Bay, the Glens of Antrim or the picturesque villages of the Antrim coast road. For tourers only, this site instantly appeals, for it is well laid out with trees, shrubs, flower beds and tarmac roads. There are now 53 serviced pitches with hardstanding, electricity (5/10A) and water points. Ballymoney is a popular shopping town and the Joey Dunlop Centre provides a high-tech fitness studio, sports hall, etc. There is much to see and do within this Borough and of interest is the Ballymoney museum in Charlotte Street.

Facilities: Modern toilet blocks, spotlessly clean when we visited, include individual wash cubicles, and facilities for disabled visitors, plus four family shower rooms. Dishwashing sinks. Washing machine and dryer. Children's play area. Volleyball and table tennis. Barbecue and picnic areas. **Off site:** Bicycle hire and golf 4 miles, riding 0.5 miles.

Charges 2002

Per unit incl. electricity	£13.00
for 7 days	£78.00
pitch without services	£10.00
for 7 days	£60.00

Tel: 028 2766 6466. Fax: 028 2766 7659. E-mail: info@ballymoney.gov.uk. **Reservations:** Essential for peak periods and weekends. **Open** Easter - 1 October.

Directions: From A26/B62 Portrush - Ballymoney roundabout continue for approx. 1 mile on the A26 towards Coleraine. Site is clearly signed - follow International camping signs.

Bush Caravan Park

835

95 Priestland Road, Bushmills BT57 8UJ

An ideal base for touring the North Antrim Coast, this family run, recently extended park is only minutes away from two renowned attractions, the Giant's Causeway and the Old Bushmills Distillery. This fact alone makes Bush a popular location, but its fast growing reputation for friendliness and top class facilities makes it equally appealing. Conveniently located just off the main Ballymoney - Portrush road, it is approached by a short drive. The site itself is partly surrounded by mature trees and hedging, but views across the countryside can still be appreciated. Tarmac roads around the site lead to 43 well laid out and spacious pitches, with hardstanding and electric hook-up (16A), or to a grass area for tents. Unique features on site are murals depicting the famed scenery, sights and legends of the Causeway Coast. The enthusiastic owners organise tours to the Distillery and coastal trips - a musical evening can't be ruled out.

Facilities: The toilet block (opened by key-pad) is modern, clean and equipped to a high standard. Facilities include controllable showers with excellent provision for people with disabilities. Washing machine, dryer and dishwashing sinks. Central children's play area. Recreation room for all ages.

Charges 2002

Per unit incl. all persons, electricity	£12.00
frame tent	£6.00 - £10.00
awning	£2.00
small tent	£6.00

Tel: 028 2073 1678. Fax: 028 7035 1998. **Reservations:** Advised for high season or weekends. **Open** Easter - 31 October.

Directions: From Ballymoney A26/B62 roundabout proceed north on B62 towards Portrush for 6.5 miles. Turn right onto B17 and site is 350 yds on the left.

Ballyness Caravan Park

40 Castlecatt Road, Bushmills BT57 8TN

Ballyness is immaculately cared for and is designed with conservation in mind. In keeping with the surrounding countryside, it is extensively planted with native trees and shrubs which attract local wildlife and birds. The overall appearance of this site, with its entrance gate, white stone pillars and broad tarmac drive are appealing. The drive leads to 30 hardstanding pitches with electric hook-ups, water and drainage. There is a dedicated area for tents and several caravan holiday homes, but these are placed away from the touring pitches. From the site you can enjoy a relaxing walk by way of the meadow ponds and winding pathway alongside the stream known as St Columb's Rill. The village of Bushmills, with its famous Whiskey Distillery, is within walking distance and the Causeway Coast a short drive.

Facilities: One spotlessly clean and well decorated, cottage style heated sanitary block (key coded) includes facilities for disabled visitors (toilet and shower), a bathroom and baby changing unit, laundry room and dishwashing area. Children's play area. Football field. Nature trail.

Charges 2002

Per unit incl. 2 persons, electricity, water and drainage	£12.00
awning or pup tent	free - £1.00
2 person tent	£8.00
extra person over 5 yrs	£0.50

Tel: 028 2073 2393. Fax: 028 2073 2713. E-mail: info@ballynesscaravanpark.com. **Reservations:** Contact site. **Open** 17 March - 31 October.

Directions: From M2 follow A26 N. At Ballymoney turn right on B66 towards Dervock and turn left. Stay on B66 and site is 5.5 miles on right.

Bellemont Caravan Park

10 Islandtasserty Road, Coleraine BT52 2PN

Close to Coleraine and Portstewart, this well kept park makes an immediately favourable impression with its white concrete roads, its perfect grass areas and well laid out appearance. The gently sloping ground rises at the far right of the park to give views over Portstewart and towards the sea. To the left of the entrance and security gate are five privately owned caravan holiday homes. There are 30 touring pitches, all with hardstanding, electric hook-up and water. These are spacious and well distributed around this open, parkland style setting. In a central position stands a gleaming white building, with flower tubs decorating the forecourt, which houses reception and heated sanitary facilities. Bellemont makes a good base for visiting the university town of Coleraine, the resorts and beaches of Portstewart and Portrush, or famous sights such as Dunluce Castle, Carrick-a-Rede rope bridge, the Giant's Causeway, plus the ports and harbours which follow the North Antrim coastline. There are no tent pitches.

Facilities: Toilet facilities with good sized showers (token operated). En-suite unit for disabled visitors. Laundry room with two washing machines, two dryers and iron (token operated), plus dishwashing sink and drainer to the outside. Play area for children with swings and slide on a bark surface. Dogs are not accepted.

Charges 2002

Per unit incl. all persons	£10.50
Per unit incl. all persons and electricity	£12.00
awning	£1.50

No credit cards. **Tel:** 028 7082 3872. **Reservations:** Contact site. **Open** Easter - 30 September.

Directions: From Lodge Road roundabout on eastern outskirts of Coleraine follow A29 north to fourth roundabout. Continue towards Portrush and site is clearly signed on left after 400 yards.

Tullans Farm Caravan Park

 46 Newmills Road, Coleraine BT52 2JB

A quality, well run family park convenient for the Causeway coast, Tullans Farm is one of the most popular in the area. It has a quiet, heart of the country feel, yet the University town of Coleraine is within a mile, the seaside resort Portrush and Portstewart five miles and a shopping centre a five minute drive. Tullans Farm has earned a reputation for its spotlessly clean toilet block, attractive flower displays and its well cared for appearance. In a central position, fronted by a parking space, stands a long white building housing the sanitary facilities and reception. Around the park roads are gravel and 32 pitches are on hardstanding, all with electric hook-ups (10A). In season the owners organise barbecues, barn dances and line dancing (funds in aid of charity).

Facilities: The toilet and shower rooms, including a family shower unit, are spacious, modern and include facilities for people with disabilities. Laundry and washing up room with sinks, washing machine, dryers and a large fridge. Play area. TV lounge and barn used for indoor recreation.

Charges 2002

Per unit incl. all persons, electricity	£10.00 - £11.00
awning	£1.00
family tent	£10.00
2 man tent	£7.00

No credit cards. **Tel:** 028 7034 2309. Fax: 028 7034 2309. **Reservations:** Advised for peak times. **Open** March - 31 October.

Directions: From the Lodge Road roundabout (south end of Coleraine) turn east onto A29 Portrush ring road and proceed for 0.5 miles. Turn right at sign for park and Windy Hall. Park is clearly signed on left.

LoanEden Caravan Park

Muckross Bay, Kesh BT93 1TX

The owners of LoanEden have built up a reputation for their park, based on a friendly, caring attitude. It is particularly suitable for those who enjoy fishing or riding. First impressions are of an overall neat and tidy appearance, with well tended shrubs, flower beds and wide tarmac driveways. There are many privately owned holiday homes on the site, but these are kept separate from the touring area. The 24 touring and 12 long-stay pitches are level with hardstanding, water, electricity, drainage, rubbish bin and a grass area for an awning. For children there are two outdoor play areas and a new indoor room for football, netball, etc. Young and old can enjoy pony and horse riding tuition under the supervision of the owners' daughter Victoria, an A.I. instructor and son Andrew who is an international rider. The owners organise barbecues and barn dances in aid of charity.

Facilities: The fully tiled central sanitary block is well equipped and includes facilities for disabled people. Laundry area with washing machines, dryers and sinks. Motorcaravan service point. Children's play areas. Riding. **Off site:** Fishing and bicycle hire nearby, golf 5 miles.

Charges 2002

Per caravan or motorcaravan incl. awning and electricity	£14.00
tent	£8.00
electricity	£1.00

Tel: 028 6863 1603. Fax: 028 6863 2300. **Reservations:** Advisable for high season and B.Hs. **Open** all year.

Directions: From Enniskillen take A32 Omagh road for 3.5 miles and branch left on B82 Kesh road. Continue for 11 miles to village of Kesh. Cross over bridge at north end of village and turn immediately left to park in 0.5 miles on the right.

Mullynascarthy Caravan Park

Lisnaskea BT92 0NZ

851

This is a well kept touring site situated on the banks of the Colebrooke River. It has instant appeal, for the setting at Mullynascarthy is more like a mature garden. The pitches to the right of reception, which are grass on hard-standing, are mostly angled between the many tree varieties, also separated by low hedging and flowering shrubs. To the left of the facility block additional pitches are spread over meadow-like terrain and all have electric hook-ups. Sanitary facilities, although not ultra modern, are kept very clean and housed alongside reception, which doubles up as a sub post office. The attention and care this site obviously receives is due to the warden who also extends a friendly warm welcome to her guests. Lisnaskea makes an ideal base for exploring this lakeland county which abounds in historic treasures, stately homes, and is excellent for watersports enthusiasts. The county town of Enniskillen is within a short drive and the Marble Arch caves are a experience not to be missed.

Facilities: The toilet block (key operated) has showers, open style washbasins, facilities for people with disabilities (washbasin/WC), laundry room and dishwashing sinks. Games and sports area. Children's play area. River fishing (licences and permits available).

Charges 2002
Per unit incl. 2 persons and electricity   £12.00

Tel: 028 6772 1040. **Reservations:** Contact site. **Open** 17 March - 31 October.

Directions: From Enniskillen take A4 towards Dungannon for 8 miles, then turn right on A34 signed Lisnaskea. Continue on A34 for 3.5 miles and turn right onto B514 where site is signed Mullynascarthy.

Tollymore Forest Caravan Park

Bryansford Village, Newcastle BT33 0PW

842

This popular park, for tourers only, is located within the parkland of Tollymore Forest. It is discreetly situated away from the public footpaths and is noted for its scenic surroundings. The forest park, which is approached by way of an ornate gateway and majestic avenue of Himalayan cedars, covers an area of almost 500 hectares. It is backed by the Mourne mountains and situated two miles from the beaches and resort of Newcastle. The site is attractively laid out with hardstanding pitches, 72 of which have electricity (6A). The Head Ranger at Tollymore is helpful and ensures that the caravan site is efficiently run and quiet, even when full. Exploring the forest park is part of the pleasure of staying here, and of note are the stone follies, bridges and entrance gates. The Shimna and Spinkwee rivers flow through the park adding a refreshing touch and tree lovers appreciate the arboretum with its many rare species.

Facilities: Toilet blocks, timbered in keeping with the setting, are clean and modern with wash cubicles, facilities for disabled people, dishwashing and laundry area. **Off site:** Confectionery shop and tea room nearby. Small grocery shop a few yards from the exit gate of the park with gas available.

Charges 2002
Per unit incl. car and occupants   £8.00 - £12.00
electricity   £1.50

Low season mid-week special rates. **Tel:** 028 4372 2428. **Reservations:** Advisable in high season and for B.Hs. and made with £10 deposit. Contact: Tollymore Forest Park (Administration), 176 Tullybrannigan Road, Newcastle, Co. Down BT33 0PW. **Open** all year.

Directions: Approach Newcastle on the A24. Before entering the town, at roundabout, turn right on to A50 signed Castlewellan and follow signs for Tollymore Forest Park.

Banbridge Touring Caravan & Camping Park

200 Newry Road, Banbridge BT32 3NB

This conveniently situated touring park on the main A1 Belfast - Newry road is an ideal place for a stopover if travelling between Southern and Northern Ireland. It is within easy towing distance of the main ports or would make an ideal base for discovering many tourist attractions such as the Bronte Homeland or Scarna Visitor Centre. A tiny site, with 8 hardstanding pitches and electrical connections (6A), it is part of the Banbridge Gateway Tourist Information Centre complex. The centre is an attractive building of modern design surrounded by a well maintained garden area and car park. Housed inside, apart from the offices of the centre and a bureau de change, is a display areas for Irish crafts. The restaurant and coffee shop within the complex (10.00-17.00 hrs daily) serves lunchtime specials, scones, cakes, etc. The touring park, located in the far left hand corner of the complex, is enclosed with ranch fencing, plus a security gate and barrier. The town of Banbridge is 1 mile.

Facilities: Excellent, ultra-modern toilet facilities, spotlessly clean and key operated, include two showers, good facilities for disabled people and an outside, covered dishwashing area. Extensive children's play area with safety base. **Off site:** Shops, restaurants, pubs and all services within 1 mile. Fishing, bicycle hire or golf within 3 miles.

Charges 2003

Per unit incl. electricity	£10.00
tent	£5.00

Max. stay 5 consecutive nights. Refundable key deposit (gate, WCs and showers) £20. **Tel:** 028 4062 3322. Fax: 028 4062 3114. E-mail: banbridge@nitic.net. **Reservations:** Contact centre during office hours (summer: Mon-Sat 09.00-19.00, Sun. 14.00-18.00; winter: Mon-Sat 10.00-17.00, Sun. closed). It is essential to arrive during opening hours to obtain keys. **Open** all year, but closed Sundays Oct - May incl.

Directions: Follow signs to Tourist Information Centre off the A1 Belfast - Newry dual carriageway, 1 mile south of Banbridge.

Banbridge Touring Caravan & Camping Park
Banbridge, Co. Down, N. Ireland

8 fully serviced pitches for Caravans. Adjacent to Banbridge Gateway Tourist Information Centre on main A1 Belfast/Dublin Euroroute.

All facilities available - toilets, showers, children's play area, restaurant, etc.

CARAVANS £10.00 per night. TENTS £5.00 per night. ELECTRICITY free

Arrivals by 7.00pm (summer) and 5.00pm (winter)

BANBRIDGE
DISTRICT COUNCIL

Telephone: (028) 4062 3322 for bookings

Delamont Country Park Camping & Caravanning Club Site

846 Delamont Country Park, Downpatrick Road, Killyleagh BT30 9TZ

This is Northern Ireland's first Camping and Caravanning Club site and although not long in existence, it is proving to one of the country's most popular sites. Within the boundaries of Delamont Country Park, it is an idyllic location for those seeking an away from it all feel, yet wanting to be within easy reach of major attractions. The country park is a designated area of outstanding natural beauty and commands from its highest point, breathtaking vistas of Strangford Lough and surrounding countryside. Facilities on the campsite itself are excellent and it has an orderly, neat and tidy appearance. Reception stands to the fore of the site and the sanitary block towards the rear. The 64 all weather pitches on level terrain all have electricity, plus water and waste hook-ups. Although the site is surrounded by trees and the rich vegetation of the country park, the young shrubs and trees around the pitches will take time to mature.

Facilities: The single modern toilet block, with heating, has wash cubicles and a baby bath. En-suite facilities for disabled visitors. Laundry sinks, washing machine and dryer; dishwashing inside. Small shop area selling basics. Adventure playground and miniature railway in country park. Free admittance to country park for campers. **Off site:** Tyrella beach 7 miles.

Charges 2002

Per adult	£3.90 - £5.50
child	free - £1.70
non-member pitch fee	£3.50
electricity	£1.75 - £2.50

Tel: 028 4482 1833. **Reservations:** No calls after 8 pm. Contact site. **Open** 15 March - 28 October.

Directions: From Belfast follow A22 southeast to village of Killyleagh. Pass through village and site entrance is on left after 1 mile.

Gortin Glen Caravan & Camping Park

856 1 Lisnaharney Road, Lislap, Omagh BT79 7UG

Pronounced 'Gorchin', this excellent, truly peaceful site is deep in Gortin Glen with splendid views of the surrounding hills and forest. The very large Gortin Glen Forest embraces the 405 ha. forest park which has a 5 mile scenic road offering breathtaking views, picnic areas, nature trails, wildlife enclosures and an indoor exhibit, all open to the public. Within the park is a camping area with 24 individually numbered pitches, all with hardstanding and electricity (13A). All pitches are spacious with room for an awning. In addition there are separate areas for tents and attractive self catering cottages. A barbecue area is located behind the main block. Reception is well stocked with tourist information on local attractions which include the Ulster History Park, Ulster American Folk Park and Sperrin Heritage Centre.

Facilities: The toilet block has four controllable hot showers and good facilities for people with disabilities, which mothers may also use for children. Laundry room with two washing machines and two dryers. Dishwashing area with free hot water. TV/games room with table tennis. Children's play area with safety base and provision for ball games. **Off site:** Shops are in Gortin village (3 miles).

Charges 2002

Per caravan	£9.00
tent acc. to size	£4.50 - £9.00
electricity	£1.50
awning	£0.50
youth groups (10 or more, per person)	£1.50

Youth groups of 10 or more £1.50 per person, per night. **Tel:** 028 8164 8108. Fax: 028 8164 8108. E-mail: gortinholidaypark@omagh.gov.uk. **Reservations:** Made with £15 fee for B.H. weekends. **Open** all year.

Directions: From Omagh take B48 road signed Gortin. Proceed north for approx. seven miles and turn left immediately after Ulster History Park into site.

IRELAND.
IT'S BETTER BY FAR – BY CAR!

For freedom, flexibility and convenience there's no better way to travel than with your own car. Irish Ferries offer you the most modern fleet, great value fares and inclusive package holidays.

Ferries & Holidays to Ireland Call 08705 17 17 17 or see your travel agent.
£5 Off On-Line Car Bookings www.irishferries.com

Ulysses, the World's Largest Car Ferry and Dublin Swift – Holyhead to Dublin   Z920

REPUBLIC OF IRELAND

For information on visiting Irelaqnd, North and South, contact:

Tourism Ireland
150 New Bond Street, London W1Y 0AQ
Tel: 0800 039 7000
E-mail: info@irelandholidays.co.uk

Internet: http://www.tourismireland.com

'You're welcome' is not said lightly to the visitor who sets foot in Ireland, it is said with sincerity. On this `Emerald Isle' you will find friendly and hospitable people, spectacular scenery and a selection of good campsites to suit your particular needs. Whether you choose to be sited by a lough shore, at the foothills of a mountain range or close by golden sands, the scenery is stunning and the pace of life slow.

With the help of information and maps available from the Tourist Office you discover for yourself, not only the beauty spots, but also many historic and interesting routes to follow. In such areas we have endeavoured to locate well run sites that range from family parks where children can find day long amusement, to the more simple site offering total relaxation, all of good quality.

British visitors born in the United Kingdom when travelling to the Republic of Ireland do not require passports or visas. However, identification is required. Residents of the UK who were not born there or those travelling to Ireland via the UK do require a passport and may require a visa.

The Euro ( ) is now the official currency of the Irish Republic. Sterling is the official currency in Northern Ireland.

Travel insurance is advisable when travelling in the south.

To telephone the Irish Republic from the UK, replace the first `0' given in the number with the country code: 00 353. For example: (094) 88100 becomes 00 353 94 88100.

The population of the Republic (26 counties) is now just over 4 million. Dublin is the largest city with 1,058,264 inhabitants, Cork is the second with 420,510 inhabitants.

Signposts are mostly bilingual. Whilst Ireland has gradually converted to metric measurements, it should be noted that most of the black on white finger-post signs are in miles and the newer green and white ones are in kilometres.

Gas cylinders in the UK and Ireland are not compatible. In Ireland the Euro-system that has a click-on regulator is used. The cylinders used in Ireland have a different shape, weight and size to those used in Britain.

Irish Caravan Council

Ireland, one of Europe's best kept secrets, is the Caravan and Camping destination for the discerning traveller. You take control of your holiday from start to finish, go as you please, and do as little or as much as you like. It's all on offer in Ireland: rugged coastlines, inland waterways, lakes and rivers, Celtic monuments, churches and castles, rolling hills and lush green valleys. Plus, of course, Ireland's legendary hostelries and the friendliest people you're ever likely to meet. Pick up a copy of the 2003 Caravan and Camping Guide at your local tourist office today - it's a breath of fresh air.

Alternatively contact ICC direct at:
Fax: 00 353 98 28237.
E-mail: info@camping-ireland.ie
Website: http//www.camping-ireland.ie
Boite Postale: ICC, Box 4443, Dublin 2, Ireland

Knockalla Caravan & Camping Park

Magherawarden, Portsalon

864

What adds to the popularity of this site is its location, nestling between the slopes of the Knockalla Mountains and Bally-mastocker Bay amidst the breathtaking scenery of County Donegal. The fact that the beach here has been named 'the second most beautiful beach in the world' is not surprising. Approached by an unclassified but short road, Knockalla's elevated situation commands a panoramic view of the famed Bay, Lough Swilly, Inishowen Peninsula and Dunree Head. The family run park is partly terraced giving an attractive, orderly layout with reception, shop and restaurant in a central position and the touring area sited to the left of reception. All 50 pitches have electrical hook-ups and hardstanding, offering a choice of tarmac only or with an adjoining grass to allow for awnings. Tents are pitched on a lower level facing reception and to the far left of the tourers, with caravan holiday homes placed around the right hand perimeter and to the rear of the park. Specialities at the shop and café are home made scones, apple cakes, jams, etc. with a takeaway or table service. Full Irish breakfasts are served.

Facilities: The main toilet block, tastefully refurbished and kept clean and fresh, can be heated. Showers (€1 token). Dishwashing area and campers' kitchen with hot water. Laundry service operated by staff. Motorcaravan service points. Gas available. Children's play area and TV/games room. Shop and cafe (both July/Aug, plus B.H. w/ends). **Off site:** Golf 3 miles, fishing, riding and bicycle hire within 10 miles.

Charges 2003

Per unit incl. 2 adults, 2 children	€17.00
awning	€2.00
small tent	€12.00
extra adult	€4.00
electricity	€2.00

No credit cards. **Tel:** 074 59108. **Reservations:** Advisable for July/Aug and B.H. w/ends. **Open** 17 March - 17 September.

Directions: From Letterkenny take R245 to Rathmelton. Continue on R245 to Milford. Turn right on R246 to Kerrykeel. In village turn left towards Portsalon and at second crossroads turn right onto Portsalon/Knockalla coast road. Turn right to park at sign.

Greenlands Caravan & Camping Park

Rosses Point

869

Just off the N15 road and 8 km. from Sligo town, this is a well run park at Rosses Point, in the sand hills adjoining a championship golf course. It is thoughtfully laid out with small tents placed to the front of reception and the hardstanding touring pitches separated from the trailer tent pitches which occupy the rear. The ground is undulating and adds interest to the overall appearance. Your view depends on where you are pitched - look towards Coney Island and the Blackrock lighthouse which guards the bay, take in the sight of Benbulben Mountain or appreciate the seascape and the water lapping the resort's two bathing beaches. Electric hook-ups (10A) are available for touring units. This is an excellent base from which to explore the 'Yeats Country' and discover the beauty spots immortalised in his poems, such places as Lissadell, Dooney Rock, the Isle of Innisfree and the poet's burial place at Drumcliffe.

Facilities: Modern toilet facilities, recently extended and refitted, are kept exceptionally clean, with hot showers (token) dishwashing and laundry sinks, washing machine, dryer and iron. Motorcaravan service point. New campers' kitchen. Information point and TV room beside reception. Sand pit for children and outdoor chess and draughts sets. Night security. **Off site:** Mini-market, restaurant and evening entertainment in the village. Fishing and boat launching 100 m, golf 50 m, bicycle hire 8 km, riding 14 km.

Charges 2002

Per unit	€12.70
Per person	€0.65
hiker/cyclist incl. tent	€8.25
awning or pup tent	€1.25
electricity	€2.50

Weekly rates available. Tel: 071 77113.
Reservations: Contact park. **Open** 29 March - 9 September.

Directions: From Sligo city travel approx. 800 m. north on N15 road, turn left onto R291 signed Rosses Point. Continue for 6.5 km. and park is on right after village.

Cong Caravan and Camping Park

Lisloughrey, Quay Road, Cong

874

It would be difficult to find a more idyllic and famous spot for a caravan park than Cong. Situated close to the shores of Lough Corrib, Cong's scenic beauty was immortalised in the film 'The Quiet Man'. This well kept park is 1.6 km. from the village of Cong, near the grounds of the magnificent and renowned Ashford Castle. The owner's house that incorporates reception, shop and the hostel, stands to the fore of the site. Toilet facilities and the holiday hostel accommodation are entered from the courtyard area. The 40 grass pitches, 36 with electricity, are placed at a higher level to the rear, with the tent areas below and to the side. The park can be crowded and busy in high season. When not spending time around the village of Cong with its picturesque river setting and Monastic relics, there is much to keep the active camper happy. Watersports, cycling, walking, climbing, caving and scenic drives can all be pursued. Not least of the on site attractions at this park is a mini cinema showing 'The Quiet Man' film nightly all season.

Facilities: Toilet facilities for the campsite are tastefully decorated, kept clean and are heated when necessary. They include include hot showers with curtains (charge), hairdryers, soap and hand towels. Dishwashing area (charge for hot water). Campers' kitchen. Launderette service. Central bin depot. Barbecue, games room and extensive children's play area. Shop. Catering is a feature - full Irish or continental breakfast, dinner or packed lunch may be ordered, or home baked bread and scones purchased in the shop. Bicycle hire. **Off site:** Riding or golf within 2 km, fishing and boat slipway 500 m.

Charges 2002

Per pitch	€10.00
adult	€2.00
child	€1.60
awning	€3.00
electricity	€3.00
hiker/cyclist incl. tent and 1 person	€8.50

Tel: 092 46089. Fax: 092 46448. E-mail: quiet.man.cong@iol.ie. **Reservations:** Contact park. **Open** all year.

Directions: Leave N84 road at Ballinrobe to join R334/345 signed Cong. Turn left at end of the R345 (opposite entrance to Ashford Castle), take next road on right (approx. 300 m) and the park is on right (200 m).

Belleek Caravan & Camping Park

Ballina

875

Belleek has a quiet woodland setting, only minutes from Ballina, a famed salmon fishing centre. With excellent pitches and toilet block, the family owners are committed to ensuring that it is immaculate at all times. From the entrance gate, the park is approached by a drive that passes reception and leads to 58 well spaced pitches. With a very neat overall appearance, 32 pitches have hardstanding, 45 have electricity hook-ups, and you may choose your pitch. Sports facilities within a short distance of the park include a swimming pool, tennis and bicycle hire. Other local attractions are the Blue Flag beach at Ross, Ceide Fields (Neolithic farm), Down Patrick Head, Mayo North Heritage Centre or a seaweed bath at Kilcullen's Bath House, Enniscrone.

Facilities: Spotlessly clean, tastefully decorated toilet block providing showers (€0.70 token), baby sink and facilities for disabled people. Laundry sink, two washing machines and two dryers. TV room and games room with table tennis and football game. Campers' kitchen and emergency accommodation with beds provided. Children's play area, ball game area, basketball and tennis courts. New barbecue area. Reception includes a shop (June-Sept) and a tea room that also serves breakfasts. **Off site:** Fishing 1 km, bicycle hire 3 km.

Charges 2002

Per unit incl. 2 persons	€13.00
motorcyclist and tent	€6.00
hiker or cyclist and tent	€5.00
extra adult	€4.00
child	€1.50
electricity	€2.00

No credit cards. **Tel:** 096 71533. E-mail: lenahan@indigo.ie. **Reservations:** Contact park. **Open** 15 March - 8 October; by arrangement all year.

Directions: Take R314 Ballina - Killala road. Park is signed on right after approx. 1.75 miles.

To **telephone** the Irish Republic from the UK, replace the first `0' given in the number with the country code: 00 353.

eg. (094) 88100 becomes 00 353 94 88100.

Parkland Caravan & Camping Park
Westport House Country Park, Westport

877

Located in the grounds of an elegant country estate, this popular park offers the choice of a 'pitch only' booking, or a 'special deal' (min. stay 3 nights). This includes free admission to Westport House and children's animal and bird park, plus other activities, such as boating and fishing on the lake and river, pitch and putt, 'slippery dip', ball pond and 'supabounce', new play adventure world, hillside train rides and a flume ride. Stay one week or more and all the above are free, plus tennis, a par-3 golf course and 20% discount on bar food in the Horse and Wagon bar on the site. From Westport Quay, you enter the grounds of the estate by way of a tree lined road that crosses the river and leads to the site. In an attractive, sheltered area of the parkland, set in the trees, are 155 pitches. There are 65 with hardstanding and 76 electric hook-ups. The gate is closed 11.30 pm.- 9 am. with good site lighting around the site. If late, vehicles must be parked in the car park. Early in the season the site may not be fully prepared, and only minimal facilities may be available. Westport is an attractive town with splendid Georgian houses and traditional shop fronts. There are many good restaurants and pubs.

Facilities: Toilet facilities are provided at various points on the site, plus a 'super-loo' located in the farmyard buildings. Facilities for disabled people. Dishwashing and laundry sinks, washing machines and dryers plus free ironing facilities. Fifties style function room and bar with food and musical entertainment (all 1/6-31/8). No dogs are accepted. **Off site:** Within 5 km. of the estate are an 18 hole golf course and deep sea angling on Clew Bay.

Charges 2002

Per pitch excl. facilities	€23.00 - €35.00
hiker or cyclist incl. 2 persons	€17.00 - €19.00

Electricity incl. No credit cards. **Tel:** 098 27766. Fax: 098 25206. E-mail: camping@westporthouse.ie. **Reservations:** Contact park. **Open** 17 May - 8 September.

Directions: Take R335 Westport - Louisburgh road and follow signs for Westport Quay, then turn right into Westport House.

Lough Lannagh Caravan Park
Castlebar

881

Lough Lannagh is an attractive lakeshore holiday village which comprises quality accommodation, self catering cottages and a caravan park. It is within walking distance of Castlebar with its many restaurant, pubs and shops. County Mayo's main attractions are also within a short drive. The caravan park has 20 touring pitches, well laid out in a separate dedicated corner of the village, all on hardstanding with electric connections. One reception area serves all and is situated to the right of the security barrier. When not out and about, there are many on site activities for all the family. The main attraction is the fitness suite, sauna and steam room, plus reflexology and therapies available (over 18s only admitted to the gym). Popular with the young is the three times weekly club held in July/August. Anglers need only travel 500 m, or if you prefer cycling, bicycles can be hired.

Facilities: One modern heated sanitary block provides washbasins and well equipped, pre-set showers. En-suite unit for disabled people. Laundry room with sink, washing machines and dryers; dishwashing area. Café (serving breakfast). Fitness suite. Tennis. Table tennis. Bicycle hire.

Charges 2002

Per unit incl. all persons, electricity and hardstanding	€18.00 - €24.00
tent incl. 2 persons	€18.00

Tel: 094 27111. Fax: 094 27295. E-mail: llv@eircom. net. **Reservations:** Advised for high season; contact site. **Open** all year, excl. 22 Dec - 2 Jan.

Directions: To get to Castlebar take the N5, N60 or N84. At Castlebar ring road follow directions for Westport. Site is signed on all approach roads to the Westport roundabout.

Co. Mayo
Knock Caravan & Camping Park
878 Claremorris Road, Knock

This park is immediately south of the world famous shrine that receives many visitors. Comfortable and clean, the square shaped campsite is kept very neat with tarmac roads and surrounded by clipped trees. Of a decent size, the pitches accommodate 50 caravans or motorcaravans, 20 tents and 18 caravan holiday homes (for rent). All pitches have hardstanding (5 doubles) and there are 52 electrical connections (13A), with an adequate number of water points. There is also an overflow field. Because of the religious connections of the area, the site is very busy in August and indeed there are unlikely to be any vacancies at all for 14-16 August. Besides visiting the shrine and Knock Folk Museum, it is also a good centre for exploring scenic Co. Mayo.

Facilities: Two heated toilet blocks have good facilities for disabled visitors and a nice sized rest room attached, hot showers (on payment) and adequate washing and toilet facilities. Laundry and dishwashing room. Gas supplies. Playground. **Off site:** Fishing 3 miles, golf or riding 7 miles.

Charges 2002

Per unit	€12.00 - €13.00
hiker or cyclist incl. tent	€6.00 - €7.00
motorcylist incl. tent	€8.00 - €9.00
adult	€2.00
child	€1.00
electricity	€2.00

No credit cards. **Tel:** 094 88100. Fax: 094 88295. E-mail: info@knock-shrine.ie. **Reservations:** Taken for any length, no deposit, but see editorial for August. **Open** 1 March - 31 October.

Directions: Take N17 to the Knock site which is just south of the village. Camp site is well signed.

Co. Mayo
Carra Caravan & Camping Park
879 Belcarra, Castlebar

This is an ideal location for those seeking a real Irish village experience on a 'value for money' park. Small, unpretentious and family run, it is located in Belcarra, a regular winner of the 'Tidiest Mayo Village' award. Nestling at the foot of a wooded drumlin, it is surrounded by rolling hills and quiet roads which offer an away from it all feeling, yet Castlebar the county's largest town is only an 8 km. drive. On the pleasant 1.5 acre park, the 20 unmarked touring pitches, 14 with electric hook-up (13A), are on flat ground enclosed by ranch fencing and shaded in parts by trees. An additional novel idea at Carra are eight horse-drawn caravans for hire. Also of interest are the talks that the owner Sean and daughter Deirdre give on the area.

Facilities: The basic toilet block has adequate, well equipped showers (charged), Combined kitchen, dishwashing, laundry area with fridge/freezer, sink, table, chairs, washing machine and dryer. Comfortable lounge with TV, books and magazines located at reception. **Off site:** Village shops, a post office and cosy bar which serves Irish breakfast and where Irish stew is a speciality. Leisure centre and tennis courts. Free fishing area and special walkway to the river. Golf 8 km.

Charges 2002

Per unit incl. all persons	€8.00
electricity	€1.50

No credit cards. **Tel:** 094 32054. Fax: 094 32351. E-mail: post@ mayoholidays.com. **Reservations:** Contact park. **Open** 8 June - 21 September.

Directions: From Castlebar take N60 Claremorris road for 8.5 km. southeast and turn right at sign for Belcarra. Continue for 4.5 km. to village and site on left at end of village.

Co. Westmeath
Lough Ree (East) Caravan & Camping Park
896 Ballykeeran, Athlone

This touring park is alongside the river, screened by trees but reaching the water's edge. Drive into the small village of Ballykeeran and the park is discreetly located behind the main street. The top half of the site is in a woodland situation and after the reception and sanitary block, Lough Ree comes into view and the remaining pitches run down to the shoreline. There are 60 pitches, 20 with hardstanding and 52 with electricity. With fishing right on the doorstep there are boats for hire and the site has its own private mooring buoys, plus a dinghy slip and harbour. A restaurant and 'singing' pub are close.

Facilities: The toilet block is clean without being luxurious. Hot showers (charged). Dishwashing sinks are outside. New laundry room. A wooden chalet houses a pool room and campers' kitchen. **Off site:** Golf or riding 4 km.

Charges 2002

Per adult	€4.00
child (under 14 yrs)	€2.00
pitch	€3.00 - €6.00
electricity	€3.00

No credit cards. **Tel:** 0902 78561. Fax: 0902 77017. E-mail: athlonecamping@eircom.net. **Reservations:** Contact park for details. **Open** 1 April - 2 October.

Directions: From Athlone take N55 towards Longford for 4.8 km. Park is in the village of Ballykeeran, clearly signed.

The Táin Holiday Village

Carlingford Lough, Omeath

889

This holiday complex is one of the most extensive in Ireland and is exactly what a family seeking non-stop entertainment might want. The touring park is within the 10-acre fun packed holiday village, overlooking Carlingford Lough with views towards the Mourne mountains, whilst nestling at the foot of the Cooley mountains. The area for tourers is situated to the far right of the main buildings with entry through a security gate (deposit required for key). There are 87 pitches with hardstanding and electrical hook-ups, plus 10 pitches for tents. Young trees are planted and will eventually add more detail to this well laid out, but open site. Included in the site fees is the use of the 40,000 sq.ft. of indoor leisure facilities. These include a heated pool with slides, flumes and rafts, an indoor water play pool, an indoor play area with free fall, ball pool, climbing room and nets, also a sports hall, gym and games room, a jacuzzi, steam room and sun beds. Not least at Táin is a hands-on Science Interactive Centre.

Facilities: The fully equipped sanitary block is kept clean and can be heated. Facilities for disabled visitors. Dishwashing and laundry sinks. Washing machines and iron. Motorcaravan services. Licensed restaurant with varied menus. Good bar and lounge (all limited opening outside July/Aug). Indoor swimming pool complex (4-9 pm daily), indoor play area and sports hall. Outdoor activities include two adventure playgrounds, tennis courts and watersports. **Off site:** Fishing, bicycle hire or riding 2 km, golf 5 km.

Charges 2002

Per unit incl. 2 persons

(fully serviced pitch)	€19.00 - €21.00
tent on grass area	€17.00 - €19.00
extra person	€4.00 - €5.00

Min. 2 nights in high season; for 1 night only prices are higher. **Tel:** 042 9375385. Fax: 042 9375417. E-mail: tainhol@eircom.net. **Reservations:** Made with deposit. **Open** 17 March - 31 October.

Directions: From Newry take B79/R173 road signed Omeath. Site is 1.6 km. south of Omeath village, on the left.

Green Gables Caravan & Camping Park

Geashill, Tullamore

906

A peaceful, relaxing environment in the heart of Ireland's Bogland, Green Gables enjoys a natural meadow-like setting in keeping with the wide open countryside that enhances this county. This park is maturing and offers top class facilities but most importantly, a friendly reception - in fact, here you experience Irish hospitality at its best. From the park entrance the drive leads to a parking area, clearly defined by a roundabout and a huge Ice Age stone from Boora Bog, known as 'Mona'. Reception, the Gables tea rooms and a patio area lie to the right, approached by a gateway and gravel path. Apart from 8 hardstanding pitches towards the rear of the park, the remainder are on grass. Electric hook-ups (10A) are provided on 20 pitches and tents are catered for. The ground is gently sloping and the perimeter is surrounded by hedging. Getting out of the village can mean taking a train from Portarlington station to Dublin city. If preferring the countryside there are cycle tours, the Grand Canal walking routes or a Bog Train tour through the historic bogland, one of Offaly's many attractions.

Facilities: The spotlessly clean heated toilet block is well cared for and includes baby changing space. There are excellent facilities for disabled people, a laundry area and a washing up sink. Motorcaravan service point. Gas supplies. **Off site:** The village of Geashill is 50 m. with old houses, stone walls, shops and three pubs. The proprietor at Hamilton's welcomes Green Gables campers in his pub where Irish culture abounds. Riding 5 km, fishing, bicycle hire or golf 10 km.

Charges 2002

Per unit	€11.00
small tent	€8.00
adult	€1.50
child	€0.75
hiker or cyclist and tent	€6.50
electricity (10A)	€2.00

No credit cards. **Tel:** 0506 43760. Fax: 0506 43760. E-mail: ggcp@iol.ie. **Reservations:** Contact park. **Open** Easter - 31 September.

Directions: From Tullamore take R420 east for 12 km. to village of Geashill. Site is on right at end of village.

Shankill Caravan and Camping Park

Shankhill

Shankill is a long-established park that makes an excellent overnight halt within easy reach of Dublin Port and Dun Laoghaire ferries. It also makes an ideal base for visiting Dublin with a bus departing from the site entrance every 15 minutes. The Dart fast train also leaves from Shankill village at 15 minute intervals. With lovely views of the Dublin mountains, the site is set in pleasant grounds with an abundance of mature trees, shrubs and well kept flower beds which gives it a park-like appearance. Additionally there are broad tarmac roads and night lighting. There are 82 unmarked pitches, 66 of which are for tourers. Some have hardstanding and 40 have electric hook-ups (10A). Reception staff are pleasant, helpful and willing to give advice on visiting the city or local tourist spots.

Facilities: The two sanitary blocks, although showing signs of age and certainly not ultra modern, offer basic but adequate facilities which are kept clean, with piping hot water to sinks and showers (on €1 payment). Laundry sinks, ironing facilities and dishwashing area. Basic foodstuffs such as milk, bread etc. can be purchased at reception. No double-axle vans are permitted. **Off site:** The site is located within a three minute walk of the village with shops, restaurants, supermarkets. The seaside resort of Bray is a 5 minute drive.

Charges 2002

Per unit	€11.00 - €12.00
adult	€2.00
child	€1.00
hiker or cyclist's tent	€8.00 - €9.00
tent and motorcycle	€11.00 - €12.00
electricity	€2.00

Tel: 01 282 0011. Fax: 01 282 0108. E-mail: shankillcaravan@eircom.net. **Reservations:** Not possible in advance. **Open** all year.

Directions: Site is 15 km. south of Dublin off the N11. From Dublin take N11 Wexford road for 15 km. and turn left at Bray, Shankill sign. Then follow signs to site on right.

Camac Valley Tourist Caravan & Camping Park

Naas Road, Clondalkin, Dublin 22

Opened in '96, this campsite is not only well placed for Dublin, but also offers a welcome stopover if travelling to the more southern counties from the north of the country, or vice versa. Despite its close proximity to the city, being located in the 300 acre Corkagh Park gives it a 'heart of the country' atmosphere. The site entrance and sign are distinctive and can be spotted in adequate time when approaching on the busy N7. Beyond the entrance gate and forecourt stands an attractive timber fronted building. Its design includes various roof levels and spacious interior layout, with large windows offering a view of the site. Housed here is reception, information, reading, TV and locker rooms plus shop and sanitary facilities. There are 163 pitches, 48 for tents placed to the fore and the hardstandings for caravans laid out in bays and avenues with electrical connections (10A), drainage and water points. Young trees separate pitches and roads are of tarmac. After a day of sightseeing in Dublin, which can be reached by bus from the site, Camac Valley offers an evening of relaxation with woodland and river walks in the park or a number of first class restaurants and pubs nearby.

Facilities: Heated sanitary facilities include good sized showers (token), facilities for disabled people, baby changing room, laundry and washing up. Children's playground with wooden play frames and safety base. Shop and coffee bar (open June, July and August). Automatic gate and 24 hour security. Dogs are not accepted in July/Aug. **Off site:** Fishing 8 km, bicycle hire 1.5 km, riding 9 km, golf 6 km.

Charges 2002

Per unit incl. 2 adults	€13.00 - €17.00
incl. 2 adults and up to 4 children	€14.00 - €19.00
extra adult	€3.00
extra child	€2.00
motorcyclist, cyclist or hiker and tent (per person)	€6.00 - €7.00
electricity	€3.00

Tel: 01 4640644. Fax: 01 4640643. E-mail: camacmorriscastle@eircom.net. **Reservations:** Advance bookings necessary (max. stay operates at certain times). **Open** all year.

Directions: From north follow signs for West Link and M50 motorway. Exit M50 at junction 9 onto N7 Cork road. Site is on right of dual carriageway (beside Green Isle Hotel) after 2 km. and is clearly signed. At City West business park, cross over bridge and return on dual-carriageway following camp signs - site is on left after 800 m.

Roundwood Caravan & Camping Park
Roundwood

In the heart of the Wicklow mountains, this park is under new management, but still maintains high standards. It is neatly laid out with rows of trees dividing the different areas and giving an attractive appearance. There are 31 hardstanding pitches for caravans and 8 motorcaravans, all with electricity (6A), plus 40 pitches for tents, arranged off tarmac access roads. There are excellent walks around the Varty Lakes and a daily bus service to Dublin city. Close by are the Wicklow and Sally Gap, Glendalough, Powerscourt Gardens, plus many other places of natural beauty. Apart from its scenic location, this site is well placed for the ferry ports.

Facilities: The newly renovated sanitary block is kept clean, with adequate washing and toilet facilities, plus spacious showers on payment. The block also houses two dishwashing sinks and good laundry facilities, but ask at reception as machines are not self service. Motorcaravan service point. Campers' kitchen and dining room. TV room. Children's adventure playground. Bicycle hire. **Off site:** Roundwood village has shops, pubs restaurants, takeaway food, and a Sunday market. Fishing or golf 1 km.

Charges 2002
Per unit	€8.90 - €10.20
adult	€2.55
child (under 14 yrs)	€1.90
electricity	€1.90

No credit cards. **Tel:** 01 2818163. Fax: 01 2818196. E-mail: roundwoodcaravancamp@yahoo.co.uk. **Reservations:** Accepted without deposit and advisable for July/Aug. **Open** 31 March - 1 October.

Directions: Turn off N11 Dublin - Wexford road at Kilmacanogue towards Glendalough and then 15 km. to Roundwood.

Valley Stopover & Caravan Park
Killough, Kilmacanogue

In a quiet, idyllic setting in the picturesque Rocky Valley, this small, neat, family run park is convenient for the Dublin ferries. Situated in the grounds of the family home, covering three-quarters of an acre, it can be used either as a transit site or for a longer stay. It will appeal to those who prefer the more basic 'CL' type site. There are 15 grassy pitches, 11 with electric hook-ups, 3 hardstandings, 2 water points, night lighting and a security gate. Staying put here you are only minutes from Enniskerry which lies in the glen of the Glencullen river. Here you can enjoy a delight of forest walks, or visit Powerscourt, one of the loveliest gardens in Ireland. To be at the sea, travel 6 km. to Bray and you are in one of the oldest seaside resorts in the country.

Facilities: Toilet facilities, clean when we visited, are housed in one unit and consist of two WCs with washbasins, mirrors, etc. and a shower on payment. Dishwashing and laundry sink, a spin dryer and a campers' kitchen. Full cooked Irish breakfast is available in the family guest house. **Off site:** Fishing 16 km, bicycle hire 7 km (can be delivered), riding 3 km, golf 7 km.

Charges 2002
Per caravan or tent with car	€8.00
motorcaravan	€7.00
tent with bike	€3.50
electricity	€1.00
awning	€1.00

No credit cards. **Tel:** 01 2829565. E-mail: suzier@gofree.indigo.ie. **Reservations:** Advised for July/Aug. **Open** Easter - 31 October.

Directions: Turn off N11 Dublin - Wexford road at Kilmacanogue, following signs for Glendalough. Continue for 1.6 km and take right fork signed 'Waterfall'. Park is first opening on the left in approx. 200 m.

River Valley Caravan & Camping Park

Redcross Village

In the small country village of Redcross, in the heart of County Wicklow, you will find this popular, family run park. Based here you are within easy reach of beauty spots such as the Vale of Avoca (Ballykissangel), Glendalough and Powerscourt, plus the safe beach of Brittas Bay. The 95 touring pitches at River Valley are mostly together in a dedicated area, all have electricity connections (6A) and offer a choice of hardstanding or grass - you select your pitch. Within this 16-acre site children can find day long amusement, whether it be Fort Apache, the adventure playground, the tiny tots playground, or at the natural mountain stream where it is safe to paddle. There is also a pets corner with a 'fat belly pig'. An attractive wine and coffee bar with a conservatory is inviting, or an alternative may be the restaurant where home-made, traditional dishes are on the menu (1/6-31/8). The late arrivals area has electricity hook-ups, water and night lighting.

Facilities: A luxurious new sanitary block has a modern, well designed appearance. Facilities for disabled visitors are excellent. Showers are on payment (€0.50). Laundry area. Campers' kitchen. Motorcaravan service points. Gas available. Wine/coffee bar and restaurant. TV and games room. Three tennis courts. Par 3 golf course. Bowling green. Sports complex with badminton courts and indoor football and basketball. Adventure and tiny tots playgrounds. Area allocated for rallies. Caravan storage. No dogs are accepted in July/Aug.

Charges 2002

Per unit incl. 2 adults	€13.00 - €15.00
small tent	€11.00 - €12.00
extra adult	€3.00
child (under 15 yrs)	€1.00
motorcyclist, cyclist or hiker and tent	€7.00 - €8.00
electricity	€2.00

Tel: 0404 41647. **Fax:** 0404 41677. **E-mail:** info@rivervalleypark.ie. **Reservations:** Made with deposit. **Open** 14 March - 21 September.

Directions: From Dublin follow N11 Wexford road. Turn right in Rathnew and left under railway bridge onto the Wexford - Arklow road. Continue for 11 km. and turn right at Doyle's Pub. Park is in Redcross village, under 5 km.

Moat Farm Caravan and Camping Park

Donard

Providing a true feel of the countryside, this park is part of a working sheep farm. It offers incredible vistas across a scenic landscape, yet is within driving distance of Dublin and Rosslare. Driving into the village of Donard you little suspect that alongside the main street lies a pleasant, well cared for and tranquil five-acre campsite. The entrance is approached by way of a short road where the ruins of a Medieval church sit high overlooking the forecourt and reception. There are 40 pitches for caravans and tents. Spacious pitches with hardstanding line both sides of a broad avenue, incorporating ample space for awning and all with 10A electricity and drainage points. A large field takes tents and further caravans. The site makes a good base for touring or going on foot, for this area is a walker's paradise with a 30 minute circular walk around the perimeter of the site.

Facilities: The toilet block is kept very clean and includes spacious showers, facilities for visitors with disabilities, and a well equipped laundry room. There is a good quality campers' kitchen and a large recreation/entertainment room with an open fire. Three large barbecues and a patio area are provided. Caravan storage. **Off site:** Mountain climbing or sites of archaeological interest nearby. Fishing 3 km, bicycle hire 15 km, golf 13 km.

Charges 2002

Per caravan, motorcaravan or family tent	€11.00
adult	€1.50
child	€0.75
tent (1 or 2 persons)	€8.00
motorcyclist, cyclist or hiker incl. tent	€7.00
electricity	€2.00

No credit cards. **Tel:** 045 404727. **Fax:** 045 404727. **E-mail:** moatfarm@ireland.com. **Reservations:** Contact site. **Open** 1 March - 31 October.

Directions: Park is 16.5 km. south of Blessington. Leave M50 Dublin ring motorway at exit 10 to join N81 southwest for 19 km. to Blessington. Continue on N81 for a further 16.5 km. And turn left at Old Toll House pub onto local road and follow signs to park in Donard village (3.5 km.)

Forest Farm Caravan and Camping Park

Dublin Road, Athy

This site makes an excellent stopover if travelling from Dublin to the southeast counties. It is signed on the N78 and approached by a 500 m. avenue of tall pines. Part of a working farm, the campsite spreads to the right of the modern farmhouse, which also provides B&B. The owners have cleverly utilised their land to create a site which offers 64 unmarked touring pitches on level ground. Of these, 32 are for caravans, all with 16A electricity connections and 10 with hardstanding, and 32 places are available for tents. Full Irish breakfasts are served at the farmhouse and farm tours are arranged on request.

Facilities: The centrally located, red brick toilet block is heated and double glazed, providing quality amenities including a spacious shower unit for disabled visitors, a family room with shower and WC. It also houses a laundry room, a campers' kitchen with dishwashing sinks, a fridge/freezer, cooker, table and chairs and a comfortable lounge/games room (a TV can be provided). Basketball net, sand pit and picnic tables. **Off site:** Golf courses nearby. Course and game fishing 4 km.

Charges 2002

Per unit incl. 2 adults	€9.00
1 or 2 person tent per person	€5.00
extra adult	€1.50
child	€0.50
hiker, cyclist or motorcyclist incl. tent	€5.00
electricity	€2.00

Tel: 0507 31231. Fax: 0507 31231. E-mail: forestfarm@eircom.net. **Reservations:** Contact site. **Open** all year.

Directions: Site is 4.8 km. northeast of Athy town off the main N78 Athy - Kilcullen road.

Tree Grove Caravan & Camping Park

Danville House, Kilkenny

The entrance gate to this small family run site is easily spotted off the R700 road. Tree Grove is within walking distance of medieval Kilkenny, known for its elegance and famed for its beer and cats. An orderly, neat park, it has instant appeal because its young owners are friendly and have insisted on a logical layout to suit both the terrain and campers needs. It is terraced with the lower terrace to the right of the wide sweeping driveway laid out with 11 hardstanding pitches for caravans. All 30 pitches have electrical hook-ups (10A) and plenty of water points are to be found. On a higher level is a grass area for hikers and cyclists with further caravan and tent pitches sited near the elevated sanitary block. If needed more grass pitches face reception, which is temporarily housed in a mobile unit. Whilst there are mature trees at the entrance and around the site perimeter, many shrubs have been effectively placed together with flower troughs. On the patio there are bench seats with tables and umbrellas. Tents to rent on site. There is much to see and do around the ancient city of Kilkenny (1.5 km) with its cobbled streets and castle. County Touring Routes are worth following.

Facilities: House plants add decoration inside the toilet block giving a cared for look to this modern building which includes a family room with shower, WC and washbasin which can be used by disabled people. Laundry room. Open, covered kitchen for campers with fridge, work-top, sink and electric kettle adjoins a comfortable games/TV room with pool table, and easy chairs. Bicycle hire. **Off site:** Fishing 500 m, riding 1 km. Golf 2 or 15 km.

Charges 2003

Per unit incl. 2 persons	€13.50
1 man tent	€7.00
2 man tent	€11.00
extra adult or child	€1.50
electricity	€2.00
awning	€1.00

No credit cards. No credit cards. **Tel:** 056 70302. Fax: 056 21512. E-mail: treecc@iol.ie. **Reservations:** Contact site. **Open** 1 March - 15 November.

Directions: Travelling north on the N10 Waterford - Kilkenny Road turn right at roundabout on ring road. Continue to 2nd roundabout and turn right onto R700. Site is 150 m. on right.

Nore Valley Park

Annamult, Bennettsbridge

923

This lovely site is set on a grassy hillock overlooking the valley and the river Nore, with a woodland setting behind. Situated on a working farm, it offers 60 pitches, 30 for caravans and motorcaravans, all with electrical hook-up and hardstanding. The owners pride themselves on their home baking and farm produce and during high season cooked breakfasts are available in the small café. An attractive courtyard houses several unusual facilities including a sand pit, pedal go-karts, tractor rides and a straw loft play area for wet weather. This is an ideal park for families, offering children and adults alike the opportunity to feed the animals (goats, lambs, ducks, chickens, and donkey). It is 11 km. from Kilkenny, renowned for its castle, history and crafts, and 3 km. from the village of Bennettsbridge, where there are shops and eating places. Note: the tractor rides, go-karts and the café are closed on Sundays.

Facilities: The modern toilet block is kept spotlessly clean and can be heated. Two units suitable for disabled visitors. Dishwashing sinks. Laundry room with washing machine and dryer. Motorcaravan services. The original block in the courtyard is used mainly in the low season. New reception, shop (basic items such as milk, bread and camping gaz) and café (June-Aug). Comfortable lounge. Games room with pool table. Fenced children's play area. Crazy golf. Bicycle hire. **Off site:** Outdoor pursuits nearby such as canoeing, walking or fishing (4 km). Riding 6 km. Golf 10 km.

Charges 2003

Per person over 2 yrs	€2.00
caravan	€10.50
family tent	€10.00
motorcaravan	€9.50
2 person tent	€7.00
3-4 person tent	€8.50
awning or extra small tent	€2.50
electricity (6A)	€2.00

Tel: 056 27229. Fax: 056 27748. E-mail: norevalleypark@eircom.net. **Reservations:** Contact park. **Open** 1 March - 31 October.

Directions: From Kilkenny take R700 to Bennettsbridge. Just before the bridge turn right at sign for Stoneyford and after approx. 3 km. site is signed Nore Valley Park.

Morriscastle Strand Caravan Park

Morriscastle, Kilmuckridge

930

Whether you use this park as a stopover, to or from Rosslare Port, or choose it for a longer stay, you will find it to be a quiet relaxing location. Note, however, that the park no longer accepts tents. Situated minutes from the pretty village of Kilmuckridge it offers well maintained and clean facilities. There are 145 privately owned caravan holiday homes on site but these are unobtrusive and kept separate by high hedging. The entrance to the touring park is to the right of reception by way of a tarmac drive. This leads to the secluded, gently sloping, grass pitches which enjoy an open aspect. They overlook marshland which attracts wild geese and ducks, whilst the sea brings in crabs, eels and fish. To the right of the site lie the sand-hills and pathways to the beach which is supervised by lifeguards in high season. The 100 pitches are numbered and marked by concrete slabs, each with an electrical hook-up (5A) and drainage point. Spacing can be a little tight in high season when the park gets very busy. Kilmuckridge is approximately 3 km. with an assortment of shops, pubs offering nightly entertainment and top class restaurants, such as The Rafters, a picturesque spot which helps characterise this charming village.

Facilities: Two toilet blocks house all the toilet facilities, including unisex showers (on €1 payment). There is provision for disabled people, a baby bath, kitchen, dishwashing area, launderette, and outside cold showers. Good night lighting. Shop, snacks and takeaway in high season. Games room. Two tennis courts. Football field and children's play area. Dogs are only accepted in certain areas. Tents are not accepted. **Off site:** Golf 5 km.

Charges 2003

Per unit incl. 2 persons	€15.00 - €18.00
family unit incl. 4 children	€17.00 - €20.00
extra person	€5.00
child (under 7 yrs)	€3.00
awning	€3.00
electricity	€2.00

Tel: 053 30124 or 30212 (off season 01 4952219). Fax: 053 30365. E-mail: camacmorriscastle@eircom.net. **Reservations:** Made with deposit; contact site by phone or letter (use off season number Oct - April). **Open** 2 May - 28 September.

Directions: Site is 25 km. east of Enniscorthy. Travelling south on N11 Dublin/Wexford road branch onto R741 at Gorey. Continue for 19 km. to Ballyedmund. Turn left at petrol station and follow signs for Kilmuckridge and site.

Newtown Cove Camping & Caravan Park

934 Tramore

Well run and friendly, this small park is only five minutes walk from the beautiful Newton Cove. It offers views of the famous and historic Metal Man and is 2.5 km. from Tramore beach and 11 km. from Waterford. Neatly set out on gently sloping grass with an abundance of shrubs and bushes, there are 40 pitches. All have electrical connections (10A), some hardstanding also, with access by well lit tarmac roads. There are around 50 privately owned caravan holiday homes. A modern building at the entrance houses reception, the amenities and further sanitary facilities. The village of Tramore, with a wide range of shops and eating houses, is close and there is a choice of many delightful cliff walks in the immediate vicinity.

Facilities: The main sanitary block at the bottom end of the site is not very modern but has been retiled and provides good facilities including a bathroom. Showers on payment (token from reception). Also here are a campers' kitchen with cooking facilities, lounge, dishwashing room and small laundry. Small shop (1/7-30/8). TV room. Games room. Small children's play area in centre of park. **Off site:** Golf 800 m. Fishing 400 m, riding 3 km.

Charges 2002

Per unit incl. 2 persons	€12.50 - €14.00
extra adult	€1.50 - €2.00
child	free - €1.50
hiker, cyclist or motorcyclist	€5.00 - €6.50
awning	€1.50 - €2.50
electricity	€2.00

No credit cards. No single sex groups. **Tel:** 051 381979. E-mail: newtown_cove@iol.ie. **Reservations:** Not necessary or accepted but for information contact park. **Open** Easter, then 1 May - 30 September.

Directions: From Tramore on R675 coast road to Dungarvan. Turn left 2 km. from town centre, following signs.

Casey's Caravan Park

933 Clonea, Dungarvan

Set on 20 acres of flat grass, edged by mature trees, this family run park offers 284 pitches which include 154 touring pitches, 118 with electrical hook-ups (5A) and 30 with hardstanding. The remainder are occupied by caravan holiday homes. There is direct access from the park to a sandy, Blue Flag beach with a resident lifeguard during July/Aug. A highly recommended leisure centre is adjacent should the weather be inclement. The park is 5.5 km. from Dungarvan, a popular town for deep sea angling, from which charter boats can be hired and three 18 hole golf courses are within easy distance. Recommended drives include the scenic Vee, the Comeragh Drive and the coast road to Tramore.

Facilities: The central toilet block (key system), has good facilities kept spotlessly clean, with showers on payment (€1), washing up sinks and small laundry with machine and dryer. A further luxurious and modern block provides an excellent campers' kitchen, laundry room and toilet for disabled visitors. Large children's adventure play area with bark surface in its own field (not supervised by staff). Games room with pool table, table tennis and amusements. TV lounge. Crazy golf. Gas supplies. Full time security staff in high season. **Off site:** Two village stores near the beach. Golf.

Charges 2002

Per unit incl. all persons	€16.50
hiker, cyclist or m/cyclist incl. tent	€6.35
electricity	€1.50

No credit cards. **Tel:** 058 41919. **Reservations:** Are made in low season, but not between 9 July - 15 Aug; contact park. **Open** 3 May - 14 September.

Directions: From Dungarvan centre follow R675 east for 3.5 km. Look for signs on the right to Clonea Bay and site. Site is approx. 1.5 km.

★ ★ ★ ★
△ ⚷ ♿

Casey's Caravan & Camping Park

Clonea, Dungarvan, Co Waterford Tel: 058 41919

Top class facilities	Two ablution blocks
Playground	with laundry & kitchen
Electric sites for tents & tourers (5A)	Games room and TV room
Dungarvan town 3fi miles	EU Blue Flag beach
Choice of scenic views to visit	Two nearby shops with takeaway
Adjacent hotel with 19 metre pool	Deep sea and river angling
and leisure centre with bowling alley	18 hole golf course in easy reach

Streamstown Caravan & Camping Park

Streamstown, Roscrea

942

This family run site, set on a dairy farm in the centre of Ireland, is conveniently situated off the N7 Dublin - Limerick road. It makes a good overnight halt or for a longer stay if you are seeking a quiet, restful location with little to disturb the peace. This is a working farm and the owners, who are friendly and welcoming, are in the process of improving and developing their site. What impresses most here is the tidy overall appearance with neatly trimmed hedging, tables placed around the grass areas and with flower baskets a special feature. There are 27 pitches, 10 with hardstanding and separated by low hedges. The remainder are on grass and more suitable for units with awnings. Nearby pubs offer traditional music evenings and mountain walking and fishing can be enjoyed in the area.

Facilities: The sanitary facilities, which were of an acceptable level of cleanliness when we visited, are housed in a modern block, although showers, toilets and washbasins are of the older type and slightly out of keeping with the outside appearance. Good camper's kitchen with fridge/freezer and electric cooker. Good quality children's play area with safety surface. TV and pool room.

Charges 2002

Per unit	€8.25
adult	€2.54
child	€1.27
motorcyclist, cyclist or hiker incl. tent	€7.62
electricity (10A)	€1.90

Tel: 0505 21519. Fax: 0505 21519. E-mail: streamstowncaravanpark@eircom.net. **Reservations:** Contact site. **Open** 1 April - 1 November.

Directions: From Roscrea centre follow signs for R491 Shirone. Continue towards Shirone following camp signs for approx. 2.5 km and site entrance is on left.

Carrick-on-Suir Camping & Caravan Park

Carrick-on-Suir

939

This memorable site is not only conveniently situated off the main N24 between Waterford and Clonmel, but its owner, Frank O'Dwyer, is an excellent ambassador for his county. On his quiet, family run site campers are guaranteed the finest example of 'Cead Mile Failte' it is possible to encounter - personal attention and advice on where to go and what to see in the area is all part of the service. The entrance to the park is immediately past the O'Dwyers' shop, through a gate which is closed at 11 pm. The tarmac drive leads past tall hedges and well kept shrubs to the right and several caravan holiday homes (for hire) to the left. The touring park lies to the rear with scenic views to the wooded hills. At present there are 40 level pitches, 33 with electricity (6/10A) and several with hardstanding, but this number is to be extended. What makes this site distinctive is its excellent, well designed sanitary block which has a sparkling clean freshness. Within a short drive is the 'magic road', the Mahon Falls, a slate quarry or a romantic river walk. Carrick is well placed en-route to the west, only 90 minutes from Rosslare.

Facilities: Toilet facilities are kept clean and fresh with plenty of hot water. Showers cost 50p. Laundry room with washing machine. Camper's kitchen with dishwashing area and TV (no cooker). Motorcaravan service point. Good grocery shop with a hot snacks to take away and a selection of fine wines. Gas supplies. Good night lighting. **Off site:** Fishing 1 km, riding 6 km, golf 3 km. Carrick town centre is five minutes walk for shops, pubs, restaurants, etc. plus a castle which is open to the public.

Charges 2002

Per unit incl. 2 adults	€17.00
extra adult	€3.50
child	€3.00
electricity	€2.00
hiker/cyclist incl. tent	€4.00

Tel: 051 640461. E-mail: coscamping@eircom.net. **Reservations:** Contact site. **Open** 1 March - 1 November.

Directions: Approaching town on N24 road, follow signs for R690 in the direction of Kilkenny. Site is north of town, clearly signed at junction with R697.

The Apple Camping & Caravan Park

Moorstown, Cahir

This fruit farm and campsite combination offers an idyllic country holiday venue in one of the most delightful situations imaginable. For tourers only, it is located off the N24, midway between Clonmel and Cahir. Entrance is by way of a 300 m. drive which follows straight through the heart of the farm. Apple trees guard the route, as do various non-fruit tree species, which are named and of interest to guests who are free to spend time walking the paths around the farm. When we visited, strawberries were being gathered - the best we had tasted all season. Reception is housed with the other site facilities in a large farmyard barn. Although a rather unusual arrangement, it is very effective. The 32 pitches are in a secluded situation behind the barns and are mostly grass with a few hardstandings, with electricity connections (13A) to 24. The towns of Cahir and Clonmel are of historic interest and the countryside around boasts rivers, mountains, Celtic culture and scenic drives.

Facilities: Toilet facilities, kept very clean, quite modern in design and with heating, comprise showers, washbasins with mirrors, electric points, etc. in functional units occupying two corners of the large floor space with an attractive, well maintained appearance. Facilities for disabled visitors. Also in the barn are dishwashing sinks, washing machine and a fridge/freezer for campers to use. Motorcaravan service point. Tennis court, basketball/football pitch and play area. Dogs are not accepted. **Off site:** Fishing, golf, bicycle hire and riding within 6 km.

Charges 2002

Per person	€4.50 - €5.00
child (0-12 yrs)	€2.50 - €3.00
electricity	€2.00

No charge per unit. Less 20% for groups of 4 or more. No credit cards. **Tel:** 052 41459. Fax: 052 42774. E-mail: con.traas@ theapplefarm.com. **Reservations:** Contact site. **Open** 1 May - 30 September.

Directions: Park is 300 m. off main N24, 9.6 km. northwest of Clonmel, 6.4 km. southeast of Cahir.

Parsons Green Caravan & Camping Park

Clogheen

In a tranquil and scenic location, this small, family run park commands panoramic views toward the Vee Gap and Knockmealdown Mountains. In open style, surrounded by low ranch fencing, it offers 34 pitches with hardstanding for caravans and motorcaravans and 10 on grass, all with electrical connections (6A), plus 20 pitches for tents. There is a range of things to do and see including a garden area, river walks, picnic area, an extensive farm museum, a pet field with selection of domestic and rare animals and birds, pony and trap rides, boating on the small lake and trout fishing river. If not sitting back enjoying the scenic surroundings or participating in the many activities, there is much to see and do in this area. The manager at Parson's Green would be more than pleased to pinpoint places of interest.

Facilities: Toilet facilities to the top right of the site close to reception are kept clean and include good facilities for disabled people (shower and toilet). Laundry area with washing machines, dryer and sinks, plus dishwashing sinks. Coffee shop and takeaway. Children's playground. Minigolf. Fishing. TV/games room. Campers' kitchen and function room. **Off site:** Village within 500 m. (footpath and lighting) with shops, pubs, bank, post office, etc. Riding and golf 8 miles.

Charges 2002

Per caravan, family tent or motorcaravan	€6.50
small tent	€5.00
adult	€2.60
child	€1.30
awning	€1.30
electricity	€1.30
hardstanding	€1.50

Tel: 052 65290. Fax: 052 65504. E-mail: pjkn@ eircom.net. **Reservations:** Contact site. **Open** all year.

Directions: Site is in the village of Clogheen, 200 m. off the R665, 24 km. west of Clonmel, 19 km. east of Mitchelstown.

Curraghchase Caravan & Camping Park

945 c/o Coillte Teoranta, Plassey Technological Park, Limerick

Approached by a long, tree-lined avenue that sets it well back from the main road, this tranquil 39 acre park is set in 600 acres of beech forest (known as the Coillte Forest Park), 21 km. from Limerick City. Touring pitches have hardstanding with drainage and electric hook-ups, with a separate grassy area allocated for 40 tents. Behind the main block is a small 'sun trap' picnic area. There are many lovely forest walks, a nature trail and a number of rare orchids can be found. Adjacent to the site are the ruins of Curragh (or Currah) Chase House, once the home of the poet Aubrey de Vere, set in parkland with lakes and making a lovely place to wander.

Facilities: One large building houses the amenities including clean, but basic, toilet facilities. Hot water is free and showers are separated by a partition, sharing a large base with single drain and a communal dressing area with hooks and benches. There is also a small shop for essentials, a TV lounge with wood-burning stove, a games room and a good campers' kitchen with dishwashing sinks. Small laundry with washing machines, dryers and iron. Children's play area with a bark safety base. **Off site:** Fishing, riding, golf and Adare village, with its interesting historical buildings and shopping facilities, are within 10 km.

Charges 2002

Per caravan or family tent	€15.00
tent incl. 1 or 2 persons	€10.00
electricity	€2.00

No credit cards. **Tel:** 061 396349. Fax: 061 338271. E-mail: okeeffe_e@coillte.ie. **Reservations:** Advisable in high season - contact site. **Open** 1 May - 10 September.

Directions: From Limerick city take N69 Foynes road; park entrance is at Kilcornan. Park also signed from Adare on the N20.

Blarney Caravan & Camping Park

948 Stone View, Blarney

There is a heart of the country feel about this 'on the farm' site, yet the city of Cork is only an 8 km. drive. What makes this friendly, family run park so appealing is its secluded location and neatly laid out, open appearance. The terrain on the three acre park is elevated and gently sloping, commanding views towards Blarney Castle and the surrounding mountainous countryside. The 40 pitches, 30 of which have hardstanding and 10A electrical connections, are with caravans sited to the centre and left and tents pitched to the right. There are gravel roads, well tended young shrubs, and a screen of mature trees and hedging marks the park's perimeter. In the Blarney area, apart from the castle, house and gardens, there are shops, restaurants, pubs with traditional music and an abundance of outdoor pursuits such as walking, riding and fishing.

Facilities: Well kept toilet areas, one new, are housed in converted farm buildings with reception and small shop. Facilities for disabled visitors. Laundry room with sinks, washing machine, dryer and ironing. Dishwashing area in the large campers' kitchen. Motorcaravan service point. Shop (1/6-31/8). TV lounge. 18 hole golf and pitch and putt course. Night lighting. **Off site:** Public bar and restaurant 100 m. serving food all day. Within easy reach of the ports of Cork and Rosslare.

Charges 2003

Per caravan, family tent or motorhome	€6.50 - €8.00
car and small tent	€5.50 - €6.50
adult	€4.00
child	€2.00
hiker/cyclist and tent	€5.50 - €6.00
motorcyclist (per person)	€5.50 - €6.00
electricity	€3.00
awning	€1.50 - €2.00

7 nights for price of 6, if pre-paid. **Tel:** 021 451 6519. Fax: 021 438 5167. E-mail: con.quill@camping-ireland.ie. **Reservations:** Contact park. **Open** 1 February - 15 November.

Directions: Site is 8 km. northwest of Cork, just off the N20. Take N20 from Cork for approx. 6 km. and then left on R617 to Blarney. Site clearly signed at Esso station in village, in approx. 2 km.

The Meadow Camping Park
Glandore

950

The stretch of coast from Cork to Skibbereen reminds British visitors of Devon before the era of mass tourism. This is rich dairy country, the green of the meadows matching the emerald colours of the travel posters. Thanks to the warm and wet Gulf Stream climate, it is also a county of gardens - and keen gardeners. The Meadows is best described not as a site, but as a one acre garden surrounded, appropriately, by lush meadows. It lies 1.5 km. east of the fishing village of Glandore. A further 5 km. west is the regional centre, Skibbereen, beyond which the landscape moves from unspoilt Devon to unspoilt Cornwall. The owners, who live on the park, have cunningly arranged accommodation for 19 pitches among the flower beds and shrubberies of their extended garden. Space is rather tight and only small caravans are encouraged. There are 6 hardstandings for motorcaravans with 5A electric hook-ups. Among the homely features are a sitting room and a well equipped kitchen. Note: tents, small caravans and motorcaravans only.

Facilities: Facilities are limited but well designed and immaculately maintained. Showers on payment. Washing machine and dryer. American motorhomes accepted with additional charge according to length. Dogs are not accepted. **Off site:** Fishing or riding 2 km, fishing, swimming, boat launching and sailing at Glandore (2 km).

Charges 2003

Per unit incl. 2 persons	€13.00
extra adult	€4.00
child under 12 yrs	€2.00
hiker or cyclist incl. tent (per person)	€6.50
electricity	€2.00

No credit cards. **Tel:** 028 33280. E-mail: the_meadow@oceanfree.net. **Reservations:** Please phone site for details. **Open** 15 March - 30 September.

Directions: Park is 1.5 km. east of Glandore, off N71 road, on R597 mid-way between Leap and Rosscarbery (coast road).

Barleycove Holiday Park
Crookhaven, Skibbereen

952

This long established, family owned park enjoys an idyllic situation tucked between the golden sands of Barleycove and Crookhaven Harbour on the scenic Mizen Peninsula. It is within an 8 km. drive of Mizen Head, Ireland's most south-westerly point, and approached along a route of unspoilt rugged countryside, offering the ideal 'away from it all' environment. It is a well cared for park with a neat and tidy appearance. Mobile homes are sited around the perimeter and within a field to the right. The 85 touring pitches all have electricity hook-ups (5A). Some are on grass in bays of 12, divided by timber fencing, others are unfenced on hardstanding with drainage and rubbish disposal. Tents have a dedicated grass area. Apart from discovering the natural beauty of this peninsula, of interest is Mizen Head Signal Station visitor centre, reached by a suspension bridge. Alternatively, the local friendly pubs and quality seafood restaurant at Heron's Cove offer a memorable evening out.

Facilities: Three toilet blocks, kept clean and well maintained, provide free hot showers, open style wash areas, plus a vanity unit. Laundry, with washing machines, dryer and spin dryer, washing-up sinks. Motorcaravan service point. Cafe/takeaway (July/Aug) with outside seating. Well stocked mini-market. Ice packs at reception. Games room with table tennis, pool tables and games machines. Tennis court (free). Pitch and putt on payment. Activities for children are organised in high season. Security gate and night watchman. Dogs are not accepted.

Charges 2002

Per family unit	€13.50 - €17.00
2 person unit	€12.00 - €14.00
awning	free - €3.00
hiker, cyclist or motorcyclist with tent	€4.00 - €5.00
hardstanding	free - €1.25
electricity	free - €1.25

Tel: 028 35302. Fax: 021 430 7230. **Reservations:** Contact park. **Open** Easter, then 3 May - 15 September.

Directions: Site is 35 km. southwest of Bantry. From N71 Bantry/Cork road join R591 (3.2 km. south of Bantry) and follow signs for Crookhaven via Durrus, Toormore and Goleen. Site on right before Crookhaven village.

Eagle Point Caravan & Camping Park

Ballylickey, Bantry

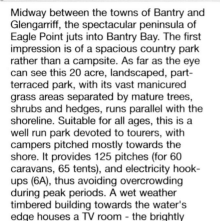

Midway between the towns of Bantry and Glengarriff, the spectacular peninsula of Eagle Point juts into Bantry Bay. The first impression is of a spacious country park rather than a campsite. As far as the eye can see this 20 acre, landscaped, part-terraced park, with its vast manicured grass areas separated by mature trees, shrubs and hedges, runs parallel with the shoreline. Suitable for all ages, this is a well run park devoted to tourers, with campers pitched mostly towards the shore. It provides 125 pitches (for 60 caravans, 65 tents), and electricity hook-ups (6A), thus avoiding overcrowding during peak periods. A wet weather timbered building towards the water's edge houses a TV room - the brightly decorated interior is guaranteed to brighten the dullest of days. Eagle Point makes an excellent base for watersports enthusiasts - swimming is safe and there is a slipway for small craft.

Facilities: Three well maintained, well designed toilet blocks are above expected standards. Laundry and dishwashing. Motorcaravan services. Children's play area. Tennis courts. Football field to the far right, well away from the pitches. Fishing. Supermarket at park entrance. Dogs are not accepted. **Off site:** Bicycle hire 6 km, riding 10 km, golf 2 km.

Charges 2002

Per family unit	€17.50 - €18.50
unit incl. 2 persons	€15.00 - €16.00
motorcyclist, hiker or cyclist (per person)	€6.50
extra car	€2.50
electricity	€1.50

Tel: 027 50630. E-mail: eaglepointcamping@eircom.net. **Reservations:** Bookings not essential. **Open** 26 April - 30 September.

Directions: Take N71 to Bandon, then R586 Bandon to Bantry, N71 Bantry to Glengarriff. 6.4 km. from Bantry; park entrance is opposite Burmah petrol station.

Creveen Lodge Caravan & Camping Park

Healy Pass, Lauragh

The address of this park is rather confusing, but Healy Pass is the well known scenic summit of the road (R574) crossing the Beara Peninsula, which lies between Kenmare Bay to the north and Bantry Bay to the south. Several kilometres inland from the north coast road (R571), the R574 starts to climb steeply southward towards the Healy Pass. Here, on the mountain foothills, is Creveen Lodge, a working hill farm with a quiet, homely atmosphere. Although not so famed as the Iveragh Peninsula, around which runs the Ring of Kerry, the northern Beara is a scenically striking area of County Kerry. Creveen Lodge, commanding views across Kenmare Bay, is divided among three gently sloping fields separated by trees. To allow easy access, the steep farm track is divided into a simple one-way system. There are 20 pitches, 16 for tents, 4 for caravans, with an area of hardstanding for motorcaravans, and electrical connections (5A) are available. The park is carefully tended with neat rubbish bins and rustic picnic tables informally placed. This is walking and climbing countryside or, of interest close by, is Derreen Gardens.

Facilities: Well appointed and immaculately maintained, the small toilet block provides showers on payment (€0.65), plus a communal room with a fridge, freezer, TV, ironing board, fireplace, tables and chairs. Reception is in the farmhouse which also offers guests a comfortable sitting room. Full Irish breakfast is served on request. Children's play area. **Off site:** Water sports, riding, 'Seafare' cruises, shops and a restaurant nearby. Fishing 2 km, bicycle hire 9 km, boat launching 9 km.

Charges 2002

Per unit	€9.00
adult	€1.50
child	€0.75
motorcyclist incl. tent	€5.00
hiker or cyclist incl. tent	€4.75
electricity	€1.50

No credit cards. **Tel:** 064 83131. Fax: 064 83998. E-mail: info@creveenlodge.com. **Reservations:** Write to site with an S.A.E. **Open** Easter - 31 October.

Directions: Park is on the Healy Pass road (R574) 1.5 km. southeast of Lauragh.

Wave Crest Caravan & Camping Park
Caherdaniel

It would be difficult to imagine a more dramatic location than Wave Crest's on the Ring of Kerry coast. Huge boulders and rocky outcrops tumble from the park entrance on the N70 down to the seashore which forms the most southern promontory on the Ring of Kerry. There are spectacular southward views from the park across Kenmare Bay to the Beara peninsula. Sheltering on grass patches in small coves that nestle between the rocks and shrubbery, are 65 hardstanding pitches and 55 on grass offering seclusion. Electricity connections are available (13A). A unique feature is the TV room, an old stone farm building with a thatched roof. Its comfortable interior includes a stone fireplace heated by a converted cast iron marker buoy. Caherdaniel is known for its cheerful little pubs and distinguished restaurant. The Derrynane National Park Nature Reserve is only a few kilometres away, as is Derrynane Cove and Bay. This park would suit families or older people looking for a quiet, relaxed atmosphere.

Facilities: Two blocks house the sanitary facilities and include hot showers on payment (€1), toilet for disabled people and dishwashing sinks. Laundry service. Fully stocked shop and takeaway service (May - 1 Sept). Children's play area. Fishing and boat launching. **Off site:** Riding 1 km, bicycle hire or golf 10 km. Small beach near and Derrynane Hotel with bar and restaurant.

Charges 2003

Per unit	€12.00
small tent	€11.00
adult	€2.00
child	€1.00
hiker or cyclist incl. tent	€5.50
motorcyclist incl. tent	€6.50
electricity	€2.00
awning	€4.00

Tel: 066 9475188. Fax: 066 9475188. E-mail: wavecrest@eircom.net. **Reservations:** Write for details. **Open** all year.

Directions: On the N70 (Ring of Kerry), 1.5 km. east of Caherdaniel.

Anchor Caravan Park
Castlegregory

Of County Kerry's three long, finger like peninsulas which jut into the sea, Dingle is the most northerly. Tralee is the main town and Anchor Caravan Park is 20 km. west of this famed town and under 4 km. south of Castlegregory on Tralee Bay. A secluded and mature, five acre park, it is enclosed by shrubs and trees, with a gateway leading to a beautiful, sandy beach which is safe for bathing, boating and shore fishing. There are 30 pitches, all with 6A electric hook-ups and some also with drainage and water points. Although there are holiday homes for hire, these are well apart from the touring pitches. In this area of great beauty, miles of sand abounds and taking in the panorama of mountain scenery from the top of the Conor Pass is a wonderful experience.

Facilities: Toilet facilities (entry by key) are kept clean (three or four times daily in busy periods) providing showers on payment (€0.50), two private cabins, toilet with handrail, dishwashing and laundry facilities (incl. clothes lines). Motorcaravan services. Two play areas. Games/TV room. Night lighting. **Off site:** Beautiful sandy beach 2 minutes. Fishing 2 km. Riding or bicycle hire 3 km. Golf 4 km.

Charges 2003

Per unit incl. all persons	€13.00 - €14.00
small tent incl. 1 or 2 persons	€11.00 - €12.00
motorcyclist, hiker or cyclist incl. tent	€10.00
electricity	€2.00
awning	€2.50

No credit cards. **Tel:** 066 7139157. Fax: 066 7139157. E-mail: anchorcaravanpark@eircom.net. **Reservations:** Contact site. **Open** Easter - 30 September.

Directions: From Tralee follow the Dingle coast road for 19 km. Park is signed from Camp junction.

Fossa Caravan & Camping Park

Killarney

959

This mature, well equipped park is in a scenic location, ten minutes drive from the town centre. Fossa Caravan Park is recognisable by its forecourt on which stands a distinctive building housing a roof top restaurant, reception area, shop and petrol pumps. The well laid out park is divided in two - the touring area to the right, tucked behind the main building, and to the left an open grass area mainly for campers. Touring pitches, with electricity and drainage, have hardstanding and are angled between shrubs and trees in a tranquil, well cared for garden setting. To the rear at a higher level and discreetly placed are 50 caravan holiday homes, unobtrusive and sheltered by the thick foliage of the wooded slopes which climb high behind the park. Fossa is convenient for Killarney (5.5 km) and is also en-route for the famed 'Ring of Kerry', making it an ideal base for walkers and golfers.

Facilities: Modern toilet facilities kept spotlessly clean include showers on payment. Laundry room, washing up area. Campers' kitchen. Shop (April - Sept). Restaurant (1 June - end Aug) and takeaway (July/Aug). TV lounge. Play area. Picnic area. Games room. Bicycle hire. Night lighting and security patrol. **Off site:** Fishing or golf 2 km, riding 3 km.

Charges 2002

Per unit	€5.00 - €6.50
adult	€4.50
child (under 14 yrs)	€1.50
motorcycle and tent per person	€6.75 - €7.50
hiker/cyclist and tent per person	€5.00 - €6.00
awning	€3.00
electricity (5/10A)	€3.00

Tel: 064 31497. Fax: 064 34459. E-mail: fossaholidays@eircom.net. **Reservations:** Advisable in high season and made for min. 3 nights with deposit. **Open** 1 April - 30 September.

Directions: Approaching Killarney from all directions, follow signs for N72 Ring of Kerry/Killorglin. At last roundabout join R562/N72. Continue for 5.5 km. and Fossa is the second park to the right.

FOSSA CARAVAN & CAMPING PARK

★ Ample hardstanding & electric hook-up ★ Separate tent area
★ Modern toilets ★ Shaving points ★ Hairdryers ★ Hot showers
★ Facilities for the disabled ★ Full laundry facilities ★ Campers kitchen
★ Free wash-up facilities ★ On site shop open 7 days Easter to Sept.
★ Restaurant (June-Aug) ★ Take away (July/Aug)
★ Children's playground ★ Tennis court ★ Games room ★ TV room ★ Bicycles for hire
★ Mobile homes for hire ★ Hostel accommodation

FOR FREE COLOUR BROCHURE WRITE TO:

Brosnan Family, Fossa Caravan & Camping Park, Fossa, Killarney, Co. Kerry, Ireland
Telephone: (064) 31497   Fax: (064) 34459

Glenross Caravan & Camping Park

Glenbeigh, Ring of Kerry

960

Its situation on the spectacular Ring of Kerry and the Kerry Way gives Glenross an immediate advantage, and scenic grandeur around every bend of the road is guaranteed as Glenbeigh is approached. Quietly located before entering the village, the park commands a fine view of Rossbeigh Strand, which is within walking distance. On arrival, a good impression is created with the park well screened from the road and with new stone entrance and gates. There are 34 touring pitches including hardstanding pitches with 10A electricity and 6 caravan holiday homes, and the park is attractively laid out. There is no catering on site but the Glenbeigh Hotel next door is popular and the shops are near. Not least is the Kerry Bog Village where you can go back in time in this reconstructed pre-famine village.

Facilities: Well maintained modern toilet block includes facilities for laundry and dishwashing. Motorcaravan service point. Games room. Bicycle hire. Shelter for campers. Sun lounge and barbecue patio. **Off site:** Watersports and tennis near, riding and fishing 200 m. and golf 500 m.

Charges 2002

Per unit	€4.50 - €5.50
adult	€5.50
child (under 14 yrs)	€1.50
motorcycle and tent	€7.00 - €7.50
hiker or cyclist and tent	€6.25 - €6.75
electricity	€3.00
awning	€2.00

No credit cards. **Tel:** 066 97 68451. Fax: 064 37474. E-mail: glenross@eircom.net. **Reservations:** Write to site for details. **Open** 3 May - 15 September.

Directions: Park is on the N70 Killorglin - Glenbeigh road, on the right just before entering the village.

Mannix Point Camping & Caravan Park

Cahirciveen

961

A quiet and peaceful, beautifully located seashore park, it is no exaggeration to describe Mannix Point as a nature lovers' paradise. Situated in one of the most spectacular parts of the Ring of Kerry, overlooking the Portmagee Channel towards Valentia Island, the park commands splendid views in all directions. It is flat and open being right on marshland which teems with wildlife (a two acre nature reserve) with direct access to the beach and seashore. The owner has planted around 500 plants with plans for around 1,000 more trees and shrubs. There are 42 pitches, 15 for tourers and 27 for tents, with electricity (6A) available. A charming old fisherman's cottage has been converted to provide reception. A cosy sitting room with turf fire, and 'emergency' dormitory for campers, is a feature of this site. There is no television, but compensation comes in the form of a knowledgeable, hospitable owner who is a Bord Fáilte registered local tour guide. This park retains a wonderful air of Irish charm aided by occasional impromptu musical evenings. Watersports, bird watching, walking and photography can be pursued. Local cruises to Skelligs Rock with free transport to and from the port for walkers and cyclists. This is also an ideal resting place for people walking the Kerry Way.

Facilities: Toilet facilities, now upgraded and immaculate, have well designed showers (on €0.80 payment). Modern campers' kitchen. Laundry facilities with washing machines and dryer. Motorcaravan service facilities. Dogs are not accepted in July and August. **Off site:** Bicycle hire 800 m. riding 3 km, golf 14 km. Pubs, restaurants and shops 15 minutes walk.

Charges 2002

Per adult	€5.50
child (1 or 2 children)	€3.00
extra child	€1.20
caravan or motorcaravan	€3.50
electricity	€1.50
motorcycle	€1.00

Book 7 nights, pay 6. Reductions for groups if pre-paid. No credit cards. **Tel:** 066 9472806. Fax: 066 9472028. E-mail: mannixpoint@mail.com. **Reservations:** Made with deposit of one night's fee. **Open** 15 March - 1 October.

Directions: Park is 250 m. off the N70 Ring of Kerry road, 800 m. southwest of Cahirciveen (or Cahersiveen) on the road towards Waterville.

White Villa Farm Caravan & Camping Park

Killarney-Cork Road (N22), Killarney

963

This is a very pleasing small touring park in scenic surroundings on the N22 Killarney-Cork road. It is set on a 100 acre family operated dairy farm which stretches as far as the River Flesk, yet is only five minutes away from Killarney town. Trees and shrubs surround the park but dominant is a magnificent view of the MacGillicuddy's Reeks. There are 25 pitches for caravans and tents, 15 with hardstanding and a grass area for awnings, electricity (10A), water points and night lighting. An unusual novelty is old school desks placed around the site, plus an antique green telephone box. One can also enjoy walking through the oak wood, fishing on the Flesk or visiting the site's own National Farm Museum.

Facilities: The toilet block, a sandstone coloured building to the rear of the park, is kept spotlessly clean and houses showers on payment, a good toilet/shower room for disabled visitors, laundry room, clothes lines and dishwashing sinks. Motorcaravan service area. Campers' kitchen with TV. Children's play area and basketball. Bicycle hire. Max. 2 dogs per pitch are accepted (not certain breeds). **Off site:** Riding, golf and boat launching 5 km. Killarney town 5 minutes, the National Park 10 minutes away.

Charges 2003

Per unit	€2.00 - €3.50
adult	€4.50
child (under 14 yrs)	€2.00
child (14-18 yrs)	€2.50
motorcyclist incl. tent	€5.00 - €6.00
hiker or cyclist incl. tent	€5.00
electricity	€2.00

No credit cards. Seven nights for the price of six. **Tel:** 064 20671 or 32456. E-mail: killarneycamping@eircom.net. **Reservations:** Made with deposit (€15 or UK£10). **Open** 1 April - 16 October.

Directions: Park is 3 km. east from Killarney town on N22 Cork road. Park entrance is 500 m. east of N22/N72 junction. From Killarney follow N22 Cork road signs and 'White Villa Farm' finger signs from Park Road roundabout. From Kenmare take R569 via Kilgarvan to the N22, then as above.

The Flesk Muckross Caravan & Camping Park

Muckross Road, Killarney

At the gateway to the National Park and Lakes, near Killarney town, this family run, seven acre park has undergone extensive development and offers high quality standards. Pitches are well spaced and have electricity (10A), water, and drainage connections; 21 also have hardstanding with a grass area for awnings. The grounds have been well cultivated with further shrubs, plants and an attractive barbecue and patio area. This is to the left of the sanitary block and is paved and sunk beneath the level roadway. Surrounded by a garden border, it has tables and chairs, making a pleasant communal meeting place commanding excellent views of Killarney's mountains.

Facilities: Modern, clean toilet blocks are well designed and equipped. Baby bath/changing room. Laundry room. Campers' kitchen with dishwashing sinks. Comfortable games room. Other on site facilities include petrol pumps, supermarket (all year), delicatessen and café (March - Oct) with extra seating on the sun terrace. Night lighting and night time security checks. Winter caravan storage. **Off site:** Fishing 300 m, boat launching 2 km.

Charges 2002

Per unit	€4.50 - €5.00
adult	€5.75
child (under 14 yrs)	€1.50
small tent	€4.00 - €4.50
motorcyclist incl. tent	€6.50 - €7.00
hiker or cyclist incl. tent	€6.00 - €6.50
awning	€2.00
electricity	€3.00

Tel: 064 31704. Fax: 064 35439. E-mail: killarneylakes@eircom.net. **Reservations:** Advisable in peak periods, write to park. **Open** 29 March - 30 September.

Directions: From Killarney town centre follow the N71 and signs for Killarney National Park. Site is 1.5 km. on the left beside the Gleneagle Hotel.

FLESK MUCKROSS
CARAVAN PARK

Family run, 7 acre park, situated at the gateway to 25,000 acres of National Park and lakes.

AA award winning sanitation facilities 1994/5

Just 1 mile (1.5 km) from Killarney town on the N71 south of Kenmare,

adjacent to Gleneagle Hotel and leisure centre

MUCKROSS, KILLARNEY
CO. KERRY, IRELAND   Prop: Johnny & Sinead Courtney

Phone: 064-31704
Fax: 064-35439

Flemings White Bridge Caravan Park

Ballycasheen Road, Killarney

Once past the county border, the main road from Cork to Killarney (N22) runs down the valley of the Flesk river. On the final approach to Killarney off the N22 Cork road, the river veers away from the road to enter the Lower Lake. On this prime rural position, between the road and the river, and within comfortable walking distance of the town, is Fleming's White Bridge, a nine acre woodland park. The ground is flat, landscaped and generously adorned with flowers, shrubs and trees. There are now 92 pitches (46 caravans and 46 tents) that extend beyond a wooden bridge to an area surrounded by mature trees and where a new toilet block, one of three, is sited. This is obviously a park of which the owners are very proud, and the family personally supervise the reception and grounds, maintaining high standards of hygiene, cleanliness and tidiness. The park's location so close to Ireland's premier tourism centre makes this park an ideal base to explore Killarney and the southwest.

Facilities: Three toilet blocks are maintained to high standards. Dishwashing sinks. Motorcaravan service point. Campers' drying room and two laundries. Shop (1/6-1/9). Two TV rooms and a games room. Fishing (advice and permits provided). Canoeing (own canoes). Bicycle hire. Woodland walks. **Off site:** Riding 3 km, golf 2 km.

Charges 2002

Per unit	€4.50 - €5.50
adult	€5.50
child (under 14 yrs)	€1.50
motorcyclist incl. tent	€7.00 - €7.50
hiker or cyclist incl. tent	€6.00 - €6.50
electricity (10A)	€3.00
awning	€1.50 - €2.00

No credit cards. **Tel:** 064 31590. Fax: 064 37474. E-mail: fwbcamping@eircom.net. **Reservations:** Advised for high season; contact site. **Open** 15 March - 31 October.

Directions: From Cork and Mallow: at N72/N22 junction continue towards Killarney and take first turn left (signed Ballycasheen Road). Proceed for 300 m. to archway entrance on left. From Limerick: follow N22 Cork road. After passing Super Valu and Killarney Heights Hotel take first right (signed Ballycasheen Road) and continue as above. From Kenmare: on N71, pass Gleneagles Hotel and Flesk Bridge. Turn right before Shell filling station into Woodlawn Road and Ballycasheen Road continue for 2 km. to archway.

Woodlands Park Touring Caravan & Camping Park

Dan Spring Road, Tralee

Tralee is not only the Capital of County Kerry and gateway to the Dingle Peninsula, it is also Ireland's fastest growing visitor destination, with Woodlands its newest touring caravan park. Although only a ten minute walk from the town centre, this park is located on a 16 acre elevated site approached by a short roadway and bridge that straddles the River Lee. Once on site the town seems far removed, with a countryside environment taking over. Hedging, trees, grazing fields and the distant Slieve Mish Mountain create the setting. The owners of Woodlands have designed and equipped their park to a high standard. A distinctive feature is its impressive yellow coloured building which houses an 'on top' family dwelling and ground floor services. There are 92 pitches with hardstanding, electricity (10A), water and drainage plus night light, to the left and centre behind the main building, and a grass area for 40 tents to the right. Young shrubs, cordyline trees and flower beds have been planted around the park and a security barrier is in operation. Interesting is the award winning 'Kerry the Kingdom' museum with its incredible time car trip through the Middle Ages. Evening entertainment in Tralee means a selection of singing pubs, restaurants and the National Folk Theatre.

Facilities: Heated sanitary facilities include sizeable showers (€1 token) and provision for disabled guests. Campers' kitchen and dishwashing sinks. Laundry room with washing machines and dryer. Café/snack bar. Shop. Games room. TV and adult room. Fenced adventure play area. **Off site:** The nearby Aqua Dome offers half price admission after 6 pm. Golf 6 km, riding 2 km. Blue flag beaches on the Dingle Peninsula.

Charges 2002

Per unit incl. 2 adults	€15.50 - €16.00
Per unit incl. 2 adults, 2 children	€18.50 - €19.00
small tent and car incl. 2 adults	€15.00 - €15.50
motorcyclist incl. tent	€6.50 - €7.00
hiker or cyclist incl. tent	€6.00 - €6.50
extra adult	€5.50
child (under 14 yrs)	€1.50
electricity	€3.00

Tel: 066 7121235. Fax: 066 7181199. E-mail: wdlands@eircom.net. **Reservations:** Advisable for high season. **Open** Easter - 30 September.

Directions: Site is 1 km. southwest of Tralee town centre. From N21/N69/N86 junction south of Tralee follow camp signs for 2.4 km. to park, 200 m. off the N86 Tralee - Dingle road.

CHANNEL ISLANDS

Jersey

Jersey Tourism
Liberation Square, St Helier, Jersey JE1 1BB
Tel: (01534) 500700 Fax: (01534) 500899
E-mail: info@jersey.com   Internet: www.jersey.com

Guernsey and Herm

States of Guernsey Tourist Board
PO Box 13, White Rock, Guernsey
Tel: (01481) 723552

Sark

Sark Tourism Office
Sark (via Guernsey), Channel Islands.
Tel: (01481) 832345

A visit to the Channel Islands offers a holiday in part of the British Isles, but in an area which has a definitely continental flavour. Of course, you don't need a passport (except foreign nationals) or to change your money, although the proximity of the islands to the French coast might tempt one to take a day trip, where you will need to have Euros. All the islands have beautiful beaches and coves, pretty scenery and fascinating histories. Jersey is probably more commercially orientated, with more entertainment provided, while Guernsey will suit those who prefer a quieter, more peaceful holiday. For total relaxation, one of the smaller islands, such as Sark or Herm, where no cars are allowed, might appeal. Shopping in all the islands has the advantage of no mainland VAT – particularly useful for buying cameras, watches, jewellery and clothes.

Camping holidays on the islands are limited to TENTS only - caravans and motor-caravans are not permitted due to the narrow and sometimes crowded nature of the roads. Trailer tents (with canvas roof and walls) are permitted but on Jersey advance reservations must be made. Contact the Island Tourism authorities for more detailed information. Some of the parks we feature offer tents and camping equipment for hire, which may prove a popular option for some, and cars are also easily rented on the main islands.

Since all the parks cater solely for tents, rather than caravans or motorcaravans, this means that there tend to be very limited waste water emptying points and almost no chemical disposal facilities. We are advised that on both Jersey and Guernsey, that political pressure is being placed for a change of policy in order to develop tourism. Guernsey is trying for caravans on the basis that, once they are on site, then only the car will run around the island, while Jersey is pushing for motorcaravans under a certain length. Both developments are under consideration – contact the relevant tourist board for the latest information.

Travel between mainland Britain and the Channel Islands is not cheap, particularly if you take your car. However the Condor wave-piercing catamaran service has made travelling to the Channel Islands a very easy and much quicker proposition than ever before. We used this service, which now carries cars, and were most impressed, in respect of the speed (From Poole, Guernsey is only some 2.5 hours travelling time, Jersey 1 hour longer), the comfort and the onboard service. These craft are surprisingly spacious with room to walk around (and even to go outside), a bar and snack bar and duty-free shopping facilities. Condor offer a range of fares, including a Family Saver deal. Condor may be contacted on tel: (01305) 761551.

Photo: Jersey Tourism

Jersey, Guernsey and St. Malo

The fast car ferry service

If you're travelling to the Channel Islands or Western France for your holiday next year, the first thing you need is your copy of a Condor 2002 Car Ferries Brochure.

With services up to 3 times daily from Weymouth or Poole you can be in Jersey in 3 hours, Guernsey in 2 hours or St. Malo in as little as $4^1/_2$ hours.

Information & Booking 0845 345 2000

ONLY WE DUTY FREE

CONDOR Ferries

Jersey
Rozel Camping Park
Rozel, St Martin, Jersey JE3 6AX

971

This family owned park is within walking distance of the famous Jersey Zoo and the pretty harbour and fishing village of Rozel, where the north coast cliff path commences. The surrounding countryside is quieter than many areas of the island. A car is probably necessary to reach the main island beaches, although a bus service does run to St Helier from close by. The park itself is quietly situated at the top of a valley (the French coast can be seen on a clear day) and is surrounded by trees providing shelter. There are two main camping areas providing 100 pitches, of which some 15 are used for fully equipped tents to hire. Some pitches, mainly for smaller tents are arranged on terraced areas. The remainder are on a higher, flat field where pitches are arranged in bays with hedges growing to separate them into groups. Parking is permitted by the tents and some electrical connections are available. In addition to package deals for tent hire and travel, the site offers a good range of camping equipment for hire on a daily basis. Boats are accepted by prior arrangement.

Facilities: Two heated sanitary buildings offer first rate facilities including a bathroom for disabled people with a shower, toilet and washbasin in the lower block with an access ramp. Family shower room in the upper block with a small heater for cooler weather. Dishwashing facilities under cover. Laundry and make up room. Shop. Attractive, sheltered swimming pool (June-Sept) with children's pool and sunbathing areas. Play equipment. Crazy golf. Games room, reading and TV room. Torches useful. Dogs are not accepted. **Off site:** Fishing 1 mile, riding 3 miles, golf 4 miles.

Charges 2002

Per person	£5.20 - £7.50
child (4-11 yrs)	£2.60 - £3.75
electricity	£1.50

Tent hire and travel packages available. **Tel:** 01534 856 797. Fax: 01534 856 127. E-mail: rozelcamping@ jerseyhols.com. **Reservations:** Made for any length with £40 deposit; balance due 14 days before arrival. **Open** 1 May - 7 September.

Directions: On leaving the harbour by Route du Port Elizabeth, take A1 east through the tunnel and the A17. At the fourth set of traffic lights turn left on A6. Keep in the middle lane. Continue to Five Oaks and on to St Martin's church. Turn right, then immediately left at the 'Royal' onto the B38 to Rozel and the park is on the right.

Jersey
Beuvelande Camp Site
St Martin, Jersey JE3 6EZ

972

This pleasant site with an outstanding sanitary building gives campers facilities normally associated with top class hotels. A licensed restaurant with covered terrace area is also situated in this building, open morning and evening all season, but perhaps a few less hours at quiet times. There are 150 pitches, 60 with fully equipped tents for hire, but with plenty of space for those with their own tents. Some electric hook ups are available and cars may be parked next to your tent. Torches would be useful. Car hire can be arranged and bicycle hire is possible from the site. This family run park prides itself on quality, cleanliness and hospitality.

Facilities: The toilet block is tiled top to bottom and spotlessly clean, with controllable showers, two fully equipped bathrooms for disabled people, and a baby room. Plenty of dishwashing facilities and a laundry can now be found in the original sanitary building. Games room and TV room. Well stocked shop open 8 am. - 7 pm. during peak times and stocks gas. Ice pack and battery charging services for a small charge. Outdoor heated swimming pool (41 x 17 ft) with a sun terrace. Simple play equipment for children. **Off site:** Fishing, golf or riding within 3 km.

Charges 2002

Per adult	£6.00 - £8.00
child (8-14 yrs)	£4.50
child (2-8 yrs)	£3.50
dog	£2.00

Single sex groups not accepted. No credit cards. **Tel:** 01534 853 575. Fax: 01534 857 788. **Reservations:** Made with £30 deposit; contact park for details. **Open** 1 May - 15 September.

Directions: On leaving the harbour by Route du Port Elizabeth, take A1 east through the tunnel and the A17. At the fourth set of traffic lights turn left on A6. Continue to Five Oaks and on to St Martin's RC church, then right into La Longue Rue, right again Rue de L'Orme then left to site.

Guernsey

Fauxquets Valley Farm Campsite

978 Castel, Guernsey GY5 7QA

Situated in the rural centre of the island, Fauxquets is in a pretty sheltered valley, hidden down narrow lanes away from busy roads and is run by the Guille family. A car would be useful here to reach the beaches, St Peter Port and other attractions, although there is a bus service each day (20 minutes walk). It was once a dairy farm, but the valley side has now been developed into an attractive camp site, with the old farm buildings as its centre. Plenty of trees, bushes and flowers have been planted to separate pitches and to provide shelter around the various fields which are well terraced. The 86 touring pitches are of a good size, most marked, numbered and with electricity, and there is lots of open space. There are also 15 smaller places for backpackers. The site has 23 fully equipped tents for hire, but there are no tour operators. The Haybarn licensed restaurant and bar provides (15/6-31/8) breakfast, morning coffee and cake and evening meals. There is plenty of room to sit around the heated swimming pool, including a large grassy terrace with sun-beds provided.

Facilities: The toilet facilities are good with free, controllable hot showers, some washbasins set in flat surfaces, with others in private cabins and with a shower, baby bath and changing unit for children. Hairdryers and irons are free. Dishwashing facilities under cover (free hot water) and a tap to take away hot water. Laundry room with free iron. Heated swimming pool (20 x 45 ft.) with paddling pool. Restaurant. Bar. Small shop (Easter-15/9) with ice-pack hire and gas. TV room and table tennis rooms. Small children's play area and play field. Nature walk. Bicycle hire. A torch would be useful. **Off site:** Fishing and boat launching 3 miles, riding and golf 2 miles

Charges 2003

Per adult	£4.80 - £5.50
child (at school)	£2.40 - £2.75
electricity	£2.50

Fully equipped tents with fridge for hire - details form park. **Tel:** 01481 255 460. Fax: 01481 251 797. E-mail: info@fauxquets.co.uk. **Reservations:** Made for independent campers for any length, with £50 deposit. **Open** Easter - 15 September.

Directions: From St Peter Port harbour take second exit from roundabout. At top of hill, turn left at 'filter in turn' into Queens Road, then right at next filter. Follow straight through traffic lights and down hill past Hospital, through pedestrian lights and straight on at another set of lights at top of hill. Continue for 0.75 miles, then turn right opposite at sign for German Underground Hospital. Fourth left is pedestrian entrance, cars carry on for 400 yds to gravel entrance on left.

Guernsey

Vaugrat Camping

977 St Sampson's, Guernsey GY2 4TA

Vaugrat Camping is a neat, well tended site, close to the beach in the northwest of the island. Owned and run by the Laine family, it is centred around attractive and interesting old granite farm buildings dating back to the 15th century, with a gravel courtyard and colourful flower beds. It provides 150 pitches on flat grassy meadows, that are mostly surrounded by trees, banks and hedges to provide shelter. Tents are arranged around the edges of the fields, giving open space in the centre, and while pitches are not marked, there is sufficient room and cars may be parked next to tents. Only couples and families are accepted and the site is well run and welcoming. It also offers 25 fully equipped tents for hire. Housed in the old farmhouse, now a listed building, are the reception area, shop and upstairs Coffee Barn, with views to the sea and where breakfast is served; one can also sit here in the evenings. A cider room complete with the ancient presses is now the games/TV room.

Facilities: Well kept sanitary facilities are in two buildings, one of which is in the courtyard, with hot showers on payment. Unit for disabled visitors with shower, basin and toilet (although there is a 6" step into the building). Laundry room with washing machine, dryer and iron. Second block near the camping fields provides one private cabin for ladies and dishwashing facilities. Shop with ice pack hire (main season only). Café. Dogs are not accepted. Torches may be useful. **Off site:** Bus service within easy reach. Car or bicycle hire can be arranged. Fishing, riding and golf within 1.5 miles. Hotel and bar nearby.

Charges 2002

Per adult	£5.50
child (under 14 yrs)	£4.40
car or boat	£1.05

Families and couples only. Fully equipped tents to hire (details from site). **Tel:** 01481 57468. Fax: 01481 51841. **Reservations:** Made for independent campers for any length, with £10 deposit and balance on arrival. **Open** 1 May - 30 September.

Directions: On leaving St Peter Port, turn right onto coast road for 1.5 miles. At filter turn left into Vale Road. Straight over at two sets of lights then first left turn by church. Follow to crossroads (garage opposite) turn right. Carry on past Peninsula Hotel, then second left, signed for site. Site on left after high stone wall (400 yds) with concealed entrance.

Herm

Seagull Campsite

983 The Administration Office, Herm Island GY1 3HR

This tiny site, and indeed the island of Herm, will appeal to those who are looking for complete tranquillity and calm. Reached by boat (20 minutes and approx. £6 return fare for adults, £3 for children) from Guernsey, the 500 acre island allows no cars, only tractors on its narrow roads and paths (no bicycles either). One is free to stroll around the many paths, through farmland, heath and around the coast, where there are beautiful beaches. The campsite is a 20 minute uphill walk from the harbour, but your luggage will be transported for you by tractor. It consists of several terraced areas offering a total of 80 pitches, and 30 fully equipped tents for hire on flat grass areas. There are no electricity hook-ups. One may bring one's own tent and equipment or hire a tent and equipment (but not bedding, crockery and lighting) from the site. Herm is definitely not for those who like entertainment and plenty of facilities, but for total relaxation, with the absence of any bustle and noise it takes some beating!

Facilities: Small, modern, but open, toilet block on site. Hot showers (£1 payment - there is a shortage of water on Herm). Freezer for ice-packs. The harbour village is about ten minutes walk down the hill where there is a small shop for provisions, gas, a post office, pub, restaurants and café. Fishing on the island. No dogs or pets are allowed. Torches useful.

Charges 2002

Per adult	£4.40
child (under 14 yrs)	£2.40
transportation of luggage £6.50	

Equipped tents for hire. Groups of single people not accepted. **Tel:** 01481 722 377. Fax: 01481 700 334. E-mail: camping@herm-island.com. **Reservations:** Made for any length with £20 deposit. Details of hire tents from above address. **Open** 14 May - first w/end in September.

Directions: Reached by boat from St Peter Port - report to Administration Office on arrival. Do not take your car as it is unlikely you will be able to park long term in St Peter Port.

Sark

Pomme de Chien Campsite

987 Sark, Channel Islands

'The island where time stands still' is an apt description of Sark, one of the smallest inhabited Channel Islands, some 45 minutes from Guernsey by boat. There is no airport, no cars or motorcycles and (apart from a tractor-drawn 'train' up Harbour Hill) the only transport is by bicycle or horse-drawn carriage. However everything you are likely to need for a tranquil holiday is provided with several small shops, pubs, hotels, restaurants, a Tourist Office and even two banks! Situated five minutes from the shops and ten from the beach, the Pomme de Chien campsite on Sark is tiny in terms of the number of pitches, totalling only 20, of which 8 are occupied by large, fully equipped frame tents (of excellent quality) for rent. The remainder are for campers with their own tents (no caravans, motorcaravans or trailer tents of course). The pitches themselves are large, on fairly level ground, but none have electricity hook-ups. There is a warm welcome from the owners Chris and Jill Rang with the famous charm of Sark. Although you cannot take your car to the island, transport by the Condor service via Guernsey means you can get there in a little over three hours either with your own small tent or of course you could hire one of the site's own fully equipped ones.

Facilities: A new sanitary block was added in 1999 with free hot showers (large, with bench and hook), toilets and washbasins. Dishwashing sinks are outside. Dogs are not accepted and torches are necessary. Baggage can be transferred from the harbour right to the site by tractor trailer, at a cost of 60p per item. **Off site:** Fishing 10 mins. walk, bicycle hire 5 mins.

Charges guide

Per adult	£5.00
child	£3.00
hire tent (per week)	£160.00

No credit cards. **Tel:** 01481 832 316. **Reservations:** Write to site. **Open** all year - ind. campers Jun-Sep for hire tents.

Directions: Take the tractor drawn 'train' up Harbour Hill (60p; you can walk but it is a ten minute hike). Once at the top take road leading off left, then second right, and follow the lane to the site entrance. Reception is at house with white gates.

Open All Year

The following parks are understood to accept caravanners and campers all year round, although the list also includes some parks open for at least 10 months. These parks are marked with a star ( ) – please refer to the park's individual entry for details. It is always wise to phone the park to check as, for example, facilities available may be reduced.

ENGLAND

002 Cardinney
018 Carnon Downs
037 Budemeadows
044 Dolbeare
053 Trethiggey
071 Hidden Valley
080 Higher Longford
081 Riverside
091 Ross Park
092 Finlake
135 Quantock Orchard
140 Isle of Avalon
142 Southfork
144 Baltic Wharf Caravan Club
148 Home Farm
150 Long Hazel
151 Bath Chew Valley
152 Waterrow
155 Bucklegrove
163 Brokerswood
164 Greenhill Farm
165 Coombe
167 Alderbury
170 C&C Club Devizes
177 Binghams Farm
181 Newlands
182 Bagwell Farm
202 Ulwell Cottage
203 Wareham Forest
208 Merley Court
216 Harrow Wood Farm
227 Oakdene
228 Lytton Lawn
229 Sandy Balls
236 Hill Cottage Farm
245 The Orchards
260 Barnstones
262 Wysdom
275 Highclere Farm
281 C&C Club Chertsey
289 White Rose
293 Sheepcote Caravan Club
294 Honeybridge Park
295 Washington
303 Tanner Farm
304 Broadhembury
305 Pine Lodge
307 C&C Club Canterbury
309 Black Horse Caravan Club
323 Lee Valley
326 Abbey Wood

327 Crystal Palace
331 Low House
333 Moat Farm
340 Old Brick Kilns
342 Two Mills
347 Breckland Meadows
355 Old Manor
358 Ferry Meadows
369 Bainland
373 Skegness Sands
376 Tallington Lakes
385 Rivendale
390 Bosworth Water Trust
391 Shardaroba
392 Riverside
394 Smeaton's Lakes
407 Somers Wood
413 Moreton-in-Marsh
414 C&C Club Winchcombe
415 Croft Farm
417 Tudor
421 Lickhill Manor
430 Poston Mill
439 Westbrook Park
440 Stanmore Hall
441 Beaconsfield Farm
442 Severn Gorge
443 Oxon Hall
454 St Helens
460 Vale of Pickering
464 Goose Wood
474 Jasmine Park
523 Chester Southerly
528 Abbey Farm
535 Holgates
536 Willowbank
556 Sykeside
557 Wild Rose
574 White Water Caravan Club
576 Percy Wood
580 Ord House

WALES

590N   Tything Barn Naturist
591 St Pierre
593 Cwmcarn Forest Drive
595 Afon Lodge
601 Cenarth Falls
604 Pencelli Castle
606 Tredegar Caravan Club
624 Cringoed
633 Daisy Bank

637 Hendre Mynach
659 Beddgelert
660 Bryn Gloch
668 James

SCOTLAND

687 Glenearly
692 Cressfield
693 Brandedleys
695 Brighouse Bay
702 Aird Donald
703 Gibson Park Caravan Club
705 Edinburgh Caravan Club
724 Lomond Woods
727 Auchterarder
768 Glenmore
785 Linnhe Lochside

NORTHERN IRELAND

842 Tollymore Forest
843 Banbridge
850 LoanEden
856 Gortin Glen

IRISH REPUBLIC

874 Cong
881 Lough Lannagh
908 Forest Farm
910 Camac Valley
911 Shankill
938 Parsons Green
948 Blarney
961 Mannix Point

CHANNEL ISLANDS

987 Pomme de Chien

No Dogs!

For the benefit of those who want to take their dogs with them and for those who do not like dogs on the parks they visit, we list here the parks which have indicated to us that they do not accept dogs. If you are planning to take your dog we do, however, advise that you phone the park first to check - there may be limits on numbers, breeds, etc. or times of the year when they are excluded.

NEVER - these parks do not accept dogs at any time:

020	Newquay Holiday Park	312	Gate House Wood	860	Bellemont
025	Pentewan Sands	327	Crystal Palace	877	Parkland
087	Beverley Park	410	Hoburne Cotswold	881	Lough Lannagh
113	Hoburne Torbay	416	Christchurch	889	The Tain
138	Hoburne Blue Anchor	422	Riverside	941	The Apple
149	Greenacres	453	Northcliffe	950	The Meadow
182	Bagwell Farm	555	Limefitt	951	Eagle Point
213	Grove Farm Meadow	598	Moreton Farm	952	Barleycove
216	Harrow Wood Farm	604	Pencelli Castle	971	Rozel
230	Ashurst	635	Barcdy	977	Vaugrat
305	Pine Lodge	729	Craigtoun Meadows	983	Seagull
306	Yew Tree	782	Oban Divers	987	Pomme de Chien

SOMETIMES - these parks do not accept dogs at certain times of the year:

072	Easewell Farm	not high season, max 1	251	Whitecliff Bay	not high season
085	Galmpton	not high season, max 2	629	Glan-y-Mor	not 4/7-31/8
155	Bucklegrove	not high season	910	Camac Valley	not July/Aug
208	Merley Court	not 14/7-31/8	915	River Valley	not July/Aug
210	Sandford Park	not high season, max 1	961	Mannix Point	not July/Aug
211	Pear Tree	not July/Aug			

MAYBE - accepted at any time but with certain restrictions:

001	Chacewater	not all breeds	398	Longnor Woods	max 2
003	Ayr	Max 1	420	The Boyce	max 2 not all breeds
006	River Valley	certain areas	440	Stanmore Hall	max 2
015	Sea View	not all breeds	441	Beaconsfield	max 2
048	Boscrege	max 3	442	Severn Gorge	max 2
049	Mullion	max 1	443	Oxon Hall	max 2
069	Stowford	max 2	452	Flower of May	by arrangement
071	Hidden Valley	max 2	463	Ripley	max 2
090	Widdicombe	not all breeds	464	Goose Wood	max 2
092	Finlake	only in some areas	467	Wood Nook	no cats
093	Ashburton	not all breeds	470	Nostell Priory	max 2
095	River Dart	max 2	476	Riverside	by arrangement
102	Oakdown	not all breeds	530	Kneps Farm	max 2
141	Broadway	not all breeds	535	Holgates	not all breeds
154	Batcombe Vale	max 1, not all breeds	554	Fallbarrow	max 1
168	Plough Lane	max 2	557	Wild Rose	not all breeds
181	Newlands	max 2	571	Doe Park	by arrangement
204	Manor Farm	owner's discretion	575	Waren	by arrangement
225	Hoburne Bashley	max 1	576	Percy Wood	not all breeds
228	Lytton Lawn	max 1	580	Ord House	by arrangement
229	Sandy Balls	certain fields only	593	Cwmcar	by arrangement
247	Southland	by arrangement	628	Aeron Coast	max 1
248	Appuldurcombe	max 2	636	Pen-y-Garth	by arrangement
257	Lincoln Farm	max 2	664	Home Farm	max 2
290	Horam Manor	max 2	665	Hunters Hamlet	max 2
304	Broadhembury	max 2	693	Brandedleys	max 2
311	Quex	max 2 by arrangement	699	Mortonhall	by arrangement
342	Two Mills	max 2	706	Tantallon	by arrangement
343	Kelling Heath	max 2	730	Blair Castle	max 2
351	Liffens	max 1	731	Twenty Shilling	max 2
355	Old Manor	max 2	764	Dunroamin	max 2
367	Lakeside Park	max 2	769	Torvean	max 1
376	Tallington Lakes	max 2	770	Pitgrudy	max 2
396	Silvertrees	not all breeds	785	Linnhe	max 2
397	Glencote	max 2	963	White Villa	max 2, not all breeds

Fishing

We are pleased to include details of parks which provide facilities for fishing on the site. Many other parks, particularly in Scotland and Ireland, are in popular fishing areas and have facilities within easy reach. Where we have been given details, we have included this information in the individual site reports. It is always best to contact individual parks to check that they provide for your individual requirements.

ENGLAND

006	River Valley
017	Trevella
022	Trevornick
025	Pentewan Sands
038	Wooda Farm
053	Trethiggey
075	Minnows
077	Clifford Bridge
079	Harford Bridge
081	Riverside
092	Finlake
095	River Dart
097	Cofton
106	Yeatheridge Farm
109	Peppermint
138	Blue Anchor
139	The Old Oaks
142	Southfork
148	Home Farm
152	Waterrow
154	Batcombe Vale
157	Northam Farm
159	Exe Valley
163	Brokerswood
164	Greenhill Farm
174	Golden Cap
176	Wood Farm
178	Freshwater Beach
201	Sandyholme
213	Grove Farm
215	Woolsbridge Manor
216	Harrow Wood Farm
229	Sandy Balls
236	Hill Cottage Farm
245	The Orchards
251	Whitecliff Bay
252	Thorness Bay
253	Waverley Park
261	Bo Peep
269	Wellington
270	Hurley
281	Chertsey
282	Horsley
290	Horam Manor
292	Bay View
303	Tanner Farm
321	Lee Valley
329	Fen Farm
340	Old Brick Kilns

ENGLAND

343	Kelling Heath
344	Gatton Waters
348	Little Lakeland
359	Yarwell Mill
367	Lakeside
375	Foreman's Bridge
376	Tallington Lakes
390	Bosworth
394	Smeaton's Lakes
397	Glencote
408	Riverside
409	Island Meadow
410	Hoburne Cotswold
414	Winchcombe
415	Croft Farm
417	Tudor
419	Kingsgreen
420	The Boyce
421	Lickhill Manor
422	Riverside
430	Poston Mill
431	Luck's All
432	Broadmeadow
433	The Millpond
434	Pearl Lake
438	Fernwood
439	Westbrook
441	Beaconsfield
444	The Green
450	Burton Constable
451	Thorpe Hall
461	Moorside
464	Goose Wood
466	Woodhouse Farm
470	Nostell Priory
472	Knight Stainforth
473	Far Grange
480	Brompton on Swale
528	Abbey Farm
554	Fallbarrow
555	Limefitt
560	Pennine View
571	Doe Park

WALES

593	Cwmcarn
604	Pencelli Castle
625	Dolswydd
629	Glan-y-Mor
659	Beddgelert
660	Bryn Gloch
667	The Plassey

SCOTLAND

689	Mossyard
691	Hoddom Castle
695	Brighouse Bay
700	Strathclyde
727	Auchterarder
726	Ardgartan
766	Spindrift
771	Ardmair Point
772	Woodend
774	Loch Greshornish
779	Invercoe
780	Resipole Farm
784	North Ledaig
785	Linnhe
786	Glendaruel

NORTHERN IRELAND

834	Drumaheglis
842	Tollymore
851	Mullynascarthy

IRISH REPUBLIC

877	Parkland
889	The Tain
896	Lough Ree
930	Morriscastle
938	Parsons Green
951	Eagle Point
956	Wave Crest
962	Flemings
963	White Villa

INSPECTED CAMPSITES & SELECTED

Bicycle Hire

We understand that the following parks have bicycles to hire on site or can arrange for bicycles to be delivered. However, we would recommend that you contact the park to check as the situation can change.

ENGLAND

011	Calloose
014	Penrose Farm
022	Trevornick
025	Pentewan Sands
026	Penhaven
033	Killigarth Manor
036	Lakefield
069	Stowford Farm
100	Forest Glade
135	Quantock Orchard
139	The Old Oaks
140	Isle of Avalon
141	Broadway House
148	Home Farm
149	Greenacres
155	Bucklegrove
205	Rowlands Wait
210	Sandford
213	Grove Farm
225	Hoburne Bashley
227	Oakdene
229	Sandy Balls
235	Red Shoot
258	Cotswold View
339	Dower House

ENGLAND

340	Old Brick Kilns
343	Kelling Heath
351	Liffens
356	Highfield Farm
375	Foreman's Bridge
380	Highfields
391	Shardaroba
430	Poston Mill
441	Beaconsfield Farm
454	St Helens
456	Golden Square
462	Upper Carr
466	Woodhouse Farm
471	Rudding
472	Knight Stainforth
555	Limefitt Park
557	Wild Rose
580	Ord House

WALES

604	Pencelli Castle

SCOTLAND

695	Brighouse Bay
696	Crossburn
700	Strathclyde
723	Trossachs
724	Lomond Woods
774	Loch Greshornish

IRISH REPUBLIC

874	Cong
879	Carra
881	Lough Lannagh
908	Forest Farm
913	Roundwood
923	Nore Valley
952	Barleycove
959	Fossa
960	Glenross
962	Flemings White Bridge
963	White Villa Farm
964	Flesk Muckross

CHANNEL ISLANDS

972	Beuvelande
977	Vaugrat
978	Fauxquets Valley

Photo: Jersey Tourism

Golf

We understand that the following parks have facilities for playing golf on site. Where facilities are within easy reach and we have been given details, we have included this information in the individual site reports. However, we recommend that you contact the park to check that the facility meets your requirements.

022	Trevornick	369	Bainland	695	Brighouse Bay
038	Wooda Farm	407	Somers Wood	706	Tantallon
069	Stowford Farm	430	Poston Mill	769	Torvean
072	Easewell Farm	434	Pearl Lake	780	Resipole Farm
101	Lady's Mile	452	Flower of May	831	Carnfunnock
102	Oakdown	471	Rudding	915	River Valley
107	Woolacombe Bay	473	Far Grange	948	Blarney
175	Highlands End	633	Daisy Bank		
225	Hoburne Bashley	667	The Plassey		
323	Lee Valley	690	Seaward		
367	Lakeside Park	691	Hoddom Castle		

Horse Riding

We understand that the following parks have horse riding stables on site. Where facilities are within easy reach and we have been given details, we have included this information in the individual site reports. However, we would recommend that you contact the park to check that the facility meets your requirements.

036	Lakefield	178	Freshwater	695	Brighouse Bay
038	Wooda Farm	210	Sandford Park	850	LoanEden
069	Stowford Farm	229	Sandy Balls	851	Mullynascarthy
092	Finlake	252	Thorness Bay	916	Moat Farm
106	Yeatheridge Farm	290	Horam Manor		
112	Napps Park	295	Washington		
137	Burrowhayes	480	Brompton on Swale		

Boat Launching

We understand that the following parks have boat slipways on site. Where facilities are within easy reach and we have been given details, we have included this information in the individual site reports. However, we would recommend that you contact the park to check that the facility meets your requirements.

025	Pentewan Sands	376	Tallington Lakes	780	Resipole Farm
075	Minnows	390	Bosworth	784	North Ledaig
153	Slimeridge Farm	408	Riverside	785	Linnhe
154	Batcombe Vale	415	Croft Farm	831	Carnfunnock
175	Highlands End	421	Lickhill Manor	834	Drumaheglis
251	Whitecliff Bay	450	Burton Constable	889	The Tain
252	Thorness Bay	554	Fallbarrow	896	Lough Ree
253	Waverley Park	689	Mossyard	951	Eagle Point
269	Wellington	695	Brighouse Bay	956	Wave Crest
270	Hurley	726	Ardgartan	961	Mannix Point
329	Fen Farm	771	Ardmair Point		
359	Yarwell Mill	774	Loch Greshornish		

Naturist Parks

We feature just two naturist sites in this guide: 024 Southleigh Manor Naturist Club and 590 Tything Barn. In addition, 029 Carlyon Bay provides a separate area for naturist campers.

Adults Only

The following parks have made the decision not to accept children.

001	Chacewater (30 yrs+)	345	Little Haven (14 yrs+)
139	The Old Oaks (18 yrs+)	398	Longnor Woods (18 yrs+)
151	Bath Chew Valley	407	Somers Wood
152	Waterrow (18 yrs+)	441	Beaconsfield Farm (25 yrs+)
159	Exe Valley (18 yrs+)	461	Moorside (16 yrs+)
168	Plough Lane	551	The Larches
177	Binghams Farm	565	The Ashes
342	Two Mills	633	Daisy Bank
344	Gatton Waters (18 yrs+)		

The following parks also do not accept children at certain times or in certain areas of their site:

380	Highfields Camping and Caravan Park	- in one area only
438	Fernwood Caravan Park	- in one area only
440	Stanmore Hall Touring Park (21 yrs)	- 31 grass pitches only
479	Bronte Caravan Park	- in certain areas
443	Oxon Hall Touring Park	- in one area only

The Right Honourable Margaret Beckett MP was the principal guest speaker at the Caravan Writers Guild Chairman's Event in June 2002, held at Rivendale Caravan & Leisure Park. The second speaker was Michael Leete of Dometic (Electrolux).

Reports by Readers

We always welcome reports from readers concerning parks which they have visited. Generally reports provide us with invaluable feedback on parks already featured in the Guide or, in the case of those not featured in our Guide, they provide information which we can follow up with a view to adding them in future editions.

However, if you have a complaint about a site, this should be addressed to the campsite owner, preferably in person before you leave.

Please make your comments either on this form or on plain paper. It would be appreciated if you would indicate the approximate dates when you visited the park and, in the case of potential new parks, provide the correct name and address and, if possible, include a park brochure. Send your reports to:

Alan Rogers' Guides, Manor Garden, Burton Bradstock, Bridport DT6 4QA

Name of Park and Ref. No. (or address for new recommendations):

....

....

Dates of Visit: ....

Comments:

Reader's Name and Address: ....

....

....

....

Gerry and Chris Bullock's Page

Who are they and why give them a page?

Gerry and Chris are both disabled. Chris has been a wheelchair user for many years and Gerry has, as he puts it, a bionic leg and wrist! (He says "I use Chris's wheelchair as my zimmer frame".) For many years they have been involved with many aspects of camping and motor caravanning for the disabled with various publications - they were the original authors of the MMM Mobility Guide. They also assist people such as the National Trust regarding access difficulties and problems that arise. They visit cities around the country and assist local tourist boards regarding access reports. They have over the years become 'experts' in finding parks that also offer good facilities for the wheelchair users which are truly useable.

They have also looked very carefully at the Disabled Discrimination Act, which comes into force in 2004 and have tried (as with most Acts, quite a minefield) to note any points that may be of relevance to site owners and of which they should be aware. Site owners need to be aware that from 2004 any services they offer to the general public, must also be accessible to the disabled, or at least the owner must offer an alternative - 'make reasonable adjustment to the service offered.

For example:

A park with steps up to the shop - if a person in a wheelchair comes to the site the shop assistant will come out to greet the wheelchair user and get whatever they require and bring it to the customer. This is reasonable.

A park has an upstairs restaurant below which is the reception - if persons staying on the site using a wheelchair want a meal and a table and chairs are available in the reception and the site owner allows this to be used and food and drinks are brought down to them. Again, reasonable adjustment...

Here are some of the things they look for when inspecting sites:

Access to the facilities block.

Are there special facilities either for wheelchair users or walking disabled?

What facilities are on offer?	En-suite or separate or just a W.C.?
What does the room offer and is it suitable?	The shower and its access for users?
Handrails - are they adequate?	Sink - its height and the type of taps?
Height of mirrors and other accessories?	Is there an emergency cord?

They also look at the site from the wheelchair user's (non powered) point of view.

Kerbs and paths	Roads and their surfaces
Grass and general condition of the pitches	Access to other areas

Of course they look at all parks with the attitude that you cannot expect a small (say 20 to 30 pitch, private park) to offer the same quality or range of equipment as a large commercial or club owned site. They recommend that disabled campers join one of the larger clubs, as their disabled rooms are usually of a very high standard. They try to make disabled campers aware of one point - that they must remember that "camping is still sleeping in a field", whether you are in a tent, a caravan or a motorhome; that you will not find the same facilities as you may find in your converted home, it will not be all concrete and tarmac, with all rooms and areas accessible. These are things that may only be found in a specialist hotel and if essential, that should be the type of holiday you should look at.

What they try to do is offer a list of sites that have been inspected and that readers can rely on. Please note: To ensure suitable pitching when you visit a campsite chosen as most suitable for its facilities for disabled visitors, we would advise booking. Giving information of your requirements to the site means that they can place you as best as possible (but please be patient as it is hard to please everyone no matter how hard they try).

If readers require any further information, or have any suggestions, or any site owners need any assistance, Gerry and Chris would like to hear from you. Their address is:

97 Stalham Road, Hoveton, Norwich, Norfolk NR12 8EF Telephone: 01603 784152

NOTE. They are not looking at facilities for persons with special needs. They leave this to the such people as the Sue Ryder Foundation, etc. which cater very well in this field.

Following visits this year, Chris and Gerry have made the following comments:

ENGLAND

102 Oakdown Holiday Park

Excellent en-suite disabled room; adequate handrails; bath for those with enough mobility; roadways tarmac; keys with reception; level site; access to donkey sanctuary; access to lake and bird hive.

270 Hurley Riverside Park

Spacious en-suite disabled room; adequate handrails; radar key; roadways hardcore; level site.

321 Lee Valley Caravan Park

Excellent en-suite unit; roadways tarmac; level site; access to river.

324 Lee Valley Caravan & Camping Park

Two excellent en-suite units; access all areas; roadways tarmac; level site; hardstandings; key access.

325 Lee Valley Campsite

En-suite disabled room; access to shop and reception; roadways tarmac; roadways steep in places; key at reception.

326 Abbey Wood

Excellent en-suite disabled room; walking disabled cubicles; access all areas; roadways tarmac; some parts sloping; level pitches; shallow gravel.

329 Fen Farm Caravan Site

Excellent en-suite disabled room; handrails; roadways hardcore (assistance recommended).

344 Polstead Touring Park

Male and female disabled WCs and showers in able bodied rooms; adequate handrails; shingle roads (assistance recommended); access to washing-up area.

352 Searles Holiday Park

Excellent en-suite disabled rooms; roadways tarmac; access to all areas; site level; disabled friendly site.

340 The Old Brick Kilns

Excellent en-suite disabled room; good handrails; roads hardcore; some gravel areas on site (shallow); access other areas.

339 The Dower House

Good en-suite disabled room; roadways hardcore; paths concrete; dedicated pitches; access reception-bar; assistance on site recommended.

343 Kelling Heath

En-suite disabled room; also separate shower-wc rooms; roadways hardcore; access all areas; assistance on site recommended.

WALES

588 Springwater Lakes

Disabled WC; washroom; good handrails; soap and towels; roadways hardcore; access to fishing lakes; assistance recommended; level site.

597 Noble Court

En-suite disabled room; good handrails; access most areas including poolside; roadways and paths tarmac and concrete; roadways very steep in some areas, strong helper needed.

603 Brynich Caravan Park

Two en-suite disabled rooms; adequate handrails; access shop-reception; roadways and paths tarmac and concrete; level site; wheelchair friendly site.

604 Pencelli Castle

Two superb en-suite units; handrails well placed; soap and towels; roadways and paths tarmac- concrete; access all areas including reception; level site; wheelchair friendly site.

629 Glan-Y-Mor Holiday Park

En-suite disabled room; WC-washroom; adequate handrails; access all areas including indoor pool; roadways tarmac; roadways steep in places assistance recommended.

633 Daisy Bank Touring Caravan Park

Excellent en-suite disabled units x 6; soap and towels; adequate handrails; slightly sloping paths and roads; roadways shallow gravel or hardcore.

660 Bryn Gloch Touring Park

Separate disabled shower - washroom and WC; adequate handrails; roadways tarmac; level site; access most areas; bridge from reception to main site; disabled friendly.

Chris and Gerry have visited the following parks in previous years. Please contact them if you are interested in their coments:

England
011 Calloose Caravan Park
016 Newperran Tourist Park
018 Carnon Downs Caravan Park
021 Hendra Holiday Park
075 Minnows Camping and Caravan Park
088 Dornafield
091 Ross Park
144 Baltic Wharf Caravan Club Site
145 Bath Marina and Caravan Park
203 Wareham Forest Tourist Park
258 Cotswold View Caravan Site
347 Breckland Meadows
348 Little Lakeland Caravan Park
365 Cherry Tree Site

373 Skegness Sands Touring Site
404 C&C Club Site Clent Hills
411 Tewksbury Caravan Club Site
442 Seven Gorge Caravan Park
Scotland
691 Hoddom Castle Caravan Park
699 Mortonhall Caravan Park
704 Slatebarns Caravan Park
724 Lomond Woods Holiday Park
726 Ardgartan Caravan and Camping Site
732 Witches Craig Caravan Park
Ireland
905 Green Gables Caravan Park
915 River Valley Caravan Park
930 Morriscastle Strand

APPLE MOTORHOME HIRE LTD

Lucky-Lite Farm, 217-219 Catherington Lane, Catherington, Portsmouth PO8 0TB
Tel: 023 9257 1155   Fax: 023 9257 1155   website: www.apple-motorhome.co.uk
e-mail: hire@apple-motorhome.co.uk

APPLE MOTORHOME HIRE

Choice of right / left hand drive

European breakdown cover

Comprehensive insurance

Unlimited mileage

THE SOUTH'S ONLY SUPPLIER OF BENIMAR MOTORHOMES

All models supplied by Apple Motorhome Hire include as standard – 2.8 Turbo Diesel engine, PAS, central heating, double-glazing, blinds, screens and curtains, shower compartment, 90 litre 3-way fridge, water heater, 125 litre fresh water capacity, Thetford cassette with electric flush, electric step, rear corner steadies, roof rack and ladder.

TRY BEFORE YOU BUY

One week money-back test hire if you subsequently decide to buy a brand new Benimar motorhome from us within three months. (ask for details)

COLLECTION and DELIVERY

Collect your motorhome from our offices in Portsmouth or, alternatively, let us deliver to a destination of your choice, (a small charge may be applied for delivery outside of a 50 mile radius of Portsmouth).

P&O PORTSMOUTH

A FULL COLOUR BROCHURE AND PRICE LIST AVAILABLE ON REQUEST

Also available from RDH Motorhome Hire, Nottingham Tel: (0870) 752727 (Sales) 7585050 (Hire) Fax: 7583030
e-mail: motorhomes@rdh.co.uk website: www.rdh.co.uk

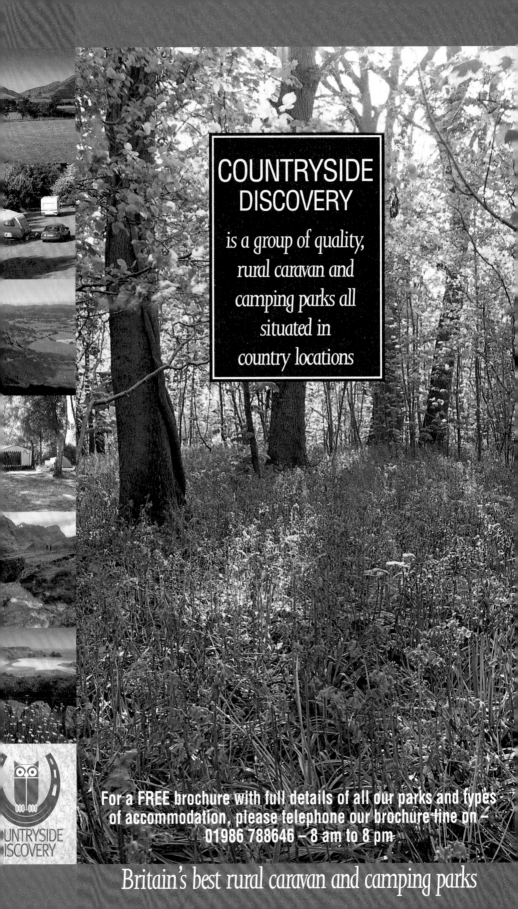

COUNTRYSIDE DISCOVERY

is a group of quality, rural caravan and camping parks all situated in country locations

For a FREE brochure with full details of all our parks and types of accommodation, please telephone our brochure line on – 01986 788646 – 8 am to 8 pm

COUNTRYSIDE DISCOVERY

Britain's best rural caravan and camping parks

www.insure4europe.com

Taking your own tent, caravan or motorhome abroad?

Looking for the best cover at the best rates?

Our prices considerably undercut most high street prices and the 'in-house insurance' of many tour operators whilst offering equivalent (or higher) levels of cover.

Our annual multi-trip policies offer superb value, covering you not only for your european camping holiday but also subsequent trips abroad for the next 12 months.

Total Peace of Mind

To give you total peace of mind during your holiday our insurance policies have been specifically tailored to cover most potential eventualities on a self-drive camping holiday. Each is organised through Voyager Insurance Services Ltd who specialize in travel insurance for Europe and for camping in particular. All policies are underwritten by UK Insurance, part of the Green Flag Group.

24 Hour Assistance

Our personal insurance provides access to the services of International Medical Rescue (IMR), one of the UK's largest assistance companies. Experienced multi-lingual personnel provide a caring and efficient service 24 hours a day.

European vehicle assistance cover is provided by Green Flag who provide assistance to over 3 million people each year. With a Europe-wide network of over 7,500 garages and agents you know you're in very safe hands.

Both IMR and green flag are very used to looking after the needs of campsite-based holidaymakers and are very familiar with the location of most European campsites, with contacts at garages, doctors and hospitals nearby.

Save with an Annual policy

If you are likely to make more than one trip to Europe over the next 12 months then our annual multi-trip policies could save you a fortune. Personal cover for a couple starts at just £90 and the whole family can be covered for just £110.

Cover for up to 17 days wintersports participation is included.

Low Cost Annual multi-trip insurance

Premier Annual Europe self-drive
including 17 days wintersports

£90 per couple

Premier Annual Europe self-drive
including 17 days wintersports

£110 per family

Low Cost Combined Personal and Vehicle Assistance Insurance

Premier Family Package
10 days cover for vehicle, 2 adults plus dependent children under 16.

£71-50*

Premier Couples Package
10 days cover for vehicle and 2 adults

£57-75*

* Motorhomes, cars towing trailers and caravans, all vehicles over 4 years old and holidays longer than 10 days attract supplements – ask us for details. See leaflet for full terms and conditions.

South West England

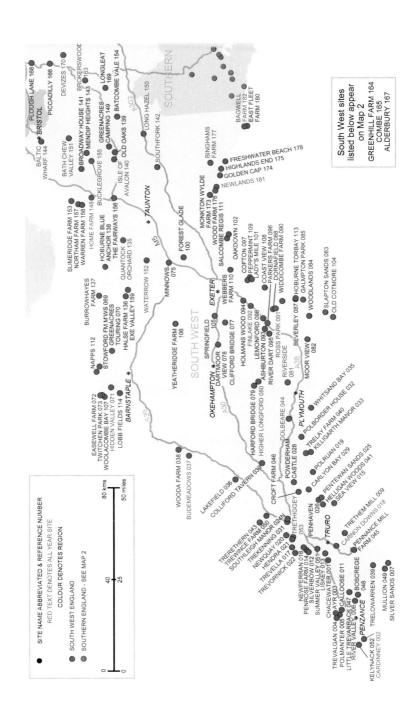

South West sites listed below appear on Map 2
GREENHILL FARM 164
COMBE 165
ALDERBURY 167

SITE NAME ABBREVIATED & REFERENCE NUMBER
RED TEXT DENOTES ALL YEAR SITE
COLOUR DENOTES REGION

SOUTH WEST ENGLAND
SOUTHERN ENGLAND - SEE MAP 2

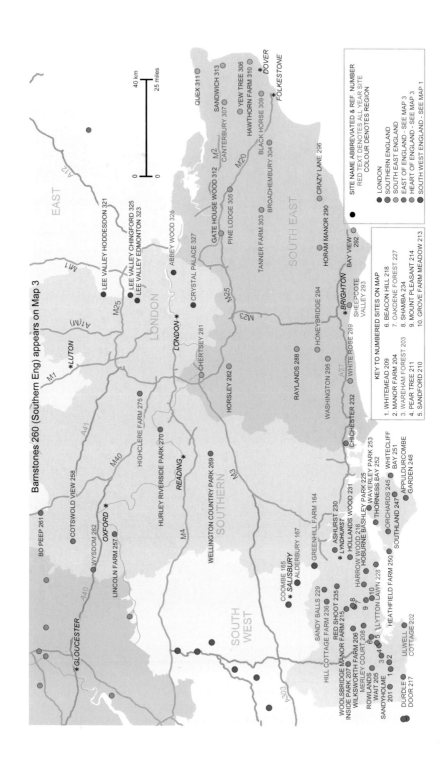

Barnstones 260 (Southern Eng) appears on Map 3

SITE NAME ABBREVIATED & REF. NUMBER
RED TEXT DENOTES ALL YEAR SITE
COLOUR DENOTES REGION

LONDON
SOUTHERN ENGLAND
SOUTH EAST ENGLAND
EAST OF ENGLAND - SEE MAP 3
HEART OF ENGLAND - SEE MAP 3
SOUTH WEST ENGLAND - SEE MAP 1

KEY TO NUMBERED SITES ON MAP

1. WHITEMEAD 209
2. MANOR FARM 204
3. WAREHAM FOREST 203
4. PEAR TREE 211
5. SANDFORD 210
6. BEACON HILL 218
7. OAKDENE FOREST 227
8. SHAMBA 234
9. MOUNT PLEASANT 214
10. GROVE FARM MEADOW 213

40 km
25 miles
0
0

QUEX 311
SANDWICH 313
CANTERBURY 307
YEW TREE 306
HAWTHORN FARM 310
BLACK HORSE 309
DOVER
FOLKESTONE

EAST

GATE HOUSE WOOD 312
PINE LODGE 305
TANNER FARM 303
BROADHEMBURY 304
CRAZY LANE 296
HORAM MANOR 290
BAY VIEW 292

LEE VALLEY HODDESDON 321
LEE VALLEY CHINGFORD 325
LEE VALLEY EDMONTON 323
ABBEY WOOD 326

LONDON

LONDON *
CRYSTAL PALACE 327
CHERTSEY 281
HORSLEY 282
RAYLANDS 288
HONEYBRIDGE 294
WASHINGTON 295
SHEEPCOTE VALLEY 293
WHITE ROSE 289
BRIGHTON *

SOUTH EAST

LUTON *

HIGHCLERE FARM 275
HURLEY RIVERSIDE PARK 270
READING *
WELLINGTON COUNTRY PARK 269

BO PEEP 261
COTSWOLD VIEW 258
WYSDOM 262
OXFORD *
LINCOLN FARM 257

GLOUCESTER *

SOUTHERN

CHICHESTER 232

GREENHILL FARM 164
ASHURST 230
LYNDHURST *
HOLLANDS WOOD 231
HOBURNE BASHLEY PARK 225
WAVERLEY PARK 253
THORNESS BAY 252
WHITECLIFF BAY 251
ORCHARDS 245
APPULDURCOMBE GARDEN 248
SOUTHLAND 247
HARROW WOOD 216

COOMBE 165
SALISBURY *
ALDERBURY 167

SANDY BALLS 229
RED SHOOT 235
HILL COTTAGE FARM 236
WOOLSBRIDGE MANOR FARM 207
INSIDE PARK 206
WILKSWORTH FARM 206
MERLEY COURT 208
ROWLANDS WAIT 205
LYTTON LAWN 228
HEATHFIELD FARM 250
SANDYHOLME 201
DURDLE DOOR 217
ULWELL COTTAGE 202

SOUTH WEST

For latest information visit www.alanrogers.com

Wales

SITE NAME ABBREVIATED & REFERENCE NUMBER
RED TEXT DENOTES ALL YEAR SITE
COLOUR DENOTES REGION

WALES
HEART OF ENGLAND - SEE MAP 3
NORTH WEST ENGLAND - SEE MAP 5

0   40   80 kms
0   25   50 miles

BLACKPOOL *
PRESTON*

NORTH WEST

LIVERPOOL *

HOLYHEAD *   HOME FARM 664

BRON-Y-WENDON 669
HUNTERS HAMLET 665

BRYN GLOCH 660

BEDDGELERT (FC) 659

THE PLASSEY 667
JAMES' 668
TY-UCHA FARM 670

LLANYSTUMDWY 658
BARCDY 635   PENYBONT 634 PEN-Y-GARTH 636

HENDRE MYNACH 637

CRINGOED 624   LLWYN CELYN 623

BACHELDRE WATERMILL 631
DAISY BANK 633

GLAN-Y-MOR 629

WALES   HEART

AERON COAST 628   DOLSWYDD 625

FFOREST FIELDS 632

CENARTH FALLS 601 SPRINGWATER LAKES 588   RHANDIRMWYN 607

GWAUN VALE 600

ABERMARLAIS 596   BRYNICH 603
PENCELLI CASTLE 604

AFON LODGE 595

GLEN TROTHY 589

TYTHING BARN 590N   MORETON FARM 598
FRESHWATER   PEMBREY 594
EAST 599

SWANSEA *   CWMCARN FOREST DRIVE 593
ST PIERRE 591
NEWPORT
M4   TREDEGAR HOUSE 606
CARDIFF

SITE NAME (ABBREVIATED) & REF. NUMBER
RED TEXT DENOTES ALL YEAR SITE
COLOUR OF SYMBOL DENOTES REGION

○ CUMBRIA
● NORTHUMBRIA
● NORTH WEST ENGLAND
● SCOTLAND
● YORKSHIRE

0   40   80 kms
0   25   50 miles

SCOURIE 773 ●

WOODEND 772 ●
DUNROAMIN 764 ●
ARDMAIR POINT 771 ●
PITGRUDY 770 ●

STAFFIN 775 ●
● LOCH GRESHORNISH 774   SPINDRIFT 766
TORVEAN 769 ● *INVERNESS*   ADEN COUNTRY PARK 753
                    ABERLOUR GARDENS 754
RERAIG 776 ●   GRANTOWN-ON-SPEY 767
                    HUNTLY CASTLE 755
                    GLENMORE (FC) 768
FAICHEM PARK 778 ●   *ABERDEEN*

LINNHE LOCHSIDE 785 ●
RESIPOLE FARM 780 ●   GLEN NEVIS 783   BLAIR CASTLE 730
                INVERCOE 779   NETHER CRAIG 728 ●
OBAN 781 ●
NORTH LEDAIG 784 ●
OBAN DIVERS 782 ●   *DUNDEE*
                TWENTY SHILLING 731 ●   CRAIGTOUN MEADOWS 729
                AUCHTERARDER 727 ●
ARDGARTAN (FC) 726 ●
        TROSSACHS 723 ●   WITCHES CRAIG 732   TANTALLON 706
GLENDARUEL 786 ●
        LOMOND WOODS 724 ●   EDINBURGH
                EDINBURGH 705   DRUM MOHR 698
                GLASGOW   MORTONHALL 699   SLATEBARNS 704
        STRATHCLYDE 700 ●
                            ORD HOUSE 580
                CROSSBURN 696
                GIBSON PARK 703 ●   WAREN 575
                            DUNSTAN HILL 577
CULZEAN CASTLE 701 ●   PERCY WOOD 576

                            NORTHUMBRIA
                        BROWN RIGG 578
            HODDOM CASTLE 691   CRESSFIELD 692
        BRANDEDLEYS 693 ●   FALLOWFIELD DENE 581   *NEWCASTLE UPON TYNE*
AIRD DONALD 702 ●   GLENEARLY 687
        MOSSYARD 689 ●   SANDYHILLS BAY 688
        BRIGHOUSE BAY 695 ●   SEAWARD 690
                THE LARCHES 551
                FLUSCO WOOD 567
        WATERFOOT 561   WHITE WATER 574
CASTLERIGG HALL 566   COVE 562   DOE PARK 571
        CUMBRIA   SYKESIDE 556   WILD ROSE 557   BARNARD CASTLE 572
                LIMEFITT 555   PENNINE VIEW 560
        SKELWITH FOLD 552   WESTMORLAND 559   BROMPTON ON SWALE 480
        WALLS 553   CONSTABLE BURTON HALL 469
FALLBARROW PARK 554   STREET HEAD 468
                THE ASHES 565   RIVERSIDE MEADOWS 476
        HOLGATES 535   WOODHOUSE FARM 466
        KNIGHT STAINFORTH HALL 472   WOOD NOOK 467   RIPLEY 463
                HOWGILL LODGE 475   RUDDING 471   *YORK*
        KNEPS FARM 530
        BLACKPOOL   PIPERS HEIGHT 531   BRONTE 479
MARTON MERE 533   *PRESTON*   *BRADFORD*
                            NOSTELL PRIORY 470
        WILLOWBANK 536   ABBEY FARM 528

        YORKSHIRE
NORTH WEST
LIVERPOOL *   *MANCHESTER*
                        SHEFFIELD *
Chester Southerly 252 (North West Eng) appears on Map 3

SPIERS HOUSE (FC) 457   NORTHCLIFFE 453
ROSEDALE 477   ST HELENS IN THE PARK 454
VALE OF PICKERING 460   JACOBS MOUNT 459
        UPPER CARR 462   *SCARBOROUGH*
FOXHOLME 458   CAYTON VILLAGE 455
GOLDEN SQUARE 456   FLOWER OF MAY 452
                LEBBERSTON 478
        JASMINE PARK 474
GOOSE WOOD 464   THORPE HALL 451   *BRIDLINGTON*
        MOORSIDE 461   FANGFOSS OLD   FAR GRANGE 473
        YORK   STATION 465
PART OF YORKSHIRE
        BURTON CONSTABLE 450
BRADFORD   *HULL*

Ireland and the Channel Islands

SITE NAME ABBREVIATED & REF NUMBER

■ TRAVEL SERVICE SITE

RED TEXT DENOTES ALL YEAR ROUND SITE

COLOUR OF SYMBOL DENOTES REGION

○ NORTHERN IRELAND
○ REPUBLIC OF IRELAND
● CHANNEL ISLANDS

0 — 40 — 80 kms
0 — 25 — 50 miles

KNOCKALLA 864

BUSH 835
BELLEMONT 860 — BALLYNESS 836
COLERAINE — TULLANS FARM 859
LONDONDERRY — DRUMAHEGLIS 834

STRABANE
BALLYMENA — LARNE
CARNFUNNOCK 831
CURRAN COURT 832

DONEGAL
GORTIN GLEN 856 — OMAGH — COOKSTOWN — BANGOR
LOANEDEN 850 — BELFAST

NORTHERN IRELAND

GREENLANDS 869 — SLIGO
ENNISKILLEN — ARMAGH — DELAMONT 846
BELLEEK 875 — MULLYNASCARTHY 851 — BANBRIDGE 843
NEWRY — TOLLYMORE FOREST 842
TAIN 889

PARKLAND 877 — LOUGH LANNAGH 881
CARRA 879 — KNOCK 878
CAVAN — DUNDALK

CONG 874

GALWAY — ATHLONE — LOUGH REE (EAST) 896

CAMAC VALLEY 910 — DUBLIN
GREEN GABLES 906
SHANKHILL 911
NAAS
VALLEY 914
PORTLAOISE
ROUNDWOOD 913
STREAMSTOWN 942 — FOREST FARM 908
MOAT FARM 916 — WICKLOW
RIVER VALLEY 915

IRELAND

CURRAGHCHASE 945 — LIMERICK
KILKENNY — TREE GROVE 924
NORE VALLEY 923
ANCHOR 955 — TRALEE
WOODLANDS PARK 965 — TIPPERARY
APPLE 941
MORRISCASTLE STRAND 930
PARSONS GREEN 938 — CLONMEL — CARRICK-ON-SUIR 939
FOSSA 959 — KILLARNEY
WEXFORD
GLENROSS 960
WHITE VILLA FARM 963 — WATERFORD
ROSSLARE
THE FLESK 964 — FLEMING'S WHITEBRIDGE 962
MANNIX POINT 961
NEWTOWN COVE 934
BLARNEY 948 — CORK — CASEY'S 933
WAVE CREST 956
CREVEEN LODGE 957 — EAGLE POINT 951
THE MEADOW 950
BARLEYCOVE 952

VAUGRAT 977 ●   ● SEAGULL (HERM) 983
FAUXQUETS ●✳ ST PETER PORT
VALLEY 978
                     ● POMME DE CHIEN
                       (SARK) 987

GUERNSEY

CHANNEL ISLANDS

ROZEL 971 ●
BEUVELANDE 972 ●

JERSEY   ✳ ST HELIER

Town and Village Index

Town and Village Index

Town and Village Index

Index by Campsite Number

Index by Campsite Number

NORTHERN IRELAND

IRISH REPUBLIC

CHANNEL ISLANDS

INSPECTED CAMPSITES & SELECTED

Campsite Index

ENGLAND

South West England

Heart of England

Yorkshire

North West England

Cumbria

Northumbria

WALES

New Parks: Parks that are new to the guide this year are highlighted in bold type in this index.